A-Z GLASGOW

CONTENTS

Key to Map Pages		66-254
Large Scale City Centre	4	
Map Pages	6-1	55-256

REF

Motorway	**M8**	Map Continuation	**86**	Large Scale City Centre **4**
A Road	**A77**	Car Park Selected		P
Under Construction		Church or Chapel		†
Proposed		Cycle Route		
B Road	**B812**	Fire Station		■
Dual Carriageway		Hospital		H
One Way Street	→	House Numbers (A and B Roads only)		13 8
Traffic flow on A Roads is also indicated by a heavy line on the driver's left.	→	Information Centre		i
Junction Name	TOWNHEAD INTERCHANGE	National Grid Reference		660
Restricted Access		Police Station (Open 24 Hours)		▲
Pedestrianized Road		Post Office		★
Track/Footpath		Toilet		▽
Residential Walkway		with facilities for the Disabled		♿
Railway	Level Crossing Station Tunnel	Viewpoint		
Underground Station	U	Educational Establishment		
Local Authority Boundary		Hospital or Hospice		
Posttown Boundary		Industrial Building		
Postcode Boundary within Posttowns		Leisure or Recreational Facility		
		Place of Interest		
Built-up Area	MILL ST.	Public Building		
		Shopping Centre or Market		
		Other Selected Buildings		

SCALE

Map Pages 6-165 1:18,103

0	¼	½ Mile
0	250	500	750 Metres

3½ inches (8.89 cm) to 1 mile   5.52 cm to 1 km

Map Pages 4-5 1:9051

0	⅛	¼ Mile
0	100	200	300	400 Metres

7 inches (17.78 cm) to 1 mile   11.05 cm to 1 km

Copyright of Geographers' A-Z Map Company Limited

Head Office:
Fairfield Road, Borough Green, Sevenoaks, Kent TN15 8PP
Telephone 01732 781000 (General Enquiries & Trade Sales)

Showrooms:
44 Gray's Inn Road, London WC1X 8HX
Telephone 020 7440 9500 (Retail Sales)
www.a-zmaps.co.uk

Ordnance Survey® This product includes mapping data licensed from Ordnance Survey® with the permission of the Controller of Her Majesty's Stationery Office.

© Crown Copyright 2002. Licence number 100017302
Edition 2   2002
Copyright © Geographers' A-Z Map Co. Ltd. 2002

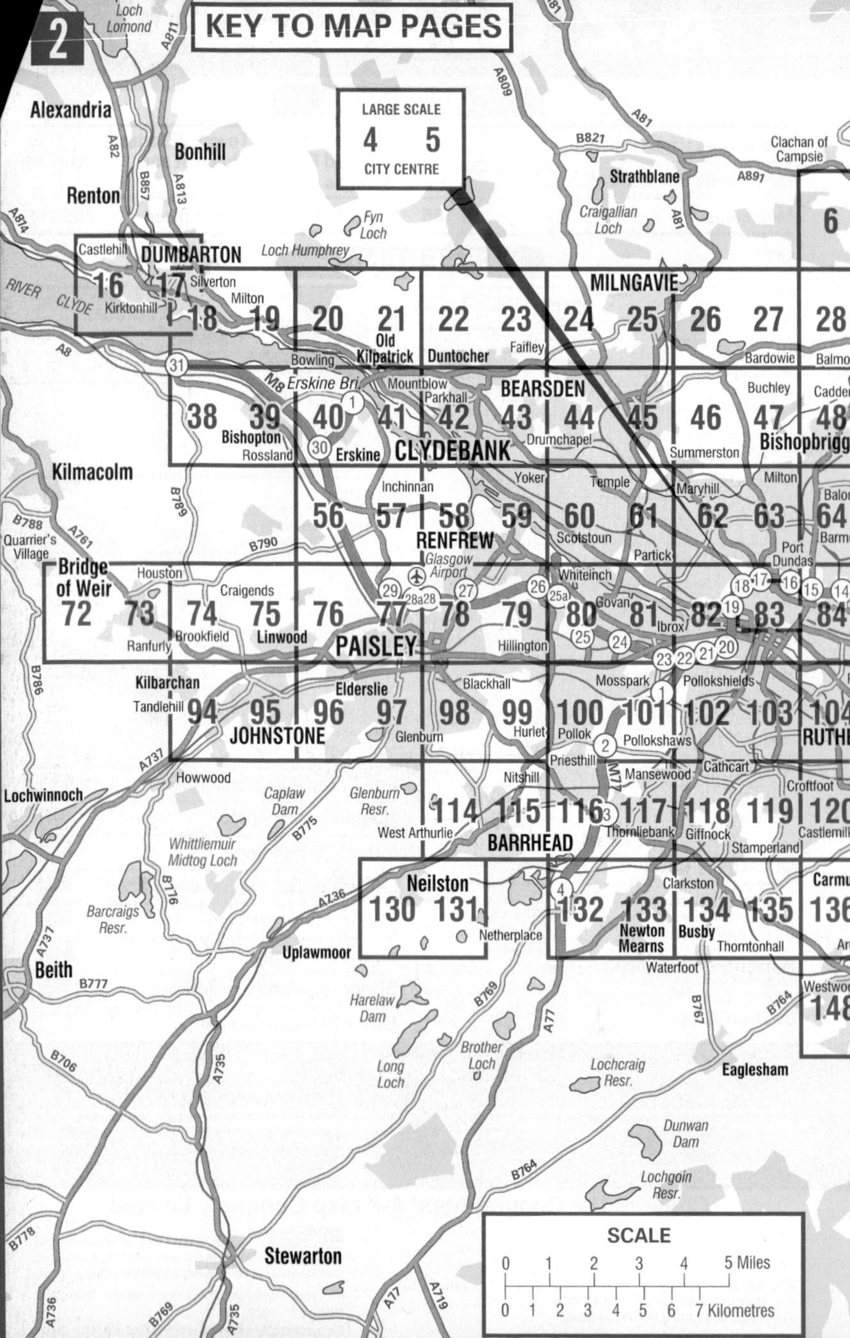

KEY TO MAP PAGES

2

LARGE SCALE
4   5
CITY CENTRE

Loch Lomond

Alexandria

Bonhill

Renton

Clachan of Campsie

Strathblane

Craigallian Loch

Castlehill

DUMBARTON

Silverton

Kirktonhill

Milton

Loch Humphrey

Fyn Loch

MILNGAVIE

16	17							6

RIVER CLYDE

18	19	20	21	22	23	24	25	26	27	28

Bowling

Old Kilpatrick

Duncher

Faifley

Bardowie

Balmore

Erskine Bri.

Mountblow Parkhall

BEARSDEN

Buchley

Cadder

38	39	40	41	42	43	44	45	46	47	48

Bishopton

Rossland

Erskine

CLYDEBANK

Drumchapel

Summerston

Bishopbriggs

Kilmacolm

Inchinnan

Yoker

Temple

Maryhill

Milton

Balorno

		56	57	58	59	60	61	62	63	64

Quarrier's Village

Houston

RENFREW

Glasgow Airport

Scotstoun

Partick

Port Dundas

Barmull

Bridge of Weir

Craigends

Whiteinch

72	73	74	75	76	77	78	79	80	81	82	83	84

Ranfurly

Brookfield

Linwood

PAISLEY

Hillington

Govan

Ibrox

Kilbarchan

Tandlehill

Eldersle

Blackhall

Mosspark

Pollokshields

Par

94	95	96	97	98	99	100	101	102	103	104

JOHNSTONE

Glenburn

Hurlet

Pollok

Pollokshaws

Cathcart

RUTHER

Lochwinnoch

Howwood

Nitshill

Priesthill

Mansewood

Crofftoot

Castlemilk

Caplaw Dam

Glenburn Resr.

		114	115	116	117	118	119	120

Whittliemuir Midtog Loch

West Arthurlie

BARRHEAD

Thornliebank

Giffnock

Stamperland

Barcraigs Resr.

Neilston

Clarkston

Carmunn

		130	131	132	133	134	135	136

Beith

Uplawmoor

Netherplace

Newton Mearns

Busby

Thorntonhall

Arrot

Waterfoot

Westwood

Harelaw Dam

Brother Loch

Lochcraig Resr.

						148

Long Loch

Eaglesham

Dunwan Dam

Stewarton

Lochgoin Resr.

SCALE

0	1	2	3	4	5 Miles

0	1	2	3	4	5	6	7 Kilometres

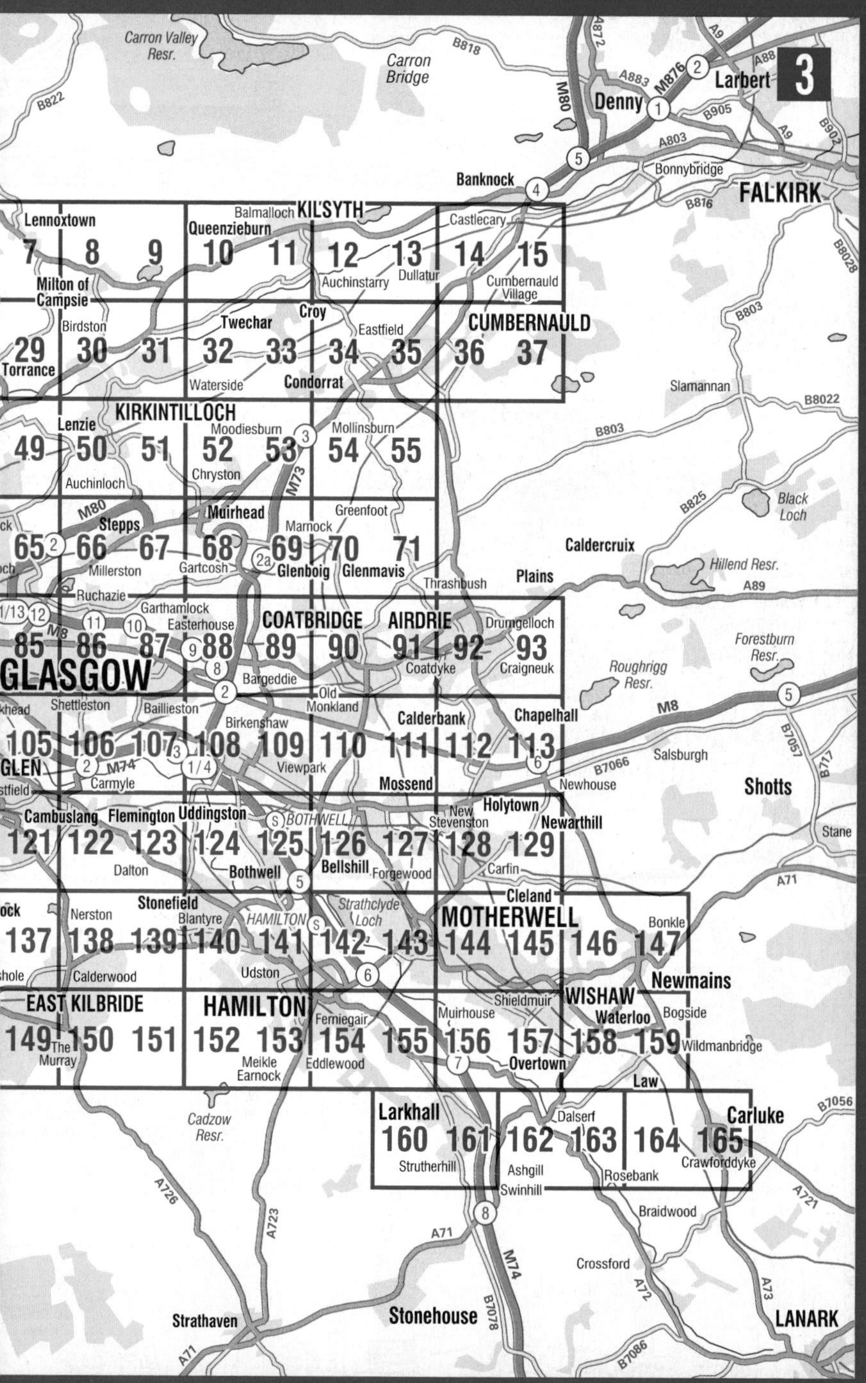

3

Carron Valley Resr.

Carron Bridge

B818

B822

A872 A876 A88

A883 M876 ② Larbert
Denny ① A88

B905 A9

B803

Bonnybridge

FALKIRK

B816

B803

B8028

B8022

Lennoxtown
7 8 9

Milton of Campsie

Birdston
29 30 31
Torrance

Balmalloch KILSYTH
Queenzieburn
10 11

Auchinstarry Dullatur

Castlecary

14 15
Cumbernauld Village

Banknock ④

⑤

Slamannan

Twechar
32 33

Croy
34

Eastfield
35

CUMBERNAULD
36 37

Waterside Condorrat

B825

Black Loch

KIRKINTILLOCH
Lenzie
49 50 51

Moodiesburn
52 53 ③

Chryston

Mollinsburn
54 55

B803

Auchinloch

M80 Stepps
65 ② 66 67

Millerston Ruchazie

Muirhead
68 69 70 71
Marnock
2a Glenboig Glenmavis
Greenfoot

Caldercruix

Hillend Resr.
A89

Gartcosh Thrashbush Plains

1/13 12
85 86 87 88
GLASGOW

11 10
Garthamlock Easterhouse
9
8 Bargeddie

COATBRIDGE AIRDRIE
89 90 91 92 93
Coatdyke Craigneuk Drumgelloch

Forestburn Resr.

⑤

Shettleston Baillieston
②

Old Monkland
Calderbank Chapelhall

Roughrigg Resr.

M8

B7057 B717

105 106 107 108 109 110 111 112 113
GLEN ② M74 ③ 1/4 Viewpark Mossend ⑥

Birkenshaw

Carmyle

B7066 Salsburgh Newhouse Shotts Stane

Cambuslang Flemington Uddingston
121 122 123 124 125 126 127 128 129

S BOTHWELL Holytown
New Stevenston Newarthill

A71

Dalton Bothwell Bellshill Forgewood Carfin

⑤

Cleland

ock Nerston Stonefield
137 138 139 140 141 142 143 144 145 146 147
Blantyre HAMILTON S Strathclyde Loch MOTHERWELL Bonkle

Calderwood Udston ⑥ Shieldmuir WISHAW Newmains

EAST KILBRIDE HAMILTON
149 150 151 152 153 154 155 156 157 158 159
The Murray Ferniegair Muirhouse Waterloo Bogside Wildmanbridge

Meikle Earnock Eddlewood ⑦ Overton Law

Cadzow Resr.

Larkhall Dalserf Carluke
160 161 162 163 164 165
Strutherhill Ashgill Rosebank Crawforddyke B7056

Swinhill

⑧ A71 M74

Braidwood

Crossford

A726 A723 B7078 A72 A73

Strathaven Stonehouse LANARK

A71 B7086 A721

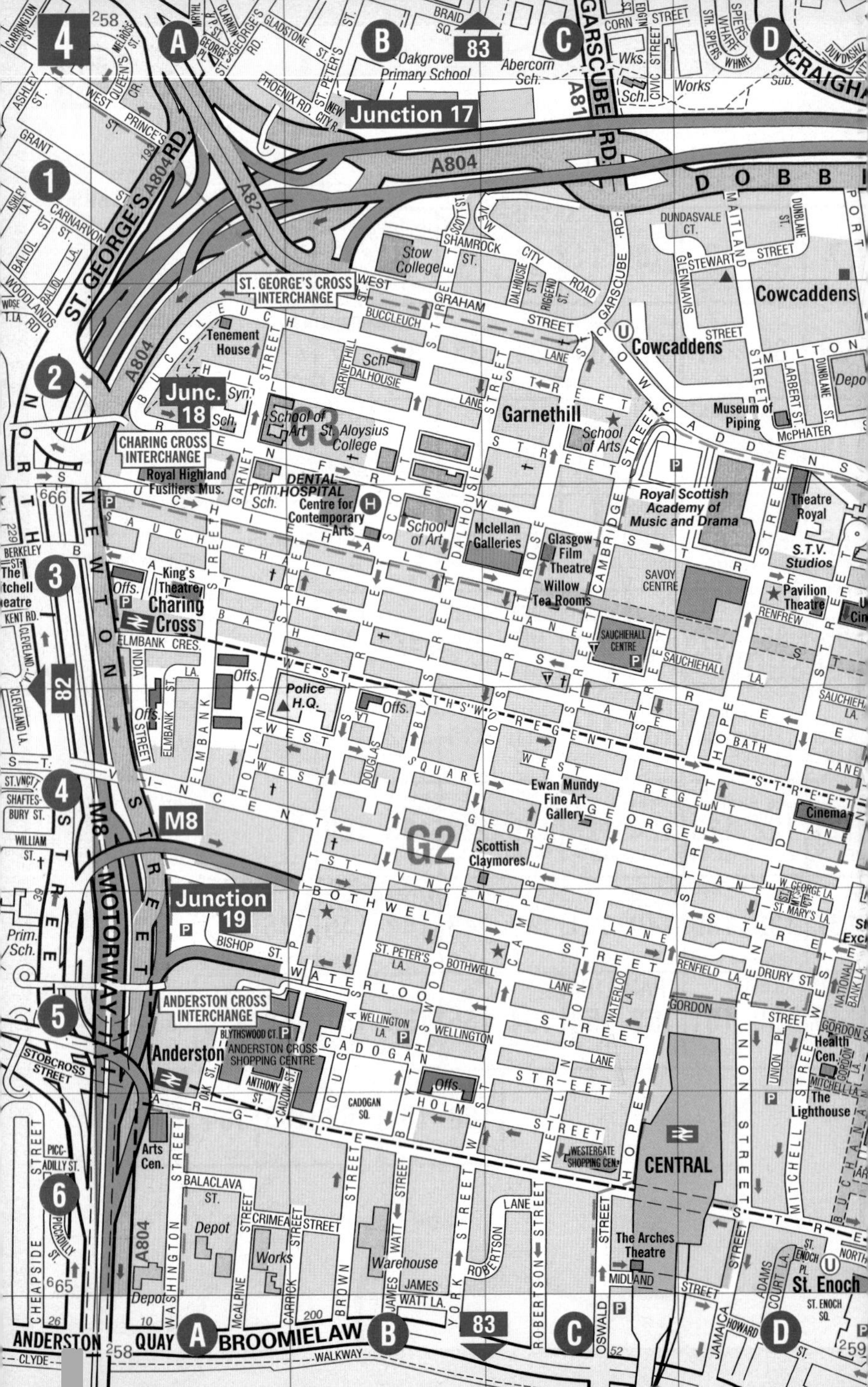
Junction 17
Junc. 18
Junction 19
CHARING CROSS INTERCHANGE
ST. GEORGE'S CROSS INTERCHANGE
ANDERSTON CROSS INTERCHANGE
M8 MOTORWAY
Garnethill
Cowcaddens
Charing Cross
Anderston
CENTRAL
St. Enoch
G2
G3
Royal Scottish Academy of Music and Drama
Theatre Royal
S.T.V. Studios
Pavilion Theatre
King's Theatre
Tenement House
School of Art
St. Aloysius College
DENTAL HOSPITAL
Centre for Contemporary Arts
Mclellan Galleries
Glasgow Film Theatre
Willow Tea Rooms
SAUCHIEHALL CENTRE
SAVOY CENTRE
Police H.Q.
Ewan Mundy Fine Art Gallery
Scottish Claymores
Cinema
Royal Highland Fusiliers Mus.
Stow College
Oakgrove Primary School
Abercorn Sch.
Museum of Piping
The Arches Theatre
The Lighthouse
Health Cen.
ANDERSTON CROSS SHOPPING CENTRE
WESTERGATE SHOPPING CEN.
Arts Cen.
Warehouse
ANDERSTON QUAY
BROOMIELAW
CLYDE
WALKWAY
83
82

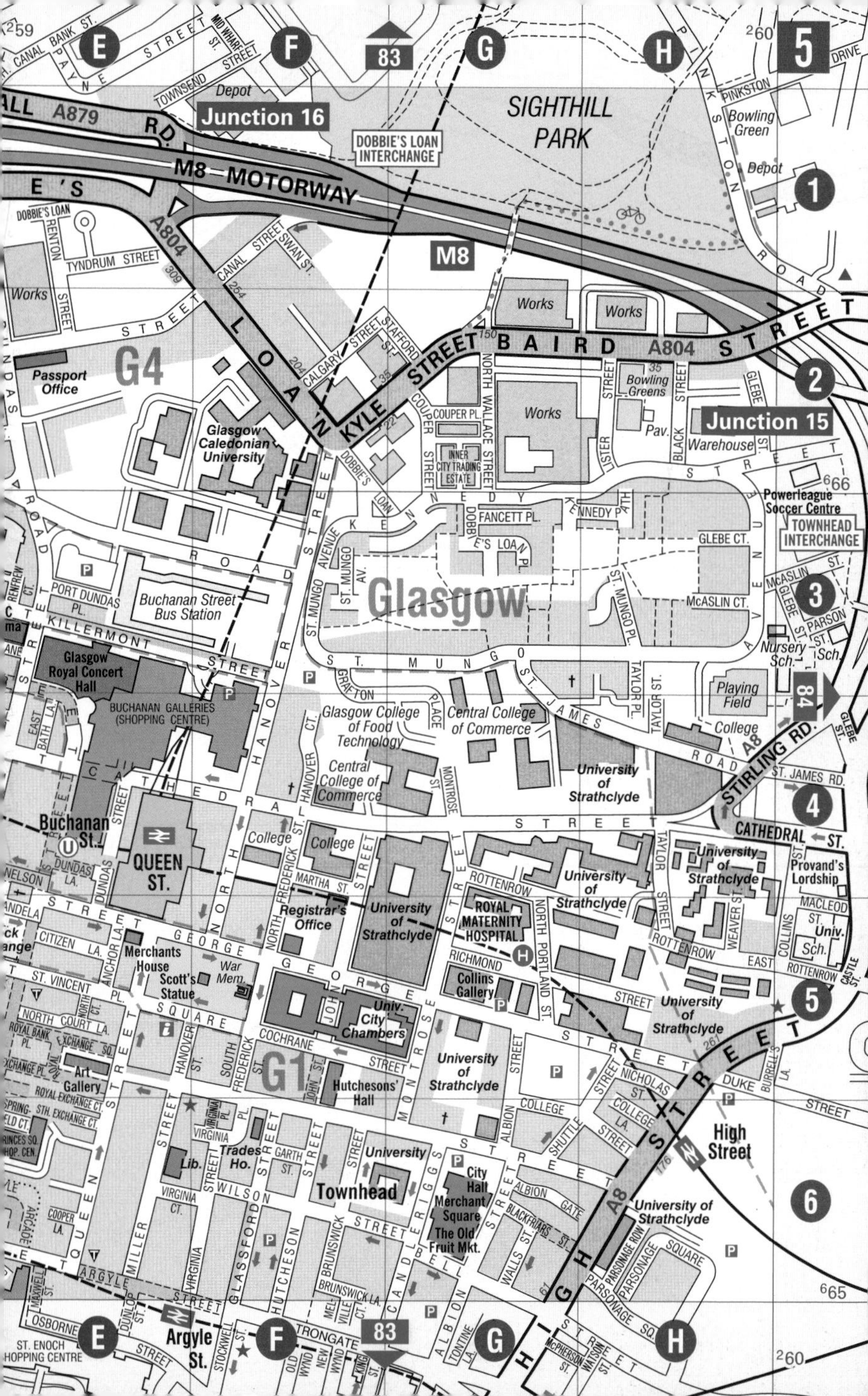

Crosshouse
Kier Hill
Rosedene
Wellbank
Baillie Hill
Kilwinnet
Hall
Kirkton Ter.
Castleview
Cricket Grd.
Weir
Hall
Haughhead
Balcorrach
Strathblane Road
A891
Glen
East Lodge
Finglen Burn
Kirk Burn
Hole
Capieston House
A891
Pow Burn
West Lodge
Glazert Wood
Riverside
Glazert Drive
The Boulevard
Castle View Drive
Crossan
Tennis Ct.
Bank Wood
Lovers' Leap
Ten. Cts.
Nurses Home
Pavilion
LENNOX CASTLE HOSPITAL
Bowl Grns.
Oval
Netherton Oval
Netherton Hill
Netherton
Craigend Wood
Filter House
The White House
Campsie House
South Lodge
Clochcore Wood
Baldow
Reservoir
Baldow Plantation
Drum Plantation
Glen
Mounthuillie
Baldow
Glasgow
G66
Cattle Grid
Newlands
Peathill Wood
Glenwynd Wood
G64
Glenwhapple
Waterfall
Up. Carle.
Muir
Balgla Farm
Sev Wo
79
78
77
76
60
61
A
B
C
D
1
2
3
4
5
6

28

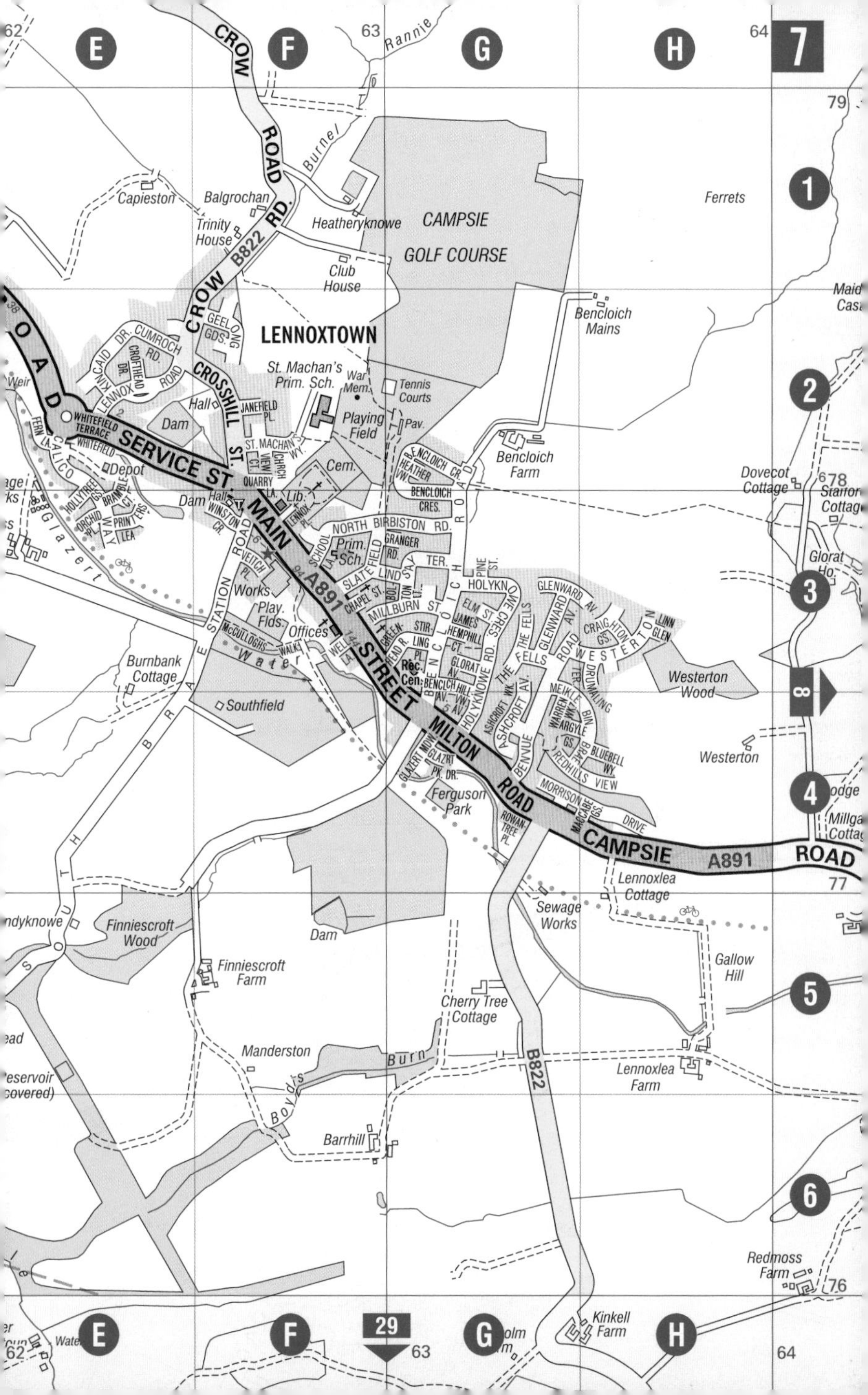

7
E
F
G
H
LENNOXTOWN
CAMPSIE GOLF COURSE
CROW ROAD
CROW B822 RD.
SERVICE ST.
MAIN STREET
A891
MILTON ROAD
CAMPSIE ROAD
Capieston
Balgrochan
Trinity House
Heatheryknowe
Club House
Ferrets
Bencloich Mains
Bencloich Farm
St. Machan's Prim. Sch.
Tennis Courts
Playing Field
Dovecot Cottage
Glorat Ho.
Westerton Wood
Westerton
Burnbank Cottage
Southfield
Ferguson Park
Lennoxlea Cottage
Sewage Works
Finniescroft Wood
Finniescroft Farm
Gallow Hill
Cherry Tree Cottage
Manderston
Lennoxlea Farm
Barrhill
Redmoss Farm
Kinkell Farm
Dam
29

Glasgow
G66
MILTON OF CAMPSIE
CAMPSIE ROAD
ANTERMONY ROAD
A891
BIRDSTON ROAD
B757
Waterfall
Knockybuckle
Forking Burn
Red Cleuch Burn
Waterfalls
Maiden Castle
Garmore
Spouthead
Shields
Dovecot Cottage
Stafford Cottage
Old Workings Wood
Glorat Ho.
Home Wood
Ashenwell
Ashenwell Dams
North Derry Wood
Shields Cottage
Girdle Hill
Boat Ho.
Alloch Dam
Westerton
Brash Burn
Quarry Wood
Lodge
Millgate Cottage
Mill Wood
South Derry Wood
Darnaconner
Mount Dam
West Baldorran
Baldorran Wood
Cowies Glen
Newmill
Craighead Prim. Sch.
East Baldorran
Gallow Hill
Waltry
Works
Alton Holdings
Rec. Grd.
Kincaid Field
Braeside
Bowling Green
Redmoss Farm
Glazert
Water
REDMOSS ROAD
Lib.
64
265
79
678
77
76
30

E
F
G
H
66
67
68
79
78
77
76
Brown Hill
Corrie Spout
(Waterfall)
Corrie
Burn
NORTH LANARKSHIRE
EAST DUNBARTONSHIRE
G65
1
2
3
4
5
6
Waterfall
Woodburn
Reservoir
Water
Treatment
Works
Reservoir
Kierhill
Wood
Burn
Weir
10
Waterfall
Upper
Woodburn
The
Pavilion
Woodburn
House
Burniebrae
Farm
Dyke
Farm
Jetty
Viewfield
ANTERMONY LOCH
Antermony
House
Nursery
Lodge
King's Hill
Lochmill
Farm
ROAD
Sunnyside
Cott.
Auchenreoch
Kennels Mains
Auchenreoch
A891
A803
Alton
Farm
Alton
Smallholdings
Lochmill
Smallholdings
Burnside
Cottage
31

68
69
A
B
C
D
Corrie Plantation
Corrie
79
Drumheldric
Corrie
Burn
Waterfall
1
Waterfalls
Cairnbog Farm
Stoneree Glen
Napp
2
DYKEHEAD
Burnhead Farm
Weir
Waterfall
Glasgow
678
WHIN
Dykehead
Old Place Farm
Lossit Wood
Lossit
Queenzieburn
3
Wham Glen
Playground
Kierhill
ROAD
LOSSIT PL.
ANDERSON CR.
HILLCREST RD.
ROAD
DUMBRECK TE.
MEADOWSIDE
ROAD
9
Burn
Weir
RD.
MILL
Sch.
2
52
Upper Woodburn
Gallow Hill
Queenzieburn Farm
Recreation Ground
Upper Inchwood Farm
Weir
4
Woodburn House
Cast
LOAN
Gavell Farm
KILSYTH
Waterfall
Gavell
Queenzie
GAVELL
77
Burn
Inchwood Cottage
Sewage Works
A803
Inchwood Farm
5
Taigh Chan
Wood
Kennels
Auchenreoch
G66
Netherinch Farm
Burn
6
Netherinch Refuse Tip
Kelvin
River
Works
76
Twechar
A
B
C
D
Burn
68
69
ROAD

32

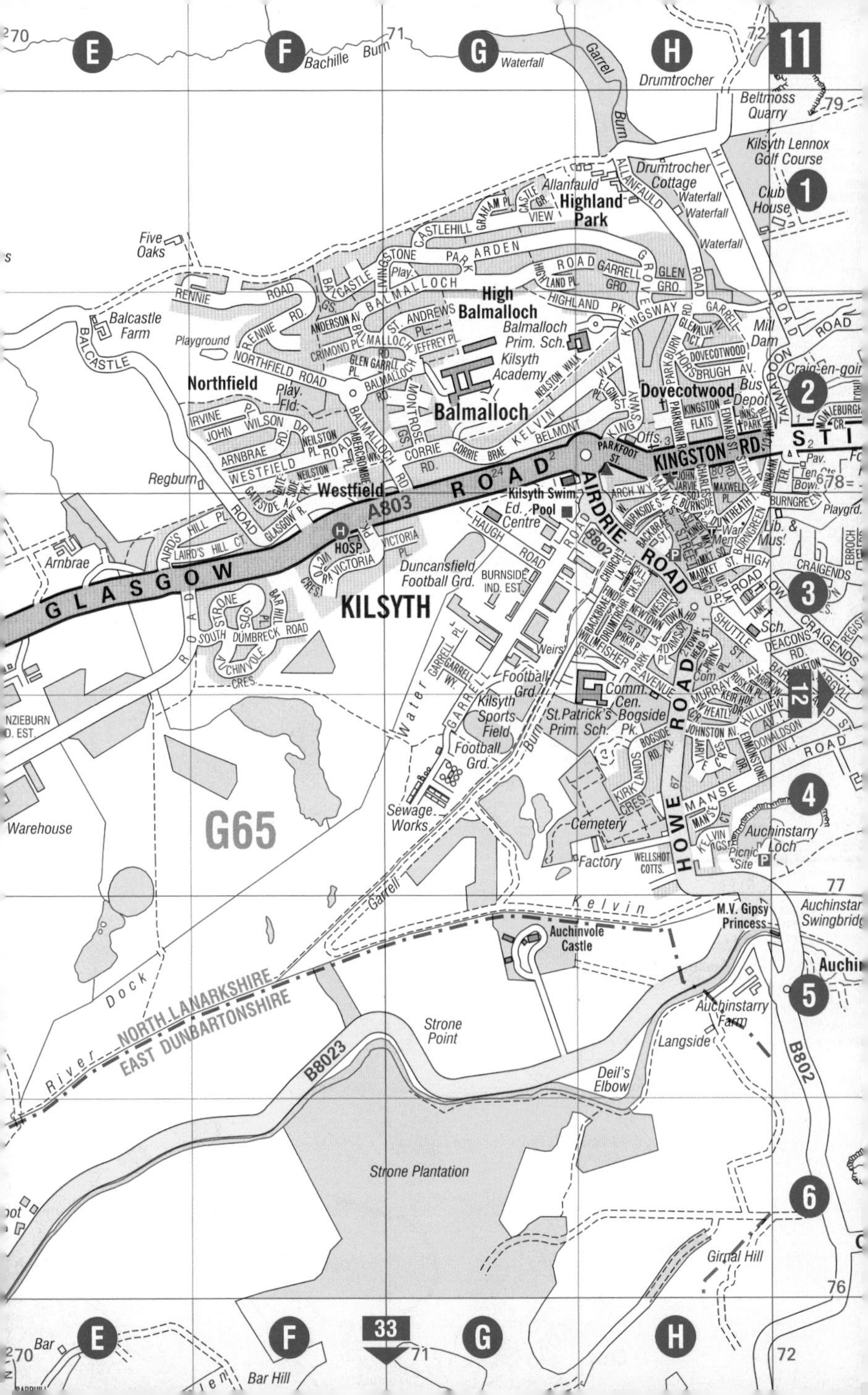

11
E
F
G
H
Bachille Burn
Waterfall
Garrel Burn
Drumtrocher
Beltmoss Quarry
Kilsyth Lennox Golf Course
Club House
Drumtrocher Cottage
Highland Park
Allanfauld
Five Oaks
Balcastle Farm
Playground
Northfield
High Balmalloch
Balmalloch Prim. Sch.
Kilsyth Academy
Balmalloch
Dovecotwood
Bus Depot
Mill Dam
Craigenḡoin
KINGSTON RD.
Regburn
Westfield
GLASGOW ROAD
A803
HOSP.
Kilsyth Swim. Pool
Ed. Centre
AIRDRIE ROAD
B802
Arnbrae
Duncansfield Football Grd.
BURNSIDE IND. EST.
KILSYTH
Lib. & Mus.
War Mem.
Football Grd.
Kilsyth Sports Field
St.Patrick's Prim. Sch.
Comm. Cen.
Bogside Pk.
HOWE ROAD
Sewage Works
Warehouse
G65
Cemetery
Factory
WELLSHOT COTTS.
Auchinstarry Loch
Picnic Site
Garrell Water
Kelvin
M.V. Gipsy Princess
Auchinvole Castle
Auchinstarry Swingbridge
Auchinstarry Farm
Langside
Deil's Elbow
Strone Point
Dock
River
NORTH LANARKSHIRE
EAST DUNBARTONSHIRE
B8023
B802
Strone Plantation
Girnal Hill
Bar Hill
Bar
12
33
1
2
3
4
5
6
70
71
72
76
77
78
79

12
A
B
C
D
Quarry
Beltmoss Quarry
The Strip
Stable Wood
KILSYTH LENNOX GOLF COURSE
Club House
Waterfalls
Riskend
Colzium Castle (Rems. of)
Colzium Glen
Merryton Nursery
Colzium Ho. (Comm. Cen.)
North Lodge
Bandstand
Avenue Strip
Riskend Strip
Dam Wood
Boat House
Spiers Island
Lochside Cottage
Colzium-Margaret Lennox Memorial Estate
Craigstone Wood
Bank Wood
Neilston
Colzium Burn
Colzium
Factory
Craig-en-goin
Mill Dam
TAKMADOON ROAD
STIRLING ROAD
A803
Lodge
Castle Hill
Currymire
Weir
Colzium
Endwood
Mill
North Barrwood
KILSYTH
Football Pitch
G65
Woodend
CADGER'S SHEUCH
HIGH BARRWOOD RD.
Barrwood
COACH ROAD
BARRWOOD
Aqueduct
Glasgow
Craigmarloch Drawbridge
Kings Seat
South Barrwood
MAL FLEMING'S COACH BRAE
STH. BARRWOOD RD.
MANSE AV.
Barr
Auchinstarry Loch
Picnic Site
River Kelvin
Craigmarloch Wood
M.V. Gipsy Princess
Auchinstarry Swingbridge
Forth and Clyde Canal
Auchinstarry
Langhill
B802
Nethercroy Quarry (disused)
Croy Hill
Quarries (disused)
Bowling Green
Playgrd.
Club
CONSTARRY ROAD
Croy Quarry
Auchinbee Quarry (disused)
Craigmarloch
Girnal Hill
Croy
Football
34
11

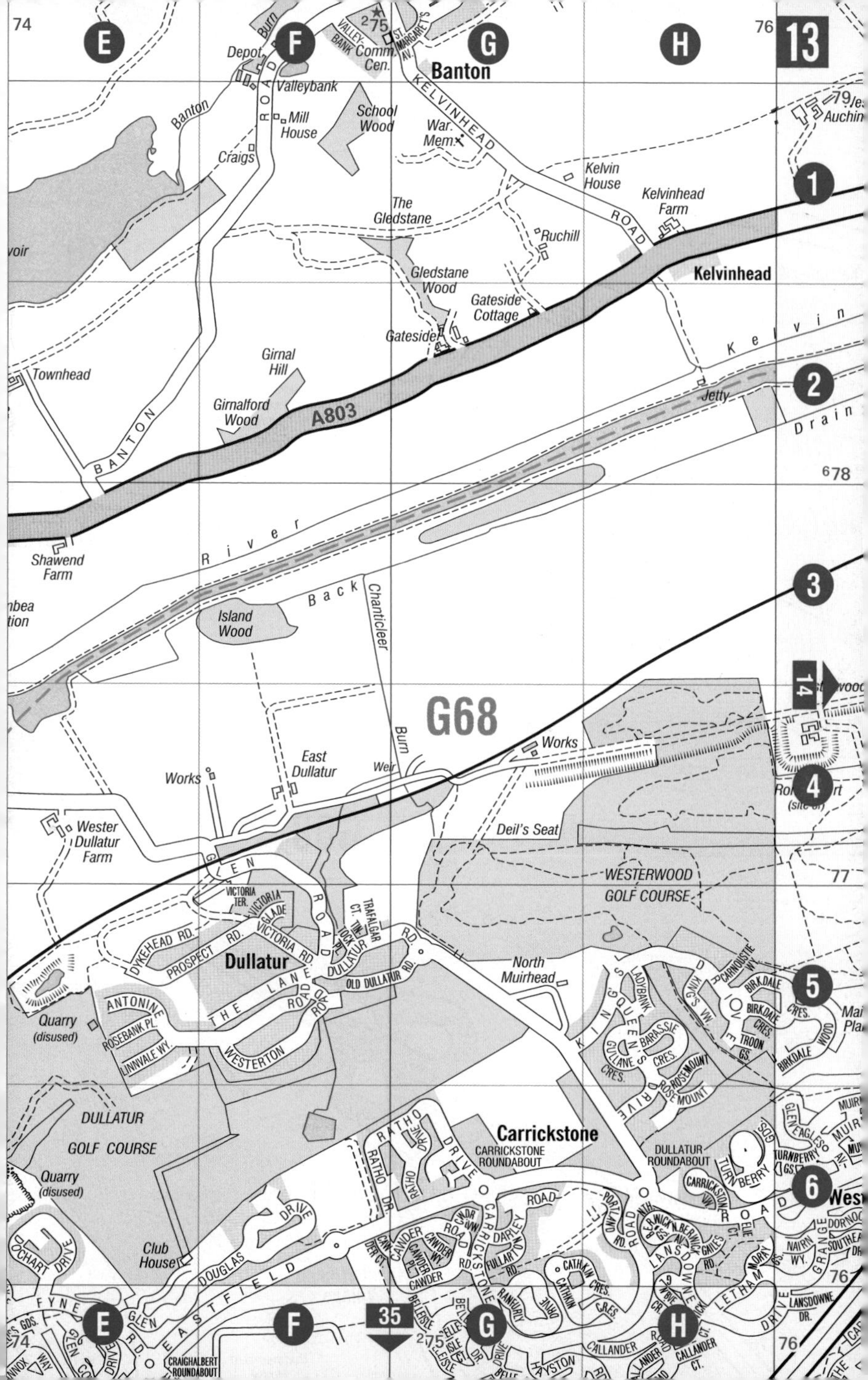
E
F
G
H
74
76
Banton
Depot
Burn
Valleybank
VALLEY-BANK
Comm. Cen.
ST. MARGARET'S AV.
ROAD
KELVINHEAD
Mill House
School Wood
War. Mem.
Craigs
Kelvin House
Kelvinhead Farm
The Gledstane
Ruchill
Kelvinhead
Gledstane Wood
Gateside Cottage
Gateside
Kelvin
Townhead
Girnal Hill
Girnalford Wood
A803
BANTON
Jetty
Drain
678
River
Shawend Farm
Island Wood
Back
Chanticleer
Burn
G68
Works
East Dullatur
Weir
Wester Dullatur Farm
Deil's Seat
WESTERWOOD GOLF COURSE
77
GLEN ROAD
VICTORIA TER.
VICTORIA GLADE
TRAFALGAR CT.
DYKEHEAD RD.
PROSPECT RD.
VICTORIA RD.
Dullatur
DULLATUR RD.
OLD DULLATUR RD.
North Muirhead
THE LANE
ROAD
ANTONINE
ROSEBANK PL.
LINNVALE WY.
WESTERTON
Quarry (disused)
KING'S
LADYBANK
QUEEN'S DRIVE
CARNOUSTIE WY.
KING'S WY.
BIRKDALE
BIRKDALE CRES.
TROON GS.
BIRKDALE WOOD
BARASSIE CRES.
GULLANE CRES.
ROSEMOUNT
DULLATUR GOLF COURSE
Carrickstone
CARRICKSTONE ROUNDABOUT
DULLATUR ROUNDABOUT
RATHO DRIVE
RATHO DR.
DRIVE
TURNBERRY
GLENEAGLES
CARRICKSTONE VW.
Club House
DOUGLAS
DRIVE
DOCHART DRIVE
ROAD
CARRICKSTONE
DARLEY
FULLARTON RD.
CAWDER
BERWICK
LANSDOWNE
LETHAM
NAIRN WY.
GRANGE
CATHKIN CRES.
CATHKIN
FYNE
GLEN
EASTFIELD
RD.
CRAIGHALBERT ROUNDABOUT
CALLANDER
CALLANDER CT.
HAYSTON
BELLEISLE
LANSDOWNE DR.
1
2
3
4
5
6
76
14
35
275
Auchin
Mai Pla
Wes

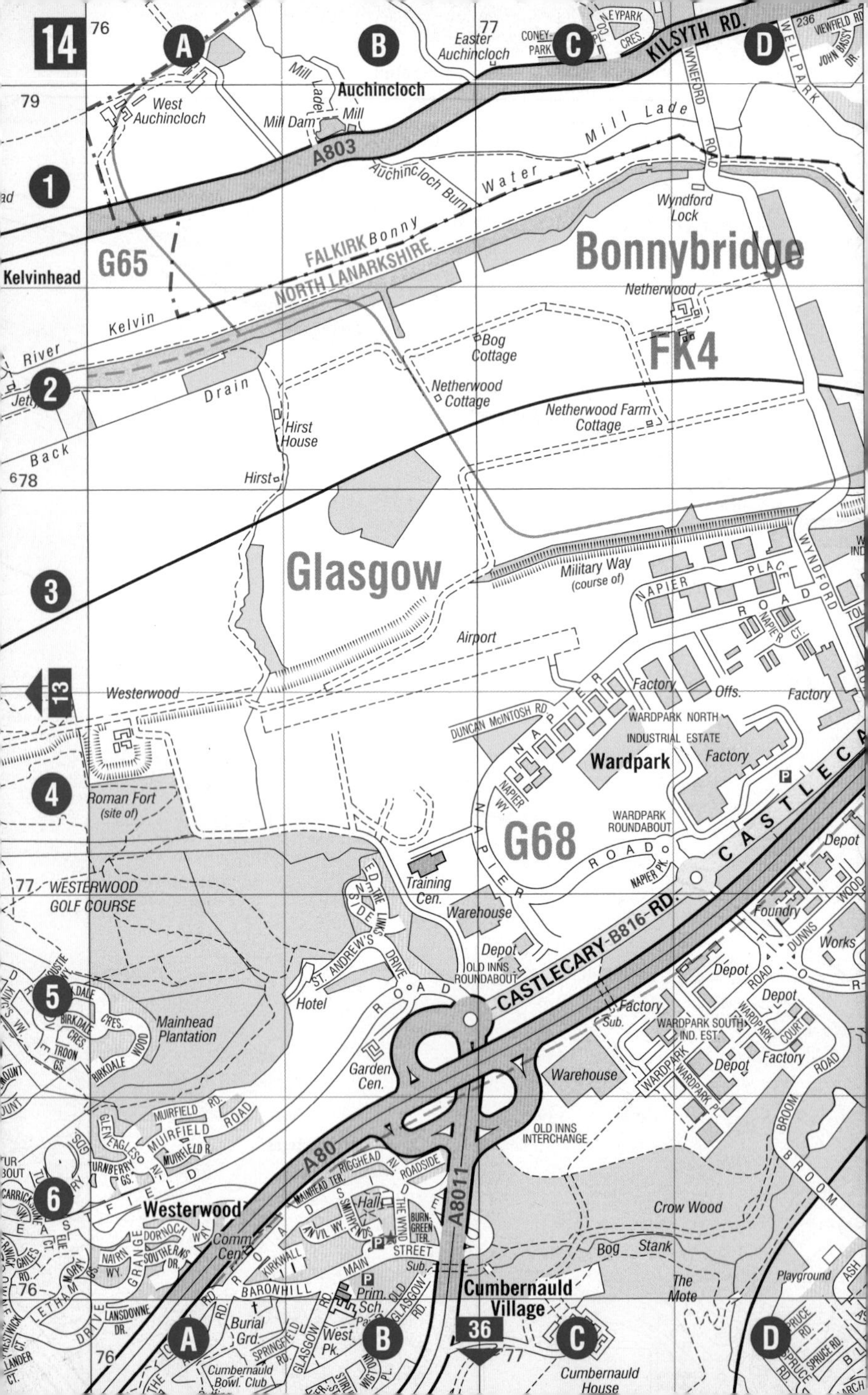
Bonnybridge
Glasgow
Airport
Kelvinhead
G65
FK4
G68
Wardpark
Westerwood
Cumbernauld Village
Auchincloch
West Auchincloch
Easter Auchincloch
KILSYTH RD.
A803
A80
A8011
CASTLECARY-B816-RD.
FALKIRK
NORTH LANARKSHIRE
Wyndford Lock
Netherwood
Bog Cottage
Netherwood Cottage
Netherwood Farm Cottage
Hirst House
Hirst
Military Way (course of)
Roman Fort (site of)
WESTERWOOD GOLF COURSE
Mainhead Plantation
WARDPARK NORTH INDUSTRIAL ESTATE
WARDPARK ROUNDABOUT
OLD INNS ROUNDABOUT
OLD INNS INTERCHANGE
WARDPARK SOUTH IND. EST.
Crow Wood
Bog Stank
The Mote
Training Cen.
Warehouse
Depot
Factory
Foundry
Works
Hotel
Garden Cen.
Burial Grd.
West Pk.
Prim. Sch.
Cumbernauld Bowl. Club
Cumbernauld House
Playground
13
36

BANKNOCK
Castlecary
Haggs
Longcroft
Longcroft Holdings
Allandale
Woodend
Thorn
CASTLECARY LOW WOOD
West Craig
Bandominie Strip
Bandominie
Bandominie South Wood
Kilt Farm
Kilt Bridge
Walton Burn
Red Burn
Castle Glen
Castle Cary
Dunns Wood
Upper Glen Plantation
Waterfalls
Waterfall
Purification Works
Factory
Depot
Works
Woodneuk
Castlecary Bridge
Castlecary Mill Farm
Bonny Water
Forth and Clyde Canal
Bowling Green
Rec. Grd.
Pav.
DUNDAS COTTS.
ALLANDALE COTTS.
THORNDALE GDNS.
A80
B816
G67
Whitelees Prim. Sch.
WHITELEES ROUNDABOUT
St. Lucy's Prim. Sch.
Prim. Sch.
Bowling Greens
Football Grd

37

A   B   38   C   Dalmoak House   D   Sewage Pumping Station

77

Works

1

KIPPEROCH   Underpass

Weir   Mains Lodge   Dalmoak Farm   Weir

Whiteleys Burn   ROAD   Weir   Curling

Whiteleys

Perrays Wood   **Dumbarton**   Dalreoch Prim. Sch.

VALE OF LEVEN   A812

Knowetop Comm Farm   King's WAY   ARRAN   KNOWE

Lea Farm   **Castlehill**   CUMBRAE   RATHLIN   TERRACE   CASTLEBRAE   QUARRY

2   TEL. AV.   MAPLE AV.   Rec. Grd.   CRES. NTH.   ZERBRA   CASTLEHILL ROAD

PERRAYS CRES.   PERRAY AV.   CRESCENT   SOUTH   CASTLEHILL   **Dalreoch**

SERRAYS DRIVE   HAWTHORN HILL   G62   PLAC   RS

Leabrae   HORN   CR   Pitch   RYLET   CARRICK   High Sch   SUNDERLAND ST   LEVEN VALLEY ENTERPRISE CEN.

CARDROSS   76   RONAN   HAWTHORN WY.   200   A814   137   126   **DUMBARTON JOINT HOSP.**   Merns Park   BLACKBURN RD   St.Michaels Prim. Sch.

Leabank   210   TURNBERRY PL.   H   Fftball Pitch

Cats Castle   ASHTON VIEW   WATERLEY   65   48   R O A D

3   Sewage Works   WESTCLIFF   Westfield   CHAR... CLOTTE... RD

Playing Field   Pav   Convent   BRUCEHILL ROAD   ARDOCH   OXHILL   **Dennystown**   COME... RD

Football Pitches   P   Havoc Hole   CRAIGEND HO.   BONTINE ROAD   GRAHAM RD   Activity Cen. AV.   CHARTREE...

P   Football Pitches   HAVOC ROAD   Play. Fld   GLENCAIRN   NAPIER   HILL ST.   CRESCENT   HELENSLEE   Lib

P   Playing Field   FIRTHVIEW   CALEDONIA TER.   KEIL CRES   OXHILL PL.   HELENSLEE CT.   HELENSLEE ROAD

4   WEST DUNBARTONSHIRE   ARGYLL & BUTE   OXHILL TERRACE   **Kirtonhill**   KIRKTON

675   Keil Sch.   Monastery   HELENSLEE   DIXON

5   R I V E R   Playing Field

74   C L Y D E

6   Timber Ponds (Disused)

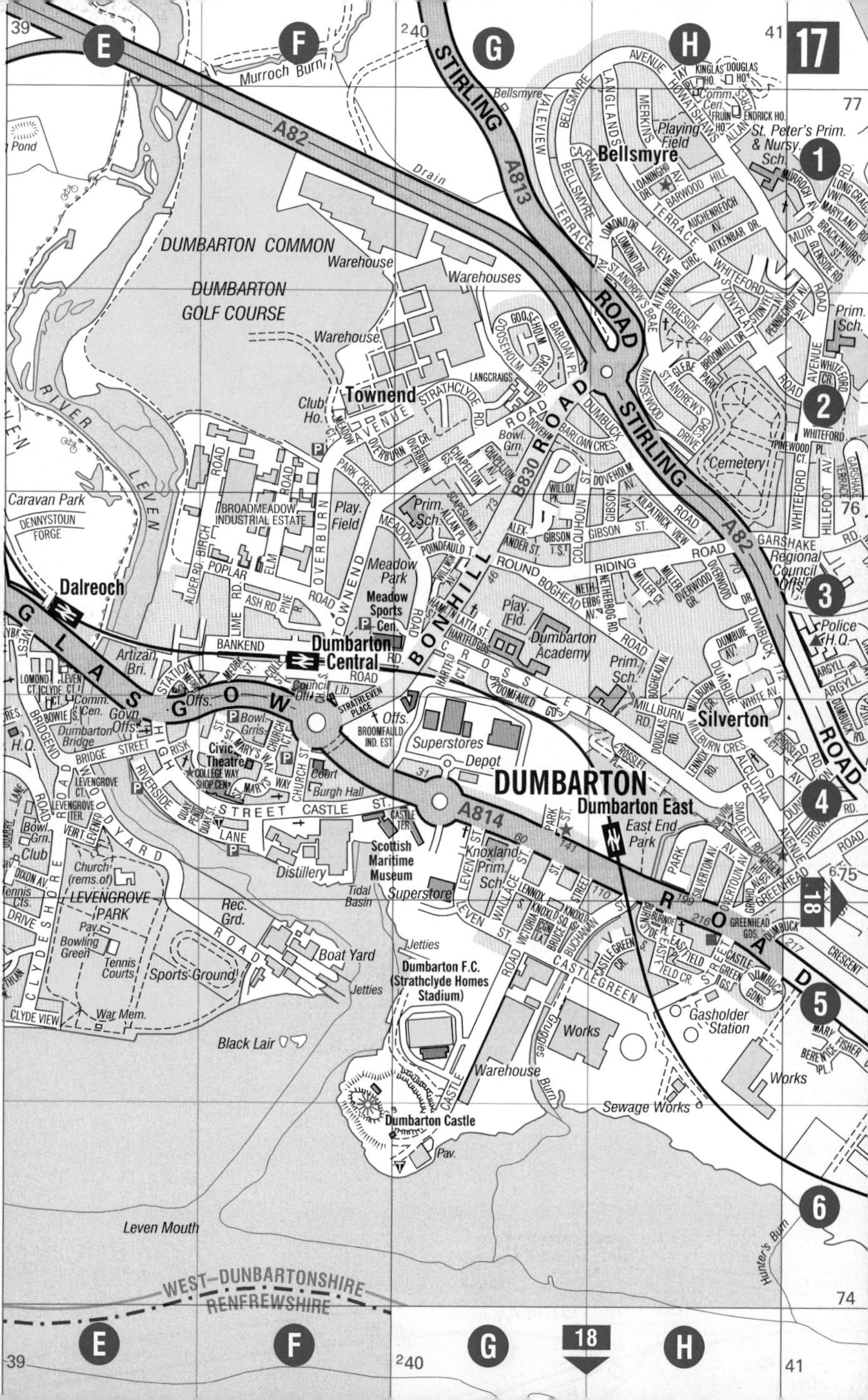
DUMBARTON
Dumbarton Central
Dumbarton East
Dalreoch
Bellsmyre
Townend
Silverton
DUMBARTON COMMON
DUMBARTON GOLF COURSE
RIVER LEVEN
STIRLING ROAD
GLASGOW ROAD
BONHILL ROAD
Dumbarton Academy
Scottish Maritime Museum
Dumbarton F.C. (Strathclyde Homes Stadium)
Dumbarton Castle
LEVENGROVE PARK
Black Lair
Leven Mouth
Gasholder Station
Sewage Works
WEST–DUNBARTONSHIRE
RENFREWSHIRE
A82
A813
A814
B830
18
18

DUMBARTON
Dumbarton Central
Dumbarton East
Silverton
Crosslet
Dumbarton Academy
Dumbarton Castle
Dumbarton F.C. (Strathclyde Homes Stadium)
Scottish Maritime Museum
Superstores
Gasholder Station
Sewage Works
Warehouses
Works
Council Offs.
Police H.Q.
Meadow Park
Meadow Sports Cen.
Knoxland Prim. Sch.
East End Park
Boat Yard
Jetties
Cemetery
A82
A814
B830
GLASGOW ROAD
STIRLING ROAD
RIVER LEVEN
RIVER
Dumbuck Perch
Dumbuck Lighthouse
Long Dyke
Gruggies Burn
Hunter's Burn
WEST FERRY INTERCHANGE
Junction 31
M8
M8 MOTORWAY
A8
Caravan Park
FERRYHILL PLANTATION

17
38

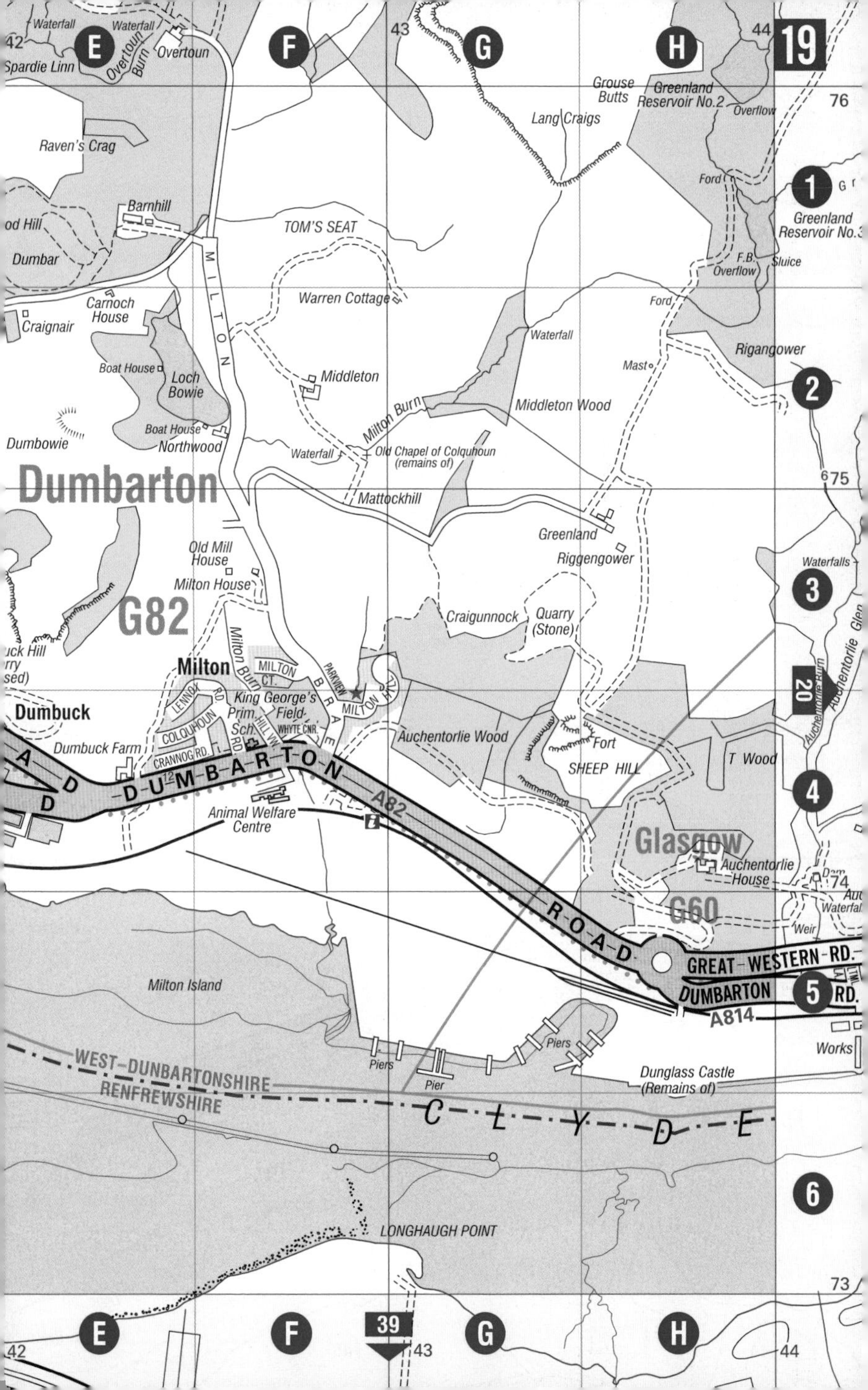

Waterfall
Waterfall
Spardie Linn
Overtoun
Overtoun
Burn
E
F
G
H
44
76
Grouse Butts
Greenland Reservoir No.2
Overflow
Lang Craigs

Raven's Crag
Ford
Greenland Reservoir No.3
od Hill
Barnhill
TOM'S SEAT
F.B Overflow
Sluice
1
Dumbar
Warren Cottage
Ford
Milton
Waterfall
Rigangower
Craignair
Carnoch House
Middleton
Mast
2
Boat House
Middleton Wood
Loch Bowie
Milton Burn
675
Dumbowie
Boat House
Northwood
Waterfall
Old Chapel of Colquhoun
(remains of)

Dumbarton
Mattockhill
Greenland
Waterfalls

Old Mill House
Riggengower
3
G82
Milton House
Craigunnock
Quarry (Stone)

Auchentorlie Glen

Auchentorlie Burn

Milton
MILTON CT.
PARKING RD.
MILTON HL.
20
uck Hill arry sed)
LENNOX
King George's Field
Auchentorlie Wood
Fort
T Wood
Dumbuck
COLQUHOUN
HILL RD.
WHITE CNR.
SHEEP HILL
4
Dumbuck Farm
CRANNOG RD.
A
D
DUMBARTON
A82
Animal Welfare Centre
Glasgow
Auchentorlie House
674
Aut Waterfall

G60
Weir
ROAD
GREAT WESTERN RD.
Milton Island
DUMBARTON RD.
5
A814
Works
Piers
WEST DUNBARTONSHIRE
RENFREWSHIRE
Pier
Piers
Dunglass Castle (Remains of)
C L Y D E
6
73
LONGHAUGH POINT

E
F
39
G
H
42
43
44

A B C D

LOCH HUMPHREY
(Reservoir)

Boat Shed

1

For
ir 762   Overflow

Grouse Butts

Dam

Greenland
Reservoir No.3

C R A I G A R E S T I E

K I L P A

F.B.
Overflow   Sluice

2

Rigangower

675

3

Bow Linn

Waterfalls

Reservoir

Waterfall

McKellar's
Wood

Waterfall

Quarry (Disused)

19

Auchentorlie Glen

Auchentorlie Burn

Lonendale
Wood

Glenarbuck

Haw Craig

4

T Wood

Hill of Dun

K I L P A

Auchentorlie
Cottage

74   Auchentorlie
House

Dam

High
Auchentorlie

East Wood

Bowling

Torwood Villa

Lodge

Waterfalls

Glenbuck House

Gavinburn Co

Waterfall   Weir

A82   W E S T E R N

Dunabuck
Cottage

Lodge

5

G R E A T

D U M B A R T O N

SCOTT AVENUE

MANSE

Weir

R O A D   D U M B A R

Works

Bowling

Jetty   Frisky
Wharf

P

A814

Bowling Harbour

Lock

Basin

Lodge

Gavinburn

ss Castle
ns of)

Pier

Jetty

Lock

R I V E R

WEST–DUNBARTONSHIRE

Library Ga
Pr

RENFREWSHIRE

C L Y D E

ROMAN CRESCENT

6

Jetty

Chapel Hill

ROMAN CRESCENT

Depot

GAVIN

OLDPATRICK

73

Donald's Quay
Light

Beacon

A B

245

C D

E
F
G
H
46
47
48
Dirty Leven
76
TRICK HILLS
1
GREENSIDE RESERVOIR
Loch Humphrey Burn
Dumbarton
G82
OGAIROCH
2
THE SLACKS
75
3
Loch Humphrey Burn
22
4
Ford
Waterfall
RICK BRAES
Cattle Grid
74
Glasgow
Craigleith
Blackmailing
Blackmailing Reservoir (Covered)
G60
Filter Beds
Waterfall
5
Drums
Lodge
Hole Cottage
Mount Pleasant
Netherclose
A82 ROAD
6
Carleith
Cemy.
A814 ROAD
THISTLENEUK
MOUNT PLEASANT RD.
PEACOCK PL.
Halls
Old Kilpatrick
STA. RD.
41
Kilpatrick
North Dalnottar Cemetery
Clydebank Crematorium
73
Carleith Prim. Sch.
GAVINBURN PL.
KIRKTON
ERSKINE VIEW
MT. PLEASANT HO.
ASHTREE
LUSSET RD.

A   B   C   D

COCHNO LOCH
(Reservoir)

49

JAW RESERVOIR

Overflow
Boat House

Dam

76

1

COCHNO HILL

2

6 75

Bog Wood

3

Loch Humphrey Burn

21

Adam's Well

Dam

Auchenduich
Wood

Waterfall

Ford

Waterfalls

Sheepfold

Cochnohill

Cochno

4

Waterfall

Wester Cochno

Clydebank

G81

74

Cochno Filters

Tanks

5

Waterfalls

WESTER COCHNO
HOLDINGS

Cave

Dam

Waterfalls

COCHNO

Duntiglennan
Farm

FARM

CRAIGHURST DR.

HEATHER RD.

BIRNIEHILL
CT.

GLENHEAD

BURNMOOR AV.

WISHBURN DR.

GREENSIDE

Cochno Burn

MIRREN

DRIVE

CRESCENT

HILL RD.

6

Carleith

RUSSELL RD.

RUSSELL CT.

PINLOCH PL.

BLANTYRE RD.

CRAIGIELEA

BEECHES

REDWOOD

BIRCH

CRES.

ROAD

BREVAL

CRES.

BRAEHEAD AV.

BRAEHEAD

HILL CRES.

IDLEWILD

LINE

DUNELLAN DR.

CROFTPARK RD.

RONNAN

ROAD

SPINNERS LA.

AUCHINLECK PL.

Carleith
Prim.

BEECHES

STARK

DALGLEISH

BISHOP

CARLEITH

BEECHES AV.

CARLEITH

HILLEND

DUNN'S

AV.

HOGAN

ROAD

VEITCHE'S
CT.

BRAEHEAD

ROAD

GARDENS

DUMBARTON
ROAD

BURNSIDE

CRES.

GLASGOW

VICTORIA
PL.

ROAD

bank
torium

A   B   **42**   C   D

St. Mary's

49

Pav.   Football

Weir

Golden Hill

HELENA

48

73
ttar

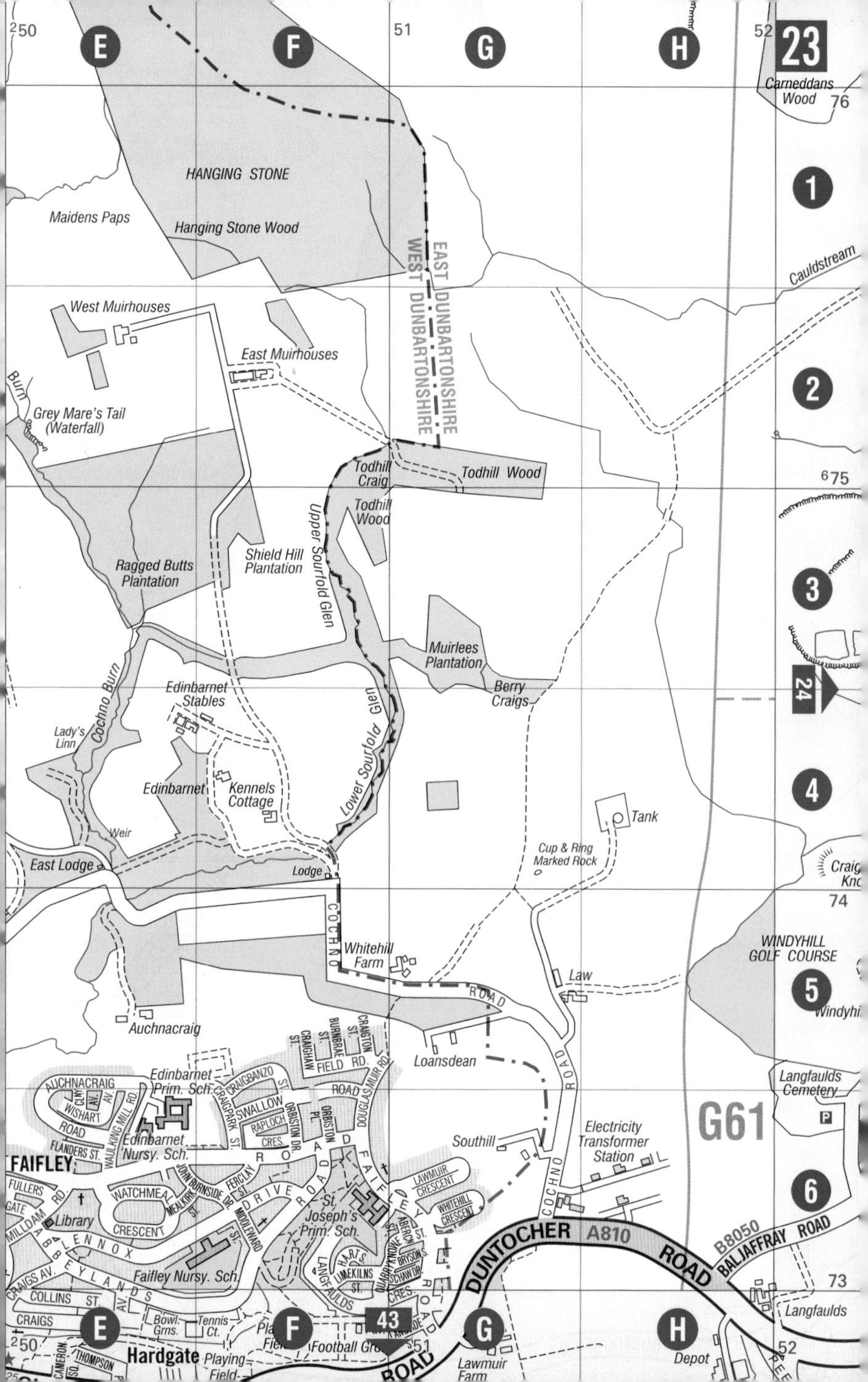

HANGING STONE
Hanging Stone Wood
Maidens Paps
EAST DUNBARTONSHIRE
WEST DUNBARTONSHIRE
Carneddans Wood
Cauldstream
West Muirhouses
East Muirhouses
Burn
Grey Mare's Tail (Waterfall)
Todhill Craig
Todhill Wood
Todhill Wood
Upper Sourfold Glen
Shield Hill Plantation
Ragged Butts Plantation
Muirlees Plantation
Berry Craigs
Cochno Burn
Edinbarnet Stables
Lady's Linn
Lower Sourfold Glen
Edinbarnet
Kennels Cottage
Weir
Tank
Cup & Ring Marked Rock
East Lodge
Lodge
Craig Kno
WINDYHILL GOLF COURSE
Windyhi
COCHNO ROAD
Whitehill Farm
Law
Auchnacraig
Loansdean
Langfaulds Cemetery
Southill
Electricity Transformer Station
G61
AUCHNACRAIG ROAD
CLWYD
AV.
WISHART
Edinbarnet Prim. Sch.
Edinbarnet Nursy. Sch.
WAULKING MILL RD.
CRAIGBANZO ST.
CRAIGPARK ST.
SWALLOW RD.
RAPLOCH
CRES.
ORBISTON DR.
ORBISTON PL.
CRAIGHAW ST.
BURNBRAE ST.
CRAIGTON ST.
FIELD RD.
DOUGLASMUIR RD.
FAIFLEY
FLANDERS ST.
FULLERS GATE
MILLDAM RD.
Library
WATCHMEAL CRESCENT
MEALKIRK ST.
JOHN BURNSIDE DR.
FERCLAY ST.
MIDDLEWARD ST.
DRIVE
FAIFLEY ROAD
St. Joseph's Prim. Sch.
LAWMUIR CRESCENT
WHITEHILL CRESCENT
LENNOX
ABBEYLANDS
CRAIGS AV.
Faifley Nursy. Sch.
COLLINS ST.
CRAIGS
AV.
LANGFAULDS
HARTS.
LIMEKILNS ST.
QUARRYKNOWE ST.
ABERCAIRN ST.
BRYSON'S
SCHAW DR.
CRES.
DUNTOCHER ROAD A810
B8050 BALJAFFRAY ROAD
Langfaulds
Bowl. Grns.
Tennis Ct.
Playing Fields
Football Gr.
Hardgate
Playing Field
CAMERON SQ.
THOMPSON
Lawmuir Farm
Depot
ROAD
24
43
E F G H
1 2 3 4 5 6
50 51 52
76 75 74 73

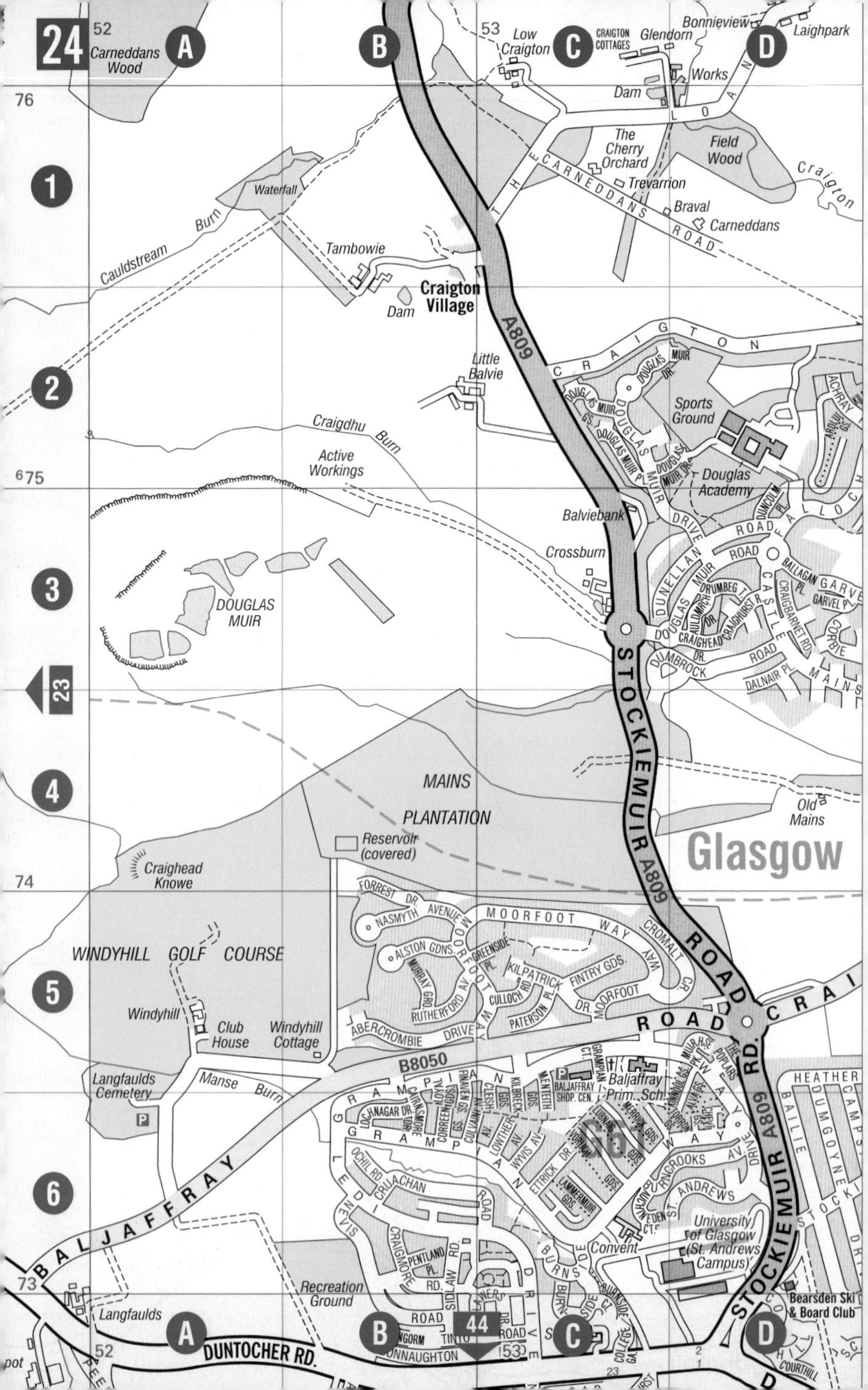
Carneddans Wood
Low Craigton
Craigton Cottages
Glendorn
Bonnieview
Laighpark
Works
Dam
The Cherry Orchard
Field Wood
Trevarrion
Braval
Carneddans
The Carneddans Road
Waterfall
Cauldstream Burn
Tambowie
Craigton Village
Dam
A809
Little Balvie
Craigdhu Burn
Active Workings
Craigton Road
Sports Ground
Douglas Academy
Balviebank
Crossburn
Douglas Muir
Stockiemuir Road A809
Mains Plantation
Reservoir (covered)
Old Mains
Glasgow
Craighead Knowe
Windyhill Golf Course
Windyhill
Club House
Windyhill Cottage
Langfaulds Cemetery
Manse Burn
B8050
Baljaffray Road
Baljaffray Prim. Sch.
Baljaffray Shop. Cen.
G61
University of Glasgow (St. Andrews Campus)
Convent
Recreation Ground
Langfaulds
Duntocher Rd.
Bearsden Ski & Board Club

23
44

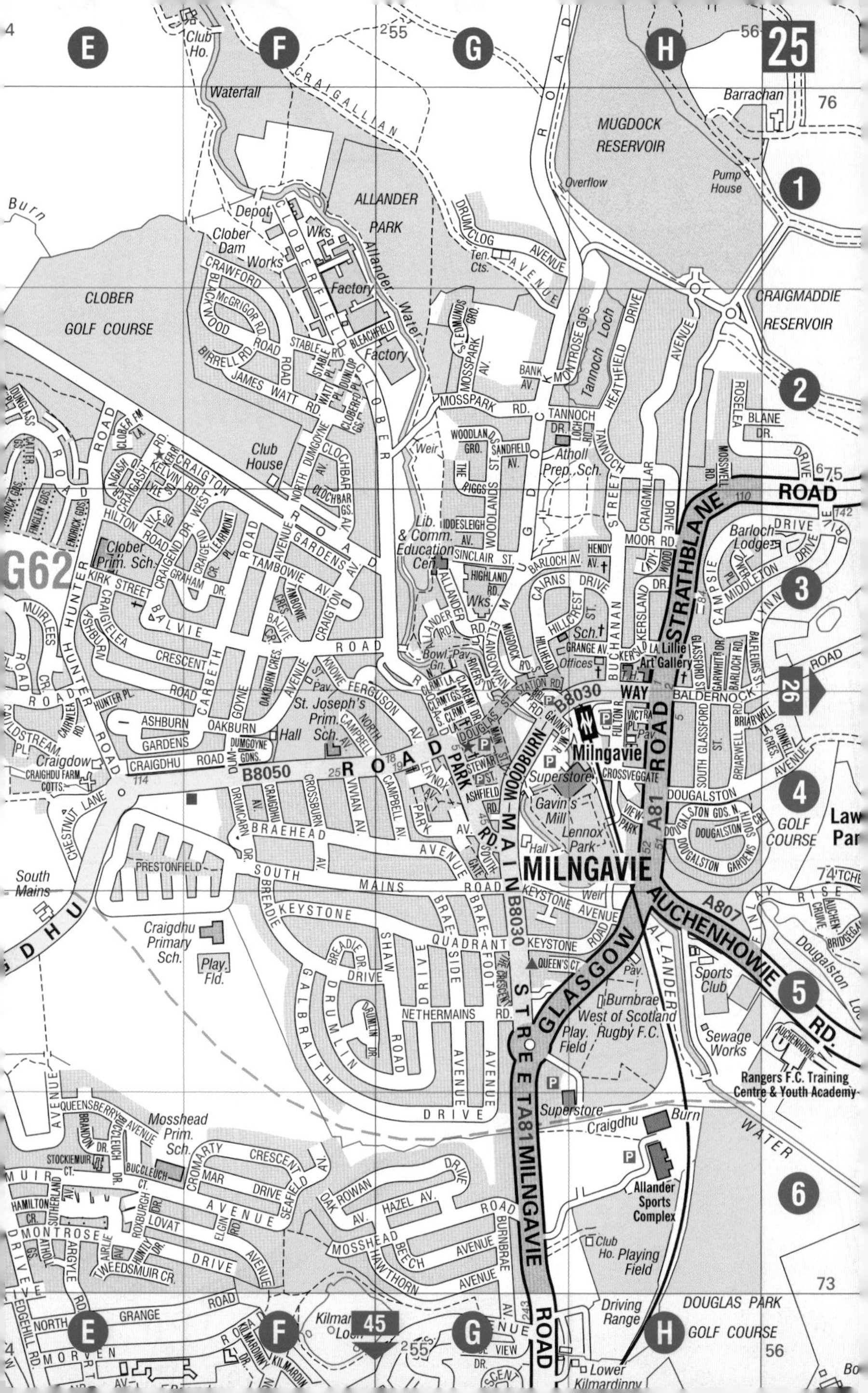

MUGDOCK RESERVOIR
CRAIGMADDIE RESERVOIR
CLOBER GOLF COURSE
ALLANDER PARK
MILNGAVIE
Milngavie
G62
STRATHBLANE ROAD
AUCHENHOWIE RD.
GLASGOW ROAD
MILNGAVIE ROAD
CRAIGDHU ROAD
B8050
B8030
A81
A807
Lillie Art Gallery
Clober Prim. Sch.
St. Joseph's Prim. Sch.
Craigdhu Primary Sch.
Mosshead Prim. Sch.
Atholl Prep. Sch.
West of Scotland Rugby F.C.
Rangers F.C. Training Centre & Youth Academy
Allander Sports Complex
DOUGLAS PARK GOLF COURSE
DOUGALSTON GOLF COURSE
Superstore
Gavin's Mill
Lennox Park
Tannoch Loch
Allander Water
Craigdhu Burn
Sewage Works
Sports Club
Driving Range
Lower Kilmardinny
Kilmardinny Loch
26
45

A
B
C
D
1
2
3
4
5
6
56
57
76
75
74
73
Barrachan
Craigash
Bankend Cottage
Craighead
Measuring Pond
Craigmaddie Lodge
ROAD
MUGDOCK RESERVOIR
CRAIGMADDIE RESERVOIR
A81
BANKELL LANE
Bankell House
Hollybank Cottages
Bankell Farm
Craigmaddie
Burn
Baldernock Wood
Manse
Glasgow
Tinkers Burn
Esporta Health & Racquets
ESPORTA DOUGALSTON GOLF COURSE
STRATHBLANE
AVENUE
BLANE DR.
ROSELEA DR.
MOSSWELL
DRIVE
Weir
The Kirkhouse
Baldernock House
Baldernock Mill
Saw Mill
Baldernoc
Kettlehill
BACK WOOD
Barloch Lodge
CAMPSIE DRIVE
MIDDLETON DR.
LYNN
Dowan
Stable Wood
BALDERNOCK ROAD
Woodhouse Cottage
Lillie Gallery
GLASSFORD ST.
BALFEURS ST.
BRIARWELL
CONNELL CRES.
DOUGALSTON AV.
SOUTH GLASSFORD ST.
G62
Craigmaddie
Boghall
DOWAN ROAD
GOLF COURSE
Lawn Park
Wards Wood
Ladies Pond
Beech Wood
Ladies Ride Wood
DOUGALSTON
DOUGALSTON GARDENS
MITCHELL DR.
LAWN PK.
LAWN PARK
EWING WK.
FINLAY RISE
AUCHENHOWIE ROAD
MURDOCH DR.
DUNMORE DR.
Jaw
Dougalston Loch
Sports
Sewage Works
Weir
Aqueduct
Rangers F.C. Training Centre & Youth Academy
Pow Burn
Bardowie Castle
BARDOWIE LOCH
Langbank Holdings
Lodge
A807
Langbank Farm
Hayhill
ALLANDER WATER
G61
BALMORE ROAD
DOUGLAS PARK GOLF COURSE
Boclair

25
46

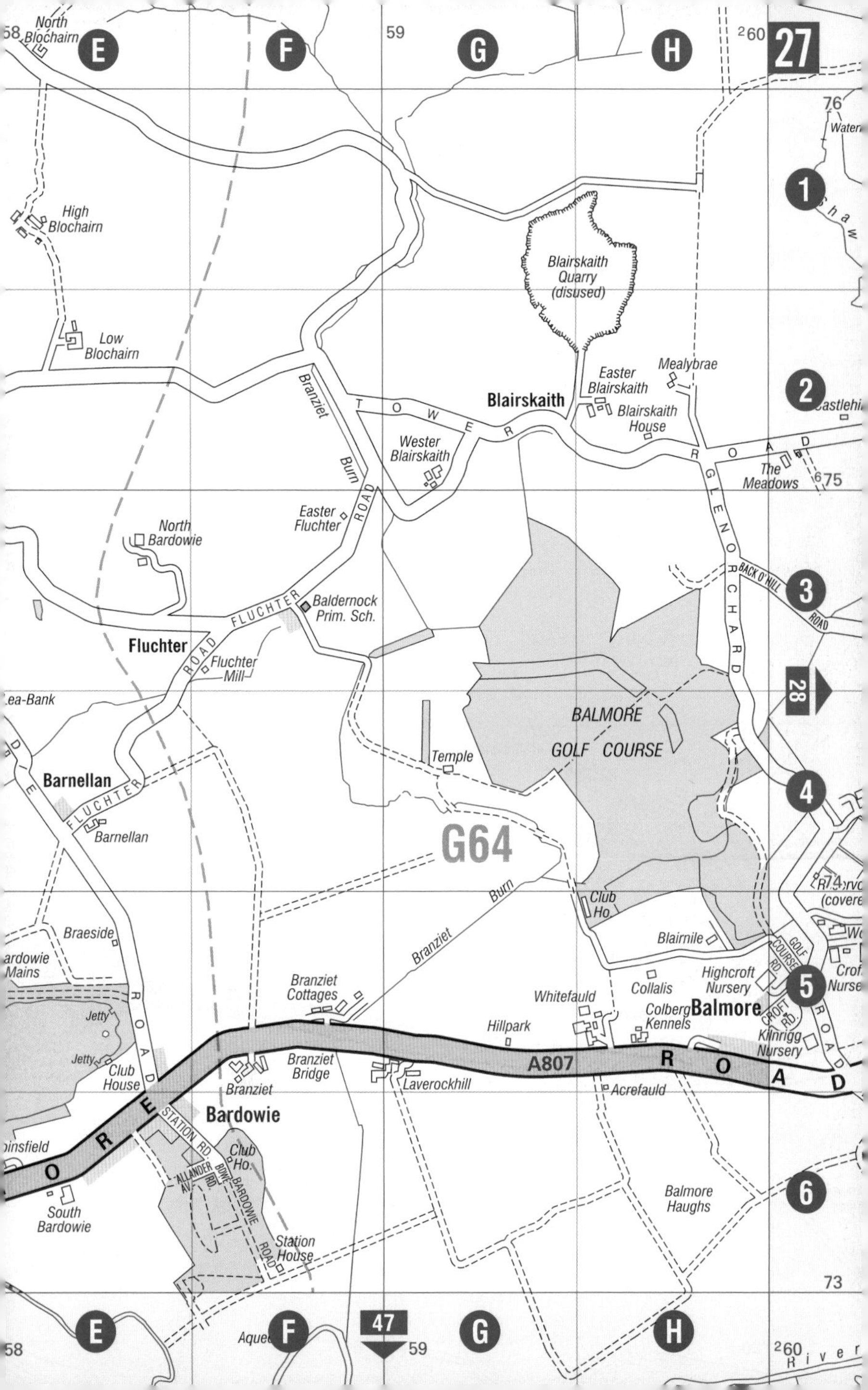

North Blochairn
58

High Blochairn

Low Blochairn

Branziet Burn

Blairskaith Quarry (disused)

Easter Blairskaith

Mealybrae

Blairskaith

Blairskaith House

Castlehi

The Meadows

675

TOWER ROAD

Wester Blairskaith

GLEN ORCHARD ROAD

BACK O'MILL ROAD

North Bardowie

Easter Fluchter

1

2

3

76
Water

260

Fluchter

FLUCHTER ROAD

Baldernock Prim. Sch.

Fluchter Mill

28

Lea-Bank

Barnellan

FLUCHTER

Barnellan

BALMORE GOLF COURSE

Temple

G64

4

Braeside

Burn

Branziet

Club Ho.

Blairnile

Branziet

Collalis

Highcroft Nursery

H14 rvo (covere

We

Crof Nurse

ardowie Mains

ROAD

Jetty

Jetty

Club House

Branziet Cottages

Whitefauld

Hillpark

Colberg Kennels

Balmore

Klinrigg Nursery

GOLF COURSE RD

CROFT RD

Crof Nurse

5

insfield

Branziet Bridge

Laverockhill

A807 ROAD

Acrefauld

Branziet

STATION RD

Bardowie

ALLANDER AV

BRAE

BARDOWIE ROAD

Club Ho.

South Bardowie

Station House

Balmore Haughs

6

73

Glenwynd Wood
6
Waterfalls
Waterfall
Shaw Burn
Barraston Farm
Barraston Holdings
Nursery
Barraston Cottages
BARRASTON ROAD
Castlehill
TOWER ROAD
The Meadows
Hillhead
Barraston House
Leitchbank
Drumbain Cottage
Dounne
Ford
Langshot Farm
Acre Valley
ACRE VALLEY ROAD
Resr. (cov.)
Drumfarm
GLENORCH
BACK O' HILL ROAD
Back o' Hill Farm
Hillacre
Craighead
TOWER ROAD
West Balgrochan Farm
West Balgrochan
WARDEND ROAD
W. BALGROCHAN RD.
BLAIR GDS.
CAMPBELL PL.
NEVIS DR.
BUCHANAN PL.
MORAY DR.
WALLACE
ATHOLL AV.
WEST RD.
Torrance Prim. Sch.
TORRANCE
Tower Farm
Glenside
G64
27
Water Works
Reservoirs (covered)
Resr. (cov.)
Works
Works
Croft Nursery
Balmore Golf Course
GOLF COURSE RD.
Nursery
CROFT RD.
Kilnrigg Nursery
Balmore
CRAIGMADDIE GDS.
FORTH RD.
SMEATON AV.
CLYDE AV.
FORTH ROAD
DUNDAS AV.
CHARLOTTE AV.
JOHN McEWAN WY.
MICHAEL McPARLAND DR.
CRAIGMARLOCH AV.
QUEENS WY.
ALLANDER DR.
CRAIGBARNET AV.
MAIN B822
FIRBANK
ROAD
KELVINBRIDGE ROUNDABOUT
Torrance Bridge
BALMORE ROAD
A807
BALMORE ROAD
PATERSON'S LAUN
Bogside Farmhouse
Sewage Works
Kelvin
River
KEIR GOLF COURSE
48
A B C D
1 2 3 4 5 6
260 61 76 75 74 73

E
F
G
H
7
63
62
64
76
Kinkell Farm
Braeholm Farm
Waterfall
Waterfall
B822
Whitehill
Balquharrage Cottages
Balquharrage
Wetsho
rdbank
Glasgow
ROAD
KIRKINTILLOCH ROAD
675
East Balgrochan Farm
Weir
Craigen Glen Cottage
Carlston Cottages
Carlston
EASTERTON COTTAGES
East Balgrochan
Red Burn
B822
West Carlestoun
Ferrymill House
Balgrochan House
HAYSTON GOLF COURSE
Hayston
30
CAMPSIE
SCHOOL ROAD
MILL CRES.
KING'S PK.
Bowl. Gn.
KELVINDALE
WOODMILL DR.
PARK CRES.
Playing Field
Wardhill
Meadowbank Farm
G66
Kelvin
74
HAWTHORN DR.
CORMACK AV.
ST.
DALRIADA DR.
GUTHRIE PL.
VIOLA PL.
HEARN DR.
KELVIN VIEW ROAD
River
Meadowbank House
KELVIN
KELCLARK
Hayst
Sewage Works
ADAMSLIE CR.
Sandy Knowes
GLASGOW RD
A803
RANCE ROAD
A807
Easter Cadder
Glasgow Bri.
Hungryside Bridge (Drawbridge)
Slipway
EASTER CADDER COTTAGES
Forth and Clyde Canal
73
KIRKINTILLOCH ROAD
Leafield
49
1
2
3
4
5
6

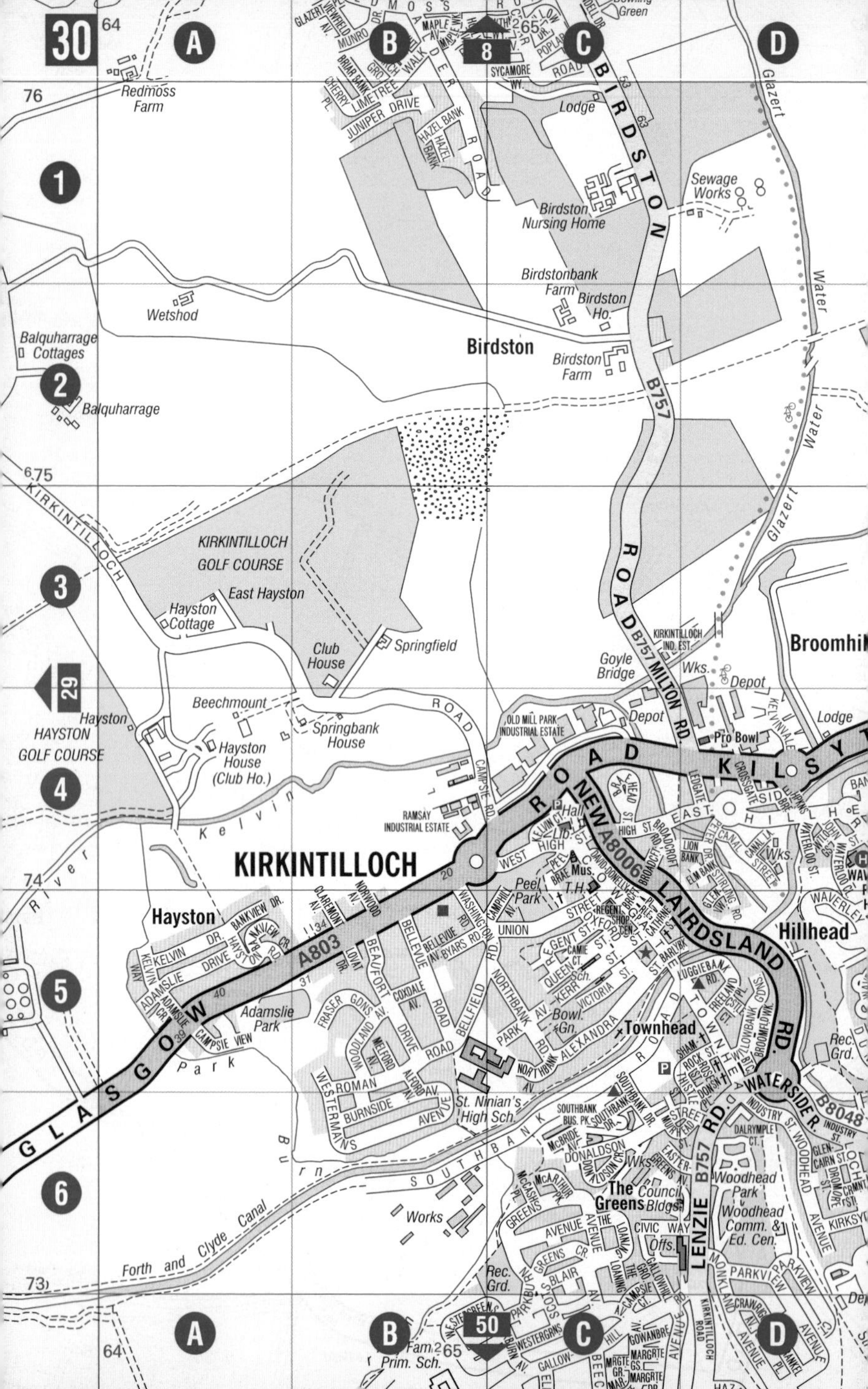

Redmoss Farm
Wetshod
Balquharrage Cottages
Balquharrage
Birdston
Birdston Nursing Home
Birdstonbank Farm
Birdston Ho.
Birdston Farm
Sewage Works
Glazert Water
BIRDSTON ROAD
B757
KIRKINTILLOCH GOLF COURSE
East Hayston
Hayston Cottage
Club House
Springfield
Beechmount
Springbank House
Hayston House (Club Ho.)
Hayston
HAYSTON GOLF COURSE
River Kelvin
KIRKINTILLOCH
Goyle Bridge
KIRKINTILLOCH IND. EST.
OLD MILL PARK INDUSTRIAL ESTATE
RAMSAY INDUSTRIAL ESTATE
Broomhil
Pro Bowl
Depot
Hillhead
Townhead
Adamslie Park
GLASGOW ROAD
A803
NEW LAIRDSLAND RD.
A8006
St. Ninian's High Sch.
SOUTHBANK ROAD
Forth and Clyde Canal
Works
The Greens
Council Bldgs.
Woodhead Park
Woodhead Comm. & Ed. Cen.
LENZIE RD.
B8048
Rec. Grd.

Glasgow
G66
Alton Smallholdings
Inchbelle Farm
Inchbreck
Bridgend Farm
Shirva Dyke
Auchendavie Farm
NORTH LANARKSHIRE
EAST DUNBARTONSHIRE
Inchbelly Bri.
A803
B8023
B8048
BROOMHILL INDUSTRIAL ESTATE
Kelvinbank Training Cen.
Wks.
Playing Field
Cleddans
Harestanes
Langmuir
Merkland
Rosebank
Comm. Cen.
Merkland Sch.
St.Flannan's Prim. Sch.
Oxgang Prim. Sch.
Kirkintilloch High Sch.
Monastery
Duntiblae
Waterside
Oxgang
Cemetery
Sports Ground
Oxgang Bri.
St. Ninian's Bridge
St. Agatha's Prim. Sch.
Gartconner Prim. Sch.
Playground
Braes of Yetts
Black Burn
Lodge
Club
Ford
Caurnie View
Wallace Cottage
MUIRHEAD COTTAGES
WOODILEE INDUSTRIAL ESTATE
Recreat Groun
Tint
AUCHENDAVIE
TINTOCK RD.
ELLISLAND DR.
BURNS ROAD
LANGMUIR ROAD
NEWDYKE ROAD
WOODSTOCK ROAD
MUIRSIDE AVENUE
BARRHILL ROAD
GARTCONNER AV.
HIGHFIELD ROAD
KENILWORTH
FRIARS CROFT
MERKLAND DRIVE
CROSSDYKES
DUNTIBLAE RD
MARKET
BANKHEAD
CALFMUIR ROAD
RUTHERFORD AV.
76
675
74
73
68
66
67
9
51
32
E
F
G
H
1
2
3
4
5
6

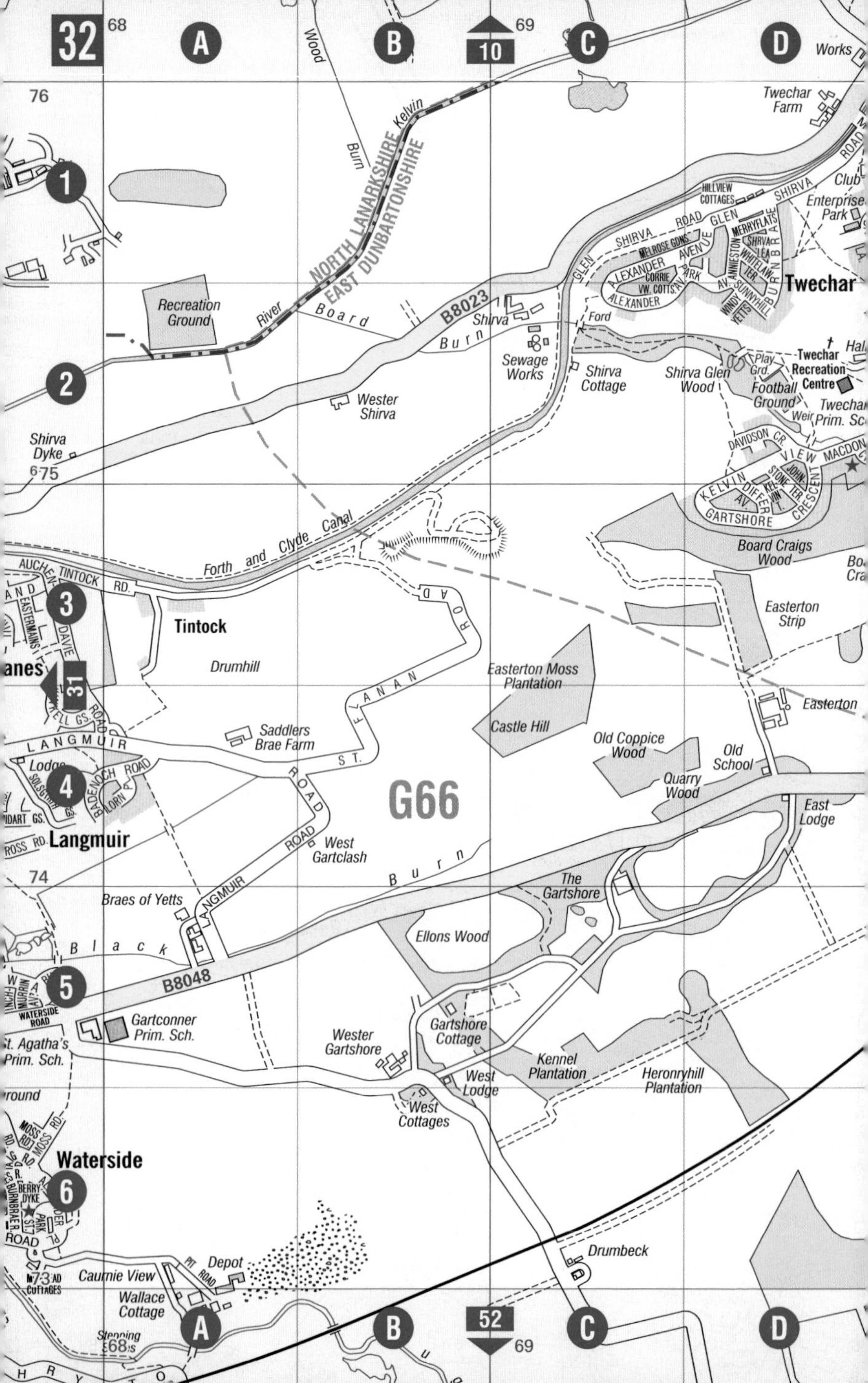

A
B
C
D
10
52
31
68
69
76
75
74
73
1
2
3
4
5
6
NORTH LANARKSHIRE
EAST DUNBARTONSHIRE
River Kelvin
Wood Burn
Board Burn
Shirva Burn
Recreation Ground
B8023
B8048
Shirva
Sewage Works
Shirva Cottage
Wester Shirva
Shirva Dyke
Forth and Clyde Canal
Ford
Shirva Glen Wood
Twechar
Twechar Farm
Works
Club
Enterprise Park
Twechar Recreation Centre
Play Grd.
Football Ground
Weir
Twechar Prim. Sc
Board Craigs Wood
Easterton Strip
Easterton
Old School
Quarry Wood
Old Coppice Wood
Castle Hill
Easterton Moss Plantation
East Lodge
The Gartshore
Ellons Wood
Kennel Plantation
Heronryhill Plantation
Gartshore Cottage
Wester Gartshore
West Lodge
West Cottages
Drumbeck
Tintock
Drumhill
Saddlers Brae Farm
G66
West Gartclash
Braes of Yetts
Black Burn
Langmuir
Lodge
Gartconner Prim. Sch.
St. Agatha's Prim. Sch.
Waterside
Caurnie View
Wallace Cottage
Depot
PIT ROAD
AUCHENTINTOCK RD.
LANGMUIR
LANGMUIR ROAD
FLANAN ST.
ROAD
BADENOCH ROAD
LORN
SHIRVA ROAD
GLEN SHIRVA ROAD
HILLVIEW COTTAGES
MELROSE GDNS.
ALEXANDER AVENUE
CORRIE
VW. COTTS.
PARK AV.
MERRYFLATS
ANNIESTON
SHIRVA LEA
WHITELAW TER.
SUNNYHILL
WINDY YETTS
BURNBRAE
DAVIDSON CR.
VIEW
MACDON
KELVIN
DIFFER AV.
GARTSHORE
CRESCENT
JOHN. STONE TER.
KEL VIN T.
WATERSIDE ROAD
MOSS RD.
BERRY DYKE
BURNBRAER ROAD
PARK ST.

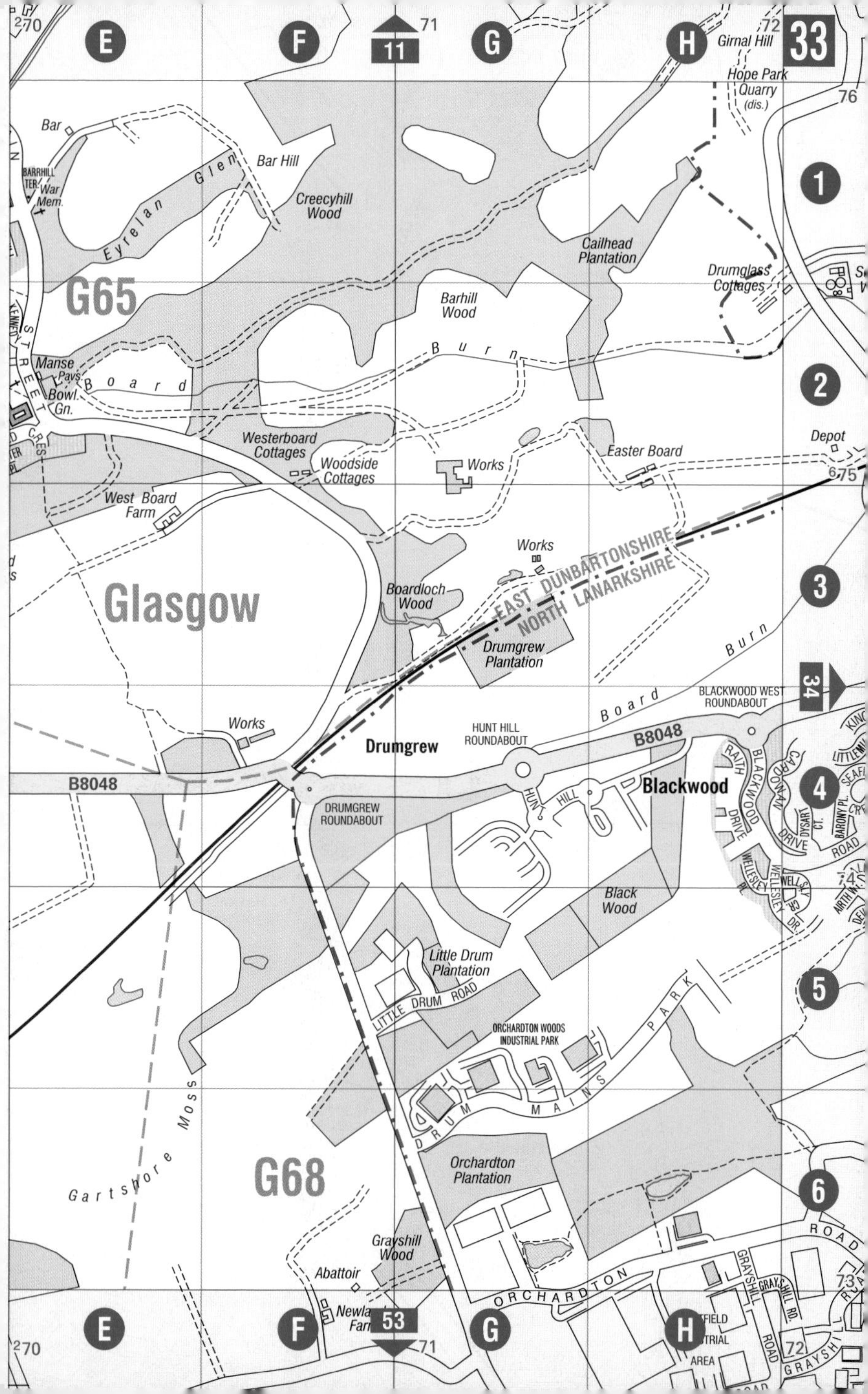
E
F
11
G
H
Girnal Hill
Hope Park
Quarry
(dis.)
Bar
Bar Hill
BARRHILL TER.
War Mem.
Eyrelan Glen
Creecyhill Wood
Cailhead Plantation
Drumglass Cottages
G65
Barhill Wood
KENNEDY STREET
Manse
Pavs.
Bowl. Gn.
Board Burn
Westerboard Cottages
Woodside Cottages
Works
Easter Board
Depot
West Board Farm
Works
EAST DUNBARTONSHIRE
NORTH LANARKSHIRE
Glasgow
Boardloch Wood
Drumgrew Plantation
Board Burn
BLACKWOOD WEST ROUNDABOUT
34
Works
HUNT HILL ROUNDABOUT
B8048
Drumgrew
B8048
Blackwood
DRUMGREW ROUNDABOUT
HUNT HILL
RAITH
BLACKWOOD DRIVE
CARDOWAN DRIVE
DYSART CT.
BARONY PL.
ROAD
WELLESLEY PL.
WELLESLEY DR.
Black Wood
Little Drum Plantation
LITTLE DRUM ROAD
ORCHARDTON WOODS INDUSTRIAL PARK
DRUM MAINS PARK
Gartshore Moss
G68
Orchardton Plantation
Grayshill Wood
Abattoir
ORCHARDTON ROAD
GRAYSHILL ROAD
GRAYSHILL RD.
AREA
53
1
2
3
4
5
6
70
71
72
73
74
75
76

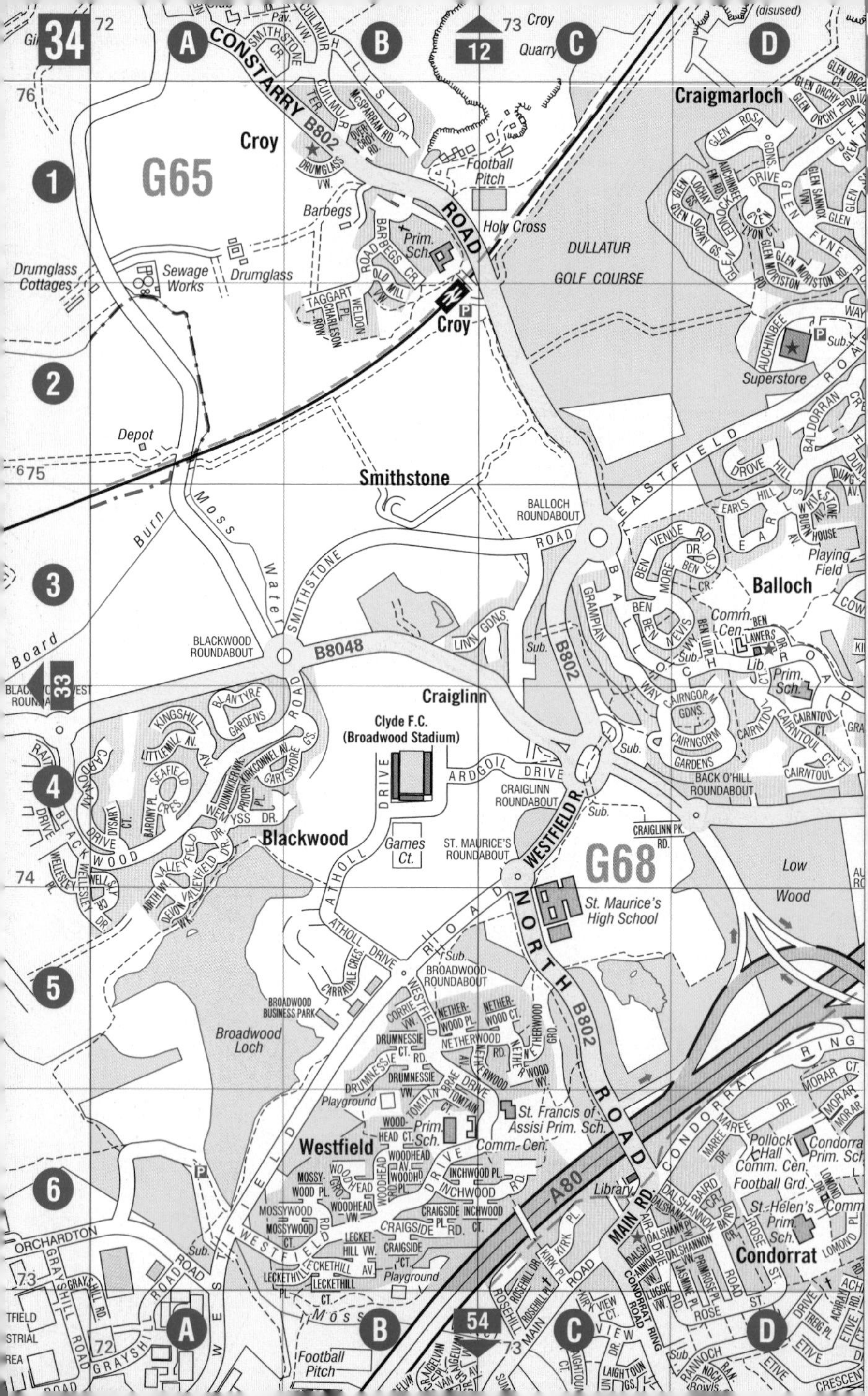
34
12
33
54
G65
G68
Croy
Croy Quarry
Craigmarloch
Barbegs
Drumglass
Drumglass Cottages
Sewage Works
Football Pitch
Holy Cross
Prim. Sch.
DULLATUR GOLF COURSE
Superstore
Depot
Smithstone
BALLOCH ROUNDABOUT
BLACKWOOD ROUNDABOUT
Balloch
Playing Field
Comm. Cen.
Lib.
Craiglinn
Clyde F.C. (Broadwood Stadium)
CRAIGLINN ROUNDABOUT
BACK O'HILL ROUNDABOUT
Blackwood
Games Ct.
ST. MAURICE'S ROUNDABOUT
St. Maurice's High School
Low Wood
BROADWOOD ROUNDABOUT
BROADWOOD BUSINESS PARK
Broadwood Loch
Westfield
Playground
St. Francis of Assisi Prim. Sch.
Comm. Cen.
Library
Pollock Hall Comm. Cen.
Condorrat Prim. Sch.
Football Grd.
St. Helen's Prim. Sch.
Condorrat
Football Pitch
CONSTARRY ROAD B802
B8048
B802
NORTH ROAD B802
A80
WESTFIELD DR.
SMITHSTONE ROAD
EASTFIELD ROAD
BALLOCH ROAD
ARDGOIL DRIVE
ATHOLL DRIVE
BLACKWOOD DRIVE
WESTFIELD ROAD
CONDORRAT RING ROAD
MAIN RD.
Burn
Moss Water
Board
A
B
C
D
1
2
3
4
5
6
72
73
74
75
76

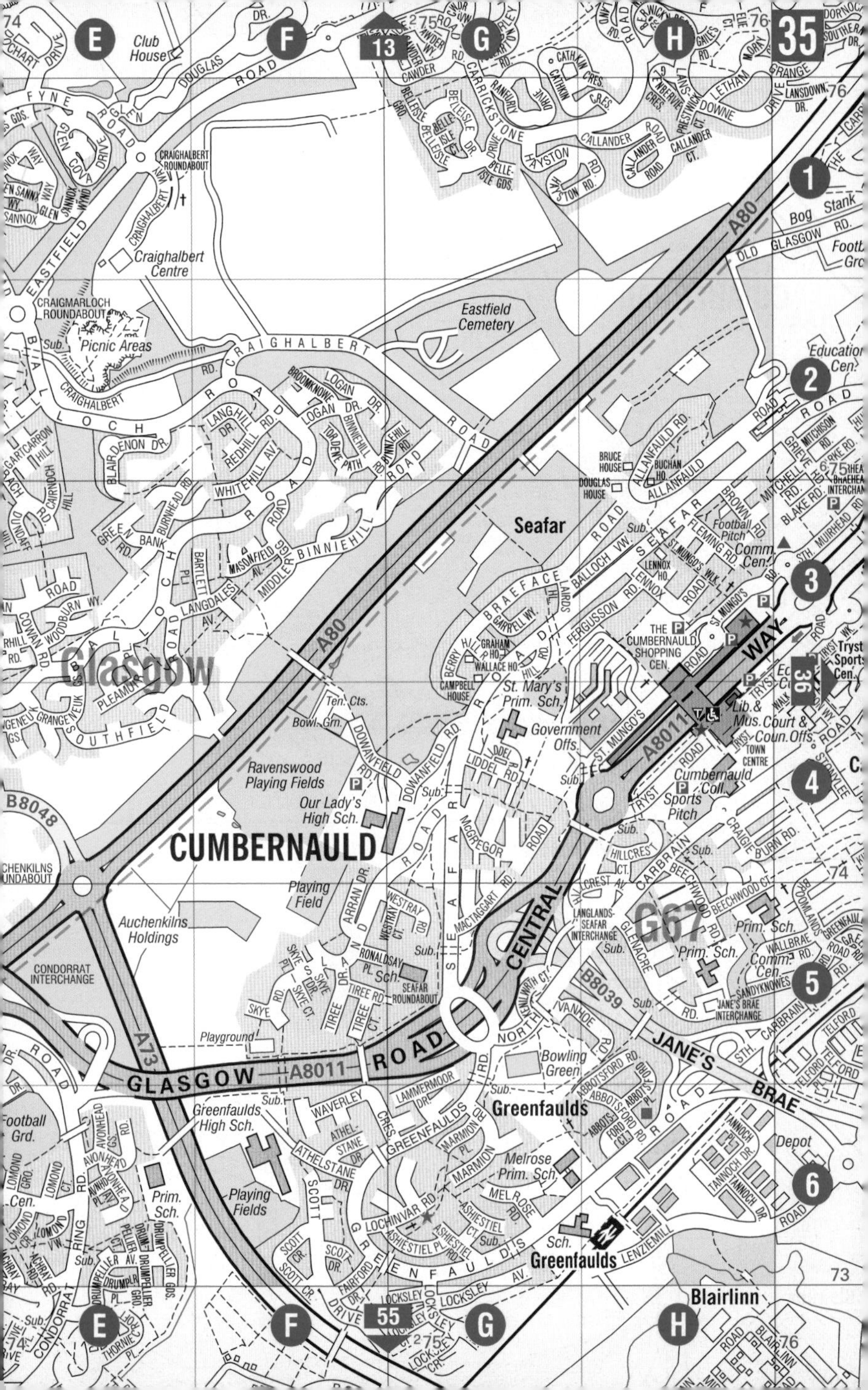

CUMBERNAULD
Seafar
Greenfaulds
Blairlinn
Glasgow
G67
A80
A8011
A73
B8048
B8039
GLASGOW ROAD
CENTRAL WAY
JANE'S BRAE
Eastfield Cemetery
Craighalbert Centre
Picnic Areas
Ravenswood Playing Fields
Our Lady's High Sch.
Auchenkilns Holdings
CONDORRAT INTERCHANGE
Greenfaulds High Sch.
The Cumbernauld Shopping Cen.
Cumbernauld Coll.
Government Offs.
St. Mary's Prim. Sch.
Melrose Prim. Sch.
Bowling Green
Lib. & Mus. Court & Coun. Offs.
Town Centre
Langlands-Seafar Interchange
Jane's Brae Interchange
Seafar Roundabout
Craighalbert Roundabout
Craigmarloch Roundabout
Depot
13
55
36

CUMBERNAULD
Cumbernauld Village
Cumbernauld House
Kildrum
Carbrain
Lenziemill
Blairlinn
Glasgow G67
Cumbernauld Theatre
Kildrum Prim. Sch.
Sacred Heart Prim. Sch.
Carbrain Prim. Sch.
Redburn School
Kildrum Plantation
Cumbernauld High School
Abronhill Prim. Sch.
Tryst Sports Cen.
Superstore
Educational Cen.
Football Grd.
Wilderness Brae
Burial Grd.
Cumbernauld Bowl. Club
Glencryan Plantation
Quarry (disused)
Greenyards Interchange
Carbrain Ind. Est.
Works
Depot
Factory
Cumbernauld
Reservoir (covered)
Greenside
West Waterhead
Waterhead Farm
Golf Driving Range
Sandyknowes
Luggie Bridge
Tannoch Farm
The Mote
Bog Stank
A80
A8011
B8054
B8039
Central Wy.
Lenziemill Road
Forest Road
Kildrum Road
Lye Brae
Seafar Road
Jane's Brae
Vault Glen
Red Burn
Glencryan Burn
Waterfall
Kelvin Ind. Estate
Muirhead Roundabout
Kildrum South Roundabout
14
35
76
77
75
74
73

Abronhill
Abronhill High Sch.
Football Grd.
Tennis Cts.
St. Lucy's Prim. Sch.
Prim. Sch.
Lib.
Comm. Cen.
Bowling Greens
Kilt Bridge
Walton
Crowbank
Glenhead
Glenhead Wood
BLACKTHORN ROUNDABOUT
Mid Forest
Forest Plantation
FANNYSIDE MUIR
FANNYSIDE LOCHS
Glencryan Burn
PALACERIGG GOLF COURSE
PALACERIGG COUNTRY PARK
Palacerigg Cottage
Visitor Cen.
Palacerigg House
Cattle Grid
Club House
PALACERIGG (CUMBERNAULD) GOLF COURSE
Picnic Area
Cherrybank Nurseries
Herd's Hill
MOSS ROAD
FOREST ROAD
OAK ROAD
PINE RD.
ALMOND RD.
ELM DR.
HAWTHORN RD.
GEAN CT.
BIRCH RD.
LIME CRESCENT
HORNBEAM RD.
MAPLE CT.
15

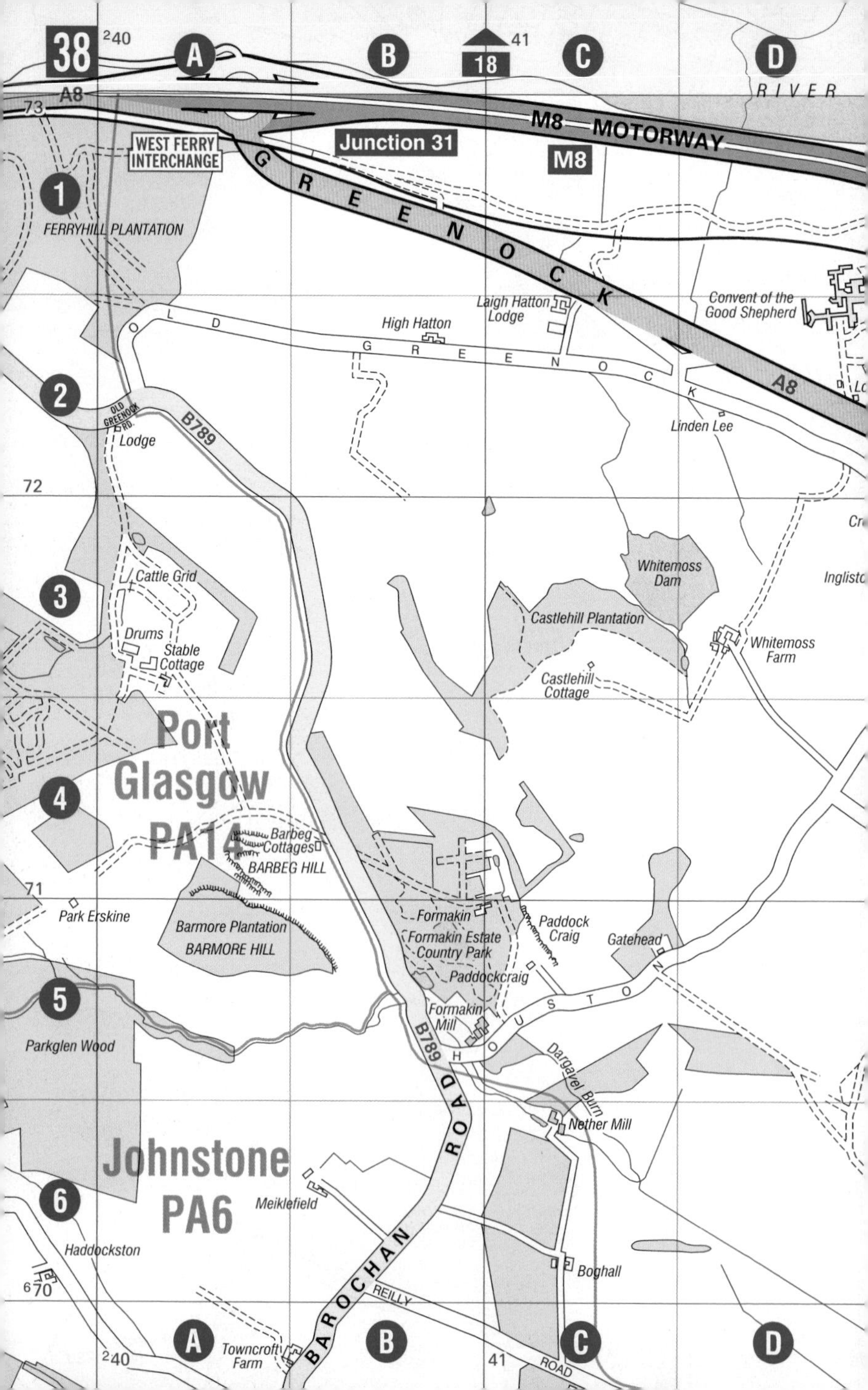

A
B
C
D
18
RIVER
A8
M8 MOTORWAY
M8
Junction 31
WEST FERRY INTERCHANGE
GREENOCK
FERRYHILL PLANTATION
OLD GREENOCK
High Hatton
Laigh Hatton Lodge
Convent of the Good Shepherd
A8
Linden Lee
OLD GREENOCK RD.
Lodge
B789
Whitemoss Dam
Castlehill Plantation
Inglisto
Whitemoss Farm
Castlehill Cottage
Cattle Grid
Drums
Stable Cottage
Port Glasgow PA14
Barbeg Cottages
BARBEG HILL
Park Erskine
Barmore Plantation
BARMORE HILL
Formakin
Formakin Estate Country Park
Paddock Craig
Paddockcraig
Gatehead
HOUSTON
Formakin Mill
B789
Dargavel Burn
Parkglen Wood
Nether Mill
Johnstone PA6
Meiklefield
ROAD
BAROCHAN
Haddockston
Boghall
REILLY
Towncroft Farm
ROAD

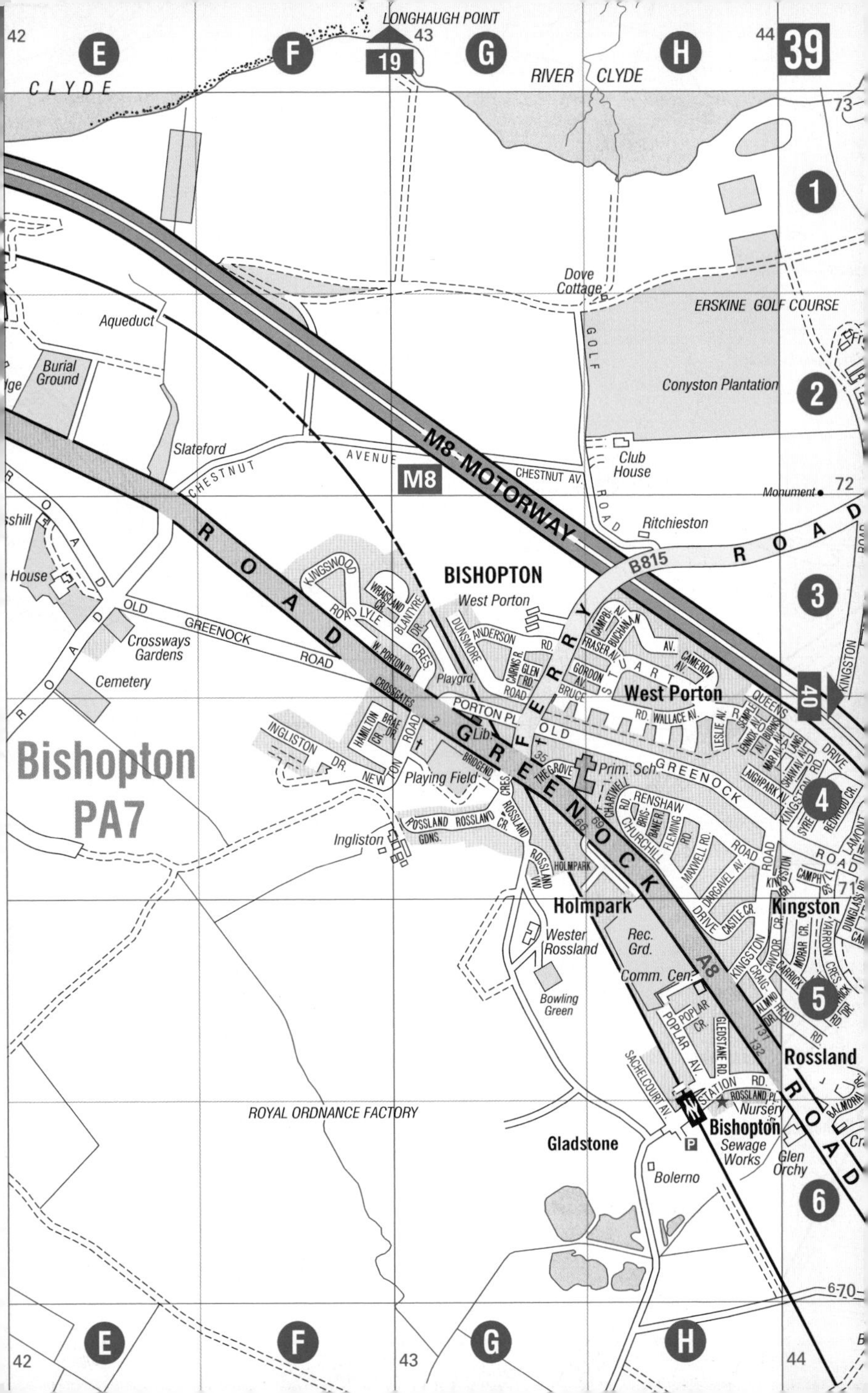

LONGHAUGH POINT
19
RIVER CLYDE
CLYDE
ERSKINE GOLF COURSE
Conyston Plantation
Dove Cottage
Aqueduct
Burial Ground
Slateford
CHESTNUT AVENUE
M8
M8 MOTORWAY
CHESTNUT AV.
Club House
Monument
Ritchieston
B815 ROAD
BISHOPTON
West Porton
Crossways Gardens
Cemetery
OLD GREENOCK ROAD
GREENOCK ROAD
West Porton
40
Bishopton PA7
INGLISTON DR.
Playing Field
Prim. Sch.
Ingliston
Holmpark
Wester Rossland
Rec. Grd.
Comm. Cen.
Bowling Green
Kingston
Rossland
ROYAL ORDNANCE FACTORY
Gladstone
Bishopton
Nursery
Sewage Works
Glen Orchy
Bolerno
A8
E
F
G
H
1
2
3
4
5
6
42
43
44
73
72
71
70

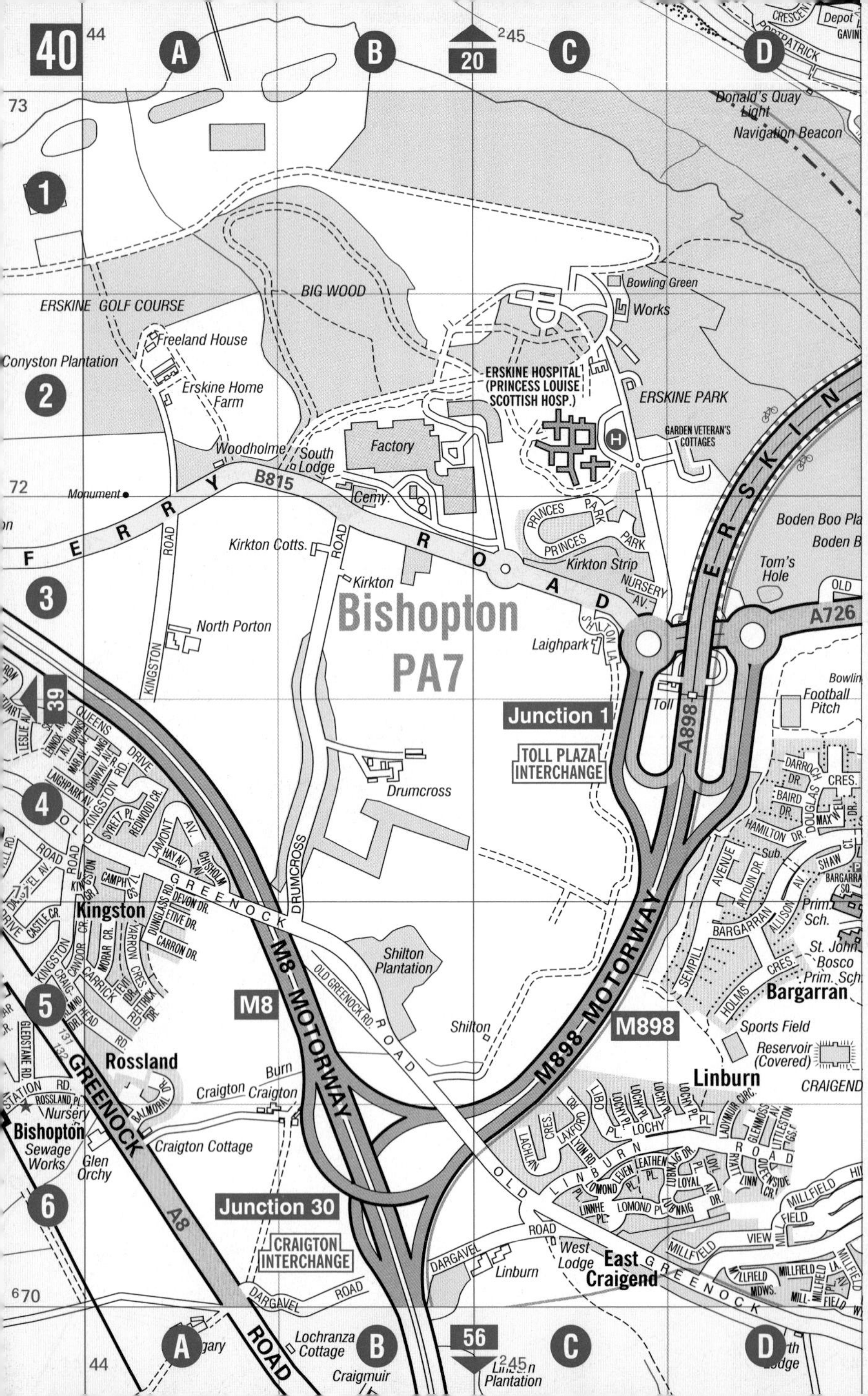

A
B
C
D
20
56
39
1
2
3
4
5
6
44
245
73
72
71
670
Donald's Quay Light
Navigation Beacon
ERSKINE GOLF COURSE
BIG WOOD
Freeland House
Conyston Plantation
Erskine Home Farm
Woodholme
South Lodge
Factory
ERSKINE HOSPITAL (PRINCESS LOUISE SCOTTISH HOSP.)
ERSKINE PARK
GARDEN VETERAN'S COTTAGES
Bowling Green
Works
Monument
FERRY ROAD
B815
Cemy.
PRINCES PARK
Kirkton Strip
NURSERY AV.
Kirkton Cotts.
Kirkton
Bishopton
PA7
North Porton
KINGSTON ROAD
Laighpark
SHILTON LA.
Boden Boo
Tom's Hole
A726
ERSKINE
A898
Toll
Junction 1
TOLL PLAZA INTERCHANGE
Football Pitch
Drumcross
DRUMCROSS ROAD
QUEENS DRIVE
OLD ROAD
Kingston
GREENOCK
M8 MOTORWAY
M8
M898 MOTORWAY
M898
Shilton Plantation
OLD GREENOCK RD.
Shilton
Bargarran
Sports Field
Reservoir (Covered)
St. John Bosco Prim. Sch.
Prim. Sch.
Rossland
Craigton Burn
Craigton
Bishopton Sewage Works
Nursery
Craigton Cottage
Glen Orchy
Junction 30
CRAIGTON INTERCHANGE
A8
GREENOCK ROAD
DARGAVEL ROAD
Linburn
West Lodge
East Craigend
LINBURN ROAD
CRAIGEND
Lochranza Cottage
Craigmuir
Plantation
MILLFIELD

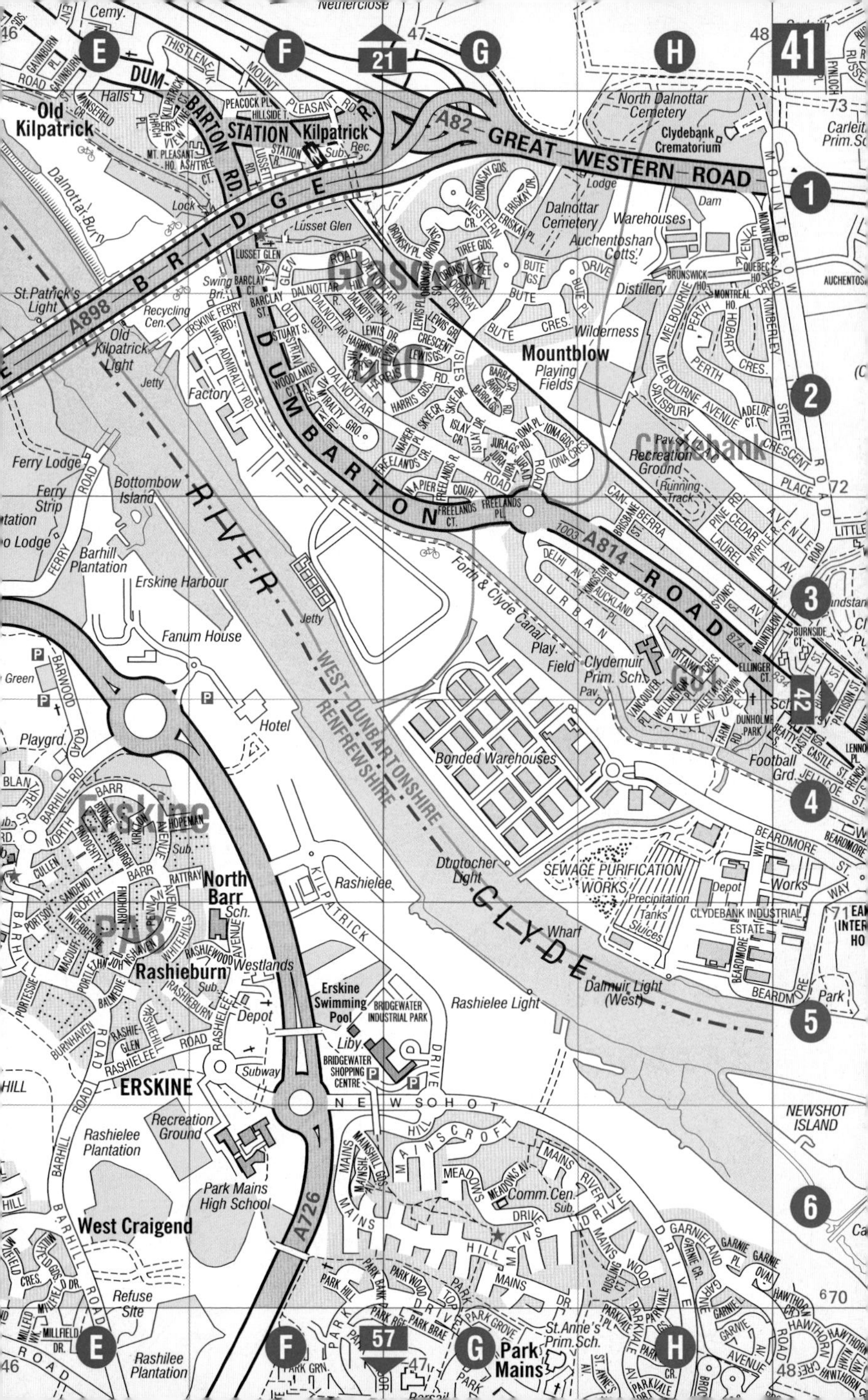
Old Kilpatrick
Kilpatrick
STATION
GREAT WESTERN ROAD
North Dalnottar Cemetery
Clydebank Crematorium
Dalnottar Cemetery
Auchentoshan Cotts.
Distillery
Mountblow
Playing Fields
Clydebank
Recreation Ground
A898
BRIDGE
A82
A814
ROAD
DUMBARTON
RIVER CLYDE
WEST DUNBARTONSHIRE
RENFREWSHIRE
Bonded Warehouses
SEWAGE PURIFICATION WORKS
CLYDEBANK INDUSTRIAL ESTATE
Erskine Harbour
Fanum House
Hotel
Erskine
North Barr
Rashieburn
ERSKINE
Erskine Swimming Pool
BRIDGEWATER INDUSTRIAL PARK
BRIDGEWATER SHOPPING CENTRE
Park Mains High School
West Craigend
NEWSHOT ISLAND
Park Mains
A726
21
57
42

22
58
41
A
B
C
D
1
2
3
4
5
6
GREAT WESTERN ROAD
A82
DUMBARTON ROAD
A810
GLASGOW ROAD
KILBOWIE ROAD
A8014
DUNTOCHER ROAD
B814
A814
DUNTOCHER
Antonine Sports Cen.
Golden Hill Park
Golden Hill
Goldenhill Prim. Sch.
St. Mary's Sch.
Football Park
Carleith Prim. Sch.
Kilpatrick Sch.
Auchentoshan Occupational Centre
AUCHENTOSHAN ESTATE
Ocean Field
DALMUIR (CLYDEBANK) MUNICIPAL GOLF COURSE
Duntocher Burn
Parkhall
Clydebank G81
Library
Boquhanran Park
Radnor Park
Clydebank High Sch.
Playing Field
Kilbowie Prim. Sch.
Clydebank Coll.
KILBOWIE
Singer
DALMUIR
Dalmuir
Club House
Bandstand
Putting Grn.
Clydebank Public Park
Bowl. Green
St. Stephen's Prim. Sch.
Sports Ground
Nursing Home
Works
Depot
CLYDEBANK INDUSTRIAL ESTATE
HEALTH CARE INTERNATIONAL HOSPITAL
Park
Helipad
RIVER CLYDE
WEST DUNBARTONSHIRE
RENFREWSHIRE
Newshot Light
Dalmuir Light
Erskine PA8
NEWSHOT ISLAND
Causeway
CLYDEBANK BUSINESS PARK
Forth & Clyde Canal
Coun. Offs.
CLYDE SHOP. CEN.
CLYDEBANK
Clydebank District Museum
Clydebank

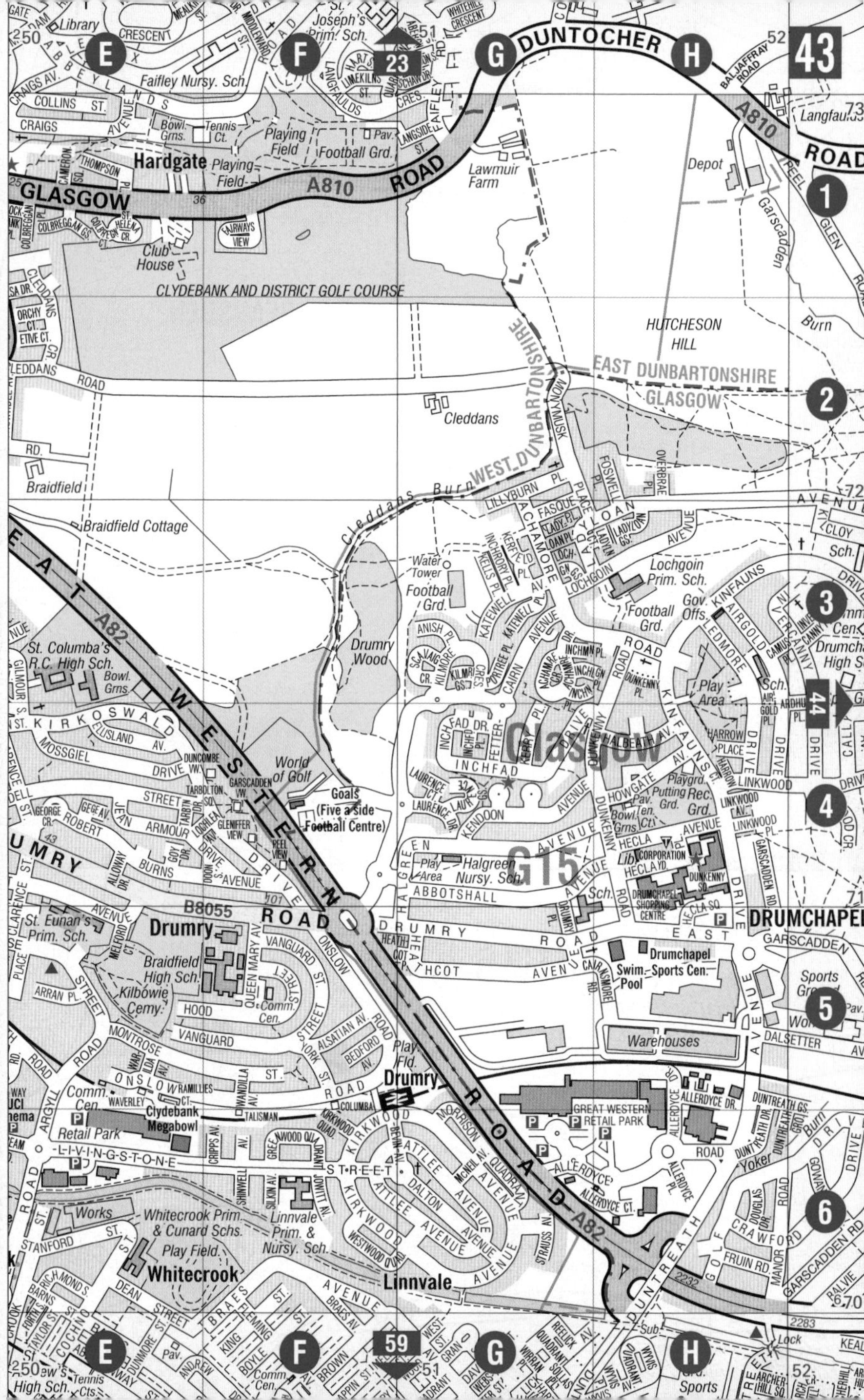
43
23
59
44
E
F
G
H
1
2
3
4
5
6
Library
CRESCENT
Faifley Nursy. Sch.
Joseph's Prim. Sch.
WHITEHILL CRESCENT
DUNTOCHER
BALJAFFRAY ROAD
A810
ROAD
Langfaulds
CRAIGS AV.
COLLINS ST.
CRAIGS
AVENUE
Bowl. Grns.
Tennis Ct.
Playing Field
Football Grd.
LANGSIDE ST.
FAIFLEY
LANGFAULDS
Hardgate
THOMPSON PL.
CAMERON SQ.
Playing Field
GLASGOW
A810
ROAD
Lawmuir Farm
Depot
Garscadden
REEL GLEN
COLBREGGAN GS.
ST. HELENA CR.
FAIRWAYS VIEW
Club House
CLYDEBANK AND DISTRICT GOLF COURSE
CLEDDANS
ORCHY CT.
ETIVE CT.
HUTCHESON HILL
Burn
EAST DUNBARTONSHIRE
GLASGOW
WEST DUNBARTONSHIRE
CLEDDANS ROAD
Cleddans
Braidfield
Cleddans Burn
LILLYBURN PL.
FASQUE PL.
FOSWELL PL.
OVERBRAE PL.
ACHAMORE
LADYLOAN
AVENUE
CLOY
Sch.
DRIVE
Braidfield Cottage
Water Tower
Football Grd.
INCHCRORY PL.
KERFIELD PL.
KELLS PL.
LOCHGOIN
Lochgoin Prim. Sch.
Gov. Offs.
KINFAUNS
AIRGOLD
LEDMORE
Football Grd.
Comm. Cen.
Drumchapel High Sch.
GREAT WESTERN ROAD
A82
St. Columba's R.C. High Sch.
Bowl. Grns.
KIRKOSWALD
ELLISLAND AV.
MOSSGIEL DRIVE
Drumry Wood
KATEWELL AV.
ANISH PL.
SCALVAIG CR.
KILMORE CRES.
CAIRN AVENUE
INCHMURRIN DR.
DUNKENNY PL.
Play Area
Sch.
AIRGOLD PL.
ARDHUE PL.
Glasgow
INCHFAD DR.
FETTERCAIRN
HALBEATH AV.
HARROW PLACE
KINFAUNS DRIVE
DUNCOMBE VW.
TARBOLTON SQ.
GARSCADDEN VW.
STREET
World of Golf
Goals (Five a side Football Centre)
INCHFAD
HOWGATE AV.
Playgrd. Putting Grd.
Rec. Grd.
LINKWOOD
LINKWOOD AV.
GEORGE CR.
ROBERT
JEAN ARMOUR
GLENIFFER VIEW
LAURENCE CT.
LAURENCE DR.
KENDOON AVENUE
Pav. Ten. Cts.
Bowl. Grns.
HECLA AVENUE
DRUMRY
BURNS AVENUE
PEEL VIEW
HALGREEN AVENUE
Play Area
Halgreen Nursy. Sch.
G15
Lib.
CORPORATION
HECLA YD.
DUNKENNY SQ.
GARSCADDEN RD.
ABBOTSHALL AVENUE
Sch.
DRUMCHAPEL SHOPPING CENTRE
HECLA SQ.
St. Eunan's Prim. Sch.
B8055
ROAD
Drumry
DRUMRY ROAD EAST
DRUMCHAPEL
GARSCADDEN
MELFORD CT.
VANGUARD ST.
ONSLOW
HEATHCOT AVENUE
CAIRNSMORE RD.
Drumchapel Sports Cen.
Swim. Pool
Braidfield High Sch.
QUEEN MARY AV.
Sports Ground
ARRAN PL.
STREET
Kilbowie Cemy.
HOOD
Comm. Cen.
Warehouses
DALSETTER AV.
MONTROSE
VANGUARD
ALSATIAN AV.
BEDFORD AV.
Play. Fld.
ONSLOW
RAMILLIES CT.
WANDILLA AV.
ROAD
Drumry
Comm. Cen.
WAVERLEY
COLUMBA
GREAT WESTERN RETAIL PARK
ALLERDYCE DR.
DUNTREATH GS.
Clydebank Megabowl
Retail Park
TALISMAN
KIRKWOOD
MORRISON
LIVINGSTONE STREET
ATTLEE AVENUE
ROAD
Yoker Burn
CRIPPS AV.
GREENWOOD QUAD.
DRANT
STREET
McNEIL AV.
QUADRANT
ALLERDYCE
ALLERDYCE CT.
ALLERDYCE PL.
Works
Whitecrook Prim. & Cunard Schs.
SHINWELL
SILKIN AV.
Linnvale Prim. & Nursy. Sch.
JOWITT AV.
DALTON AVENUE
KIRKWOOD AVENUE
STRAUSS AV.
DUNTREATH
GOLF
CRAWFORD
DOUGLAS DR.
MANOR ROAD
GARSCADDEN RD.
STANFORD ST.
Play Field
Whitecrook
WESTWOOD QUAD.
AVENUE
FRUIN RD.
RICHMOND S.
DEAN STREET
BRAES AVENUE
FLEMING ST.
BRAES AV.
Linnvale
2232
RALVIE
2283
Lock
KEAL
Sub.
KING ST.
BOYLE ST.
BROWN
Comm. Cen.
Pav.
DUNMORE ST.
CRANSTON
REELICK QUADRANT
REELICK AV.
Sports
Tennis Cts.
High Sch.
ARCHERHILL SQ.
50
51
52
70
71
72
73

44
A
B
C
D
24
60
43
1
2
3
4
5
6
Langfaulds
Recreation Ground
University of Glasgow (St. Andrews Campus)
Convent
Bearsden Ski & Board Club
DUNTOCHER ROAD
A810
A809
DRYMEN ROAD
Castle Hill (Roman Fort)
Castlehill
CASTLEHILL ROAD
BEARSDEN
BEARSDEN GOLF COURSE
Club House
GARSCADDEN WOOD
EAST DUNBARTONSHIRE
GLASGOW
Glasgow
HUTCHESON HILL
Ford
PEEL GLEN ROAD
Garscadden Burn
LADYLOAN AVENUE
DRUMMORE ROAD
KINFAUNS DRIVE
SUMMERHILL ROAD
St. Pius' Primary School
Drumchapel High Sch.
Comm. Cen.
Spts Grd.
Drummore School
Scotus College
Public Park
The High Sch. of Glasgow Jun. Sch.
COLQUHORN PARK
Football Grd.
Playing Field
STATION ROAD
WESTBOURNE DRIVE
GLENBURN ROAD
WHITEHILL LANE
Broadholm Prim. Sch.
Hall
DRUMCHAPEL
LINKWOOD DRIVE
TALLANT ROAD
SOUTHDEEN AVENUE
Colquhoun Park Prim. Sch.
CANNIESBURN ROAD
Stonedyke Prim. Sch.
Play. Fld.
G15
G13
GARSCADDEN ROAD
Sports Ground
Works
DRUMCHAPEL HOSPITAL
DRUMCHAPEL ROAD
Drumchapel
Youth Cen.
Milngavie Junction
Library
Nursery Sch.
ROTHERWOOD AVENUE
Rec. Grd.
Blairdardie Prim. Sch.
Comm. Cen.
A82
Playgrd.
Trinley Brae
GREAT WESTERN ROAD
Lock
Forth & Clyde Canal (dis.)

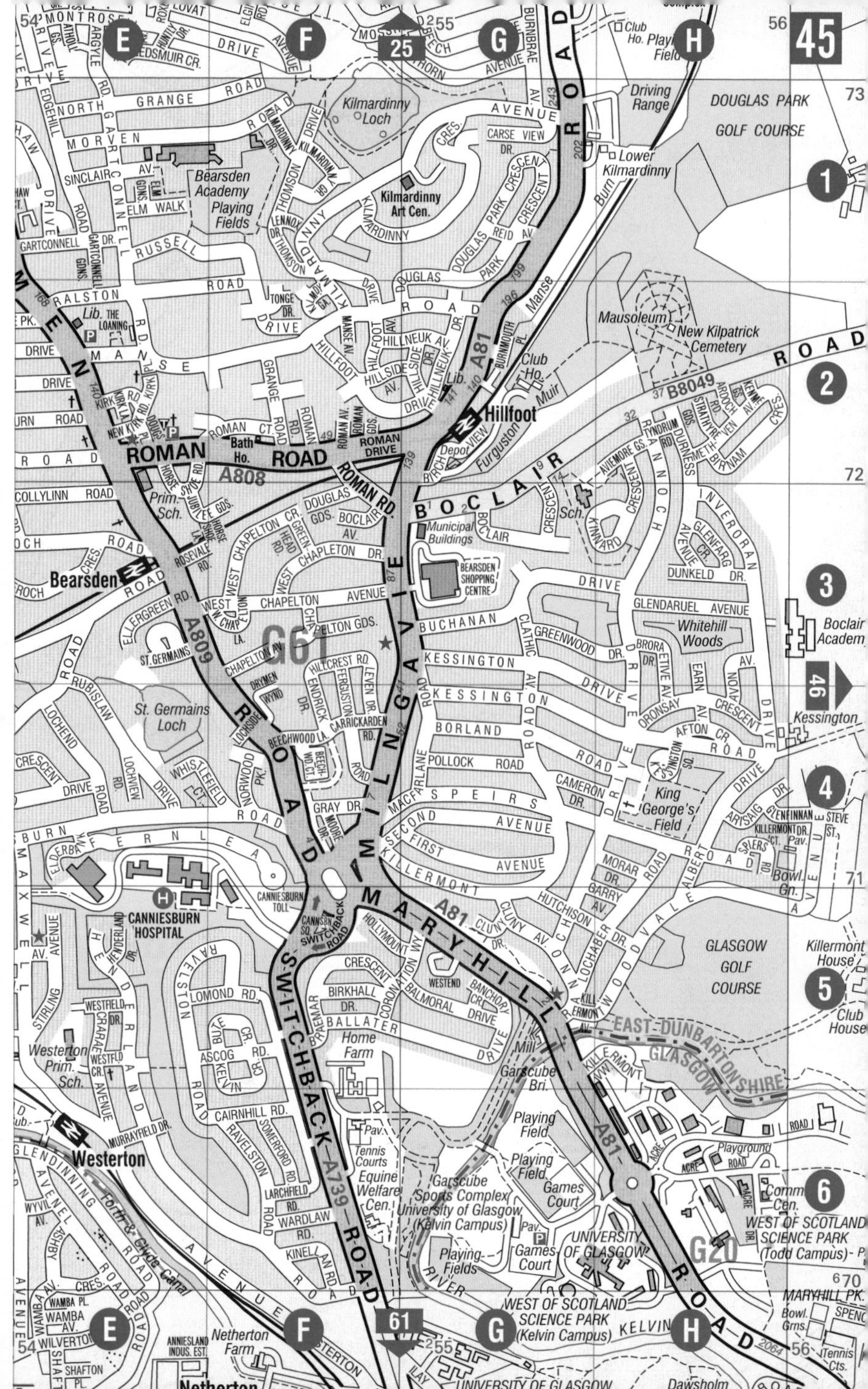
25
DOUGLAS PARK GOLF COURSE
Driving Range
Kilmardinny Loch
Bearsden Academy Playing Fields
Kilmardinny Art Cen.
Lower Kilmardinny
Mausoleum
New Kilpatrick Cemetery
Hillfoot
ROMAN ROAD
A808
A81
A809
B8049
BOCLAIR ROAD
Bath Ho.
Municipal Buildings
BEARSDEN SHOPPING CENTRE
Bearsden
G61
St. Germains Loch
Whitehill Woods
Boclair Academy
46
Kessington
King George's Field
MILNGAVIE ROAD
MARYHILL ROAD
CANNIESBURN HOSPITAL
CANNIESBURN TOLL
SWITCHBACK ROAD
A739
GLASGOW GOLF COURSE
Killermont House
Club House
EAST DUNBARTONSHIRE
GLASGOW
Garscube Bri.
Home Farm
Playing Field
Games Court
Garscube Sports Complex University of Glasgow (Kelvin Campus)
Playing Fields
UNIVERSITY OF GLASGOW
Equine Welfare Cen.
Tennis Courts
WEST OF SCOTLAND SCIENCE PARK (Todd Campus)
WEST OF SCOTLAND SCIENCE PARK (Kelvin Campus)
Comm Cen.
G20
Westerton
Westerton Prim. Sch.
Forth & Clyde Canal
Netherton Farm
ANNIESLAND INDUS. EST.
61
MARYHILL PK.
Dawsholm
RIVER KELVIN

DOUGLAS PARK GOLF COURSE
Boclair
ALLANDER WATER
G62
AUCHENHOWIE ROAD
A807
BALMORE RD
BALMORE ROAD
B8049
BOCLAIR ROAD
Crow Hill
Hillside
Temple of Boclair
West Millichen
East Millichen Cotts.
ROAD
Summerston Farm
A879
Kelvin View
Rosehill
East Millichen
G61
EAST DUNBARTONSHIRE
GLASGOW
Birkwood
MILLICHEN
KELVIN
Boclair Academy
Shielburn
Glasgow
Kessington
TEMPLEHILL WOOD
RIVER
GLASGOW GOLF COURSE
G23
Blackhill Farm
Killermont House
Club House
Cawder Cuilt
BLACKHILL
Summerston
Sandyflat Riding Sch.
Playing Field
John Paul Academy
G20
WEST OF SCOTLAND SCIENCE PARK (Todd Campus)
Comm. Cen.
Caldercuilt Play. Field
Pav.
MARYHILL PARK
St. Blane's Prim. Sch.
Football Grd.
LAMBHILL CEMETERY
WESTERN NECROPOLIS
ST. KENTIGERN CEMETERY
MARYHILL RD.
Bowl. Grns.
Tennis Cts.
Comm. Cen.
Shopping Cen.
St. Agnes

26
45
62

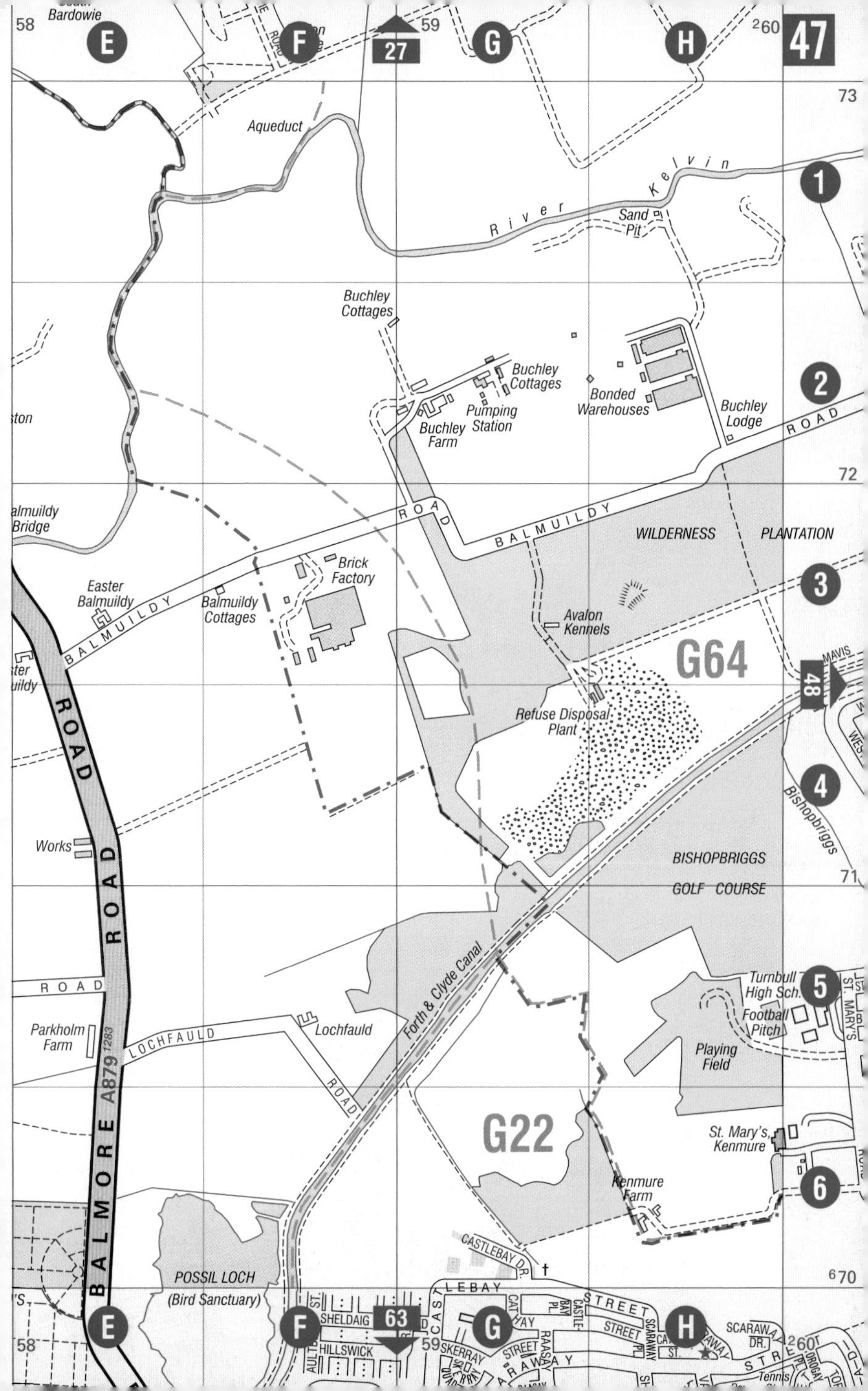

E   F   27   G   H

South Bardowie

58   59   260   73

Aqueduct

River Kelvin

Sand Pit

1

Buchley Cottages

Buchley Cottages

Pumping Station

Buchley Farm

Bonded Warehouses

Buchley Lodge

ROAD

2

72

...ton

ROAD

BALMUILDY

WILDERNESS   PLANTATION

almuildy Bridge

Easter Balmuildy

Balmuildy Cottages

BALMUILDY

Brick Factory

Avalon Kennels

3

G64

...ster ...uildy

ROAD

Refuse Disposal Plant

48   MAVIS

Bishopbriggs

4

WEST

BISHOPBRIGGS

GOLF   COURSE

71

Works

ROAD

Forth & Clyde Canal

Turnbull High Sch.

Football Pitch

ST. MARY'S

5

Parkholm Farm

A879   1283

LOCHFAULD

Lochfauld

ROAD

Playing Field

St. Mary's, Kenmure

6

G22

Kenmure Farm

BALMORE   ROAD

POSSIL LOCH (Bird Sanctuary)

CASTLEBAY DR.

CASTLEBAY DR.

E   F   63   G   H

SHELDAIG ST.

HILLSWICK

AULT...

SKERRAY

A... A WAY

CAST

LEBAY

SKERRAY   STREET

CATT AY

RAASAY   ST.

STREET

CASTLE

BAY   PL.

STREET

SCARAWAY   PL.

ST.

STREET

SCARAWAY   DR.

SCARAWA...

STRE...

Tennis

58   59   260   670

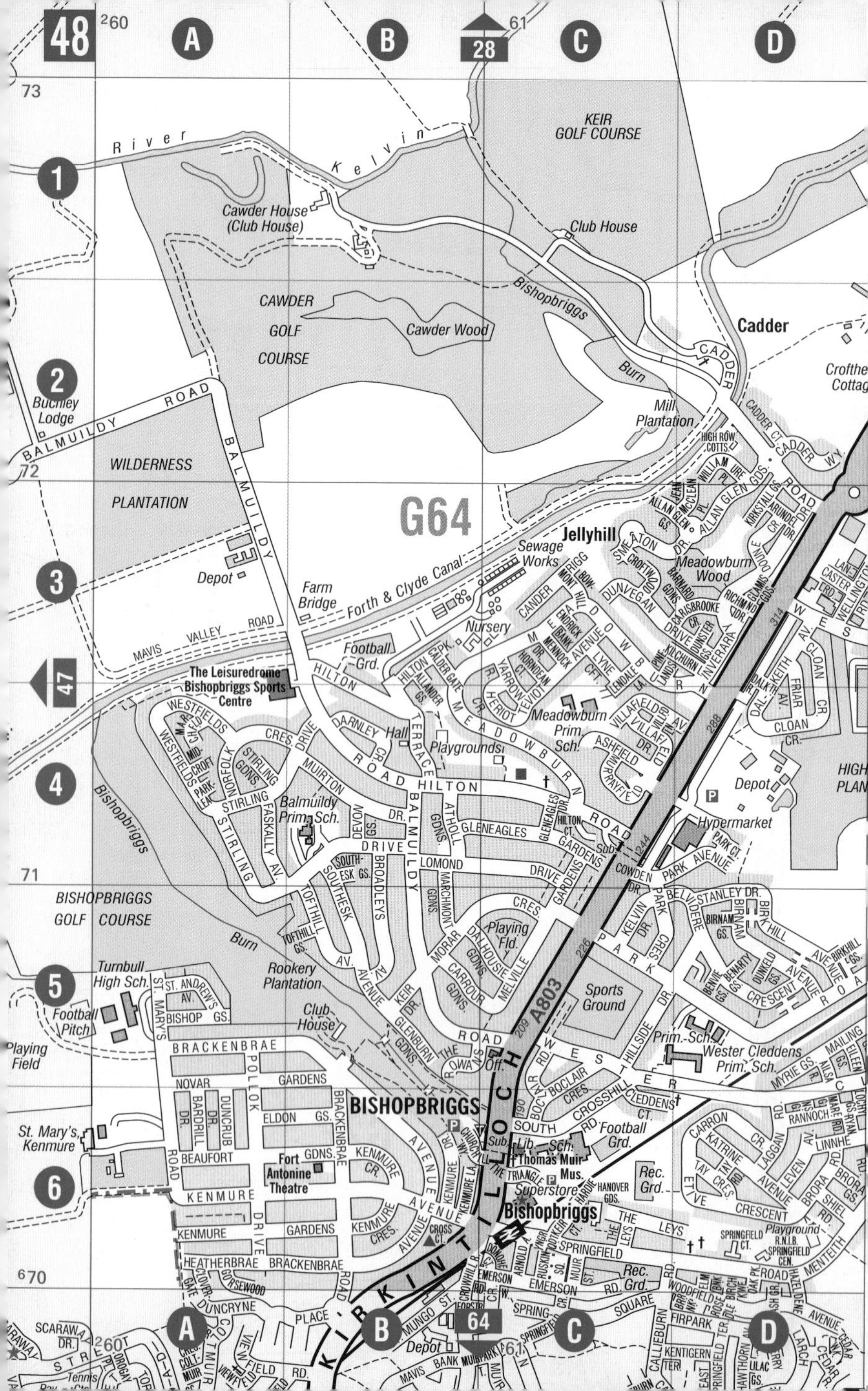

A
B
C
D
28
47
64
1
2
3
4
5
6
River Kelvin
KEIR GOLF COURSE
Cawder House (Club House)
Club House
CAWDER GOLF COURSE
Cawder Wood
Bishopbriggs Burn
Cadder
Mill Plantation
WILDERNESS PLANTATION
G64
Jellyhill
Sewage Works
Forth & Clyde Canal
Farm Bridge
Depot
Meadowburn Wood
Nursery
Football Grd.
The Leisuredrome Bishopbriggs Sports Centre
Meadowburn Prim. Sch.
Playgrounds
Balmuildy Prim. Sch.
Hypermarket
BISHOPBRIGGS GOLF COURSE
Playing Fld.
Sports Ground
Rookery Plantation
Turnbull High Sch.
Football Pitch
Playing Field
Club House
Wester Cleddens Prim. Sch.
BISHOPBRIGGS
St. Mary's, Kenmure
Fort Antonine Theatre
Thomas Muir Mus.
Superstore
Bishopbriggs
Rec. Grd.
A803

Hungryside Bridge (Drawbridge)
Glasgow Bri.
Slipway
EASTER CADDER COTTAGES
Forth and Clyde Canal
TORRANCE RD.
A807
KIRKINTILLOCH A803 ROAD
Leafield
G66
Golf Driving Range
Club Ho.
Meiklehill
Works
Pav.
Loretto Playing Field
CROSSHILL
H.M.P. LOW MOSS
A803
Cadder Cemetery
Vehicle Testing Centre
Bearhill Farm
Hazel Cottage
Works
Driver Testing Centre
B819
STRATHKELVIN RETAIL PARK
LOW MOSS PLANTATION
Playing Field
Park Burn
Mid Boghead Cottage
Boghead
Wester Boghead
Sewage Works
LOW MOSS INDUSTRIAL ESTATE
Glasgow
ROAD
Wester Boghead Holdings
Football Grd.
Lochgrog
Works
Sub.
Works
Depot
MOSS
TATION
Cottage
Cadder Yard
Depot
ROAD
BURRA GS.
ROAD
SELLA RD.
RONALDSAY
WESTRAY PL.
STRONSAY DR.
COLLA GS.
DORNOCH PLACE
PENTLAND
LORNE CR.
CROMARTY AV.
SOLWAY
MONYMUSK GS.
SPYNIE PL.
TWEEDSMUIR
BEMERSYDE
MOORFOOT
St. Helen's Prim. Sch.
KINTESSACK PL.
PITMEDDEN RD.
HARLAW GDS.
AVENUE
FLORA GDS.
SANDRA RD.
ABBOTSFORD
BEAULY PL.
DR.
ELSPETH
EDDEN
NORTH LANARKSHIRE
EAST DUNBARTONSHIRE
WESTERHILL
Rushyhill
ROBROYSTON B812
KIRRIEMUIR GS.
Woodhill Prim. Sch.
Thomas Muir High Sch.
MEARNS WY.
DUN
NOTTAR ST.
GRAINGER RD.
Westerhill
AVENUE
WOODHILL
KIRRIEMUIR RD.
THRUMS GDS.
OCHIL RD.
CLAIR
TORR RD.
CARESTON PL.
CORTACHY PL.
SUNART GS.
CARRADALE
AVENUE
TORR
MNA.
NEWTLE
CARNOUSTIE
ARDBEG AV.
CRES.
CARRICK RD.
ROAD
CREE AV.
PL.
MUIRHEAD WY.
MONIKIE GS.
DUNNICHEN GS.
CRINAN
BRECHIN
GANNOCHY DR.
MORAY PL.
FINTRY
TINTO R.
ROAD
ST. CYRUS RD.
RANSON WY.
FETTERCAIRN GS.
MORVINA
ANGUS
BALMERINO PL.
CERES GS.
ROBROYSTON ROAD
AUCHINAIRN ROAD
Lumloch
Wester Lumloch
WOOD LA.
GREENHILL
VALE WLK.
FORFAR
EDZELL
LUNAN
LETHA
LUNDIE GS.
LIFF GS.
FALKLAND
FORGAN
DAIRSIE GDS.
FIFE WY.
PINEWOOD CT.
GLENWOOD PL.

29
50
65

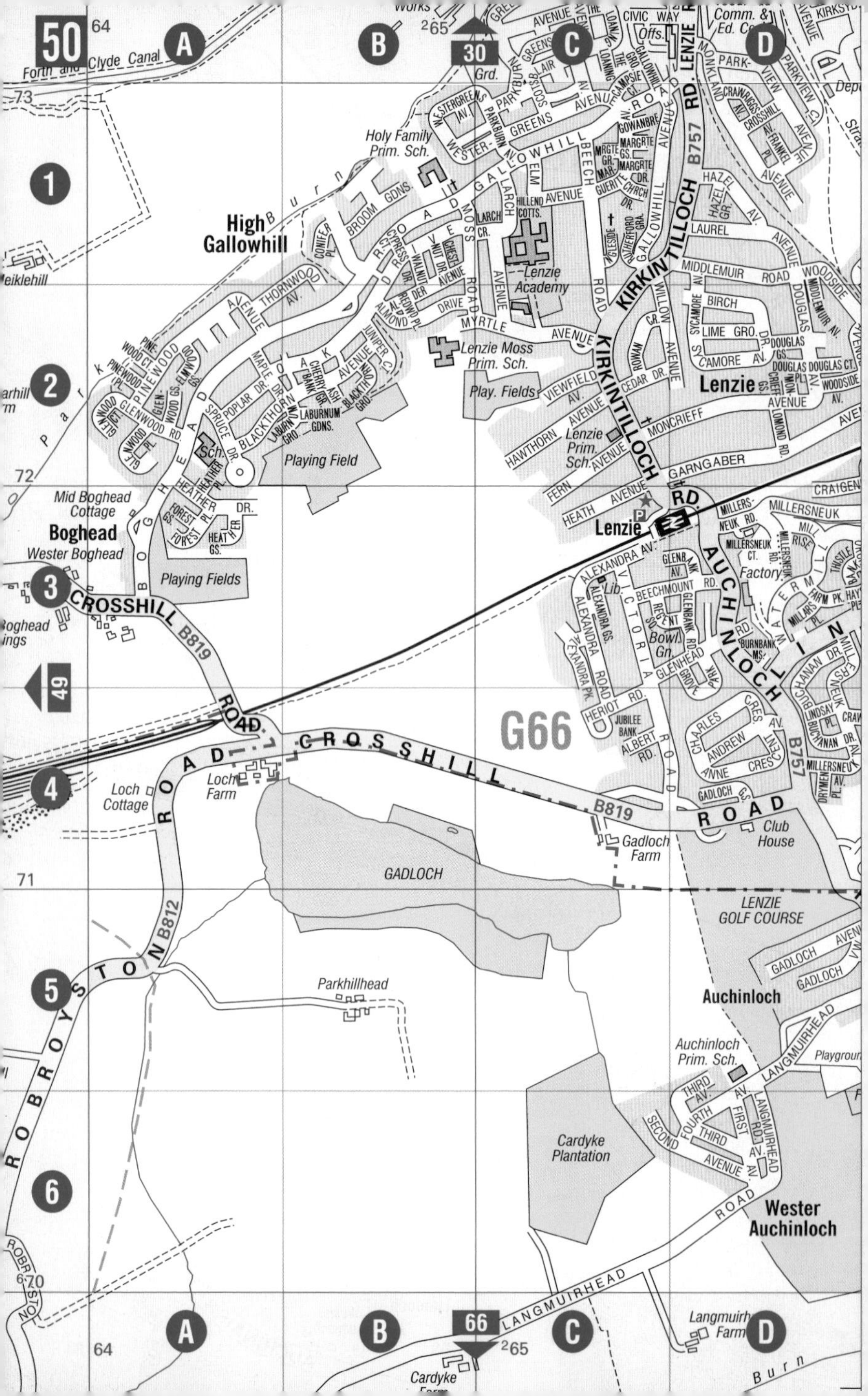

Forth and Clyde Canal
High Gallowhill
Holy Family Prim. Sch.
Lenzie Academy
Lenzie Moss Prim. Sch.
Play. Fields
Lenzie Prim. Sch.
Lenzie
Playing Field
Mid Boghead Cottage
Boghead
Wester Boghead
Playing Fields
CROSSHILL ROAD
B819
KIRKINTILLOCH ROAD
B757
AUCHINLOCH ROAD
G66
Loch Cottage
Loch Farm
Gadloch Farm
GADLOCH
Club House
LENZIE GOLF COURSE
Parkhillhead
Auchinloch
Auchinloch Prim. Sch.
Cardyke Plantation
Wester Auchinloch
ROBROYSTON ROAD
B812
LANGMUIRHEAD ROAD
Langmuirhead Farm
Cardyke Farm
Factory
Lib.
Bowl. Gn.
Comm. & Ed. Ce
CIVIC WAY
Offs.
30
49
66

Oxgang
Cemetery
Woodilee Industrial Estate
Woodilee Cottages
Works
Bothlin Burn
Lodge
Chryston
Fauldhead
Caurnie View
Wallace Cottage
Stepping Stones
Muirhead Cottages
Calfmuir Road
Canal Feeder
Millersneuk
Bothlin Bank
Weir
Muckcroft Road
Claddens Smallholdings
Claddens
Lindsaybeg Kennels
Burnbrae Road
Burnbrae Farm
Orchard Park
Glasgow
Netherhouses
G69
Davidston
East Dunbartonshire
North Lanarkshire
Easter Auchinloch
Cult Burn
Fair Winds
Blacklands
B819
Garnkirk Burn
North Broomknowes
South Broomknowes
Peathill
Greenlea Cott.
Lindsaybeg Ho.
Lindsaybeg Road
Stepps Road B757
Lenzie Golf Course
Football Grd.
Drumsack
Arronhill Plantation
M80
Garnkirk

31
52
67

A
B
C
D
1
2
3
4
5
6
32
51
68
Fauldhead
Caurnie View
Wallace Cottage
Stepping Stones
Depot
Luggie
CHRYSTON ROAD
Drumshanty
Sauchen
G66
Wester Bedcow Cottage
EAST DUNBARTONSHIRE
NORTH LANARKSHIRE
Braeside Farm
MUCKCROFT ROAD
VIEWFIELD
Glasgow
Bothlin Burn
AUCHENGEICH ROAD
Pav.
Bowl.
Football Grd.
Burnbrae Farm
Sewage Works
Works
Bridgend
Davidston
GARTFERRY ROAD
Hill of Chryston
Glenmanor Prim. Sch.
Play. Fld.
Com. Liby. Cen.
Moodiesburn
Garnkirk Burn
LINDSAYBEG ROAD
Lindsaybeg Ho.
G69
The Glen
Millbrae Nursery
Millbrae Farm
Lanrigg
Chryston
Bedlay Castle
Bedlay Cemetery
Chryston Mains
Chryston Prim. Sch.
Chryston High. Sch.
CUMBERNAULD ROAD
A80
B819 ROAD
MAIN STREET
CHRYSTON VALLEY BUSINESS CEN.
Playground

E
F
G
H
Grayshill
33
Abattoir
Newlands Farm
ORCHARDTON
WESTFIELD INDUSTRIAL AREA
GRAYSHILL ROAD
GRAYSHILL RD.
Playhill
Barbeth Farm
MOLLINS RD.
Works
WESTFIELD
WEST-FIELD PL.
VIEW
WESTFIELD INDUSTRIAL ESTATE
DEERDYKES VW.
DEERDYKES
MOLLINS CT.
Badenheath Bungalow
DEERDYKES ROUNDABOUT
G68
Deerdykes
Factory
QUARRY RD.
OLD RD.
ORCHARDTON RD.
Sewage Works
Badenheath Bridge
My Lord's Bridge
MOLLINS ROUNDABOUT
Mollin Craigs
A80
Mollins Farm
ROAD
Barrs
CROFTMORAIG AV.
THE LARCHES
CRES.
DALCRUIN GDS.
STRATHORD PL.
GLENISLA
ALLANA
LISMORE PL.
CREAG GS.
CUMBERNAULD
AIRDRIE RD.
BADENHEATH TER.
Mollinsburn
54
G67
Adamswell
Factory
Junction 3
MOLLINSBURN JUNCTION
Mollinhillhead
GLENLUCE GDS.
BRADY CR.
DRYBURGH
LOCHWOOD LOAN
CULROSS
GLENTROOL
INCHCOLM GS.
BEDLAY
AVENUE
MOSSVALE
STRATHORE
ATHOLL LA.
RANNOCH LA.
ADAMSWELL T.
SEAFORTH LA.
TORWOOD LA.
GLENTANAR DRIVE
DUNELLAN CR.
DUNLIN GS.
Peat Works
M73
M73 MOTORWAY
AULD ROAD
Coatbridge
ML5
Mollins Burn
Football Ground
Leckethill
Cloverhill
BIRKENSHAW ROAD
Woodend
Avenuehead
ROAD
Refuse Site
69
70
71
72
73
1
2
3
4
5
6

Condorrat
Dalshannon
Glasgow
G68
G67
Mollinsburn
Annathill
Coatbridge
ML5
Westfield Industrial Estate
Badenheath Bridge
Badenheath Park
North Medrox
Spouty Braes
Craigend Nursery
Wester Myvot
Annathill Farm
Muirend
Wardhead
Gain Wood
Gain Farm
Woodend
Medrox Quarry (Disused)
Sewage Works
Football Ground
Luggie Water
A80
B802

34
53
70

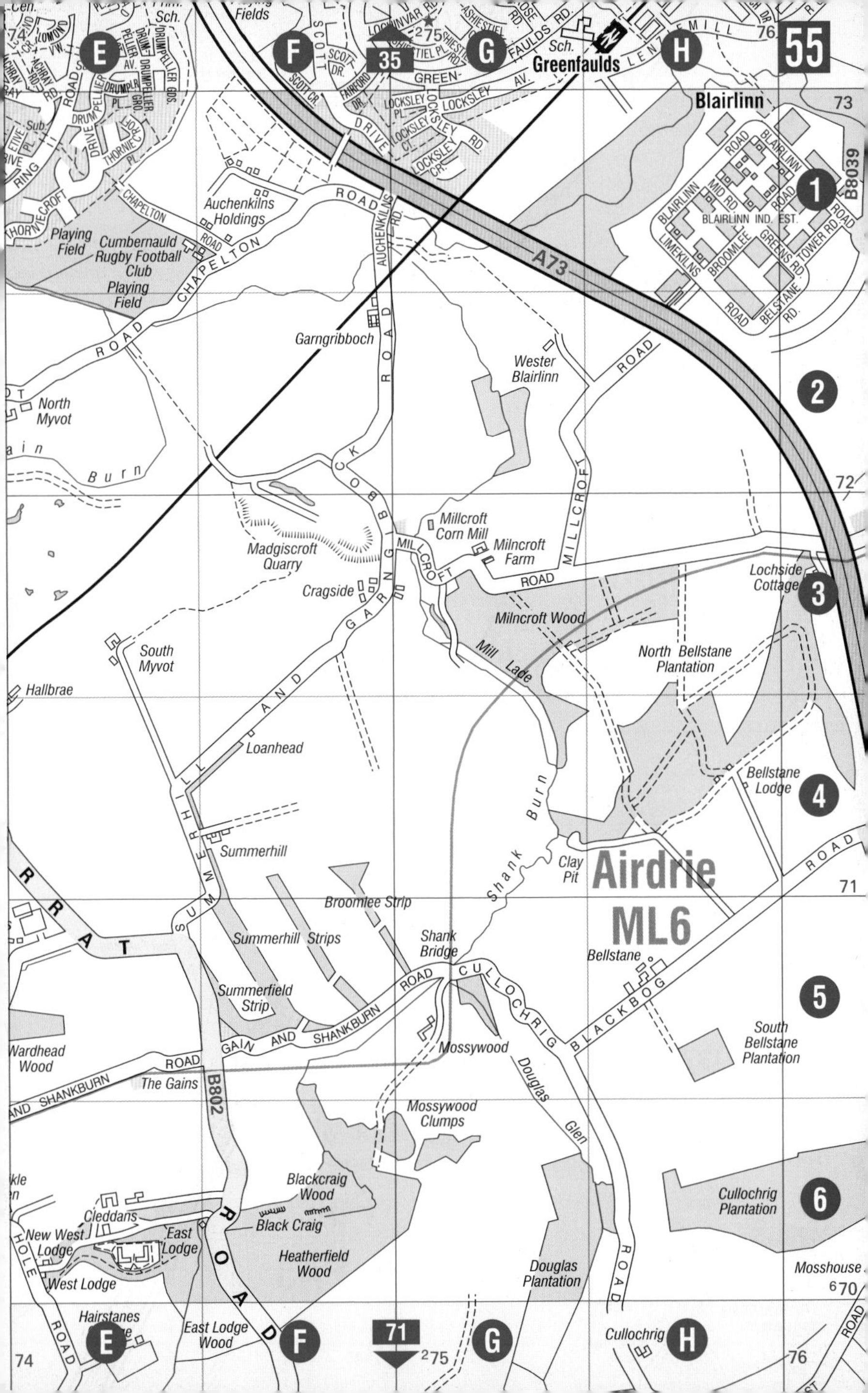
E
F
G
H
35
Greenfaulds
Blairlinn
Blairlinn Ind. Est.
B8039
A73
Playing Field
Cumbernauld Rugby Football Club
Playing Field
Auchenkilns Holdings
Chapelton Road
Auchenkilns Rd.
Garngribboch
Wester Blairlinn
North Myvot
Millcroft Corn Mill
Milncroft Farm
Millcroft Road
Madgiscroft Quarry
Cragside
Lochside Cottage
Milncroft Wood
Mill Lade
North Bellstane Plantation
South Myvot
Hallbrae
Loanhead
Garngibbock Road
Bellstane Lodge
Summerhill
Summerhill Road
Broomlee Strip
Clay Pit
Airdrie
ML6
Summerhill Strips
Shank Bridge
Shank Burn
Bellstane
Blackbog Road
Summerfield Strip
Cullochrig Road
Gain and Shankburn Road
Wardhead Wood
Mossywood
South Bellstane Plantation
The Gains
B802
Douglas Glen
Mossywood Clumps
Blackcraig Wood
Cullochrig Plantation
Cleddans
Black Craig
New West Lodge
East Lodge
Heatherfield Wood
West Lodge
Douglas Plantation
Mosshouse
Hairstanes
East Lodge Wood
Cullochrig
71
1
2
3
4
5
6
72
73
70
74
75
76

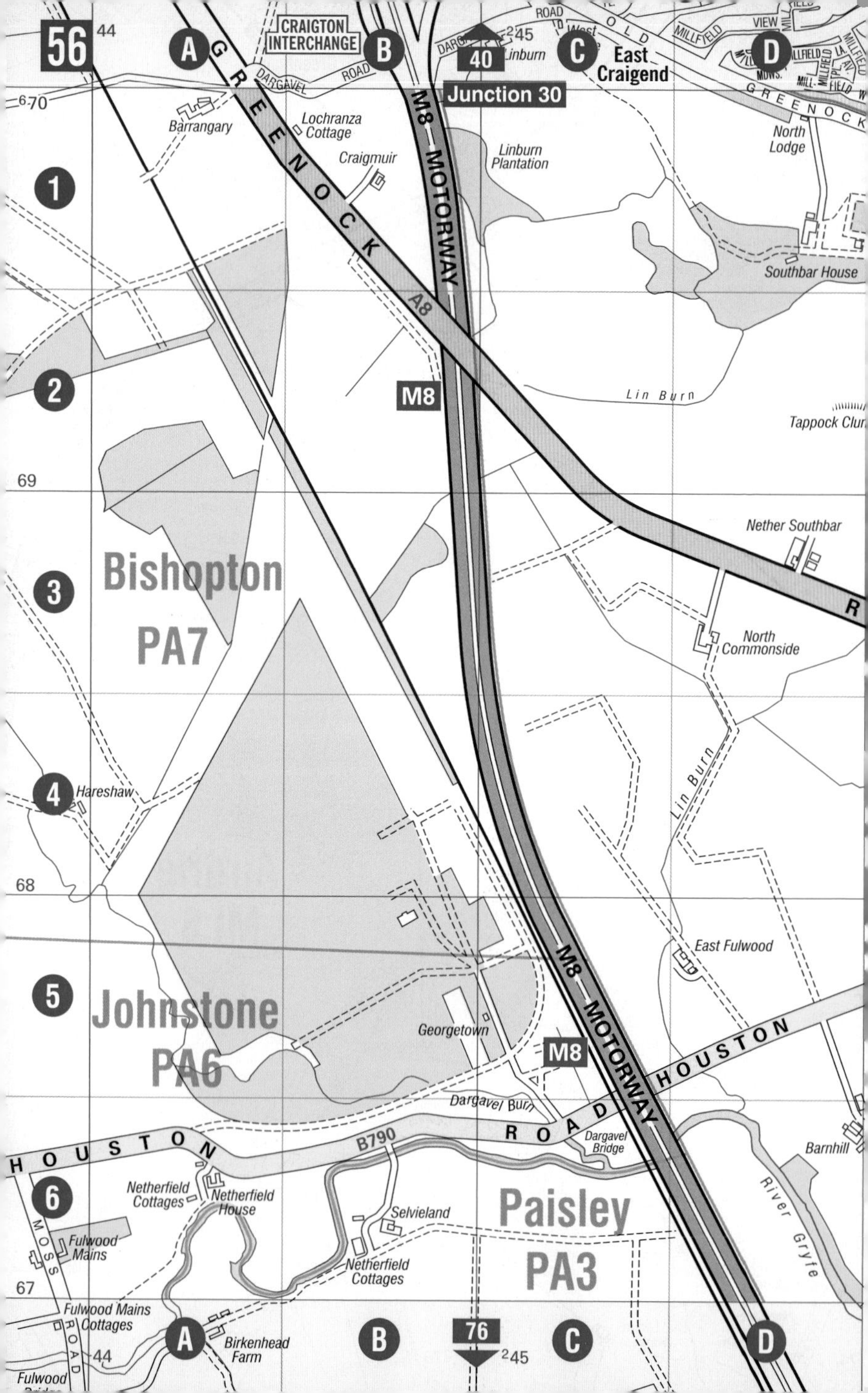

44
A
B
C
D
CRAIGTON INTERCHANGE
40
Junction 30
Linburn
West
East Craigend
OLD
MILLFIELD
VIEW
GREENOCK
DARGAVEL ROAD
670
Barrangary
Lochranza Cottage
Craigmuir
Linburn Plantation
North Lodge
1
GREENOCK
M8 MOTORWAY
Southbar House
A8
2
M8
Lin Burn
Tappock Cl
69
Nether Southbar
3
Bishopton
PA7
North Commonside
Lin Burn
4
Hareshaw
68
East Fulwood
5
Johnstone
PA6
Georgetown
M8
M8 MOTORWAY
HOUSTON
Dargavel Burn
ROAD
HOUSTON
Dargavel Bridge
B790
Barnhill
6
Netherfield Cottages
Netherfield House
Selvieland
Paisley
River Gryfe
MOSS
Fulwood Mains
Netherfield Cottages
PA3
67
Fulwood Mains Cottages
ROAD
Birkenhead Farm
76
245
44
Fulwood

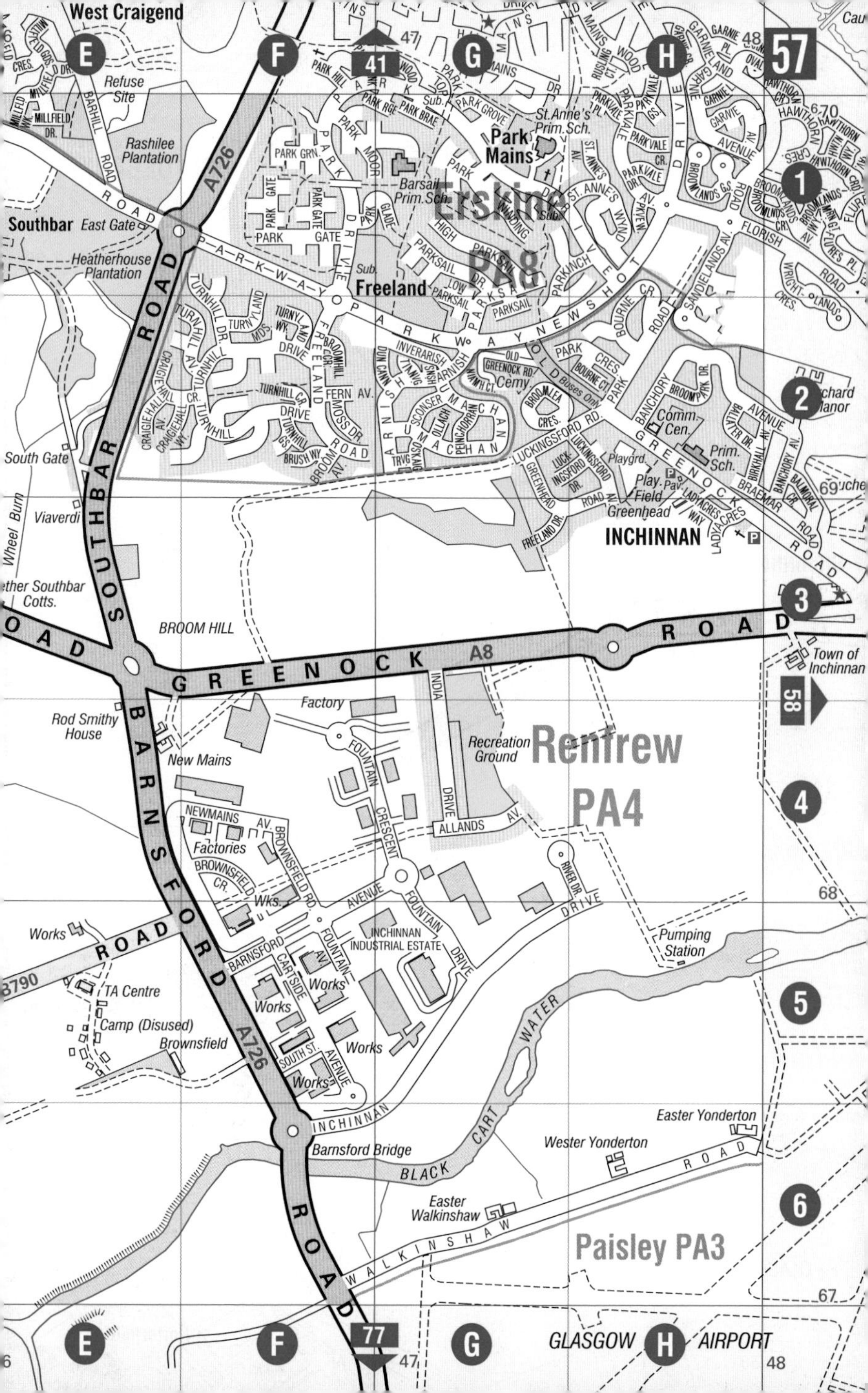
West Craigend
E
F
G
H
41
47
48
Refuse Site
Rashilee Plantation
Southbar
East Gate
Heatherhouse Plantation
A726
PARKWAY
Park Mains
St. Anne's Prim. Sch.
Barsail Prim. Sch.
Erskine PA8
Freeland
Sub.
NEWSHOT DRIVE
GREENOCK RD.
Cemy.
Comm. Cen.
Prim. Sch.
Playgrd.
Play. Field
Pav.
Greenhead
INCHINNAN
Orchard Manor
1
2
3
4
5
6
670
69
68
67
South Gate
Viaverdi
Wheel Burn
Heather Southbar Cotts.
BROOM HILL
SOUTHBAR ROAD
GREENOCK ROAD
A8
Town of Inchinnan
58
Rod Smithy House
New Mains
Factory
Recreation Ground
Renfrew PA4
BARNSFORD ROAD
INDIA DRIVE
FOUNTAIN CRESCENT
ALLANDS AV.
NEWMAINS AV.
Factories
BROWNSFIELD CR.
BROWNSFIELD RD.
Wks.
RIVER DR.
INCHINNAN INDUSTRIAL ESTATE
Pumping Station
Works
TA Centre
Camp (Disused)
Brownsfield
B790
SOUTH ST.
INCHINNAN
Barnsford Bridge
BLACK CART WATER
Easter Yonderton
Wester Yonderton
Easter Walkinshaw
WALKINSHAW ROAD
Paisley PA3
77
GLASGOW AIRPORT

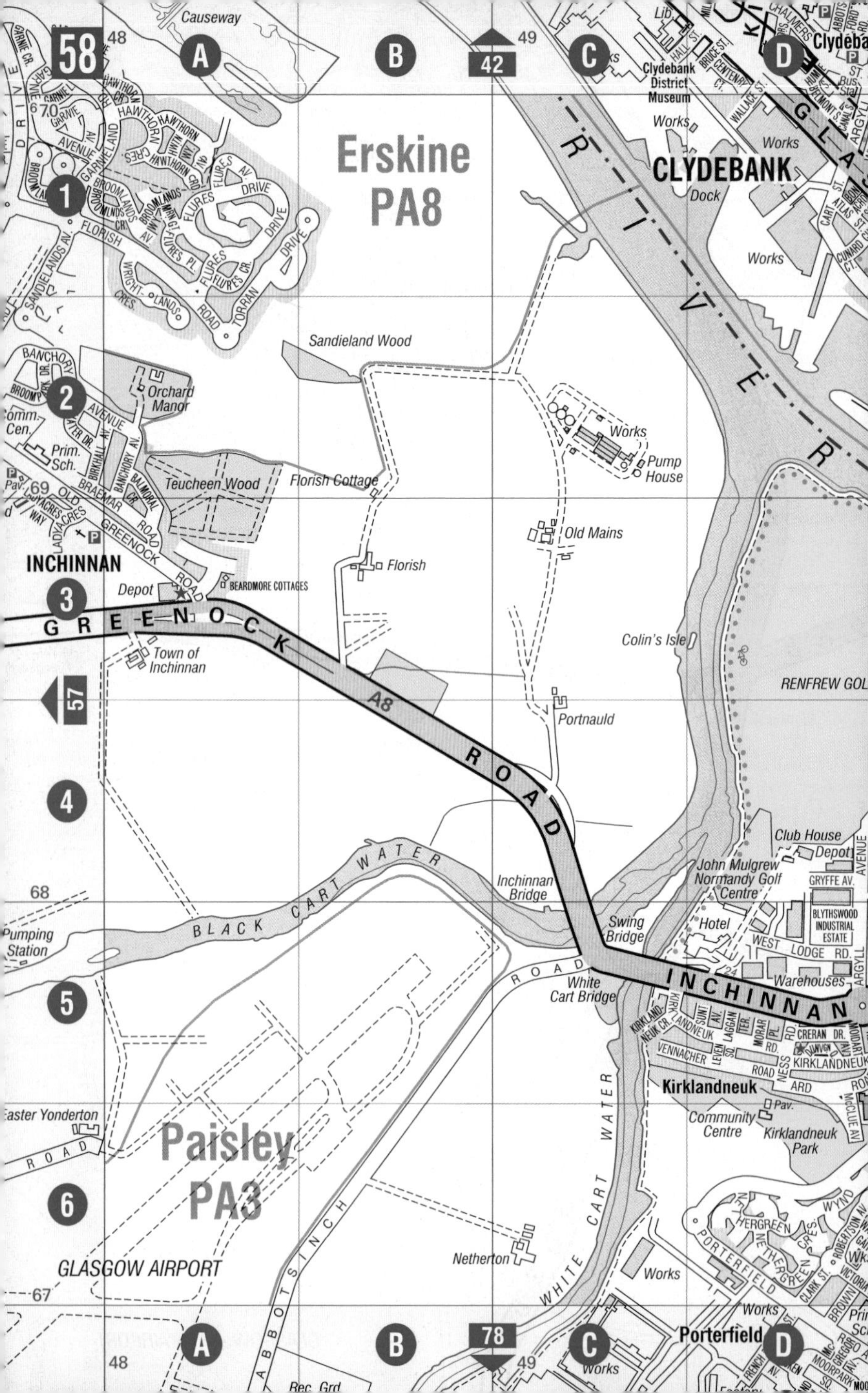
Erskine
PA8
CLYDEBANK
Clydebank District Museum
Sandieland Wood
Orchard Manor
Teucheen Wood
Florish Cottage
Florish
Old Mains
Works
Pump House
INCHINNAN
Depot
BEARDMORE COTTAGES
Town of Inchinnan
GREENOCK ROAD
A8
Portnauld
Colin's Isle
RENFREW GOL
Inchinnan Bridge
Swing Bridge
White Cart Bridge
BLACK CART WATER
WHITE CART WATER
INCHINNAN
John Mulgrew Normandy Golf Centre
Club House
Hotel
BLYTHSWOOD INDUSTRIAL ESTATE
Warehouses
Kirklandneuk
Community Centre
Kirklandneuk Park
Pumping Station
Easter Yonderton
Paisley
PA3
GLASGOW AIRPORT
ABBOTSINCH
Netherton
Works
Porterfield
Rec. Grd

42
57
78

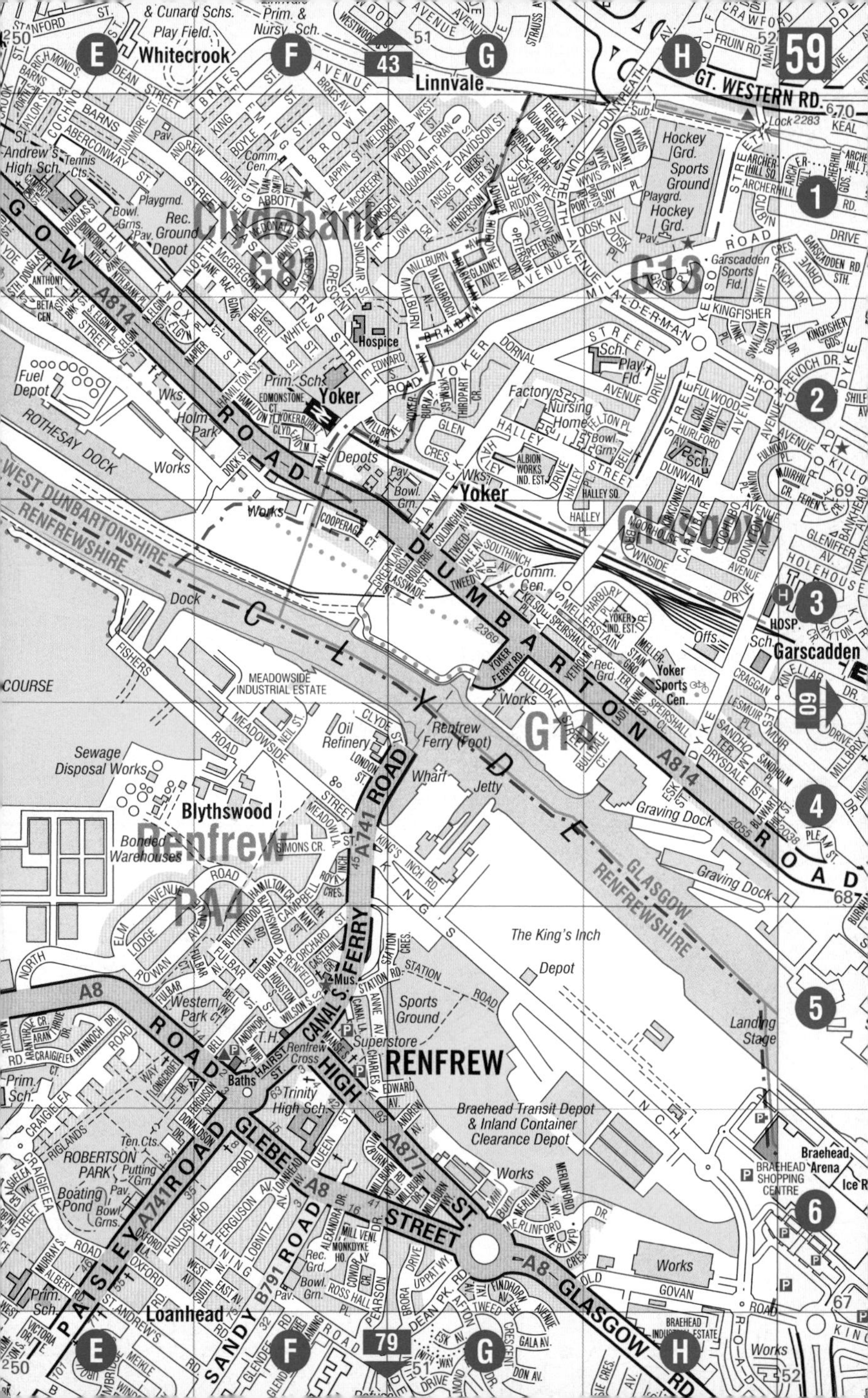

59
43
79
60
E
F
G
H
1
2
3
4
5
6
Whitecrook
Linnvale
Clydebank
G81
G13
G14
Yoker
Glasgow
Garscadden
Renfrew
PA4
RENFREW
Blythswood
Loanhead
GT. WESTERN RD.
DUMBARTON ROAD
A814
A741
A8
A877
B791
CLYDE
WEST DUNBARTONSHIRE
RENFREWSHIRE
GLASGOW
ROTHESAY DOCK
Fuel Depot
Hospice
Hockey Grd.
Sports Ground
Garscadden Sports Fld.
Yoker Sports Cen.
MEADOWSIDE INDUSTRIAL ESTATE
Sewage Disposal Works
Oil Refinery
Renfrew Ferry (Foot)
Bonded Warehouses
Graving Dock
The King's Inch
Braehead Transit Depot
& Inland Container
Clearance Depot
BRAEHEAD SHOPPING CENTRE
Braehead Arena
BRAEHEAD INDUSTRIAL ESTATE
ROBERTSON PARK
Boating Pond
Trinity High Sch.
Renfrew Cross
Superstore
Sports Ground
Landing Stage
GLASGOW RD
PAISLEY ROAD
GLEBE STREET
HIGH ST.
CANAL ST.
FERRY ROAD
KING'S INCH RD

GREAT WESTERN ROAD
A82
G15
Forth & Clyde Canal (Dis.)
High Knightswood
KNIGHTSWOOD GOLF COURSE
Garscadden Burn
Knightswood
Glasgow
G13
Garscadden
Scotstounhill
Scotstoun
DUMBARTON ROAD
A814
G14
RIVER CLYDE
Shipbuilding Yard
Braehead Arena
Ice Rinks
BRAEHEAD SHOPPING CENTRE
Clydebuilt (Scottish Maritime Museum)
Retail Park
G51
Whiteinch
VICTORIA PARK DRIVE (CLYDESIDE E...
UNIVERSITY STRATHCLYDE (Jordanhill Cam...
Scotstoun Leisure Cen.
Scotstoun Athletic Running Track
Laurel Pk. Spts. Club
Knightswood Sec. Sch.
Knightswood Park
Fossil Grove
44
59
80
52
53
67
68
69

E
F
G
H
45
81
62
1
2
3
4
5
6
Netherton
Temple
Anniesland
Anniesland
Jordanhill
Broomhill
Hyndland
Kelvinside
Kelvindale
Maryhill
Partickhill
PARTICK
G61
G20
G12
G11
UNIVERSITY OF GLASGOW
WEST OF SCOTLAND SCIENCE PARK (Kelvin Campus)
UNIVERSITY OF GLASGOW (Veterinary Medicine)
DAWSHOLM PARK
DALSHOLM INDUSTRIAL ESTATE
Refuse Destructors
Forth & Clyde Canal
Glasgow Hawks RUFC
The High Sch. of Glasgow
Anniesland Coll.
Kelvinside Academy War Mem. Grd.
GARTNAVEL ROYAL HOSPITAL
GARTNAVEL GENERAL HOSPITAL
GLASGOW HOMOEOPATHIC HOSPITAL
Next Generation Health Club
ANNIESLAND INDUS. EST.
Netherton Farm
Rowena Nursy. Sch.
Cleveden Sec. Sch.
VICTORIA PARK
Cross Park
MARYHILL PARK
MARYHILL A81
GREAT WESTERN A82
A739
CROW ROAD
BEARSDEN ROAD
BALSHAGRAY AV.
SWITCHBACK ROAD
MAXWELL AVENUE
WESTERTON AVENUE
TEMPLE ROAD
SKAETHORN ROAD
DALSHOLM ROAD
CLEVEDEN ROAD
CHURCHILL DRIVE
CLARENCE DRIVE
HYNDLAND ROAD
KELVINDALE ROAD
SHELLEY ROAD
WOODEND DRIVE
PARK DRIVE
Dawsholm Bri.
KELVIN

62
A
B
C
D
46
82
61
1
2
3
4
5
6
56
57
67
69
G23
G20
G12
MARYHILL PARK
Play. Field
St. Blane's Sch. Football Grd.
WESTERN NECROPOLIS
Glasgow Crematorium
War Mem.
St. Agnes Prim. Sch.
Comm. Cen.
Youth Cen.
Shopping Cen.
Prim. Sch.
Summerston
Maryhill
Gilshochill
Cadder
Cadder Prim. Sch.
Play. Fld.
Nurs. Sch.
Works
Forth & Clyde Canal
Stockingfield Junction
RUCHILL PARK GOLF COURSE
Ruchill Prim. Sch.
Club House
Ruchill Sports Cen.
Ruchill
Warehouses
Offs.
Lochburn Park
Lib.
Locks
Depot
Playground
DALSHOLM INDUSTRIAL ESTATE
Weir
RIVER KELVIN
Kelvindale
Cleveden Sec. Sch.
Halls of Residence
Theatre
Football Grds.
Rec. Cen.
Rec. Grd.
Academy
Kirklee Bri.
Play. Field Pav.
North Kelvin
East Park Home Sch.
MARYHILL SHOP. CEN.
CHAPEL ST. INDUS. EST.
T.A. Cen.
Bowling Greens
Glasgow Botanic Gardens
Winter Gardens
Queen Margaret Bri.
B.B.C.
Dowanhill
Hillhead
Glasgow Academy
Kelvinbridge
Hunterian Gall.
Univ.
Coll.
MARYHILL ROAD
A81
A82
B808
GREAT WESTERN RD.
QUEEN MARGARET DRIVE
BILSLAND DRIVE
SKAETHORN ROAD
BALCARRES AVENUE
KELVINDALE RD.
CLEVEDEN RD.
BYRES RD.
UNIVERSITY AV.
CRESTA
HERMA
SKIRSA
TRESTA
ARROCHAR DR.
SANDBANK ST.
GLENAVON ROAD
KNOWETAP ST.
GLENBURN ST.
THORNTON ST.
LANGA ST.
CADDER RD.
FEARNMORE RD.
DUNCRUIN ST.
VIEWMOUNT DRIVE
FINGAL ST.
LOCHBURN RD.
BRASSEY
LEIGHTON
CURZON ST.
SHUNA ST.
RUCHILL ST.
CRAIGMONT ST.
GAIRBRAID AV.
COLLINA ST.
BURNHOUSE ST.
NIVEN ST.
GUTHRIE ST.
WYNDFORD RD.
GARRIOCH RD.
SHAKESPEARE ST.
OBAN DR.
KELVINSIDE
HAMILTON DRIVE
OBSERVATORY RD.
VICTORIA CIRCUS
KENSINGTON RD.
HYNDLAND RD.
KINGSBOROUGH GDS.
DOWANSIDE RD.
WOODSIDE
WILTON ST.
RAEBERRY ST.
HENDERSON ST.
MURANO ST.
BENVIEW
SHANNON ST.
MAYFIELD

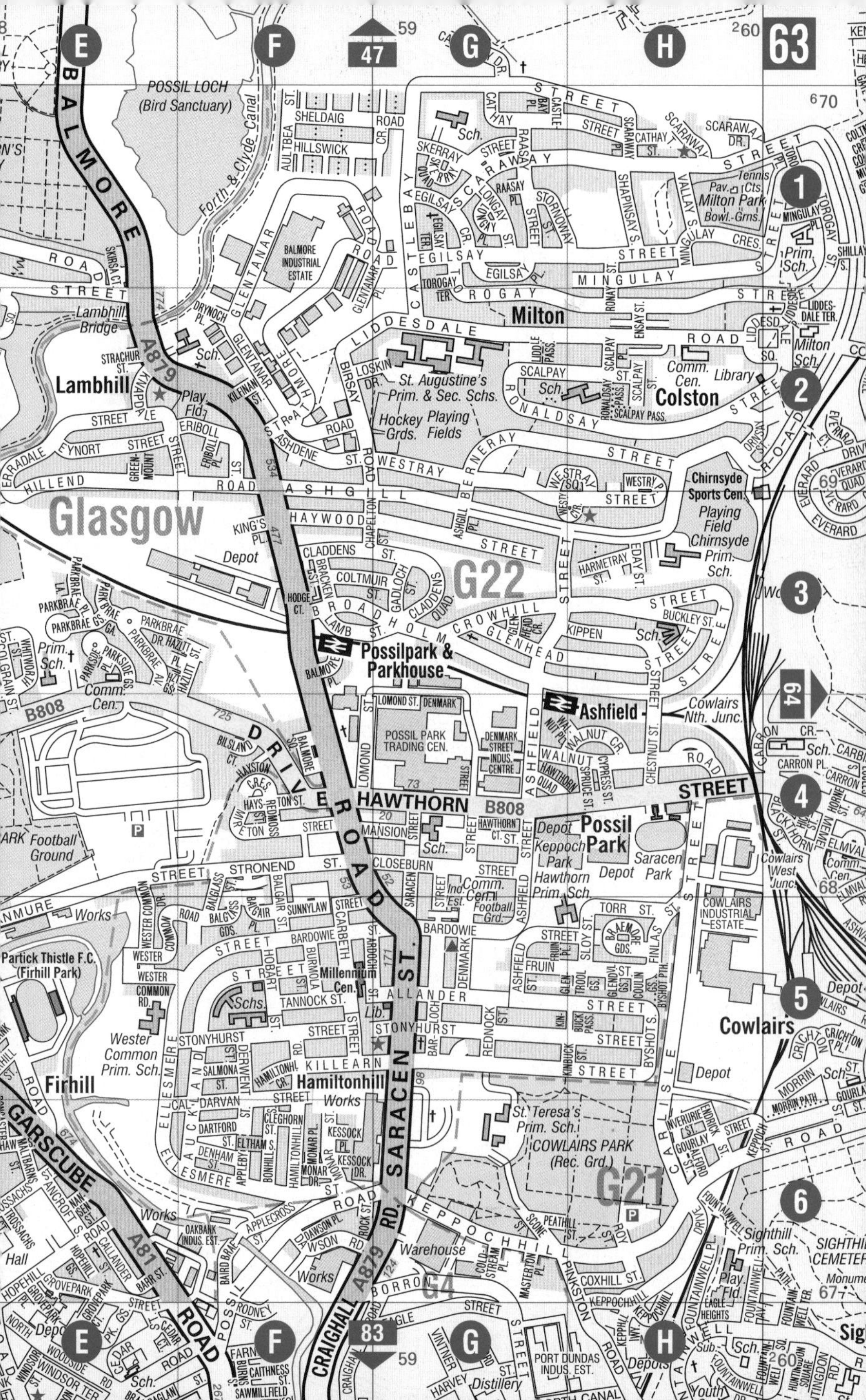
63
47
83
64
59
E
F
G
H
1
2
3
4
5
6
POSSIL LOCH
(Bird Sanctuary)
Forth & Clyde Canal
BALMORE
A879
Lambhill
Lambhill Bridge
BALMORE INDUSTRIAL ESTATE
Milton
Colston
Milton Park
Tennis Cts.
Bowl.-Grns.
Milton Sch.
Comm. Cen.
Library
St. Augustine's Prim. & Sec. Schs.
Hockey Grds.
Playing Fields
Chirnsyde Sports Cen.
Playing Field
Chirnsyde Prim. Sch.
Glasgow
G22
Depot
Possilpark & Parkhouse
Ashfield
Cowlairs Nth. Junc.
POSSIL PARK TRADING CEN.
DENMARK STREET INDUS. CENTRE
HAWTHORN
B808
Possil Park
Keppoch Park
Hawthorn Prim. Sch.
Saracen Park
COWLAIRS INDUSTRIAL ESTATE
Cowlairs West Junc.
Cowlairs
Partick Thistle F.C. (Firhill Park)
Football Ground
Wester Common Prim. Sch.
Firhill
Millennium Cen.
Hamiltonhill
Works
St. Teresa's Prim. Sch.
COWLAIRS PARK (Rec. Grd.)
G21
SARACEN ST.
GARSCUBE ROAD
A81
OAKBANK INDUS. EST.
Warehouse
G4
PORT DUNDAS INDUS. EST.
Distillery
Sighthill Prim. Sch.
SIGHTHILL CEMETERY
CRAIGHALL RD.
KEPPOCHHILL ROAD
PINKSTON ROAD
CARLISLE STREET
ROYSTON ROAD

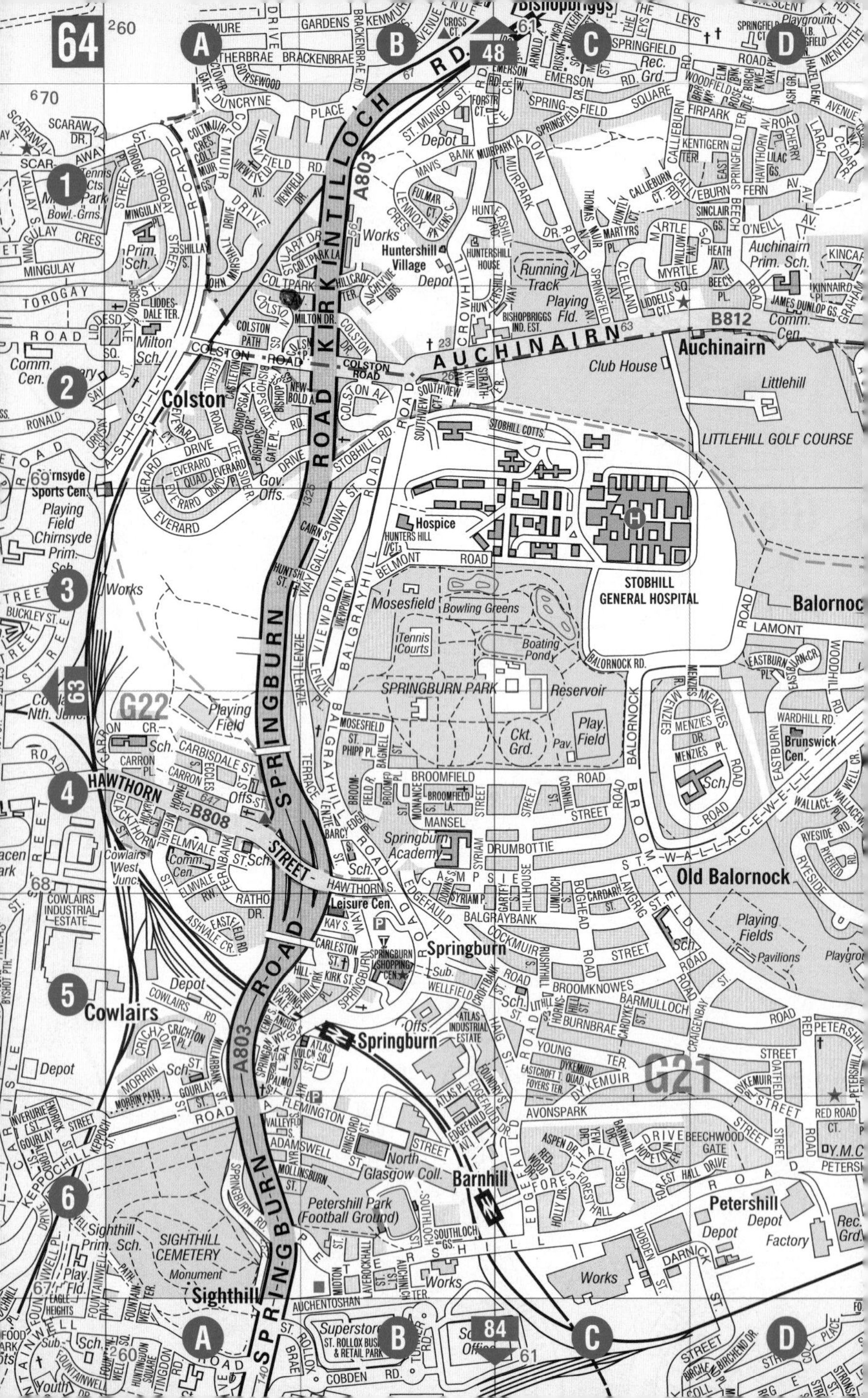

Bishopbriggs
48
Colston
Auchinairn
Littlehill
LITTLEHILL GOLF COURSE
STOBHILL GENERAL HOSPITAL
Balornock
Old Balornock
SPRINGBURN PARK
Springburn
Cowlairs
Sighthill
SIGHTHILL CEMETERY
Barnhill
Petershill
Petershill Park (Football Ground)
North Glasgow Coll.
KIRKINTILLOCH ROAD
SPRINGBURN ROAD
AUCHINAIRN ROAD
HAWTHORN STREET
G21
G22
63
84

G64
Lumloch
Wester Lumloch
Wester Lumloch Cottage
B812
AUCHINAIRN ROAD
EAST DUNBARTONSHIRE
GLASGOW
ROBROYSTON ROAD
LANGMUIRHEAD RD.
Robroyston Mains
Robroyston Farm Cottages
Auchinleck Cottages
Auchinleck
AUCHINLECK ROAD
HILLHEAD RD.
B765
STANDBURN RD.
BROOMTON ROAD
NORTHGATE
FERNESS OVAL
Sch.
Youth Cen.
Water Tower
Corporation Yd.
Robroyston
Superstore
MONUMENT DR.
SAUGHS ROAD
ROBROYSTON INTERCHANGE
Junc. 2
M80
M80 MOTORWAY
G33
Glasgow
Gadburn Sch.
Lib.
Prim. Sch.
College Play. Fields
All Saints Sports Sec. Cen. Sch.
Barmulloch
QUARRYWOOD ROAD
RYEHILL
BROOMFIELD
Football Grd.
St. Philomena's Prim. Sch.
ROYSTON RD.
ROYSTON ROAD
LANGDALE ST.
Provanmill
Provanhill Park Pav.
Littlehill Prim. Sch.
Playing Field
Gasholder
Blackhill
RIDDRIE PARK CEMETERY
Molendinar Burn
Superstore
CUMBERNAULD ROAD
A80
HOGGANFIELD LOCH
Slipway
Club House
Landing Stage
Miniature Golf Course
LETHAMHILL GOLF COURSE
MOSSBANK AVENUE
LOCHVIEW DRIVE
STATION ROAD
E
F
G
H
1
2
3
4
5
6
49
85
99

A
B
C
D
50
LENZIE GOLF COURSE
LANGMUIRHEAD ROAD
Langmuirhead Farm
Cardyke Farm
G66
Cult Burn
Hillview Farm
Auchengree Farm
Nursery
M80 MOTORWAY
M80
ROBROYS
ROBROYSTON ROAD
Auchinleck Cottages
Auchinleck
AUCHINLECK ROAD
SAUGHS AVENUE
SAUGHS DRIVE
SAUGHS ROAD
SAUGHS GATE
SAUGHS PL.
SAUGHS AV.
Saughs
BOGSIDE ROAD
Whitehill Farm
LENZIE ROAD
BOTHLIN DR.
WHITEHILL FARM ROAD
ALEXANDRA AV.
CHURCH AV.
ANNIESDALE AV.
Pav.
Bowl. Grn.
Rec. Gr.
War Me
VICTORIA RD.
WEST AV.
STATION RD.
STEPPS
65
ROBROYSTON INTERCHANGE
Junction 2
Garnkirk Burn
DUNALASTAIR CRES.
MILLERSNEUK CRES.
INGLENEUK AV.
LOCHEARNHEAD RD.
ST. FILLANS RD.
ALMOND DRIVE
BALLAIG CRESCENT
LAUNDRY LA.
CLARENDON PL.
G33
LEDNOCK RD.
COMRIE RD.
STEPPSHILL TER.
Works
LOCH ROAD
STATION ROAD
FIFTH AV.
FOURTH AV.
FIRST AV.
SECOND AV.
THIRD AV.
COSHNEUK RD.
Coshneuk Hall
CESSNOCK RD.
LOUDON RD.
Millerston
Craigendmuir Park
BLANEVIEW
CAMPSIE VW.
CRAIGENDMUIR CARAVAN SITE
68
CASTLEFIELD CT.
ROWALLAN TER.
Running Track
Playing Field
Frankfield Loch
Ogilvie Athletic Ground
Games Court
Molendinar Burn
Playing Fields
Games Ct.
Pav.
CUMBERNAULD ROAD
A80
MOSSBANK DRIVE
AVENUE
ROYSTON ROAD
DRIVE
LOCHVIEW DRIVE
AVENUE END ROAD
CARDOWAN MO
HOGGANFIELD LOCH
Bird Sanctuary
Landing Stage
Club House
67
Miniature Golf Course
Lethamhill Golf Course
64
Hogganfield Park
Hogganfield
Ashcraig School
MOSSVALE
CARDRONA ST.
POWRIE ST.
GLENRAITH WLK.
Football Grd.
Sch.
Craigend
MOSSVALE PATH
Football Pitch
Football Ground
GILBERTFIELD PATH
BIGTON
86
265
GRANGE RD.

67
51
67
STEPPS RD.
Arronhill Plantation
Drumsack Plantation
Garnkirk
Burn
RICHMOND GDS.
PEATHILL
BARCALDINE
HILLVIEW
GLEN AV.
GLENTNEY
LANRIG PL.
DRUMSACK
THE EVERGLADES
GREENLEA ROAD
CROW WOOD GOLF COURSE
Playground
Play Fld.
CAMPSIE VIEW
JOHN BROWN PL.
KNOWE
BERRYKNOWE
FLEMING AV.
Glen Plantation
Glen Cott.
M80
Junction 3
HORNSHILL INTERCHANGE
Hornshill
Garnkirk Ho. (Club Ho.)
Sub.
Glen Plantation
Crow Wood
Crow Wood House Hotel
Burn
Glasgow
Lodge
CUMBERNAULD ROAD
A80
WOODHEAD TER.
CROW WD TER.
LAURELBANK RD.
CROW WOOD RD
BELHAVEN PARK
LILYBANK
POTASSIUM
69
DRIVE
HORNSHILL FARM RD.
HARRIET
MINT
Pav.
Warehouse
Gateside
Playground
Recreation Grd.
PARKVIEW DR.
ROAD
A80
DEWAR ROAD
Highpit Plantation
Woodhead Farm
Depot
BUCHANAN CT.
BUCHANAN BUSINESS PARK
Lib.
Sch.
SCHOOL RD.
CARDOWAN DR.
COURT
Works
Garnkirk
WOODHEAD IND. EST.
WOODHEAD
Woodhead Cottage
Cardowan Cottage
68
Stepps
GARNKIRK LA.
MULLEN CT.
REYNOLDS PL.
HALL DR.
WHITEFORD
KIRKWOOD AV.
ROAD
KIRKPATRICK
Gartloch Cottages
Club
St. Joseph's Prim. Sch.
DRIVE
JACKSON DR.
ARDTOE
ARDTOE PL.
DRIMNIN RD.
CR.
ROAD
FRANKFIELD
MOSS VIEW
RESIPOL
GASKIN PTH.
DORLIN RD.
Craigendmuir
CRAIGENDMUIR RD.
COMEDIE RD.
68
G69
NORTH LANARKSHIRE
GLASGOW
CRAIGENDMUIR CARAVAN SITE
Drain
ROAD
TOWERVIEW
Mid Cotts
West Cottages
GARTLOCH B806
Recreation Ground
Lodge
67
Blackfaulds Farm
87
67
68
E
F
G
H
1
2
3
4
5
6

Chryston
Lanrigg
Muirhead
Glasgow
G69
Gartcosh
Mount Ellen
Cumbernauld Road
A80
Drumcavel Road
A752
Lochend Road
Gartloch Road
B806
B819
Lindsaybeg Rd.
Station Road
M73 Motorway
North Lanarkshire
Glasgow
Chryston High. Sch.
Chryston Prim. Sch.
Chryston Valley Business Cen.
Iain Nicolson Rec. Cen.
Bedlay Castle
St. Barbara's Prim. Sch.
Slakiewood
Glaudhall Farm
Garnkirk Moss
Mossvale Nurseries
Heathfield Moss
Heathfield Farm
Station Cott.
Mossview Cotts.
Works
Holms
Lochend House
Lochend Nursery
Johnston Loch
Comm. Cen.
Football Grd.
Depot
Woodhead Ind. Est.
Mid Cotts.
Recreation Ground
Lodge
Lochview Cottages
Gartloch Cottages
Bothlin Burn
Drain
Bishop Loch
52
67
88

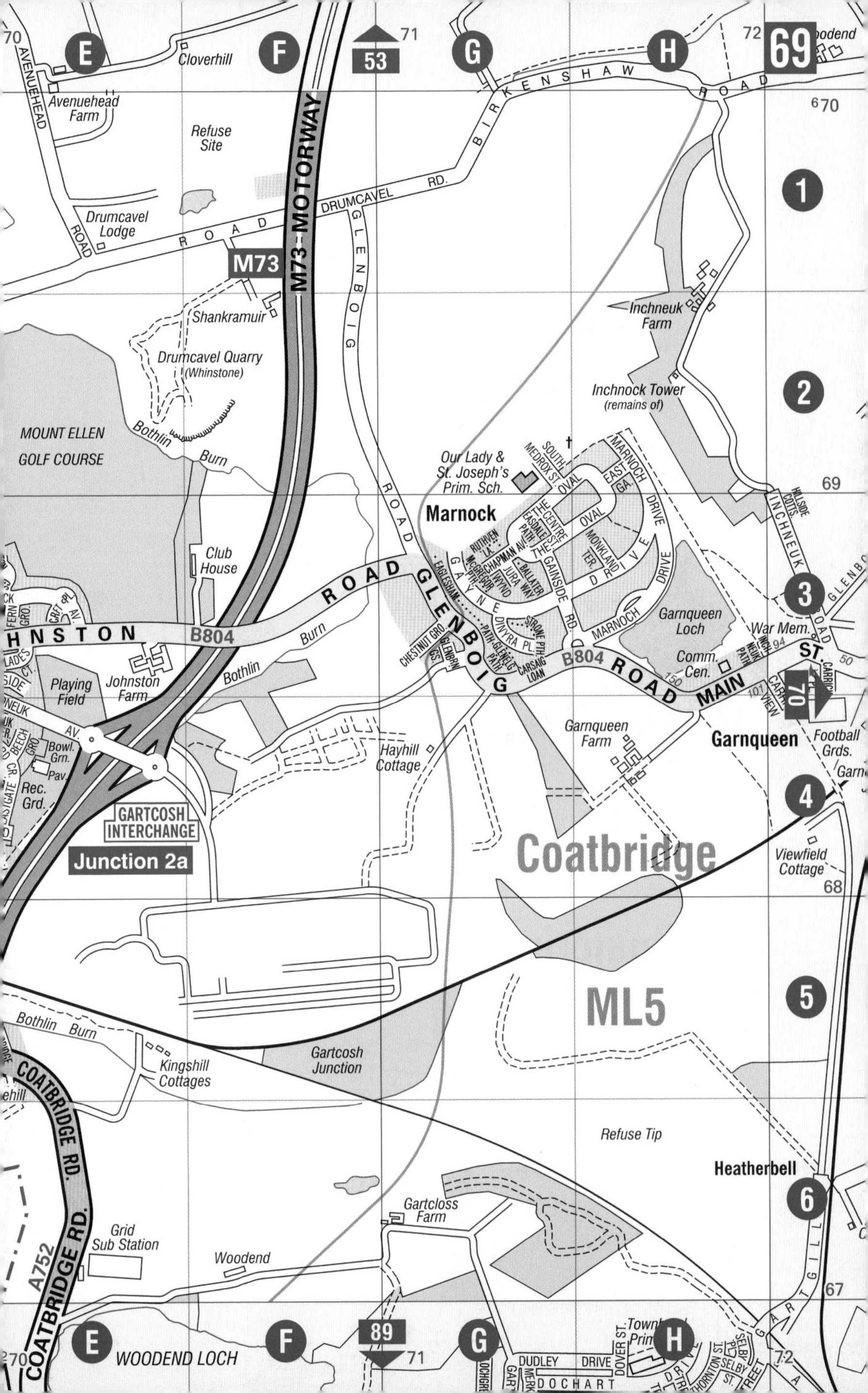

69
53
89
70
E
F
G
H
1
2
3
4
5
6
Cloverhill
Avenuehead Farm
AVENUEHEAD ROAD
Refuse Site
M73-MOTORWAY
M73
BIRKENSHAW ROAD
DRUMCAVEL RD.
DRUMCAVEL ROAD
Drumcavel Lodge
Shankramuir
Drumcavel Quarry (Whinstone)
MOUNT ELLEN GOLF COURSE
Bothlin Burn
GLENBOIG ROAD
Inchneuk Farm
Inchnock Tower (remains of)
Our Lady & St. Joseph's Prim. Sch.
Marnock
MARNOCH DRIVE
Club House
JOHNSTON ROAD
B804
Playing Field
Johnston Farm
Bowl. Grn.
Pav.
Rec. Grd.
Garnqueen Loch
Comm. Cen.
War Mem.
MAIN ST.
INCHNEUK ROAD
Garnqueen Farm
Garnqueen
Football Grds.
Hayhill Cottage
GARTCOSH INTERCHANGE
Junction 2a
Coatbridge
Viewfield Cottage
ML5
Kingshill Cottages
Gartcosh Junction
Refuse Tip
Heatherbell
COATBRIDGE RD.
A752
Grid Sub Station
Woodend
Gartcloss Farm
GARTGILL
WOODEND LOCH
DUDLEY DRIVE
DOCHART
DOVER ST.
THORNTON ST.
SELBY ST.

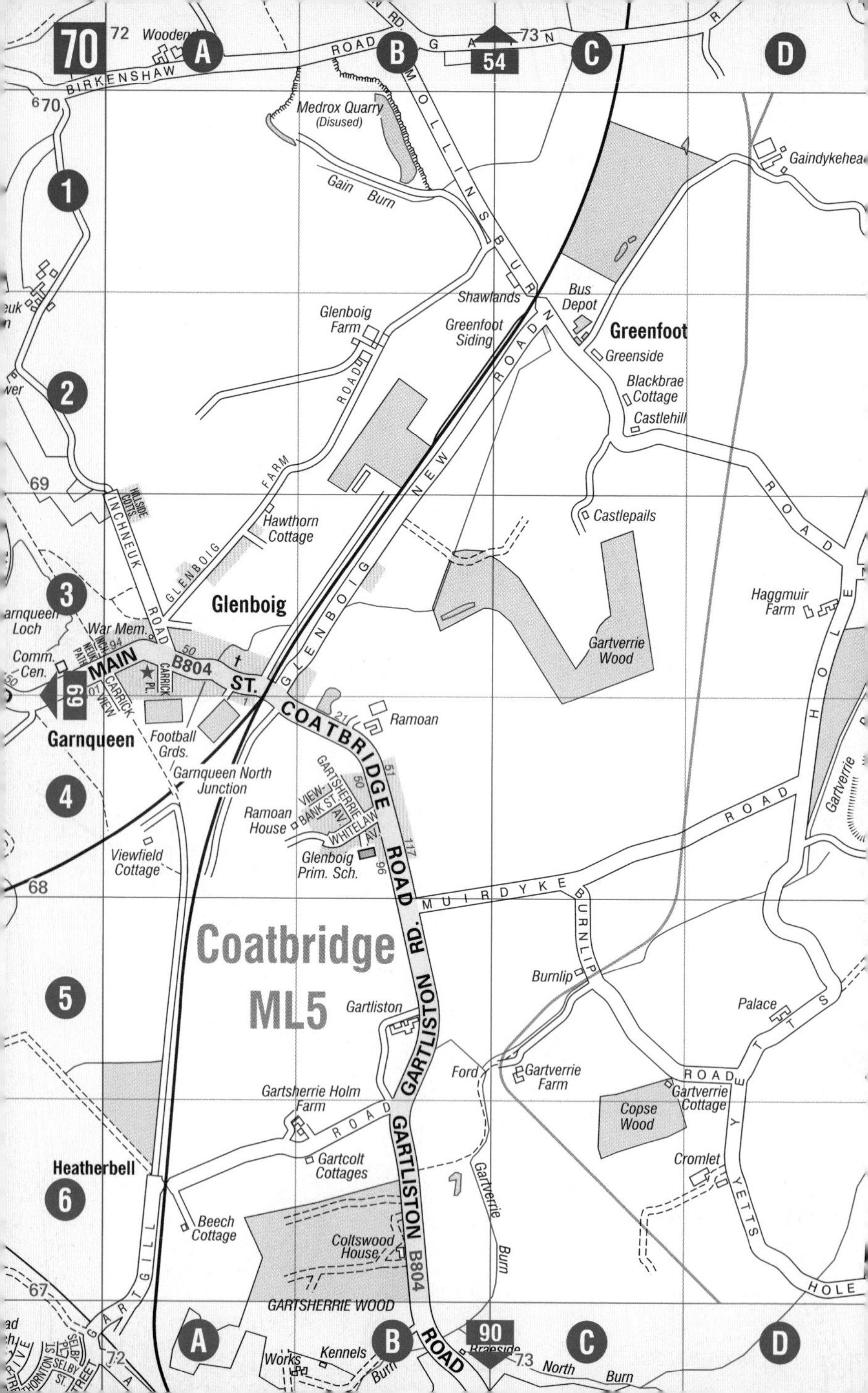

Woodend

A

BIRKENSHAW

670

M ROD

ROAD

B

M O L L I N S B U R N

G

A

73 N

54

R

C

D

Medrox Quarry
(Disused)

Gaindykehea

Gain Burn

1

Glenboig
Farm

Shawlands

Greenfoot
Siding

Bus
Depot

Greenfoot

Greenside

ROAD

N

2

F A R M

Blackbrae
Cottage

Castlehill

ROAD

69

Hawthorn
Cottage

Castlepails

Haggmuir
Farm

H
O
L
E

Gartverrie
Wood

HILLSIDE
COTTAGE

INCHNEUK

Glenboig

G
L
E
N
B
O
I
G

ROAD

3

Garnqueen
Loch

War Mem.

NEW
ROW

CRAIGIE
PARK

B804

50

t

Comm.
Cen.

69

MAIN

CARRICK
PL.

CARRICK
VIEW

ST.

COATBRIDGE

211

Ramoan

ROAD

Castlepails

Gartverrie

Garnqueen

Football
Grds.

Garnqueen North
Junction

VIEW

GARTSHERRIE
BANK ST.

50

51

117

ROAD

4

Ramoan
House

WHITELAW AV.

96

Glenboig
Prim. Sch.

MUIRDYKE

ROAD

Viewfield
Cottage

68

**Coatbridge
ML5**

Gartliston

Ford

Gartverrie
Farm

Burnlip

Burnlip

Palace

BURNLIP

ROAD

Y
E
T
T
S

5

GARTLISTON

Copse
Wood

Gartverrie
Cottage

Cromlet

Gartsherrie Holm
Farm

ROAD

Gartcolt
Cottages

RD.

B804

Gartverrie

Burn

Heatherbell

6

Beech
Cottage

Coltswood
House

67

CART GILL

GARTSHERRIE WOOD

GARTLISTON

ROAD

A

Kennels

B

72

Works

Burn

HORNTON

THORNTON ST.
SELBY

72A

STREET

90

Breaside

73

North

Burn

C

HOLE

D

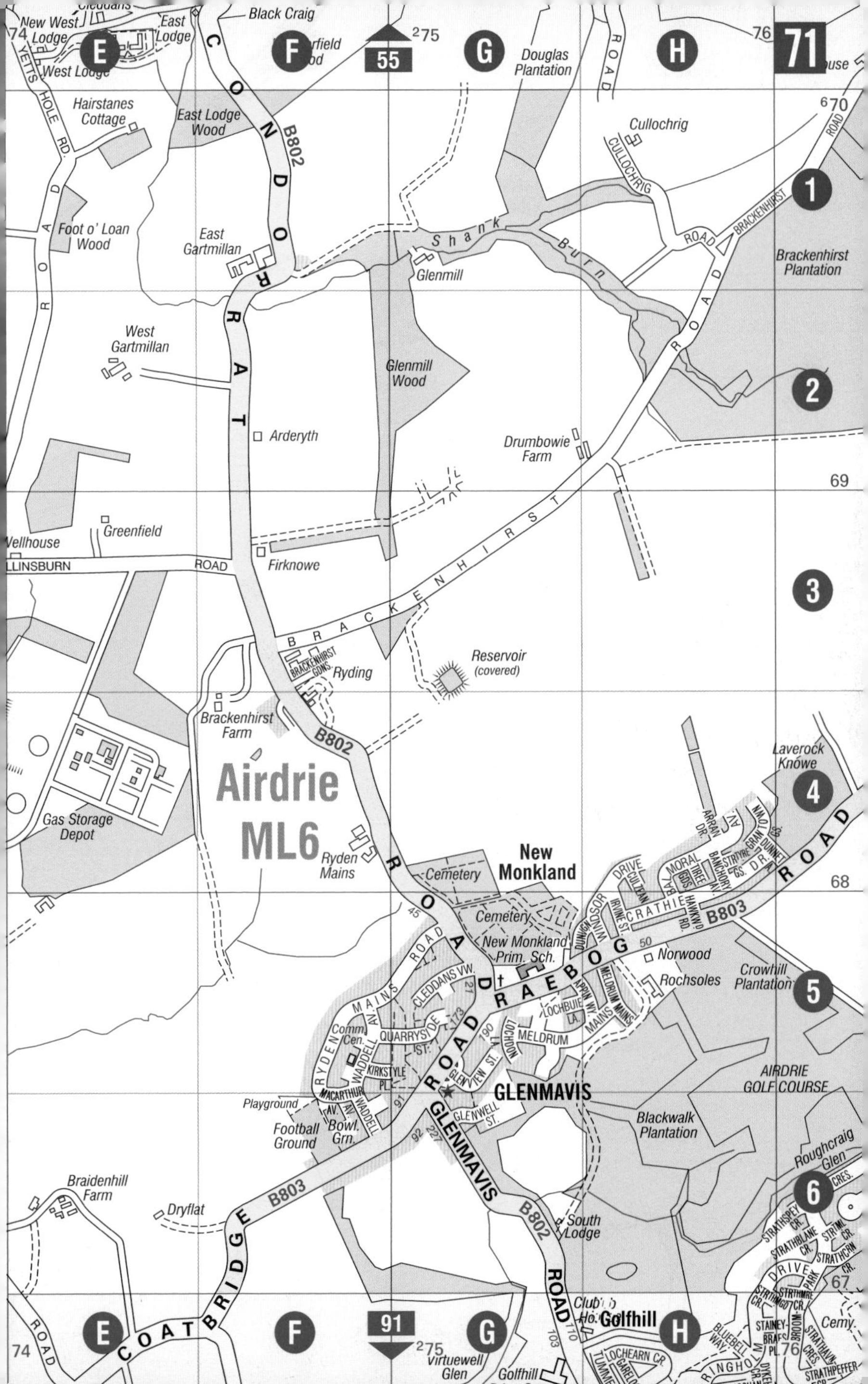
55
275
76
E
F
G
H
New West Lodge
East Lodge
West Lodge
Black Craig
Douglas Plantation
Hairstanes Cottage
East Lodge Wood
YETTS HOLE RD.
B802
CONDORRAT ROAD
Cullochrig
CULLOCHRIG
670
1
Foot o' Loan Wood
East Gartmillan
Shank Burn
Glenmill
BRACKENHIRST ROAD
Brackenhirst Plantation
West Gartmillan
Glenmill Wood
2
Arderyth
Drumbowie Farm
69
Greenfield
Wellhouse
LLINSBURN ROAD
Firknowe
3
BRACKENHIRST GDNS.
Ryding
Reservoir (covered)
Brackenhirst Farm
Laverock Knowe
Airdrie ML6
4
Gas Storage Depot
Ryden Mains
New Monkland
Cemetery
68
New Monkland Prim. Sch.
B803
RAEBOG ROAD
CRATHIE DR.
Norwood
Rochsoles
Crowhill Plantation
5
MAINS ROAD
CLEDDANS VW.
QUARRYSIDE ST.
MELDRUM
LOCHBUIE LA.
MELDRUM MAINS
Comm. Cen.
KIRKSTYLE PL.
GLENVIEW ST.
AIRDRIE GOLF COURSE
GLENMAVIS
Playground
GLENWELL ST.
Football Ground
Bowl. Grn.
Blackwalk Plantation
Roughcraig Glen
Braidenhill Farm
Dryflat
GLENMAVIS ROAD
6
South Lodge
COATBRIDGE ROAD
Club Ho.
Golfhill
67
Cemy.
91
74
Virtuewell Glen
Golfhill

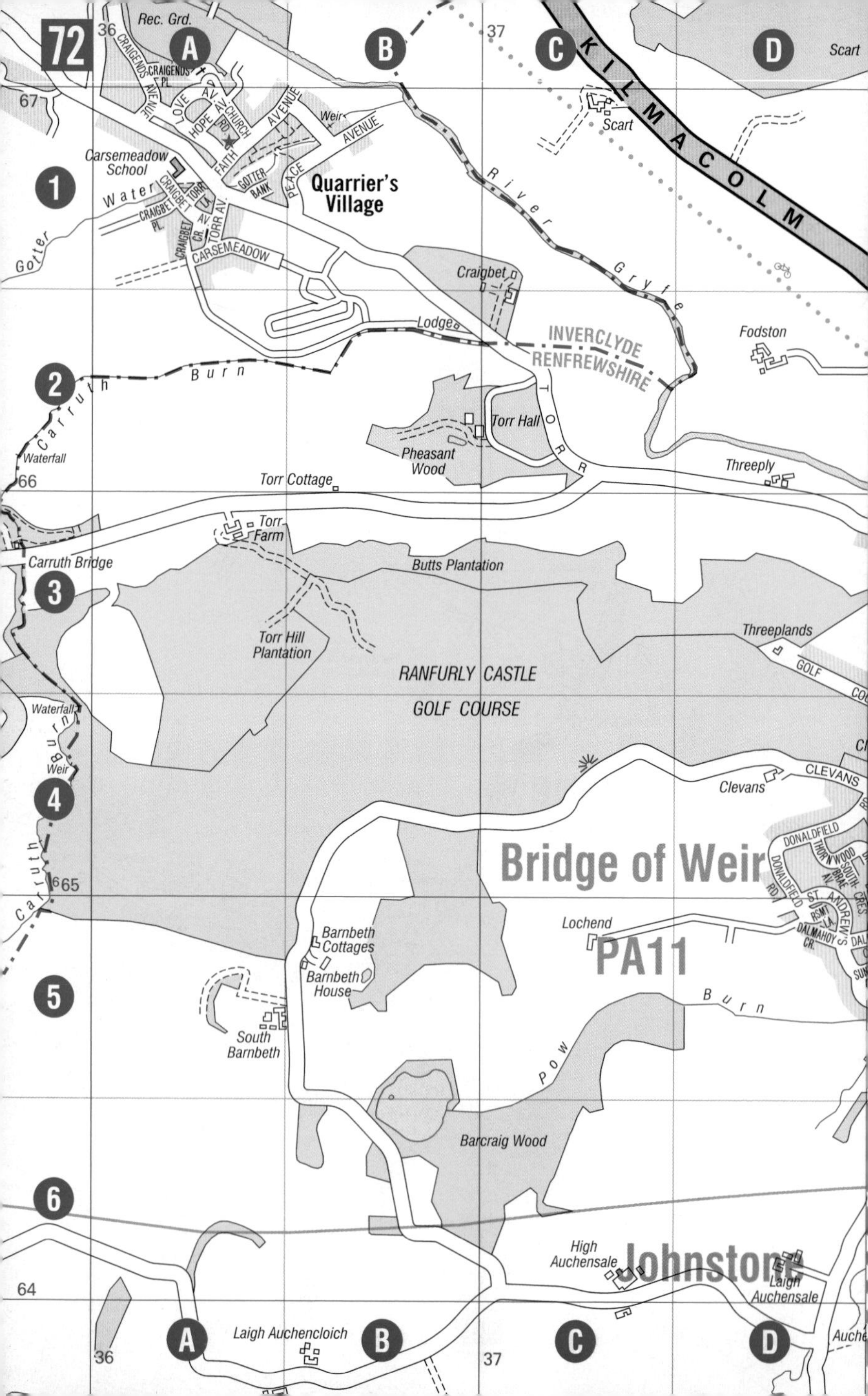

A
B
C
D
36
37
67
66
65
64
1
2
3
4
5
6
Rec. Grd.
CRAIGENDS AVENUE
CRAIGENDS PL.
LOVE AV.
HOPE AV.
CHURCH RD.
FAITH
AVENUE
Weir
AVENUE
Carsemeadow School
Water
CRAIGBET AV.
TORR LA.
GOTTER BANK
PEACE
Quarrier's Village
CRAIGBET PL.
CR.
TORR AV.
CRAIGBET
CARSEMEADOW
Gotter
KILMACOLM
Scart
Scart
River
Gryfe
Craigbet
Lodge
INVERCLYDE
RENFREWSHIRE
Fodston
Carruth
Burn
Torr Hall
TORR
Pheasant Wood
Waterfall
Torr Cottage
Threeply
Torr Farm
Carruth Bridge
Butts Plantation
Threeplands
Torr Hill Plantation
GOLF
RANFURLY CASTLE
GOLF COURSE
Waterfall
Burn
Weir
CLEVANS
Clevans
DONALDFIELD
THORNWOOD AV.
SOUTH BRAE
Bridge of Weir
DONALDFIELD RD.
ST. ANDREW'S CRES.
Carruth
Barnbeth Cottages
Lochend
RSMT. LA.
DALMAHOY CR.
PA11
Barnbeth House
Burn
South Barnbeth
Pow
Barcraig Wood
High Auchensale
Johnstone
Laigh Auchensale
Laigh Auchencloich

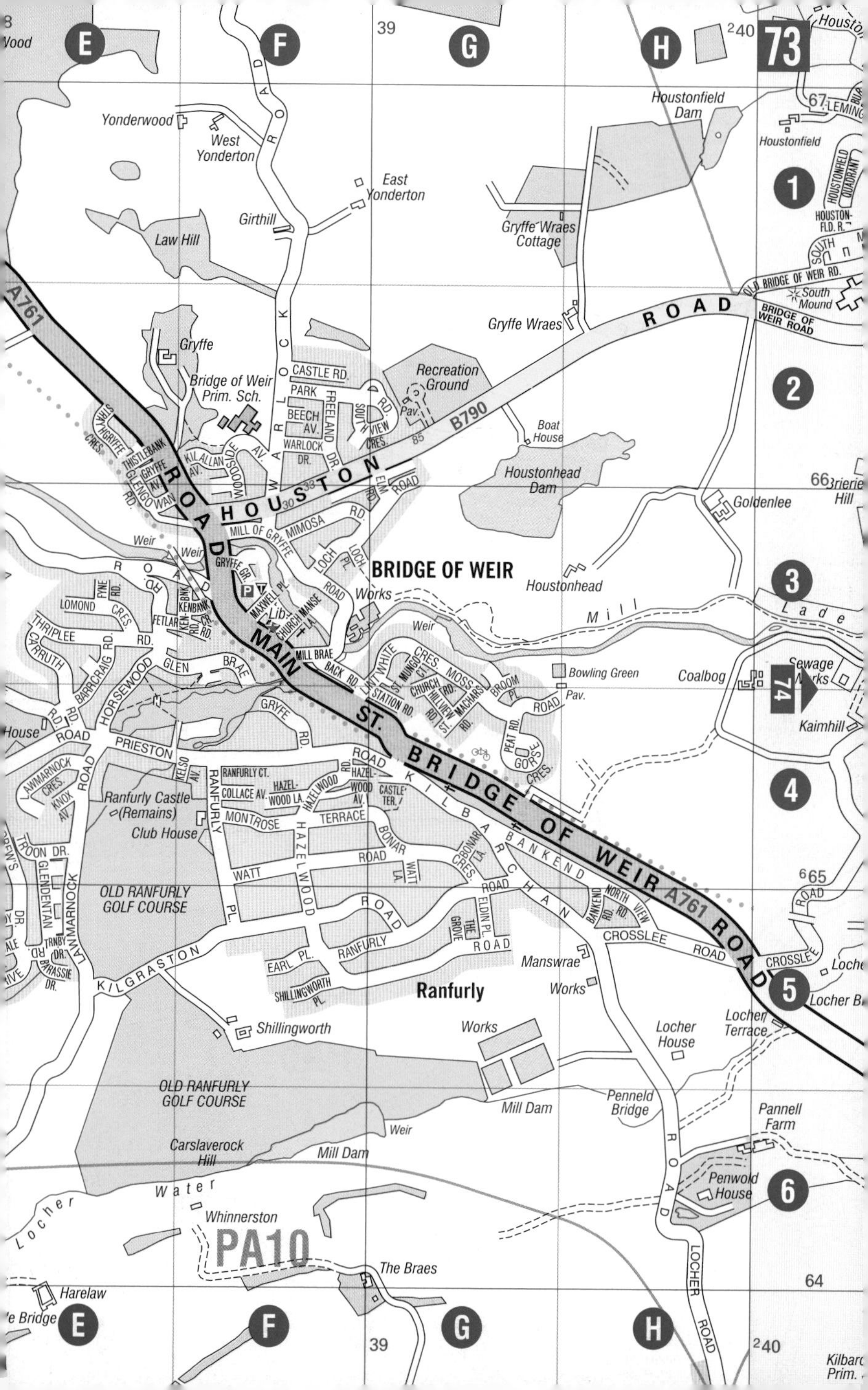

E
F
G
H
39
240
Wood
Yonderwood
West Yonderton
East Yonderton
Girthill
Law Hill
Houstonfield Dam
Houstonfield
67
HOUSTONFIELD QUADRANT
HOUSTON-FLD. R.
Gryffe Wraes Cottage
OLD BRIDGE OF WEIR RD.
South Mound
BRIDGE OF WEIR ROAD
ROAD
Gryffe Wraes
A761
Gryffe
Bridge of Weir Prim. Sch.
CASTLE RD.
PARK
BEECH AV.
FREELAND DR.
SOUTH VIEW CRES.
Recreation Ground
Pav.
B790
85
Boat House
Houstonhead Dam
WARLOCK DR.
WARLOCK ROAD
KILALLAN AV.
WOODSIDE AV.
THISTLEBANK
GRYFFE AV.
GLENGO RD.
WAN
STRATHGRYFFE CRES.
HOUSTON ROAD
33
30
ELM RD.
MIMOSA RD.
MILL OF GRYFFE
LOCH RD.
LOCH PL.
66
Brierie Hill
Goldenlee
Weir
ROAD
RD.
GRYFFE GR.
MAXWELL PL.
Lib.
CHURCH MANSE LA.
BRIDGE OF WEIR
Works
Houstonhead
Mill Lade
3
LOMOND
FYNE RD.
CRES.
THRIPLEE RD.
FETLAR
KENBANK RD.
KENBANK CR.
CARRUTH
BARRCRAIG RD.
HORSEWOOD RD.
GLEN BRAE
MAIN ST.
MILL BRAE
BACK RD.
LINTWHITE
ST. MUNGO CT.
CHURCH RD.
HILLVIEW RD.
MOSS RD.
ST. MACHARS RD.
BROOM PL.
STATION RD.
Bowling Green
Pav.
Coalbog
Sewage Works
74
Kaimhill
House
ROAD
PRIESTON
GRYFFE RD.
PEAT RD.
GORSE CRES.
LAWMARNOCK CRES.
KNOX AV.
KELSO AV.
RANFURLY CT.
COLLACE AV.
HAZELWOOD LA.
HAZELWOOD AV.
CASTLE TER.
KILBARCHAN ROAD
BRIDGE OF WEIR ROAD
4
Ranfurly Castle (Remains)
Club House
MONTROSE TERRACE
HAZELWOOD ROAD
BONAR ROAD
BONAR CRES.
BONAR LA.
WATT LA.
BANKEND
TROON DR.
GLENDENTAN
LAWMARNOCK
WATT
OLD RANFURLY GOLF COURSE
RANFURLY PL.
ELDIN PL.
THE GROVE
NORTH VIEW
BANKEND RD.
665
ROAD
A761
CROSSLEE ROAD
CROSSLEE
TRNBY DR.
BARASSIE DR.
KILGRASTON
EARL PL.
RANFURLY ROAD
SHILLINGWORTH PL.
Manswrae
Works
Ranfurly
5
Locher
Shillingworth
Works
Locher House
Locher Terrace
OLD RANFURLY GOLF COURSE
Mill Dam
Penneld Bridge
Pannell Farm
Weir
Carslaverock Hill
Mill Dam
Locher Water
Whinnerston
Penwold House
6
PA10
LOCHER ROAD
The Braes
Harelaw
64
Bridge
Kilbarc Prim.

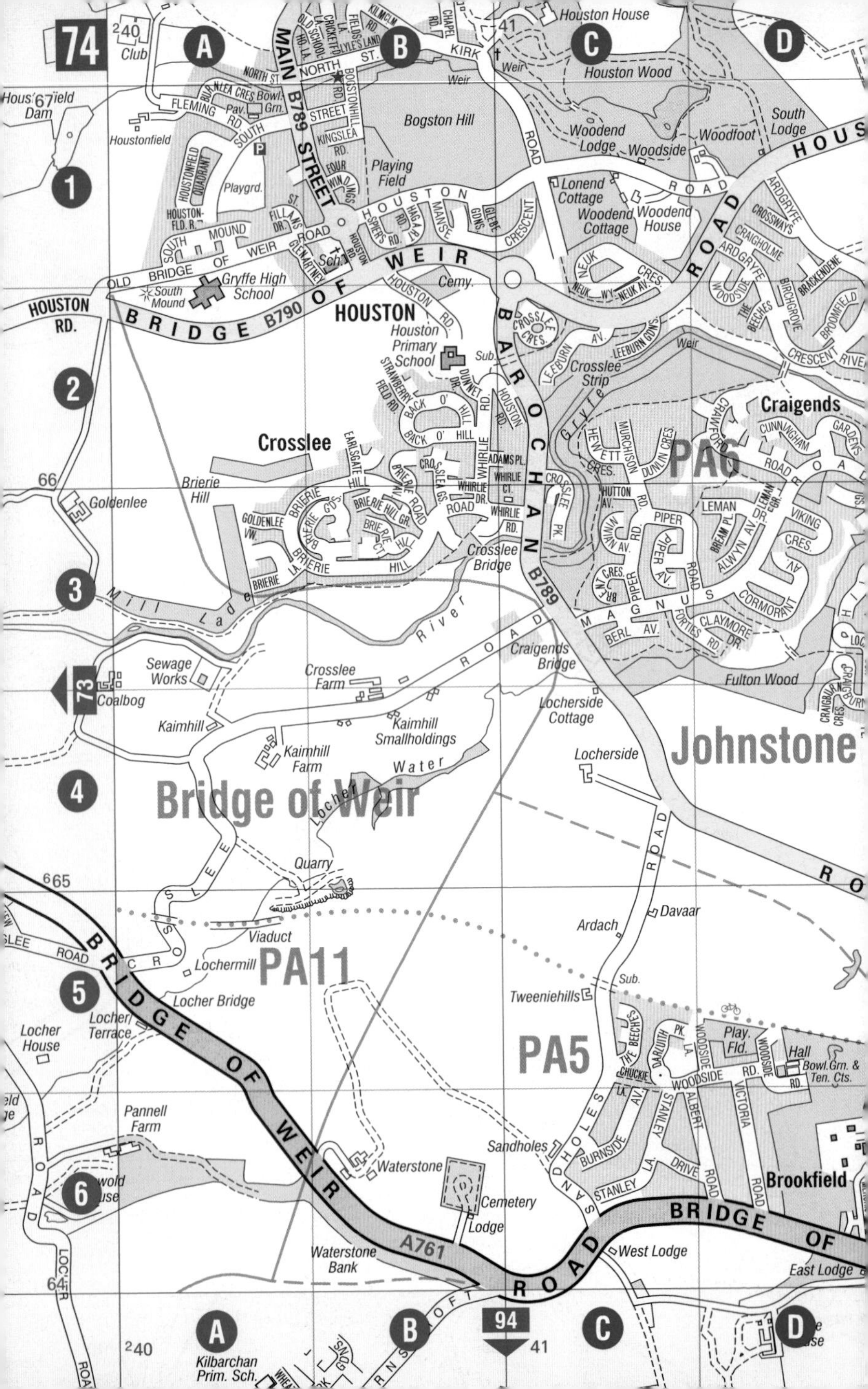

Houston House
Houston Wood
Bogston Hill
Woodend Lodge
Woodside
Woodfoot
South Lodge
Lonend Cottage
Woodend Cottage
Woodend House
Houstonfield Dam
Houstonfield
Club
Playing Field
Playgrd.
Gryffe High School
South Mound
HOUSTON
Houston Primary School
Cemy.
BRIDGE OF WEIR ROAD
HOUSTON RD.
Crosslee
Brierie Hill
Goldenlee
Crosslee Strip
Craigends
PA6
Crosslee Bridge
Craigends Bridge
Mill Lade
River Gryfe
Sewage Works
Coalbog
Crosslee Farm
Kaimhill
Kaimhill Smallholdings
Kaimhill Farm
Locherside Cottage
Locherside
Fulton Wood
Johnstone
Bridge of Weir
Locher Water
Quarry
Viaduct
PA11
Lochermill
Locher Bridge
Locher Terrace
Locher House
Pannell Farm
Ardach
Davaar
Tweeniehills
PA5
Play. Fld.
Hall
Bowl.Grn. & Ten. Cts.
Sandholes
Waterstone
Cemetery
Lodge
Waterstone Bank
West Lodge
East Lodge
Brookfield
Kilbarchan Prim. Sch.
A761
B789
B790
73
94

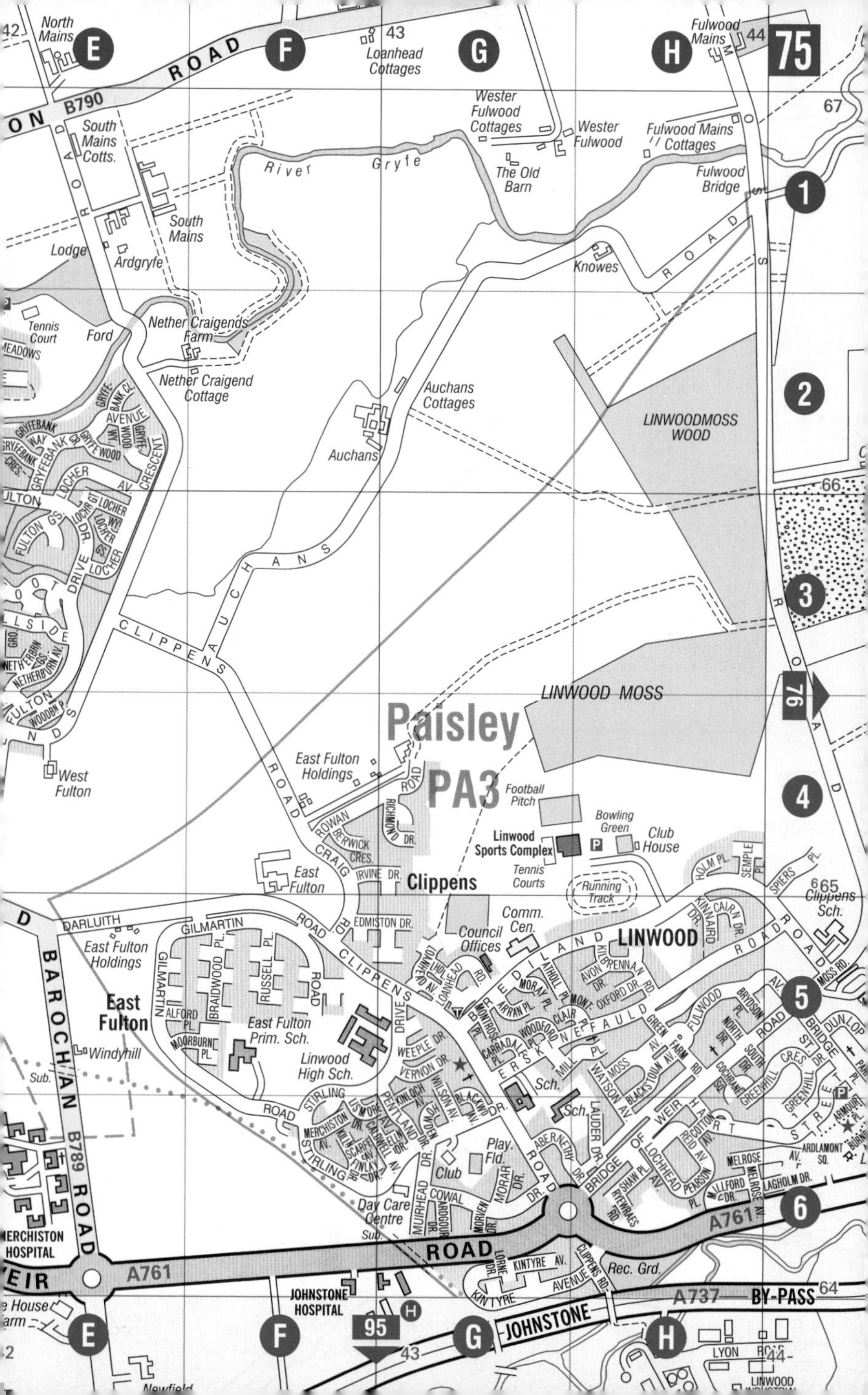

North Mains
Loanhead Cottages
Wester Fulwood Cottages
Wester Fulwood
Fulwood Mains
Fulwood Mains Cottages
Fulwood Bridge
South Mains Cotts.
South Mains
River Gryfe
The Old Barn
Knowes
Lodge
Ardgryfe
Tennis Court
Ford
Nether Craigends Farm
Nether Craigend Cottage
Auchans Cottages
Auchans
LINWOODMOSS WOOD
LINWOOD MOSS
Paisley
PA3
Football Pitch
Bowling Green
Club House
Linwood Sports Complex
Tennis Courts
Running Track
East Fulton Holdings
East Fulton
Clippens
Comm. Cen.
Council Offices
LINWOOD
Clippens Sch.
East Fulton
Windyhill
East Fulton Prim. Sch.
Linwood High Sch.
Sch.
Play. Fld.
Club
Day Care Centre
JOHNSTONE HOSPITAL
Rec. Grd.
MERCHISTON HOSPITAL
West Fulton
CLIPPENS ROAD
AUCHANS ROAD
BAROCHAN ROAD
B790
B789
A761
A737 BY-PASS
JOHNSTONE
76
95

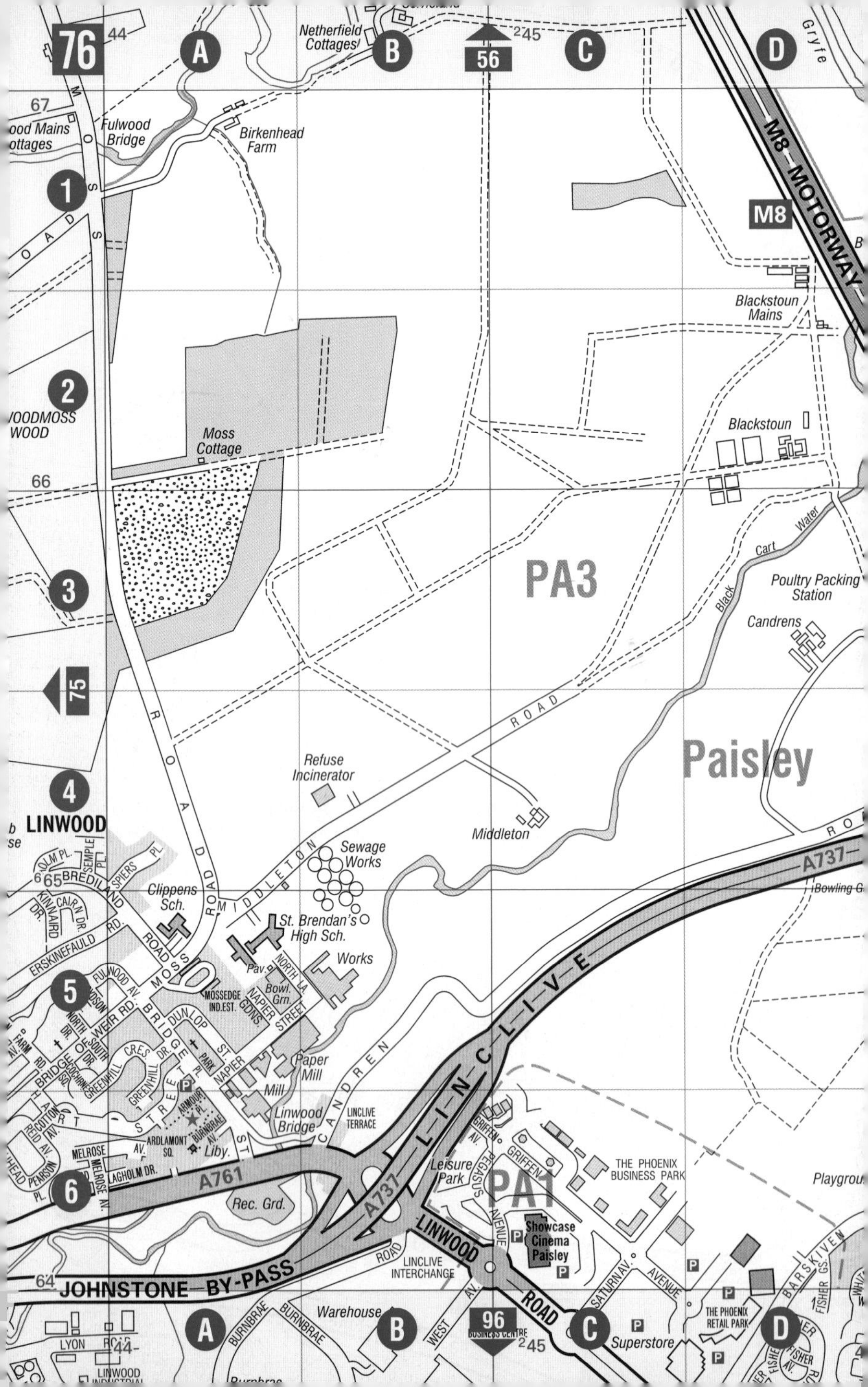

Netherfield Cottages
56
Gryfe
Fulwood Bridge
Birkenhead Farm
M8 MOTORWAY
M8
Blackstoun Mains
Blackstoun
Moss Cottage
Cart Water
Black
Poultry Packing Station
Candrens
PA3
75
Paisley
Refuse Incinerator
Middleton
LINWOOD
Sewage Works
MIDDLETON ROAD
MOSS ROAD
A737
Bowling G
Clippens Sch.
St. Brendan's High Sch.
Works
ERSKINEFAULD RD.
BREDILAND RD.
SPIERS PL.
SEMPLE PL.
KINNAIRD DR.
CAIRN DR.
MOSSEDGE IND.EST.
NAPIER GDNS.
NAPIER STREET
NORTH LA.
Bowl. Grn.
Pav.
FULWOOD AV.
BRIDGE OF WEIR RD.
BRIDGE STREET
DUNLOP ST.
PARK PL.
GREENHILL CRES.
GREENHILL DR.
COCHRANE SQ.
NORTH DR.
SOUTH DR.
Paper Mill
Mill
CANDREN ROAD
LINCLIVE
LINCLIVE TERRACE
Linwood Bridge
ARMOUR PL.
BURNBRAE AV.
ARDLAMONT SQ.
Liby.
COTTON AV.
MELROSE AV.
LAGHOLM DR.
PEARSON PL.
A761
Rec. Grd.
Leisure Park
GRIFFEN AV.
GRIFFEN
PEGASUS AVENUE
PA1
THE PHOENIX BUSINESS PARK
Showcase Cinema Paisley
Playgrou
LINWOOD ROAD
LINCLIVE INTERCHANGE
SATURN AV.
AVENUE
BARSKIVEN
FISHER GS.
JOHNSTONE BY-PASS
THE PHOENIX RETAIL PARK
Warehouse
BURNBRAE
WEST AV.
96
BUSINESS CENTRE
Superstore
FISHER AV.
LINWOOD INDUSTRIAL
LYON

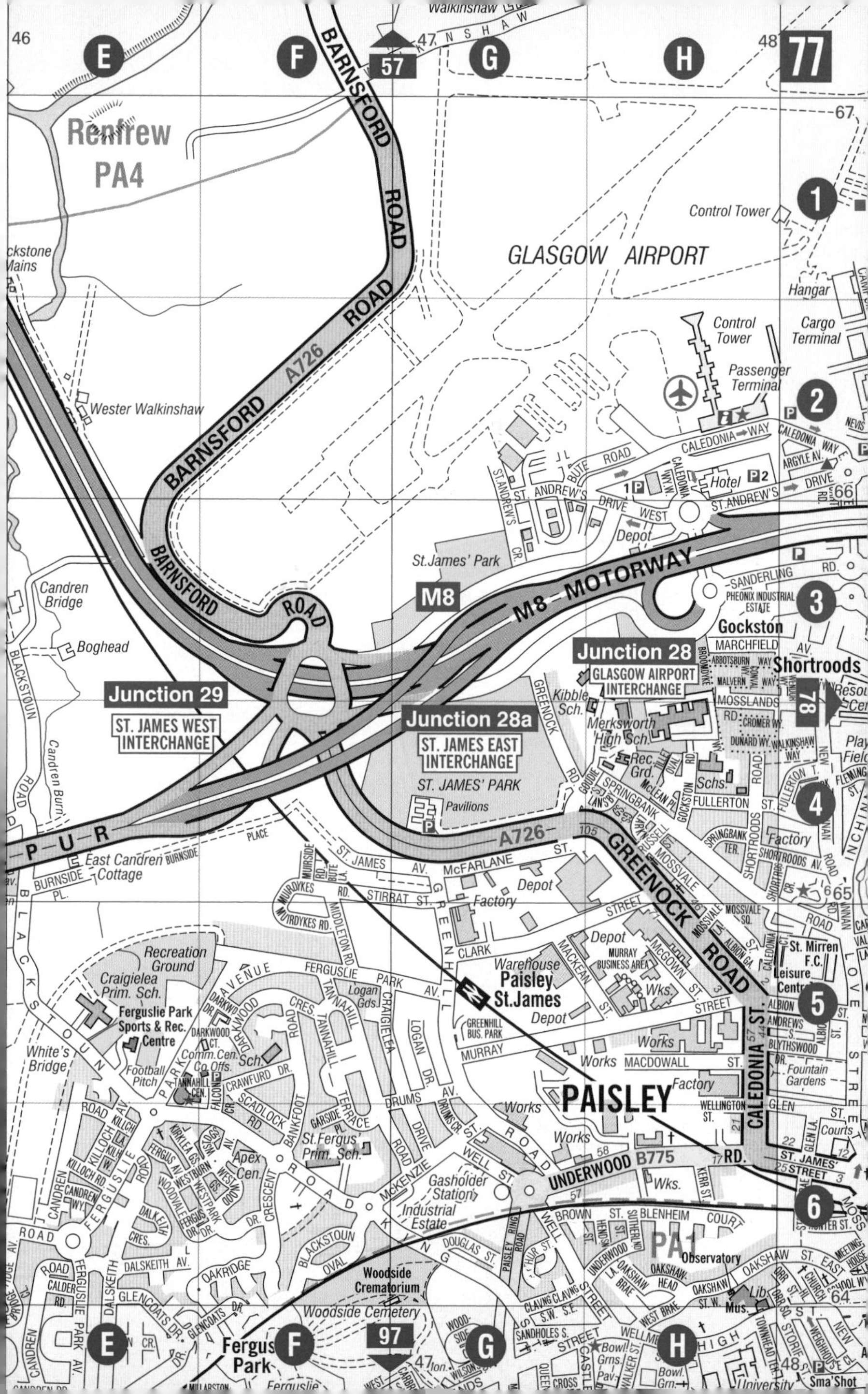

Renfrew
PA4
GLASGOW AIRPORT
Control Tower
Hangar
Cargo Terminal
Passenger Terminal
Wester Walkinshaw
BARNSFORD ROAD
A726
M8 MOTORWAY
Junction 29
ST. JAMES WEST INTERCHANGE
Junction 28a
ST. JAMES EAST INTERCHANGE
Junction 28
GLASGOW AIRPORT INTERCHANGE
St.James' Park
ST. JAMES' PARK
Pavilions
Gockston
Shortroods
Candren Bridge
Boghead
East Candren Cottage
Recreation Ground
Craigielea Prim. Sch.
Ferguslie Park Sports & Rec. Centre
White's Bridge
Paisley St.James
PAISLEY
GREENOCK ROAD
CALEDONIA ST.
UNDERWOOD B775
Gasholder Station
Industrial Estate
Woodside Crematorium
Woodside Cemetery
Ferguslie Park
St.Mirren F.C.
Fountain Gardens
Observatory
PA1
St.Fergus' Prim. Sch.
Merksworth High Sch.
Kibble Sch.

57
78
97

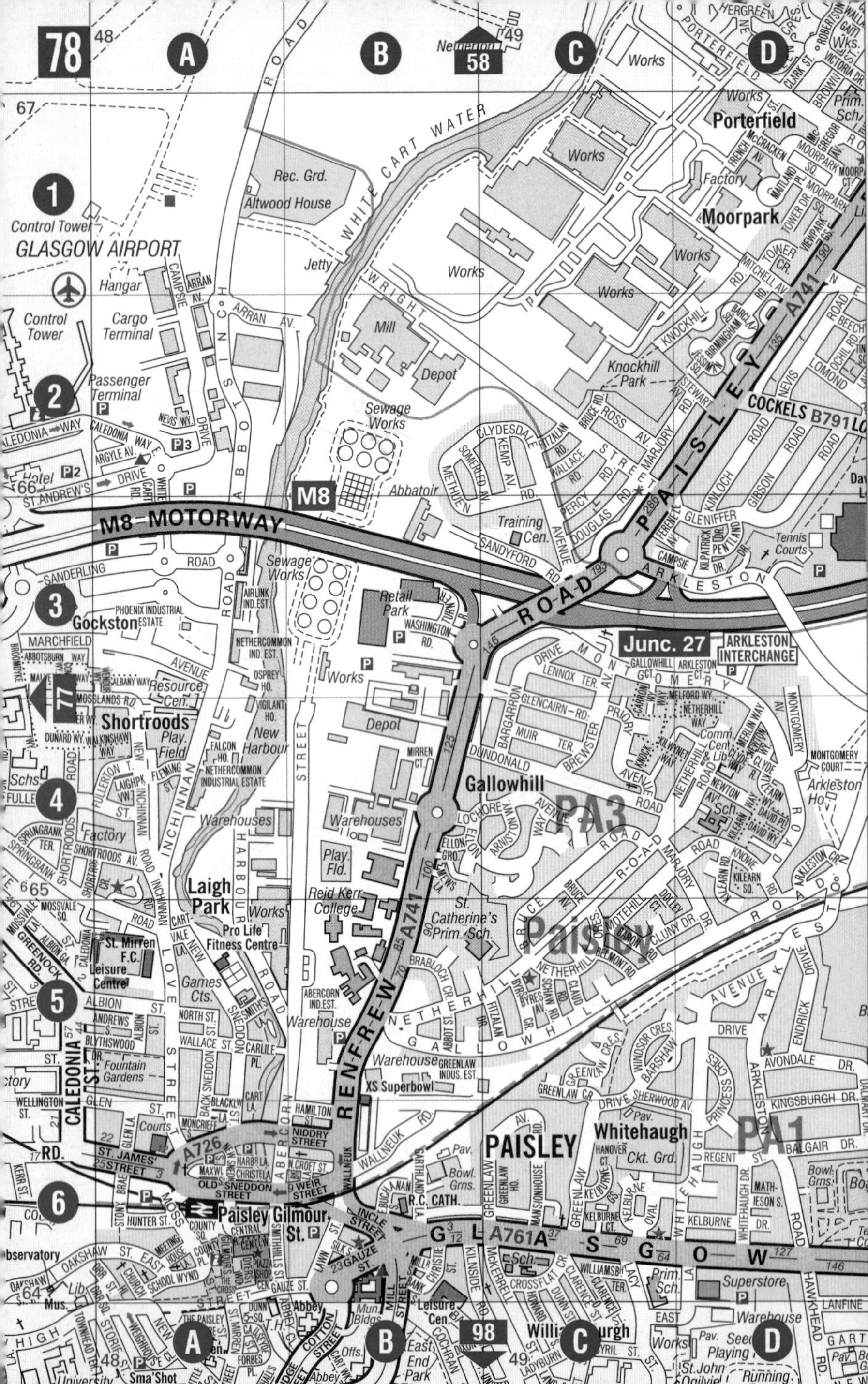
GLASGOW AIRPORT
Control Tower
Hangar
Cargo Terminal
Passenger Terminal
Rec. Grd.
Altwood House
WHITE CART WATER
Works
Porterfield
Moorpark
Jetty
Mill
Depot
Knockhill Park
Sewage Works
Abbatoir
Training Cen.
M8 MOTORWAY
PAISLEY ROAD
A741
Junc. 27
ARKLESTON INTERCHANGE
Gockston
Phoenix Industrial Estate
Airlink Ind. Est.
Nethercommon Ind. Est.
Retail Park
Resource Cen.
Shortroods
Play. Field
New Harbour
Nethercommon Industrial Estate
Gallowhill
Arkleston Ho.
PA3
Laigh Park
Warehouses
Factory
Play. Fld.
Reid Kerr College
St. Catherine's Prim. Sch.
Paisley
Pro Life Fitness Centre
St. Mirren F.C.
Leisure Centre
Games Cts.
Abercorn Ind. Est.
Warehouse
Fountain Gardens
Greenlaw Indus. Est.
XS Superbowl
Whitehaugh
Ckt. Grd.
PA1
PAISLEY
Courts
A726
Paisley Gilmour St.
R.C. CATH.
Bowl. Grns.
GLASGOW ROAD
A761
Observatory
Mus.
Abbey
Mun. Bldgs
Leisure Cen.
Superstore
Warehouse
Playing
University
Sma'Shot
East End Park
Williamsburgh
St. John Ogilvie
Running Track
RENFREW ROAD
GALLOWHILL ROAD
NETHERHILL RD.
ARKLESTON ROAD
CALEDONIA ST.
LOVE STREET
INCHINNAN ROAD
ABBOTSINCH ROAD
SNEDDON
HARBOUR ROAD
ABERCORN
WALLNEUK RD.
CAUSEYSIDE ST.
GAUZE ST.
OAKSHAW ST. EAST
HIGH ST.
NEW ST.
MOSS ST.
COUNTY SQ.
NIDDRY STREET
OLD SNEDDON STREET
WEIR STREET
INCLE STREET
MILL STREET
COTTON STREET
KILNSIDE RD.
McKERRELL ST.
WHITEHAUGH DR.
HAWKHEAD ROAD
KINGSBURGH DR.
AVONDALE DR.
BALGAIR DR.
KELBURNE DR.
BARSHAW
WINDSOR CRES.
GREENLAW CRES.
SHERWOOD AV.
PRINCESS CRES.
ENDRICK DRIVE
MONTGOMERY ROAD
MONTGOMERY COURT
MARJORY ROAD
BRUCE RD.
DUNDONALD
GLENCAIRN RD.
BARGARRON
LENNOX TER.
GALLOWHILL CT.
ARKLESTON CT.
CAMPSIE DR.
GLENIFFER DR.
KINLOCH ROAD
GIBSON ROAD
COCKELS B791 LOAN
LOMOND
NEVIS
STEWART AV.
KNOCKHILL RD.
MITCHELL AV.
TOWER CR.
VIEWPARK
MOORPARK SQ.
McCRACKEN AV.
FRENCH AV.
PORTERFIELD RD.
CLARK ST.
VICTORIA DR.
ROBERTSON
WRIGHT ST.
ROSS AV.
DOUGLAS
PERCY RD.
WALLACE RD.
FITZALAN RD.
CLYDESDALE
KEMP AV.
SOMERLED AV.
METHUEN
SANDYFORD RD.
WASHINGTON RD.
TURNER
MIRREN CT.
SANDERLING ROAD
MARCHFIELD
ABBOTSBURN WAY
MOSSLANDS RD.
WALKINSHAW WAY
DUNARD WY.
FULLERTON T.
LAIGHPARK VW.
FLEMING ST.
SPRINGBANK TER.
SHORTROODS AV.
SHORTROODS RD.
MOSSVALE SQ.
GREENOCK RD.
ALBION ST.
ANDREWS S.
BLYTHSWOOD DR.
WELLINGTON ST.
GLEN ST.
ST. JAMES' STREET
HUNTER ST.
STONY BRAE
KERR ST.
NORTH ST.
WALLACE ST.
CARLILE PL.
CART LA.
BACK SNEDDON
MONCRIEFF
HAMILTON ST.
ARRAN AV.
CAMPSIE DRIVE
NEVIS WY.
CALEDONIA WAY
ARGYLE AV.
ST. ANDREW'S DRIVE
WHITE CART RD.
Hotel
Schs.
Tennis Courts
Comm. Cen. & Lib.
Sch.
Prim. Sch.
Pav.
Offs.
Lib.
77
58
98
M8

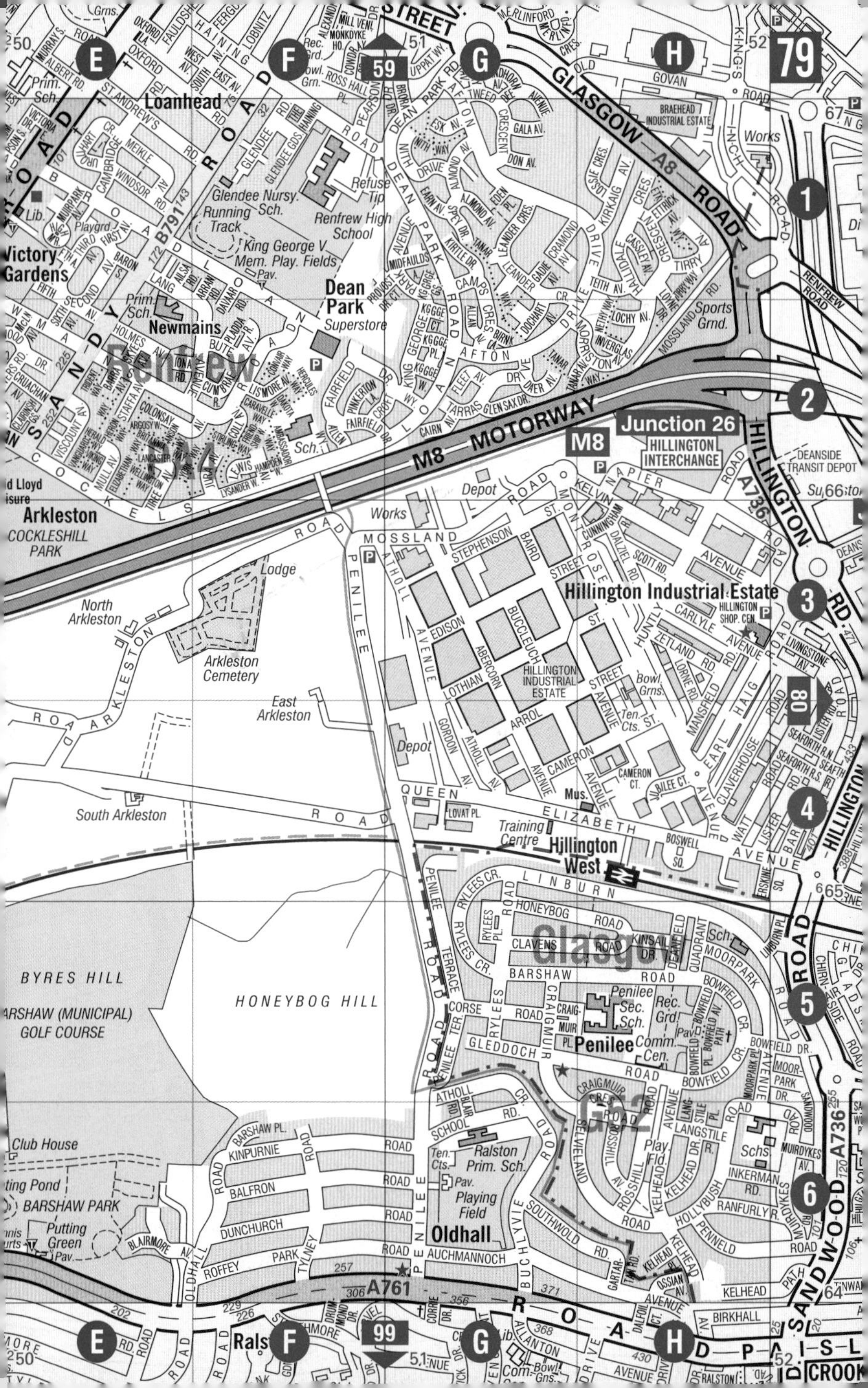
Loanhead
Victory Gardens
Newmains
Renfrew
PA4
Arkleston
COCKLESHILL PARK
North Arkleston
Arkleston Cemetery
East Arkleston
South Arkleston
Lodge
Dean Park
Superstore
Renfrew High School
Refuse Tip
Glendee Nursy. Sch.
Running Track
King George V Mem. Play. Fields
M8 MOTORWAY
Junction 26
HILLINGTON INTERCHANGE
DEANSIDE TRANSIT DEPOT
BRAEHEAD INDUSTRIAL ESTATE
GLASGOW A8 ROAD
GOVAN
Sports Grnd.
Hillington Industrial Estate
HILLINGTON SHOP. CEN.
Hillington West
Glasgow
Penilee
G52
Penilee Sec. Sch.
Ralston Prim. Sch.
Playing Field
Oldhall
BYRES HILL
HONEYBOG HILL
BARSHAW (MUNICIPAL) GOLF COURSE
Club House
BARSHAW PARK
Putting Green
A761
A736
PAISLEY ROAD
HILLINGTON RD.
SANDWOOD RD.
Training Centre
Mus.
Depot
Works
59
99
80
E F G H
1 2 3 4 5 6
50 51 52

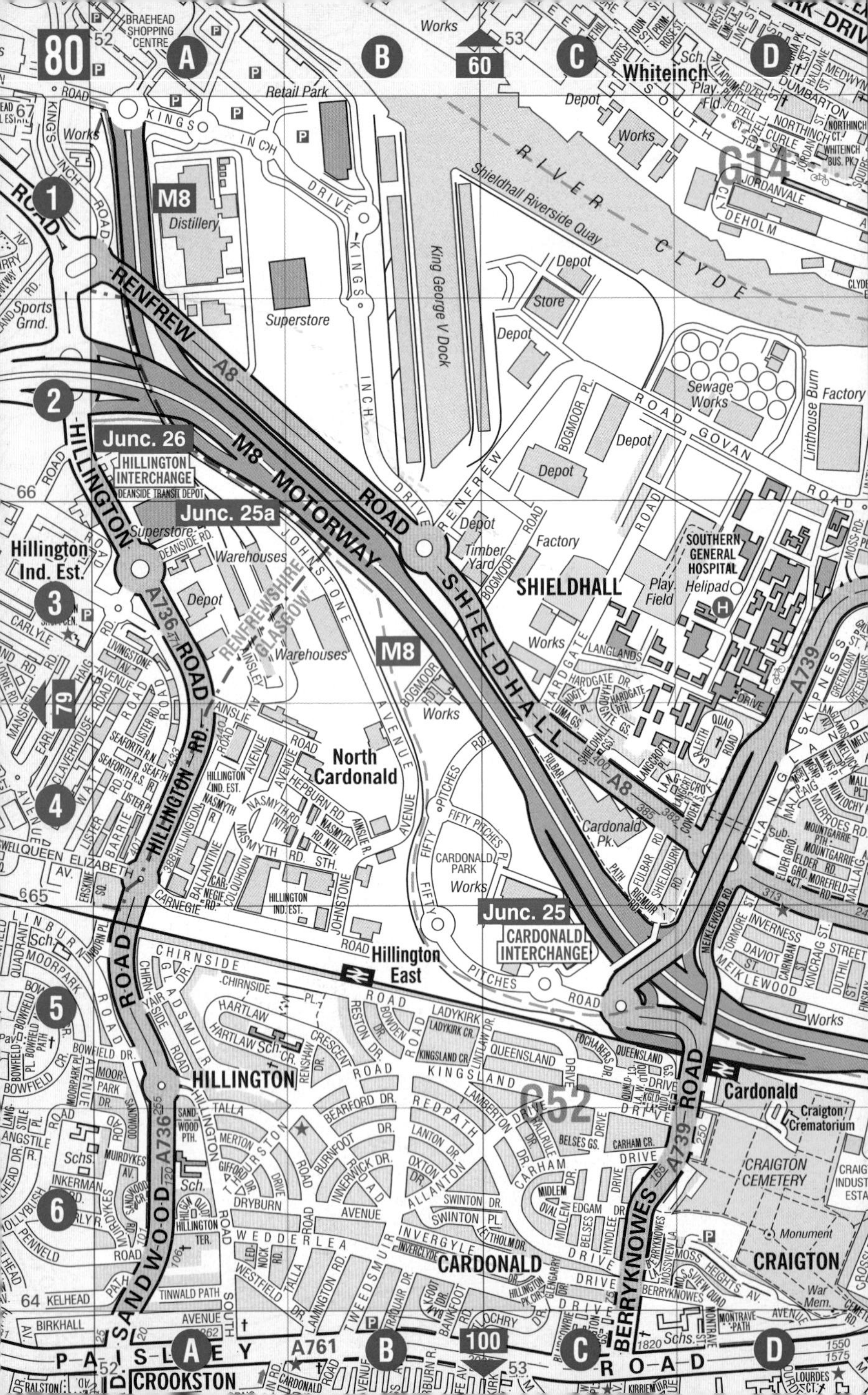

A
B
C
D
60
Whiteinch
BRAEHEAD SHOPPING CENTRE
Retail Park
Distillery
Superstore
King George V Dock
Shieldhall Riverside Quay
RIVER CLYDE
G14
Sewage Works
Linthouse Burn
Factory
GOVAN ROAD
RENFREW ROAD
M8 MOTORWAY
M8
A8
Junc. 26
HILLINGTON INTERCHANGE
Junc. 25a
Hillington Ind. Est.
RENFREWSHIRE GLASGOW
SHIELDHALL
SOUTHERN GENERAL HOSPITAL
Helipad
North Cardonald
Cardonald Pk.
CARDONALD PARK
Junc. 25
CARDONALD INTERCHANGE
Hillington East
HILLINGTON
G52
Cardonald
Craigton Crematorium
CRAIGTON CEMETERY
CRAIGTON
CARDONALD
A736
A739
A761
79
100
PAISLEY ROAD
CROOKSTON

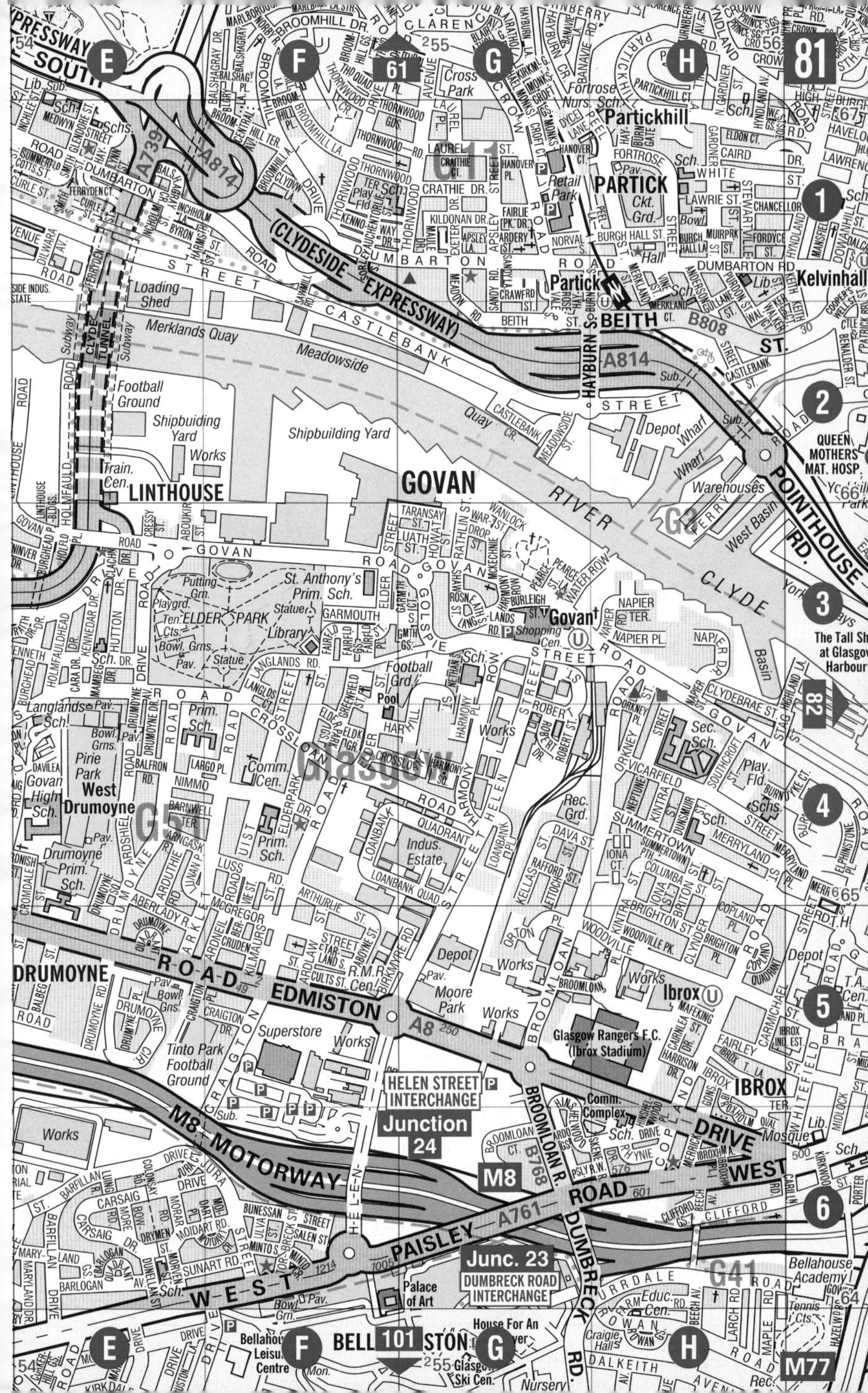81
61
101
82
E
F
G
H
E
F
G
H
1
2
3
4
5
6
54
255
56
67
66
65
64
54
255
EXPRESSWAY
SOUTH
A739
A814
CLYDESIDE EXPRESSWAY
Partickhill
PARTICK
Partick
Kelvinhall
Cross Park
Fortrose Nurs. Sch.
Retail Park
Ckt. Grd.
DUMBARTON ROAD
DUMBARTON RD
BEITH ST.
B808
A814
HAYBURN ST.
CASTLEBANK STREET
Loading Shed
Merklands Quay
Meadowside
Quay
CLYDE TUNNEL
Subway
Football Ground
Shipbuiding Yard
Shipbuilding Yard
Works
Train. Cen.
LINTHOUSE
GOVAN
RIVER CLYDE
Depot
Wharf
Warehouses
West Basin
POINTHOUSE RD.
QUEEN MOTHERS MAT. HOSP.
The Tall Ship at Glasgow Harbour
GOVAN ROAD
ELDER PARK
Putting Grn.
Playgrd.
Ten. Cts.
Bowl. Grns.
Pav.
Statue
Library
St. Anthony's Prim. Sch.
Govan
Shopping Cen.
NAPIER TER.
NAPIER PL.
Basin
Football Grd.
Pool
Langlands Sch.
Pirie Park
West Drumoyne
Govan High Sch.
Drumoyne Prim. Sch.
G51
Glasgow
Comm. Cen.
Prim. Sch.
Indus. Estate
Works
Rec. Grd.
Sec. Sch.
Play. Fld.
Schs.
SUMMERTOWN
DRUMOYNE
EDMISTON ROAD
A8
Depot
Moore Park
Works
Ibrox
Glasgow Rangers F.C. (Ibrox Stadium)
IBROX
Superstore
Tinto Park Football Ground
HELEN STREET INTERCHANGE
Junction 24
M8 MOTORWAY
M8
B768
BROOMLOAN R.
WEST DRIVE
PAISLEY ROAD WEST
A761
Junc. 23
DUMBRECK ROAD INTERCHANGE
DUMBRECK RD.
Comm. Complex
Works
Palace of Art
Educ. Cen.
G41
Bellahouse Academy
Tennis Cts.
Mosque
Lib.
House For An Art Lover
BELLAHOUSTON
Craigie Hall
DALKEITH AVENUE
Glasgow Ski Cen.
Nursery
Rec.
M77

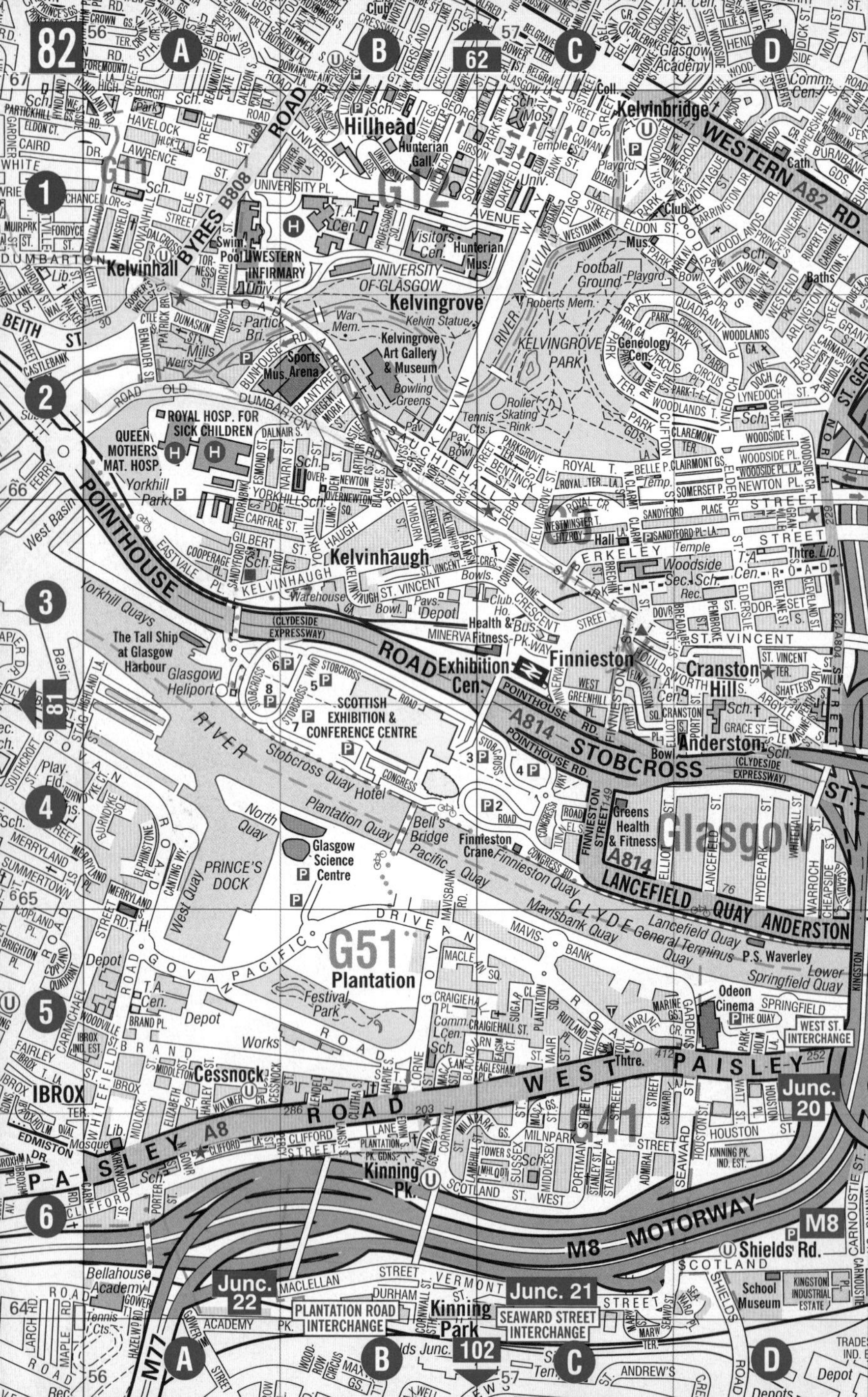

82
A
B
C
D
1
2
3
4
5
6
56
57
62
81
102
Hillhead
Hunterian Gall.
Kelvinbridge
Glasgow Academy
WESTERN A82 RD.
UNIVERSITY AVENUE
Visitors Cen.
Hunterian Mus.
UNIVERSITY OF GLASGOW
WESTERN INFIRMARY
Swim. Pool
Kelvinhall
BYRES B808 ROAD
DUMBARTON
BEITH ST.
Kelvingrove
Kelvin Statue
War Mem.
Kelvingrove Art Gallery & Museum
Bowling Greens
Sports Arena
Mus.
Partick Bri.
Mills
Weirs
KELVINGROVE PARK
Football Ground
Playgrd.
Roberts Mem.
Roller Skating Rink
Tennis Cts.
Geneology Cen.
PARK CIRCUS
ROYAL HOSP. FOR SICK CHILDREN
QUEEN MOTHERS MAT. HOSP.
Yorkhill Park
POINTHOUSE
West Basin
Yorkhill Quays
Kelvinhaugh
SAUCHIEHALL
ROYAL T.
SANDYFORD PLACE
Woodside Sec. Sch.
Cen.
Thtre.
Lib.
(CLYDESIDE EXPRESSWAY)
ROAD
Exhibition Cen.
Finnieston
Health & Fitness
Bus Pk.
Depot
The Tall Ship at Glasgow Harbour
Glasgow Heliport
SCOTTISH EXHIBITION & CONFERENCE CENTRE
RIVER
Stobcross Quay
Hotel
Plantation Quay
Bell's Bridge
North Quay
Glasgow Science Centre
PRINCE'S DOCK
West Quay
Finnieston Crane
Pacific Quay
Finnieston Quay
Cranston Hill
Anderston
A814 STOBCROSS
Greens Health & Fitness
Glasgow
LANCEFIELD QUAY ANDERSTON
CLYDE
Lancefield Quay
General Terminus Quay
Mavisbank Quay
P.S. Waverley
Lower Springfield Quay
G11
G12
G3
G51
G41
Plantation
Festival Park
GOVAN PACIFIC ROAD
Works
Odeon Cinema
WEST ST. INTERCHANGE
Cessnock
IBROX
WEST PAISLEY ROAD
PAISLEY A8
Junc. 20
Kinning Pk.
M8 MOTORWAY
M8
Shields Rd.
SCOTLAND
Junc. 22
PLANTATION ROAD INTERCHANGE
Kinning Park
Junc. 21
SEAWARD STREET INTERCHANGE
School Museum
KINGSTON INDUSTRIAL ESTATE
Bellahouse Academy
M77
Depot
Depots

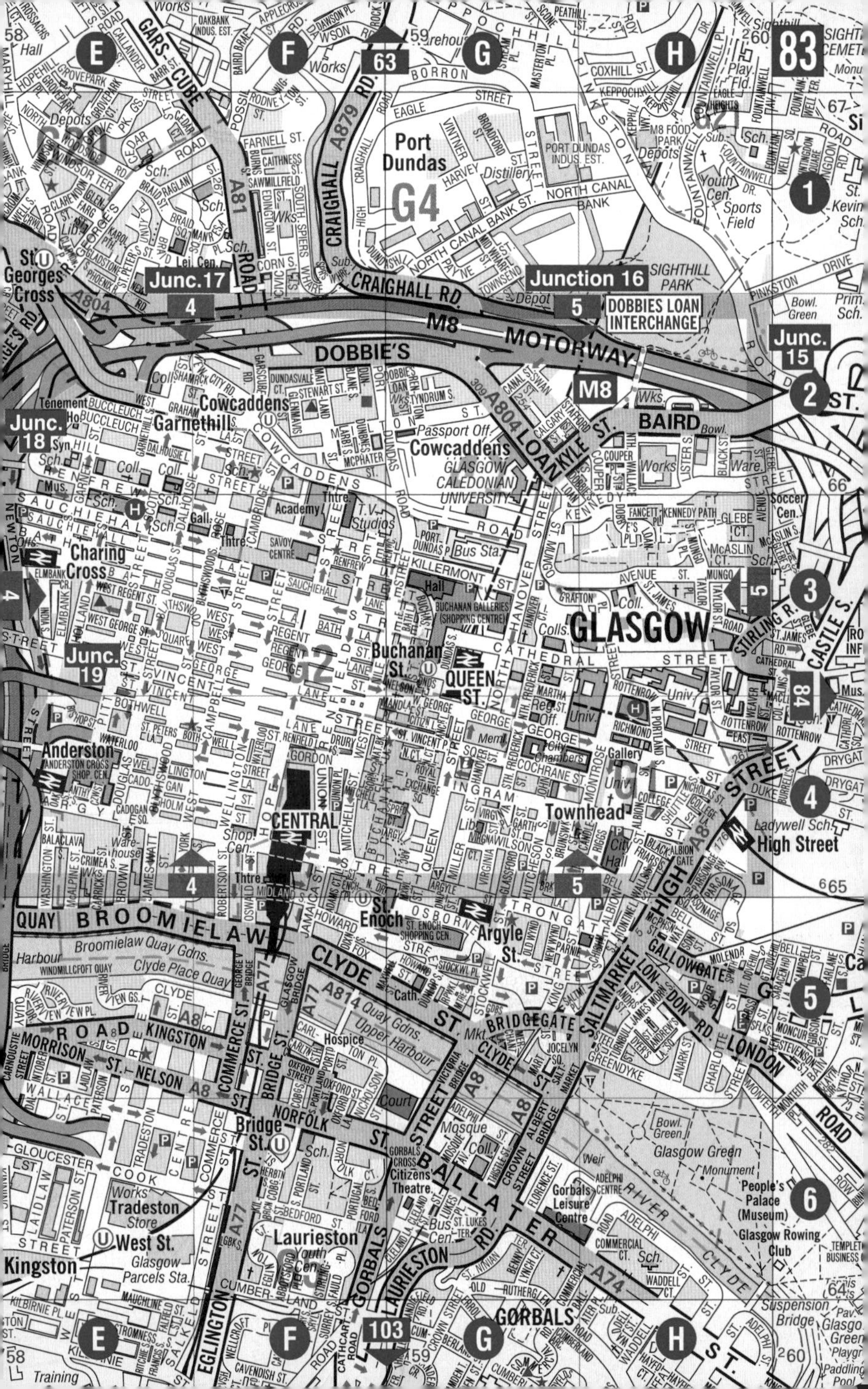

E
F
G
H
63
Port Dundas
G4
CRAIGHALL RD.
A879
A81
GARSCUBE ROAD
G20
St. Georges Cross
Junc. 17
4
Junction 16
5
DOBBIES LOAN INTERCHANGE
SIGHTHILL PARK
Sighthill
PORT DUNDAS INDUS. EST.
NORTH CANAL BANK
Distillery
M8 FOOD PARK
Youth Cen.
Sports Field
1
G21
A804
M8
DOBBIE'S
MOTORWAY
Junc. 15
2
Cowcaddens
Garnethill
Junc. 18
Passport Off.
GLASGOW CALEDONIAN UNIVERSITY
BAIRD
KENNEDY PATH
Soccer Cen.
66
COWCADDENS
RENFREW
SAUCHIEHALL
Academy
T.V. Studios
Charing Cross
SAVOY CENTRE
Bus Sta.
Hall
BUCHANAN GALLERIES (SHOPPING CENTRE)
GLASGOW
CATHEDRAL
STREET
3
4
5
G2
Buchanan St.
QUEEN ST.
Junc. 19
Univ.
84
Anderston
ANDERSTON CROSS SHOP. CEN.
City Chambers
G1
Townhead
Gallery
High Street
Ladywell Sch.
CENTRAL
Shop. Cen.
City Hall
4
5
665
QUAY
BROOMIELAW
Broomielaw Quay Gdns.
Clyde Place Quay
Harbour
WINDMILLCROFT QUAY
CLYDE
St. Enoch
ST. ENOCH SHOPPING CEN.
Argyle St.
TRONGATE
SALTMARKET
GALLOWGATE
LONDON RD.
5
A77
A814
A8
Upper Harbour
Hospice
Quay Gdns.
BRIDGEGATE
KINGSTON
MORRISON
NELSON
Court
Mosque
Bowl. Green
Glasgow Green
Monument
Weir
Bridge St.
NORFOLK
STREET
COMMERCE ST.
GLOUCESTER
COOK
Tradeston
Store
Works
West St.
Kingston
Glasgow Parcels Sta.
Laurieston
Youth Cen.
GORBALS
GORBALS CROSS
Citizens' Theatre.
Bus Cen.
BALLATER
Gorbals Leisure Centre
ADELPHI CENTRE
RIVER CLYDE
People's Palace (Museum)
Glasgow Rowing Club
6
A74
EGLINTON
LAURIESTON RD.
103
CATHCART ROAD
Suspension Bridge
58
59
260
Training

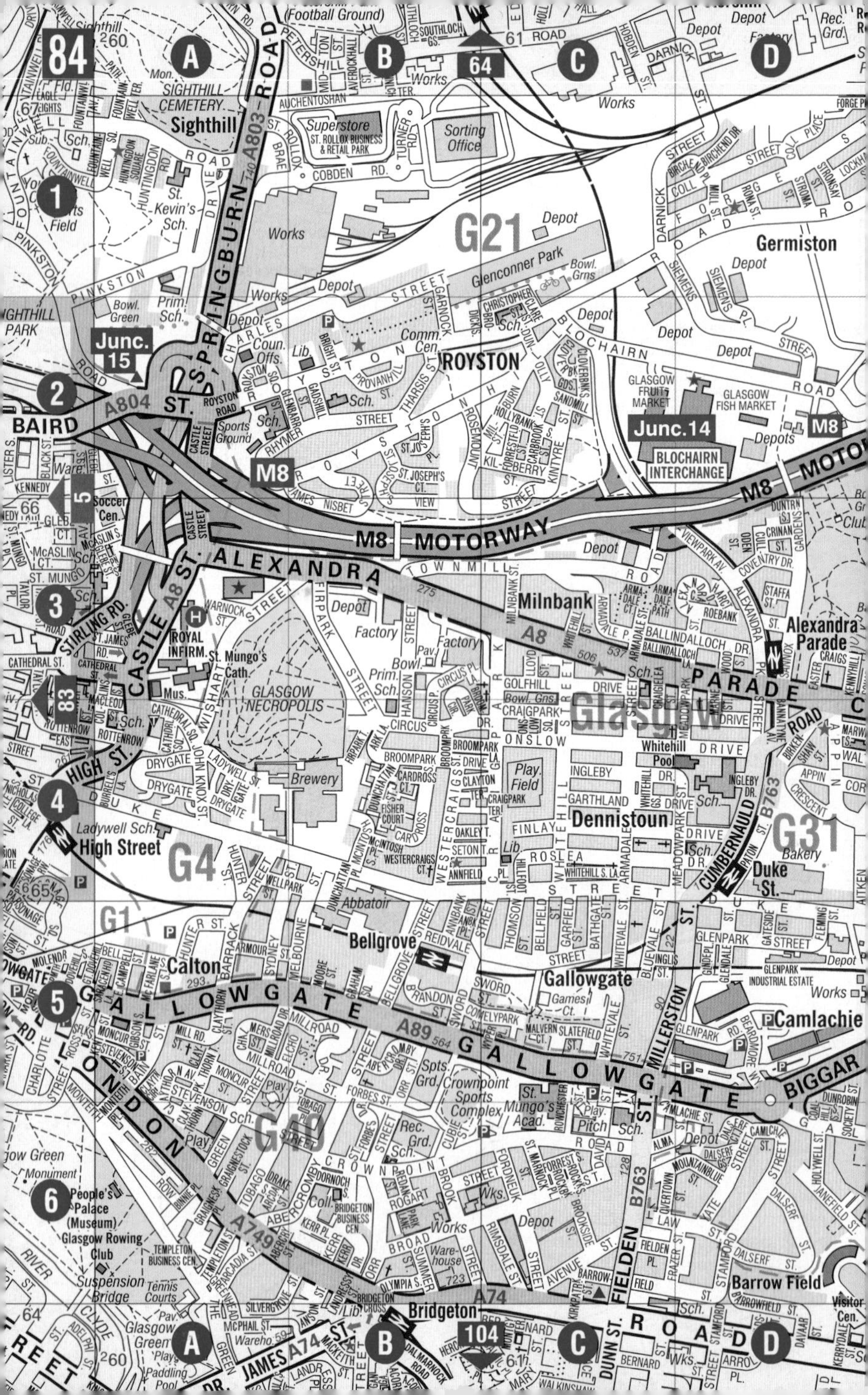

A
B
C
D
1
2
3
4
5
6
64
83
104
5
(Football Ground)
Sighthill
SIGHTHILL CEMETERY
Superstore
ST. ROLLOX BUSINESS & RETAIL PARK
Sorting Office
G21
Glenconner Park
Germiston
Junc. 15
ROYSTON
GLASGOW FRUIT MARKET
GLASGOW FISH MARKET
Junc.14
BLOCHAIRN INTERCHANGE
M8
M8 MOTORWAY
ALEXANDRA
Milnbank
A8
Alexandra Parade
PARADE
ROYAL INFIRM.
St. Mungo's Cath.
GLASGOW NECROPOLIS
Glasgow
Brewery
Dennistoun
G31
Duke St.
High Street
G4
G1
Abbatoir
Bellgrove
Calton
Gallowgate
Camlachie
GALLOWGATE
A89
BIGGAR
Crownpoint Sports Complex
St. Mungo's Acad.
G40
People's Palace (Museum)
Glasgow Rowing Club
Suspension Bridge
Tennis Courts
Glasgow Green
Barrow Field
Visitor Cen.
Bridgeton
A74
A749
B763
LONDON
FIELDEN
CUMBERNAULD
SPRINGBURN ROAD
A803
A804
BAIRD ST.
CASTLE ST.
HIGH ST.
DUKE
Works
Depot
Factory

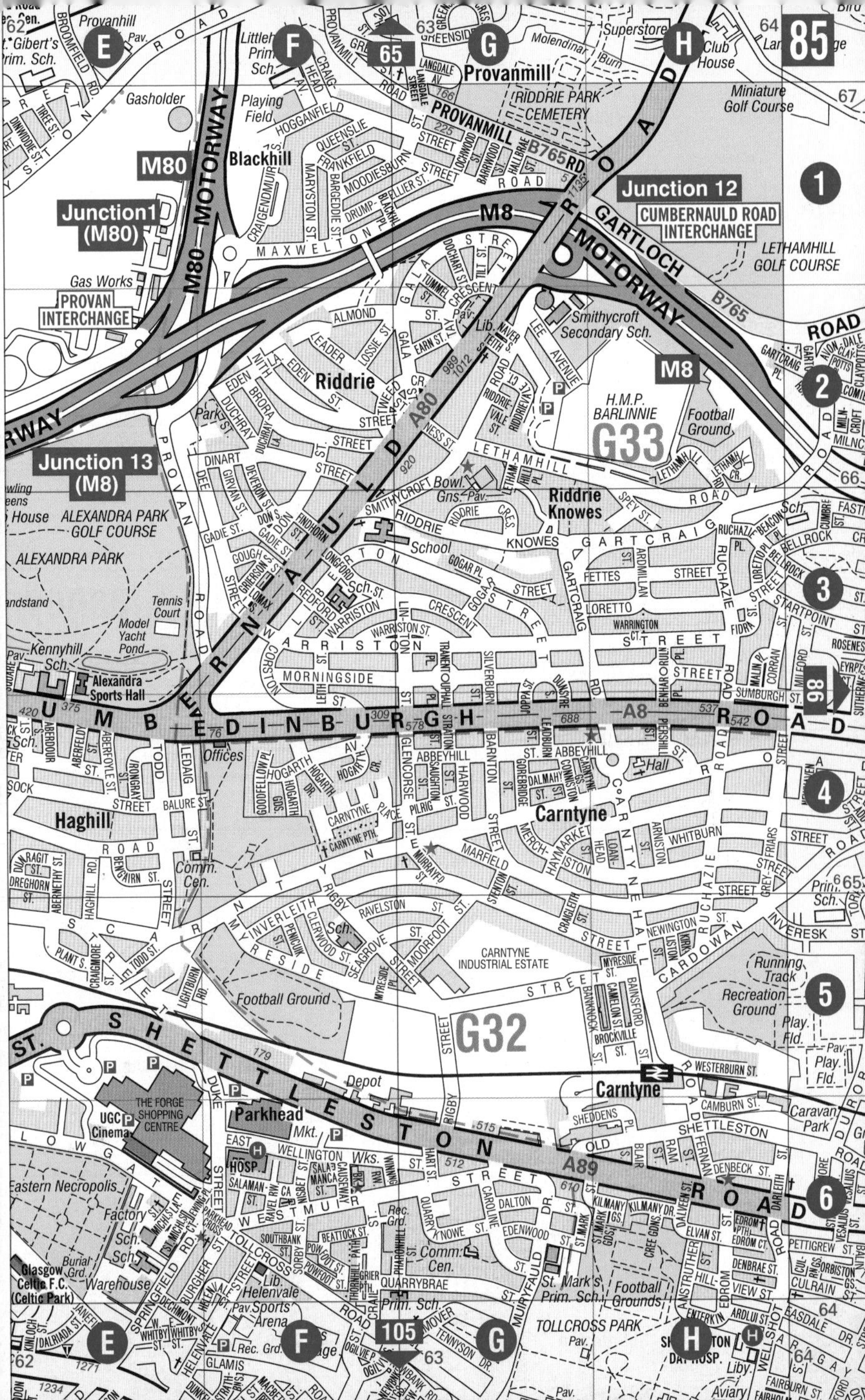
Provanhill
St. Gilbert's Prim. Sch.
E
F
G
H
65
Provanmill
Superstore
Club House
Molendinar Burn
Miniature Golf Course
Gasholder
Playing Field
Blackhill
M80
M80 MOTORWAY
Junction1 (M80)
PROVANMILL RD.
RIDDRIE PARK CEMETERY
B765
Junction 12
CUMBERNAULD ROAD INTERCHANGE
GARTLOCH MOTORWAY
LETHAMHILL GOLF COURSE
M8
MAXWELTON
Gas Works
PROVAN INTERCHANGE
Smithycroft Secondary Sch.
Riddrie
H.M.P. BARLINNIE
G33
Football Ground
Junction 13 (M8)
ALEXANDRA PARK GOLF COURSE
ALEXANDRA PARK
A80
CUMBERNAULD ROAD
Riddrie Knowes
School
Tennis Court
Model Yacht Pond
Kennyhill Sch.
Alexandra Sports Hall
EDINBURGH ROAD
A8
Offices
Haghill
Carntyne
CARNTYNE INDUSTRIAL ESTATE
Running Track
Recreation Ground
Play. Fld.
Football Ground
G32
SHETTLESTON ROAD
A89
Carntyne
Caravan Park
THE FORGE SHOPPING CENTRE
UGC Cinema
Parkhead
Depot
Mkt.
HOSP.
Eastern Necropolis
Factory
Glasgow Celtic F.C. (Celtic Park)
Warehouse
Burial Grd.
Helenvale Sports Arena
Rec. Grd.
Comm. Cen.
St. Mark's Prim. Sch.
Football Grounds
TOLLCROSS PARK
Shettleston Day Hosp.
Liby.
Aviary
105
1
2
3
4
5
6
98
62
63
64

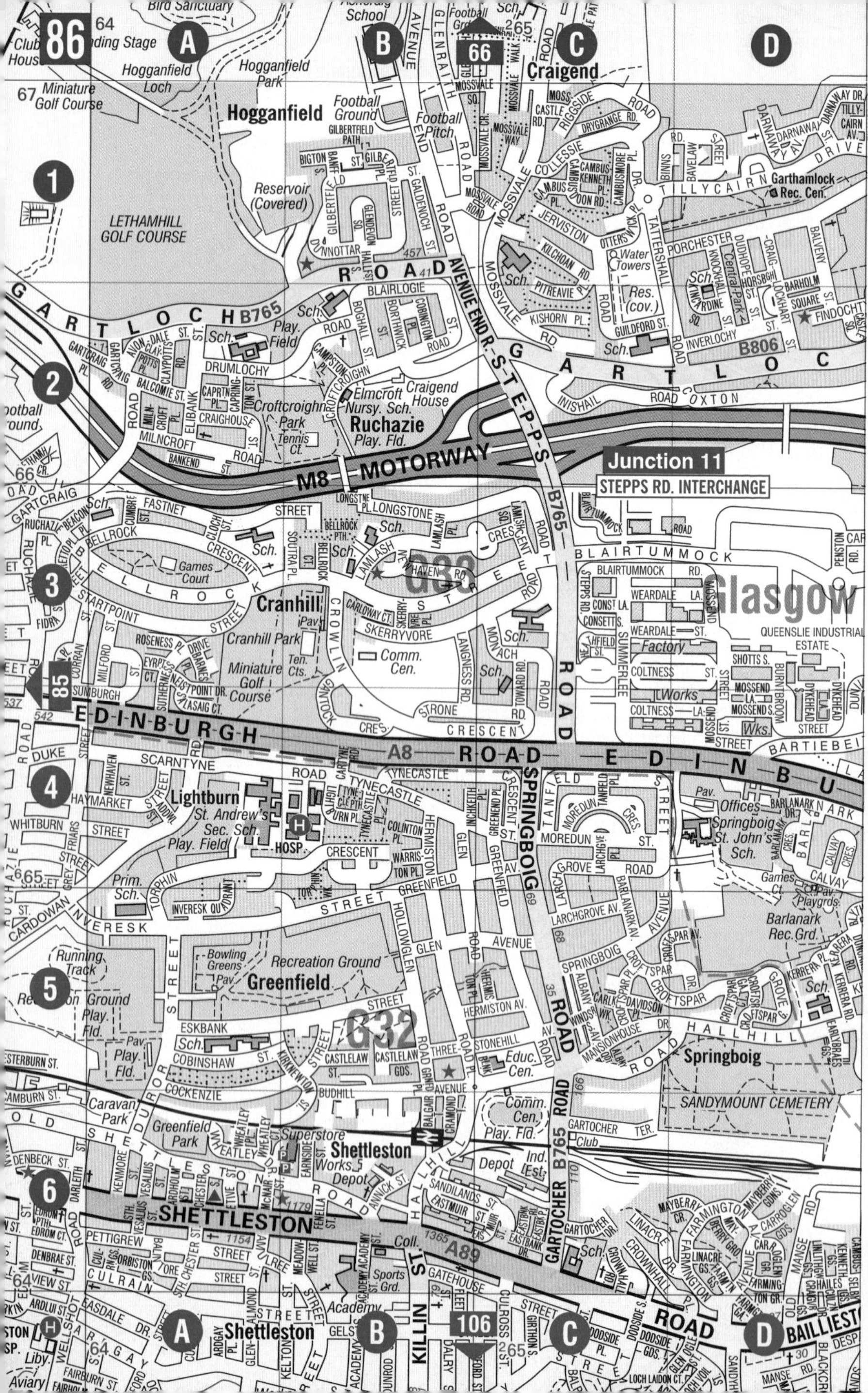
86
66
106
85
A
B
C
D
1
2
3
4
5
6
Bird Sanctuary
Landing Stage
Club House
Hogganfield Loch
Hogganfield Park
Miniature Golf Course
Hogganfield
Football Ground
Football Pitch
Craigend
Reservoir (Covered)
LETHAMHILL GOLF COURSE
GARTLOCH ROAD
B765
B806
MOSSVALE RD.
COLLESSIE DR.
TILLYCAIRN DRIVE
Garthamlock Rec. Cen.
Water Towers
Res. (cov.)
Central Park
Craigend House
Elmcroft Nursy. Sch.
Croftcroighn Park
Ruchazie
Play. Fld.
M8 MOTORWAY
Junction 11
STEPPS RD. INTERCHANGE
STEPPS ROAD
AVENUE END R.
BELLROCK CRESCENT
BELLROCK STREET
Games Court
Cranhill
Cranhill Park
Miniature Golf Course
Comm. Cen.
G33
BLAIRTUMMOCK RD.
Glasgow
QUEENSLIE INDUSTRIAL ESTATE
Factory
Works
EDINBURGH ROAD
A8
Lightburn
St. Andrew's Sec. Sch.
HOSP.
Play. Field
SPRINGBOIG ROAD
Springboig St. John's Sch.
Barlanark Rec. Grd.
Running Track
Recreation Ground
Bowling Greens
Greenfield
G32
Educ. Cen.
Springboig
SANDYMOUNT CEMETERY
Caravan Park
Greenfield Park
Superstore
Shettleston
Works Depot
Ind. Est.
GARTOCHER ROAD
SHETTLESTON ROAD
A89
Sports Grd.
Academy
BAILLIESTON ROAD
Aviary
Liby.

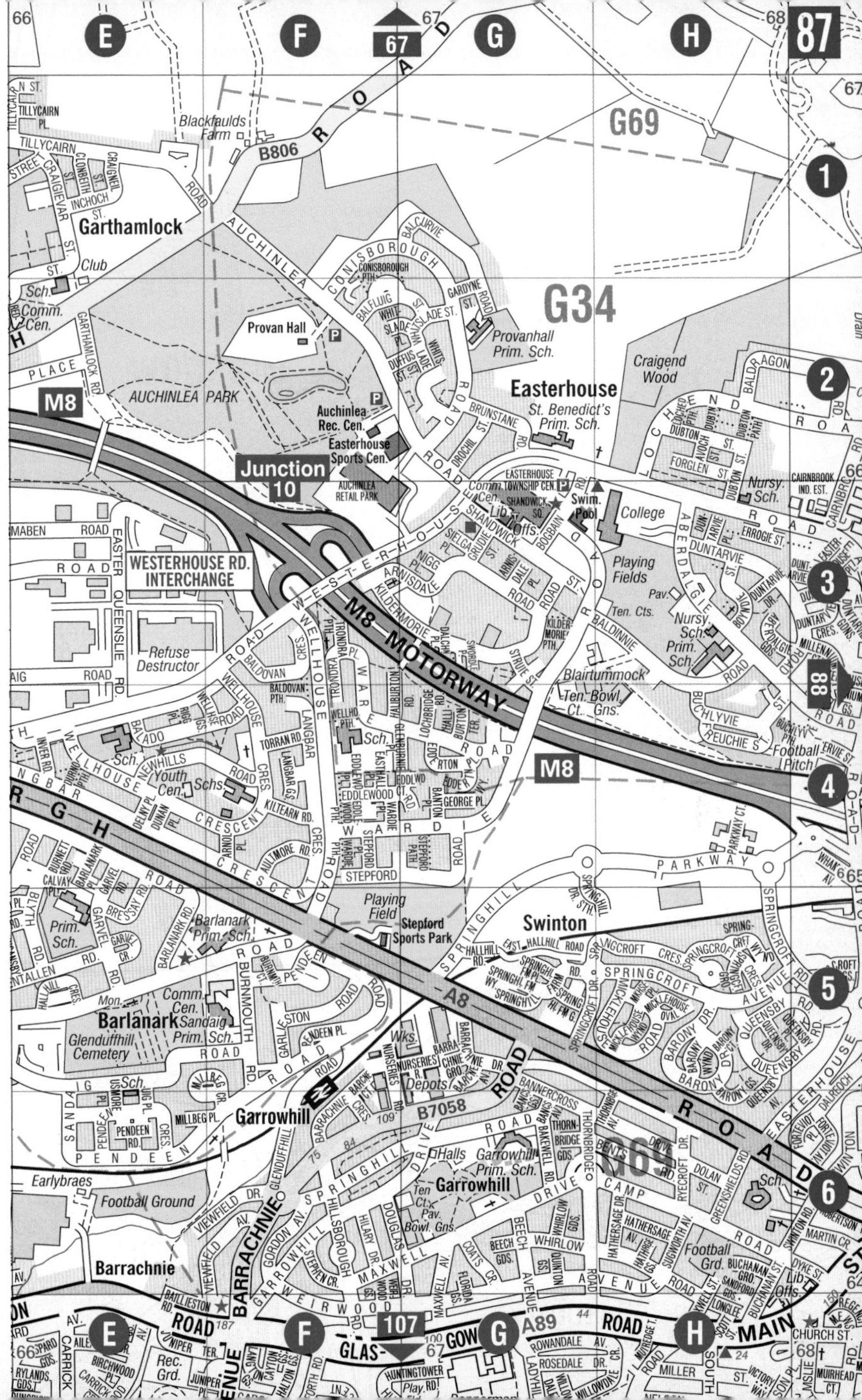
E
F
67
G
H
Tillycairn Pl.
Blackfaulds Farm
B806
Road
G69
1
Garthamlock
Club
Sch.
Comm. Cen.
Auchinlea Road
Conisborough
Balcurvie
Provan Hall
Provanhall Prim. Sch.
G34
Craigend Wood
2
Garthamlock Rd.
Place
M8
Auchinlea Park
Easterhouse
St. Benedict's Prim. Sch.
Auchinlea Rec. Cen.
Easterhouse Sports Cen.
Junction 10
Auchinlea Retail Park
Brunstane Rd.
Drochil St.
Lochend Road
Dubton St.
Forglen St.
Nursy. Sch.
Cairnbrook Ind. Est.
Easterhouse Township Cen.
Shandwick Sq.
Swim. Pool
Lib.
Offs.
College
Road
Westerhouse Rd. Interchange
Easter Queenslie Rd.
Refuse Destructor
Westerhouse Road
Bogbain Rd.
Playing Fields
Aberdalgie Rd.
Duntarvie
3
M8 Motorway
Wellhouse Cres.
Baldovan Cres.
Arnisdale Road
Kildermorie
Ten. Cts.
Pav.
Nursy. Sch.
Prim. Sch.
Baldinnie
Blairtummock
Ten. Bowl. Ct. Gns.
88
Buchlyvie St.
Freuchie St.
Football Pitch
Wellhouse Road
Youth Cen.
Schs
Newhills Road
Torran Rd.
Langbar Cres.
Wardie Road
M8
4
Kiltearn Rd.
Crescent
Eddlewood
Stepford
George Pl.
Parkway
Springhill
Barlanark Road
Crescent
Playing Field
Stepford Sports Park
Swinton
Springcroft Cres.
Springcroft Avenue
5
Barlanark Prim. Sch.
Pendeen
Burnmouth Rd.
A8
Comm. Cen.
Barlanark
Sandaig Prim. Sch.
Glenduffhill Cemetery
Garlieston
Wks.
Nurseries
Depots
Queensby Rd.
Barony Dr.
Mickle house Oval
Road
Garrowhill
B7058
Sandaig Rd.
Pendeen
Millbeg Pl.
Springhill Drive
Road
Garrowhill Prim. Sch.
Thornbridge
G69
Easterhouse
Earlybraes
Football Ground
Viewfield Dr.
Barrachnie
Garrowhill
Camp
Dolan St.
Sch.
6
Hillsborough
Douglas
Maxwell
Whirlow
Hathersage
Football Grd.
Barrachnie
Weirwood
Avenue
Road
Lib. Offs.
Road
E
F
107
G
A89
Road
H
Main
Glasgow
Church St.
Rec. Grd.
Juniper
Huntingtower
Rowandale Av.
Rosedale Dr.
Miller
66
67
68

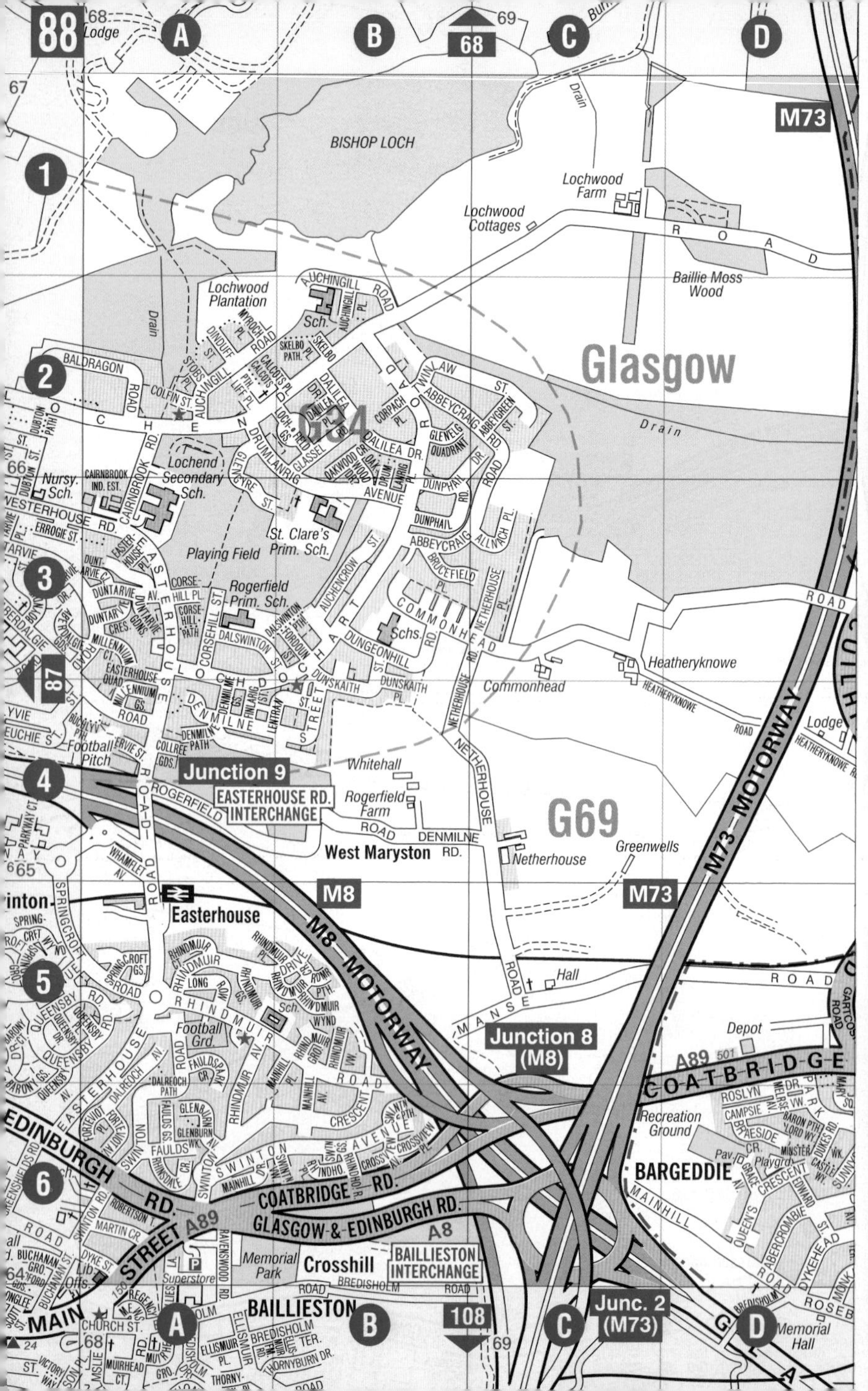

A
B
C
D
1
2
3
4
5
6
68
87
108
BISHOP LOCH
Lochwood Farm
Lochwood Cottages
Baillie Moss Wood
Glasgow
G34
G69
Lochwood Plantation
Lochend Secondary Sch.
St. Clare's Prim. Sch.
Rogerfield Prim. Sch.
Playing Field
Heatheryknowe
Commonhead
Whitehall
Rogerfield Farm
West Maryston
Netherhouse
Greenwells
Junction 9
EASTERHOUSE RD. INTERCHANGE
M8
M73
M8 MOTORWAY
M73 MOTORWAY
Easterhouse
Junction 8 (M8)
A89
COATBRIDGE
Recreation Ground
BARGEDDIE
Depot
Memorial Park
Crosshill
BAILLIESTON INTERCHANGE
BAILLIESTON
Junc. 2 (M73)
Memorial Hall
EDINBURGH RD.
COATBRIDGE RD.
GLASGOW-&-EDINBURGH RD.
A8
MAIN STREET
Superstore
Football Pitch
Football Grd.
Hall
Lodge

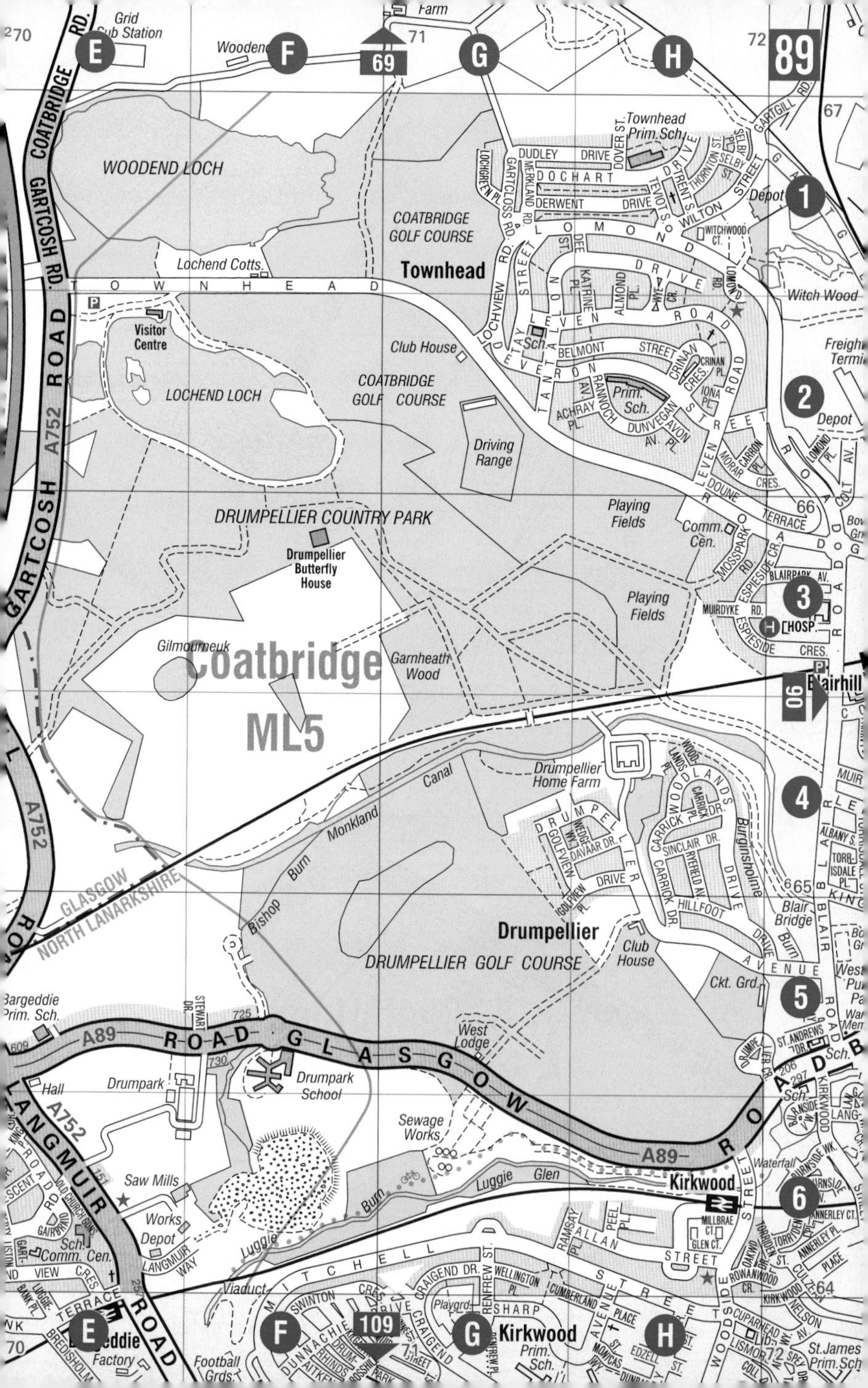

WOODEND LOCH
COATBRIDGE GOLF COURSE
Townhead
Lochend Cotts.
TOWNHEAD
Visitor Centre
LOCHEND LOCH
Club House
Driving Range
DRUMPELLIER COUNTRY PARK
Drumpellier Butterfly House
Gilmourneuk
Coatbridge
ML5
Garnheath Wood
Playing Fields
Comm. Cen.
HOSP.
Blairhill
Monkland Canal
Drumpellier Home Farm
Bishop Burn
GLASGOW
NORTH LANARKSHIRE
Drumpellier
DRUMPELLIER GOLF COURSE
Club House
Ckt. Grd.
Bargeddie Prim. Sch.
A89 ROAD GLASGOW ROAD
Drumpark
Drumpark School
West Lodge
Sewage Works
Saw Mills
Works Depot
Luggie Glen
Luggie Burn
Kirkwood
Viaduct
MITCHELL STREET
Kirkwood Prim. Sch.
St.James Prim.Sch.
Factory
Football Grds.
GARTCOSH ROAD
COATBRIDGE RD.
LANGMUIR ROAD
A752
Grid Sub Station
Woodend
Farm
Townhead Prim.Sch.
Depot
Witch Wood
Freight Termi
Blair Bridge
Waterfall
69
90
109

72
A
B
C
D
73
70
1
2
3
4
5
6
67
66
65
64
Beech Cottage
Coltswood House
GARTSHERRIE WOOD
YETTS
GARTGILL ROAD
Works
Kennels
Burn
Braeside
North Burn
Blacklands
Depot
Gartsherrie
Wks.
Witch Wood
Hollandhurst
Freightliner Terminal
Gartsherrie
Works
COATBRIDGE INDUS. EST.
North Burn
Greenhill
GREENHILL IND. EST.
Factory
Works
Depot
Janefield
Kipps
METHVEN TER.
HORNOCK
GARTSHERRIE INDUSTRIAL ESTATE
HOLLANDHURST ROAD
GARTSHERRIE ROAD
GARTLISTON B804 RD.
COLTSWOOD ROAD
Cemetery
Playing Field
Sunnyside
WAVERLEY
B803 ST.
BURNBANK
Gas Works
Works
Dunbeth
CHASSELS ST.
GILCHRIST
INVERESK PL.
Hornock Cotts.
GEORGE STREET
COLTSWOOD CT.
RED BRI. CT.
RONALD ST.
COLT STREET
RUSSELL
ROAD
Red Bri.
ALEXANDER STREET
LUGAR ST.
DUNBETH
EGLINTON AV.
LAIRD STREET
STUARTVILLE
KILDONAN
Council Offs.
Sch.
MUIRYHALL
STREET
Depot
TOWNHEAD TERRACE
Comm. Cen.
GARTSHERRIE ROAD
Bowl. Grn.
Pav.
Sch.
BLAIRPARK AV.
ALEXANDER HOSPITAL
NORTH SQ.
COULTER AV.
CORNISH CT.
ORLINGTON CT.
HERRIOT ST.
ESPIESIDE CRES.
Blairhill
Sch.
CORNHILL
KELSO
QUADRANT
CORSEWALL
Summerlee Heritage Trust
Coatbridge Sunnyside
Summerlee
Heritage Park
SUMMERLEE COTTS
BOTHWELL PL.
CULROSS PL.
DUNROBIN PL.
DRYBURGH PL.
MELROSE PL.
LENNOX AV.
MOUNT VERNON
PARKVIEW DR.
MUIR STREET
LEFROY STREET
Coatbridge Central
SUMMERLEE ST.
CANAL STREET
SUNNYSIDE
B803
CHURCH STREET
ACADEMY ST.
Lib.
Koko's
BAIRD
MAIN
THE QUADRANT SHOP. CEN.
DUNBETH ROAD
B804
Sub.
A89
STH. CIRCULAR
Blairhill
TORRISDALE ST.
FINLAYSTONE ST.
KING STREET
WEST STREET
A89 STREET
Blair Bridge
Bowling Greens
BLAIRGROVE CT.
MERRYSTON CT.
West End Public Park
War Mem.
The Time Capsule
DUNDYVAN
BANK
RD.
GLASGOW
Sch.
ST. ANDREWS
DRUMPELLIER AVENUE
HILLFOOT
SINCLAIR DR.
Burn
KIRKWOOD STREET
Comm. Cen.
Coatbridge Outdoor Sports Complex
Langloan
Waterfall
Weir
Kirkwood
Luggie
Works
Burn
Coatbridge
COATBRIDGE
Works
FARADAY RETAIL PARK
A725
COATBANK
MAIN ST.
RD.
CENTRE PARK CT.
Wks.
COATBANK
GROVE
REDWOOD
ORCHARD
ALDER GR.
MEADOW
LABURNUM
MILLER GR.
CALDEEN
TENNENT
Foundry
Whifflet
Whifflet Junction
ROAD
B753
CECIL
DUNDYVAN GATE
MAULDSLIE ST.
BROWN ST.
Langloan Junction
Works
Dundyvan
SOUTERHOUSE
DUNDYVAN IND. EST.
Bowl. Grn.
HAMILTON CR.
DUNDYVAN GDNS.
LEE'S
WALLACE
Sch.
HOZIER STREET
Sports Complex
Barrowfield
Sch.
WHIFFLET ST.
EASTON PL.
GILSON
ROBERT
CARFIN
Lib.
Old Monkland
Comm. Cen.
Playing Field
110
ANNERLEY CT.
ANNERLEY PL.
TORRIDEN
ROWANWOOD CR.
CULZEAN
NELSON
AVENUE
KIRKWOOD
CUPARHEAD
MILLBRAE CT.
GLEN CT.
STREET
St. James Prim. Sch.
LISMORE
OLD SCHOOL
Ten. Cts.
Whifflet Public Park

Airdrie
ML6
AIRDRIE
Golfhill
Thrashbush
Burnfoot
Whinhall
Coatdyke
Cliftonville
Cairnhill
Sikeside
Whifflet
Greenend
Monklands District General Hospital
Albion Rovers F.C. (Cliftonhill Stadium)
Coatbridge Indoor Bowling Club
Powerdrome Bowl
Dunbeth Public Park
Airdrie Academy
Virtuewell Glen
Golfhill Prim. Sch.
Kippsbyre
Mosside
Depot
Centenary Park
Rochsolloch Prim. Sch.
Devonview Sch.
Sikeside Prim. Sch.
St. Stephen's Prim. Sch.
Engineering Works
Works
ALEXANDER ST.
DEEDES ST.
AITCHISON ST.
HIGH ST.
GLENMAVIS ROAD
GARTBRIDGE ROAD
CAIRNHILL ROAD
LOCKS ST.
SIKESIDE ST.
A89
B803
B802
B753
A8010
71
92
111

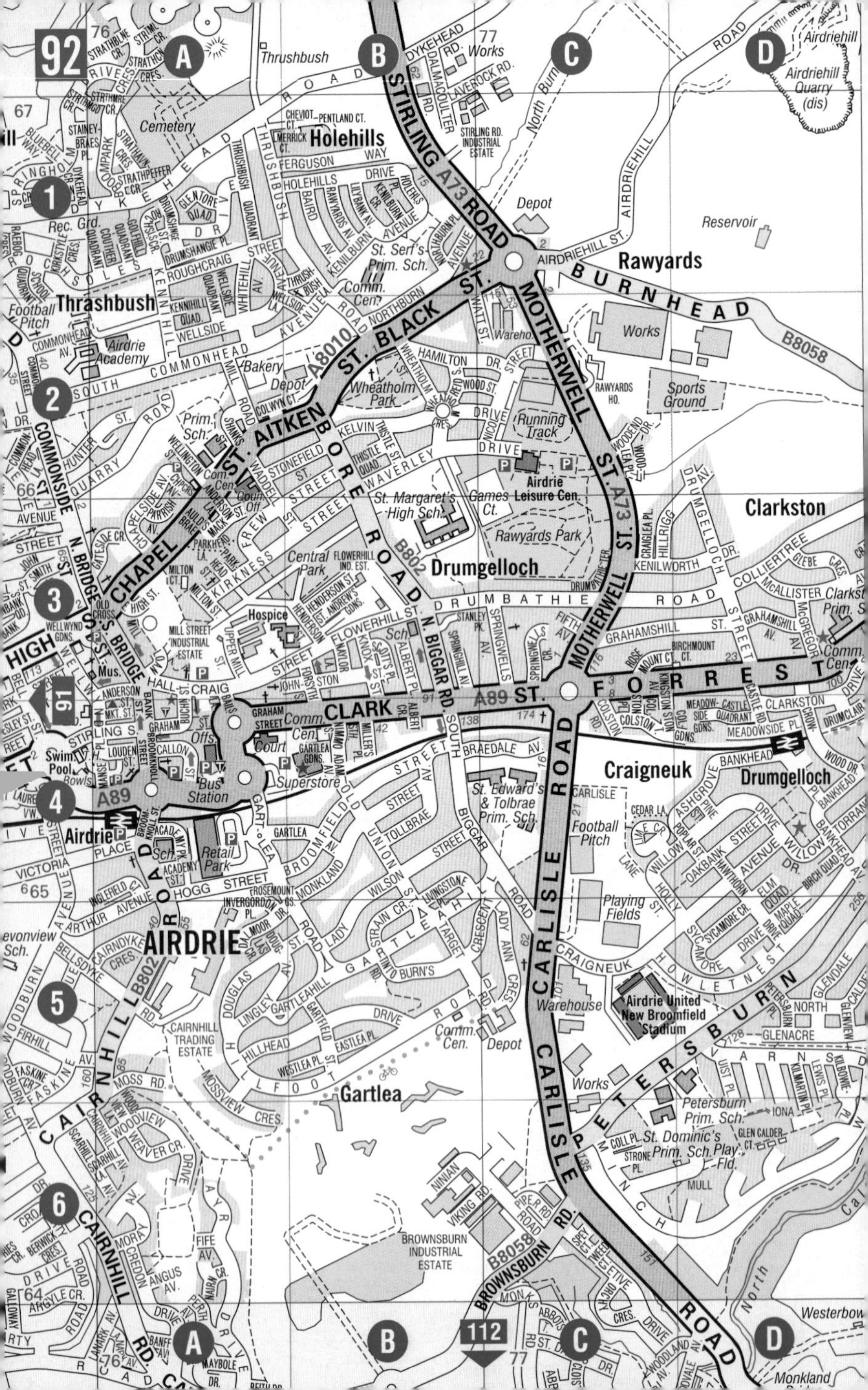

A
B
C
D
1
2
3
4
5
6
76
77
67
66
65
64
Thrushbush
Holehills
Works
Airdriehill
Airdriehill Quarry (dis)
Cemetery
DYKEHEAD ROAD
STIRLING ROAD
A73
DALMACOULTER RD.
LAVEROCK RD.
STIRLING RD. INDUSTRIAL ESTATE
North Burn
AIRDRIEHILL ROAD
CHEVIOT CT.
PENTLAND CT.
MERRICK CT.
FERGUSON WAY
HOLEHILLS DRIVE
KENILBURN AVENUE
BAIRD AV.
RAWYARDS AV.
LILYBANK AV.
KENILBURN CR.
HOLEHILLS PL.
THRUSHBUSH QUADRANT
THRUSHBUSH RD.
Depot
Reservoir
AIRDRIEHILL ST.
Rawyards
BURNHEAD
B8058
Works
Sports Ground
RAWYARDS HO.
Running Track
Airdrie Leisure Cen.
Games Ct.
Rawyards Park
Clarkston
Drumgelloch
St. Serf's Prim. Sch.
Comm. Cen.
NORTHBURN AVENUE
NORTHBURN PL.
Thrashbush
Football Pitch
Airdrie Academy
COMMONHEAD AV.
SOUTH COMMONHEAD AVENUE
WELLSIDE
KENNIHILL
WHITEHILL AV.
ROUGHCRAIG
DRUMSHANGIE PL.
GLENTORE QUAD.
STRATHPEFFER CR.
Rec. Grd.
SPRINGHOLM DR.
BLUEBELL WAY
STAINEY BRAES PL.
BROOMPARK CRES.
STRATHAVEN CRES.
STRATHBLANE CR.
STRATHON CRES.
ST. BLACK ST.
A8010
ST. AITKEN ST.
WATT ST.
Wareho.
HAMILTON DR.
WHEATHOLM ST.
Wheatholm Park
Bakery
Depot
MILL ROAD
COLWYN CT.
Prim. Sch.
HUNTER ST.
QUARRY ST.
COMMONSIDE ST.
WELLINGTON
Com. Cen.
Coun. Off.
KELVIN
THISTLE ST.
STONEFIELD ST.
WAVERLEY STREET
FREW ST.
BORE ROAD
B802
St. Margaret's High Sch.
Drumgelloch
Central Park
FLOWERHILL IND. EST.
KIRKNESS ST.
CHAPEL ST.
PARKHEAD LA.
MILTON ST.
HENDERSON ST.
Hospice
DRUMBATHIE ROAD
MOTHERWELL ST.
KENILWORTH
CRAIGLEA PL.
HILLRIGG
DRUMGELLOCH DR.
COLLIERTREE
GLEBE CRES.
McALLISTER
GRAHAMSHILL ST.
GRAHAMSHILL AV.
McGREGOR AV.
Clarkston Prim. Sch.
Comm. Cen.
FORREST ST.
A89
CLARK ST.
N. BIGGAR RD.
FLOWERHILL STREET
STANLEY PK.
SPRINGWELLS AV.
FIFTH AV.
ROSE
MOUNT CT.
BIRCHMOUNT CT.
COLSTON RD.
MEADOWSIDE GDNS.
CASTLE QUADRANT
CLARKSTON
MEADOWSIDE PL.
HIGH ST.
N. BRIDGE ST.
S. BRIDGE ST.
MILL STREET INDUSTRIAL ESTATE
UPPER MILL ST.
HALLCRAIG ST.
Mus.
ANDERSON ST.
MKT. ST.
91
GRAHAM STREET
Comm. Cen.
Court
GARTLEA GDNS.
Superstore
Bus Station
Offs.
STIRLING ST.
Swim. Pool
Bowls
LOUDEN ST.
CALLON ST.
BROOMKNOLL ST.
Airdrie
ACADEMY PL.
Sch.
Retail Park
SOUTH BRAEDALE AV.
BRIDGE ST.
St. Edward's & Tolbrae Prim. Sch.
Craigneuk
CARLISLE ROAD
Football Pitch
Playing Fields
BANKHEAD
Drumgelloch
ASHGROVE
PINE ST.
CEDAR LA.
LIME CR.
POPLAR ST.
WILLOW DRIVE
OAKBANK STREET
HAWTHORN AVENUE
HOLLY ST.
SYCAMORE CR.
SYCAMORE DRIVE
ELM QUAD.
MAPLE QUAD.
BIRCH QUAD
VICTORIA PLACE
HOGG STREET
ARTHUR AVENUE
INGLEFIELD CT.
INVERGORDON PL.
ROSEMOUNT GS.
MONKLAND
WILSON
TOLLBRAE AV.
UNION ST.
BROOMFIELD AV.
GARTLEA AV.
OLD STREET
LIVINGSTONE ST.
STRAIN CR.
TARGET
CRESCENT
LADY ANN CRES.
GARTLEA ROAD
AIRDRIE
B802
BELLSDYKE RD.
CAIRNDYKE CRES.
CAIRNHILL ROAD
DOUGLAS
LINGLEY AV.
GARTLEAHILL
GARTFIELD
HILLHEAD
EASTLEA PL.
WESTLEA PL.
BURN'S
Comm. Cen.
Depot
CAIRNHILL TRADING ESTATE
Gartlea
HILLFOOT
MOSSVIEW CRES.
MOSS RD.
FIRHILL
FASKINE AV.
WOODBURN
CRAIGNEUK
Warehouse
Airdrie United New Broomfield Stadium
HOWLETNEST
PETERSBURN ROAD
NORTH
GLENACRE
VARNS
Works
Petersburn Prim. Sch.
St. Dominic's Prim. Sch.
Play Fld.
IONA
GLEN CALDER CT.
MULL
MINCH
STRONE PL.
COLL PL.
CARLISLE ROAD
NINIAN
VIKING RD.
PIPER ROAD
BROWNSBURN INDUSTRIAL ESTATE
BROWNSBURN RD.
B8058
WOODVIEW
WEAVER CR.
SCARHILL
CAIRNHILL
MORAY AV.
CREDON
FIFE AV.
ANGUS AV.
AYR
PERTH
BERWICK CRES.
ARGYLE CR.
GALLOWAY
LANARK AV.
BANFF AV.
MAYBOLE DR.
NAIRN
CAIRNHILL RD.
DRIVE
MONKS
ABBOTS
112
77
Westerbow
Monkland
North Calder

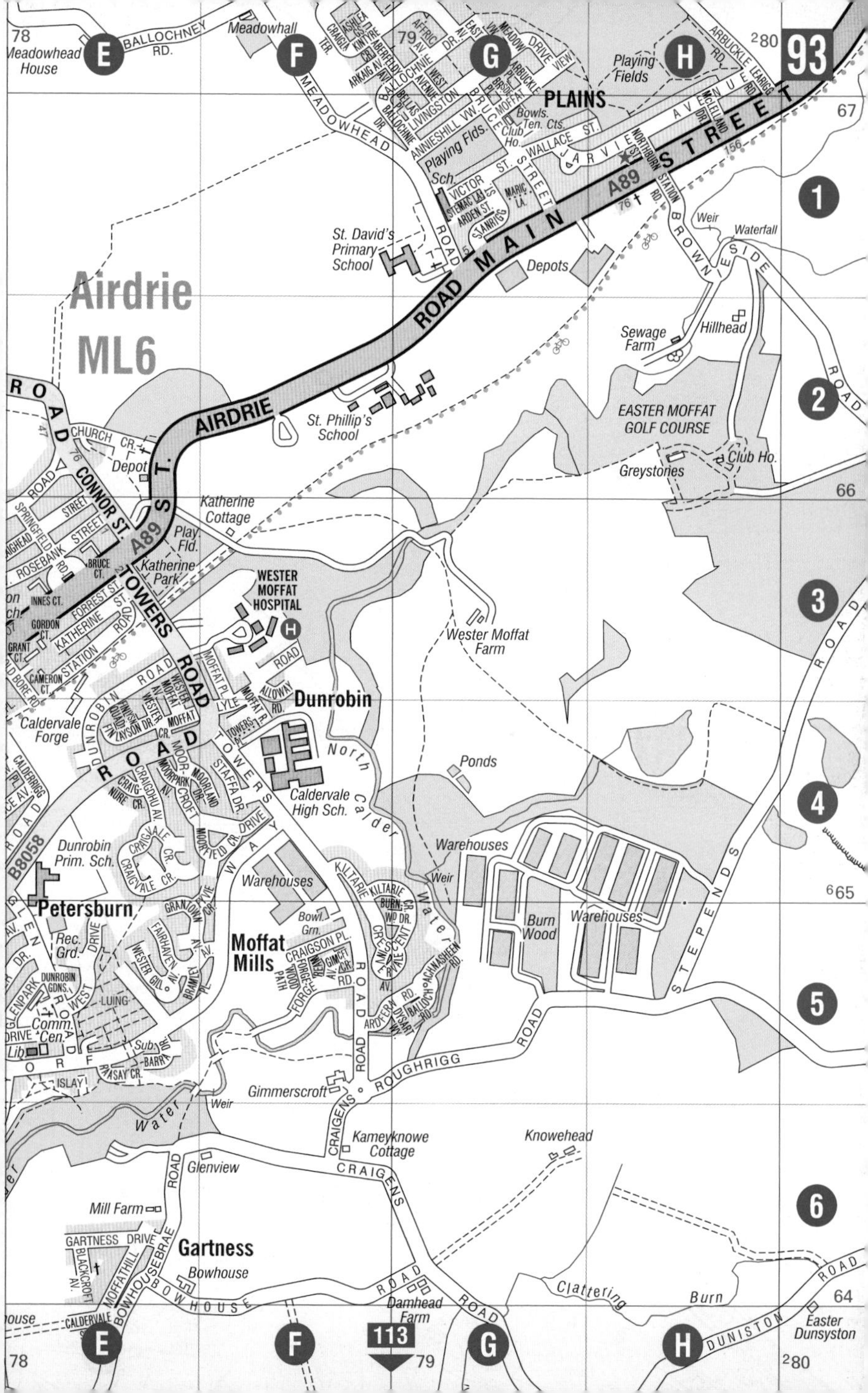
Airdrie
ML6
PLAINS
Meadowhead House
Meadowhall
BALLOCHNEY RD.
MEADOWHEAD DR.
Playing Fields
ARBUCKLE RD.
MAIN STREET
ROAD
AIRDRIE
ST.
A89
Playing Flds.
Sch.
St. David's Primary School
Depots
Weir
Waterfall
BROWNIESIDE
Sewage Farm
Hillhead
EASTER MOFFAT GOLF COURSE
Club Ho.
Greystones
St. Phillip's School
Katherine Cottage
Play. Fld.
Katherine Park
WESTER MOFFAT HOSPITAL
Wester Moffat Farm
TOWERS ROAD
CONNOR ST.
Depot
Dunrobin
North Calder Water
Caldervale High Sch.
Ponds
Warehouses
Burn Wood
STEPENDS ROAD
Caldervale Forge
DUNROBIN ROAD
B8058
Dunrobin Prim. Sch.
Petersburn
Rec. Grd.
Moffat Mills
Bowl. Grn.
Comm. Cen.
Lib.
ROUGHRIGG ROAD
Gimmerscroft
CRAIGENS ROAD
Kameyknowe Cottage
Knowehead
Glenview
Mill Farm
Gartness
Bowhouse
BOWHOUSE ROAD
Damhead Farm
Clattering Burn
DUNISTON ROAD
Easter Dunsyston
E
F
G
H
1
2
3
4
5
6
78
79
280
67
66
665
64

113

74
A
B
C
D
1
2
3
4
5
6
Johnstone
KILBARCHAN
PA10
PA9
Tandlehill
Millikenpark
Cartside
Corseford
Spateston
Waterstone Bank
Cemetery Lodge
West Lodge
East Lodge
BRIDGE OF
White House
Barrhill Wood
Barr Hill
Tower
Kilbarchan Prim. Sch.
Public Park
Pav.
Forehouse
The Cross
Football Grd.
Bank Brae
Foremount House
The White House
Abbanoy
Auchenames Cottage
Wardend
Mosside
Burnbrae
Muirfaulds Cottage
Cartside
Kibbleston
Faulds
Bus Depot
Fordbank Prim. Sch.
Fordbank
Fordbank Stables
Corseford School
St. Cuthbert's High Sch.
St. Anthony's Prim. Sch.
Playing Field
Playing Fields
Johnstone High Sch.
Red House
Piggery
Hospice
West Corseford Farm
Thirdpart Hall
Warbowie
Lib.
Shop. Cen.
Bowl. Gn. Club
THE FAIRWAYS
Black Cart Water
Burn
Midtown Burn
JOHNSTONE BY-PASS
A737
A761
B787
BEITH ROAD
COCHRANEMILL ROAD
KILBARCHAN ROAD
BARNSCROFT
KIBBLESTON ROAD
TANDLEHILL
LOCHER RD.
SHUTTLE ST.
NEW ST.
HIGH BARHOLM
LOW BARHOLM
CHURCHILL
AUCHENGREOCH AV.
CRAIGVIEW AV.
SPATESTON RD.
MIDTON RD.
OLD HOWWOOD RD.

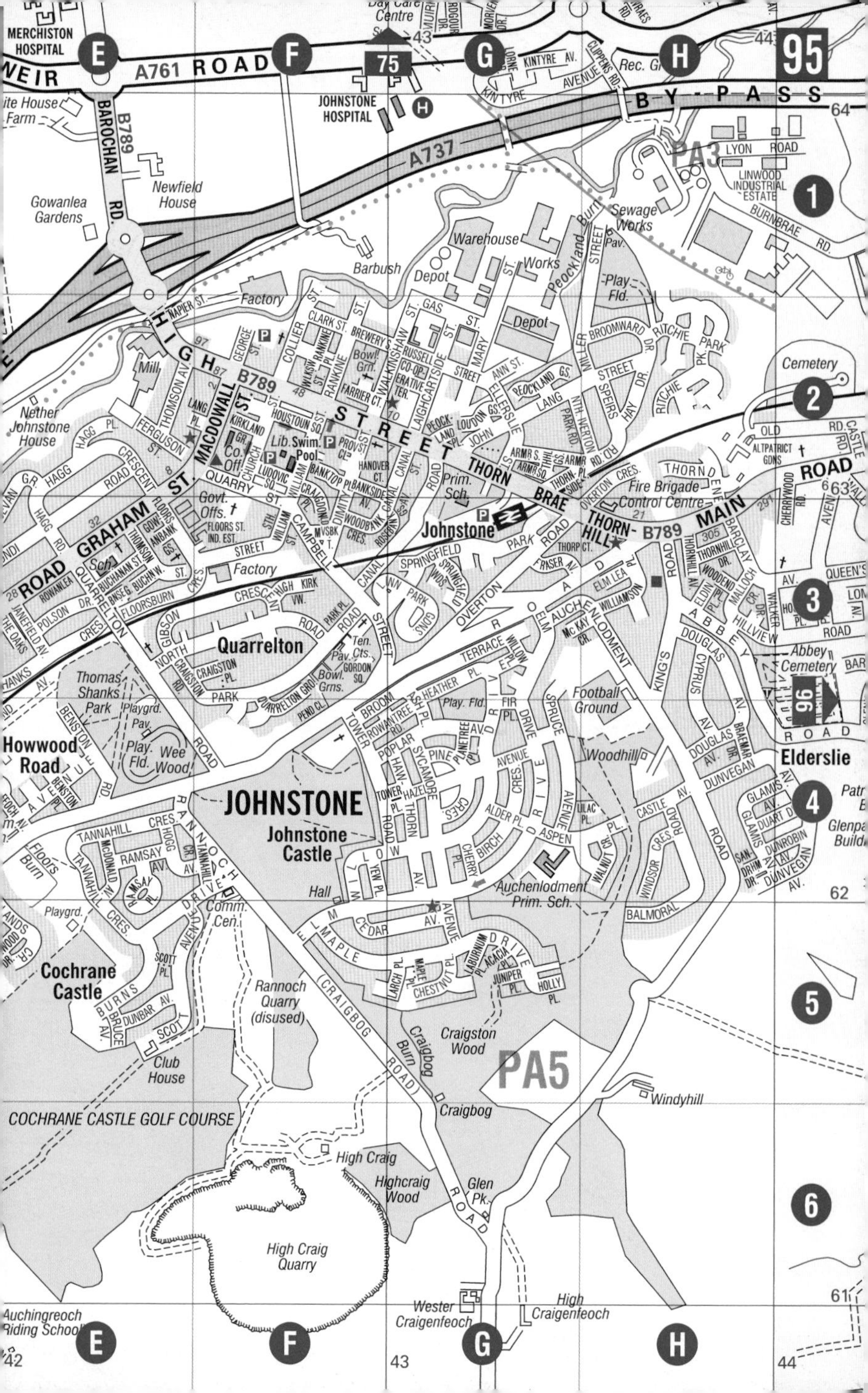

JOHNSTONE BY-PASS
A737
LYON ROAD
LINWOOD INDUSTRIAL ESTATE
BURNBRAE
Burnbrae Bridge
Old Patrick Water
Depots
Depot
Cemetery
Warehouse
PA3
Depot
Works
Warehouse
ST. JAMES BUSINESS CENTRE
LINWOOD A761
Showcase Cinema Paisley
Superstore
THE PHOENIX RETAIL PARK
B789 ROAD
CANAL GDS.
CANAL ST.
Club House
Hall
Elderslie Leisure Centre
Lib.
Roundhill Plantation
Newton Cottage
ELDERSLIE GOLF COURSE
Lex Wood
Newton Wood
MAIN
Wallace Prim. Sch.
Play. Flds.
Football Grd.
Abbey Cemetery
Elderslie
Patrick Bank Bridge
Glenpatrick Buildings
Works
Johnstone PA5
Leitchland Farm
Glenpatrick
Leethland
Gleniffer Ho.
LEITCHLAND
Mackiesmill Bridge No.2
Mackiesmill Bridge No.1
Mackiesmill
Old Foxbar
Low Bardrain
Old Patrick Water
Heriot Prim. Sch.
Prim. Sch.
Comm. Cen.
Play. Field
Playgrd.
HOLLOWS
FOXBAR
Roaden Burn
GLEN

77
Crematorium
Woodside Cemetery
Ferguslie Park
Ferguslie Gardens
St. Mirin's High Sch.
GEORGE ST.
A761
CANAL STREET
FERGUSLIE
Sports Ground
MILLARSTON INDUSTRIAL ESTATE
Millarston
Maxwellton Sch. Pk.
MAXWELLTON ST.
B775
Castlehead High Sch.
PAISLEY
Univ. of Paisley
University of Paisley
Tannahill's Cott.
Bowl. Grns.
Observatory
Lib.
Mus.
PA1
Castlehead
Maternity Hospital
ROYAL ALEXANDRA HOSPITAL
Rec. Ground
Lounsdale
Comm. Cen.
Playing Field
Meikleriggs
Paisley
Brodie Park Pitch & Putt Course
Carriagehill
98
Brediland
Stanely
CORSEBAR RD
MOREDUN RD
Crosbie Newark
Playing Field
Pav.
Donald's Wood
Potterhill
Super Factory
PA2
Bushes Prim. Sch.
Glenburn
Comm. Cen.
Bowling Green
Prim. Sch.
FOXBAR
Playing Field
Gleniffer High Sch.
STANELY RESERVOIR
Stanely Castle (Remains of)
Harelaw Aqueduct
Comm. Cen.
Water Works
Waterfall
Weir
Limecraigs
Langcraigs Sch.
Gateside Sch.
Cattle Market
GLENIFFER BRAES COUNTRY PARK
Gleniffer Burn
E
F
G
H
1
2
3
4
5
6
46
47
48
61
62
63
64

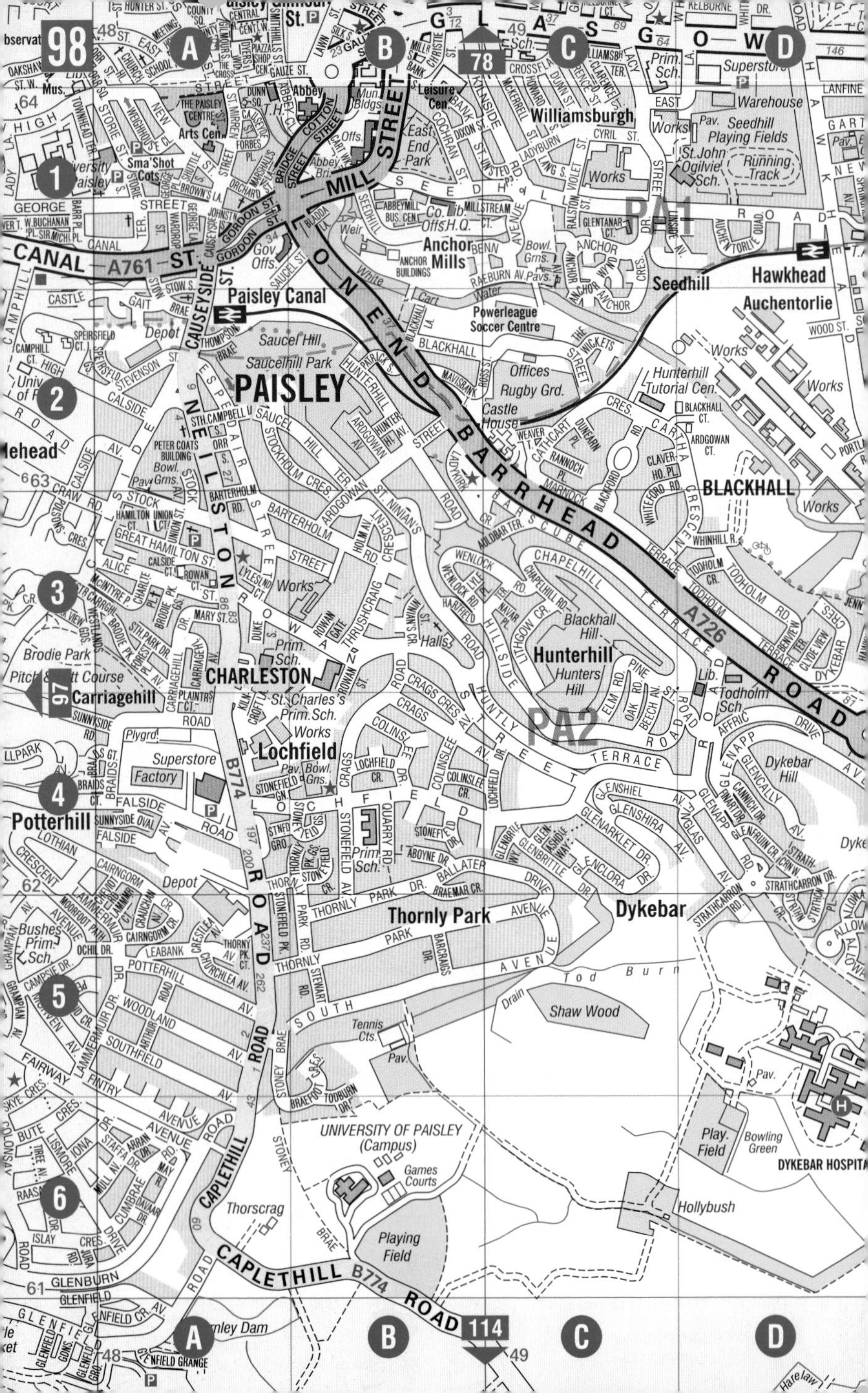
A
B
C
D
1
2
3
4
5
6
78
97
114
PAISLEY
Williamsburgh
Anchor Mills
Paisley Canal
Saucel Hill
Saucelhill Park
Seedhill
Hawkhead
Auchentorlie
BLACKHALL
CHARLESTON
Carriagehill
Lochfield
Potterhill
Hunterhill
Hunters Hill
Blackhall Hill
Thornly Park
Dykebar
Dykebar Hill
Brodie Park
Pitch & Putt Course
Shaw Wood
Tod Burn
Hollybush
Thorscrag
UNIVERSITY OF PAISLEY (Campus)
Games Courts
Playing Field
Play. Field
Bowling Green
DYKEBAR HOSPITAL
Seedhill Playing Fields
Running Track
St.John Ogilvie Sch.
Superstore
Warehouse
Works
Abbey
Arts Cen.
Sma'Shot Cots.
University of Paisley
THE PAISLEY CENTRE
Leisure Cen.
East End Park
Powerleague Soccer Centre
Offices
Rugby Grd.
Castle House
Hunterhill Tutorial Cen.
St.Charles's Prim.Sch.
Todholm Sch.
Factory
Depot
Tennis Cts.
Bushes Prim. Sch.
PA1
PA2
CANAL A761 ST.
MILL STREET
LONEND
BARRHEAD ROAD A726
NEILSTON ROAD B774
CAPLETHILL B774 ROAD
CAPLETHILL ROAD
CAUSEYSIDE ST.
SEEDHILL ROAD
HUNTLY TERRACE
THORNLY PARK AVENUE
SOUTH AVENUE
STONEY BRAE
GEORGE STREET
HIGH STREET
CALSIDE
ESPEDAIR STREET
BARTERHOLM
ARDGOWAN STREET
ROWAN STREET
LOCHFIELD ROAD
FALSIDE ROAD
POTTERHILL AV.
WOODLAND AV.
SOUTHFIELD AV.
FINTRY AVENUE
GLENBURN
GLENFIELD
GLENFIELD GRANGE
AFFRIC DRIVE
STRATHCARRON RD.
GLENAPP
CHAPELHILL
BLACKHALL
Stanely Dam
Harelaw
48
49
61
62
63
64
146

Oldhall
Ralston
Paisley
Hawkhead
Rosshall
Crookston
Glasgow
G52
G53
Hurlet
A761
PAISLEY RD.
CROOKSTON RD.
A736
A726
BARRHEAD ROAD
HURLET ROAD
GRAHAMSTON RD.
B771
BATHGO HILL
RALSTON GOLF COURSE
Rosshall Cottage
HAWKHEAD CEMETERY
The Mary Russell Sch.
Hawkhead Bri.
HAWKHEAD HOSPITAL
Hospice
St. Andrew's Academy
Kersland School
White Cart Water
Playing Field
BULL WOOD
Hawkhead House Farm
RENFREWSHIRE
GLASGOW
LEVERNDALE HOSPITAL
LEVERNDALE GOLF COURSE
LEVERNDALE INDUSTRIAL CENTRE
Howford Bridge
Howford Sch.
Rosshall Estate Gds.
TEMPLE HILL
Oldbarhills Bridge
Tongues Hill
Hurlethill Plantation
Low Oldbar
Oldbar Hills
Hurlet Hill
Roughmussel
West Hurlet Ho.
Levern Bridge
Works
Depot
79
100
115
E
F
G
H
1
2
3
4
5
6

CARDONALD
CRAIGTON
Craigton Cemetery
80
53
PAISLEY ROAD
A761
CROOKSTON
Crookston
South Cardonald
Mosspark
G52
Cardonald College
Convent
Lourdes Sec. Sch.
Our Lady of the Rosary Prim. Sch.
Cardonald Cemetery
Cardonald Place Farm
Crookston Wood
CROOKSTON WOOD
Bonnyholm Prim. Sch.
Play. Fields
ROSS HALL BMI HOSPITAL
Rosshall Estate Gds.
Rosshall
Rosshall Park
Howford Bridge
Howford Sch.
LEVERNDALE HOSPITAL
99
McGill Prim. Sch.
White Cart Water
Lochar Park
Nethercraigs Playing Field
Corkerhill
Running Track
Crookston Castle (Remains of)
Crookston Castle Sec. Sch.
Glasgow
Nethercraigs Play. Fld.
St. Edmund's Prim. Sch.
G53
Comm. Cen.
Leithland Prim. Sch.
Haugh Hill
POLLOK
M77
St. Paul's High Sch.
Junc. 2
CROOKSTON ROAD A736
BARRHEAD ROAD B762
Levern Water
Househill Park
Househillwood
Pollok Leisure Pool
POLLOK TOWNSHIP CENTRE (SHOPPING CEN.)
M77 MOTORWAY
PRIESTHILL
Prim. Sch.
Works
Bowl. Green
Levern Bridge
116
Bellarmine Secondary School
Recreation Ground
COWGLEN HOSPITAL
A B C D
1 2 3 4 5 6

M8 MOTORWAY
Junc. 23
81
BELLAHOUSTON
BELLAHOUSTON PARK
Bellahouston Leisure Centre
Palace of Art
House For An Art Lover
Glasgow Ski Cen.
Pitch & Putt Course
Running Track
Nursery
Lodge
Dumbreck
Mosspark
MOSSPARK BOULEVARD
M77 MOTORWAY
Junc. 1
DUMBRECK INTERCHANGE
DUMBRECK ROAD
B768
Club House
Dumbreck Riding Sch.
Rugby Football Club Playing Fields
Engine Shed
HAGGS CASTLE GOLF COURSE
Corkerhill
Lochinch Sports Field
NORTH WOOD
POLLOK COUNTRY PARK
Burrell Collection Museum
Knowehead Cottage
NETHER POLLOK PLAYING FIELDS
Pollok House
White Cart Water
Weir
Cricket Ground
Tennis Courts
Pollokshaws
Pollokshaws West
G41
G43
POLLOK GOLF COURSE
Hippingstones
South Lodge
BARRHEAD ROAD
B762
Broompark Farm
Club House
Bowling Greens
POLLOKSHAWS ROAD
B769
NETHER AULDHOUSE RD.
SHAWBRIDGE INDUSTRIAL EST.
AULDHOUSE RETAIL PARK
COWGLEN GOLF COURSE
KENNISHEAD
117
102
Pollok Wood

102
A
B
C
D
1
2
3
4
5
6
M8
M77
M77 MOTORWAY
Junc. 22
Junc. 21
82
118
101
Shields Rd.
Bellahouse Academy
PLANTATION ROAD INTERCHANGE
SEAWARD STREET INTERCHANGE
Kinning Park
Shields Junc.
Depots
Sikh Temple
Depot
Dumbreck
NITHSDALE
MAXWELL DRIVE
ST. ANDREW'S DRIVE
POLLOKSHIELDS
Craigholme Sch.
Dumbreck
G41
Maxwell Park
Burgh Hall
Maxwell Pk.
TERREGLES AVENUE
FOTHERINGAY
Pollokshields West
Strathbungo
Haggs Castle
DUMBRECK RD. B768
TITWOOD 768 RD.
Superstore
Crossmyloof
DARNLEY B763
Crossmyloof
HAGGS ROAD B769
POLLOKSHAWS
MINARD ROAD
PARK
Playing Fields
NETHER POLLOK PLAYING FIELDS
Shawlands Academy
Waverley Pk.
Shawlands
Shawlands
LANGSIDE B768 AVENUE
Goals Football Centre
Camp Hill
QUEEN'S
Pollokshaws
Pollokshaws West
Pollokshaws East
A77
KILMARNOCK
Langside
HOSP.
Langside
Millbrae Bri.
Albert Park
Bowling Greens
G43
AULDHOUSE
NETHER RD.
Superstore
Warehouse Works
SHAWBRIDGE INDUSTRIAL EST.
AULDHOUSE RETAIL PARK
Mosque
Nursery

E
F
G
H
83
119
104
1
2
3
4
5
6
West St.
Kingston
Laurieston
Glasgow Parcels Sta.
GORBALS
BALLATER
A74 STREET
Suspension Bridge
CLYDE
Glasgow Green
Hutchesontown
PLAYING FIELDS
Port Eglington
Gasholder Station
Training Cen.
Works
EGLINTON
A77
ROAD
POLLOKSHAWS
Freightliner Terminal
CALEDONIA
A728
CATHCART
Cemetery
A730
ROAD RUTHERGLEN
Gushetfaulds Junction
DIXONS BLAZES INDUSTRIAL ESTATE
Richmond Park School
G5
POLMADIE
B763
Oatlands
Govanhill
Bus Depot
Tramway East
AIKENHEAD
STREET
Health Club
Swim. Pool
Queen's Pk.
Crosshill
Glasgow
G42
Holyrood Sec. Sch.
Holyrood Sports Cen.
Hangingshaw
Polmadie Marshalling Yard
WORKS
TORYGLEN PARK
Superstore
Playing Fields
Cathkin Rec. Cen.
Cathkin Park
Cycle Track
Miniature Golf Course
Football Grounds
Recreation Ground
VICTORIA INFIRMARY
PROSPECTHILL
ROAD
B768
Mt. Florida
Battlefield
Queens Park F.C. (Hampden Park)
Mount Florida
Playing Fields
Hampden Sch.
St. Brigid's Prim. Sch.
Toryglen
CURTIS AV.
KERRYCROY
ARDMORY
MONTFORD AVENUE
Public Park
KINGSACRE ROAD
B766
King's Park
Cart Water
Rec. Grd.
Works
G44

104
A
B
C
D
84
1
2
3
4
5
6
103
120
LONDON ROAD
Bridgeton
Hutchesontown
Glasgow Green
Playground
Paddling Pool
KING'S DR.
JAMES ST.
A74
DALMARNOCK ROAD
Barrow Field
G40
PLAYING FIELDS
Polmadie Bridge
RIVER CLYDE
Richmond Park
Model Yacht Pond
RUTHERGLEN ROAD
SHAWFIELD DR.
Shawfield Stadium
DUNN ST.
Dalmarnock
DALMARNOCK
Glasgow
A749
Oatlands
West of Scotland Indoor Bowling Club
Polmadie Industrial Estate
GLASGOW ROAD
A730
Shawfield Ind. Est.
Sewage Works
Bridgeton Bank
Trading Estate
Polmadie Marshalling Yard
Adult Training Centre
Community Centre
G42
Burnhill Sports Cen.
Rutherglen
FARMELOAN RD.
DALMARNOCK RD.
PROSPECTHILL RD.
B768
BURNHILL ST.
MAIN ST.
STONELAW ROAD
MILL STREET
Toryglen
Clincarthill
Bankhead
Overtoun Park
King's Park
KINGSBRIDGE DRIVE
KINGSHEATH

Glasgow Celtic F.C. (Celtic Park)
Helenvale Sports Arena
Bus Garage
G31
Celtic Sports Grd.
Westthorn Recreation Ground
Cuningar
Sand Pit
Bonded Stores
Cemetery
Braidfauld
Dalbeth
G32
Tollcross Park
Tollcross Leisure Centre
Shettleston Day Hosp.
St. Mark's Prim. Sch.
St. Paul's Prim. Sch.
A74
London Road
River Clyde
Glasgow South Lanarkshire
Clyde Workshops
Drumhead Rd.
Junc. 1
Fullarton Dr.
Cambuslang Road
Cambuslang Ind. Park
Clydesmill Rd.
Recreation Ground
Playing Field
Hamilton Farm
Works
Rutherglen
Farme Cross
A724
Gallowflat
G72
Eastfield
Trinity High Sch.
Bogleshole Rd.
Glasgow Rd.
Somervell Park
Bridge Street
Sports Centre
85
106
121

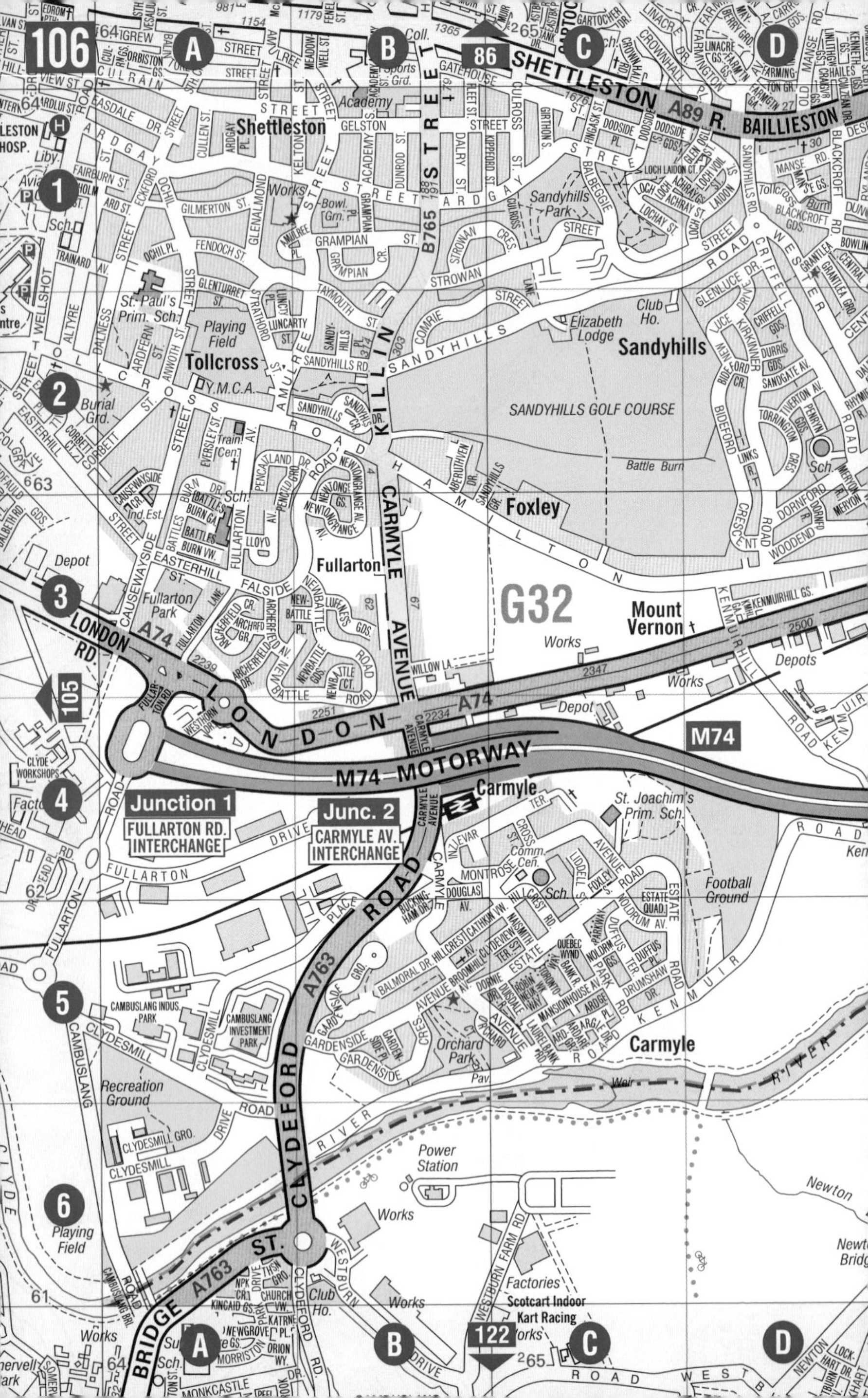

Shettleston
Tollcross
Sandyhills
SANDYHILLS GOLF COURSE
Foxley
Fullarton
G32
Mount Vernon
Carmyle
Junction 1
FULLARTON RD. INTERCHANGE
Junc. 2
CARMYLE AV. INTERCHANGE
M74 MOTORWAY
LONDON ROAD
A74
SHETTLESTON RD.
A89
BAILLIESTON
HAMILTON ROAD
CARMYLE AVENUE
CLYDEFORD ROAD
A763
BRIDGE ST.
KENMUIR ROAD
RIVER CLYDE
Power Station
Recreation Ground
Playing Field
Orchard Park
Football Ground
St. Joachim's Prim. Sch.
St. Paul's Prim. Sch.
Scotcart Indoor Kart Racing
Factories
Works
Depot
Depots
CAMBUSLANG INDUS. PARK
CAMBUSLANG INVESTMENT PARK
CLYDE WORKSHOPS
86
105
122

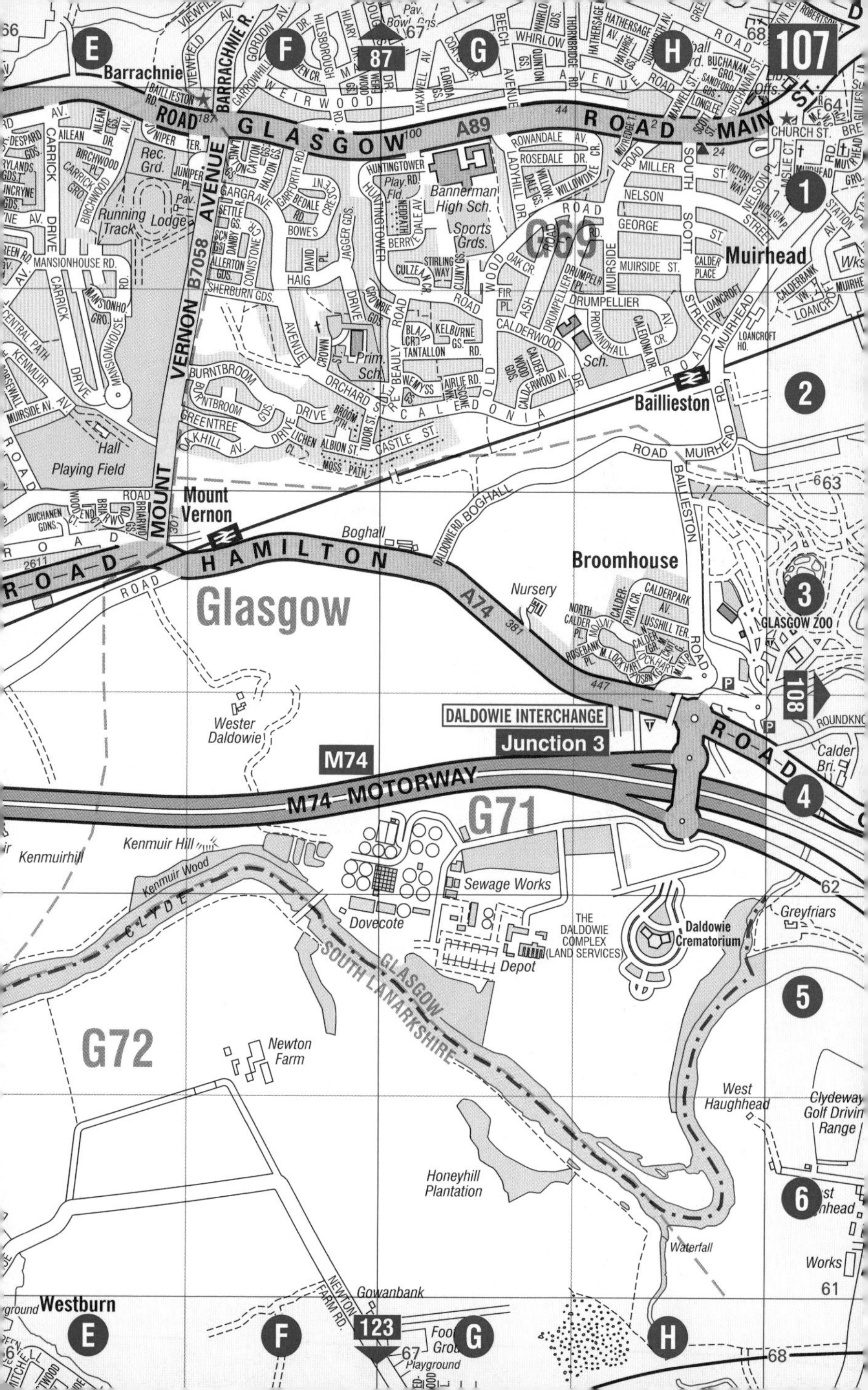
Barrachnie
Glasgow Road
A89
Bannerman High Sch.
Muirhead
Baillieston
Mount Vernon
Hamilton Road
A74
Glasgow
Broomhouse
Glasgow Zoo
Daldowie Interchange
Junction 3
M74
M74 Motorway
G69
G71
G72
Sewage Works
Dovecote
The Daldowie Complex (Land Services)
Daldowie Crematorium
Depot
Kenmuir Hill
Kenmuirhill
Wester Daldowie
Newton Farm
Honeyhill Plantation
West Haughhead
Clydeway Golf Driving Range
Greyfriars
Waterfall
Gowanbank
Westburn
Playing Field
Running Track
Glasgow South Lanarkshire
87
108
123

GLASGOW-&-EDINBURGH RD.
A8
88
Memorial Park
Crosshill
Superstore
BAILLIESTON
MAIN ST.
A89
CHURCH ST.
BREDISHOLM RD.
BREDISHOLM TER.
ELLISMUIR PL.
THORNYBURN DR.
THORNYBURN PL.
STATION PARK
BRACADALE DR.
BRACADALE GDS.
Muirhead
CALDER PLACE
LOANCROFT PL.
MUIRHEAD GDS.
Wks.
Baillieston
Junc. 8 (M8)
Junction 2 (M73)
Cattle Grid
Memorial Hall
Ellismuir
G69
Waterfall
GLASGOW
NORTH LANARKSHIRE
Newlands Glen
Thornyburn
Calderbank House
North Calder Water
Woodhead Farm
M73
M73 MOTORWAY
Newlands Farm
CALDERBRAES GOLF COURSE
GLASGOW ZOO
Glasgow
107
HAMILTON RD. A721 GLASGOW
ROUNDKNOWE RD.
Junction 1 (M73)
Calder Bri.
MARYVILLE INTERCHANGE
Club Ho.
Warehouses
BIRKENSHAW INDUSTRIAL ESTATE
Depots
MARYVILLE VW.
OLD EDINBURGH ROAD
B7001
Calderbraes
Playgrd.
Birkenshaw Sports Hall
Aitkenhead Prim. Sch.
Birkenshaw
Recreation Grd.
KILMUIR ROAD
SECOND AVENUE
M74 MOTORWAY
M74
Greyfriars
Daldowie Crematorium
Junction 4 (M74)
GREYFRIARS RD.
FARM ROAD
Powburn
NEW EDINBURGH ROAD
A721
HOLMBRAE RD.
A752
West Haughhead
Clydeway Golf Driving Range
BLANTYRE FARM RD. B758
RIVER CLYDE
GLASGOW ROAD B7071
East Haughhead
Works
Waterfall
Kylepark
KYLEPARK DRIVE
Uddingston
MILL ROAD
Uddingston Junc.
124
Playing Fields
Sch.
A B C D
1 2 3 4 5 6
61 62 63 68 69

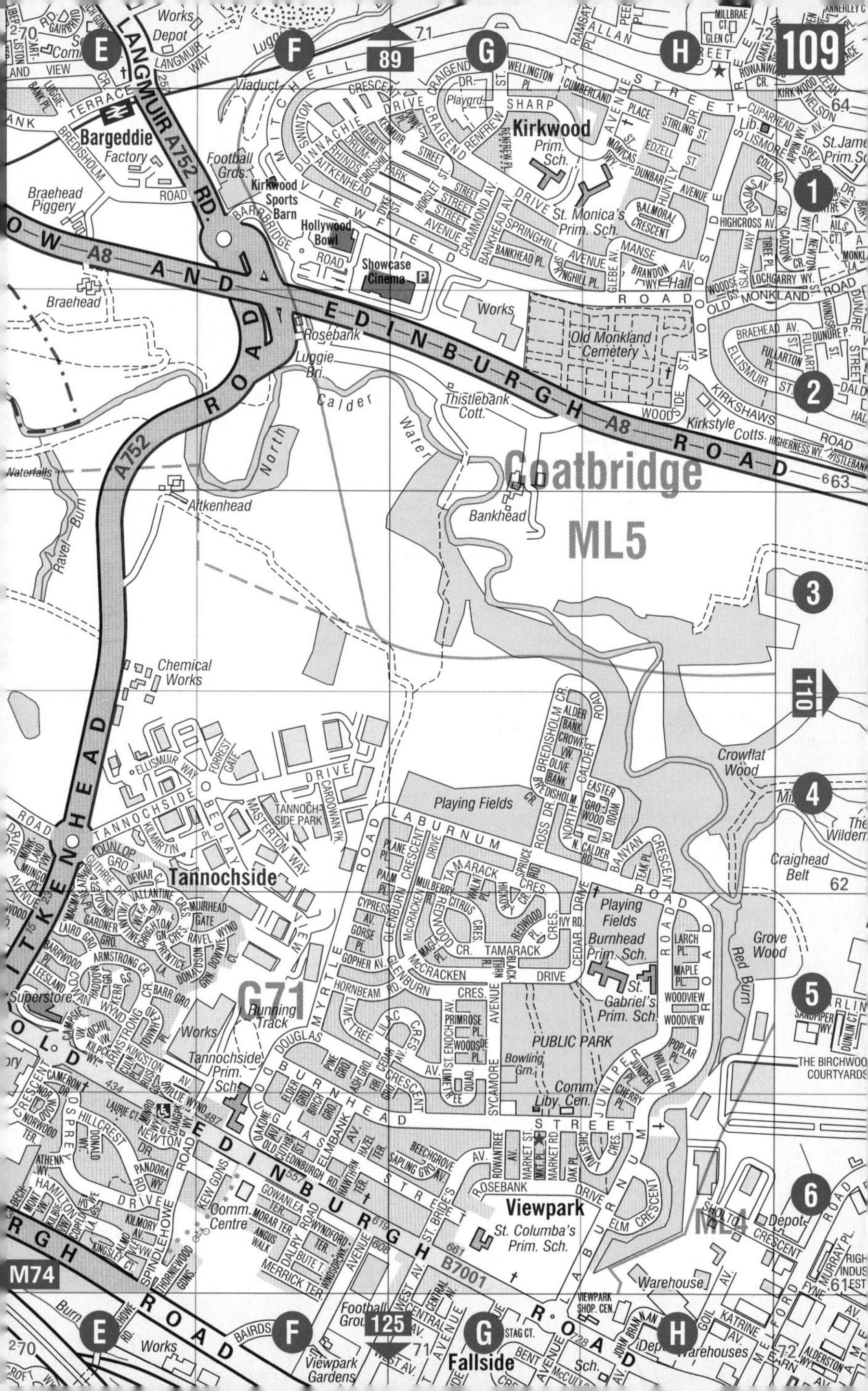

Bargeddie
Kirkwood
Coatbridge
ML5
Tannochside
G71
Viewpark
Fallside
ML4
Kirkwood Sports Barn
Hollywood Bowl
Showcase Cinema
Old Monkland Cemetery
Rosebank
Luggie Bri.
Calder Water
North Calder
Thistlebank Cott.
Bankhead
Aitkenhead
Braehead
Braehead Piggery
Chemical Works
Crowflat Wood
Craighead Belt
Grove Wood
Playing Fields
Public Park
Running Track
Tannochside Prim. Sch.
Burnhead Prim. Sch.
St. Gabriel's Prim. Sch.
St. Columba's Prim. Sch.
Kirkwood Prim. Sch.
St. Monica's Prim. Sch.
Viewpark Gardens
The Birchwood Courtyards
Superstore
Warehouse
Warehouses
GLASGOW AND EDINBURGH ROAD
EDINBURGH ROAD
AITKENHEAD ROAD
LANGMUIR A752 RD.
M74
89
125
110

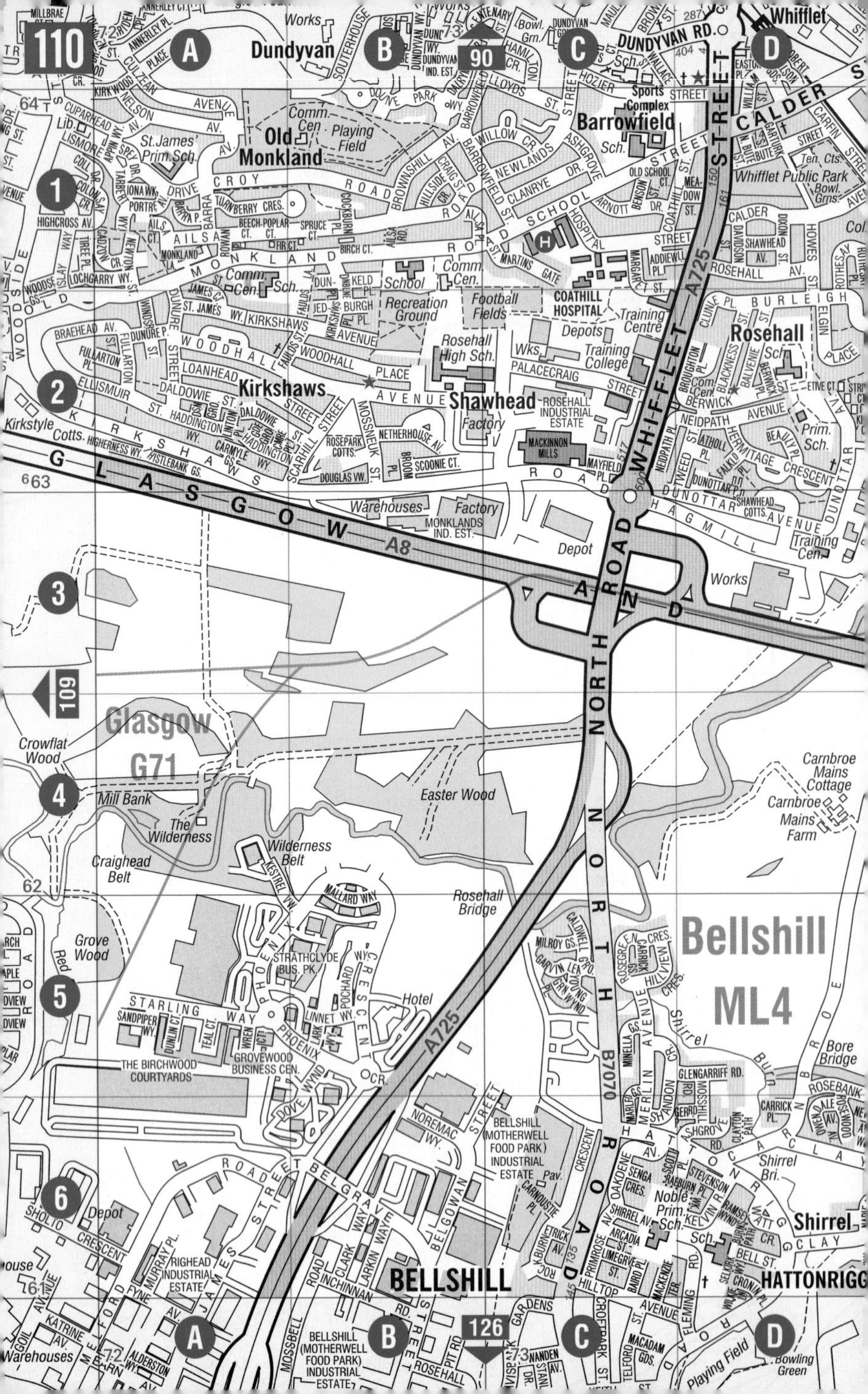
Dundyvan
Old Monkland
Barrowfield
Whifflet
Rosehall
Kirkshaws
Shawhead
Glasgow G71
Bellshill ML4
BELLSHILL
Shirrel
HATTONRIGG
Easter Wood
Carnbroe Mains Cottage
Carnbroe Mains Farm
Crowflat Wood
Mill Bank
The Wilderness
Wilderness Belt
Craighead Belt
Grove Wood
Rosehall Bridge
Bore Bridge
COATHILL HOSPITAL
ROSEHALL INDUSTRIAL ESTATE
MONKLANDS IND. EST.
STRATHCLYDE BUS. PK.
THE BIRCHWOOD COURTYARDS
GROVEWOOD BUSINESS CEN.
BELLSHILL (MOTHERWELL FOOD PARK) INDUSTRIAL ESTATE
RIGHEAD INDUSTRIAL ESTATE
GLASGOW ROAD
A8
A725
B7070
NORTH ROAD
WHIFFLET STREET
CALDER STREET
MONKLAND ROAD
SCHOOL ROAD
90
109
126

Coatbridge
ML5
Whifflet
Greenend
Sikeside
91
Airdrie
ML6
High Palacecraig
Low Palacecraig
Brickwork Cottage
Monkland Canal (disused)
North Calder Water
Faskine Farm
Maggieshaugh
Fox Covert
Stank Brae
Carnbroe
East Shawhead
Shawhead Ind. Estate
Works
Weir
Comm. Centre
Playing Fields
Sch.
Heathery Lea Covert
112
EDINBURGH ROAD
A8
Orchard Farm
The Mount
Carnbroe Rd.
Townhead Avenue
Woodside
Eurocentral
Reset Plantation
Byramsmuir Plantation
Motherwell
ML1
Coddington Crescent
Eurocentral Industrial Estate
Mossend Sidings
Eurocentral Rail Terminal
127
Sykeside Street
Sutherland Drive
Cairnhill Road
Calderview Av.
Earlston Crescent
Drummore Av.
Hawick Dr.
Peebles Path
Cairnhill Cres.
Brittain Way
McNeil
Condor Glen
E
F
G
H
1
2
3
4
5
6
74
275
76
64
63
62
61

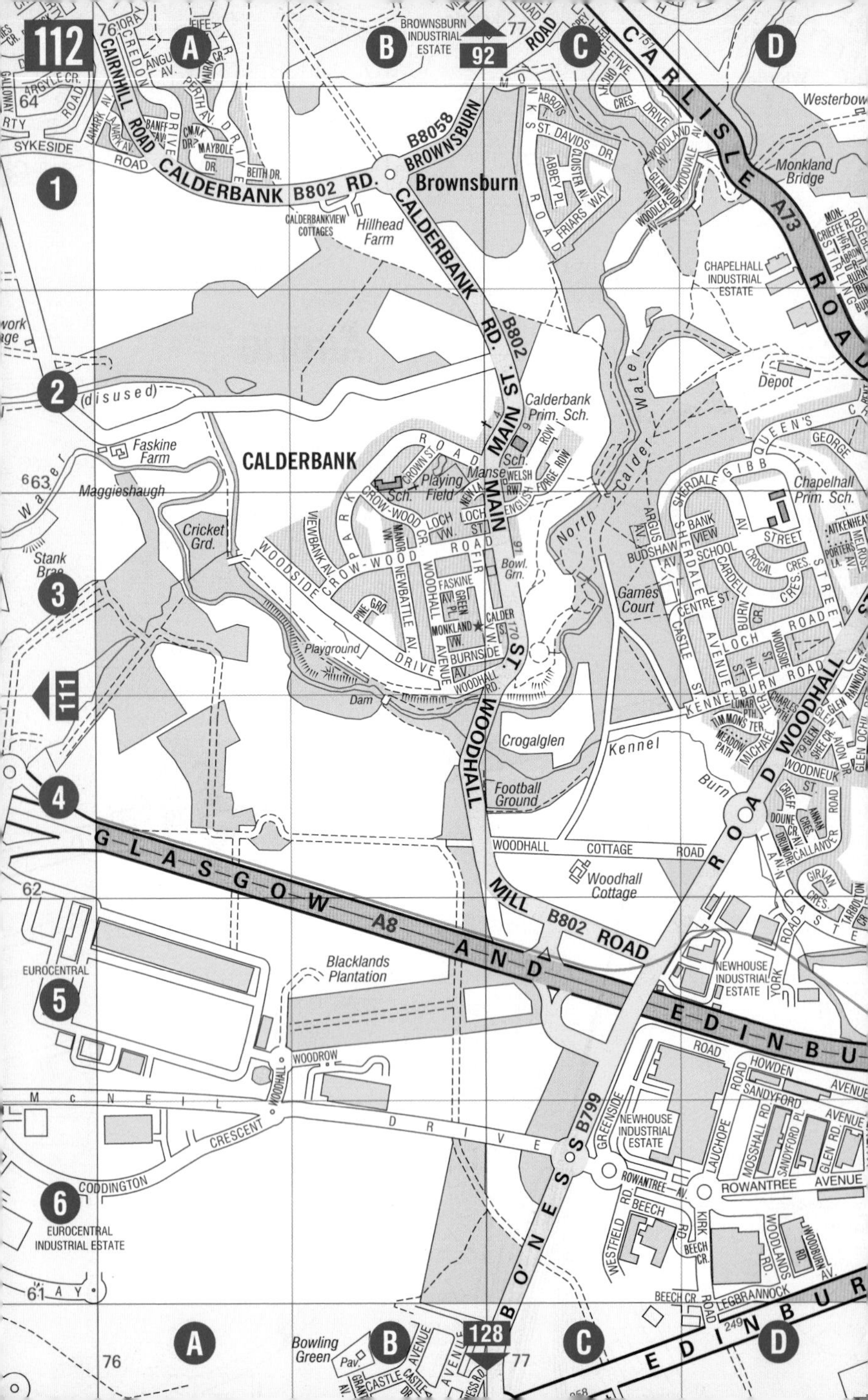

A
B
C
D
1
2
3
4
5
6
BROWNSBURN INDUSTRIAL ESTATE
92
111
128
CALDERBANK B802 RD.
B8058 BROWNSBURN ROAD
Brownsburn
CALDERBANKVIEW COTTAGES
Hillhead Farm
CALDERBANK RD.
B802
MAIN ST.
CALDERBANK
Calderbank Prim. Sch.
Faskine Farm
Maggieshaugh
Cricket Grd.
Stank Brae
(disused)
Playing Field
Playground
Dam
Bowl. Grn.
Crogalglen
Football Ground
WOODHALL COTTAGE ROAD
Woodhall Cottage
MILL B802 ROAD
WOODHALL ST.
North Calder Water
Kennel Burn
Games Court
Chapelhall Prim. Sch.
CHAPELHALL INDUSTRIAL ESTATE
Depot
Monkland Bridge
Westerbow
CARLISLE A73 ROAD
GLASGOW A8 AND EDINBURGH ROAD
Blacklands Plantation
EUROCENTRAL
EUROCENTRAL INDUSTRIAL ESTATE
McNEILL DRIVE
CRESCENT
CODDINGTON
WOODROW
NEWHOUSE INDUSTRIAL ESTATE
BO'NESS B799 ROAD
ROWANTREE AVENUE
HOWDEN AVENUE
SANDYFORD AVENUE
LEGBRANNOCK ROAD
EDINBURGH ROAD
WOODHALL ROAD
Bowling Green
SYKESIDE ROAD
CAIRNHILL ROAD
ARGYLE CR.
GALLOWAY
64
63
62
61
76
77

Gartness
Bowhouse
BOWHOUSE ROAD
93
Damhead Farm
CRAIGENS ROAD
Clattering Burn
DUNISTON ROAD
Easter Dunsyston
Works
Sauchenbog Bridge
BOWHOUSEBRAE
Airdrie
ML6
Shotts Burn
Craigends
Gartness Farm
GARTNESS ROAD
LAWHOPE MILL ROAD
Burn
Wester Dunsyston
MAIN ST.
LAUCHOPE ST.
B799
BELLSIDE ROAD
A73
Budshaw
Football Ground
St. Aloysius Prim. Sch.
CHAPELHALL
Bailside Farm
Waterfall
M8
M8 MOTORWAY
Junction 6
NEWHOUSE INTERCHANGE
Sandyford Farm
Reservoir
A8 ROAD
B7066
GLASGOW AND EDINBURGH ROAD
BELLSIDE RD.
Newhouse
Motel
Pollockshill
Motherwell
ML1
A775 ROAD
BIGGAR ROAD
Greenside
CARLISLE ROAD
MOTHERWELL RD.
B7066
129
Burn
E
F
G
H
1
2
3
4
5
6

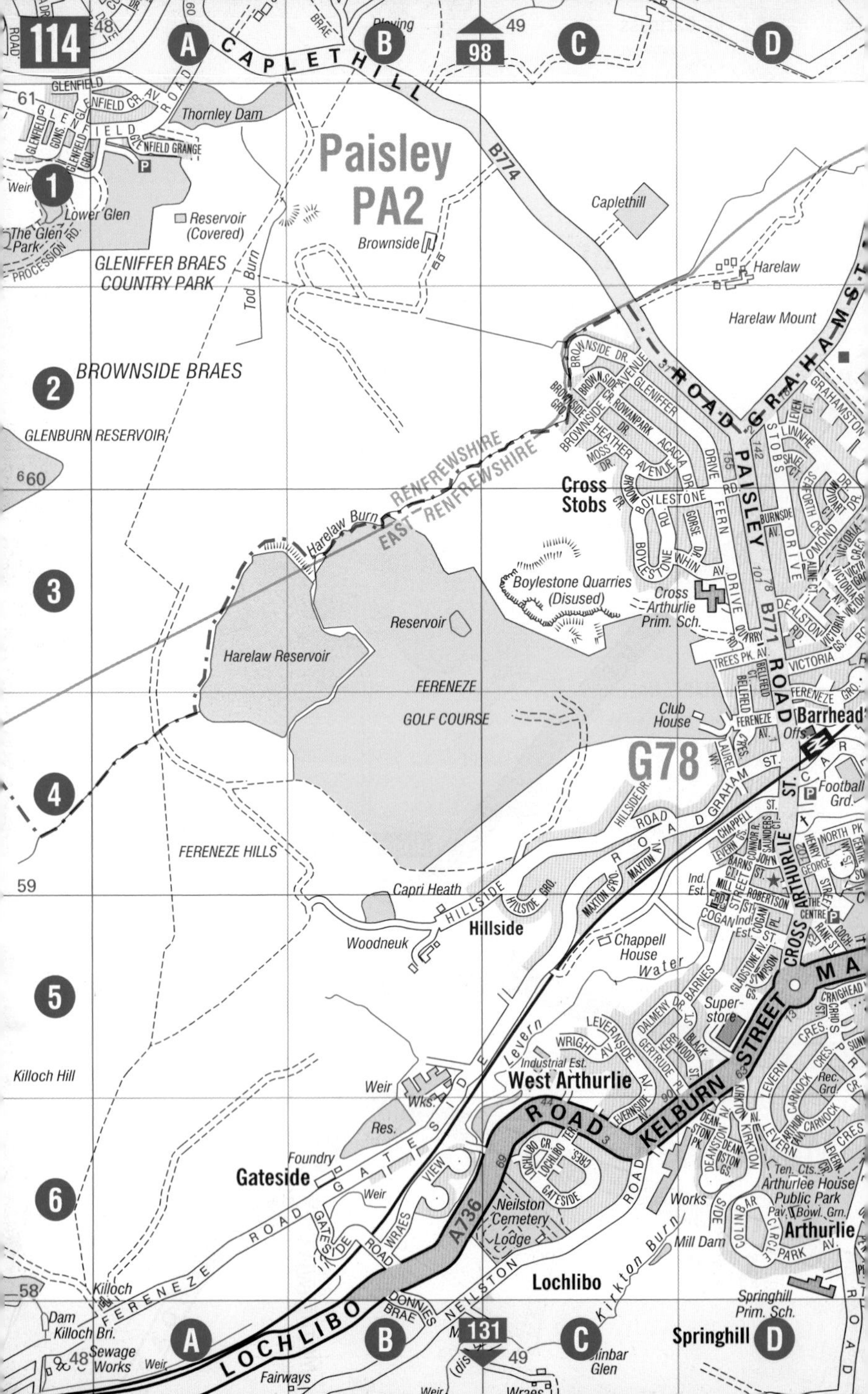

98
131
Paisley PA2
G78
CAPLETHILL ROAD
B774
Thornley Dam
Caplethill
Brownside
Harelaw
Harelaw Mount
GRAHAM ST.
Lower Glen
The Glen Park
PROCESSION RD.
Reservoir (Covered)
GLENIFFER BRAES COUNTRY PARK
BROWNSIDE BRAES
GLENBURN RESERVOIR
Tod Burn
RENFREWSHIRE
EAST RENFREWSHIRE
Harelaw Burn
Cross Stobs
Boylestone Quarries (Disused)
Cross Arthurlie Prim. Sch.
PAISLEY ROAD
B771
Reservoir
Harelaw Reservoir
FERENEZE GOLF COURSE
Club House
Barrhead
Football Grd.
FERENEZE HILLS
Capri Heath
Hillside
Woodneuk
Chappell House
Levern Water
Super-store
Killoch Hill
West Arthurlie
Industrial Est.
Weir
Wks.
Res.
Foundry
Gateside
GATESIDE ROAD
A736
Neilston Cemetery
Lodge
Lochlibo
LOCHLIBO ROAD
KELBURN STREET
MAIN ST.
CROSS ARTHURLIE ST.
Works
Mill Dam
Kirkton Burn
Arthurlie House Public Park
Arthurlie
Springhill Prim. Sch.
Springhill
Killoch
Dam
Killoch Bri.
Sewage Works
FERENEZE ROAD
Fairways
Glen

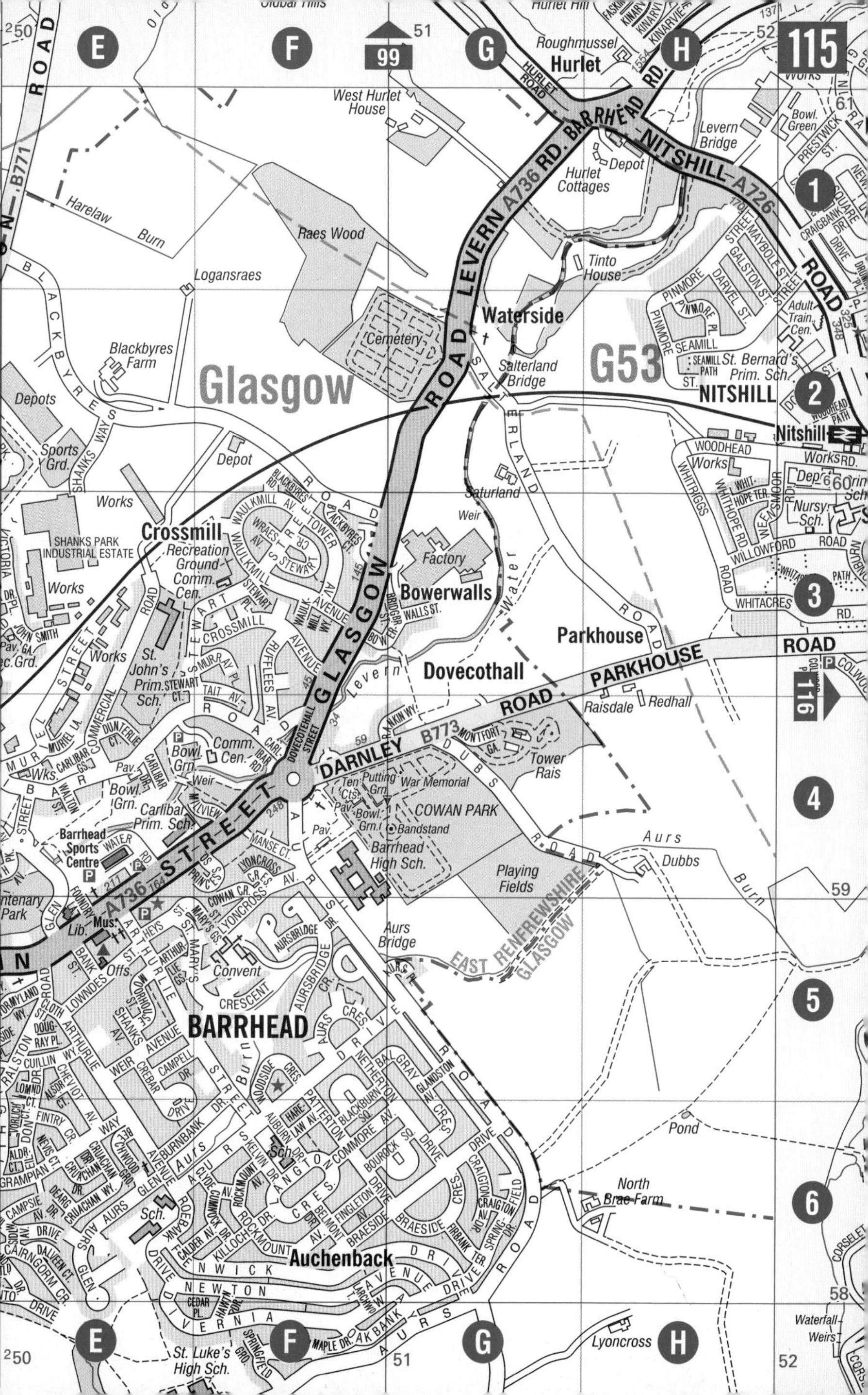

E
F
G
H
99
Hurlet
Roughmussel
West Hurlet House
Levern Bridge
Hurlet Cottages
Depot
NITSHILL
A726
BARRHEAD RD.
LEVERN RD. A736
Harelaw Burn
Raes Wood
Logansraes
Tinto House
Waterside
Cemetery
Blackbyres Farm
Glasgow
G53
Salterland Bridge
St. Bernard's Prim. Sch.
Nitshill
Depots
Sports Grd.
Depot
Works
Crossmill
Recreation Ground
Comm. Cen.
SHANKS PARK INDUSTRIAL ESTATE
Saturland
Weir
Factory
Bowerwalls
Parkhouse
Dovecothall
PARKHOUSE ROAD
116
Raisdale
Redhall
DARNLEY ROAD B773
GLASGOW ROAD
St. John's Prim. Sch.
Tower Rais
War Memorial
COWAN PARK
Bandstand
Barrhead High Sch.
Playing Fields
Aurs Dubbs
Barrhead Sports Centre
Carlibar Prim. Sch.
Aurs Bridge
EAST RENFREWSHIRE
GLASGOW
Convent
BARRHEAD
Pond
North Brae Farm
Auchenback
Lyoncross
St. Luke's High Sch.
Waterfall Weirs
1
2
3
4
5
6
50
51
52
58
59
60
61

PRIESTHILL
NITSHILL
Nitshill
South Nitshill
Priesthill & Darnley
G53
G78
G77
Glasgow
GLASGOW
EAST RENFREWSHIRE
M77 MOTORWAY
A726
B773
PARKHOUSE ROAD
Bellarmine Secondary School
Recreation Ground
COWGLEN HOSPITAL
Kennishead Wood
St. Robert's Prim. Sch.
Burnbrae Prim. Sch.
St. Bernard's Prim. Sch.
DARNLEY IND. EST.
Nursing Home
Superstore
Junction 3
ARDEN
Jenny Lind
Waukmill Glen
WAULKMILL GLEN RESERVOIR
Patterton
Levern Bridge
STEWARTON

100
115
132

117
E
F
G
H
101
133
118
1
2
3
4
5
6
COWGLEN GOLF COURSE
Pollok Wood
Pollokwood House
Kennishead
KENNISHEAD
King George's Field
Busby Junction
Auldhouse Burn
Auldhouse Playing Field
Eastwood Cemy.
Thornliebank
Cemetery
Mansewood
G43
Industrial Estate
Carnwadric
Thornlaw Nursery Sch.
Thornliebank
THORNLIEBANK INDUSTRIAL ESTATE
Woodfarm High Sch.
Orchard Park
Playing Fields
Giffnock
G46
St. Ninian's High Sch.
Eastwood Park
Eastwood Rec. Cen.
Municipal Offices
Spiers Bri.
Driving Range
Club House
Eastwood Butterfly Kingdom
ROUKEN GLEN PARK
Miniature Golf Course
DEACONSBANK GOLF COURSE
Boating Lake
BARRHEAD ROAD
NETHER AULDHOUSE RD.
KENNISHEAD ROAD
BOYDSTONE ROAD
THORNLIEBANK ROAD B769
MAIN STREET
SPIERSBRIDGE ROAD
ROUKEN GLEN ROAD A726
FENWICK ROAD
AYR RD. A77
MANSEWOOD ROAD
BURNFIELD ROAD
ROBSLEE ROAD
ORCHARD PARK AVENUE
EASTWOODMAINS ROAD
54
55
56
59
60
61
58

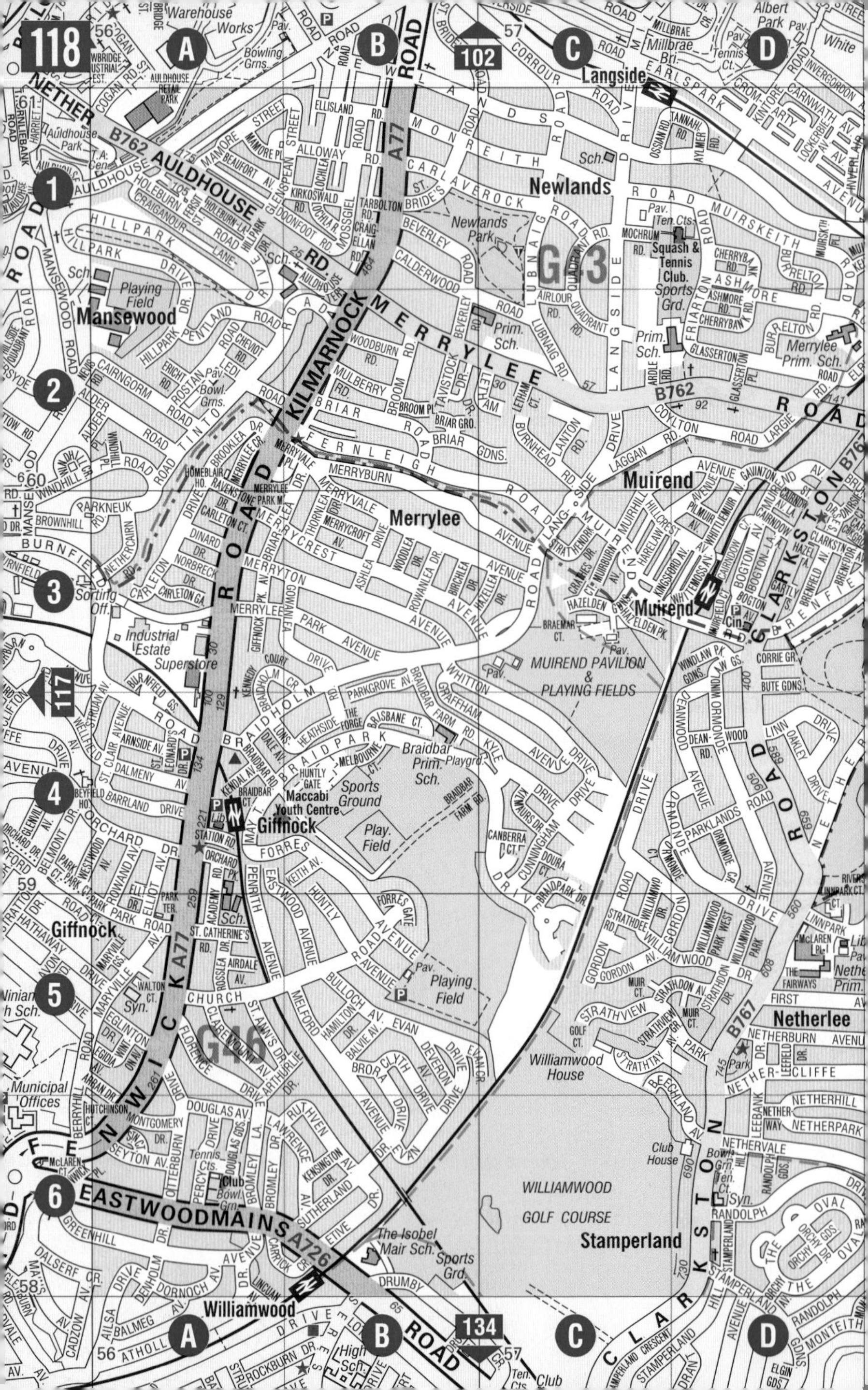

102
134
117
A
B
C
D
1
2
3
4
5
6
Newlands
Newlands Park
Mansewood
Merrylee
Muirend
Giffnock
Netherlee
Stamperland
Williamwood
Langside
G43
G46
Auldhouse Retail Park
Warehouse Works
Muirend Pavilion & Playing Fields
Williamwood Golf Course
Williamwood House
Industrial Estate
Superstore
Sorting Off.
Maccabi Youth Centre
Braidbar Prim. Sch.
Merrylee Prim. Sch.
Squash & Tennis Club.
The Isobel Mair Sch.
Municipal Offices
Kilmarnock Road
Fenwick Road
Eastwoodmains Road
Merrylee Road
Auldhouse Rd.
Clarkston Road
A77
A726
B762
B767

CATHCART
Cathcart
King's Park
KING'S PARK
Aikenhead House
Croftfoot
KING'S PARK GOLF COURSE
LINN PARK
LINN PARK GOLF COURSE
Mansion House
Linn Crematorium
LINNPARK INDUSTRIAL ESTATE
Castlemilk
Glasgow
G44
G45
G76
Mid Netherton
KING'S PARK AVENUE
CARMUNNOCK ROAD
AIKENHEAD ROAD
MENOCK RD.
CROFTFOOT ROAD
DOUGRIE ROAD
ARDENCRAIG ROAD
CARMUNNOCK BY-PASS
LAINSHAW DRIVE
DRAKEMIRE DRIVE
CASTLE ROAD
CROFTPARK AVENUE
103
120
135

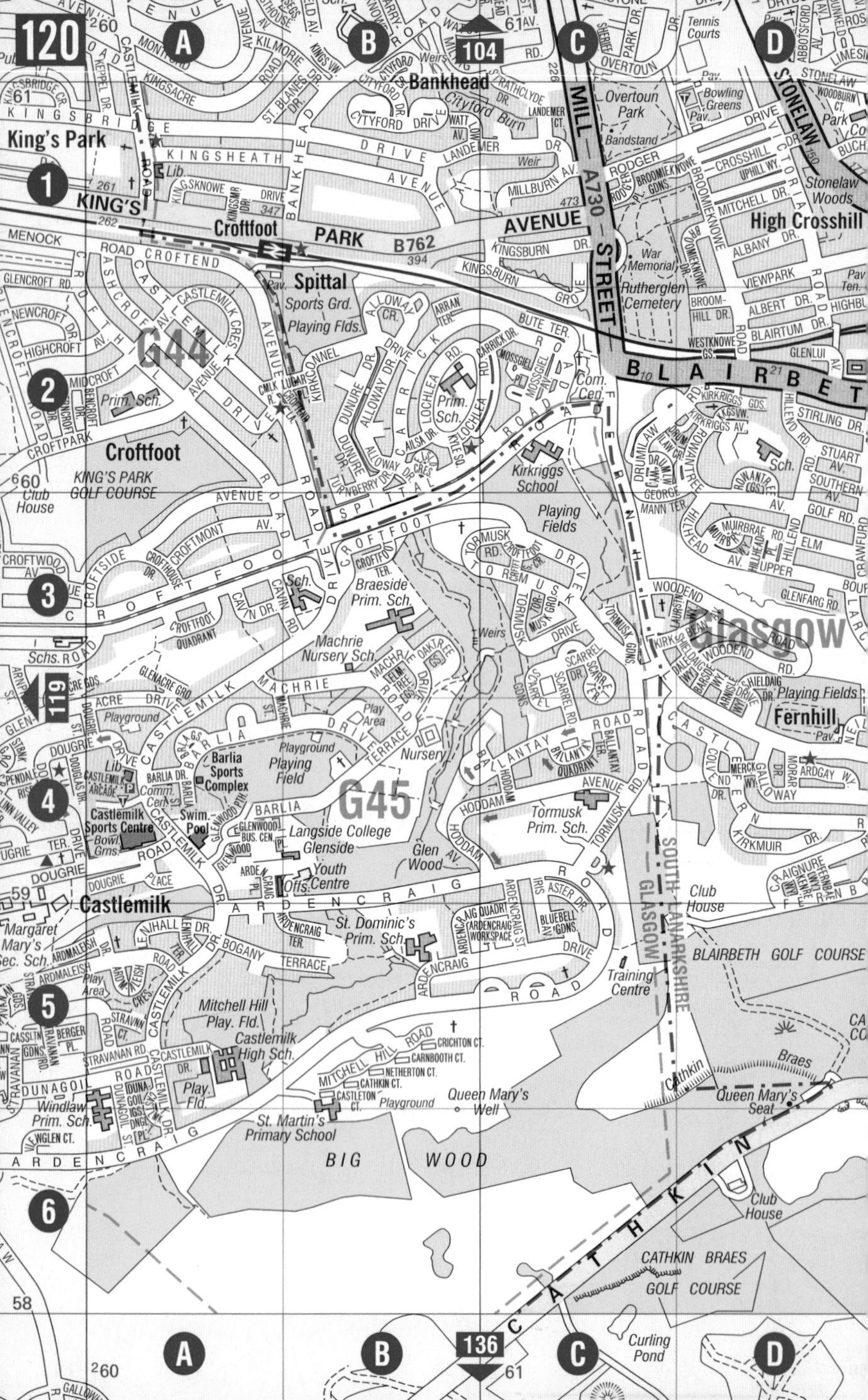
King's Park
Croftfoot
Bankhead
Spittal
Overtoun Park
Rutherglen Cemetery
High Crosshill
Stonelaw Woods
KING'S PARK GOLF COURSE
Castlemilk
Glasgow
Fernhill
BLAIRBETH GOLF COURSE
BIG WOOD
CATHKIN BRAES GOLF COURSE
Queen Mary's Seat
Queen Mary's Well
G44
G45
KING'S PARK AVENUE
B762
MILL STREET
A730
SOUTH LANARKSHIRE
GLASGOW
CASTLEMILK ROAD
CROFTFOOT ROAD
ARDENCRAIG ROAD
CATHKIN ROAD
Barlia Sports Complex
Castlemilk Sports Centre
Langside College Glenside
Castlemilk High Sch.
St. Martin's Primary School
St. Dominic's Prim. Sch.
Kirkriggs School
Braeside Prim. Sch.
Tormusk Prim. Sch.
Windlaw Prim. Sch.
104
119
136

E
F
G
H
Eastfield
105
63
64
Trinity High Sch.
Works
Playing Field
Recreation Grd.
Tennis Ct.
Bowls.
Sports Centre
High Sch.
Calderwood Prim. Sch.
CALDERWOOD AVENUE
GREYSTONE
SOUTHHILL
STONELAW TWRS.
BULLIONSLAW
COLVILLE DR.
HILLARY AV.
OVERLEA AV.
GLENSIDE
CRAIGWELL AV.
Eastfield Burn
DUKE'S ROAD
B762
HAWTHORN WK.
GLENBURN
KENT DR.
BROWNSIDE
Play-grd.
Pav.
Comm.Cen.
Football Grd.
Silverbank
GLASGOW ROAD
A724
Somervell Park
Offs.
Lib.
Cambuslang
MAIN
STREET
Super Sch.
Y.M.C.A.
Ten.Cts.
Pav.
CENTRAL
PROSPECT
CAMBUSLANG
BUCHANAN DR.
WELLSHOT
WEST COATS ROAD
HAMILTON
CADZOW
DOUGLAS DR.
DOUGLAS GA.
West Coats Prim. Sch.
Kirkh
60
Burnside
EAST KILBRIDE ROAD
A749
A730
Burnside
Burnside Sports Ground
STEWARTON
LANGLEA
LANGLEA AVENUE
HUNTERFIELD DR.
Kirkhill Bowling Club
GRENVILLE
DOUGLAS DRIVE
G72
Holmhills Wood
Holmhills Farm
3
Cathkin High School
WHITLAWBURN RD.
Subs.
High Burnside
St. Anthony's Prim. Sch.
Loch Prim. Sch.
Springhall
Com. Cen.
Lib.
LOCHABER
WESTERN ROAD
Shop. Cen.
RONA T.
LORNE TER.
Play-Grd.
STAFFA
GREENLEES
KIRKHILL
4
122
CATHKIN BY-PASS
ST. STEPHEN'S
AVENUE
Cathkin Prim. Sch.
SKYE ROAD
TROSSACHS ROAD
Fernhill Sch.
Sub.
Whitlawburn
Greenlees Nursing Home
Playing Field
EAST
B759
59
Club House
Cathkin House
Cathkin
G73
MENTEITH DR.
INCHMURRIN DRIVE
The Mid Gardens
East Farm
West Greenlees Cottage
GREENLEES ROAD
5
KIRKHILL GOLF COURSE
B759
Cathkin Quarry
Easthills Farm
Motte
GLASGOW ROAD
A749
6
Greenleeshill
Turnlaw Cotts
58
CAIRNMUIR RD.
South Cathkin Farm
137
Kirk Burn
62
63
64
1
2

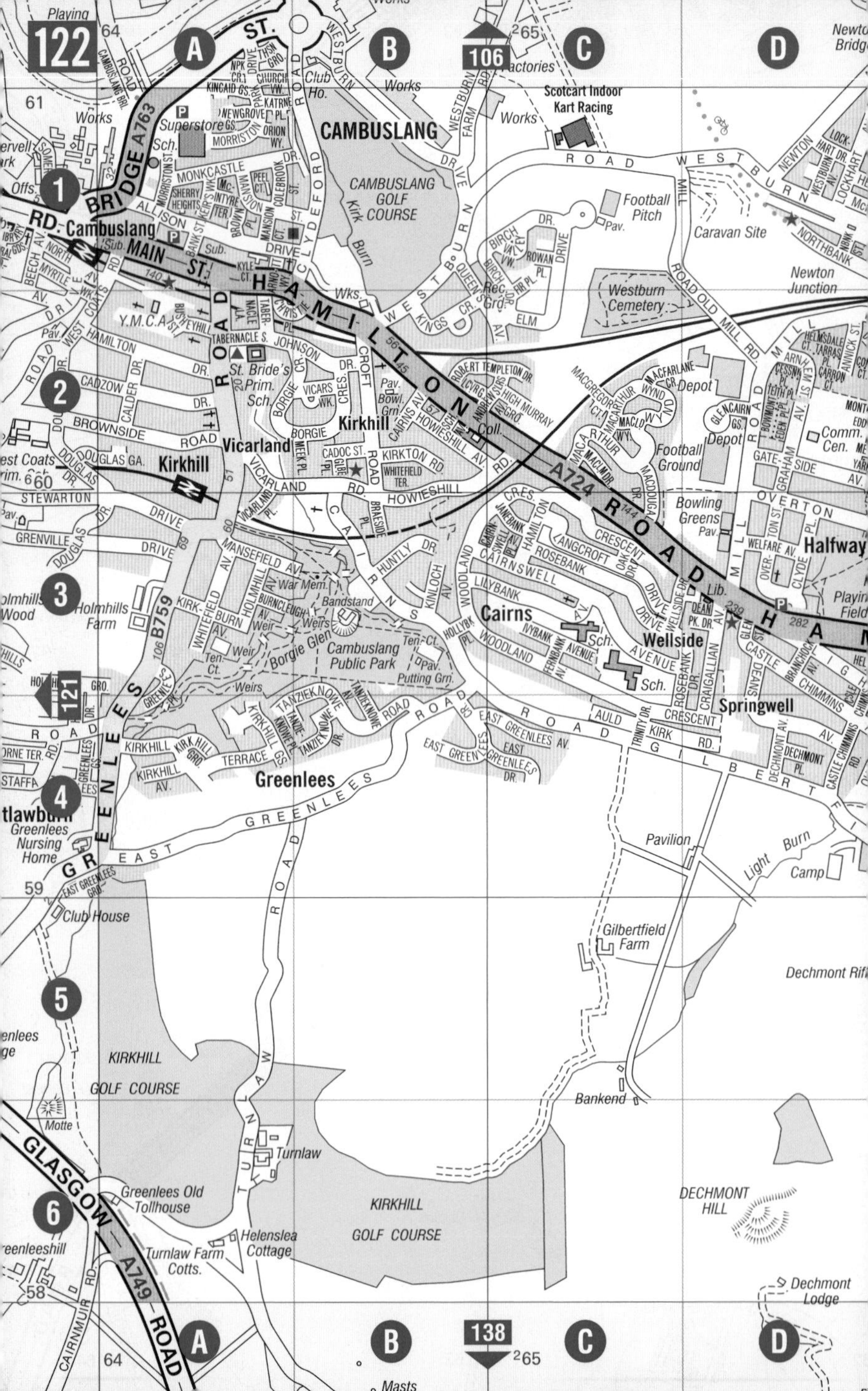
A
B
C
D
106
138
121
1
2
3
4
5
6
CAMBUSLANG
CAMBUSLANG GOLF COURSE
Kirk Burn
Scotcart Indoor Kart Racing
Football Pitch
Caravan Site
Newton Junction
Westburn Cemetery
Cambuslang
Superstore
Y.M.C.A.
St. Bride's Prim. Sch.
Kirkhill
Vicarland
Depot
Comm. Cen.
Football Ground
Bowling Greens
Halfway
Cairns
Wellside
Springwell
Holmhills Farm
War Mem.
Bandstand
Borgie Glen
Cambuslang Public Park
Putting Grn.
Greenlees
Greenlees Nursing Home
Club House
Pavilion
Light Burn
Camp
Gilbertfield Farm
Dechmont Rifle
Bankend
KIRKHILL GOLF COURSE
Motte
Turnlaw
Greenlees Old Tollhouse
Helenslea Cottage
Turnlaw Farm Cotts.
DECHMONT HILL
Dechmont Lodge
Masts
MAIN ST.
HAMILTON ROAD
A724
A763
BRIDGE ST.
B759
GREENLEES ROAD
EAST GREENLEES ROAD
GILBERTFIELD ROAD
TURNLAW ROAD
WESTBURN ROAD
GLASGOW ROAD
A749
CAIRNS ROAD
BROWNSIDE ROAD
WESTBURN FARM RD.
MILL ROAD
OLD MILL RD.

107
139
124
Westburn
Newton
Gowanbank
Football Ground
Playground
St. Charles' Prim. Sch.
Hallside Newhouse Farm
Brackenbrae
Redlees
Bogend
Hamilton Junction
Glasgow
G72
Redlees Bridge
Rotten Calder
East Hallside
Hallside
FLEMINGTON
Lightburn
Back O'Hill
Calderglen Nursing Home
Hallside Farm
Spittal Burn
Hallside Manse
Spittalhill
Cairnsmore
Dalton
Bardykes Bing
Works
Flemington House
Flemington Farm
Flemington Farm Cottage
Spittal Farm
Quarry Wood
LOANEND COTTAGES
Lodge
Priory Bri.
Caldergrove
Bardykes
BLANTYRE
Calder House
A724
GLASGOW RD.
WESTBURN ROAD
CALDER ROAD
HALLSIDE ROAD
VILLAGE ROAD
HAMILTON ROAD
FLEMINGTON ROAD
NEWTON FARM ROAD
STRATHCLYDE BUSINESS CENTRE
FLEMINGTON IND. EST.
DECHMONT COTTAGES

Kylepark
Uddingston
UDDINGSTON
Glasgow
G72
Blantyreferme
Townfoot Farm
Blantyreferme Cottage
Meadowbank
Playing Fields
Football Pitch
Rugby Football Grd.
Cricket Grd.
Tennis Cts.
Bowling Grns.
BOTHWELL CASTLE PARK
Bothwell Castle (rems. of)
BOTHWELL CASTLE PARK GOLF COURSE
Dechmont House
Craigknowe
Coatshill
Community Hall
Prim. Sch.
Priory Plantation
David Livingstone Centre
Livingstone Memorial Park
Wooddean House
Low Blantyre
Bothwellbank
BLANTYRE
Calder House
Wheatlands
Bardykes
Priory Bri.
Redlees
Redlees Bridge
Rotten Calder
RIVER CLYDE
BLANTYRE FARM ROAD B758
GLASGOW ROAD A724
BOTHWELL ROAD
MAIN STREET B7071
CALDER RD.
CASTLE AVENUE
Uddingston Junc.
108
123
140

E
F
G
H
109
141
126
1
2
3
4
5
6
Viewpark
St. Columba's Prim. Sch.
Comm. Centre
OLD EDINBURGH ROAD
NEW EDINBURGH ROAD
B7001
A721
ML4
Depots
Depot
Warehouses
Factory
Sch.
VIEWPARK SHOP. CEN.
Football Ground
Viewpark Gardens
Fallside
BAIRDS AVENUE
WEST AVENUE
EAST AVENUE
CENTRAL AV.
LANGSIDE AV.
FALLSIDE AVENUE
ROSEPARK AV.
ROMAN WY.
SANDERSON AV.
MURRAY RD.
PHILIP
KATRINE AV.
GOIL AVENUE
MELFORD
ALDERSTON WY.
LABURNUM RD.
ELM CRES.
Works
Burn
SPINDLEHOWE RD.
M74 MOTORWAY
M74
Sub.
Prim. Sch.
Muiredge Prim. Sch.
SHERWOOD AV.
GRAY'S RD.
B7071
ROAD
Industrial Estate
ASHLEY DR.
COALBURN RD.
HALPIN CL.
NEW GRO.
THOMSON
CRIGHTON
Bothwell Cemetery
BELZIEHILL RD.
BOTHWELLPARK ROAD
HILL
FLAX RD.
WILKIE
MYERS CR.
Bowling Green
BOTHWELL PARK INDUSTRIAL ESTATE
Mains Park
GOLDIE ROAD
JOHN HENDRY RD.
G71
St. Bride's Prim. Sch.
Play. Field
Monastery
Rec. Grd.
Comm. Cen.
KIRKLANDS HOSPITAL
FARM COURT
MERLEWOOD AV.
ROWANS GS.
WORDSWORTH
McPHERSON DR.
WHITELOANS
THORNTREE WY.
OLIFARD AV.
SHELLEY
KEATS PK.
COLERIDGE AV.
BYRON CT.
AVENUE DRIVE
WAY
NORTH LANARKSHIRE
SOUTH LANARKSHIRE
Bothwell Service Area
BOTHWELLPARK
Bothwell Park Farm
Bothwell Park Wood
BOTHWELLPARK ROAD
Bothwell Park
Kilmallie House
BELLSHILL ROAD
A725
Junction 5
Camping Site
Caravan Park
RAITH INTERCHANGE
A725
BELLSHILL RD.
Motherwell
ML1
Pav.
Play. Flds.
Raith Cott. Visitor's Cen.
Strathclyde Country Park
Pontoons
Mem.
M & D Theme
Strathclyde Loch
RAITH HAUGH
M74 MOTORWAY
Laighland
LAIGHLANDS ROAD
BOTHWELLPARK RD.
GLEBE
GLEBE WYND
GLEBE HOLLOW
BOTHWELL
Works
Manse
Hall
Depot
Elmwood Manor
MAIN ST.
ROAD
HAMILTON ROAD
B7071
Lib.
FAIRYKNOWE GS.
SWEETHOPE GS.
FAIRFIELD PLACE
CROFTBANK CR.
HAMILTON DR.
STRATHCLYDE VW.
CLYDEVIEW
LANGSIDE RD.
ORCHARD AV.
Works
Silverwells
DOUGLAS DR.
ST. ANDREW'S CRESCENT
SILVERWELLS CT.
SILVERWELLS
DUNLOP CRES.
FIFE CRES.
FERRY RD.
BLANTYRE
STATION RD.
CLYDE TER.
MILL ROAD
FERNHILL GRGE
DUNCLUTHA DR.
BLAIRSTON
CLYDEBRAE DR.
RIVER CLYDE
Craighead
BOTHWELL RD.
WOODHEAD GS.
NTH. DEAN PK. AV.
DEAN PARK AV.
S. DEAN PK. AV.
MANSE AV.
WAVERLEY CT.
CASTLE WAY
HUME DR.
KIRKFIELD RD.
HOMESTON AV.
KNOCKBURNIE RD.
ST. BRIDES
MORAVIA AV.
MURRAY RD.
BAILLIE
WOODLANDS AV.
PEEL PL.
70
71
72
660
59
58

A
B
C
D
110
1
2
3
4
5
6
BELLSHILL
BELLSHILL (MOTHERWELL FOOD PARK) INDUSTRIAL ESTATE
RIGHEAD INDUSTRIAL ESTATE
Works
Warehouses
Depots
OLD EDINBURGH RD.
B7001
NEW EDINBURGH RD.
A721
A725
GARTCOSH WALK
A775
CAMPBELL ST.
NORTH ROAD
B7070
MAIN STREET
HATTONRIGG
HATTONRIGG ROAD
Playing Field
Bowling Green
Playing Fields
Bellshill Academy
Comm. Cen.
Y.M.C.A.
Cultural Cen. & Lib.
Mkt.
Bellshill
Sir Matt Busby Sports Complex
Cardinal Newman High Sch.
Recreation Ground
Playground
Bellshill ML4
MOTHERWELL RD.
HAMILTON ROAD
Bowling Greens
Comm. Cen.
Orbiston
Public Park
Sacred Heart Prim. Sch.
Lawmuir Prim. Sch.
Adult Train. Cen.
Viewfield
125
G71
BELLSHILL ROAD
Kilmallie House
Mary Rae's Well
Douglas Park Cottages
Rec. Grd.
Club House
Works
Fairways
Corby Craig
Camping Site
BELLSHILL GOLF COURSE
STRATHCLYDE COUNTRY PARK
M & D's Theme Park
Bothwellhaugh
Bothwellhaugh Plantation
BOTHWELLHAUGH ROAD
Pontoons
Mem.
Strathclyde Loch
South Calder Water
142
Roman Bath Ho. (site of)
Football Pitch
St. Bernadette's Prim. Sch.
WATLING ST.
61
60
59
58
72
73

Motherwell
ML1
Mossend
Wester Holytown
Clydesdale
Milnwood
Forgewood
Thankerton
Riccardjohnston
Eurocentral Rail Terminal
EUROCENTRAL INDUSTRIAL
HOLYTOWN RD.
A775
STREET
B7029 ROAD CLYDESDALE
CLYDESDALE
A721
BELLSHILL ROAD
CALDER RD.
JERVISTON ROAD
JERVISTON STREET
CORONATION ROAD
KIRK LEE ROAD
COBBLETON ROAD
GLEN STREET
BRAIDHURST STREET
NEW HUT ROAD
CARDEAN ROAD
CONDOR GLEN
Works
Depot
King George's Field
Woodend
Mossend W. Junct.
Fullwood Junction
Foundry
Milnwood Junct.
Jerviston Junction
Kirklee Cottage
Biggins
Cemetery
St. Patrick's Prim. Sch.
Bus. Cen.
Holm Forge Bridge
Dam
Rec. Grd.
Playing Field
Keir Hardie Sports Centre
COLVILLE PARK GOLF COURSE
Sports Field
Jerviston House
Club Ho.
Bowls
New Jerviston House
Burial Ground
Braidhurst Sports Barn
Braidhurst High Sch.
BRAIDHURST INDUSTRIAL ESTATE
Com. Cen.
Playgrd.
Gilly's Burn
Playground
Prim. Sch.
111
128
143
E F G H
1 2 3 4 5 6
61 60 59 58
74 75 76

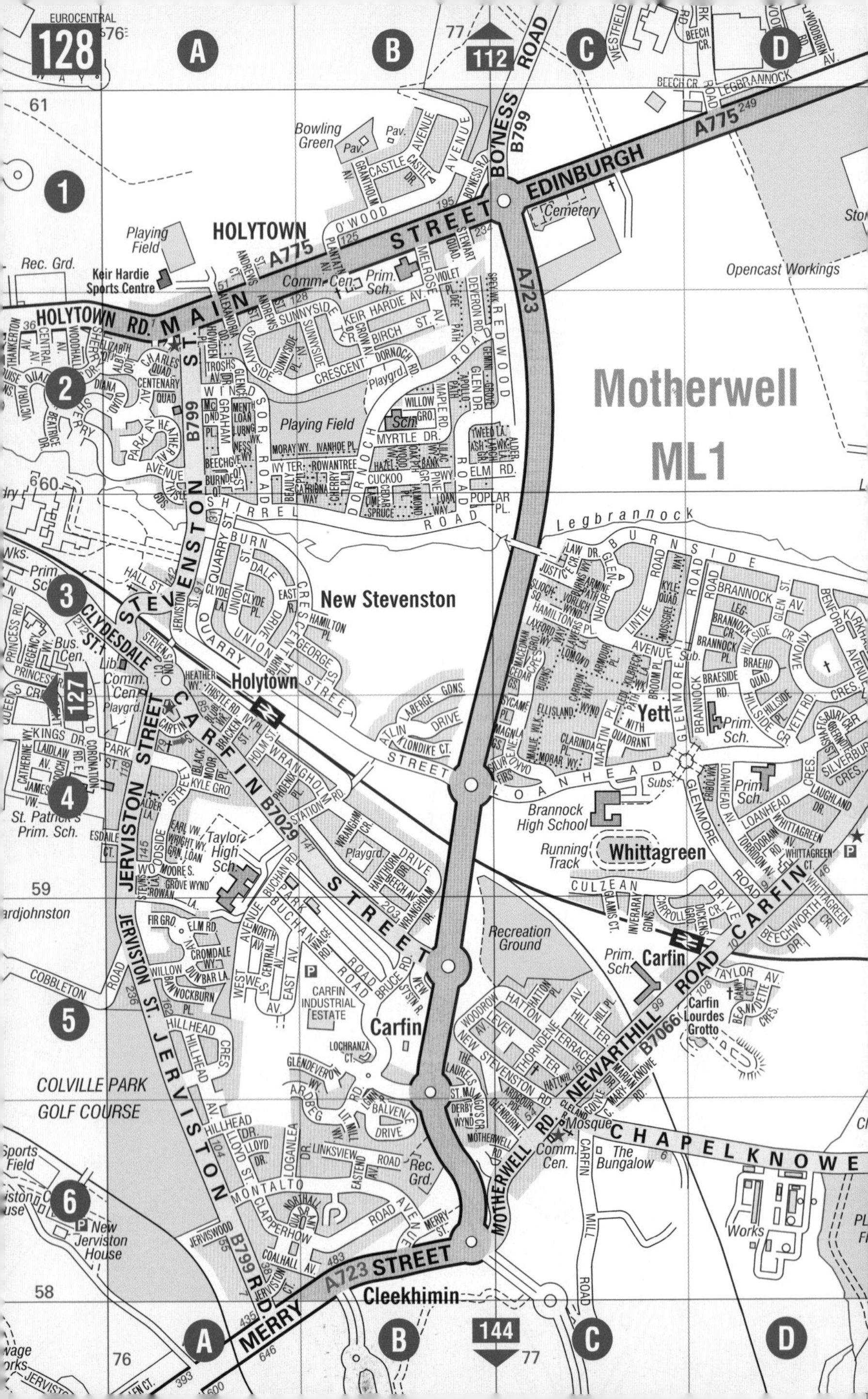
EUROCENTRAL
A
B
C
D
112
1
2
3
4
5
6
HOLYTOWN
Playing Field
Rec. Grd.
Keir Hardie Sports Centre
Bowling Green
HOLYTOWN RD.
MAIN STREET
A775
EDINBURGH
BO'NESS ROAD
B799
A723
Cemetery
Opencast Workings
Motherwell
ML1
Playing Field
New Stevenston
Holytown
Yett
Brannock High School
Running Track
Whittagreen
Recreation Ground
Carfin
CARFIN INDUSTRIAL ESTATE
Carfin Lourdes Grotto
Taylor High Sch.
St. Patrick's Prim. Sch.
COLVILLE PARK GOLF COURSE
New Jerviston House
Cleekhimin
The Bungalow
Mosque
Works
CHAPELKNOWE
NEWARTHILL ROAD
B7066
CARFIN STREET
B7029
JERVISTON STREET
MERRY STREET
MOTHERWELL RD.
LOANHEAD
Legbrannock
CLYDESDALE ST.
127
144

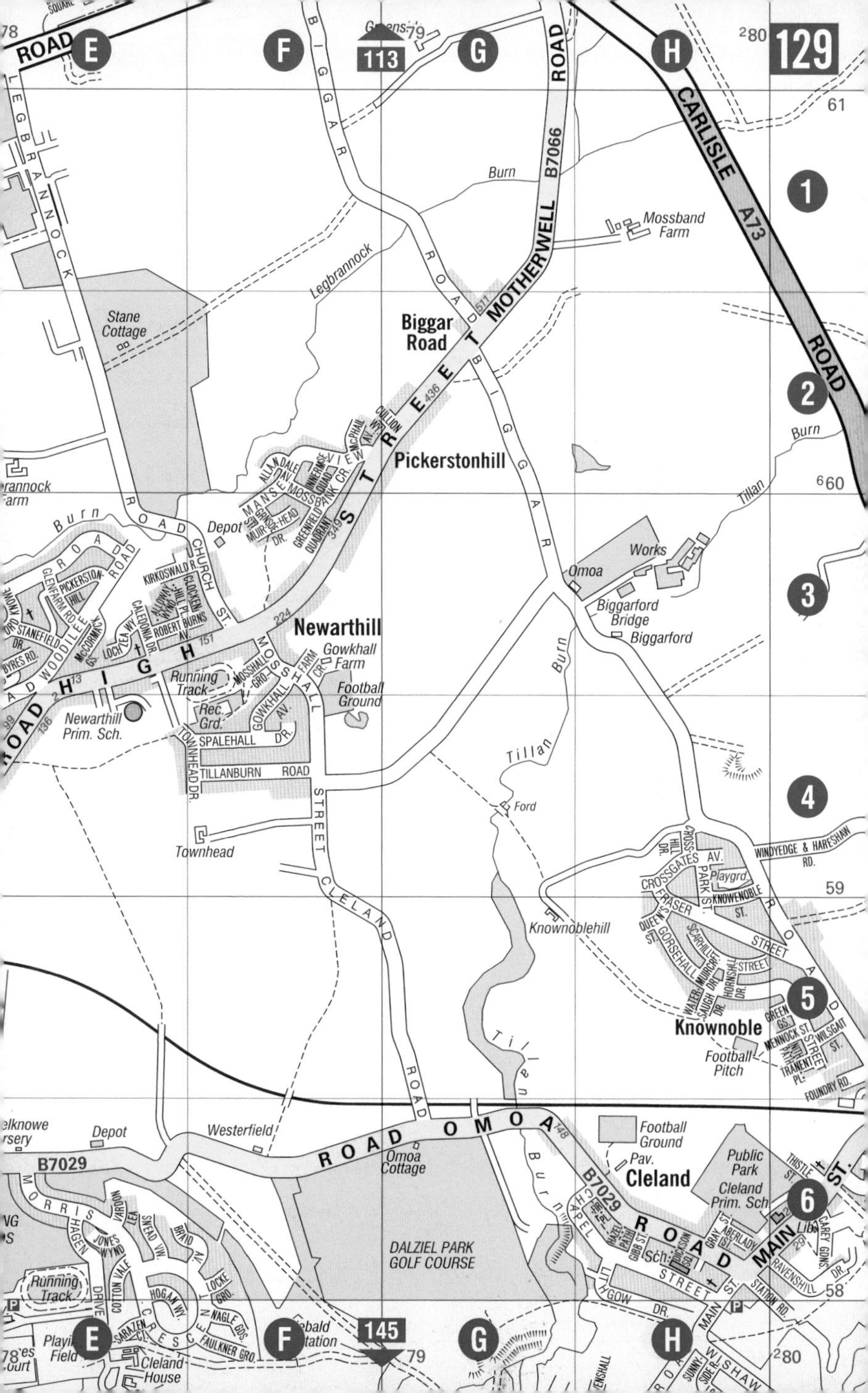
113
145
E
F
G
H
1
2
3
4
5
6
61
60
59
58
280
79
CARLISLE A73 ROAD
MOTHERWELL ROAD B7066
BIGGAR ROAD
Burn
Mossband Farm
Legbrannock
LEGBRANNOCK ROAD
Stane Cottage
Biggar Road
STREET
Pickerstonhill
Newarthill
HIGH
CHURCH ST.
Depot
Works
Omoa
Biggarford Bridge
Biggarford
Tillan Burn
Gowkhall Farm
Football Ground
Running Track
Rec. Grd.
Newarthill Prim. Sch.
SPALEHALL DR.
TILLANBURN ROAD
TOWNHEAD DR.
Townhead
CLELAND ROAD
Ford
Knownoblehill
WINDYEDGE & HARESHAW RD.
CROSSGATES AV.
Playgrd.
KNOWENOBLE ST.
FRASER STREET
Knownoble
Football Pitch
FOUNDRY RD.
Depot
Westerfield
ROAD OMOA
B7029
Omoa Cottage
DALZIEL PARK GOLF COURSE
Football Ground
Pav.
Cleland
Public Park
Cleland Prim. Sch
MAIN ST.
STATION RD.
RAVENSHILL DR.
Running Track
Playing Field
Cleland House
MORRIS
DRIVE
Tibbald Plantation
LITHGOW DR.
CHAPEL STREET
WISHAW

Killoch Water
Killoch Glen
Waterfall
Waterfalls
Dam
Killoch Bri.
Auchentiber
FERENEZE ROAD
Witch Burn
Foreside
Works
STA. BRAE
BROADLIE ROAD
G78
Mill (Dis.)
Res.
Lodge
HOLEHOUSE
CROFTHEAD COTTAGES
Weir
Dam
Holehouse Farm
High Crofthead House
Holehouse
Sidney Cottage
Neilston
Playing Field
Prim. Sch.
STATION RD.
CALL OF NEILSTON? A736
Cowdon Burn
Smiddyhill
Brimstone Bridge
Lodge
Football Grd.
Crumyards Cottage
Crumyards
UPLAWMOOR ROAD
Levern Water
GLEN SHEE AVENUE
KINGSTON AV.
HAREKAW AV.
DOUBLE HEDGES ROAD
KINGSTON ROAD
Kilburn
Water Works
Midgehole Glen
MUIRHEAD ROAD
Neilstonside Cottage
Jaapston Farm
Neilstonside Bridge
Neilstonside Hill
Links of Levern
Craig of Neilston
Craig Cottage
Craig Wood
Water Works
Braeface Farm
Neilstonside
Overflow
Boat House
NEILSTON PAD
CRAIGHALL DAM
Waterside
Aboon the Brae
Levern Water

114
Lochlibo
Arthurlie
Springhill Prim. Sch.
Springhill
A736 ROAD
Sewage Works
Weir
Fairways
Mill (dis.)
Kirkton Burn
Colinbar Glen
Wraes Farm
Newhouse
Newhouse Cottages
Springhill Villa
Mill Dam
Nether Kirkton Farm
Nether Kirkton
Sewage Works
Waterfall
Kirktonfield Bri.
Leisure Centre
Lib.
Playgrd.
Lodge
Factory
Neilston Prim. Sch.
NEILSTON
Netherton
Dam
Spierston Burn
Neilston House
Kirkton
Kirkton Mill
Waterfall
Kirkton Dam
Kirkton Bridge
Loanfoot
Greenhill
Dyke
Glasgow
Glanderston Bridge
Glanderston Mains
GLANDERSTON DAM
Fort
Reservoir (covered)
Dyke Hill
Muirhead
Boat Ho.
WALTON DAM
Burnside
SNYPES DAM
Boat House
Snypes
Overflow
Low Walton
North Walton
G77
Drumler Craigs
North Craigton
South Craigton
SPRINGHILL ROAD
GLANDERSTON ROAD
CRAIGTON ROAD
KIRKTON ROAD
NEILSTON ROAD
SPRINGFIELD ROAD
E F G H
1 2 3 4 5 6
48 49 50
55 56 57 58

116
G78
WAULKMILL GLEN
RESERVOIR
Littleton
Reservoir
Works
Waterfall
Weirs
CORSELET RD.
Patterton
B769
Walden
CAPELRIG
M77
Towerwood
Thornhill
Ho.
RYAT LINN
RESERVOIR
Ryat
Craigend
MORAR PL.
Glasgow
Crookfur
Prim. Sch.
Junction 4
Greenlaw
Weir
Waterfall
CROOKFUR
RD.
LAGGAN
ROAD
Crookfur
Pollock
Lodge
STEWARTON
M77 MOTORWAY
West
Lodge
Rugby
Club
ROAD
Polloktown
BARRHEAD
DODSIDE
FINGALTON RD.
St. Cadoc's
Prim. Sch.
G77
MEADOWBURN AV.
MEADOWBANK
PL.
Crookfur
Play. Flds.
NEWTON
MEARNS
GLEBE RD.
GLEBE LA.
Netherplace
Netherplace
Farm
Works
Res.
Netherplace
House
Netherplace
Cottage
Lodge
Bridge
Lofts
THE AVENUE
(SHOP. CEN.)
Mearns
Cross
EAGLESHAM
HUNTERS
NETHERPLACE
NETHERPLACE
East
Malletsheugh
Mearns
Primary
School
Malletsheugh
MALLETSHEUGH
ROAD
AYR
A77
Lodge
Faside House
AYR ROAD
PAIDMYRE
ROAD
LANGRIG
NEWTON
BELFORD
52
53
56
57
58
55
A
B
C
D
1
2
3
4
5
6

DEACONSBANK GOLF COURSE
117
Rouken Glen Park
Boating Lake
Whitecraigs
G46
WHITECRAIGS GOLF COURSE
CATHCART CASTLE GOLF COURSE
G76
Eastwood High Sch.
Barcapel Holm Farm
Sewage Works
Greenbank House
134
Greenbank Gardens
Broom
Kirkhill
Mearns Castle
Mearns Castle High Sch.
Castle Farm
Barrance
Mearns
Mearns Cemetery
Burnhouse
White Hill
A77
AYR ROAD
WATERFOOT ROAD
MEARNS ROAD
E F G H
1 2 3 4 5 6

118
133
Williamwood
Stamperland
WILLIAMWOOD GOLF COURSE
Clarkston
CATHCART CASTLE GOLF COURSE
Club House
Greenbank House
East Lodge
Greenbank Gardens
Flenders Farm
Ravenswood
Newford
Housecraigs
Millerston
Kirkhill
Barrance
Waterfoot Farm
Hill of Birches
Meikle Dripps
Townhead of Dripps
Waterfoot Bridge
Dripps Mill
Letham
Waterfoot
Earn Bridge
Cartside
Busby Glen Park
EAST RENFREWSHIRE
SOUTH LANARKSHIRE
EASTWOODMAINS ROAD
CLARKSTON ROAD
BUSBY ROAD
EAGLESHAM ROAD
GLASGOW RD.
WATERFOOT ROAD
HIGH FLENDERS ROAD
LOW FLENDER ROAD
FLENDER ROAD
MEARNS ROAD
GREENWOOD ROAD
G46
G45
G76
G77
A726
B767

CARMUNNOCK
Glasgow
BUSBY
NETHERTON BRAES
Carmunnock By-Pass
B766
Busby Road
B759
Carmunnock Road
Kilbride Road
A726
East Kilbride Road
Waterside Road
Windlaw Road
Carmunnock Road
Westerfield Road
Waterbank Road
Braehead Road
Thornton Road
Pedmyre House
Nurseries
Pedmyre Lane
Works
Carnbooth House
Glasgow
East Renfrewshire
Kittoch Water
Kittoch Bridge
Clyth House
Easter Busby
Busby
Castle Hill
The Peel
Lodge
Waterside
Stepends Bridge
Bystone
Busbyside
Bystone Farm Cottage
Playground
Electricity Switching Station
Thorntonhall Burn
Laigh Braehead
Braehead Court
Kingsknowe
Braehead
Craigpark
Thorntonhall
North Hill of Dripps
Birkwood
Picketlaw Farm
Prim. Sch.
Parklea
Cemetery
G74
119
136

CATHKIN BRAES GOLF COURSE
Curling Pond
G45
CATHKIN ROAD
B759
GLASGOW
SOUTH LANARKSHIRE
Muir Farm
CARMUNNOCK
Bellcraig
Highflat Farm
Parklea
Braefoot
Rockcrest
G76
Wester Kittochside
Kittochside
Kittochside Farm
Eastend
Dykehead Farm
KITTOCHSIDE ROAD
CAIRNMUIR
CARMUNNOCK
Kittochside
Waterbank
Philipshill Sewage Works
Stepends Bridge
Cemetery
Museum of Scottish Country Life
Mill Cottage
Philipshill
EAST KILBRIDE ROAD
A726
QUEENSWAY
Kingsknowe
Hotel
Castle Hill
Castleglen
Kittoch Water
Rough Hill
Government Offices
Industrial Estate
College Milton
West Mains
Supermarket
STEWARTFIELD
CASTLEGLEN ROAD
HAWBANK ROAD
GLENBURN
WESTGARTH PLACE
SPRINGBURN PL.
DIXON
JAMES
WATT PLACE
ARROTSHOLE ROAD
MACLEAN
McCALLUM AVENUE
MACDONALD
MACKENZIE GDNS.
REDWOOD
BARBANA ROAD
PEEL PARK IND. EST.
WATERSIDE

Easthills Farm
121
South Cathkin Farm
G73
Kirk Burn
CAIRNMUIR ROAD
Refuse Tip
Works
Nerston
West Nerston Farm
West Nerston
NERSTON ROAD
Rogerton
East Rogerton
West Rogerton
Barley Well
KINGSGATE RETAIL PARK
Ardoch Ho.
Allanvale
138
Glasgow
High Mains
MARKETHILL ROAD
MAINS ROAD
Training Cen.
G74
Lee's Burn
Law Knowe
Laigh Mains
Mains Castle
Heritage Cen
James Hamilton Heritage Park
STEWARTFIELD WAY
PLACE
Training Cen.
Games Cts.
LAW ROUNDABOUT
Stewartfield
Nerston
East Kilbride Burial Grd.
Rec. Grd.
Pav.
MARKETHILL ROUNDABOUT
MAVOR ROUNDABOUT
MAINS
B783
Art Cen.
ROSSLYN
OLD COACH ROAD
CAIRNRYAN ROAD
St. Kenneth's Prim. Sch.
149
Cambus Coll.
Depot
Halfmerke Primary Sch. & West Mains Sch.
Show Park
MAINS

KIRKHILL GOLF COURSE
Helenslea Cottage
Dechmont Lodge
Masts
Cocks Burn
Crookedshields
G73
Nerston Residential School
Letterickhills Cotts.
East Nerston
Scottsmuir Nursery
Letterickhills
Nerston
West Nerston Farm
West Nerston
Glasgow
EAST KILBRIDE GOLF COURSE
KINGSGATE RETAIL PARK
Ardoch Ho.
Allanvale
Club House
Chapelside
GLASGOW ROAD
A749
CROOKEDSHIELDS ROAD
CHAPELSIDE ROAD
STONEYMEADOW ROAD
STEWARTFIELD WY.
HAMILTON ROAD
A725
KINGSWAY
Industrial Estate
Works
THE WHIRLIES ROUNDABOUT
MAINS ROAD
B783
MAVOR ROUNDABOUT
East Kilbride Burial Grd.
Football Pitch
Calderwood
Playing Fields
Miniature Golf Course
Brankumhall
G74
Lib.
Football Pitch
Hunter Prim. School
Greenburn Sch.
Halfmerke Primary Sch. & West Mains Sch.
Show Park
Hunter High
Art Cen.
Mus.
Prim. Sch.
Nurs. Home
Playgrd.
122
137
150

66 E F G H

LOANEND COTTAGES
123
67

Caldergrove
Bardyk
58
1

Calder House
GR
CEDAR
DR
HAZEL
FER

Dechmont Farm
Dechmont Farm Cott.
Spy Wood

Malcolmwood

Barnhill
FRIG
CST.
DUNDONALD
KINTYRE
GLENFRUIN
IONA PATH
Prim. Sch.
2

Mid Lettrick
Mid Lettrick Farm Cott.

BLANTYRE

HUNTHILL
BARDYKES RD.
GLENFIELD RD.
WATSON
STONEFIELD PL.
PINEFIELD
GREENHALL
PARK
BROOM
TA
57

Weir

Playing Field

Playing Fields

Rotten Calder

Crossbow Ho.
Spring

Greenhall Estate
B7012
ROAD MAIN
3

Crossbasket

West Lodge
East Lodge
Greenhall View

Shott Farm
Shott Ho.
CRAIGMUIR GDNS.
Mem.
Kirk
Par

EYMEADOW
Burn
Allers
Allers Cotts.
Dam
Lodge
General's L Bridge

HAMILTON ROAD

ELLISLAND DR
AFTON
SEYMOUR CT.
CRAIGMUIR RD.
ST.
140
WESTFIELD
CAITH
SUT
ST.

R O A D

A725

G72

HILLHOUSE ROAD
HILL
HOUSE ROAD
HILL
4

Allers Sewage Purification Works

WORTH Pav

Craigmuir

Newhouse

SYDES

TECHNOLOGY AV.
TECHNO
WAY
56
5

South Lanarkshire College
CRAIG
NEITH
CT.
CALDERSIDE GRO.
STALMRINGS

Rotten Calder

Basket

HAMILTON DR
BRAE
Red Burr
Park Hous

Park Farm
Blantyre Park Farm
6

Craigneith Castle (Ruins)

DERGLEN COUNTRY PARK

Saw Mill

AUCHENTIBBER

Auchentibber Farm

Auchentibber

Clyde Cottage

Waterfalls
E
Calderside
F
151
67
Springbank
War Mem.
G
PARK
ROAD
6 55
68
H

Calder
CALDERSIDE

A
B
C
D
1
2
3
4
5
6
124
139
152
68
69
58
57
56
55
Low Blantyre
Bothwellbank
Works
Blantyre
Glasgow
Wheatlands
Calder House
Barnhill
St. Joseph's Prim. Sch.
Woodean Home Children's Home
Stonefield
Blantyre Public Park
Playground
Blantyre Sports Cen.
Council Offs.
Ind. Est.
Football Grd.
Craighead Park Football Ground
Depot
Clydeview Shopping Cen.
Lib.
Comm. Cen.
Y.M.C.A.
Gov. Offs.
Blantyre High Sch.
Hall
Playing Field
Prim. Sch.
BLANTYRE
Auchinraith
G72
Blantyre Cemy.
War Mem.
Kirkton Park
Offs.
Springwells
Whistleberry Retail Park
High Blantyre
KIRKTON
Priestfield Cemetery
Hamilton International Technology Park
Priestfield Industrial Estate
Blantyre Industrial Estate
Training Centre
Burnbrae
John Ogilvie High Sch.
Udston Hospital
Bowling Green
Udston Prim. Sch
Hillhouse
Sports Grd.
Jock Stein Sports Barn
St. Ninian's Prim. Sch.
Civic Cen.
Red Burn
Park Farm
Park House
Blantyre Park Farm
Blantyre Park House
Udston Cottage
Townhill Prim. Sch.
Dykehead
GLASGOW ROAD
A724
A725
B758
B7012
BARDYKES ROAD
HUNTHILL RD.
MAIN ST.
DOUGLAS ST.
STONEFIELD ROAD
BROOMPARK ROAD
CALDER ST.
STATION ROAD
MAIN B7012 ST.
HIGH BLANTYRE
HILLHOUSE ROAD
HUDSTON WAY
EAST KILBRIDE ROAD

E
F
G
H
125
153
142
1
2
3
4
5
6
Strathclyde Country Park
Raith Cott. Visitor's Cen.
RAITH HAUGH
M74 MOTORWAY
M74
RIVER CLYDE
G71
Craighead Retreat Ho.
Craighead
Manresa
Works
Craighead Sch.
STATION RD.
BELLSHILL RD.
A725 RD.
BOTHWELL BRIDGE
A725
A724
WHISTLEBERRY ROAD
Auchinraith Gardens
Park Burn
Gow's Linn
Training Cen.
Fire Brigade H.Q.
Black Muir Plantation
Sewage Works
Bothwell Bridge Animal Welfare Centre (Scottish SPCA)
Barmichael Plantation
Duchess Bridge
Stables
STRATHCLYDE COUNTRY PARK
Grandstand
HAMILTON PARK RACE COURSE
BOTHWELL ROAD
B7071
WHISTLEBERRY INDUSTRIAL PARK
St. Paul's Prim. Sch.
Whitehill
Powerleague Soccer Centre
Football Pitches
Rec. Grd.
Public Park
War Mem.
Bandstand
STRATHCLYDE PARK GOLF COURSE
PARK BURN INDUSTRIAL ESTATE
Sports Barn
Lib.
Burnbank
Beckford Prim. Sch.
Hamilton ML3
MAY GARDENS
Depots
Hamilton College
Playing Field
Tennis Cts.
HAMILTON BUS. PK.
Bell Coll.
T.A. Cen.
Council Offs.
Bell College
BECKFORD ST. BUS. CEN.
HAMILTON RETAIL PARK
Hamilton West
BURNBANK ROAD
FULLWOOD IND. EST.
PEACOCK CROSS IND. EST.
CLYDESDALE STREET
ALMADA STREET
A72
ALMADA GROVE
MUIR ST.
Holy Cross High Sch.
Udston
HILLHOUSE PK. INDUSTRIAL EST.
Well Hall
Wellhall Bri.
WELLHALL RD.
B755
Gov. Off.
UNION ST.
A724
St. Mary's Prim. Sch.
Playgrd.
AUCHINGRAMONT RD.
Offices
Council Offices
ALLANSHAW IND. EST.
Hamilton Grammar Sch.
West Cemetery
Superstore
CHANTINGHALL RD.
HAMILTON
St. John's Prim. Sch.
Rec. Grd.
Bent Cemetery
Chantinghall
Chantinghall Bridge
Hamilton Central
Bus Sta.
Gasholder Sta.
Factory
Bent Playing Field
70
71
72
55
56
57
58

Strathclyde Country Park
Strathclyde Loch
M74 Motorway
Hamilton Service Area
Motel
Strathclyde Park Golf Course
Roman Bath Ho. (site of)
Roman Fort (remains of)
Picnic Area
South Calder Water
North Motherwell
Playing Fields
Football Pitch
St. Bernadette's Prim. Sch.
Logans Prim. Sch.
Piper Alpha Memorial
Water Sports Centre
Weir
Braedale
Clyde Park
North Lanarkshire
South Lanarkshire
North Haugh
Hamilton Mausoleum
Golf Range
Hamilton Palace Sports Ground
Esporta Health & Fitness Club
Palace Pavilion
Ice Rink
Low Parks Mus.
HAMILTON
ML3
Palace Gardens Retail Park
Hamilton Interchange
Junction 6
Motherwell Road
Clydebridge Lodge
Ross House
South Haugh
Avon Water
Holy Cross High Sch.
St. Mary's Prim. Sch.
Council Offices
Bus Sta.
Hamilton Central
Carlisle Road
Muir St.
Cadzow Street
Union St.
Duke St.
Keith St.
Quarry St.
Gasholder Sta.
Coyan Burn
Bowling Greens
126
141
154

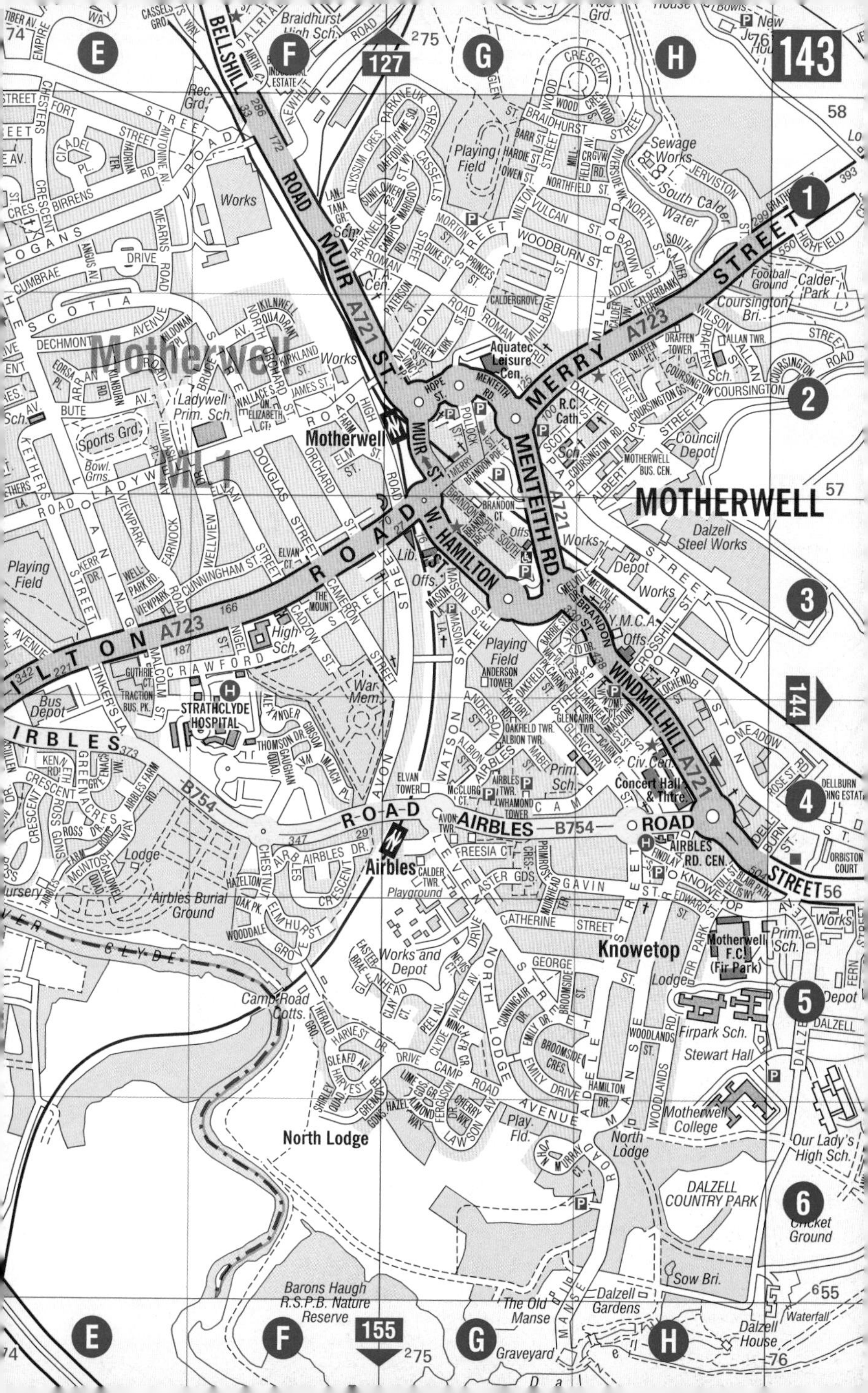
127
144
155
Motherwell
MOTHERWELL
ML1
Knowetop
North Lodge
Strathclyde Hospital
Dalzell Country Park
Barons Haugh R.S.P.B. Nature Reserve
Motherwell College
Motherwell F.C. (Fir Park)
Dalzell Steel Works
River Clyde

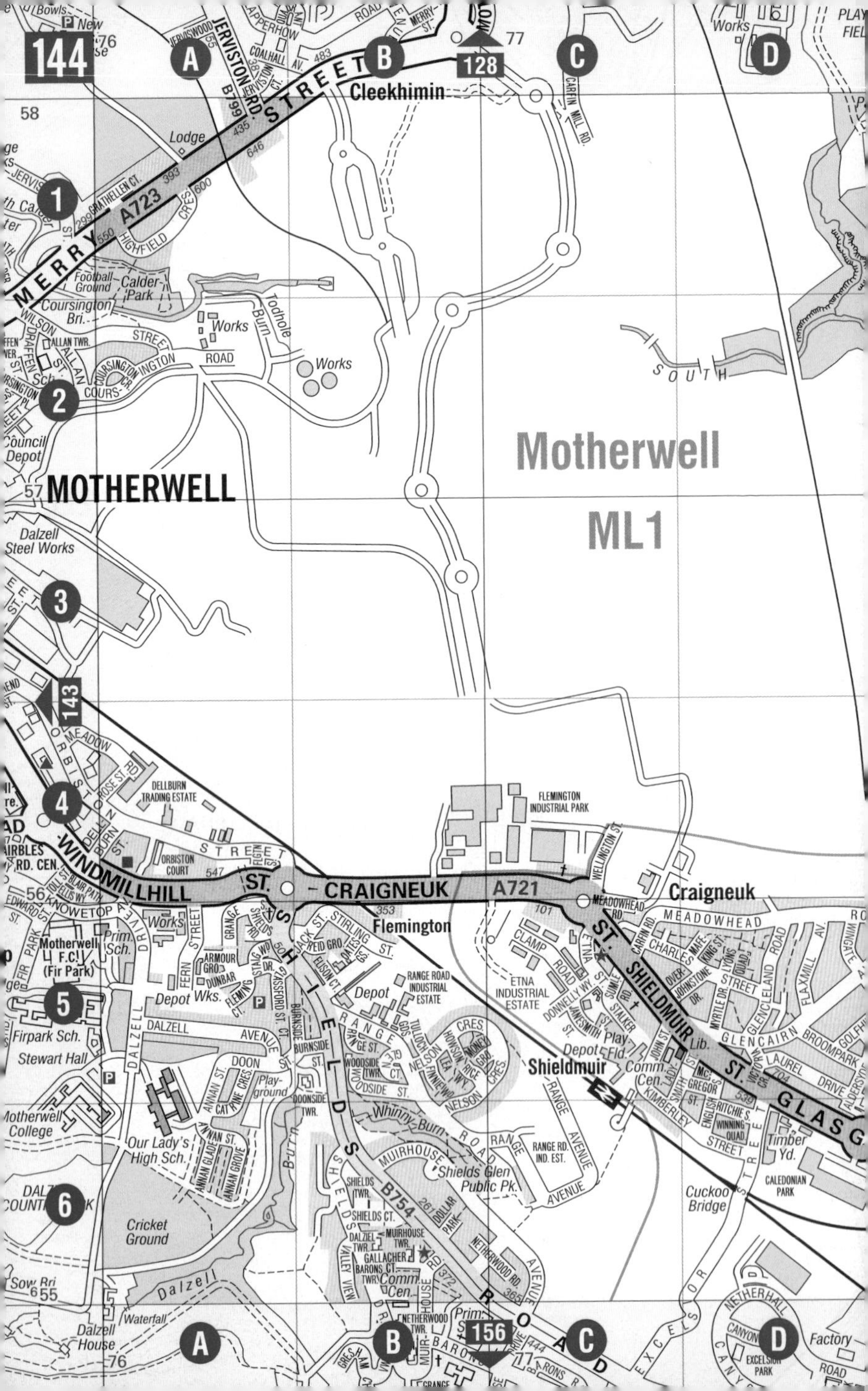

MOTHERWELL
Motherwell
ML1
Cleekhimin
Craigneuk
Flemington
Shieldmuir
MERRY STREET
A723
CRAIGNEUK ST.
A721
WINDMILLHILL ST.
SHIELDMUIR ST.
SHIELDS ROAD
B754
B799
JERVISTON RD.
Lodge
Football Ground
Calder Park
Coursington Bri.
Works
Todhole Burn
Council Depot
Dalzell Steel Works
DELLBURN TRADING ESTATE
ORBISTON COURT
FLEMINGTON INDUSTRIAL PARK
ETNA INDUSTRIAL ESTATE
RANGE ROAD INDUSTRIAL ESTATE
Depot
Motherwell F.C. (Fir Park)
Firpark Sch.
Stewart Hall
Motherwell College
Our Lady's High Sch.
Cricket Ground
Shields Glen Public Pk.
Cuckoo Bridge
Timber Yd.
CALEDONIAN PARK
Waterfall
Dalzell House
Sow Bri
Factory
EXCELSIOR PARK
128
143
156

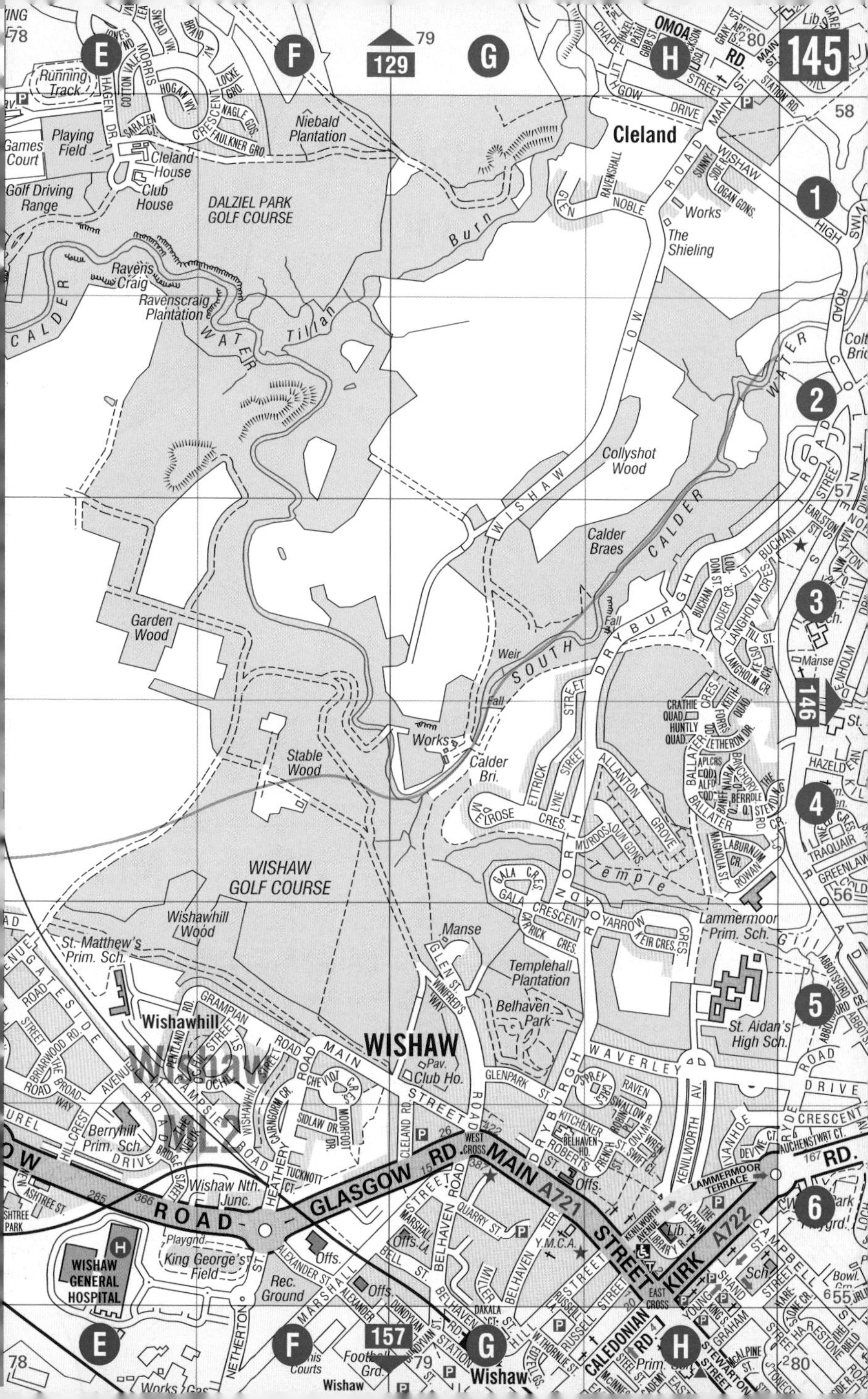

129
Cleland
Niebald Plantation
Playing Field
Games Court
Running Track
Cleland House
Club House
Golf Driving Range
DALZIEL PARK GOLF COURSE
Ravens Craig
Ravenscraig Plantation
CALDER WATER
Tillan Burn
The Shieling
Works
Collyshot Wood
Calder Braes
SOUTH CALDER WATER
WISHAW LOW ROAD
Garden Wood
Stable Wood
Calder Bri.
WISHAW GOLF COURSE
Wishawhill Wood
St. Matthew's Prim. Sch.
Wishawhill
Templehall Plantation
Belhaven Park
WISHAW
Lammermoor Prim. Sch.
St. Aidan's High Sch.
Berryhill Prim. Sch.
Wishaw Nth. Junc.
WISHAW GENERAL HOSPITAL
King George's Field
Rec. Ground
GLASGOW RD.
MAIN STREET A721
KIRK RD. A722
CALEDONIAN RD.
146
157
Wishaw

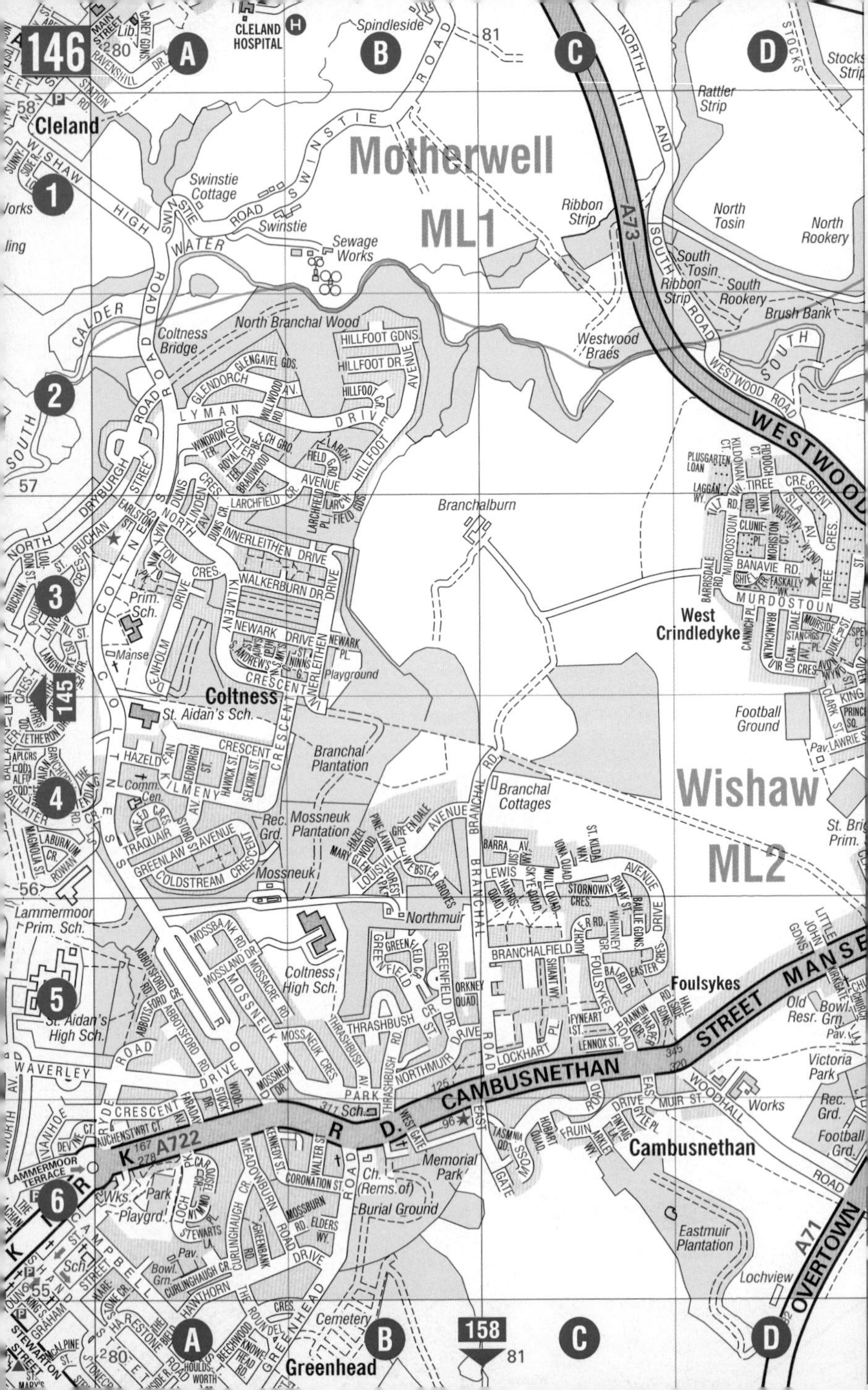
Cleland
CLELAND HOSPITAL
Spindleside
Motherwell
ML1
Swinstie Cottage
Swinstie
Sewage Works
Ribbon Strip
Rattler Strip
North Tosin
North Rookery
South Tosin
South Rookery
Brush Bank
Westwood Braes
North Branchal Wood
Coltness Bridge
Branchalburn
West Crindledyke
Coltness
St. Aidan's Sch.
Branchal Plantation
Mossneuk Plantation
Branchal Cottages
Wishaw
ML2
Football Ground
Mossneuk
Northmuir
Coltness High Sch.
Lammermoor Prim. Sch.
St. Aidan's High Sch.
Foulsykes
Cambusnethan
Memorial Park
Burial Ground
Eastmuir Plantation
Lochview
Victoria Park
Cemetery
Greenhead
CAMBUSNETHAN
A722
A73
A71
OVERTOWN
WESTWOOD
145
158

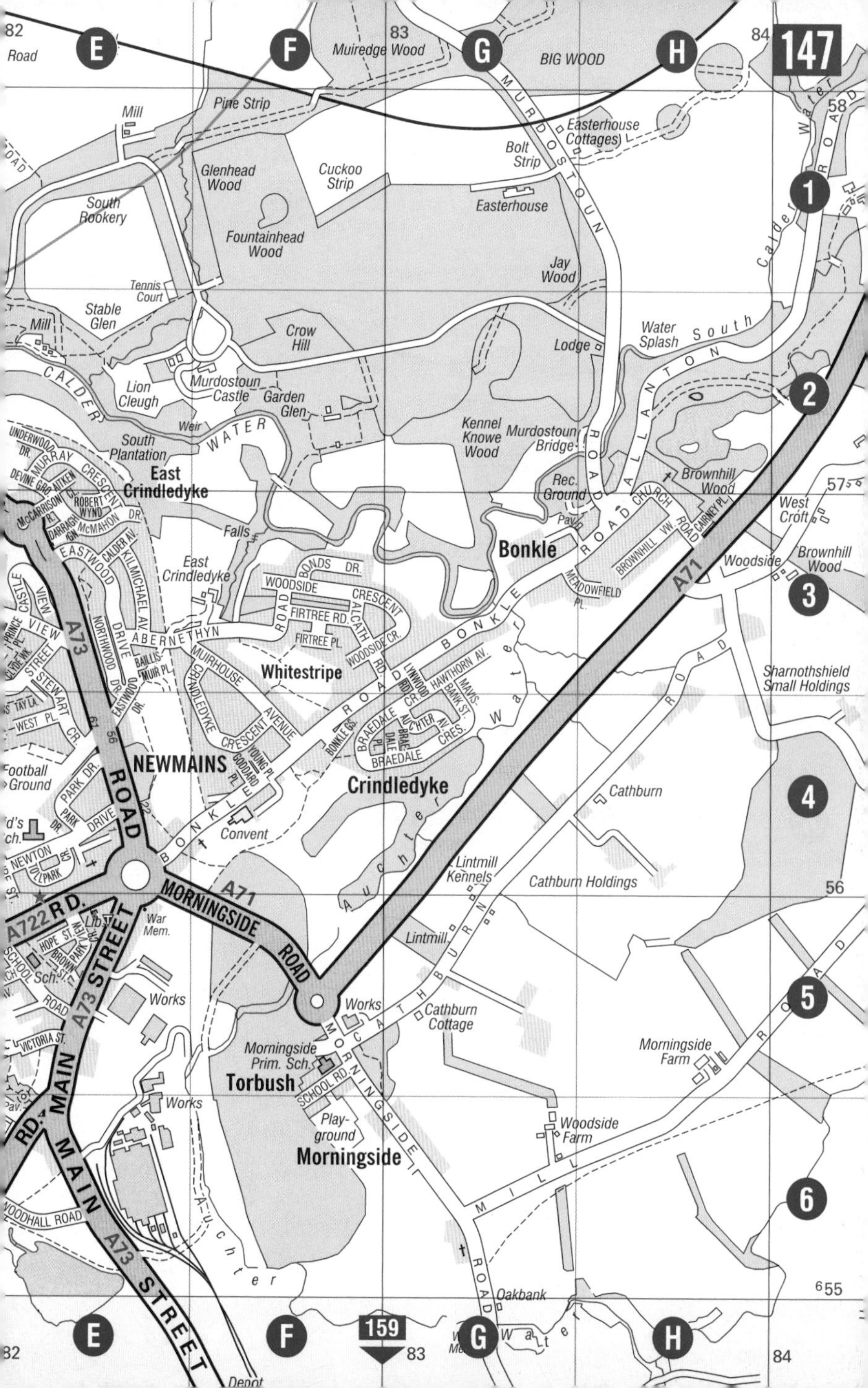
Muiredge Wood
BIG WOOD
Pine Strip
Mill
Easterhouse Cottages
Bolt Strip
Glenhead Wood
Cuckoo Strip
South Rookery
Easterhouse
Fountainhead Wood
Jay Wood
Tennis Court
Stable Glen
Crow Hill
Water Splash
Lodge
Lion Cleugh
Murdostoun Castle
Garden Glen
Weir
South Plantation
Kennel Knowe Wood
Murdostoun Bridge
Rec. Ground
Brownhill Wood
East Crindledyke
Falls
Bonkle
West Croft
Woodside
Brownhill Wood
Whitestripe
Sharnothshield Small Holdings
NEWMAINS
Crindledyke
Football Ground
Convent
Cathburn
Lintmill Kennels
Cathburn Holdings
War Mem.
Lintmill
Works
Cathburn Cottage
Morningside Prim. Sch.
Morningside Farm
Torbush
Play-ground
Woodside Farm
Morningside
Oakbank
MURDOSTOUN ROAD
CALDER WATER
South CALDER WATER
ALLANTON ROAD
CHURCH ROAD
BONKLE ROAD
MORNINGSIDE ROAD
MAIN STREET
MAIN ROAD
WOODHALL ROAD
CATHBURN ROAD
MORNINGSIDE
MILL ROAD
Auchter Water
A71
A73
A722 RD.
159
Depot

136
A
B
C
D
1
2
3
4
5
6
260
61
655
54
53
52
Craigpark
Industrial Estate
Peel Park Ind. Est.
GLASGOW SOUTHERN ORBITAL (PROPOSED)
Peel Park
College Milton
West Mains
Hawbank Roundabout
Travelling People's Site
QUEENSWAY
A726
B761
B764
Hairmyres
Hairmyres Roundabout
Abercrombie House
Hairmyres Hospital
Millbrae
Works
The Tennant Complex
EAGLESHAM ROAD
WESTWOOD ROAD
Glasgow
G75
Westwood
Rec. Ground
Playground
Duncanrig Sec. Sc.
Duncanrig Sports Cen.
Canberra Prim. Sch.
Comm. Cen.
Playing Field
Water Tower
Hairmyres
Mossneuk
Gardenhall
Newlandsmuir
Greenhills
Castlefield Prim. Sch.
Crosshouse Prim. Sch.
St. Vincent's Primary School
Ballerup High School
Newlands Farm
Newlands Dairy
Dunrobin
Dorniebank
Trunlehill
Netherton Lodge
JACKTON RD.
NEWLANDS
GREENHILLS ROAD
LICKPRIVICK RD.
CROSSHOUSE ROAD
NEWLANDSMUIR ROAD
MOSSNEUK AVENUE
GREENHILL ROAD

149
137
150
E
F
G
H
1
2
3
4
5
6
62
63
64
55
54
53
52
CAIRNRYAN
EAST MAINS RD.
B783
OLD COACH RD.
St. Kenneth's Prim.Sch.
Halfmerke Primary & West Mains Sch.
The Show Park
Football Grd
Village Theatre
East Mains
Cambuslang Coll.
Depot
M A I N S
B761
Kirktonholme Prim. Sch.
Kirktonholme Park
Comm. Cen.
East Kilbride
DOUGLASDALE
HOUSTON TER.
ABERNETHY PK.
KIRKTONHOLME CRES.
M A X W E L L
KIRKTON
LINDSAY
WHITEMOSS AV.
A725
R O A D
DRYBURGH
G74
BALMORAL PL.
Playgrd.
HARRINGTON
CUNNINGHAME ROAD
BROUSTER
TERRACE
Putting Green
Town Centre
Civic Centre
Gov. Off.
Atholl Ho.
PLATTHORN DR.
St. Bride's High Sch.
E. Milton Prim. Sch.
Q U E E N S W A Y
A726
Dollan Aqua Cen.
Ten. Ct.
RIGHEAD ROUNDABOUT
THE CENTRE ROUNDABOUT
THE PLAZA (SHOP. CEN.)
OLYMPIA (SHOP. CEN.)
Ice Rink
Lib.
Cin.
Bus Sta.
CORNWALL
ROTHESAY
HESAY
STREET
EAST KILBRIDE
Kittoch Bridge
AVONDALE
CHURCHILL
ROXBURGH
Subs.
MONTREAL PK.
QUEBEC DRIVE
SHERBROOKE
BANFF PL.
LE FROY LA.
FROY GARDENS
FRAZER RIVER TWR.
ALBERTA
PENFOLD
HOSP.
EDMONTON TER.
CALGARY
BOWDEN
MACRIMMON PL.
FORD
MID
HEADHOUSE
Headhouse Greenway
DEN-HOLM
THE MURRAY ROUNDABOUT
BIRNIEHILL ROUNDABOUT
Gov. Offs.
Birniehill
BRUNEL WY.
SCOTTISH ENTERPRISE TECHNOLOGY PARK
NASMYTH AV.
MURRAY
MUNGO PK.
Prim. Sch.
KIMBERLEY
DARWIN RD.
MELBOURNE
SYDNEY DR.
BRISBANE T.
HOBART RD.
CANBERRA AVENUE
BAIRD
BAIRD HILL
QUARRY PK.
Hall
MURDOCH
NAPIER
RUTHERFORD SQ.
SYMINGTON SQ.
BALFOUR
Sch.
ARMSTRONG GR.
PATERSON TER.
SIMPSON
GLEN GR.
STEVENSON
Murray Prim. Sch.
The Murray
LAIRHILLS
KELVIN ROAD
CHALMERS DRIVE
STRATHCONA PL.
CHATHAM
RUSSELL PL.
BLENHEIM AV.
HILL PLACE
REITH DRIVE
OWEN AVENUE
GALT
DALE AVENUE
LIDDELL GRO.
Rec. Grd.
St. Louise's Prim. Sch.
Ten. Cts.
Heathery Knowe Prim. Sch.
Playground
WHITEHILLS PL.
WHITEHILLS DR.
WHITEHILLS TER.
SOMERVILLE
SLESSOR DR.
ELPHINSTONE
BRUCE T.
CRESCENT
WARDLAW CR.
KELVIN PL.
LONG DR.
CANTERBURY
ANNIVERSARY AV.
NETHERTON
South Park Prim. Sch.
Robert Owen Centre
GREENHILLS WY.
BRYCE PL.
Playgrd.
LABURNUM AV.
ASH
AVENUE
Hostel
Sub.
STROUD ROAD
St. Andrew's Sports Cen.
St. Andrew's High Sch.
SCHOLAR'S GATE
COPENHAGAN
VIKING TER.
ODENSE CT.
SKOVLUNDE
Playing Fields
Whitehills
Pav.
Industrial Estate
Kelvin
CARRON
CARRON PL.
PLACE
COLVILLES
SYCAMORE
CRESCENT
JUNIPER AVENUE
CHESTNUT
Greenhills Sports Cen.
Greenhills Prim. Sch.
CEDAR
CEDAR COURT
CYPRESS
LAUREL
LAVENDER DR.
BROOM
ALDER
MULBERRY DR.
MULBERRY WAY
POPLAR GS.
Kittoch Water
QUARRYHILL
GRANTOFTEN PATH
KRONBORG
ELSINORE
HIGH
MILLRIG
DECHMONT
AUCHENGILLOCH
AVONHEAD
PARKFIELD
ARDOCHRIG
ARABURN DR.
W H I T E H I L L S
HAWKWOOD
DRUMDUFF
LOMOND
LOUDON
BROUGHTON
MIDDLEFIELD
CRAIGLEE
FORTIETH AV.
CADENCE GR.
ALBION WAY
ROAD
GREENHILLS ROAD
LANGLANDS
LANGLANDS AV.
KELVIN SOUTH BUSINESS PARK
SAYFIELD
AULDHOUSE RD.
SHIELDS RD.

A
B
C
D
1
2
3
4
5
6
138
149
Halfmerke Primary Sch. & West Mains Sch.
The Show Park
East Mains
Villa Theatre
Greenburn Sch.
Prim. Sch.
Hunter Prim. School
Football Pitch
Lib.
Sch.
Play. Fld.
Hunter High School
John Wright Sports Cen.
Whitemoss Rec. Area
Bowl. Grns.
G74
St. Leonards
CLAREMONT HO.
ST. LEONARDS SQ.
WHITEMOSS ROUNDABOUT
WHITEMOSS
B761 AV.
QUEENSWAY
KINGSWAY
A725
A726
STRATHAVEN
T.A. Cen.
St. Bride's High Sch.
Atholl Ho.
Weir
Subs.
Sub.
EAST KILBRIDE
Kittoch Bridge
BIRNIEHILL ROUNDABOUT
Gov. Offs.
Birniehill
Blacklaw Prim. Sch.
Play. Area
Recreation Ground
Playing Fields
Calderglen Country Park
Calder Glen
Grey M
Waterfalls
Black Linn
Trough Linn
St. Hilary's R.C. Prim. Sch.
Claremont High & Sanderson High Schs.
CLYDE TOWER
CALDER TOWER
Prim. Sch.
SCOTTISH ENTERPRISE TECHNOLOGY PARK
Rec. Grd.
Glasgow
Weir
Torrance Linn
Edge
G75
Pro Lane Bowl
Lodge
Playing Field
East Kilbride Sports Centre
Playing Fields
Children's Zoo & Aviary
Club Ho.
Weir
Calderglen Country Park Visitors Centre
Torrance House
The Tor
Industrial Estate
Kelvin
Parkhead
Newfarm
TORRANCE PARK GOLF COURSE
TORRANCE ROUNDABOUT
Cruthe Far
KELVIN SOUTH BUSINESS PARK
KELVIN PARK SOUTH
GREENHILLS ROAD
STROUD
COLVILLES ROAD
YOUNG PLACE
KELVIN DRIVE
NEWHOUSE MILL ROAD
CALDERGLEN ROAD
ST. LEONARDS DRIVE
CALDERWOOD RD.
BLACKLAW
COMMON
64
55
54
53
52
65
265

Auchentibber
AUCHENTIBBER
Clyde Cottage
139
Springbank
War Mem.
Parkneuk
Calderside
Calderside
Camp Knowe
Broomhouse
Greenblairs
Waterfalls
G72
Newfield
Braehead Cottage
Reservoir (covered)
PARKNEUK ROAD
Stewartfield
Earnock
Burn
NEWHOUSEMILL ROAD
MUTTONHOLE ROAD
Laigh Muirhouses
152
High
Lodgehill
Hamilton
ML3
BLANTYRE MUIR
Rotten Burn
East Drumloch
E
F
G
H
1
2
3
4
5
6
66
67
68
55
54
53
52

A
B
C
D
68
69
140
151
655
54
53
52
1
2
3
4
5
6
Udston Cottage
Dykehead
Dykehead House
Reservoir
(covered)
Newfield
NEWHOUSEMILL ROAD
EARNOCK ROAD
WELLHALL ROAD
LUSS BRAE
TOWNHILL RD.
Earnock
Townhill Prim. Sch.
Earnock Burn
Weir
SKYE
TIREE
GRANGE
St. Mark's Prim. Sch.
Hamilton
ML3
Muirmains
Kennedies
Wellbrae Cottage
MUTTON HOLE
High Muirhouses
HIGHSTONEHALL ROAD
Dykend
Electricity Sub Station
Mast
Sherriff Faulds
Beechfield House
Muirhall
Devonhill
Earnockmuir
Earnockmuir Cottage
East Drumloch
Cadzow Burn
Haspielaw

HAMILTON
Chantinghall
Laighstonehall
Little Earnock
Fairhill
Low Waters
Eddlewood
Meikle Earnock
Bent Cemetery
Laigh Bent Playing Field
Chantinghall Bridge
Earnock High Sch.
Factory
Works
Earnock Burn
Cadzow Burn
Neilsland Park
Woodhead Green
Woodhead Prim. Sch.
St. Peter's Prim. Sch.
Football Grd.
Playing Field
Bowling Green
Cadzow Industrial Estate
Eddlewood Sports Barn
Games Crt.
Play. Field
Eddlewood Fm.
Gasholder Sta.
Brackenhill
Whitecraigs
Broomknowe
Cornhills
Oaklea
Annsfield
Simpsonland
Simpsonland Glen
Hillcrest
Depot
Blue Waters Cottage
Blackbog
Blackbog Glen
Waterfall
MILL ROAD
NEILSLAND ROAD
WOODFOOT ROAD
LAIGHSTONEHALL ROAD
EARNOCK ROAD
MEIKLE EARNOCK ROAD
STRATHAVEN ROAD
LOW WATERS ROAD
CARSCALLAN ROAD
A723
B755
141
154

A
B
C
D
1
2
3
4
5
6
72
73
55
54
53
52
142
153
Central
CARLISLE A72 RD.
CARLISLE
AVON BRIDGE
PORTLAND PL.
LOW WATERS A723 RD.
Gasholder Sta.
Prim. Sch.
Claudsburn
Covan Burn
Haughhead
Avon Mill
Avon Mill Ho.
Old Avon Bridge
Weir
Nursery
Rec. Grd.
Avon Mill Cottage
Ferniegair
Silvertonhill
Barncluith Lodge
Monument
HAMILTON
Meikle Burn
Laverock Hill
Cattle Grid
CHATELHERAULT COUNTRY PARK
AVENUE
Chatelherault Visitor Centre
Cadzow Castle (remains of)
Chatelherault Prim. Sch.
Low Waters
CADZOW INDUSTRIAL ESTATE
Cave
Waterfall
Eddlewood Glen
Cadzow House
Hamilton ML3
Old Oaks
High Parks Farm
AVON WATER
GOLF
Eddlewood
Games Crt.
Eddlewood Sports Barn
Pav.
Meikle Glen
HAMILTON HIGH PARKS
Simpsonland
Simpsonland Glen
Thorney Glen
RAMSAY'S PLANTATION
Divoty Wood
CARSCALLAN ROAD
Blue Waters Cottage
Blackbog
Carscallan
Annax Lodge
Clover Cottage

E
F
G
H
143
275
76
Cricket Ground
Bow Bri.
MANSE ROAD
The Old Manse
Dalzell Gardens
Dalzell House
Burn
Barons Haugh R.S.P.B. Nature Reserve
M74
Graveyard
Dalzell
Motherwell
ML1
RIVER
CLYDE
NORTH LANARKSHIRE
SOUTH LANARKSHIRE
55
1
2
3
4
5
6
M74 MOTORWAY
Depot
Hall
PARK DR.
FAIRHOLM AV.
ROSS TER.
AVENUE
CASTLE HILL CR.
CLYDE
Saw Mill
Allanton
Sewage Works
Allanton Ter.
54
A72
Club House
ARTON
COURSE
156
Low Merryton
BELVIDERE PLANTATION
ROAD
Merryton Farm Cotts.
LANARK RD. END
LANARK
A72
ROAD
53
CARLISLE
Garden Centre
Larkhall
ML9
MERRYTON ROAD
Go-Kart Track
Dykehead Cottage
B7078
High Merryton
CRESCENT
ETIVE
MORR CT.
LINNHE CT.
SHIEL DR.
FYNE
Lodge
SIDLAW WY.
PENTLAND
LAMMERMUIR WYND
CAMPSIE CT.
WEST FAIRHOLM
HAMILTON RD.
DAVE BARRIE AV.
SUMMERLEE
MAPLE
BROOM DR.
CHEST-NUT
BEECH
WOOD
BIRCH GRO.
ELM
52
HAMILTON ST.
Lodge
Fairholm Bridge
160
LARKHALL
BEATON
SUNNYSIDE
MERRYTON ST.
STREET
War Mem.
GLEN VIEW
DOUGLAS S.
CADZOW ST.
NORTH
Sewage Works
Playground
Avon Braes

Motherwell
Muirhouse
ML1
Hamilton
ML3
Larkhall
ML9
Netherton
A
B
C
D
1
2
3
4
5
6
144
155
161
Cricket Ground
Waterfall
Dalzell House
Easterbraes Plantation
Adders' Gill
Pumping Station
Weir
Adders' Gill Wood
Muirhouse Farm
Upper Muirhouse Farm
Kirkhill Orchard
Monument
Graveyard
Sewage Works
Randalls Orchard
Carbarns Orchard
Carbarnswood
Lower Carbarns
Carbarns Wood
NORTH LANARKSHIRE
SOUTH LANARKSHIRE
RIVER CLYDE
M74
LARKHALL INTERCHANGE
Hall Gill
Tammy's Burn
Upper Carbarns
Junction 7
LANARK ROAD
A72
M74 MOTORWAY
Go-Kart Track
Dykehead Cottage
Highlees
Prince's Lodge
Whittrick Burn
Skelly Gill
Sewage Works
Tilework Cottage
Cemetery
EAST STATION INDUSTRIAL ESTATE
Rec. Grd.
War Mem.
Playground
SHIELDS ROAD
EXCELSIOR STREET
EXCELSIOR PARK
NETHERHALL
CANYON RD.
CANYON
Factory
Depot
B754
MERRYTON ROAD
KIRKNETHAN
CARBARNS ROAD
KIRKHILL ROAD
HAMILTON RD.
HAMILTON ST.
Prim. Sch.
GRANGE TOWER
BARONS ROAD

Major roads and references:
- A721
- A72
- A71
- A72 ROAD
- B754 ROAD
- B7032 ROAD
- CLYDE ROAD
- HORSLEY BRAE
- MAIN STREET
- STEWARTON STREET
- CASTLEHILL ROAD
- CALEDONIAN ROAD
- OLD MANSE ROAD
- NETHERTON ROAD

Area labels:
- Wishaw ML2
- WISHAW
- NETHERTON
- Pather
- Gowkthrapple
- Castlehill
- OVERTOWN
- Wemysshill

Named features:
- WISHAW GENERAL HOSPITAL
- King George's Field
- Wishaw Sports Cen.
- Wishaw Sports Grd.
- Community Centre
- Phyliss Jane Court
- St. Thomas Prim. Sch.
- Prim. Sch.
- Castlehill Prim. Sch.
- Clyde Valley High Sch.
- Garrion Business Park
- Electricity Sub Station
- Durhambank Mausoleum
- Highmainshead Wood
- Lucindabank
- West Belmont
- East Belmont
- Pathhead Orchard
- Laurelbank
- Trotterbank
- Stewartbank
- Wemysshill Orchard
- Laurel Bank Lodge
- Upper Callender
- Lower Callender
- Henleyhead
- Blair Orchard
- Gowkthrapple Burn
- Gowthrapple Burn
- Allershaw
- Birkshaw Braes
- Football Ground
- Football Grd.
- Tennis Courts
- Gas Sta.
- Bowling Green
- Playing Field
- Play Field
- Presby Playing Field
- RIVER CLYDE

Grid references around the edges: 1, 2, 3, 4, 5, 6 (right side); 54'im; 52; E, F, G, H (top and bottom)

Page connections: 78, 79, 80, 145, 158, 162, 655

A
B
C
D
1
2
3
4
5
6
146
157
163
Greenhead
Cemetery
OPENCAST WORKINGS
PARK
Recreation Ground
Waterloo
Wishaw
ML2
Dimsdale
Pather Farm
Rec. Ground
Works
Ponds
Eastmuir Plantation
STEWARTON STREET
A721
WISHAW RD.
OVERTOWN ROAD
WISHAW
A71
ROAD
Overtown Prim. Sch.
Bowling Green
Garriongill Junction
Garrion Burn
Castlehill
OVERTOWN
Rosebank
Ford Gill
Garrion
Wemyssbank
Horsleyhead Nursy.
Blairs Orchard
Upper Callender
Lower Callender
Shawgill
Birks
BROWNLEE ROAD
B7011
MAIN STREET
HORSLEY BRAE
CASTLEHILL RD.
B754
Depot
Playing Field
Comm. Cen.
Hall
Play. Field
Lanniemuir
PHYLISS JANE COURT
DRUMMOND

147
83
E
F
G
H
84
655
MAIN STREET
A73
Depot
Auchter Water
Oakbank
War Mem.
MORNINGSIDE ROAD
CHAPEL ROAD
Chapel
Holmhill
Herdshill
Bogside Farm
54
Bogside
A721 ROAD
517
NORTH LANARKSHIRE
SOUTH LANARKSHIRE
Twelve Acre Plantation
Wildmanbridge
Works
WILDMAN ROAD B7011
89
Subway
Gillhead
GILLHEAD LA.
Wildman Bridge
53
STATION PL.
MUIRHEAD DR.
WALLACE WYND
DOBBIES CT.
BUCHANAN DR.
STATION ROW
126
WATERLANDS ROAD
Waterlands Nursery
Depot
Waterlands
Carluke
PATTERSON DR.
BRACKENHILL RD.
Brackenhill
Garrion Burn
Old Toll House
A73
ML8
LAW
Football Ground
Works
OLD WISHAW ROAD
Castlehill Bridge
AIRDRIE RD.
Works
Law Primary Sch.
52
Castlehill
MANSE CT.
164
83
84
1
2
3
4
5
6

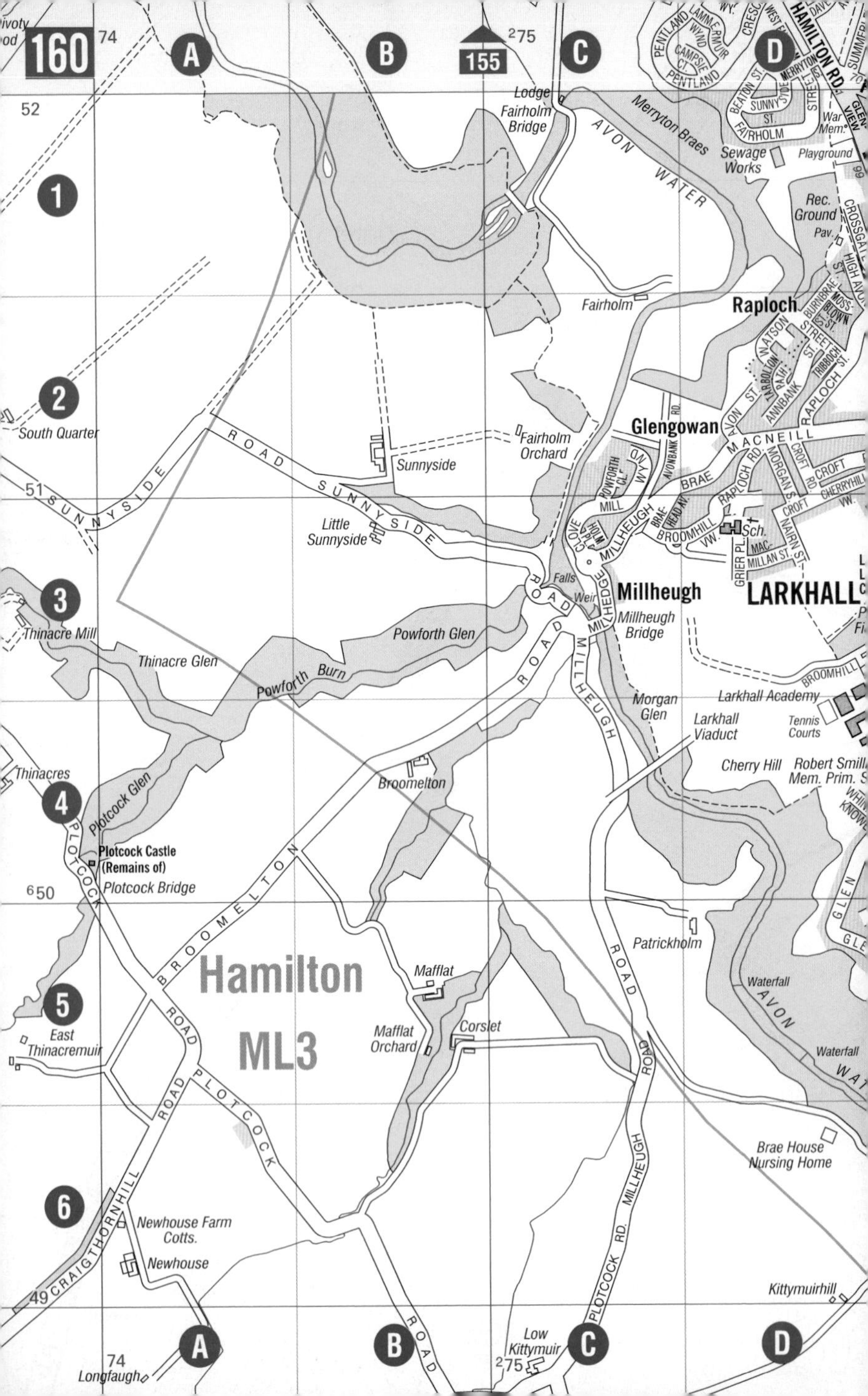
155
Hamilton
ML3
LARKHALL
Raploch
Glengowan
Millheugh
Lodge
Fairholm Bridge
Merryton Braes
AVON WATER
Sewage Works
Playground
War Mem.
Rec. Ground
Pav.
Fairholm
Fairholm Orchard
Sunnyside
Little Sunnyside
South Quarter
SUNNYSIDE ROAD
Thinacre Mill
Thinacre Glen
Powforth Glen
Powforth Burn
Falls
Weir
Millheugh Bridge
MILLHEUGH ROAD
Morgan Glen
Larkhall Viaduct
Larkhall Academy
Tennis Courts
Cherry Hill
Robert Smillie Mem. Prim. Sch.
Thinacres
Plotcock Glen
Plotcock Castle (Remains of)
Plotcock Bridge
Broomelton
BROOMELTON ROAD
PLOTCOCK ROAD
Mafflat
Mafflat Orchard
Corslet
Patrickholm
Waterfall
AVON WATER
Brae House Nursing Home
East Thinacremuir
Newhouse Farm Cotts.
Newhouse
CRAIGTHORNHILL ROAD
PLOTCOCK RD.
MILLHEUGH ROAD
Kittymuirhill
Low Kittymuir
Longfaugh
MACNEILL
BRAE
RAPLOCH RD.
BROOMHILL VW.
Sch.
GRIER PL.
MACMILLAN ST.
NAIRN ST.
MORGAN ST.
CROFT RD.
CHERRYHILL VW.
AVONBANK RD.
POWFORTH CL.
MILL WYND
BRAEHEAD AV.
CLOVE MILL
BROOMHILL
PENTLAND
LAMMERMUIR WYND
CAMPSIE CT.
BEATON ST.
SUNNYSIDE ST.
MERRYTON STREET
FAIRHOLM
HAMILTON RD.
CROSSGATES
HIGH AVON ST.
BURNBRAE ST.
MOSSBLOWN ST.
WATSON STREET
TARBOLTON PATH
ANNBANK ST.
TRIBBOCH ST.
RAPLOCH ST.
AVON ST.
GLEN
A
B
C
D
1
2
3
4
5
6
74
275
52
51
650
49

M74 MOTORWAY
Larkhall
Meadowhill
Burnhead
Hareleeshill
Machan
Machan Ind. Estate
Shawsburn
Strutherhill
Birkenshaw
Swinhill
LARKHALL GOLF COURSE
Skellyton Wood
Skelly Bridge
Millburn Cottage
Millburn
Shawsburn House
Shawsrigg
Hareleeshill Sports Barn
LARKHALL INDUSTRIAL ESTATE
STRUTHERHILL INDUSTRIAL ESTATE
EAST STATION INDUSTRIAL ESTATE
Craigbank Prim. Sch.
Machanhill Prim. Sch.
Ringsdale Castle
Birkenshaw Farm
Travelling People's Site
Hills Farm Cottage
Bogside
Hailstonemyre
Little Shaws
Shaws
Robert Smillie Memorial Park
Running Track
Sewage Works
DRYGATE
B7019
B7078
A71
AYR ROAD
BURNHEAD ROAD
CARLISLE ROAD
STRUTHERHILL
MACHAN ROAD
UNION ST.
CHURCH ST.
JOHN STREET
HARDIE ROAD
DONALDSON
SHAWS ROAD
STRUTHER & SWINHILL ROAD
TINTO VIEW
156
162
E F G H
1 2 3 4 5 6
77 78
49 50 51 52

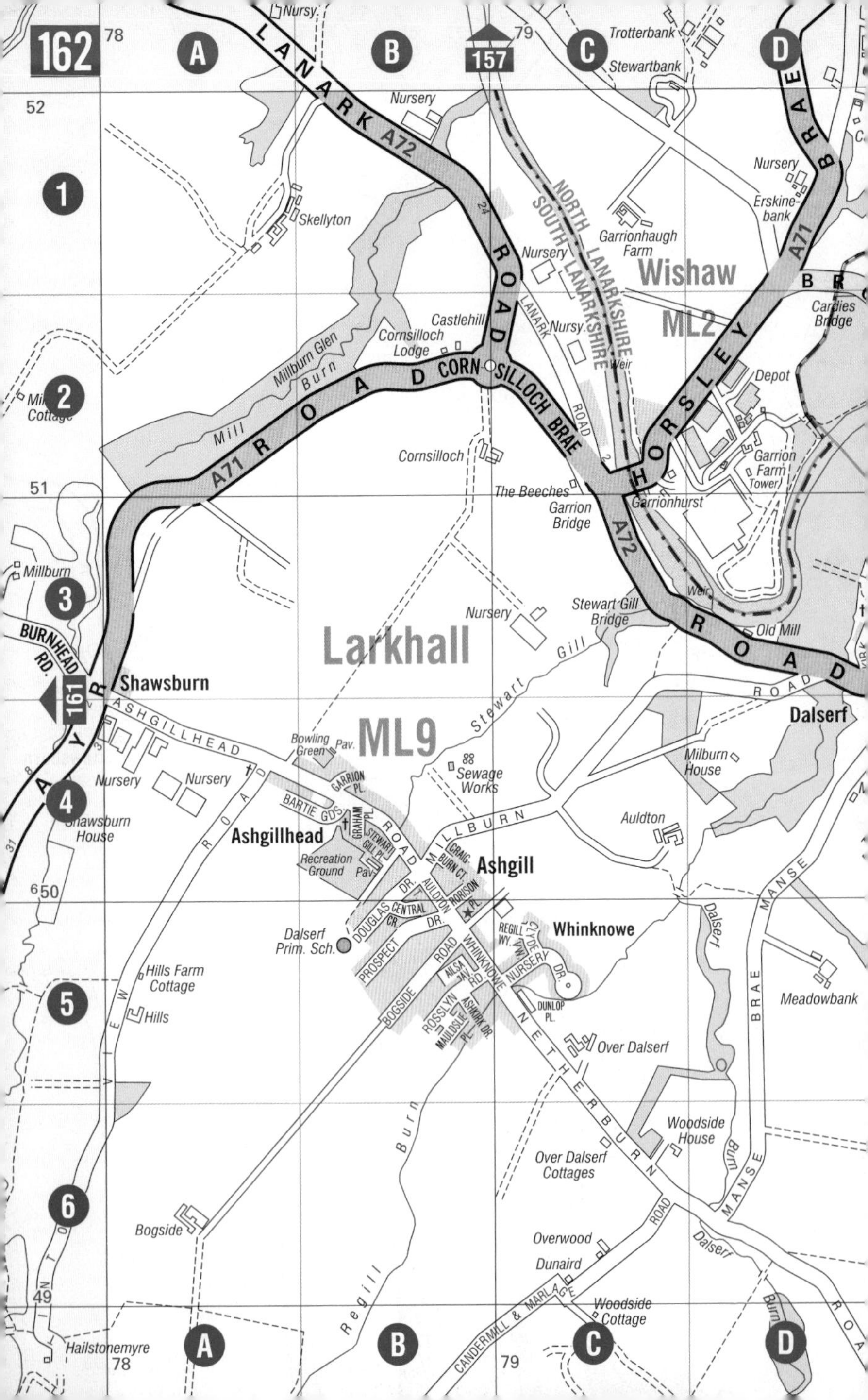
A
B
C
D
1
2
3
4
5
6
78
79
52
51
50
49
157
161
LANARK A72 ROAD
A71 ROAD CORNSILLOCH BRAE
HORSLEY BRAE A71
A72 ROAD
NORTH LANARKSHIRE
SOUTH LANARKSHIRE
Wishaw
ML2
Larkhall
ML9
Nursy.
Nursery
Trotterbank
Stewartbank
Skellyton
Erskine-bank
Garrionhaugh Farm
Castlehill
Cornsilloch Lodge
Millburn Glen
Mill Burn
Cardies Bridge
Depot
Weir
Garrion Farm Tower
Cornsilloch
The Beeches
Garrion Bridge
Garrionhurst
Millburn
BURNHEAD RD.
Mill Cottage
Stewart Gill Bridge
Old Mill
Shawsburn
ASHGILLHEAD ROAD
Dalserf
Bowling Green
Pav.
Stewart Gill
Sewage Works
Milburn House
Shawsburn House
Ashgillhead
Ashgill
Auldton
MILLBURN ROAD
Recreation Ground
Dalserf Prim. Sch.
Whinknowe
Hills Farm Cottage
Hills
Meadowbank
Over Dalserf
Woodside House
Over Dalserf Cottages
Bogside
Overwood
Dunaird
Woodside Cottage
Hailstonemyre
Regill Burn
Dalserf Burn
MANSE BRAE
MANSE ROAD
NETHERBURN ROAD
BOGSIDE ROAD
CANDERMILL & MARLAGE ROAD
GARRION PL.
BARTIE GDS.
GRAHAM PL.
STEWART GILL PL.
CRAIG. BURN CT.
AULDTON DR.
DOUGLAS DR.
CENTRAL CR.
PROSPECT DR.
RORISON PL.
REGILL WY.
CLYDE VW.
NURSERY DR.
AILSA RD.
ROSSLYN AV.
ASHKIRK DR.
MAULDSLIE PL.
DUNLOP PL.
WHINKNOWE

Carluke
ML8
Law of Mauldslie
Rosebank
B7011
A72
LANARK ROAD
MAULDSLIE ROAD
BIRKS ROAD
STRAVENHOUSE ROAD
QUARRY ROAD
QUARRY RD.
RIVER CLYDE
West Brownlee
Jollyfield
Brownlee House
Binniesbrig
Bowmanhirst
Castlehill
Nursery
Birks
Stravenhouse Farm
Comm. Cen.
Dalserf House
Rams Gill
Mauldslie Mains
Mauldslie Cottage
Mauldslie Stables
Works
Mauldslie Bridge
East Lodge
Mauldslie House
JOCK'S GILL WOOD
Jock's Burn
Mauldslie View
Hotel
Haugh Hill
Nurseries
Gillbank
Annsfield
Dalpatrick
Milton-Lockhart Farm
Hazelwood Cottage
Overton Wood
Carcain Gill
Milton Lockhart Bri.
Waterfall
Sandilandgate
Townhead
Shawgill
158
164
E F G H
1 2 3 4 5 6
80 81 82
49 50 51 52

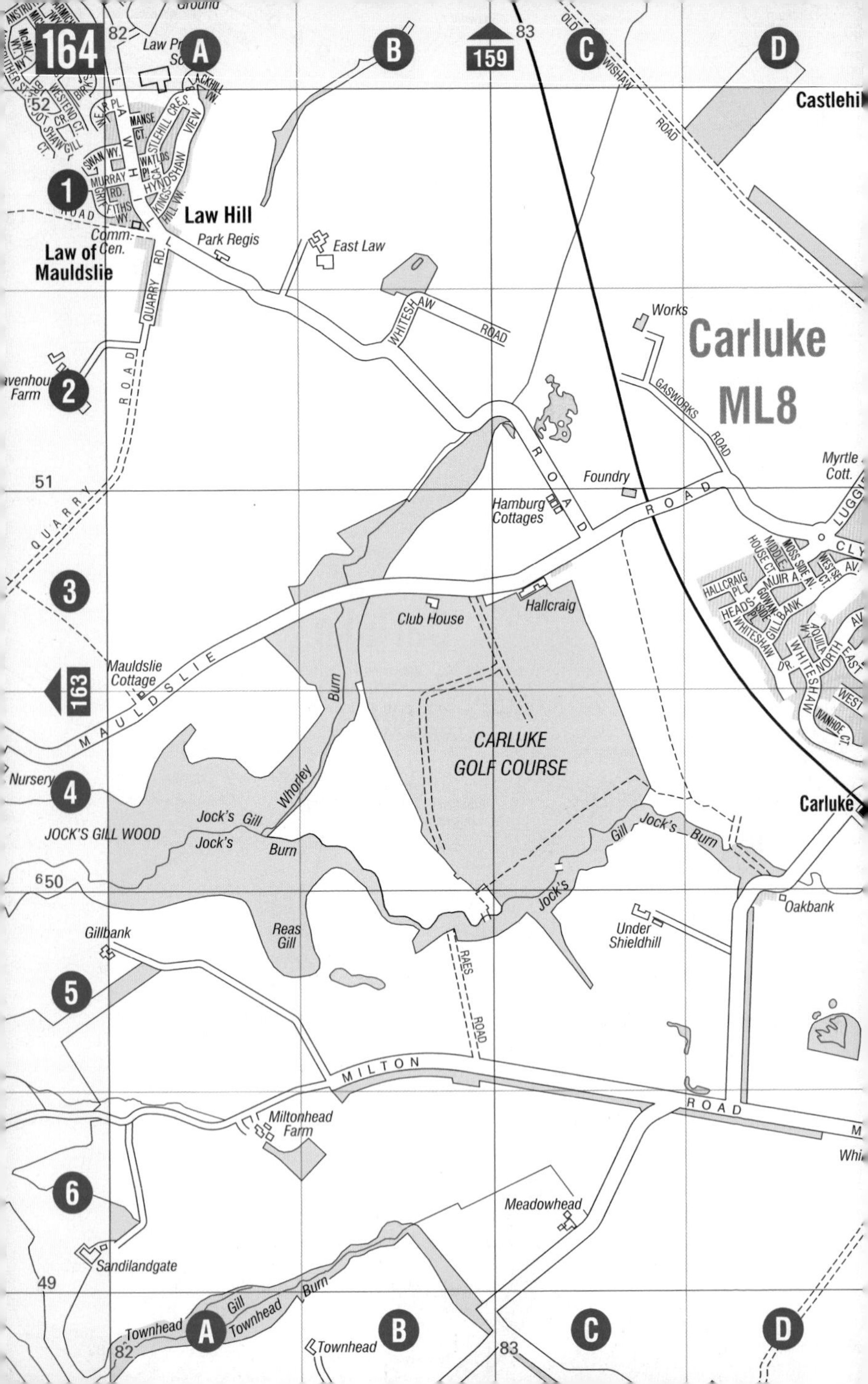

A B 159 83 C D

Castlehi

Law Pr
S

ACKHILL
VW

PL
WESTING
CR
SHAW
GILL

52

MANSE
CT
STILEHILL
CRES

WAT
WY A
PL S
STH
W

HYNDSHAW
VIEW

SWAN WY
MURRAY
TRD
THS
W

1

Law Hill

ROAD

Comm
Gen
Cen.

Law of
Mauldslie

Park Regis

East Law

QUARRY
ROAD

WHITESHAW
ROAD

Works

Carluke
ML8

ravenhous
Farm

2

GASWORKS
ROAD

Myrtle
Cott.

51

ROAD

Foundry

LUGGI
CLY

QUARRY

Hamburg
Cottages

HALLCRAIG
PL
MIDDLE
HOUSE CT
MUIR
WISS ST
NORTH
WEST
AV

3

Club House

Hallcraig

HEADS
GILL BANK
WHITESHAW
AV
EAST

163

Mauldslie
Cottage

MAULDSLIE

Burn

Wholey

CARLUKE
GOLF COURSE

WHITESHAW
WEST
WANSIDE

Nursery

4

Jock's Gill

Jock's

Gill

Jock's Burn

Carluke

JOCK'S GILL WOOD

Jock's

Burn

Jock's

Oakbank

6 50

Reas
Gill

RAES
ROAD

Under
Shieldhill

Gillbank

5

MILTON

ROAD

M

Miltonhead
Farm

Whi

6

Meadowhead

49

Sandilandgate

Townhead

Gill
Townhead
Burn

82

A

Townhead

B

83

C

D

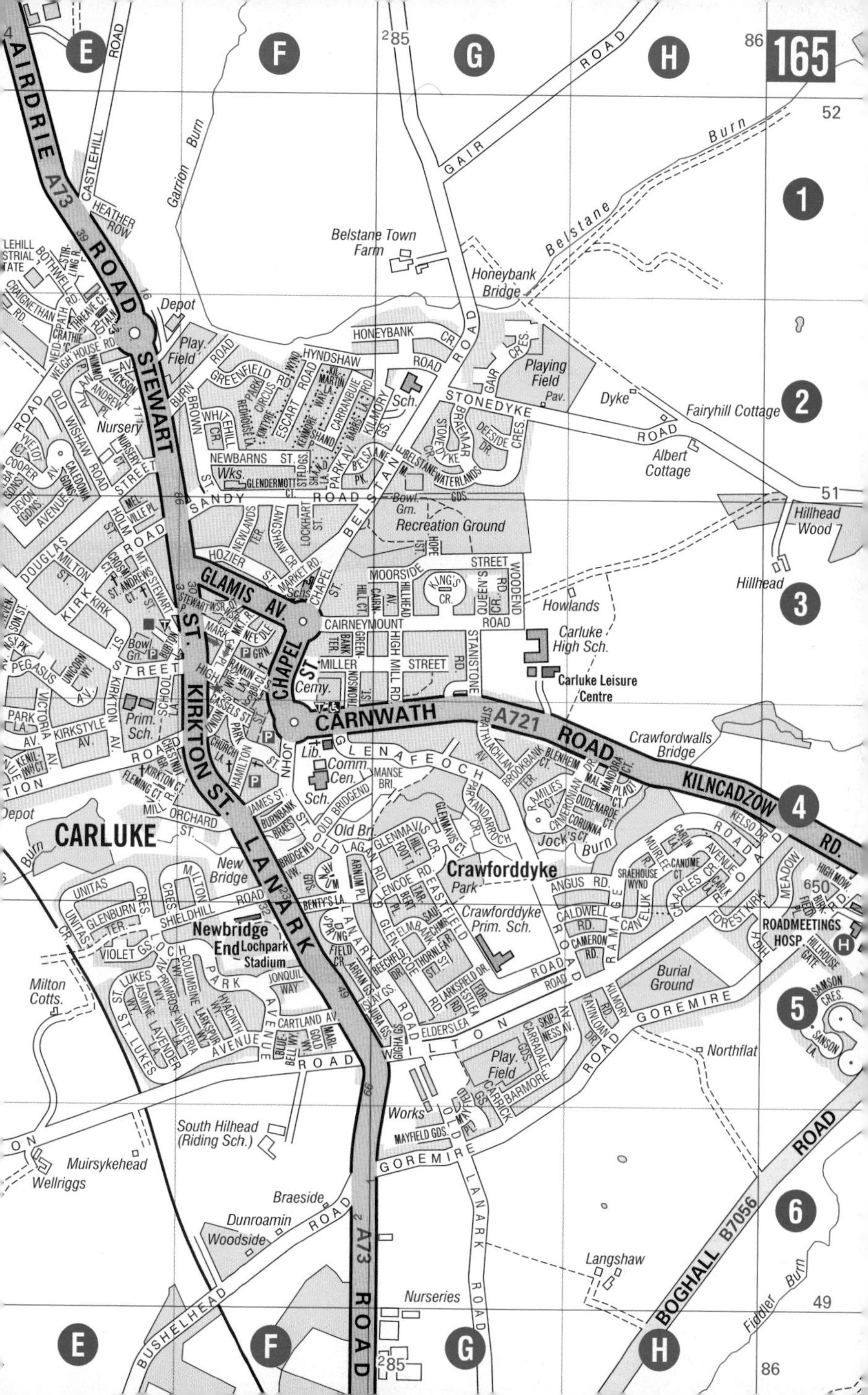

CARLUKE
AIRDRIE ROAD
A73
STEWART ST.
KIRKTON ST.
LANARK ROAD
CARNWATH ROAD
A721
KILNCADZOW RD.
GLAMIS AV.
CHAPEL ST.
GAIR ROAD
BOGHALL ROAD
B7056
BUSHELHEAD ROAD
GOREMIRE ROAD
MILTON ROAD
SANDY ROAD
STONEDYKE ROAD
Belstane Town Farm
Honeybank Bridge
Belstane Burn
Garrion Burn
Playing Field
Fairyhill Cottage
Albert Cottage
Hillhead Wood
Hillhead
Howlands
Carluke High Sch.
Carluke Leisure Centre
Crawfordwalls Bridge
Recreation Ground
Crawforddyke
Crawforddyke Prim. Sch.
Newbridge End
Lochpark Stadium
Burial Ground
Northflat
ROADMEETINGS HOSP.
Milton Cotts.
South Hilhead (Riding Sch.)
Muirsykehead
Wellriggs
Braeside
Dunroamin
Woodside
Langshaw
Nurseries
Fiddler Burn
Works
Depot
Nursery

INDEX

Including Streets, Places & Areas, Industrial Estates, Selected Flats & Walkways,
Junction Names, Stations and Selected Places of Interest.

HOW TO USE THIS INDEX

1. Each street name is followed by its Postal District and then by its Locality abbreviation(s) and then by its map reference;
   e.g. **Abbeycraig Rd.** G34: Glas . . . .2B **88** is in the Glasgow 34 Postal District and the Glasgow Locality and is to be found in square 2B
   on page **88**. The page number is shown in bold type.

2. A strict alphabetical order is followed in which Av., Rd., St., etc. (though abbreviated) are read in full and as part of the street name;
   e.g. **Adams Pl.** appears after **Adamson St.** but before **Adamswell St**.

3. Streets and a selection of flats and walkways too small to be shown on the maps, appear in the index with the thoroughfare to which it
   is connected shown in brackets; e.g. **Abbey Wlk.** G69: Barg . . . .6D **88** (off Abercrombie Cres.)

4. Addresses that are in more than one part are referred to as not continuous.

5. Places and areas are shown in the index in **BLUE TYPE** and the map reference is to the actual map square in which the town centre or
   area is located and not to the place name shown on the map; e.g. **AIRDRIE** 3H **91**

6. An example of a selected place of interest is **Auchinvole Castle** 5G **11**

7. Junction names are shown in the index in **BOLD TYPE**; e.g. **ANDERSTON CROSS INTERCHANGE** 5A **4**

8. An example of a station is **Airbles Station (Rail)** . . . .4G **143**. Included are Rail **(Rail)** and Underground **(Und.)** Stations.

9. Map references shown in brackets; e.g. **Adams Ct. La.** G1: Glas . . . .5F **83** (6D **4**) refer to entries that also appear on the large scale
   pages **4** & **5**.

GENERAL ABBREVIATIONS

Arc. : Arcade
Av. : Avenue
Bk. : Back
Blvd. : Boulevard
Bri. : Bridge
Bldg. : Building
Bldgs. : Buildings
Bus. : Business
Cvn. : Caravan
Cen. : Centre
Chu. : Church
Circ. : Circle
Cir. : Circus
Cl. : Close
Coll. : College
Comn. : Common
Cnr. : Corner
Cott. : Cottage
Cotts. : Cottages
Ct. : Court
Cres. : Crescent
Cft. : Croft
Dpt. : Depot
Dr. : Drive
E. : East

Ent. : Enterprise
Est. : Estate
Fld. : Field
Gdn. : Garden
Gdns. : Gardens
Ga. : Gate
Gt. : Great
Grn. : Green
Gro. : Grove
Hgts. : Heights
Ho. : House
Ind. : Industrial
Intl. : International
Junc. : Junction
La. : Lane
Lit. : Little
Lwr. : Lower
Mans. : Mansions
Mkt. : Market
Mdw. : Meadow
Mdws. : Meadows
M. : Mews
Mt. : Mount
Mus. : Museum
Nth. : North

Pde. : Parade
Pk. : Park
Pas. : Passage
Pl. : Place
Quad. : Quadrant
Ri. : Rise
Rd. : Road
Rdbt. : Roundabout
Shop. : Shopping
Sth. : South
Sq. : Square
Sta. : Station
St. : Street
Ter. : Terrace
Twr. : Tower
Trad. : Trading
Up. : Upper
Va. : Vale
Vw. : View
Vs. : Villas
Vis. : Visitors
Wlk. : Walk
W. : West
Yd. : Yard

LOCALITY ABBREVIATIONS

Air : **Airdrie**
Alla : **Allandale**
Anna : **Annathill**
Ashg : **Ashgill**
Auch : **Auchinloch**
Bail : **Baillieston**
Balder : **Baldernock**
Balm : **Balmore**
Bank : **Banknock**
Bant : **Banton**
Bard : **Bardowie**
Barg : **Bargeddie**
Barr : **Barrhead**
Bear : **Bearsden**
Bell : **Bellshill**
Birk : **Birkenshaw**
B'rig : **Bishopbriggs**
B'ton : **Bishopton**
Blan : **Blantyre**
B'bri : **Bonnybridge**
Both : **Bothwell**
Bowl : **Bowling**

Bri W : **Bridge of Weir**
Brkfld : **Brookfield**
Busby : **Busby**
C'bnk : **Calderbank**
Camb : **Cambuslang**
Cam G : **Campsie Glen**
Card : **Cardross**
Carf : **Carfin**
Carl : **Carluke**
Crmck : **Carmunnock**
Carm : **Carmyle**
C'cry : **Castlecary**
Chap : **Chapelhall**
Chry : **Chryston**
Clar : **Clarkston**
Cle : **Cleland**
Clyd : **Clydebank**
Coat : **Coatbridge**
Crsfd : **Crossford**
C'lee : **Crosslee**
Croy : **Croy**
Cumb : **Cumbernauld**

Dals : **Dalserf**
Denn : **Dennyloanhead**
Dull : **Dullatur**
Dumb : **Dumbarton**
Dun : **Duntocher**
E Kil : **East Kilbride**
Eld : **Elderslie**
Ersk : **Erskine**
Faif : **Faifley**
Fern : **Ferniegair**
Flem : **Flemington**
G'csh : **Gartcosh**
Gart : **Gartness**
Giff : **Giffnock**
Glas : **Glasgow**
Glas A : **Glasgow Airport**
Glass : **Glassford**
Glenb : **Glenboig**
Glenm : **Glenmavis**
Grng : **Greengairs**
Hag : **Haggs**
Ham : **Hamilton**

Hard : **Hardgate**
Hill : **Hillington Ind. Est.**
Holy : **Holytown**
Hous : **Houston**
How : **Howwood**
Inch : **Inchinnan**
John : **Johnstone**
Kilb : **Kilbarchan**
Kils : **Kilsyth**
Kirk : **Kirkintilloch**
Lang : **Langbank**
Lark : **Larkhall**
Law : **Law**
Len : **Lennoxtown**
Lenz : **Lenzie**
Lin : **Linwood**
Loch : **Lochwinnoch**
Longc : **Longcroft**
Mille : **Millerston**
Miln : **Milngavie**
Milt : **Milton**
Milt C : **Milton of Campsie**
Mollin : **Mollinsburn**
Mood : **Moodiesburn**
Moss : **Mossend**
Moth : **Motherwell**
Muirh : **Muirhead**
Neil : **Neilston**
Ners : **Nerston**
Neth : **Netherlee**
N'hill : **Newarthill**
N'hse : **Newhouse**
Newm : **Newmains**
New S : **New Stevenston**
Newt : **Newton**
Newt M : **Newton Mearns**
Old K : **Old Kilpatrick**
Over : **Overtown**
Pais : **Paisley**
Plain : **Plains**
Q'riers : **Quarriers Village**
Quar : **Quarter**
Queen : **Queenzieburn**
Renf : **Renfrew**
Rent : **Renton**
Rigg : **Riggend**
Roger : **Rogerton**
Rose : **Rosebank**
Ruth : **Rutherglen**
Shaw : **Shawsburn**
Step : **Stepps**
Tann : **Tannochside**
T'bnk : **Thornliebank**
T'hall : **Thorntonhall**
Torr : **Torrance**
Twe : **Twechar**
Udd : **Uddingston**
View : **Viewpark**
Water : **Waterfoot**
Wis : **Wishaw**

A

Abbey Cl. PA1: Pais 1A **98**
Abbeycraig Rd. G34: Glas 2B **88**
Abbeydale Way G73: Ruth 4E **121**
Abbey Dr. G14: Glas 5E **61**
Abbeyfield Ho. G46: Giff 4H **117**
ML5: Coat 5A **90**
Abbeygreen St. G34: Glas 2C **88**
Abbeyhill St. G32: Glas 4G **85**
Abbeylands Rd. G81: Faif 6E **23**
Abbeymill Bus. Cen. PA1: Pais 1B **98**
Abbey Pl. ML6: Air 1C **112**
Abbey Rd. PA5: Eld 3H **95**
Abbey Wlk. *G69: Barg 6D 88*
(off Abercrombie Cres.)
ML9: Lark 1F 161
(off Duncan Graham St.)
Abbotsburn Way PA3: Pais 3H **77**
Abbotsford G64: B'rig 5E **49**
Abbotsford Av. G73: Ruth 6D **104**
ML3: Ham 3F **141**
ML9: Lark 4E **161**
Abbotsford Brae G74: E Kil 6G **137**
Abbotsford Ct. G67: Cumb 6H **35**
Abbotsford Cres. ML2: Wis 5A **146**
ML3: Ham 3F **141**
PA2: Pais 6B **96**
Abbotsford Dr. G66: Kirk 5E **31**
Abbotsford La. ML4: Bell 1B **126**
Abbotsford Pl. G5: Glas 1F **103**
(not continuous)
G67: Cumb 6H **35**
ML1: Holy 2A 128
(off Ivy Ter.)
Abbotsford Rd. G61: Bear 1C **44**
G67: Cumb 6H **35**
G81: Clyd 6D **42**
ML2: Wis 5A **146**
ML3: Ham 3E **141**
ML6: Chap 4E **113**
Abbotshall Av. G15: Glas 4G **43**
Abbotsinch Rd. PA4: Renf 6A **58**
Abbotsinch Rd. PA3: Glas A 2A **78**
Abbots Ter. ML6: Air 1C **112**
Abbot St. G41: Glas 4C **102**
PA3: Pais 5B **78**
Abbott Cres. G81: Clyd 1F **59**
ABC Cinema **3D 118**
Aberconway St. G81: Clyd 1E **59**
Abercorn Av. G52: Hill 3G **79**
Abercorn Cres. ML3: Ham 1B **154**
Abercorn Dr. ML3: Ham 6B **142**
Abercorn Ind. Est. PA3: Pais 5B **78**
Abercorn Pl. G23: Glas 6C **46**
Abercorn Rd. G77: Newt M 3C **132**
Abercorn St. G81: Faif 6G **23**
PA3: Pais 6A **78**
Abercrombie Cres. G69: Barg 6D **88**
Abercrombie Dr. G61: Bear 5B **24**
Abercrombie Ho. G75: E Kil 2A **148**
Abercrombie Pl. G65: Kils 2F **11**
Abercromby Cres. G74: E Kil 6B **138**
Abercromby Dr. G40: Glas 5B **84**
Abercromby Pl. G74: E Kil 6B **138**
Abercromby St. G40: Glas 6A **84**
(not continuous)
Aberdalgie Path *G34: Glas 3H 87*
(off Aberdalgie Rd.)
Aberdalgie Rd. G34: Glas 3H **87**
Aberdeen Rd. ML6: Chap 1D **112**
Aberdour St. G31: Glas 4E **85**
Aberfeldy Av. ML6: Plain 1F **93**
Aberfeldy St. G31: Glas 4E **85**
Aberfoyle St. G31: Glas 4E **85**
Aberlady Rd. G51: Glas 4E **81**
Aberlady St. ML1: Cle 6H **129**
Abernethy Dr. PA3: Lin 6G **75**
Abernethyn Rd. ML2: Newm 3E **147**
Abernethy Pk. G74: E Kil 1F **149**
Abernethy Pl. G77: Newt M 5H **133**
Abernethy St. G31: Glas 5E **85**
Aberuthven Dr. G32: Glas 2B **106**
Abiegail Pl. G72: Blan 6B **124**
Aboukir St. G51: Glas 3E **81**
Aboyne Dr. PA2: Pais 4B **98**
Aboyne St. G51: Glas 5F **81**
ABRONHILL **1E 37**
Acacia Dr. G78: Barr 2C **114**
PA2: Pais 4F **97**
Acacia Pl. PA5: John 5G **95**
Acacia Way G72: Flem 2E **123**
Academy Ct. ML5: Coat 4C **90**
Academy Pk. G51: Glas 1A **102**
ML6: Air 4A **92**
Academy Pl. ML5: Coat 4C **90**
Academy Rd. G46: Giff 5A **118**
Academy St. G32: Glas 1B **106**
ML5: Coat 4C **90**
ML6: Air 4A **92**
ML9: Lark 2E **161**
Academy Ter. ML4: Bell 2D **126**
Acer Cres. PA2: Pais 4E **97**
Acer Gro. ML6: Chap 2E **113**
Achamore Cres. G15: Glas 3G **43**
Achamore Dr. G15: Glas 3G **43**
Achamore Rd. G15: Glas 3G **43**
Achnasheen Rd. ML6: Air 5G **93**
Achray Dr. PA2: Pais 4E **97**
Achray Pl. G62: Miln 2D **24**
ML5: Coat 2H **89**
Achray Rd. G67: Cumb 6D **34**
Acorn Ct. G40: Glas 1B **104**
Acorn St. G40: Glas 1B **104**
Acredyke Cres. G21: Glas 2E **65**
Acredyke Pl. G21: Glas 3E **65**
Acredyke Rd. G21: Glas 2D **64**
G73: Ruth 5B **104**
Acre Rd. G20: Glas 6H **45**
Acres, The ML9: Lark 3F **161**
Acre Valley Rd. G64: Torr 3D **28**
Adam Av. ML6: Air 4B **92**
Adams Ct. La. G1: Glas 5F **83** (6D **4**)
Adamslie Cres. G66: Kirk 5A **30**
Adamslie Dr. G66: Kirk 5A **30**
Adamson St. ML4: Moss 2F **127**
Adams Pl. G65: Kils 3H **11**
Adamswell St. G21: Glas 6A **64**
Adamswell Ter. G69: Mood 5E **53**
Addie St. ML1: Moth 1H **143**
Addiewell Pl. ML5: Coat 1C **110**
Addiewell St. G32: Glas 4A **86**
Addison Gro. G46: T'bnk 3F **117**
Addison Pl. G46: T'bnk 3F **117**
Addison Rd. G12: Glas 5B **62**
G46: T'bnk 3E **117**
Adelaide Ct. G81: Clyd 2H **41**
Adelaide Rd. G75: E Kil 4D **148**
Adele St. ML1: Moth 5H **143**
Adelphi Cen. G5: Glas 6H **83**
Adelphi St. G5: Glas 6H **83**
(Commercial Rd., not continuous)
G5: Glas 6G **83**
(Gorbals St.)
Admiral St. G41: Glas 6C **82**
Admiralty Gdns. G60: Old K 2F **41**
Admiralty Gro. G60: Old K 2F **41**
Admiralty Pl. G60: Old K 2F **41**
Advance Pl. *PA11: Bri W 3F 73*
(off Main St.)
Advie Pl. G42: Glas 5F **103**
Affric Av. ML6: Plain 1G **93**
Affric Dr. PA2: Pais 4D **98**
Afton Cres. G61: Bear 4H **45**
Afton Dr. PA4: Renf 6G **59**
Afton Gdns. G72: Blan 3H **139**
ML5: Coat 6F **91**
Afton Rd. G67: Cumb 2B **36**
Afton St. G41: Glas 5C **102**
ML9: Lark 3G **161**
Afton Vw. G66: Kirk 4F **31**
Afton Way PA2: Pais 4D **96**
Agamemnon St. G81: Clyd 5B **42**
Agate Ter. *ML4: Bell 3C 126*
(off Diamond St.)
Agnew Av. ML5: Coat 4E **91**
Agnew Gro. ML4: Bell 2H **125**
Agnew La. G42: Glas 4E **103**
Aigas Cotts. *G13: Glas 4F 61*
(off Fern La.)
Aikenhead Rd. G42: Glas 2F **103**
G44: Glas 1G **119**
Aikman Pl. G74: E Kil 5B **138**
Aikman Rd. ML1: Moth 4D **142**
Ailart Loan *ML2: Newm 3D 146*
(off Tiree Cres.)
Ailean Dr. G32: Glas 1E **107**
Ailean Gdns. G32: Glas 1E **107**
Aillort Pl. G74: E Kil 6G **137**
Ailort Av. G44: Glas 2E **119**
Ailsa Av. ML1: Moth 2D **142**
ML9: Ashg 5B **162**
Ailsa Ct. ML3: Ham 2B **152**
ML5: Coat 1A **110**
Ailsa Cres. ML1: Moth 2D **142**

Ailsa Dr. G42: Glas 6D **102**
G46: Giff. 1H **133**
G66: Kirk. 3F **31**
G71: Both 3E **125**
G73: Ruth 2B **120**
G81: Hard 1E **43**
PA2: Pais 6H **97**
Ailsa Pl. ML5: Coat. 1B **110**
Ailsa Rd. G64: B'rig 5D **48**
ML5: Coat 1A **110**
PA4: Renf 1E **79**
Ailsa Twr. G72: Camb 4G **121**
Ainslie Av. G52: Hill 3A **80**
Ainslie Rd. G52: Hill. 4A **80**
(not continuous)
G67: Cumb 2C **36**
Airbles Cres. ML1: Moth. 4F **143**
Airbles Dr. ML1: Moth. 4F **143**
Airbles Farm Rd. ML1: Moth . . 5E **143**
Airbles Rd. ML1: Moth 4E **143**
Airbles Station (Rail) 4G **143**
Airbles St. ML1: Moth 4G **143**
Airbles Twr. ML1: Moth 4G **143**
Airdale Av. G46: Giff. 5A **118**
AIRDRIE 3H **91**
Airdriehill Rd. ML6: Air. 1C **92**
Airdriehill St. ML6: Air. 1C **92**
Airdrie Leisure Cen. 2C **92**
Airdrie Rd ML6: Air, Plain 2F **93**
Airdrie Rd. G65: Kils 2H **11**
G67: Cumb 1D **54**
(Condorrat Ring Rd.)
G67: Cumb 6C **34**
(Main Rd.)
G67: Mollin. 3H **53**
ML8: Carl 6H **159**
Airdrie Station (Rail) 4A **92**
Airdrie United F.C. 5C **92**
Aird's La. G1: Glas 5G **83**
(off Bridgegate)
Airgold Dr. G15: Glas. 3H **43**
Airgold Pl. G15: Glas. 3H **43**
Airlie Av. G61: Bear 6E **25**
Airlie Dr. ML4: Bell. 1C **126**
Airlie Gdns. G73: Ruth 3F **121**
Airlie La. G12: Glas 6H **61**
Airlie Rd. G69: Bail. 2G **107**
Airlie St. G12: Glas 6G **61**
Airlink Ind. Est. PA3: Glas A . . 3A **78**
Airlour Rd. G43: Glas 2C **118**
Airth Ct. ML1: Moth 6F **127**
Airth Dr. G52: Glas 2F **101**
Airth La. G52: Glas 2F **101**
Airth Pl. G52: Glas 2F **101**
(off Airth La.)
Airthrey Av. G14: Glas. 6E **61**
Airthrey La. G14: Glas 5E **61**
(off Airthrey Av.)
Airth Way G68: Cumb 5A **34**
Aitchison Ct. ML6: Air 3H **91**
Aitchison St. ML6: Air 4G **91**
Aitkenbar Circ. G82: Dumb. . . . 2H **17**
Aitkenbar Dr. G82: Dumb 1H **17**
Aitken Cl. ML2: Newm 2E **147**
Aitkenhead Av. ML5: Coat 1F **109**
Aitkenhead Rd.
G69: Barg, Tann. 5E **109**
G71: Barg, Tann. 5E **109**
ML6: Chap 3D **112**
Aitken Rd. ML3: Ham 4A **154**
Aitken St. G31: Glas 4D **84**
ML6: Air 2A **92**
Alasdair Ct. G78: Barr. 5E **115**
Alba Gdns. ML8: Carl 2E **165**
Alba Ho. G81: Clyd. 5C **42**
Albans Cres. ML1: Moth. 1D **142**
Albany G74: E Kil 5C **138**
Albany Av. G32: Glas 5C **86**
Albany Cotts. G13: Glas 4F **61**
(off Fern La.)
Albany Dr. G73: Ruth 1D **120**
Albany Pl. G71: Both. 5F **125**
Albany Quad. G32: Glas 5C **86**
Albany Rd. ML3: Ham 4G **153**

Albany St. G40: Glas. 1C **104**
ML5: Coat. 4A **90**
Albany Ter. G72: Camb 4G **121**
Albany Way PA3: Pais. 3A **78**
Albany Wynd ML9: Lark 1F **161**
(off Duncan Graham St.)
Alba Way ML3: Ham. 5G **153**
ML9: Lark. 4G **161**
(off Keir Hardie Rd.)
Alberta Av. G75: E Kil 3D **148**
ML5: Coat. 3B **90**
Alberta Cres. G75: E Kil 3E **149**
Alberta Pk. G75: E Kil 3F **149**
Alberta Pl. G75: E Kil 3F **149**
Albert Av. G42: Glas 4D **102**
Albert Bri. G5: Glas 6G **83**
Albert Cres. ML6: Air 4B **92**
Albert Cross G41: Glas 2D **102**
Albert Dr. G41: Glas 3A **102**
G61: Bear 4H **45**
G73: Ruth 2D **120**
ML9: Lark 3F **161**
Albert Pl. ML6: Air 3B **92**
Albert Quad. ML1: Holy 2A **128**
Albert Rd. G12: Glas. 6H **61**
G42: Glas 4E **103**
G66: Lenz 4C **50**
G81: Clyd 4B **42**
PA4: Renf 6E **59**
PA5: Brkfld 6C **74**
Albert St. ML1: Moth 2H **143**
ML3: Ham 3F **141**
ML5: Coat. 4C **90**
(not continuous)
Albert Ter. ML3: Ham 3E **141**
Albion Ct. ML5: Coat. 1H **89**
(off Clifton Pl.)
Albion Ga. G1: Glas 4H **83** (6G **5**)
PA3: Pais 5H **77**
Albion Rovers F.C. 5E **91**
Albion St. G1: Glas 5H **83** (6G **5**)
G69: Bail 2H **107**
ML1: Moth 4G **143**
ML5: Coat. 4D **90**
PA3: Pais 5A **78**
Albion Twr. ML1: Moth 4G **143**
Albion Way G75: E Kil 6H **149**
Albion Works Ind. Est. G13: Glas . . 2G **59**
Alcaig Rd. G52: Glas. 3E **101**
Alcath Rd. ML2: Newm 3F **147**
Alclutha Av. G82: Dumb 4H **17**
Alder Av. G66: Lenz 2B **50**
Alder Bank G71: View. 4G **109**
Alder Ct. G75: E Kil 6E **149**
G78: Barr 6E **115**
Alder Cres. G75: E Kil 6E **149**
Alder Ga. G72: Flem 2E **123**
Alder Gro. ML5: Coat 5D **90**
Alder La. ML1: Holy 2C **128**
ML1: New S 4A **128**
Alderman Pl. G13: Glas 3C **60**
Alderman Rd. G13: Glas 2H **59**
Alder Pl. G43: Glas 2A **118**
G75: E Kil 6E **149**
PA5: John. 4G **95**
Alder Rd. G43: Glas 2H **117**
G66: Milt C 6B **8**
G67: Cumb 3D **36**
G81: Clyd 2B **42**
G82: Dumb 3E **17**
Alderside Gdns. G71: Udd 6C **108**
Alderside Pl. G71: Both 4E **125**
Alderstocks G75: E Kil 6G **149**
Alderston Pl. ML4: Bell. 3A **126**
Alderston Way ML4: Bell. 1A **126**
Aldersyde Av. ML2: Wis 5D **144**
Aldersyde Pl. G72: Blan 6A **124**
Alexander Av. G65: Twe 2C **32**
G71: View 1G **125**
Alexander Balfour Gdns. ML3: Ham
. . . . 2H **153**
Alexander Cres. G5: Glas 1G **103**
Alexander Gdns. ML3: Ham 1C **154**

Alexander Gibson Way ML1: Moth
. . . . 4F **143**
Alexander Pl. G66: Kirk 6H **31**
Alexander St. G81: Clyd 6D **42**
G82: Dumb 3G **17**
ML2: Wis. 6F **145**
ML5: Coat. 3D **90**
ML6: Air 4G **91**
Alexander Ter. G78: Neil 3C **130**
Alexandra Av. G33: Step. 3D **66**
G66: Lenz 3C **50**
Alexandra Ct. G31: Glas 3D **84**
Alexandra Dr. PA2: Pais 2F **97**
PA4: Renf 6F **59**
Alexandra Gdns. G66: Lenz 3C **50**
Alexandra Pde. G31: Glas. 3A **84**
Alexandra Parade Station (Rail) . . 3D **84**
Alexandra Pk. G66: Lenz 3C **50**
Alexandra Pk. St. G31: Glas . . . 3D **84**
Alexandra Rd. G66: Lenz 3C **50**
Alexandra Sports Hall 3E **85**
Alexandra St. G66: Kirk 5C **30**
Alford Av. G66: Kirk 5B **30**
Alford Pl. PA3: Lin 5E **75**
Alford Quad. ML2: Wis 4H **145**
Alford St. G21: Glas 6H **63**
Alfred La. G12: Glas 6C **62**
(off Cecil St.)
Alfred Ter. G12: Glas. 6C **62**
Algie St. G41: Glas. 5D **102**
Algoma Pl. G75: E Kil. 3D **148**
Alice Av. ML4: Bell 3C **126**
Alice St. PA2: Pais 3A **98**
Aline Ct. G78: Barr. 3D **114**
Alison Lea G74: E Kil 6B **138**
Allan Av. ML8: Carl 2E **165**
PA4: Renf 2G **79**
Allan Ct. G75: E Kil 4A **148**
Allan Cres. G82: Dumb. 1H **17**
ALLANDALE 1H **15**
Allandale Av. ML1: N'hill. 2F **129**
Allandale Cotts. FK4: Alla. 1H **15**
Allandale Path G72: Blan 2B **140**
(off Winton Cres.)
Allander Av. G62: Bard 6F **27**
Allander Dr. G64: Torr 5C **28**
Allander Gdns. G64: B'rig 3B **48**
Allander Ho. G67: Cumb 4H **35**
(in Cumbernauld Shop. Cen.)
Allander Rd. G62: Miln. 3G **25**
Allander Sports Complex 6H **25**
Allander St. G22: Glas 5G **63**
Allander Wlk. G67: Cumb 4H **35**
(in Cumbernauld Shop. Cen.)
Allands Av. PA4: Inch 4G **57**
Allanfauld Rd. G65: Kils 1H **11**
G67: Cumb 3H **35**
Allan Glen Gdns. G64: B'rig . . . 3C **48**
Allan Pl. G40: Glas 2D **104**
G75: E Kil 4A **148**
G82: Dumb 3G **17**
Allanshaw Gdns. ML3: Ham 6F **141**
Allanshaw Gro. ML3: Ham 1F **153**
Allanshaw Ind. Est. ML3: Ham . . 6G **141**
Allanshaw St. ML3: Ham 6G **141**
Allan St. G40: Glas. 3D **104**
ML1: Moth 2H **143**
ML5: Coat. 6H **89**
ALLANTON 2E **155**
Allanton Av. PA1: Pais 1G **99**
Allanton Dr. G52: Glas 6B **80**
Allanton Gro. ML2: Wis 4H **145**
Allanton Lea ML3: Ham 3G **153**
Allanton Pl. ML3: Ham 2A **154**
Allanton Rd. ML2: Newm 2H **147**
Allanton Ter. ML3: Fern. 3F **155**
Allan Twr. ML1: Moth 2H **143**
Allbany Cres. ML1: Holy. 2H **127**
Allendale G74: E Kil 6E **137**
Allender Rd. G61: Bear. 4D **44**
Allen Way PA4: Renf 2F **79**
Allerdyce Ct. G15: Glas 6G **43**
Allerdyce Dr. G15: Glas 6H **43**
Allerdyce Pl. G15: Glas 6H **43**

Allerdyce Rd.—Archerfield Cres.

Allerdyce Rd. G15: Glas 6G **43**
Allershaw Pl. ML2: Wis 3F **157**
Allershaw Rd. ML2: Wis 3F **157**
Allershaw Twr. ML2: Wis 3F **157**
Allerton Gdns. G69: Bail 1F **107**
Alleysbank Rd. G73: Ruth 4D **104**
Allison Av. PA8: Ersk 5D **40**
Allison Dr. G72: Camb 1A **122**
Allison Pl. G42: Glas 3E **103**
G69: G'csh 5C **68**
G77: Newt M 5C **132**
Allison St. G42: Glas 3E **103**
Allnach Pl. G34: Glas 3C **88**
Alloway Av. PA2: Pais 5D **98**
Alloway Ct. G66: Kirk 3G **31**
Alloway Cres. G73: Ruth 2B **120**
PA2: Pais 5D **98**
Alloway Dr. G66: Kirk 3F **31**
G73: Ruth 2B **120**
G77: Newt M 5G **133**
G81: Clyd 4E **43**
PA2: Pais 5D **98**
Alloway Gdns. G66: Kirk 3G **31**
ML3: Ham 2B **152**
Alloway Gro. G66: Kirk 3F **31**
PA2: Pais 5E **99**
Alloway Quad. G66: Kirk 4G **31**
Alloway Rd. G43: Glas 1B **118**
G74: E Kil 5D **138**
ML6: Air 3F **93**
Alloway St. ML9: Lark 3G **161**
Alloway Ter. G66: Kirk 3F **31**
Alloway Wynd ML1: N'hill 3E **129**
Almada Gro. ML3: Ham 5H **141**
Almada La. ML3: Ham 5H **141**
Almada St. ML3: Ham 5G **141**
Alma St. G40: Glas 6C **84**
Almond Av. PA4: Renf 1G **79**
Almond Bank G61: Bear 5C **44**
Almond Cres. PA2: Pais 3D **96**
Almond Dr. FK4: Bank 1E **15**
G66: Lenz 2B **50**
G74: E Kil 2B **150**
PA7: B'ton 5H **39**
Almond Pl. ML1: Holy 3B **128**
ML5: Coat 2H **89**
Almond Rd. G33: Step 4C **66**
G61: Bear 5D **44**
G67: Cumb 6F **15**
Almond St. G33: Glas 2F **85**
Almond Va. G71: Tann 6E **109**
Almond Vw. G15: Glas 5B **44**
Almond Way ML1: Moth 6G **143**
Alness Cres. G52: Glas 2E **101**
Alness St. ML3: Ham 2H **153**
Alness Ter. ML3: Ham 1H **153**
Alpine Gro. G71: Tann 6D **108**
Alsatian Av. G81: Clyd 5F **43**
Alsh Ter. ML3: Ham 2E **153**
Alston Av. ML5: Coat 3D **90**
Alston Gdns. G61: Bear 5B **24**
Altnacreag Gdns. G69: Mood 4E **53**
Alton Ct. *G66: Kirk* *5E* ***31***
(off Highfield Rd.)
Alton Rd. PA1: Pais 1E **99**
Altpatrict Gdns. PA5: Eld 2H **95**
Altyre St. G32: Glas 2H **105**
Alva Gdns. G52: Glas 3E **101**
G61: Bear 6D **24**
Alva Ga. G52: Glas 2E **101**
Alva Pl. G66: Lenz 3E **51**
Alwyn Av. PA6: C'lee 3D **74**
Alwyn Ct. G74: E Kil 6G **137**
Alyssum Cres. ML1: Moth 1F **143**
Alyth Cres. G76: Clar 1E **135**
Alyth Gdns. G52: Glas 2E **101**
G76: Clar 1E **135**
Ambassador Way PA4: Renf 2F **79**
Amber Ter. ML4: Bell 3C **126**
Ambleside G75: E Kil 5B **148**
Ambleside Ri. ML3: Ham 6G **153**
Ambrose Ct. *ML3: Ham* *5F* ***141***
(off Burnbank Rd.)
Amethyst Av. ML4: Bell 3C **126**
AMF Bowling 4D **82**
Amisfield St. G20: Glas 4C **62**
Amochrie Dr. PA2: Pais 5E **97**
Amochrie Glen PA2: Pais 5E **97**
Amochrie Rd. PA2: Pais 4D **96**
Amochrie Way *PA2: Pais* *4D* ***96***
(off Amochrie Rd.)
Amulree Pl. G32: Glas 1A **106**
Amulree St. G32: Glas 2A **106**
Ancaster Dr. G13: Glas 3F **61**
Ancaster La. G13: Glas 3F **61**
Anchor Av. PA1: Pais 1C **98**
Anchor Bldgs. PA1: Pais 1B **98**
Anchor Cres. PA1: Pais 2C **98**
Anchor Dr. PA1: Pais 1C **98**
Anchor La. G2: Glas 4G **83** (5E **5**)
ANCHOR MILLS 1C **98**
Anchor Wynd PA1: Pais 2C **98**
Ancroft St. G20: Glas 6E **63**
Andersen Ct. G75: E Kil 5G **149**
Anderside G75: E Kil 6G **149**
Anderson Av. G65: Kils 2F **11**
Anderson Ct. G77: Newt M 5C **132**
ML4: Bell 2D **126**
Anderson Cres. G65: Queen 3C **10**
Anderson Dr. G77: Newt M 5C **132**
PA4: Renf 5F **59**
Anderson Gdns. G72: Blan 6C **124**
Anderson La. ML6: Air 3A **92**
Anderson Rd. PA7: B'ton 3G **39**
Anderson St. G11: Glas 1H **81**
ML1: Moth 4G **143**
ML3: Ham 4D **140**
ML6: Air 3A **92**
Anderson Twr. ML1: Moth 3G **143**
ANDERSTON 4D **82**
ANDERSTON CROSS INTERCHANGE 5A **4**
Anderston Cross Shop. Cen.
G2: Glas 4E **83** (5A **4**)
Anderston Quay G3: Glas 5D **82** (6A **4**)
Anderston Station (Rail) 4E **83** (5A **4**)
Andrew Av. G66: Lenz 4D **50**
PA4: Renf 6G **59**
Andrew Dr. G81: Clyd 1E **59**
Andrew Pl. ML8: Carl 2E **165**
Andrew Sillars Av. G72: Camb 2B **122**
Andrews St. PA3: Pais 5A **78**
Andrew St. G74: E Kil 2H **149**
Anford Pl. G72: Blan 2C **140**
Angela Way G71: Udd 1D **124**
Angle Ga. G14: Glas 5D **60**
Angus Av. G52: Glas 2C **100**
G64: B'rig 1E **65**
G74: E Kil 1B **150**
ML1: Moth 1E **143**
ML3: Ham 6C **142**
ML6: Air 6A **92**
Angus Gdns. G71: Tann 5D **108**
Angus Oval G52: Glas 1B **100**
Angus Pl. G52: Glas 1B **100**
G74: E Kil 1B **150**
Angus Rd. ML8: Carl 4G **165**
Angus St. G21: Glas 5A **64**
G81: Clyd 1G **59**
Angus Wlk. G71: View 6F **109**
Anish Pl. G15: Glas 3G **43**
Annan Av. G75: E Kil 4A **148**
Annan Ct. ML5: Coat 5B **90**
Annan Cres. ML6: Chap 4D **112**
Annandale St. G42: Glas 2F **103**
Annan Dr. G61: Bear 4C **44**
G73: Ruth 6F **105**
Annan Glade ML1: Moth 6A **144**
Annan Gro. ML1: Moth 6A **144**
Annan Ho. *G67: Cumb* *4H* ***35***
(in Cumbernauld Shop. Cen.)
Annan Pl. PA5: John 5C **94**
Annan St. G42: Glas 5E **103**
ML1: Moth 6A **144**
Annan Way *G67: Cumb* *4H* ***35***
(in Cumbernauld Shop. Cen.)
ANNATHILL 5B **54**
Annathill Gdns. ML5: Anna 5B **54**
Annbank St. G31: Glas 5B **84**
ML9: Lark 2D **160**
Ann Ct. ML3: Ham 4E **141**
Anne Av. PA4: Renf 5F **59**
Anne Cres. G66: Lenz 4D **50**
Annerley Ct. ML5: Coat 6A **90**
Annerley Pl. ML5: Coat 6A **90**
Anne's M. ML3: Ham 6B **142**
Annette St. G42: Glas 3E **103**
Annfield Gdns. G72: Blan 6A **124**
Annfield Pl. G31: Glas 4B **84**
Annick Dr. G61: Bear 4C **44**
Annick St. G32: Glas 6B **86**
G72: Camb 2D **122**
Anniesdale Av. G33: Step 3D **66**
Annieshill Vw. ML6: Plain 1G **93**
ANNIESLAND 3F **61**
Anniesland Cres. G14: Glas 4A **60**
Anniesland Ind. Est. G13: Glas 1E **61**
Anniesland Rd. G13: Glas 3C **60**
G14: Glas 4A **60**
Anniesland Station (Rail) 3F **61**
Annieston G65: Twe 1D **32**
Anniversary Av. G75: E Kil 4E **149**
Annsfield Rd. ML3: Ham 4G **153**
Ann St. ML3: Ham 4E **141**
PA5: John 2G **95**
Ansdell Av. G72: Blan 2A **140**
Anson St. G40: Glas 1B **104**
Anson Way PA4: Renf 2E **79**
Anstruther Ct. ML8: Law 6D **158**
Anstruther St. G32: Glas 6H **85**
ML8: Law 6D **158**
Antermony Rd. G66: Milt C 5C **8**
Anthony Ct. G81: Clyd 1E **59**
Anthony St. G2: Glas 4E **83** (5A **4**)
Antigua Way G75: E Kil 2C **148**
Anton Cres. G65: Kils 3A **12**
Antonine G66: Kirk 3H **31**
Antonine Av. ML1: Moth 1E **143**
Antonine Gdns. G81: Dun 1C **42**
Antonine Rd. G61: Bear 1B **44**
G68: Dull 5E **13**
Antonine Sports Cen. 1C **42**
Antrim La. ML9: Lark 1F **161**
Anwoth St. G32: Glas 2A **106**
Apartments, The *G46: Giff* *6H* ***117***
(off Milverton Rd.)
Apollo Path ML1: Holy 2B **128**
Appin Ct. G66: Kirk 4H **31**
Appin Cres. G31: Glas 4D **84**
Appin Rd. G31: Glas 4D **84**
Appin Ter. G73: Ruth 3F **121**
ML3: Ham 5C **140**
Appin Way G71: Both 4E **125**
ML5: Coat 1A **110**
ML6: Glenm 5H **71**
Appleby Cl. G75: E Kil 5B **148**
Appleby St. G22: Glas 6F **63**
Applecross Gdns. G69: Mood 4D **52**
Applecross Quad. ML2: Wis 4H **145**
Applecross Rd. G66: Kirk 4H **31**
Applecross St. G4: Glas 6F **63**
Appledore Cres. G71: Both 4E **125**
Appleyard Ct. ML4: Bell 4B **126**
Apsley La. G11: Glas 1G **81**
Apsley St. G11: Glas 1G **81**
Aqua Av. ML3: Ham 1C **152**
Aqua Ct. ML3: Ham 1C **152**
Aquatec Leisure Cen. 2G **143**
Aquila Way ML8: Carl 3D **164**
Araburn Dr. G75: E Kil 6G **149**
Aranthrue Cres. PA4: Renf 5E **59**
Aranthrue Dr. PA4: Renf 5E **59**
Aray St. G20: Glas 3B **62**
Arbroath Av. G52: Glas 1B **100**
Arbroath Gro. ML3: Ham 1F **153**
Arbuckle Pl. ML6: Plain 1G **93**
Arbuckle Rd. ML6: Plain 1H **93**
Arcadia St. G40: Glas 6A **84**
ML4: Bell 6C **110**
Arcan Cres. G15: Glas 5B **44**
Archerfield Av. G32: Glas 3A **106**
Archerfield Cres. G32: Glas 3A **106**

Archerfield Dr. G32: Glas 3A **106**	Ardnish St. G51: Glas 4E **81**	Arnbrae Rd. G65: Kils 2F **11**
Archerfield Gro. G32: Glas 3A **106**	Ardoch Cres. G82: Dumb 3D **16**	Arngask Rd. G51: Glas 4E **81**
Archerhill Av. G13: Glas 1A **60**	Ardoch Gdns. G72: Camb 1H **121**	Arnhall Pl. G52: Glas 2E **101**
Archerhill Cotts. G13: Glas 1A **60**	Ardoch Gro. G72: Camb 1H **121**	Arnhem St. G72: Camb. 2D **122**
Archerhill Cres. G13: Glas 1B **60**	Ardoch Path ML2: Newm . . . . . _3D **146**_	Arnholm Pl. G52: Glas. 2E **101**
Archerhill Gdns. G13: Glas 1A **60**	_(off Tiree Cres.)_	Arnisdale Pl. G34: Glas 3G **87**
Archerhill Rd. G13: Glas. 1H **59**	Ardochrig G75: E Kil 6H **149**	Arnisdale Rd. G34: Glas 3G **87**
Archerhill Sq. G13: Glas. 1H **59**	Ardoch Rd. G61: Bear. 2H **45**	Arnisdale Way G73: Ruth 3D **120**
Archerhill Ter. G13: Glas. 1A **60**	Ardoch St. G22: Glas. 5F **63**	Arnish PA8: Ersk. 2G **57**
(not continuous)	Ardoch Way G69: Mood 5D **52**	Arniston St. G32: Glas 4H **85**
Arches Theatre 4F **83** (6C **4**)	Ardo Gdns. G51: Glas 6G **81**	Arniston Way PA3: Pais 4C **78**
Archibald Ter. G66: Milt C. 5B **8**	Ardressie Pl. G20: Glas 4B **62**	Arnold Av. G64: B'rig 6C **48**
Archiebald Rd. ML4: Bell . . . 3F **127**	Ard Rd. PA4: Renf 5D **58**	Arnol Pl. G33: Glas 3D **86**
Arch Way G65: Kils. 2H **11**	Ardshiel Rd. G51: Glas 4E **81**	Arnott Dr. ML5: Coat. 1C **110**
Ardargie Dr. G32: Carm 5C **106**	Ardsloy La. G14: Glas 5A **60**	Arnott Quad. ML1: Moth 6E **127**
Ardargie Gro. G32: Carm 5C **106**	Ardsloy Pl. G14: Glas. 5A **60**	Arnott Way G72: Camb. 1A **122**
Ardargie Pl. G32: Carm 5C **106**	Ard St. G32: Glas 1A **106**	Arnprior Cres. G45: Glas. 4H **119**
Ardbeg Av. G64: B'rig 6E **49**	Ardtoe Cres. G33: Step. 4E **67**	Arnprior Gdns. G69: Mood 5D **52**
G73: Ruth 4G **121**	Ardtoe Pl. G33: Step. 4E **67**	Arnprior Quad. G45: Glas 3H **119**
Ardbeg Rd. ML1: Carf 5B **128**	Arduthie Rd. G51: Glas 4E **81**	Arnprior Rd. G45: Glas 3H **119**
Ardbeg St. G42: Glas 3E **103**	Ardwell Rd. G52: Glas. 2E **101**	Arnprior St. G45: Glas 3H **119**
Ardconnel St. G46: T'bnk 3F **117**	Argosy Way PA4: Renf 2E **79**	Arnside Av. G46: Giff 4A **118**
ARDEN 3D **116**	Argus Av. ML6: Chap 3C **112**	Arnum Gdns. ML8: Carl. 4F **165**
Arden Av. G46: T'bnk 5E **117**	Argyle Av. PA3: Glas A 2A **78**	Arnum Pl. ML8: Carl 4F **165**
Ardenclutha Av. ML3: Ham 5F **141**	Argyle Cres. ML3: Ham 6D **140**	Arnwood Dr. G12: Glas 4G **61**
Arden Ct. ML3: Ham 2H **153**	ML6: Air 1H **111**	Aron Ter. G72: Camb 4H **121**
ML6: Air 3F **91**	Argyle Dr. ML3: Ham 5E **141**	Aros Dr. G52: Glas 2D **100**
(off Monkscourt Av.)	Argyle Gdns. G66: Len 4G **7**	Aros La. G52: Glas 3D **100**
Ardencraig Gdns. G45: Glas . . 6G **119**	Argyle Rd. G61: Bear 6E **25**	Arran Av. G82: Dumb 2D **16**
Ardencraig Dr. G45: Glas . . . 5B **120**	Argyle St. G1: Glas 4G **83** (6E **5**)	ML5: Coat 1F **111**
Ardencraig Pl. G45: Glas . . . 4A **120**	G2: Glas 4E **83** (6A **4**)	PA3: Glas A 1A **78**
Ardencraig Quad. G45: Glas . . 5B **120**	G3: Glas 2B **82**	_(not continuous)_
Ardencraig Rd. G45: Glas. . . . 6G **119**	PA1: Pais 1H **97**	Arran Dr. G46: Giff 5A **118**
Ardencraig St. G45: Glas . . . 4C **120**	Argyle Street Station (Rail)	G52: Glas 2F **101**
Ardencraig Ter. G45: Glas . . . 5B **120**	. . . . 5G **83** (6E **5**)	G66: Kirk. 3E **31**
Ardencraig Workspace G45: Glas. . 5C **120**	Argyll Arc. G1: Glas. 4G **83** (6D **4**)	G67: Cumb 5F **35**
Arden Dr. G46: Giff. 5H **117**	Argyll Av. G82: Dumb 1C **18**	ML6: Air 2H **91**
Arden Gro. G65: Kils. 1G **11**	PA4: Renf 5D **58**	ML6: Glenm 4H **71**
Ardenlea G71: Tann 6D **108**	Argyll Gdns. ML9: Lark 2F **161**	PA2: Pais 6A **98**
Ardenlea St. G40: Glas 2D **104**	Argyll Pl. G65: Kils. 3A **12**	PA5: John 4D **94**
Arden Pl. G46: T'bnk 5E **117**	G74: E Kil 6C **138**	Arran Gdns. ML3: Ham 2A **154**
Arden Rd. ML3: Ham 1G **153**	G82: Dumb 1C **18**	ML8: Carl 5F **165**
ML6: Plain 1G **93**	ML4: Bell 5B **126**	Arran La. G69: Mood 5E **53**
Arden Ter. ML3: Ham 1G **153**	Arisaig Dr. G52: Glas 2D **100**	Arran Path ML9: Lark . . . . _4G **161**_
Ardery St. G11: Glas. 1G **81**	G61: Bear 4H **45**	_(off Stuart Dr.)_
Ardessie St. G23: Glas 6B **46**	Arisaig Pl. G52: Glas 2E **101**	Arran Pl. G81: Clyd. 5E **43**
Ardfern Rd. ML6: Air. 5F **93**	Arisdale Cres. G77: Newt M . . 3E **133**	ML5: Coat 1F **111**
Ardfern St. G32: Glas 2A **106**	Arkaig Av. ML6: Plain 1F **93**	G75 . . . . 5G **75**
Ardgay Pl. G32: Glas 1A **106**	Arkaig Pl. G77: Newt M 5H **133**	Arran Rd. ML1: Moth 2E **143**
Ardgay St. G32: Glas 1A **106**	Arkaig St. ML2: Wis 2H **157**	PA4: Renf 1F **79**
Ardgay Way G73: Ruth 4D **120**	Ark La. G31: Glas 4B **84**	Arran Twr. G72: Camb 4G **121**
Ardgoil Dr. G68: Cumb 4B **34**	ARKLESTON 3E **79**	Arran Vw. G65: Kils 3H **11**
Ardgour Ct. G72: Blan. 3D **140**	Arkleston Ct. PA3: Pais. 3D **78**	Arranview St. ML6: Chap 4E **113**
Ardgour Dr. PA3: Lin. 6G **75**	Arkleston Cres. PA3: Pais. 4D **78**	Arran Way G71: Both 5D **124**
Ardgour Pde. ML1: Carf 6C **128**	ARKLESTON INTERCHANGE . . 3C **78**	G73: Ruth 2B **120**
Ardgowan Av. PA2: Pais 2B **98**	Arkleston Rd. PA1: Pais 5D **78**	Arrochar Ct. G23: Glas 1B **62**
Ardgowan Ct. PA2: Pais 2D **98**	PA4: Renf 3C **78**	Arrochar Dr. G23: Glas 6B **46**
Ardgowan Dr. G71: Tann. 6D **108**	Arkle Ter. G72: Camb 4G **121**	Arrochar Path G23: Glas . . . . _6B **46**_
Ardgowan St. PA2: Pais 3B **98**	Arklet Rd. G51: Glas 5E **81**	_(off Arrochar Rd.)_
Ardgowan Ter. La. G3: Glas . . . _2B **82**_	Arklet Way ML2: Wis 6C **146**	Arrochar St. G23: Glas 6B **46**
(off Radnor St.)	Arkwrights Way PA1: Pais 2F **97**	Arrol Pl. G40: Glas 1D **104**
Ardgryfe Cres. PA6: Hous. . . . 1D **74**	Arlington Baths Club. 1D **82**	Arrol St. G52: Hill. 4G **79**
Ardholm St. G32: Glas 6A **86**	Arlington St. G3: Glas. 2D **82**	_(not continuous)_
Ardhu Pl. G15: Glas 3A **44**	Armadale Ct. G31: Glas 3C **84**	Arrotshole Ct. G74: E Kil. . . . 6D **136**
Ardlamont Sq. PA3: Lin 6A **76**	Armadale Path G31: Glas 3C **84**	Arrotshole Rd. G74: E Kil 1D **148**
Ard La. ML2: Newm . . . . _3D **146**_	Armadale Pl. G31: Glas. 3C **84**	Arrowsmith Av. G13: Glas. . . . 1D **60**
(off Clunie Pl.)	Armadale St. G31: Glas 4C **84**	Arthur Av. G78: Barr 6D **114**
Ardlaw St. G51: Glas. 5F **81**	Armine Path ML1: N'hill 3C **128**	ML6: Air 5H **91**
Ardle Rd. G43: Glas 2C **118**	Armour Av. ML6: Air. 4G **91**	ARTHURLIE 6D **114**
Ard Loan ML1: Holy . . . . _2A **128**_	Armour Ct. G66: Kirk 4G **31**	Arthurlie Av. G78: Barr 5E **115**
(off Howden Pl.)	G72: Blan 3H **139**	G77: Newt M. 6D **132**
Ardlui Gdns. G62: Miln. 2D **24**	Armour Dr. G66: Kirk 4G **31**	Arthurlie Dr. G46: Giff 5A **118**
Ardlui St. G32: Glas 1H **105**	Armour Gdns. G66: Kirk 4G **31**	G77: Newt M. 6D **132**
Ardmaleish Cres. G45: Glas . . 5A **120**	Armour Gro. ML1: Moth 5A **144**	Arthurlie Gdns. G78: Barr . . . 5E **115**
Ardmaleish Dr. G45: Glas . . . 5H **119**	Armour Pl. G66: Kirk 4G **31**	Arthurlie St. G51: Glas 4F **81**
Ardmaleish Rd. G45: Glas . . . 5H **119**	ML1: N'hill 3C **128**	G78: Barr 5E **115**
Ardmay Cres. G44: Glas 6G **103**	PA3: Lin 6A **76**	Arthur Pl. G76: Busby 3C **134**
Ardmillan St. G33: Glas 3H **85**	PA5: John 2G **95**	Arthur Rd. PA2: Pais 5A **98**
Ardmory Av. G42: Glas 6H **103**	Armour Sq. PA5: John 2G **95**	Arthur St. G3: Glas 2B **82**
Ardmory La. G42: Glas 6A **104**	Armour St. G4: Glas 5A **84**	G76: Busby 3C **134**
Ardmory Pl. G42: Glas 6A **104**	PA5: John 2G **95**	ML3: Ham. 4H **141**
Ardnahoe Av. G42: Glas 5H **103**	Armstrong Cres. G71: Tann . . 5E **109**	PA1: Pais 6G **77**
Ardnahoe Pl. G42: Glas 5H **103**	Armstrong Gro. G75: E Kil 4F **149**	Arundel Dr. G42: Glas 6E **103**
Ardneil Rd. G51: Glas 5F **81**		G64: B'rig 3D **48**

Ascaig Cres. G52: Glas 3E **101**
Ascog Rd. G61: Bear 5F **45**
Ascog St. G42: Glas 3E **103**
Ascot Av. G12: Glas 3F **61**
Ascot Ct. G12: Glas 3G **61**
Ash Av. G75: E Kil 5E **149**
Ashbank Cres. ML6: Chap 2E **113**
Ashburn Gdns. G62: Miln 4E **25**
Ashburn Loan ML9: Lark 1F **161**
Ashburn Rd. G62: Miln 3E **25**
Ashburton La. *G12: Glas 3H 61*
  (off Ashburton Rd.)
Ashburton Pk. G75: E Kil 4C **148**
Ashburton Rd. G12: Glas 3H **61**
Ashbury Ct. *PA3: Lin 6H 75*
  (off Melrose Av.)
Ashby Cres. G13: Glas 6E **45**
Ash Ct. G75: E Kil 5E **149**
Ashcroft G74: E Kil 4D **138**
Ashcroft Av. G66: Lenz 4G **7**
Ashcroft Dr. G44: Glas 1A **120**
Ashcroft Wlk. G66: Len 4G **7**
Ashdale Dr. G22: Glas 2E **101**
Ashdene St. G22: Glas 2F **63**
Asher Rd. ML6: Chap 3E **113**
Ashfield G64: B'rig 4C **48**
Ashfield Rd. G62: Miln 4G **25**
  G76: Clar 3C **134**
  ML8: Law 5D **158**
Ashfield Station (Rail) 4G **63**
Ashfield St. G22: Glas 5G **63**
  (not continuous)
ASHGILL 4B **162**
ASHGILLHEAD 4A **162**
Ashgillhead Rd. ML9: Shaw 4A **162**
Ashgill Pl. G22: Glas 3G **63**
Ashgill Rd. G22: Glas 2F **63**
Ash Gro. G64: B'rig 1D **64**
  G66: Lenz 2B **50**
Ashgrove G69: Mood 6D **52**
Ash Gro. G71: View 5F **109**
Ashgrove ML5: Coat 1C **110**
  ML6: Air 4D **92**
Ash Gro. ML8: Law 5D **158**
Ashgrove Rd. ML4: Bell 6D **110**
Ashgrove St. G40: Glas 3C **104**
Ashiestiel Ct. G67: Cumb 6G **35**
Ashiestiel Pl. G67: Cumb 6G **35**
Ashiestiel Rd. G67: Cumb 6G **35**
Ashkirk Dr. G52: Glas 2E **101**
  ML9: Ashg 5B **162**
Ashland Av. ML3: Ham 5H **153**
Ashlea Dr. G46: Giff 3B **118**
Ashlea Gdns. ML6: Plain 1F **93**
Ashley Dr. G71: Both 2F **125**
Ashley La. G3: Glas 1A **4**
Ashley Pk. G71: View 1G **125**
Ashley Pl. G72: Blan 1A **140**
Ashley St. G3: Glas 2D **82** (1A **4**)
Ashmore Rd. G43: Glas 2D **118**
  G44: Glas 2D **118**
Ash Pl. FK4: Bank 1E **15**
  G75: E Kil 5E **149**
  PA5: John 4G **95**
Ash Rd. G67: Cumb 6D **14**
  (not continuous)
  G69: Bail 2G **107**
  G81: Clyd 2B **42**
  G82: Dumb 3F **17**
Ashton Gdns. G69: G'csh 3E **69**
Ashton Grn. G74: E Kil 1G **149**
Ashton La. G12: Glas 6B **62**
  (not continuous)
Ashton La. Nth. G12: Glas 1B **82**
Ashton Rd. G12: Glas 1B **82**
  G73: Ruth 4C **104**
Ashton St. ML1: Moth 5F **127**
Ashton Vw. G82: Dumb 3B **16**
Ashton Way PA2: Pais 5C **96**
Ashtree Ct. G60: Old K 1F **41**
Ashtree Gro. G77: Newt M 6C **132**
Ashtree Pk. ML2: Wis 6E **145**
Ashtree Rd. G43: Glas 5A **102**
Ashvale Cres. G21: Glas 5A **64**

Ash Wlk. G73: Ruth 4E **121**
  ML1: Holy 2B **128**
Ashwood ML2: Wis 2E **157**
Ashworth Ter. ML3: Ham 5H **141**
Ash Wynd G72: Flem 3E **123**
Aspen Dr. G21: Glas 6C **64**
Aspen Pl. G72: Flem 2E **123**
  PA5: John 4G **95**
Aspen Way ML3: Ham 1A **154**
Asquith Pl. ML4: Bell 2F **127**
Aster Dr. G45: Glas 4C **120**
Aster Gdns. G53: Glas 4C **116**
  ML1: Moth 4G **143**
Athelstane Dr. G67: Cumb 6F **35**
Athelstane Rd. G13: Glas 2C **60**
Athena Way G71: Tann 6E **109**
Athole Av. G52: Hill 3G **79**
Athole Gdns. G12: Glas 6A **62**
Athole La. G12: Glas 6A **62**
Atholl Av. G52: Hill 3G **79**
  (not continuous)
  G64: Torr 4D **28**
Atholl Ct. G66: Kirk 4H **31**
  G72: Blan 3D **140**
Atholl Cres. PA1: Pais 5G **79**
Atholl Dr. G46: Giff 1A **134**
  G68: Cumb 5B **34**
Atholl Gdns. G61: Bear 6E **25**
  G64: B'rig 4B **48**
  G73: Ruth 3G **121**
Atholl La. G69: Mood 5E **53**
Atholl Pl. ML5: Coat 2D **110**
  PA3: Lin 5G **75**
Atholl St. ML3: Ham 3F **141**
Atholl Ter. G71: Tann 4D **108**
Atlas Ind. Est. G21: Glas 5B **64**
Atlas Pl. G21: Glas 5B **64**
Atlas Rd. G21: Glas 5A **64**
Atlas Sq. G21: Glas 5B **64**
Atlas St. G81: Clyd 1D **58**
Atlin Dr. ML1: New S 4B **128**
Attercliffe Av. ML2: Wis 1C **156**
Attlee Av. G81: Clyd 6F **43**
Attlee Pl. *G81: Clyd 6F 43*
  (off Attlee Av.)
Attow Rd. G43: Glas 2H **117**
Auburn Dr. G78: Barr 6F **115**
Auchans Rd. PA6: Hous 3F **75**
AUCHENBACK 6F **115**
Auchenbothie Cres. G33: Glas . . 3G **65**
Auchenbothie Pl. G33: Glas 4F **65**
Auchencrow St. G34: Glas 3B **88**
Auchencruive G62: Miln 5A **26**
Auchendavie Rd. G66: Kirk 3H **31**
Auchengeich Rd. G69: Mood 3B **52**
Auchengilloch G75: E Kil 6G **149**
Auchengleich Gdns. G69: Mood . . 5D **52**
Auchenglen Dr. G69: Mood 5D **52**
Auchengreoch Av. PA5: John . . . 5D **94**
Auchengreoch Rd. PA5: John . . . 5D **94**
Auchenhowie G62: Miln 5A **26**
Auchenhowie Rd.
  G62: Bard, Miln 5H **25**
Auchenkilns Rd. G67: Cumb 1F **55**
AUCHENKILNS RDBT. 4E **35**
Auchenlodment Rd. PA5: John . . 3G **95**
AUCHENREOCH 5H **9**
Auchenreoch Av. G82: Dumb . . . 1H **17**
Auchenstewart Ct. ML2: Wis . . . 6A **146**
AUCHENTIBBER 6F **139**
Auchentibber Rd. G72: Blan 6F **139**
AUCHENTORLIE 2D **98**
Auchentorlie Quad. PA1: Pais . . . 1D **98**
Auchentorlie St. G11: Glas 1F **81**
Auchentoshan Av. G81: Dun 1B **42**
Auchentoshan Est. G81: Clyd . . . 1A **42**
Auchentoshan Ter. G21: Glas . . . 1B **84**
AUCHINAIRN 1D **64**
Auchinairn Rd. G64: B'rig 1F **65**
Auchinbee Farm Rd.
  G68: Cumb 1D **34**
Auchinbee Way G68: Cumb 2D **34**
Auchincampbell Rd.
  ML3: Ham 6H **141**
Auchincloch Dr. FK4: Bank 1F **15**

Auchineden Ct. G61: Bear 6C **24**
Auchingill Path *G34: Glas 2B 88*
  (off Auchingill Pl.)
Auchingill Pl. G34: Glas 2B **88**
Auchingill Rd. G34: Glas 2A **88**
  (not continuous)
Auchingramont Ct. ML3: Ham . . . 6H **141**
Auchingramont Rd. ML3: Ham . . . 5H **141**
Auchinlea Retail Pk. G34: Glas . . 3F **87**
Auchinlea Rd. G34: Glas 1F **87**
Auchinleck Av. G33: Glas 3G **65**
Auchinleck Cres. G33: Glas 3G **65**
Auchinleck Dr. G33: Glas 3G **65**
Auchinleck Gdns. G33: Glas 3G **65**
Auchinleck Rd. G33: Glas 2H **65**
  G81: Hard 6D **22**
Auchinleck Ter. G81: Hard 6D **22**
AUCHINLOCH
  Banknock 1C **14**
  Lenzie 5D **50**
Auchinloch Rd. G66: Lenz 3D **50**
Auchinloch St. G21: Glas 6B **64**
AUCHINRAITH 3C **140**
Auchinraith Av. ML3: Ham 3F **141**
Auchinraith Rd. G72: Blan 3B **140**
Auchinraith Ter. G72: Blan 3C **140**
  (not continuous)
AUCHINSTARRY 5A **12**
Auchintibber Ct. G72: Blan 4C **140**
Auchinvole Castle 5G **11**
Auchinvole Cres. G65: Kils 3F **11**
Auchmannoch Av. PA1: Pais 6G **79**
Auchnacraig Rd. G81: Faif, Hard . . 5E **23**
Auchter Av. ML2: Newm 4G **147**
Auchter Rd. ML2: Wis 5C **146**
Auckland Pk. G75: E Kil 3C **148**
Auckland Pl. G81: Clyd 3H **41**
Auckland St. G22: Glas 6F **63**
Auldbar Rd. G52: Glas 2F **101**
Auldbar Ter. PA2: Pais 3C **98**
Auldburn Pl. G43: Glas 1H **117**
Auldburn Rd. G43: Glas 1H **117**
Auldearn Rd. G21: Glas 2E **65**
Auldgirth Rd. G52: Glas 2F **101**
Auldhame St. ML5: Coat 3A **90**
Auldhouse Av. G43: Glas 1H **117**
Auldhouse Ct. G43: Glas 1H **117**
Auldhouse Gdns. G43: Glas 1H **117**
Auldhouse Retail Pk.
  G43: Glas 6A **102**
Auldhouse Rd. G43: Glas 1H **117**
  G75: E Kil 6F **149**
Auldhouse Ter. G43: Glas 1B **118**
Auld Kirk Mus. 4C **30**
Auld Kirk Rd. G72: Camb 4C **122**
Auldkirk, The G76: Busby 4E **135**
Auldmurroch Dr. G62: Miln 3D **24**
Auld Rd., The G67: Cumb 1A **36**
Auld's Brae ML6: Air 3A **92**
Auld St. G81: Clyd 4A **42**
Auldton Ter. ML9: Ashg 4B **162**
Aultbea St. G22: Glas 1F **63**
Aultmore Rd. G33: Glas 4F **87**
Aursbridge Cres. G78: Barr 5F **115**
Aursbridge Dr. G78: Barr 5F **115**
Aurs Cres. G78: Barr 5F **115**
Aurs Dr. G78: Barr 6F **115**
Aurs Glen G78: Barr 6E **115**
Aurs Pl. G78: Barr 5G **115**
Aurs Rd. G78: Barr 4F **115**
Austen La. G13: Glas 4E **61**
Austen Rd. G13: Glas 4E **61**
Austine Dr. ML3: Ham 4A **154**
Avenel Rd. G13: Glas 6E **45**
Avenue End Rd. G33: Glas 5B **66**
Avenuehead Rd. G69: Mood 6D **52**
Avenuepark St. G20: Glas 5C **62**
Avenue St. G40: Glas 6C **84**
  G73: Ruth 4D **104**
Avenue, The (Shop. Cen.)
  G77: Newt M 5D **132**
Aviemore Gdns. G61: Bear 2H **45**
Aviemore Rd. G52: Glas 3E **101**
Avoch St. G34: Glas 2H **87**

Avon Av. G61: Bear . . . 4H **45**
ML8: Carl . . . 3E **165**
Avonbank Cres. ML3: Ham . . . 3A **154**
Avonbank Rd. G73: Ruth . . . 6B **104**
ML9: Lark . . . 2C **160**
Avonbrae Cres. ML3: Ham . . . 3A **154**
Avon Bri. ML3: Ham . . . 1C **154**
Avonbridge Dr. ML3: Ham . . . 6B **142**
Avondale Av. G74: E Kil . . . 2H **149**
Avondale Dr. PA1: Pais . . . 5D **78**
Avondale Pl. G74: E Kil . . . 3A **150**
Avondale St. G33: Glas . . . 2A **86**
Avon Dr. ML4: Bell . . . 3E **127**
PA3: Lin . . . 5H **75**
Avonhead G75: E Kil . . . 6G **149**
Avonhead Av. G67: Cumb . . . 6E **35**
Avonhead Gdns. G67: Cumb . . . 6E **35**
Avonhead Pl. G67: Cumb . . . 6E **35**
Avonhead Rd. G67: Cumb . . . 6E **35**
Avon Ho. ML3: Ham . . . 4A **142**
Avon Pl. ML5: Coat . . . 2H **89**
ML9: Lark . . . 6F **161**
Avon Rd. G46: Giff . . . 5H **117**
G64: B'rig . . . 1C **64**
ML9: Lark . . . 5E **161**
Avonside Gro. ML3: Ham . . . 6B **142**
Avonspark St. G21: Glas . . . 6C **64**
Avon St. ML1: Moth . . . 4F **143**
ML3: Ham . . . 6A **142**
ML9: Lark . . . 2D **160**
Avon Twr. ML1: Moth . . . 4G **143**
Avon Wlk. *G67: Cumb . . . 3H* ***35***
(in Cumbernauld Shop. Cen.)
Avon Wynd ML2: Newm . . . 3D **146**
Aylmer Rd. G43: Glas . . . 1D **118**
Ayr Dr. ML6: Air . . . 6A **92**
Ayr Rd. G46: Giff . . . 2G **133**
G77: Newt M . . . 6A **132**
ML9: Lark, Shaw . . . 6H **161**
Ayr St. G21: Glas . . . 5B **64**
Ayton Pk. Nth. G74: E Kil . . . 6B **138**
Ayton Pk. Sth. G74: E Kil . . . 6B **138**
Aytoun Dr. PA8: Ersk . . . 4D **40**
Aytoun Rd. G41: Glas . . . 1B **102**
Azalea Gdns. G72: Flem . . . 2E **123**

B

Babylon Av. ML4: Bell . . . 4C **126**
Babylon Dr. ML4: Bell . . . 4C **126**
Babylon Pl. ML4: Bell . . . 5C **126**
Babylon Rd. ML4: Bell . . . 4C **126**
Backbrae St. G65: Kils . . . 3H **11**
(not continuous)
Back Causeway G31: Glas . . . 6F **85**
Backmuir Cres. ML3: Ham . . . 3F **141**
Backmuir Pl. ML3: Ham . . . 3F **141**
Backmuir Rd. G15: Glas . . . 3B **44**
ML3: Ham . . . 3F **141**
Bk. o'Barns ML3: Ham . . . 5A **142**
Bk. o'Dykes Rd. G66: Kirk . . . 6H **31**
Back o' Hill PA6: C'lee . . . 2B **74**
Back o' Hill Rd. G64: Balm, Torr . . . 3H **27**
BACK O'HILL RDBT. . . . **4D 34**
Back Row ML3: Ham . . . 5A **142**
Bk. Sneddon St. PA3: Pais . . . 6A **78**
Badenheath Pl. G68: Cumb . . . 2H **53**
Badenheath Ter. G67: Mollin . . . 3H **53**
Badenoch Rd. G66: Kirk . . . 4H **31**
Bagnell St. G21: Glas . . . 4B **64**
Bahamas Way G75: E Kil . . . 2C **148**
Bailie Dr. G61: Bear . . . 6D **24**
Bailie Fyfeway ML2: Over . . . 4H **157**
Baillie Dr. G71: Both . . . 4E **125**
G74: E Kil . . . 5B **138**
Baillie Gdns. ML2: Wis . . . 5C **146**
Baillie Pl. G74: E Kil . . . 5C **138**
Baillies La. ML6: Air . . . 4A **92**
Bailliesmuir Pl. ML2: Newm . . . 3E **147**
BAILLIESTON . . . **6A 88**
Baillieston Rd. G32: Glas . . . 1D **106**
G71: Udd . . . 2H **107**
Baillieston Station (Rail) . . . **2H 107**
Baillie Wynd G71: Tann . . . 5E **109**
Bainsford St. G32: Glas . . . 5H **85**
Bain St. G40: Glas . . . 5A **84**
Baird Av. G52: Hill . . . 3G **79**
ML6: Air . . . 1B **92**
ML9: Lark . . . 5F **161**
Baird Brae G4: Glas . . . 6F **63**
Baird Ct. G81: Clyd . . . 5C **42**
Baird Cres. G67: Cumb . . . 6D **34**
(not continuous)
Baird Dr. G61: Bear . . . 2D **44**
PA8: Ersk . . . 4D **40**
Baird Hill G75: E Kil . . . 3F **149**
Baird Pl. ML2: Wis . . . 5C **146**
ML4: Bell . . . 6C **110**
Bairds Av. G71: View . . . 1F **125**
Bairds Cres. ML3: Ham . . . 6G **141**
Bairdsland Vw. ML4: Bell . . . 2D **126**
Baird St. G4: Glas . . . 2H **83** (2G **5**)
ML5: Coat . . . 4C **90**
Baker St. G41: Glas . . . 4C **102**
Bakewell Rd. G69: Bail . . . 6G **87**
Balaclava St. G3: Glas . . . 4E **83** (6A **4**)
Balado Rd. G33: Glas . . . 4E **87**
Balbeggie St. G32: Glas . . . 1C **106**
Balbeg St. G51: Glas . . . 5E **81**
Balblair Rd. G52: Glas . . . 3F **101**
Balcarres Av. G12: Glas . . . 4A **62**
Balcary Pl. ML6: Chap . . . 4E **113**
Balcastle Gdns. G65: Kils . . . 1F **11**
Balcastle Rd. G65: Kils . . . 2E **11**
Balcomie St. G33: Glas . . . 2A **86**
Balcomie Ter. ML3: Ham . . . 3F **153**
Balcurvie Rd. G34: Glas . . . 1G **87**
BALDERNOCK . . . **3D 26**
Baldernock Rd. G62: Balder, Miln . . . 4H **25**
Baldinnie Rd. G34: Glas . . . 3H **87**
Baldoran Dr. G66: Milt C . . . 5B **8**
Baldorran Cres. G68: Cumb . . . 2D **34**
Baldovan Cres. G33: Glas . . . 3F **87**
Baldovan Path G33: Glas . . . 4F **87**
Baldovie Rd. G52: Glas . . . 1C **100**
Baldragon Rd. G34: Glas . . . 2H **87**
Baldric Rd. G13: Glas . . . 3C **60**
Baldwin Av. G13: Glas . . . 2D **60**
Balerno Dr. G52: Glas . . . 2E **101**
Balfleurs St. G62: Miln . . . 3H **25**
Balfluig St. G34: Glas . . . 2F **87**
Balfour St. G20: Glas . . . 3B **62**
Balfour Ter. G75: E Kil . . . 4H **149**
Balfour Wynd ML9: Lark . . . 4F **161**
Balfron Cres. ML3: Ham . . . 6D **140**
Balfron Dr. ML5: Coat . . . 2E **111**
Balfron Rd. G51: Glas . . . 4E **81**
PA1: Pais . . . 6F **79**
Balgair Dr. PA1: Pais . . . 6D **78**
Balgair Pl. G22: Glas . . . 5F **63**
Balgair St. G22: Glas . . . 4F **63**
Balgair Ter. G32: Glas . . . 6B **86**
Balglass Gdns. G22: Glas . . . 5F **63**
Balglass St. G22: Glas . . . 5F **63**
Balgonie Av. PA2: Pais . . . 4E **97**
Balgonie Dr. PA2: Pais . . . 4G **97**
Balgonie Rd. G52: Glas . . . 1E **101**
Balgonie Woods PA2: Pais . . . 4G **97**
Balgownie Cres. G46: T'bnk . . . 5G **117**
Balgraybank St. G21: Glas . . . 5B **64**
Balgray Cres. G78: Barr . . . 5F **115**
Balgrayhill Rd. G21: B'rig, Glas . . . 3B **64**
Balgray Rd. G77: Newt M . . . 4A **132**
Balintore St. G32: Glas . . . 6A **86**
Baliol La. G3: Glas . . . 2A **4**
Baliol St. G3: Glas . . . 2D **82** (1A **4**)
Baljaffray Rd. G61: Bear . . . 6H **23**
Baljaffray Shop. Cen. G61: Bear . . . 5C **24**
Ballagan Pl. G62: Miln . . . 3D **24**
Ballaig Av. G61: Bear . . . 2D **44**
Ballaig Cres. G33: Step . . . 4C **66**
Ballantay Quad. G45: Glas . . . 4C **120**
Ballantay Rd. G45: Glas . . . 4C **120**
Ballantay Ter. G45: Glas . . . 4C **120**
Ballantine Av. G52: Hill . . . 4A **80**
Ballantrae G74: E Kil . . . 1F **149**
Ballantrae Cres. G77: Newt M . . . 6G **133**
Ballantrae Dr. G77: Newt M . . . 5G **133**
Ballantrae Rd. G72: Blan . . . 4C **140**
Ballantrae Wynd *ML1: Holy . . . 2A* ***128***
(off Beauly Pl.)
Ballater Cres. ML2: Wis . . . 4H **145**
Ballater Dr. G61: Bear . . . 5F **45**
PA2: Pais . . . 4B **98**
PA4: Inch . . . 2H **57**
Ballater Pl. G5: Glas . . . 1H **103**
Ballater St. G5: Glas . . . 6G **83**
Ballater Way ML5: Glenb . . . 3G **69**
Ballayne Dr. G69: Mood . . . 4E **53**
Ballerup Ter. G75: E Kil . . . 5G **149**
BALLIESTON . . . **1A 108**
Ballindalloch Dr. G31: Glas . . . 3C **84**
Ballindalloch La. G31: Glas . . . 3C **84**
Ballinkier Av. FK4: Bank . . . 1E **15**
BALLOCH . . . **3D 34**
Balloch Gdns. G52: Glas . . . 2F **101**
Ballochmill Rd. G73: Ruth . . . 5F **105**
Ballochmyle G74: E Kil . . . 5D **138**
Ballochmyle Cres. G53: Glas . . . 5A **100**
Ballochmyle Dr. G53: Glas . . . 5A **100**
Ballochmyle Gdns. G53: Glas . . . 5A **100**
Ballochmyle Pl. G53: Glas . . . 5A **100**
Ballochney La. ML6: Air . . . 1G **91**
Ballochney Rd. ML6: Air . . . 1E **93**
Ballochney St. ML6: Air . . . 1G **91**
Ballochnie Dr. ML6: Plain . . . 1F **93**
Balloch Rd. G68: Cumb . . . 3C **34**
ML6: Air . . . 5G **93**
BALLOCH RDBT. . . . **3C 34**
Balloch Vw. G67: Cumb . . . 3H **35**
Ballogie Rd. G44: Glas . . . 6F **103**
BALMALLOCH . . . **2G 11**
Balmalloch Rd. G65: Kils . . . 2F **11**
Balmartin Rd. G23: Glas . . . 6B **46**
Balmedie PA8: Ersk . . . 5E **41**
Balmeg Av. G46: Giff . . . 1A **134**
Balmerino Pl. G64: B'rig . . . 1F **65**
Balmoral Av. ML6: Glenm . . . 4H **71**
Balmoral Cres. ML5: Coat . . . 1H **109**
PA4: Inch . . . 2A **58**
Balmoral Dr. G32: Carm . . . 5B **106**
G61: Bear . . . 5G **45**
G72: Camb . . . 2G **121**
PA7: B'ton . . . 6A **40**
Balmoral Gdns. G71: Tann . . . 4D **108**
G72: Blan . . . 5A **124**
Balmoral Path *ML9: Lark . . . 3G* ***161***
(off Alloway St.)
Balmoral Pl. G74: E Kil . . . 2E **149**
Balmoral Rd. PA5: Eld . . . 5H **95**
Balmoral St. G14: Glas . . . 6B **60**
BALMORE . . . **5A 28**
Balmore Dr. ML3: Ham . . . 3E **153**
Balmore Ind. Est. G22: Glas . . . 1F **63**
Balmore Pl. G22: Glas . . . 3F **63**
Balmore Rd. G23: Glas . . . 1D **46**
G62: Balm, Bard . . . 6D **26**
G64: Balm, Torr . . . 5H **27**
Balmore Sq. G22: Glas . . . 4F **63**
Balmuildy Rd. G23: Glas . . . 3E **47**
G64: B'rig . . . 3G **47**
BALORNOCK . . . **3D 64**
Balornock Rd. G21: Glas . . . 4C **64**
Balruddery Pl. G64: B'rig . . . 1F **65**
Balshagray Av. G11: Glas . . . 6F **61**
Balshagray Cres. G14: Glas . . . 1E **81**
Balshagray Dr. G11: Glas . . . 6F **61**
Balshagray La. G11: Glas . . . 1F **81**
Balshagray Pl. G11: Glas . . . 6F **61**
Baltic Ct. G40: Glas . . . 2C **104**
Baltic La. G40: Glas . . . 2C **104**
Baltic Pl. G40: Glas . . . 1C **104**
Baltic St. G40: Glas . . . 1C **104**
(not continuous)
Balure St. G31: Glas . . . 4E **85**
Balvaird Cres. G73: Ruth . . . 6C **104**
Balvaird Dr. G73: Ruth . . . 6C **104**
Balvenie Dr. ML1: Carf . . . 6B **128**
Balvenie St. ML5: Coat . . . 2D **110**
Balveny St. G33: Glas . . . 1D **86**
Balvicar Dr. G42: Glas . . . 4D **102**

Balvicar St. G42: Glas 3D **102**
Balvie Av. G15: Glas 6A **44**
G46: Giff 5B **118**
Balvie Cres. G62: Miln 3F **25**
Balvie Rd. G62: Miln 3E **25**
Banavie La. G11: Glas 6G **61**
Banavie Rd. G11: Glas 6G **61**
ML2: Newm 3D **146**
Banchory Av. G43: Glas 2H **117**
ML6: Glenm 4H **71**
PA4: Inch 2H **57**
Banchory Cres. G61: Bear 5G **45**
Banchory Rd. ML2: Wis 4H **145**
Baneberry Path G74: E Kil 5F **137**
Banff Av. ML6: Air 1A **112**
Banff Pl. G75: E Kil 3E **149**
Banff Quad. ML2: Wis 4H **145**
Banff St. G33: Glas 1B **86**
Bangorshill St. G46: T'bnk 3F **117**
Bank Av. G62: Miln 2G **25**
Bankbrae Av. G53: Glas 1A **116**
Bankend PA11: Bri W 4G **73**
Bankend Rd. G82: Dumb 3F **17**
PA11: Bri W 5H **73**
Bankend St. G33: Glas 2A **86**
Bankfield Dr. ML3: Ham 4H **153**
Bankfoot Dr. G52: Glas 6B **80**
Bankfoot Pl. G77: Newt M 5H **133**
Bankfoot Rd. G52: Glas 1B **100**
PA3: Pais 6F **77**
Bankglen Rd. G15: Glas 3B **44**
Bankhall St. G42: Glas 3F **103**
BANKHEAD **1B 120**
Bankhead Av. G13: Glas 3A **60**
ML4: Bell 4D **126**
ML5: Coat 1G **109**
ML6: Air 4D **92**
Bankhead Dr. G73: Ruth 6C **104**
Bankhead Pl. ML5: Coat 1G **109**
ML6: Air 4D **92**
Bankhead Rd. G66: Kirk 6G **31**
G73: Ruth 1B **120**
G76: Crmck 2H **135**
Bankholm Pl. G76: Busby 4D **134**
Bankier Rd. FK4: Bank 1E **15**
Bank La. PA1: Pais 6B **78**
BANKNOCK **1E 15**
Banknock St. G32: Glas 5G **85**
Bank Pk. G75: E Kil 3F **149**
Bank Rd. G32: Carm 5C **106**
Bankside Av. PA5: John 2F **95**
Banks Rd. G66: Kirk 4D **30**
Bank St. G12: Glas 1C **82**
G72: Camb 1A **122**
G78: Barr 5E **115**
G78: Neil 2D **130**
ML5: Coat 5A **90**
ML6: Air 3A **92**
PA1: Pais 1B **98**
(not continuous)
Banktop Pl. PA5: John 2F **95**
Bank Vw. ML6: Chap 3D **112**
Bankview Cres. G66: Kirk 5A **30**
Bankview Dr. G66: Kirk 5A **30**
Bank Way *ML9: Lark* *1F* ***161***
(off Carrick Pl.)
Bannatyne Av. G31: Glas 4D **84**
Bannercross Av. G69: Bail 6G **87**
Bannercross Dr. G69: Bail 5G **87**
Bannercross Gdns. G69: Bail 6G **87**
Banner Dr. G13: Glas 6C **44**
Bannerman Dr. ML4: Bell 2F **127**
Bannerman Pl. G81: Clyd 5D **42**
Banner Rd. G13: Glas 6C **44**
Bannockburn Dr. ML9: Lark 4G **161**
Bannockburn Pl. ML1: New S 5A **128**
Bantaskin St. G20: Glas 2A **62**
BANTON **1G 13**
Banton Pl. G33: Glas 4G **87**
Banton Rd. G65: Kils 2E **13**
Banyan Cres. G71: View 4H **109**
Barassie G74: E Kil 6F **137**
Barassie Ct. G71: Both 5D **124**
Barassie Cres. G68: Cumb 5H **13**
Barassie Dr. PA11: Bri W 5E **73**
Baraston Rd. G64: Torr 2B **28**
Barbados Grn. G75: E Kil 2C **148**
Barbana Rd. G74: E Kil 1A **148**
Barbegs Cres. G65: Croy 1B **34**
Barberry Av. G53: Glas 5B **116**
Barberry Gdns. G53: Glas 5B **116**
Barberry Pl. G53: Glas 5C **116**
Barbeth Gdns. G67: Cumb 1D **54**
Barbeth Pl. G67: Cumb 1C **54**
Barbeth Rd. G67: Cumb 1C **54**
Barbeth Way G67: Cumb 1C **54**
Barbrae Pl. G71: Both 4E **125**
Barbreck Rd. G41: Glas 3D **102**
Barcaldine Av. G69: Chry 1H **67**
Barcapel Av. G77: Newt M 2E **133**
Barchan's Rd. PA10: Kilb 3B **94**
Barclay Av. PA5: Eld 3H **95**
Barclay Ct. G60: Old K 1F **41**
Barclay Rd. ML1: Moth 3D **142**
Barclay Sq. PA4: Renf 2D **78**
Barclay St. G21: Glas 4B **64**
G60: Old K 2F **41**
Barcloy Pl. ML6: Chap 4E **113**
Barcraigs Dr. PA2: Pais 5B **98**
Bard Av. G13: Glas 1B **60**
BARDOWIE **6F 27**
Bardowie Ind. Est. *G22: Glas* *5G* ***63***
(off Bardowie St.)
Bardowie Rd. G62: Bard 6F **27**
Bardowie St. G22: Glas 5F **63**
(not continuous)
Bardrain Av. PA5: Eld 3A **96**
Bardrain Rd. PA2: Pais 6G **97**
Bardrill Dr. G64: B'rig 6A **48**
Bardykes Rd. G72: Blan 1H **139**
Barefield St. ML9: Lark 1E **161**
Barfillan Dr. G52: Glas 6E **81**
Bargany Rd. G53: Glas 4A **100**
Bargaran Rd. G53: Glas 2B **100**
BARGARRAN **5D 40**
Bargarran Rd. PA8: Ersk 5D **40**
Bargarran Sq. PA8: Ersk 4D **40**
Bargarron Dr. PA3: Pais 4C **78**
BARGEDDIE **6D 88**
Bargeddie Station (Rail) **1E 109**
Bargeddie St. G33: Glas 1F **85**
Barhill Cotts. *G65: Twe* *1D* ***32***
(off Main St.)
Barhill La. G65: Twe 1D **32**
Bar Hill Pl. G65: Kils 3F **11**
Barhill Ter. G65: Twe 1E **33**
Barholm Sq. G33: Glas 1D **86**
Barke Rd. G67: Cumb 2A **36**
Barkly Ter. G75: E Kil 3E **149**
BARLANARK **5E 87**
Barlanark Av. G32: Glas 4C **86**
Barlanark Cres. G33: Glas 4D **86**
Barlanark Dr. G33: Glas 4D **86**
Barlanark Pl. G32: Glas 5C **86**
G33: Glas 4E **87**
Barlanark Rd. G33: Glas 4D **86**
Barlandfauld St. G65: Kils 3A **12**
Barleybank G66: Kirk 5C **30**
Barlia Dr. G45: Glas 4A **120**
Barlia Gdns. G45: Glas 4A **120**
Barlia Sports Complex **4A 120**
Barlia St. G45: Glas 4A **120**
Barlia Ter. G45: Glas 4A **120**
Barloan Cres. G82: Dumb 2G **17**
Barloan Pl. G82: Dumb 2G **17**
Barloch Av. G62: Miln 3G **25**
Barloch Rd. G62: Miln 3H **25**
Barloch St. G22: Glas 5G **63**
Barlogan Av. G52: Glas 6E **81**
Barlogan Quad. G52: Glas 6E **81**
Barmore Av. ML8: Carl 5G **165**
BARMULLOCH **5E 65**
Barmulloch Rd. G21: Glas 5C **64**
Barnard Gdns. G64: B'rig 3C **48**
Barnbeth Rd. G53: Glas 3B **100**
Barncluith Ct. ML3: Ham 6B **142**
Barncluith Rd. ML3: Ham 6B **142**
BARNELLAN **4E 27**
Barnes Pl. G33: Glas 3A **86**
Barnes St. G78: Barr 5D **114**
Barnett Path *G72: Blan* *2B* ***140***
(off Winton Cres.)
Barnflat St. G73: Ruth 4D **104**
Barn Grn. PA10: Kilb 2A **94**
BARNHILL **1A 140**
Barnhill Dr. G21: Glas 6C **64**
G77: Newt M 6D **132**
ML3: Ham 1B **152**
Barnhill Rd. G82: Dumb 2C **18**
Barnhill Station (Rail) **6B 64**
Barnkirk Av. G15: Glas 4A **44**
Barns Ct. G78: Barr 4D **114**
Barnscroft PA10: Kilb 1B **94**
Barnsford Av. PA4: Inch 5F **57**
Barnsford Rd. PA3: Glas A 3E **77**
PA4: Inch 4E **57**
Barns St. G81: Clyd 6E **43**
Barnswood Pl. G71: Both 4F **125**
Barnton St. G32: Glas 4G **85**
Barnwell Ter. G51: Glas 4E **81**
Barnwood Rd. PA8: Ersk 3E **41**
Barochan Cres. PA3: Pais 1E **97**
Barochan Pl. G53: Glas 2B **100**
Barochan Rd. G53: Glas 2B **100**
PA5: Brkfld 2C **74**
PA6: Hous 2C **74**
(Bridge of Weir Rd.)
PA6: Hous 6B **38**
(Reilly Rd.)
Baronald Dr. G12: Glas 3H **61**
Baronald Ga. G12: Glas 3H **61**
Baronald St. G73: Ruth 4D **104**
Baron Ct. ML3: Ham 1C **154**
Barone Dr. G76: Clar 1A **134**
Baronhall Dr. G72: Blan 1A **140**
Baronhill G67: Cumb 6A **14**
Baron Path G69: Barg 6D **88**
Baron Rd. PA3: Pais 5C **78**
Baronscourt Dr. PA1: Pais 1D **96**
Baronscourt Gdns. PA1: Pais 1D **96**
Baronscourt Rd. PA1: Pais 1D **96**
Barons Ga. G71: Both 3C **124**
Barons Haugh R.S.P.B. Nature Reserve **1F 155**
Barons Rd. ML1: Moth 1B **156**
Barons Twr. ML1: Moth 6B **144**
Baron St. PA4: Renf 1E **79**
Barony Chambers Visitors Cen. **4C 30**
Barony Ct. G69: Bail 5H **87**
Barony Dr. G69: Bail 5H **87**
Barony Gdns. G69: Bail 6H **87**
Barony Pl. G68: Cumb 4A **34**
Barony Wynd G69: Bail 5H **87**
Barra Av. ML2: Wis 4C **146**
ML5: Coat 1A **110**
PA4: Renf 2E **79**
BARRACHNIE **6E 87**
Barrachnie Av. G69: Bail 5G **87**
Barrachnie Ct. G69: Bail 5F **87**
Barrachnie Cres. G69: Bail 6F **87**
Barrachnie Dr. G69: Bail 5G **87**
Barrachnie Gro. G69: Bail 5G **87**
Barrachnie Rd. G69: Bail 6F **87**
Barrack St. G4: Glas 5A **84**
ML3: Ham 5H **141**
Barra Cres. G60: Old K 2G **41**
Barra Dr. ML6: Air 5E **93**
Barra Gdns. G60: Old K 2G **41**
Barra Pl. ML5: Coat 1A **110**
Barra Rd. G60: Old K 2G **41**
Barras, The *5A 84*
(off Moncur St.)
Barra St. G20: Glas 1A **62**
Barr Av. G78: Neil 1E **131**
Barrbridge Rd. G69: Barg, Coat 1F **109**
ML5: Barg, Coat 1F **109**
Barrcraig Rd. PA11: Bri W 4E **73**
Barr Cres. G81: Hard 2D **42**
Barr Gro. G71: Tann 5E **109**
BARRHEAD **5E 115**
Barrhead Community Mus. **5E 115**

Barrhead Rd. G43: Glas 6E **101**
G53: Glas 1H **115**
G77: Newt M. 4A **132**
PA2: Pais 2B **98**
Barrhead Sports Cen. **4E 115**
Barrhead Station (Rail) **4D 114**
Barrhill Ct. G66: Kirk 5G **31**
Barrhill Cres. PA10: Kilb. 3B **94**
Barrhill Rd. G66: Kirk. 5G **31**
Barriedale Av. ML3: Ham 6F **141**
Barrie Quad. G81: Clyd. 3C **42**
Barrie Rd. G52: Hill 4A **80**
G74: E Kil 4D **138**
Barrie St. ML1: Moth 3G **143**
Barrington Dr. G4: Glas 1D **82**
Barrisdale Rd. G20: Glas 1B **62**
ML2: Newm 3D **146**
Barrisdale Way G73: Ruth 3D **120**
Barrland Dr. G46: Giff. 4A **118**
Barrland St. G41: Glas 2E **103**
Barrmill Rd. G43: Glas. 2G **117**
BARROWFIELD
Coatbridge **1C 110**
BARROW FIELD
Glasgow **6C 84**
Barrowfield St. G40: Glas. 6C **84**
(not continuous)
ML5: Coat. 1B **110**
Barrpath G65: Kils 4B **12**
Barr Pl. G77: Newt M 4C **132**
PA1: Pais 1H **97**
Barrs La. ML8: Carl. 2F **165**
Barr St. G20: Glas. 6E **63**
ML1: Moth 1G **143**
Barr Ter. G74: E Kil. 1G **149**
BARRWOOD **3B 12**
Barrwood Pl. G71: Tann 5E **109**
Barrwood St. G33: Glas 1G **85**
Barry Gdns. G72: Blan 3A **140**
Barscube Ter. PA2: Pais 3C **98**
Barshaw Dr. PA1: Pais 5C **78**
Barshaw Pl. PA1: Pais. 6F **79**
Barshaw Rd. G52: Glas. 5G **79**
Barskiven Rd. PA1: Pais. 1D **96**
Barterholm Rd. PA2: Pais 3A **98**
Bartholomew St. G40: Glas. 2C **104**
Bartiebeith Rd. G33: Glas. 4D **86**
Bartie Gdns. ML9: Ashg 4A **162**
Bartonhall Rd. ML2: Wis 2B **158**
Barty's Rd. ML4: Bell 2E **127**
Barwood Hill G82: Dumb 1H **17**
Bassett Av. G13: Glas 1B **60**
Bassett Cres. G13: Glas 1B **60**
Bathgate St. G31: Glas 5C **84**
Bathgo Av. PA1: Pais 1G **99**
Bath La. G2: Glas. 3E **83** (3A **4**)
(not continuous)
Bath St. G2: Glas 3E **83** (3A **4**)
Batson St. G42: Glas. 3F **103**
BATTLEFIELD **6E 103**
Battlefield Av. G42: Glas. 6E **103**
Battlefield Cres. G42: Glas 5E **103**
Battlefield Gdns. G42: Glas. 5E **103**
Battlefield Rd. G42: Glas 5D **102**
Battle Pl. G41: Glas 5D **102**
Battles Burn Dr. G32: Glas 3A **106**
Battles Burn Ga. G32: Glas. 3A **106**
Battles Burn Vw. G32: Glas. 3A **106**
Bavelaw St. G33: Glas 1D **86**
Bayfield Av. G15: Glas 4A **44**
Bayfield Ter. G15: Glas. 4A **44**
Beacon Pl. G33: Glas. 3H **85**
Beaconsfield Rd. G12: Glas 4H **61**
Beard Cres. G69: G'csh. 4E **69**
Beardmore G31: Glas 5D **84**
Beardmore Cotts. PA4: Inch 3A **58**
Beardmore Pl. G81: Clyd 4A **42**
Beardmore St. G81: Clyd 4H **41**
Beardmore Way G81: Clyd 5H **41**
Bearford Dr. G52: Glas 6B **80**
BEARSDEN **2C 44**
Bearsden Rd. G13: Glas 3F **61**
G61: Bear 3F **61**
Bearsden Shop. Cen. G61: Bear 3G **45**
Bearsden Ski & Board Club **1D 44**
Bearsden Station (Rail) **3E 45**
Beaton Rd. G41: Glas 3C **102**
Beaton St. ML9: Lark 1D **160**
Beatrice Dr. ML1: Holy 2H **127**
Beatrice Gdns. PA6: C'lee. 3D **74**
Beatson Wynd G71: Tann 4E **109**
Beattock St. G31: Glas 6F **85**
Beattock Wynd ML3: Ham. 6E **141**
Beatty St. G81: Clyd 4A **42**
Beaufort Av. G43: Glas 1A **118**
Beaufort Dr. G66: Kirk. 5B **30**
Beaufort Gdns. G64: B'rig. 6A **48**
Beauly Cres. ML2: Wis. 2H **157**
Beauly Dr. PA2: Pais. 4C **96**
Beauly Pl. G20: Glas. 4B **62**
G64: B'rig 5F **49**
G69: Chry 6B **52**
G74: E Kil 1F **149**
ML1: Holy. 2A **128**
ML5: Coat. 2D **110**
Beauly Rd. G69: Bail 2G **107**
Beaumont Ga. G12: Glas 1A **82**
Beckfield Cres. G33: Glas 2F **65**
Beckfield Dr. G33: Glas. 2F **65**
Beckfield Ga. G33: Glas 2F **65**
Beckfield Gro. G33: Glas. 2F **65**
Beckfield Pl. G33: Glas. 2F **65**
Beckfield Wlk. G33: Glas 2F **65**
Beckford St. ML3: Ham 4G **141**
Beckford St. Bus. Cen. ML3: Ham
. . . . 4H **141**
Bedale Rd. G69: Bail. 1F **107**
Bedcow Vw. G66: Kirk. 6F **31**
Bedford Av. G81: Clyd 5F **43**
Bedford La. G5: Glas. 6F **83**
Bedford St. G5: Glas 6F **83**
Bedlay Castle **6C 52**
Bedlay Ct. G69: Mood. 4E **53**
Bedlay Pl. ML5: Anna. 5B **54**
Bedlay Vw. G71: Tann 4F **109**
Bedlay Wlk. G69: Mood 4E **53**
Beech Av. G41: Glas. 1H **101**
(not continuous)
G61: Bear 6G **25**
G69: Bail. 6G **87**
G72: Camb 1H **121**
G73: Ruth 3E **121**
G77: Newt M. 5D **132**
ML1: New S 4B **128**
ML9: Lark. 3H **161**
PA11: Bri W. 2F **73**
PA2: Pais 4C **98**
PA5: Eld 3A **96**
Beechbank Av. ML6: Air 2H **91**
Beech Ct. ML5: Coat. 1A **110**
Beech Cres. G72: Flem 3E **123**
G77: Newt M. 6E **133**
ML1: N'hse. 6D **112**
(not continuous)
Beech Dr. G81: Clyd 2C **42**
Beeches Av. G81: Dun 1B **42**
Beeches Rd. G81: Dun 1A **42**
Beeches Ter. G81: Dun. 6B **22**
Beeches, The *G72: Blan 2A 140*
(off Burnbrae Rd.)
G77: Newt M 3F **133**
PA5: Brkfld 5C **74**
PA6: Hous 2D **74**
Beechfield Dr. ML8: Carl 5G **165**
Beech Gdns. G69: Bail 6G **87**
Beech Gro. G69: G'csh 4E **69**
Beechgrove G69: Mood 5D **52**
Beech Gro. G75: E Kil. 5D **148**
ML2: Wis 2A **146**
ML8: Law 5D **158**
Beechgrove Av. G71: View 6G **109**
Beechgrove Quad. ML1: Holy 2A **128**
Beechgrove St. G40: Glas. 3D **104**
Beechland Av. G44: Neth 5C **118**
Beechlands Dr. G76: Clar 3A **134**
Beechmount Rd. G66: Lenz 3C **50**
Beech Pl. G64: B'rig. 1D **64**
G72: Blan 2C **140**
Beech Rd. G64: B'rig 1D **64**
G66: Lenz 1C **50**
ML1: N'hse 6C **112**
PA5: John. 4D **94**
Beech Ter. ML9: Lark 4F **161**
Beechtree Ter. G66: Milt C 6C **8**
Beechwood ML2: Wis. 2D **156**
ML9: Lark 6A **156**
Beechwood Av. G73: Ruth. 1E **121**
G76: Clar. 3A **134**
ML3: Ham 3F **153**
Beechwood Ct. G61: Bear 4F **45**
G67: Cumb 5H **35**
Beechwood Cres. ML2: Wis 1A **158**
Beechwood Dr. G11: Glas 5F **61**
ML5: Coat. 6E **91**
PA4: Renf 2D **78**
Beechwood Gdns. G69: Mood 6D **52**
ML4: Bell. 3E **127**
BEECHWOOD GATE **6C 64**
Beechwood Gro. G78: Barr 6E **115**
Beechwood La. G61: Bear. 4F **45**
Beechwood Pl. G11: Glas 5F **61**
ML4: Bell. 3E **127**
Beechwood Rd. G67: Cumb 4H **35**
Beechworth Dr. ML1: N'hill. 5D **128**
Beecroft Pl. G72: Blan 6C **124**
Beil Dr. G13: Glas. 2H **59**
Beith Dr. ML6: Air. 1A **112**
Beith Rd. PA9: How 6A **94**
Beith St. G11: Glas. 2G **81**
Belford Ct. G77: Newt M. 6D **132**
Belford Gro. G77: Newt M 6D **132**
Belfron Pl. ML5: Coat 1E **111**
Belgowan St. ML4: Bell 6B **110**
Belgrave St. ML4: Bell 6B **110**
Belgrave Ter. G12: Glas 6C **62**
Belhaven Ho. ML2: Wis 6G **145**
Belhaven Pk. G69: Muirh 2A **68**
Belhaven Rd. ML2: Wis 6G **145**
ML3: Ham. 6C **140**
Belhaven Ter. G12: Glas 5A **62**
G73: Ruth 1E **121**
ML2: Wis 6G **145**
Belhaven Ter. W. G12: Glas 5A **62**
Belhaven Ter. W. La. G12: Glas 5A **62**
BELLAHOUSTON **1F 101**
Bellahouston Dr. G52: Glas 2E **101**
Bellahouston La. G52: Glas. 1E **101**
Bellahouston Leisure Cen. **1F 101**
Bellahouston Pk. **1G 101**
Bellairs Pl. G72: Blan 6A **124**
Bellas Pl. ML6: Plain 1G **93**
Bellcraig Ct. G76: Busby. 4F **135**
Bell Dr. G72: Blan. 5A **140**
Belleisle Av. G71: Udd 6C **108**
Belleisle Ct. G68: Cumb. 1G **35**
Belleisle Cres. PA11: Bri W 5E **73**
Belleisle Dr. G68: Cumb. 1G **35**
Belleisle Gdns. G68: Cumb 1G **35**
Belleisle Gro. G68: Cumb. 1G **35**
Belleisle St. G42: Glas 4F **103**
Bellevue Av. G66: Kirk 5B **30**
Bellevue Rd. G66: Kirk. 5B **30**
Bellfield Ct. G78: Barr 3D **114**
Bellfield Cres. G78: Barr 3D **114**
Bellfield Dr. ML2: Wis 1A **158**
Bellfield Rd. G66: Kirk 5B **30**
Bellfield St. G31: Glas 5C **84**
Bellflower Av. G53: Glas. 4C **116**
Bellflower Ct. G74: E Kil 6E **137**
Bellflower Gdns. G53: Glas. 4C **116**
Bellflower Gro. G74: E Kil. 5E **137**
Bellflower Pl. G53: Glas 4C **116**
Bell Grn. E. G75: E Kil 3H **149**
Bell Grn. W. G75: E Kil. 3G **149**
Bellgrove Station (Rail). **5B 84**
Bellgrove St. G40: Glas 5B **84**
Bellhaven Ter. La. *G12: Glas 5A 62*
(off Horslethill Rd.)
Bellisle Ter. ML3: Ham 4F **153**
Bellrock Ct. G33: Glas 3B **86**
Bellrock Cres. G33: Glas. 3A **86**
Bellrock Path G33: Glas 3B **86**

Bellrock St. G33: Glas 3A **86**
Bellscroft Av. G73: Ruth 6B **104**
Bellsdyke Rd. ML6: Air 5H **91**
Bellsfield Dr. G72: Blan 3B **140**
Bellshaugh Gdns. G12: Glas 4A **62**
Bellshaugh La. G12: Glas 4A **62**
Bellshaugh Pl. G12: Glas 4A **62**
Bellshaugh Rd. G12: Glas 4A **62**
BELLSHILL **2C 126**
Bellshill Cultural Cen. **2C 126**
Bellshill (Motherwell Food Pk.) Ind. Est.
ML4: Bell 6C **110**
(Belgowan St.)
ML4: Bell 1B **126**
(Belgrave St.)
Bellshill Rd. G71: Both 1G **141**
G71: Udd 2D **124**
ML1: Moth 4E **127**
Bellshill Station (Rail) **2C 126**
Bellside Rd. ML1: N'hse 5G **113**
ML6: Chap 3E **113**
BELLSMYRE **1H 17**
Bellsmyre Av. G82: Dumb 1G **17**
Bell St. G1: Glas 4H **83** (6G **5**)
G81: Clyd 2F **59**
ML2: Wis 6F **145**
ML4: Bell 6D **110**
ML6: Air 3H **91**
PA4: Renf 5F **59**
Belltrees Cres. PA3: Pais 1E **97**
Bell Vw. Ct. PA4: Renf 5F **59**
Bellvue Cres. ML4: Bell 3A **126**
Bellvue Way ML5: Coat 1E **111**
Bellwood St. G41: Glas 6C **102**
Bellziehill Rd. ML4: Bell 2A **126**
Belmar Ct. *PA3: Lin 6A **76***
(off Langholm Dr.)
Belmont Av. G71: Udd 6C **108**
Belmont Ct. *G66: Kirk 5D **30***
(off Willowbank Gdns.)
Belmont Cres. G12: Glas 6C **62**
Belmont Dr. G46: Giff 4H **117**
G73: Ruth 6D **104**
G75: E Kil 3D **148**
G78: Barr 6F **115**
Belmont Ho. *G75: E Kil 3D **148***
(off Riverton Dr.)
Belmont La. *G12: Glas 6C **62***
(off Gt. Western Rd.)
Belmont Rd. G21: Glas 3B **64**
G72: Camb 4G **121**
PA3: Pais 5C **78**
Belmont St. G12: Glas 6C **62**
G65: Kils 2G **11**
G81: Clyd 1D **58**
ML2: Over 5H **157**
ML5: Coat 2G **89**
Belses Dr. G52: Glas 6C **80**
Belses Gdns. G52: Glas 6C **80**
Belstane M. ML8: Carl 2G **165**
Belstane Pk. ML8: Carl 2F **165**
Belstane Pl. G71: Both 4E **125**
Belstane Rd. G67: Cumb 2H **55**
ML8: Carl 3F **165**
Belsyde Av. G15: Glas 5A **44**
Beltane St. G3: Glas 3D **82**
ML2: Wis 1G **157**
Beltrees Av. G53: Glas 4A **100**
Beltrees Cres. G53: Glas 4A **100**
Beltrees Rd. G53: Glas 4A **100**
Belvidere Cres. G64: B'rig 5D **48**
ML4: Bell 3D **126**
Belvidere Rd. ML4: Bell 3C **126**
Belvoir Pl. G72: Blan 1B **140**
Bemersyde G64: B'rig 5E **49**
Bemersyde Av. G43: Glas 2H **117**
Bemersyde Pl. ML9: Lark 4E **161**
Bemersyde Rd. PA2: Pais 5B **96**
Ben Aigan Pl. G53: Glas 3C **116**
Ben Alder Dr. PA2: Pais 4F **99**
Benalder St. G11: Glas 2A **82**
Benarty Gdns. G64: B'rig 5D **48**
Benbecula G74: E Kil 2C **150**
Benbow Rd. G81: Clyd 5B **42**
Ben Buie Way PA2: Pais 4F **99**
Bencloich Av. G66: Len 3G **7**
Bencloich Cres. G66: Len 2G **7**
Bencloich Rd. G66: Len 3G **7**
Bencroft Dr. G44: Glas 2A **120**
Ben Donich Pl. G53: Glas 3D **116**
Ben Edra Pl. G53: Glas 3D **116**
Benford Av. ML1: N'hill 3D **128**
Benford Knowe ML1: N'hill 3E **129**
Bengairn St. G31: Glas 4E **85**
Bengal Pl. G43: Glas 6A **102**
Bengal St. G43: Glas 6A **102**
Ben Garrisdale Pl. G53: Glas 3D **116**
Ben Glas Pl. G53: Glas 3D **116**
Benhar Pl. G33: Glas 4H **85**
Benholm St. G32: Glas 2H **105**
Ben Hope Av. PA2: Pais 3F **99**
Ben Laga Pl. G53: Glas 3D **116**
Ben Lawers Dr. G68: Cumb 3D **34**
PA2: Pais 3F **99**
Ben Ledi Av. PA2: Pais 3F **99**
Ben Ledi Cres. G68: Cumb 3D **34**
Ben Loyal Av. PA2: Pais 3F **99**
Ben Lui Dr. PA2: Pais 4E **99**
Ben Lui Pl. G53: Glas 3D **116**
G68: Cumb 3D **34**
Ben Macdui Gdns.
G53: Glas 3D **116**
Ben More Dr. G68: Cumb 3C **34**
PA2: Pais 3F **99**
Benmore Twr. G72: Camb 4G **121**
Bennan Sq. G42: Glas 3G **103**
Benn Av. PA1: Pais 1B **98**
Ben Nevis Rd. PA2: Pais 4E **99**
Ben Nevis Way G68: Cumb 3C **34**
Benny Lynch Ct. G5: Glas 6G **83**
Benson St. ML5: Coat 1C **110**
Benston Pl. PA5: John 4E **95**
Benston Rd. PA5: John 4E **95**
Bent Cres. G71: View 1G **125**
Bentfoot Rd. ML2: Over 5A **158**
Benthall St. G5: Glas 1H **103**
Bentinck St. G3: Glas 2C **82**
Bent Rd. ML3: Ham 1G **153**
ML6: Chap 2D **112**
Bents Rd. G69: Bail 6H **87**
Benty's La. ML8: Carl 5F **165**
Ben Uird Pl. G53: Glas 3D **116**
Ben Vane Av. PA2: Pais 4E **99**
Ben Venue Rd. G68: Cumb 3C **34**
Ben Venue Way PA2: Pais 4F **99**
Benvie Gdns. G64: B'rig 5D **48**
Benview Rd. G76: Clar 2C **134**
Benview St. G20: Glas 5D **62**
Benview Ter. PA2: Pais 3D **98**
Ben Vorlich Dr. G53: Glas 2D **116**
Ben Vorlich Pl. G53: Glas 3D **116**
Benvue Rd. G66: Len 4G **7**
Ben Wyvis Dr. PA2: Pais 4E **99**
Berelands Cres. G73: Ruth 6A **104**
Berelands Pl. G73: Ruth 6A **104**
Berenice Pl. G82: Dumb 3C **18**
Beresford Av. G14: Glas 5E **61**
Berkeley St. G3: Glas 3C **82** (3A **4**)
Berkley Dr. G72: Blan 6A **124**
Berkley Ter. La. *G3: Glas 3D **82***
(off Granville St.)
Berl Av. PA6: C'lee 3C **74**
Bernadette Cres. ML1: Carf 5D **128**
Bernadette St. ML1: N'hill 4D **128**
Bernard Path *G40: Glas 1C **104***
(off Bernard Ter.)
Bernard St. G40: Glas 1C **104**
Bernard Ter. G40: Glas 1C **104**
Berneray St. G22: Glas 2G **63**
Berridale Av. G44: Glas 2E **119**
Berriedale G75: E Kil 3A **148**
Berriedale Av. G69: Bail 1G **107**
Berriedale Quad. ML2: Wis 4H **145**
Berryburn Rd. G21: Glas 5E **65**
Berry Dyke G66: Kirk 6H **31**
Berryhill Dr. G46: Giff 5H **117**
Berryhill Rd. G46: Giff 6H **117**
Berry Hill Rd. G67: Cumb 3G **35**
Berryknowe *G66: Kirk 6H **31***
(off Bk. o'Dykes Rd.)
Berryknowe Av. G69: Chry 2A **68**
Berryknowes Av. G52: Glas 6C **80**
Berryknowes La. G52: Glas 6C **80**
Berryknowes Rd. G52: Glas 1C **100**
Bertram St. G41: Glas 4C **102**
ML3: Ham 3E **141**
ML9: Lark 4G **161**
Bervie St. G51: Glas 5F **81**
Berwick Cres. ML6: Air 6H **91**
PA3: Lin 4F **75**
Berwick Dr. G52: Glas 1B **100**
G73: Ruth 6F **105**
Berwick Pl. G74: E Kil 6C **138**
ML5: Coat 2D **110**
Berwick St. ML3: Ham 4F **141**
ML5: Coat 2D **110**
Bessemer Dr. G75: E Kil 6A **150**
Beta Cen. G81: Clyd 2E **59**
Betula Dr. G81: Clyd 2C **42**
Bevan Gro. PA5: John 3E **95**
Beveridge Ter. ML4: Bell 3F **127**
Beverley Rd. G43: Glas 1B **118**
Bevin Av. G81: Clyd 6F **43**
Bideford Cres. G32: Glas 2D **106**
Bield, The ML2: Wis 1A **158**
BIGGAR ROAD **2G 129**
Biggar Rd. ML1: N'hse 5F **113**
ML6: Chap 4E **113**
Biggar St. G31: Glas 5D **84**
Bigton St. G33: Glas 1B **86**
Billings Rd. ML1: Moth 4D **142**
Bilsland Ct. G20: Glas 4F **63**
Bilsland Dr. G20: Glas 4D **62**
Binend Rd. G53: Glas 5C **100**
Binniehill Rd. G68: Cumb 2F **35**
Binnie Pl. G40: Glas 6A **84**
Binns Rd. G33: Glas 1C **86**
Birch Av. G76: Busby 3D **134**
Birch Brae ML3: Ham 2A **154**
Birch Ct. ML5: Coat 1B **110**
Birch Cres. G76: Busby 3D **134**
PA5: John 4G **95**
Birch Dr. G66: Lenz 2D **50**
G72: Camb 1C **122**
Birchend Dr. G21: Glas 1D **84**
Birchend Pl. G21: Glas 1D **84**
Birchfield Dr. G14: Glas 5B **60**
Birchfield Rd. ML3: Ham 6F **141**
Birch Gro. G71: View 6F **109**
ML9: Lark 6A **156**
Birchgrove PA6: Hous 2D **74**
Birch Knowe G64: B'rig 1D **64**
Birchlea Dr. G46: Giff 3B **118**
Birchmount Ct. ML6: Air 3D **92**
Birch Pl. G72: Blan 1B **140**
G72: Flem 3F **123**
Birch Quad. ML6: Air 4D **92**
Birch Rd. G67: Cumb 2E **37**
G81: Clyd 3C **42**
G82: Dumb 3F **17**
Birch St. G5: Glas 2H **103**
ML1: Holy 2B **128**
Birch Vw. G61: Bear 2G **45**
Birchview Dr. G76: Busby 5D **134**
Birchwood Av. G32: Glas 1E **107**
Birchwood Courtyards, The
ML4: Bell 5A **110**
Birchwood Dr. PA2: Pais 4E **97**
Birchwood Pl. G32: Glas 1E **107**
Birdsfield Ct. ML3: Ham 3D **140**
Birdsfield Dr. G72: Blan 3B **140**
Birdsfield St. ML3: Ham 3D **140**
BIRDSTON **2C 30**
Birdstone Rd. G66: Kirk 3C **30**
Birdston Rd. G21: Glas 3E **65**
G66: Milt C 5C **8**
Birgidale Rd. G45: Glas 5H **119**
Birgidale Ter. G45: Glas 5H **119**
Birkdale G74: E Kil 6E **137**
Birkdale Ct. G71: Both 5D **124**
Birkdale Cres. G68: Cumb 5H **13**
Birkdale Wood G68: Cumb 5A **14**

Birkenburn Rd.—Boghall St.

Birkenburn Rd. G67: Cumb 5F **15**
Birken Rd. G66: Lenz 3E **51**
BIRKENSHAW
Glasgow **5D 108**
Larkhall **6F 161**
Birkenshaw Ind. Est. G71: Tann 4C **108**
Birkenshaw Rd. G69: G'csh 1G **69**
ML5: Glenb 6A **54**
Birkenshaw Sports Hall **4D 108**
Birkenshaw St. G31: Glas 4D **84**
Birkenshaw Way *PA3: Pais 3A 78*
(off Mosslands Rd.)
Birkfield Pl. ML8: Carl 4H **165**
Birkhall Av. G52: Glas 1H **99**
PA4: Inch 2H **57**
Birkhall Dr. G61: Bear 5F **45**
Birkhill Av. G64: B'rig 5D **48**
Birkhill Gdns. G64: B'rig 5D **48**
Birkhill Rd. ML3: Ham 4H **153**
Birkmyre Rd. G51: Glas 5F **81**
Birks Ct. ML8: Law 1H **163**
Birkshaw Brae ML2: Wis 3G **157**
Birkshaw Pl. ML2: Wis 3G **157**
Birkshaw Twr. ML2: Wis 3F **157**
Birks Rd. ML8: Carl 1G **163**
ML9: Lark 6F **161**
Birkwood St. G40: Glas 3D **104**
Birmingham Rd. PA4: Renf 2D **78**
Birnam Av. G64: B'rig 5D **48**
Birnam Cres. G61: Bear 2H **45**
Birnam Pl. G77: Newt M 5H **133**
ML3: Ham 6C **140**
Birnam Rd. G32: Glas 2F **105**
Birness Dr. G43: Glas 5B **102**
Birnie Ct. G21: Glas 5E **65**
BIRNIEHILL **3H 149**
Birniehill Ct. G81: Hard 6C **22**
BIRNIEHILL RDBT. **3A 150**
Birnie Rd. G21: Glas 5E **65**
Birnock Av. PA4: Renf 2G **79**
Birrell Rd. G62: Miln 2F **25**
Birrens Rd. ML1: Moth 1E **143**
Birsay Rd. G22: Glas 2F **63**
BISHOPBRIGGS **6C 48**
Bishopbriggs Ind. Est. G64: B'rig 2C **64**
Bishopbriggs Station (Rail) **6C 48**
Bishopdale G74: E Kil 6E **137**
Bishop Gdns. G64: B'rig 5A **48**
ML3: Ham 4A **154**
Bishopmill Pl. G21: Glas 5E **65**
Bishopmill Rd. G21: Glas 4E **65**
Bishops Ga. G74: T'hall 6G **135**
(not continuous)
Bishopsgate Dr. G21: Glas 2A **64**
Bishopsgate Gdns. G21: Glas 2A **64**
Bishopsgate Pl. G21: Glas 2A **64**
Bishopsgate Rd. G21: Glas 2A **64**
Bishops Pk. G74: T'hall 6F **135**
Bishop St. G2: Glas 4E **83** (5A **4**)
BISHOPTON **4G 39**
Bishopton Station (Rail) **6H 39**
Bisset Ct. *PA5: John 4E 95*
(off Tannahill Cres.)
Bissett Cres. G81: Dun 1A **42**
Blackadder Pl. G75: E Kil 4A **148**
Blackbog Rd. ML6: Rigg 5G **55**
Blackbraes Rd. G74: E Kil 5B **138**
Blackbull Cl. ML8: Carl 3F **165**
Blackburn Cres. G66: Kirk 5G **31**
G82: Dumb 3D **16**
Blackburn Sq. G78: Barr 6F **115**
Blackburn St. G51: Glas 5B **82**
Blackbyres Ct. G78: Barr 3F **115**
Blackbyres Rd. G78: Barr 1E **115**
Blackcraig Av. G15: Glas 4A **44**
Blackcroft Av. ML6: Gart 6E **93**
Blackcroft Gdns. G32: Glas 1D **106**
Blackcroft Rd. G32: Glas 1D **106**
Blackdyke Rd. G66: Kirk 5E **31**
Blackfarm Rd. G77: Newt M 5F **133**
Blackfaulds Rd. G73: Ruth 5A **104**
Blackford Rd. PA2: Pais 3C **98**
Blackfriars St. G1: Glas 4H **83** (6G **5**)
BLACKHALL **2C 98**
Blackhall Ct. PA2: Pais 2D **98**
Blackhall La. PA1: Pais 2B **98**
Blackhall St. PA1: Pais 2B **98**
BLACKHILL **1F 85**
Blackhill Pl. G33: Glas 1F **85**
Blackhill Rd. G23: Glas 5B **46**
Blackhill Vw. ML8: Law 6E **159**
Blackhouse Av. G77: Newt M 5F **133**
Blackhouse Gdns. G77: Newt M 5F **133**
Blackhouse Rd. G77: Newt M 5F **133**
Blackie St. G3: Glas 2B **82**
Blacklands Pl. G66: Lenz 3E **51**
Blacklands Rd. G74: E Kil 2F **149**
Blacklaw Dr. G74: E Kil 2B **150**
Blacklaw La. PA3: Pais 6A **78**
Blackmoor Pl. ML1: New S 4A **128**
Blackmoss Dr. ML4: Bell 3B **126**
Blackness St. ML5: Coat 2D **110**
Blackstone Av. G53: Glas 5C **100**
Blackstone Cres. G53: Glas 4C **100**
Blackstoun Av. PA3: Lin 5H **75**
Blackstoun Oval PA3: Pais 6F **77**
Blackstoun Rd. PA3: Pais 3E **77**
Black St. G4: Glas 2H **83** (2H **5**)
ML6: Air 2B **92**
Blackswell La. ML3: Ham 6B **142**
Blackthorn Av. G66: Lenz 2A **50**
Blackthorn Gro. G66: Lenz 2B **50**
Blackthorn Rd. G67: Cumb 1D **36**
G71: View 5G **109**
BLACKTHORN RDBT. **2E 37**
Blackthorn St. G22: Glas 4A **64**
BLACKWOOD **4A 34**
Blackwood G75: E Kil 6F **149**
Blackwood Av. G77: Newt M 6F **133**
PA3: Lin 6G **75**
Blackwood Gdns. ML1: Moth 6E **127**
Blackwood Rd. G62: Miln 1F **25**
G68: Cumb 4H **33**
BLACKWOOD RDBT. **3A 34**
Blackwoods Cres. G69: Mood 5D **52**
ML4: Bell 3E **127**
Blackwood St. G13: Glas 2E **61**
G78: Barr 5D **114**
Blackwood Ter. PA5: John 5D **94**
BLACKWOOD W. RDBT. **4H 33**
Bladda La. PA1: Pais 1B **98**
Blades Ct. G69: G'csh 3E **69**
Bladnoch Dr. G15: Glas 5C **44**
Blaeloch Av. G45: Glas 6G **119**
Blaeloch Dr. G45: Glas 6F **119**
Blaeloch Ter. G45: Glas 6F **119**
Blaeshill Rd. G75: E Kil 3A **148**
Blairardie Dr. G13: Glas 6B **44**
G15: Glas 6B **44**
Blairathol Av. G11: Glas 6G **61**
Blairathol Gdns. G11: Glas 6G **61**
Blairatholl Cres. G77: Newt M 5H **133**
Blair Atholl Dr. ML9: Lark 4G **161**
Blairatholl Ga. G77: Newt M 5H **133**
Blairbeth Dr. G44: Glas 6F **103**
Blairbeth Pl. *G73: Ruth 2D 120*
(off Blairbeth Rd.)
Blairbeth Rd. G73: Ruth 2C **120**
Blairbeth Ter. G73: Ruth 2E **121**
Blair Ct. G81: Clyd 5D **42**
Blair Cres. G69: Bail 2G **107**
Blairdardie Rd. G15: Glas 6B **44**
Blairdenan Av. G69: Mood 4E **53**
Blairdenon Dr. G68: Cumb 2E **35**
Blair Dr. G66: Milt C 6B **8**
Blair Gdns. G64: Torr 4D **28**
G77: Newt M 4B **132**
Blairgowrie Rd. G52: Glas 1C **100**
Blairgrove Ct. ML5: Coat 5A **90**
Blairhall Av. G41: Glas 5D **102**
BLAIRHILL **4B 90**
Blairhill Av. G66: Kirk 1G **51**
Blairhill Pl. ML5: Coat 4A **90**
Blairhill Station (Rail) **3A 90**
Blairhill St. ML5: Coat 4A **90**
Blairholm Dr. ML4: Bell 4D **126**
Blair Ho. G67: Cumb 2A **36**
BLAIRLINN **1H 55**
Blairlinn Ind. Est. G67: Cumb 1H **55**
Blairlinn Rd. G67: Cumb 1H **55**
Blairlogie St. G33: Glas 2B **86**
Blairmore Av. PA1: Pais 6E **79**
Blairpark Av. ML5: Coat 3A **90**
Blair Path ML1: Moth 4H **143**
Blair Rd. ML5: Coat 4A **90**
PA1: Pais 6G **79**
BLAIRSKAITH **2H 27**
Blairston Av. G71: Both 6E **125**
Blairston Gdns. G71: Both 6F **125**
Blair St. G32: Glas 6H **85**
Blairtum Dr. G73: Ruth 2D **120**
Blairtummock Rd. G33: Glas 3C **86**
(not continuous)
Blake Rd. G67: Cumb 3A **36**
Blane Dr. G62: Miln 2H **25**
Blane St. ML5: Coat 3C **90**
Blaneview G33: Step 5D **66**
BLANTYRE **3A 140**
Blantyre Ct. PA8: Ersk 4E **41**
Blantyre Cres. G81: Dun 6A **22**
Blantyre Dr. PA7: B'ton 3G **39**
Blantyre Farm Rd. G71: Udd 2A **124**
G72: Blan 6A **124**
BLANTYREFERME **1B 124**
Blantyre Gdns. G68: Cumb 4A **34**
Blantyre Ind. Est. G72: Blan 4C **140**
Blantyre Mill Rd. G71: Both 5D **124**
Blantyre Rd. G71: Both 5E **125**
Blantyre Sports Cen. **1C 140**
Blantyre Station (Rail) **1C 140**
Blantyre St. G3: Glas 2B **82**
Blaven Ct. G69: Bail 1A **108**
Blawart Hill St. G14: Glas 4H **59**
Bleachfield G62: Miln 2F **25**
Bleasdale Ct. G81: Clyd 5D **42**
Blenheim Av. G33: Step 3D **66**
G75: E Kil 4E **149**
Blenheim Ct. G33: Step 3D **66**
G65: Kils 2H **11**
ML8: Carl 4G **165**
PA1: Pais 6H **77**
BLOCHAIRN INTERCHANGE **3C 84**
Blochairn Rd. G21: Glas 2C **84**
Bluebell Gdns. G45: Glas 5C **120**
ML1: Moth 5E **127**
Bluebell Wlk. ML1: New S 4A **128**
Bluebell Way G66: Len 4H **7**
ML6: Air 1H **91**
ML8: Carl 5F **165**
Blueknowes Rd. ML8: Law 6D **158**
(not continuous)
Bluevale St. G31: Glas 5C **84**
Blyth Pl. G33: Glas 5D **86**
Blyth Rd. G33: Glas 5E **87**
BLYTHSWOOD **4F 59**
Blythswood Av. PA4: Renf 5F **59**
Blythswood Ct. G2: Glas 4E **83** (5A **4**)
Blythswood Dr. PA3: Pais 5H **77**
Blythswood Ind. Est. PA4: Renf 5D **58**
Blythswood Rd. PA4: Renf 5F **59**
Blythswood Sq. G2: Glas 3E **83** (4B **4**)
Blythswood St. G2: Glas 4E **83** (6B **4**)
Boardwalk, The G75: E Kil 4A **150**
Bobbins Ga. PA1: Pais 2F **97**
Boclair Av. G61: Bear 3F **45**
Boclair Cres. G61: Bear 3G **45**
G64: B'rig 5C **48**
Boclair Rd. G61: Bear 3G **45**
G62: Miln 1B **46**
G64: B'rig 6C **48**
Boclair St. G13: Glas 1E **61**
Bodden Sq. ML1: N'hse 6E **113**
Boden Ind. Est. G40: Glas 1D **104**
Boden Quad. ML1: Moth 5D **126**
Boden St. G40: Glas 1C **104**
Bodmin Gdns. G69: Mood 4D **52**
Bogany Ter. G45: Glas 5A **120**
Bogbain Rd. G34: Glas 3G **87**
Boggknowe G71: Tann 5B **108**
Boghall Rd. G71: Udd 3G **107**
ML8: Carl 6H **165**
Boghall St. G33: Glas 2B **86**

176 A-Z Glasgow

BOGHEAD 3H 49
Boghead Av. G82: Dumb 3H 17
Boghead Rd. G21: Glas. 4C 64
   G66: Lenz 3A 50
   G82: Dumb 3G 17
Bogleshole Rd. G72: Camb 6G 105
Bogmoor Pl. G51: Glas 2C 80
Bogmoor Rd. G51: Glas 3B 80
Bog Rd. FK4: Bank 1E 15
BOGSIDE 3G 159
Bogside Rd. G33: Mille 3A 66
   G65: Kils. 4H 11
   ML9: Ashg 5B 162
Bogside St. G40: Glas. 1D 104
Bogstonhill Rd. PA6: Hous 1B 74
Bogs Vw. ML4: Bell. 4B 126
Bogton Av. G43: Glas 3D 118
Bogton Av. La. G44: Glas 3D 118
Boleyn Rd. G41: Glas 3C 102
Bolingbroke G74: E Kil 5C 138
Bolivar Ter. G42: Glas 5G 103
Bolton Dr. G42: Glas. 5F 103
Bolton Ter. G66: Len. 3G 7
Bon Accord Rd. G76: Busby 3D 134
Bon Accord Sq. G81: Clyd. 1D 58
Bonar Cres. PA11: Bri W 4G 73
Bonar La. PA11: Bri W 4G 73
Bonawe St. G20: Glas. 5D 62
Bonds Dr. ML2: Newm 3F 147
Bo'ness Rd. ML1: Holy 1C 128
Boness St. G40: Glas 1D 104
Bonhill Rd. G82: Dumb 3G 17
Bonhill St. G22: Glas. 6F 63
BONKLE 3G 147
Bonkle Gdns. ML2: Newm 4F 147
Bonkle Rd. ML2: Newm 4F 147
Bonnar St. G40: Glas 2C 104
Bonnaughton Rd. G61: Bear 1B 44
Bonnyholm Av. G53: Glas 2A 100
Bonnyrigg Dr. G43: Glas 2G 117
Bonnyton La. ML3: Ham 4F 153
Bontine Av. G82: Dumb 3D 16
Bonyton Av. G13: Glas 3H 59
Boon Dr. G15: Glas 5B 44
Boquhanran Pl. G81: Clyd. 4C 42
Boquhanran Rd. G81: Clyd 5B 42
              (not continuous)
Borden La. G13: Glas 4E 61
Borden Rd. G13: Glas 4E 61
Border Way G66: Kirk 5E 31
Boreland Dr. G13: Glas. 2A 60
   ML3: Ham. 1C 152
Boreland Pl. G13: Glas. 3B 60
Bore Rd. ML6: Air. 2B 92
Borgie Cres. G52: Camb 2A 122
Borland Dr. ML9: Lark. 5F 161
Borland Rd. G61: Bear 4G 45
Borron St. G4: Glas 6G 63
Borrowdale G75: E Kil. 6B 148
Borthwick Dr. G75: E Kil 4A 148
Borthwick St. G33: Glas 2B 86
Bosfield Cnr. G74: E Kil 6H 137
Bosfield Pl. G74: E Kil 6H 137
Bosfield Rd. G74: E Kil 6G 137
Boswell Ct. G42: Glas. 6D 102
Boswell Dr. G72: Blan 2B 140
Boswell Pk. G74: E Kil 5C 138
Boswell Sq. G52: Glas 4H 79
Bosworth Rd. G74: E Kil 5B 138
Botanic Cres. G20: Glas 5B 62
Botanic Cres. La. G20: Glas 5B 62
Bothlin Dr. G33: Step 3D 66
Bothlyn Av. G66: Kirk 6E 31
Bothlyn Cres. G69: G'csh 2D 68
Bothlyn Rd. G69: Chry 1B 68
BOTHWELL 5E 125
Bothwell Bri. G71: Both 1G 141
Bothwell Castle 4B 124
Bothwellhaugh Quad. ML4: Bell . . 4B 126
Bothwellhaugh Rd. ML1: Moth . . . 6B 126
Bothwell Ho. ML3: Ham 4A 142
Bothwell La. *G12: Glas. 1C 82*
          (off Glasgow St.)
   G2: Glas 4E 83 (5B 4)

Bothwell Pk. Ind. Est. G71: Udd . . 2E 125
Bothwellpark Pl. ML4: Bell 1H 125
Bothwellpark Rd. G71: Both 5F 125
Bothwell Pl. ML5: Coat. 4B 90
   PA2: Pais 5C 96
Bothwell Rd. G71: Udd 2D 124
   ML3: Ham. 2G 141
   ML8: Carl 1E 165
Bothwell St. G2: Glas 4E 83 (5B 4)
   G72: Camb 1G 121
   ML3: Ham. 4G 141
Bothwick Way PA2: Pais 5C 96
Boulevard, The G66: Len 2C 6
Bourhill Ct. ML2: Wis. 1D 156
Bourne Cl. PA4: Inch 2H 57
Bourne Cres. PA4: Inch 2H 57
Bourne St. ML3: Ham 6B 142
Bourock Sq. G78: Barr. 6F 115
Bourtree Rd. ML3: Ham 1C 152
Bouverie St. G14: Glas. 3G 59
   G73: Ruth. 6B 104
Bowden Dr. G52: Glas. 5B 80
Bowden Pk. G75: E Kil 3E 149
Bower St. G12: Glas 6C 62
Bowerwalls St. G78: Barr 3F 115
Bowes Cres. G69: Bail. 1F 107
Bowfield Av. G52: Glas. 5H 79
Bowfield Cres. G52: Glas. 5H 79
Bowfield Path G52: Glas. 5H 79
Bowfield Pl. G40: Glas. 5H 79
Bowhousebrae Rd. ML6: Gart . . . 1E 113
Bowhouse Rd. ML6: Gart 6E 93
Bowie St. G82: Dumb 4E 17
BOWLING 5B 20
Bowling Grn. La. *G14: Glas* *6D 60*
          (off Westland Dr.)
Bowling Grn. Rd. G14: Glas 6D 60
   G32: Glas 1D 106
   G44: Glas 2E 119
   G69: Chry 1B 68
Bowling Grn. Vw. G72: Flem 3F 123
Bowling Station (Rail). 5A 20
Bowmanflat ML9: Lark 2E 161
Bowman St. G42: Glas 3E 103
Bowmont Gdns. G12: Glas. 6A 62
Bowmont Hill G64: B'rig 3C 48
Bowmont Pl. G72: Camb. 2D 122
   G75: E Kil 4A 148
Bowmont Ter. G12: Glas 6A 62
Bowmore Gdns. G71: Tann 5C 108
   G73: Ruth. 4G 121
Bowyer Vennel ML4: Bell 1B 126
Boyd Dr. ML1: Moth 2D 142
Boydstone Pl. G46: T'bnk 2G 117
Boydstone Rd. G43: Glas, T'bnk . . 1E 117
   G53: Glas 1E 117
Boyd St. G42: Glas 4F 103
Boylestone Rd. G78: Barr 3C 114
Boyle St. G81: Clyd. 1F 59
Boyndie Path G34: Glas 3H 87
Boyndie St. G34: Glas 3H 87
Brabloch Cres. PA3: Pais 5B 78
Bracadale Dr. G69: Bail. 1B 108
Bracadale Gdns. G69: Bail 1B 108
Bracadale Gro. G69: Bail 1A 108
Bracadale Rd. G69: Bail 1A 108
Brackenbrae Av. G64: B'rig. 5A 48
Brackenbrae Rd. G64: B'rig 6B 48
Brackendene PA6: Hous 2D 74
Brackenhill Dr. ML3: Ham 4F 153
Brackenhill Rd. ML8: Law 5E 159
Brackenhirst Gdns. ML6: Glenm . . 3F 71
Brackenhirst Rd. ML6: Glenm . . . 3F 71
Brackenhurst St. G82: Dumb . . . 1H 17
Brackenrig Rd. G46: T'bnk 5E 117
Bracken St. G22: Glas 3F 63
   ML1: New S 4A 128
Bracken Ter. G71: Both 4E 125
Bracken Way *ML9: Lark* *4G 161*
          (off Donaldson Rd.)

Brackla Av. G81: Clyd 1G 59
Bradda Av. G73: Ruth 3E 121
Bradfield Av. G12: Glas. 4A 62
Bradshaw Cres. ML3: Ham 6C 140
Brady Cres. G69: Mood. 4E 53
BRAEDALE 3D 142
Braedale ML3: Ham 6E 141
Braedale Av. ML1: Moth. 3D 142
   ML6: Air 4B 92
Braedale Cres. ML2: Newm 4F 147
Braedale Pl. ML2: Newm 4G 147
Braeface Rd. G67: Cumb 3G 35
Braefield Dr. G46: T'bnk 4G 117
Braefoot Av. G62: Miln 5G 25
Braefoot Ct. ML8: Law 6D 158
Braefoot Cres. ML8: Law 1H 163
   PA2: Pais 6B 98
BRAEHEAD 6H 135
Braehead G72: Blan 3B 140
Braehead Arena 6A 60
Braehead Av. G62: Miln 4F 25
   G78: Neil. 2D 130
   G81: Dun 6C 22
   ML5: Coat. 2H 109
   ML9: Lark 3C 160
Braehead Cres. G81: Dun. 6C 22
Braehead Curling & Ice Rinks. . . 6A 60
Braehead Dr. ML4: Bell. 3B 126
Braehead Ind. Est. PA4: Renf . . . 1H 79
Braehead Loan *ML8: Carl.* *5H 165*
          (off Charles Cres.)
Braehead Pl. ML4: Bell. 3B 126
Braehead Quad. G78: Neil 2D 130
   ML1: N'hill 3D 128
Braehead Rd. G67: Cumb 2B 36
   G74: T'hall 6G 135
   G81: Dun 6C 22
   PA2: Pais 6G 97
Braehead Shop. Cen. G51: Glas . . 6A 60
Braehead St. G5: Glas 2H 103
   G66: Kirk 4C 30
Braemar Av. G81: Clyd 3B 42
Braemar Ct. G44: Glas 3C 118
Braemar Cres. G61: Bear 5F 45
   ML8: Carl 2G 165
   PA2: Pais 4B 98
Braemar Dr. PA5: Eld 4H 95
Braemar Rd. G73: Ruth 4G 121
   PA4: Inch 2H 57
Braemar St. G42: Glas 6D 102
   ML3: Ham 3F 141
Braemar Vw. G81: Clyd 2B 42
Braemore Gdns. G22: Glas 5H 63
Braemount Av. PA2: Pais 6G 97
Braes Av. G81: Clyd 6F 43
Braesburn Ct. G67: Cumb 5F 15
Braesburn Pl. G67: Cumb 5F 15
Braesburn Rd. G67: Cumb 5F 15
Braeside Av. G62: Miln. 5G 25
   G69: Mood 5D 52
   G73: Ruth 6E 105
Braeside Cres. G69: Barg. 6D 88
   G78: Barr 6G 115
Braeside Dr. G78: Barr 6F 115
   G82: Dumb 2H 17
Braeside Gdns. ML3: Ham 3A 154
Braeside La. *ML9: Lark.* *1F 161*
          (off Carrick Pl.)
Braeside Pl. G72: Camb 3B 122
Braeside Rd. ML1: N'hill. 3D 128
Braeside St. G20: Glas. 5D 62
Braeside Way *ML9: Lark.* *4F 161*
        (off Keir Hardie Rd.)
Braes o'Yetts G66: Kirk. 5G 31
Braeview Av. PA2: Pais 6F 97
Braeview Dr. PA2: Pais 6F 97
Braeview Gdns. PA2: Pais 6F 97
Brae Vw. Pl. G74: E Kil 5B 138
Braeview Rd. PA2: Pais 6F 97
Braid Av. ML1: Cle 6E 129
Braidbar Ct. G46: Giff 4A 118
Braidbar Farm Rd. G46: Giff. . . . 3B 118
          (not continuous)
Braidbar Rd. G46: Giff 4A 118

Braidcraft Pl. G53: Glas 5C **100**
Braidcraft Rd. G53: Glas. 4C **100**
Braidcraft Ter. G53: Glas 4D **100**
BRAIDFAULD **2G 105**
Braidfauld Gdns. G32: Glas 2H **105**
Braidfauld Pl. G32: Glas. 3H **105**
Braidfauld St. G32: Glas. 3H **105**
Braidfield Gro. G81: Hard. 2D **42**
Braidfield Rd. G81: Hard 2D **42**
Braidholm Cres. G46: Giff. 4A **118**
Braidholm Rd. G46: Giff 4A **118**
Braidhurst Ind. Est. ML1: Moth. . . . 6F **127**
Braidhurst Sports Barn. **6F 127**
Braidhurst St. ML1: Moth 1G **143**
Braidley Cres. G75: E Kil 6G **149**
Braidpark Dr. G46: Giff 4B **118**
Braids Ct. PA2: Pais 4H **97**
Braids Dr. G53: Glas. 4H **99**
Braids Ga. PA2: Pais 4H **97**
Braid Sq. G4: Glas 1E **83** (1B **4**)
Braids Rd. PA2: Pais 4A **98**
Braid St. G4: Glas. 1E **83**
Braidwood Pl. PA3: Lin. 5F **75**
Braidwood St. ML2: Wis. 2A **146**
Bramah Av. G75: E Kil 4H **149**
Bramble Ct. G66: Len. 3E **7**
Brambling Ct. ML2: Wis 2F **157**
Bramley Pl. G66: Lenz 3E **51**
ML6: Air 5E **93**
Brampton G75: E Kil 5B **148**
Branchalfield Dr. ML2: Wis. 5C **146**
Branchalmuir Cres. ML2: Newm. . . 3D **146**
Branchal Rd. ML2: Wis. 4B **146**
Branchock Av. G72: Camb 3D **122**
Brancumhall Rd. G74: E Kil 6D **138**
Brandon Arc. ML1: Moth 3G **143**
Brandon Ct. ML3: Ham. 5G **141**
Brandon Dr. G61: Bear 6E **25**
Brandon Gdns. G72: Camb 2G **121**
Brandon Ho. ML3: Ham 4A **142**
Brandon Pde. E. ML1: Moth 2G **143**
Brandon Pde. Sth. ML1: Moth 3G **143**
Brandon Pl. ML4: Bell. 4A **126**
Brandon St. G31: Glas 5B **84**
ML1: Moth 3H **143**
ML3: Ham. 6A **142**
Brandon Way ML5: Coat. 1H **109**
Brand Pl. G51: Glas 5A **82**
Brand St. G51: Glas 5A **82**
Brankholm Brae ML3: Ham. 5B **140**
Branklyn Cl. G13: Glas 3D **60**
Branklyn Ct. G13: Glas 3D **60**
Branklyn Cres. G13: Glas 3D **60**
Branklyn Gro. G13: Glas. 3D **60**
Branklyn Pl. G13: Glas 3D **60**
BRANKUMHALL **6C 138**
Brannock Av. ML1: N'hill. 3D **128**
Brannock Pl. ML1: N'hill. 3D **128**
Brannock Rd. ML1: N'hill 4D **128**
Brassey St. G20: Glas. 3C **62**
Breadalbane Cres. ML1: Moth 6F **127**
Breadalbane Gdns. G73: Ruth. 3F **121**
Breadalbane St. G3: Glas 3D **82**
Breadie Dr. G62: Miln 5F **25**
Breamish Pl. G75: E Kil 5B **148**
Bream Pl. PA6: C'lee 3D **74**
Brechin Rd. G64: B'rig 6E **49**
Brechin St. G3: Glas. 3C **82**
Breck Av. PA2: Pais 6B **96**
BREDILAND. **4E 97**
Brediland Rd. PA2: Pais. 6C **96**
PA3: Lin 5G **75**
Bredin Way ML1: Moth. 1D **142**
Bredisholm Cres. G71: View. 4G **109**
Bredisholm Dr. G69: Bail 1A **108**
Bredisholm Rd. G69: Bail 1A **108**
(not continuous)
G69: Barg. 1D **108**
(not continuous)
Bredisholm Ter. G69: Bail. 1A **108**
Bredland Rd. PA2: Pais. 3E **97**
Bremners Cotts. G81: Dun 1B **42**
Brenfield Av. G44: Glas 3D **118**
Brenfield Dr. G44: Glas. 3D **118**
Brenfield Rd. G44: Glas 3D **118**
G44: Neth 3D **118**
Brent Av. G46: T'bnk 2F **117**
Brent Ct. G74: E Kil. 6G **137**
Brent Cres. PA6: C'lee. 3C **74**
Brent Dr. G46: T'bnk 2F **117**
Brent Gdns. G46: T'bnk. 2F **117**
Brent Rd. G46: T'bnk. 2F **117**
G74: E Kil 6G **137**
Brent Way G46: T'bnk 2F **117**
Brentwood Av. G53: Glas 3A **116**
Brentwood Dr. G53: Glas. 3B **116**
Brentwood Sq. G53: Glas 3B **116**
Brereton St. G42: Glas 4G **103**
Bressay G74: E Kil 6G **137**
Bressay Rd. G33: Glas 5E **87**
Bressay Wynd *ML2: Newm. 3D* ***146***
(off Tiree Cres.)
Breval Cres. G81: Dun, Hard. 6C **22**
Brewery St. PA5: John 2F **95**
Brewster Av. PA3: Pais 4C **78**
Briar Bank G66: Milt C 6B **8**
Briarbush Way G72: Blan 1A **140**
Briarcroft Dr. G33: Glas. 2F **65**
Briarcroft Pl. G33: Glas 3G **65**
Briarcroft Rd. G33: Glas 3F **65**
Briar Dr. G81: Clyd 3D **42**
Briar Gdns. G43: Glas. 2B **118**
Briar Gro. G43: Glas. 2B **118**
Briarlea Dr. G46: Giff 3A **118**
Briar Neuk G64: B'rig 1D **64**
Briar Rd. G43: Glas. 2B **118**
G66: Kirk. 5F **31**
Briar Wlk. G66: Kirk 5G **31**
Briarwell La. G62: Miln 4H **25**
Briarwell Rd. G62: Miln 4H **25**
Briarwood Ct. G32: Glas 3E **107**
Briarwood Gdns. G32: Glas. 3E **107**
Briarwood Rd. ML2: Wis. 5E **145**
Brick La. PA3: Pais. 6B **78**
Bridgebar St. G78: Barr 3G **115**
Bridgeburn Dr. G69: Mood 5C **52**
Bridgeford Av. ML4: Bell. 6E **111**
Bridgegait G62: Miln. 5A **26**
Bridgegate G1: Glas 5G **83**
Bridgegate Path *G1: Glas 5H* ***83***
(off Saltmarket)
BRIDGEND **4C 52**
Bridgend PA7: B'ton 4G **39**
Bridgend Cotts. G66: Kirk. 6G **31**
Bridgend Ct. G68: C'cry 2F **15**
Bridgend Cres. G69: Mood 5C **52**
Bridgend Pl. G69: Mood 5C **52**
Bridgend Rd. PA5: Eld 2A **96**
Bridgend Vw. ML8: Carl 4F **165**
BRIDGE OF WEIR **3F 73**
Bridge of Weir Rd. PA11: Bri W 4G **73**
PA3: Lin 6H **75**
PA5: Brkfld 6C **74**
PA6: Hous. 2A **74**
Bridge Pl. G62: Miln. 4G **25**
Bridge St. G5: Glas 5F **83**
G72: Camb 1A **122**
G81: Clyd 4A **42**
G82: Dumb 4E **17**
ML2: Wis 6E **145**
ML3: Ham. 1G **153**
PA1: Pais 1A **98**
PA3: Lin 5A **76**
Bridge Street Station (Und.) **6F 83**
BRIDGETON. **1B 104**
Bridgeton Bus. Cen. G40: Glas 6B **84**
Bridgeton Cross G40: Glas 6B **84**
Bridgeton Station (Rail). **1B 104**
Bridgewater Ind. Pk. PA8: Ersk 5F **41**
Bridgewater Shop. Cen.
PA8: Ersk 5F **41**
Bridgeway Ct. G66: Kirk 6F **31**
Bridgeway Pl. G66: Kirk 6F **31**
Bridgeway Rd. G66: Kirk. 6F **31**
Bridgeway Ter. G66: Kirk. 6F **31**
Bridie Ter. G74: E Kil 5C **138**
Brierie Av. PA6: C'lee 2B **74**
Brierie Gdns. PA6: C'lee 3B **74**
Brierie Hill Ct. PA6: C'lee 3B **74**
Brierie Hill Gro. PA6: C'lee 3B **74**
Brierie Hill Rd. PA6: C'lee 3A **74**
Brierie La. PA6: C'lee 3A **74**
Brigbrae Av. ML4: Bell 4E **127**
Brigham Pl. G23: Glas 1C **62**
Brighton Pl. G51: Glas 5H **81**
Brighton St. G51: Glas 5H **81**
Brightside Av. G71: Udd 2D **124**
Bright St. G21: Glas 2B **84**
Brig o'Lea Ter. G78: Neil 3D **130**
Brigside Gdns. ML3: Ham. 1C **154**
Brisbane Ct. G46: Giff. 4B **118**
Brisbane Rd. PA7: B'ton. 4H **39**
Brisbane St. G42: Glas 6E **103**
G81: Clyd 3H **41**
Brisbane Ter. G75: E Kil 4E **149**
Britannia Way G81: Clyd 5D **42**
PA4: Renf 2E **79**
Briton St. G51: Glas 4H **81**
Brittain Way ML1: Holy 6H **111**
Broadcroft G66: Kirk. 4C **30**
(not continuous)
Broadcroft Rd. G66: Kirk. 4C **30**
Broadford St. G4: Glas 1G **83**
Broadholm St. G22: Glas. 3F **63**
Broadleys Av. G64: B'rig 4B **48**
Broadlie Ct. G78: Neil. 2D **130**
Broadlie Dr. G13: Glas 3A **60**
Broadlie Rd. G78: Neil 2C **130**
Broadloan PA4: Renf. 1E **79**
Broadmeadow Ind. Est.
G82: Dumb 3F **17**
Broadmoss Av. G77: Newt M 5A **134**
Broad Sq. G72: Blan 1A **140**
Broad St. G40: Glas 6B **84**
Broadway, The ML2: Wis 5E **145**
Broadwood Bus. Pk. G68: Cumb. . . . 5B **34**
Broadwood Dr. G44: Glas 1F **119**
BROADWOOD RDBT. **5B 34**
Broadwood Stadium **4B 34**
Brockburn Cres. G53: Glas 5B **100**
Brockburn Rd. G53: Glas. 3A **100**
Brockburn Ter. G53: Glas 5C **100**
Brocklinn Pk. G75: E Kil 4A **148**
Brock Oval G53: Glas 1C **116**
Brock Pl. G53: Glas. 6C **100**
Brock Rd. G53: Glas 1B **116**
Brock Ter. G53: Glas 1C **116**
Brockville St. G32: Glas 5H **85**
Brodick Av. ML1: Moth 2D **142**
Brodick Dr. G74: E Kil 6F **137**
Brodick Pl. G77: Newt M. 5A **132**
Brodick Sq. G64: B'rig 1E **65**
Brodick St. G21: Glas 2C **84**
Brodie Pk. Av. PA2: Pais. 3A **98**
Brodie Pk. Cres. PA2: Pais 3H **97**
Brodie Pk. Gdns. PA2: Pais. 3A **98**
Brodie Pl. G74: E Kil 6F **137**
Brodie Rd. G21: Glas 2F **65**
Brogan Cres. ML1: Moth 2D **142**
Bromley Dr. G46: Giff 6A **118**
Bromley La. G46: Giff. 6A **118**
Bron Way G67: Cumb 4A **36**
Brookbank Ter. ML8: Carl 4G **165**
BROOKFIELD. **6D 74**
Brookfield Av. G33: Glas 2F **65**
Brookfield Cnr. G33: Glas 2F **65**
Brookfield Dr. G33: Glas 2F **65**
Brookfield Gdns. G33: Glas 2F **65**
Brookfield Ga. G33: Glas. 2F **65**
Brookfield Pl. G33: Glas. 2G **65**
Brooklands G74: E Kil. 2C **148**
Brooklands Av. G71: Udd 6C **108**
Brooklea Dr. G46: Giff. 2A **118**
Brooklime Dr. G74: E Kil 5E **137**
Brooklime Gdns. G74: E Kil. 5E **137**
Brooklyn Pl. ML2: Over 5H **157**
Brookside St. G40: Glas 6C **84**
Brook St. G40: Glas 6B **84**
G81: Clyd 3B **42**
BROOM **4H 133**
Broom Av. PA8: Ersk. 2F **57**
Broomburn Dr. G77: Newt M 5F **133**

Broom Cliff G77: Newt M. 6F **133**
Broom Cres. G75: E Kil 6F **149**
G78: Barr 2C **114**
Broomcroft Rd. G77: Newt M 3G **133**
Broom Dr. G81: Clyd. 3C **42**
ML9: Lark 6A **156**
Broomdyke Way PA3: Pais 3H **77**
Broomelton Rd. ML3: Ham 5A **160**
Broomfauld Gdns. G82: Dumb 3G **17**
(not continuous)
Broomfauld Ind. Est. G82: Dumb . . . 4F **17**
Broomfield PA6: Hous 2D **74**
Broomfield Av. G72: Camb 6F **105**
G77: Newt M 6F **133**
Broomfield Ct. G21: Glas 6E **65**
Broomfield La. G21: Glas 4B **64**
Broomfield Pl. G21: Glas 4B **64**
Broomfield Rd. G21: Glas. 4B **64**
G46: Giff. 3G **133**
ML9: Lark 5F **161**
Broomfield St. ML6: Air 4B **92**
Broomfield Ter. G71: Tann 4D **108**
Broomfield Wlk. G66: Kirk 5D **30**
Broom Gdns. G66: Lenz 1B **50**
BROOMHILL
Glasgow 6F 61
Kirkintilloch 3E 31
Broomhill Av. G11: Glas 1F **81**
G32: Carm 5B **106**
G77: Newt M 5F **133**
Broomhill Ct. *G66: Kirk 4D* ***30***
(off Eastside)
ML9: Lark 3E **161**
Broomhill Cres. ML4: Bell. 4B **126**
PA8: Ersk 2F **57**
Broomhill Dr. G11: Glas 6F **61**
G73: Ruth. 2D **120**
G82: Dumb 2H **17**
Broomhill Farm M. G66: Kirk 4E **31**
Broomhill Gdns. G11: Glas 6F **61**
G77: Newt M 5F **133**
Broomhill Ga. ML9: Lark. 3E **161**
Broomhill Ind. Est. G66: Kirk 3E **31**
Broomhill La. G11: Glas 6F **61**
Broomhill Path *G11: Glas 1F* ***81***
(off Broomhill Dr.)
Broomhill Pl. G11: Glas 1F **81**
Broomhill Rd. ML9: Lark 3D **160**
Broomhill Ter. G11: Glas. 1F **81**
Broomhill Vw. ML9: Lark 3C **160**
BROOMHOUSE. 3H 107
Broomieknowe Dr. G73: Ruth 1D **120**
Broomieknowe Gdns. G73: Ruth. . . . 1C **120**
Broomieknowe Rd. G73: Ruth 1D **120**
Broomielaw G1: Glas 5E **83** (6A **4**)
Broomknoll St. ML6: Air. 4A **92**
Broomknowe G68: Cumb. 2F **35**
Broomknowes Av. G66: Lenz. 3E **51**
Broomknowes Rd. G21: Glas 5C **64**
Broomlands Av. PA8: Ersk 1H **57**
Broomlands Cres. PA8: Ersk. 1H **57**
Broomlands Gdns. PA8: Ersk 1H **57**
Broomlands Rd. G67: Cumb. 5A **36**
Broomlands St. PA1: Pais 1F **97**
Broomlands Way PA8: Ersk 1A **58**
Broomlea Cres. PA4: Inch 2G **57**
Broomlee Rd. G67: Cumb. 1H **55**
Broomloan Ct. G51: Glas 6G **81**
Broomloan Pl. G51: Glas 5G **81**
Broomloan Rd. G51: Glas. 5G **81**
Broompark Av. G72: Blan 3A **140**
Broompark Cir. G31: Glas 4B **84**
Broompark Cres. ML6: Air 1A **92**
Broompark Dr. G31: Glas 4B **84**
G77: Newt M. 4G **133**
PA4: Inch 2H **57**
Broompark La. G31: Glas 4B **84**
Broompark Rd. G72: Blan 2A **140**
ML2: Wis 5D **144**
Broompark St. G31: Glas 4B **84**
Broom Path G69: Bail 2F **107**
Broom Pl. G43: Glas. 2B **118**
ML1: N'hill 3C **128**
ML5: Coat. 2B **110**
Broom Pl. PA11: Bri W. 4G **73**
Broom Rd. G43: Glas 2B **118**
G67: Cumb. 6D **14**
G77: Newt M. 3G **133**
Broom Rd. E. G77: Newt M. 6G **133**
Broomside Cres. ML1: Moth. 5G **143**
Broomside St. ML1: Moth 5G **143**
Broomstone Av. G77: Newt M 6F **133**
Broom Ter. PA5: John 4F **95**
Broomton Rd. G21: Glas. 2E **65**
Broomvale Dr. G77: Newt M 4F **133**
Broomward Dr. PA5: John 2H **95**
Brora Cres. ML3: Ham 3D **152**
Brora Dr. G46: Giff 5B **118**
G61: Bear 3H **45**
PA4: Renf. 6G **59**
Brora Gdns. G64: B'rig 6D **48**
Brora Rd. G64: B'rig. 6D **48**
Brora St. G33: Glas. 2F **85**
Broughton G75: E Kil 6G **149**
Broughton Dr. G23: Glas. 1C **62**
Broughton Gdns. G23: Glas 6D **46**
Broughton Pl. ML3: Ham. 6E **141**
ML5: Coat. 2D **110**
Broughton Rd. G23: Glas 1C **62**
Brouster Ga. G74: E Kil. 2G **149**
Brouster Hill G74: E Kil. 2G **149**
Brouster Pl. G74: E Kil 2G **149**
Brown Av. G81: Clyd 1F **59**
G82: Dumb 1C **18**
Brownhill Rd. G43: Glas. 3H **117**
Brownhill Vw. ML2: Newm 3H **147**
Brownieside Pl. ML6: Plain 1G **93**
Brownieside Rd. ML6: Plain. 1H **93**
Brownlee Rd. ML8: Carl, Law 1D **162**
Brownlie St. G42: Glas 5F **103**
Brown Pl. G72: Camb 1A **122**
Brown Rd. G67: Cumb 3H **35**
BROWNSBURN. 1C 112
Brownsburn Ind. Est. ML6: Air 6B **92**
Brownsburn Rd. ML6: Air. 1B **112**
Brownsdale Rd. G73: Ruth 6B **104**
Brownsfield Cres. PA4: Inch 4F **57**
Brownsfield Rd. PA4: Inch 4F **57**
Brownshill Av. ML5: Coat 1B **110**
Brownside Av. G72: Camb 2G **121**
G78: Barr 2C **114**
PA2: Pais 6G **97**
Brownside Cres. G78: Barr 2C **114**
Brownside Dr. G13: Glas. 3H **59**
G78: Barr 2C **114**
Brownside Gro. G78: Barr. 2C **114**
Brownside M. G72: Camb. 2G **121**
Brownside Rd. G73: Ruth 2F **121**
Brownsland Ct. G69: G'csh. 3D **68**
Brown's La. PA1: Pais. 1A **98**
Brown St. G2: Glas. 4E **83** (6B **4**)
ML1: Moth 1H **143**
ML2: Newm. 5E **147**
ML3: Ham. 1A **154**
ML5: Coat. 6C **90**
ML8: Carl 2F **165**
ML9: Lark 1E **161**
PA1: Pais 6G **77**
PA4: Renf. 1D **78**
Bruar Way *ML2: Newm. 3D* ***146***
(off Tiree Cres.)
Bruce Av. ML1: Moth. 2F **143**
PA3: Pais 4C **78**
PA5: John 5E **95**
Bruce Ct. ML6: Air 3E **93**
Brucefield Pl. G34: Glas 3B **88**
BRUCEHILL. 3C 16
Brucehill Rd. G82: Dumb 3C **16**
Bruce Ho. G67: Cumb. 2H **35**
Bruce Loan ML2: Over 5A **158**
Bruce Pl. G75: E Kil 4H **149**
Bruce Rd. G41: Glas 1C **102**
ML1: New S 5B **128**
PA3: Pais 5C **78**
PA4: Renf 2C **78**
PA7: B'ton 3G **39**
Bruce's Loan *ML9: Lark 3G* ***161***
(off Keir Hardie Rd.)
Bruce St. G81: Clyd 6D **42**
G82: Dumb. 5G **17**
ML4: Bell 2D **126**
ML5: Coat. 3D **90**
ML6: Plain 1G **93**
Bruce Ter. G72: Blan. 6C **124**
G75: E Kil 4H **149**
Brunel Way G75: E Kil 3H **149**
Brunstane Rd. G34: Glas 2G **87**
Brunswick Cen. G21: Glas 4D **64**
Brunswick Ho. G81: Clyd 1H **41**
Brunswick La. G1: Glas 4G **83** (6F **5**)
Brunswick St. G1: Glas. 4G **83** (6F **5**)
Brunton St. G44: Glas. 2D **118**
Brunton Ter. G44: Glas 3E **119**
Bruntsfield Av. G53: Glas 4B **116**
Bruntsfield Gdns. G53: Glas 4B **116**
Bryan St. ML3: Ham 4F **141**
Bryce Gdns. ML9: Lark 1E **161**
Bryce Pl. G75: E Kil. 5E **149**
Brydson Pl. PA3: Lin 5H **75**
Bryson Ct. ML3: Ham 4H **153**
Bryson St. G81: Faif 6G **23**
Buccleuch Av. G52: Hill 3G **79**
G76: Clar. 2B **134**
Buccleuch Ct. G61: Bear 6E **25**
Buccleuch Dr. G61: Bear 6E **25**
Buccleuch La. G3: Glas 2E **83** (2B **4**)
Buccleuch St. G3: Glas. 2E **83** (2A **4**)
Buchanan Av. PA7: B'ton 3H **39**
Buchanan Bus. Pk. G33: Step 3F **67**
Buchanan Ct. G33: Step 3E **67**
(not continuous)
Buchanan Cres. G64: B'rig 1E **65**
ML3: Ham 1F **153**
Buchanan Dr. G61: Bear 3G **45**
G64: B'rig 1E **65**
G66: Lenz. 4D **50**
G72: Camb 1G **121**
G73: Ruth. 1D **120**
G77: Newt M. 2E **133**
ML8: Law 5E **159**
Buchanan Galleries (Shop. Cen.)
G1: Glas. 3G **83** (4E **5**)
Buchanan Gro. G69: Bail 6H **87**
Buchanan Pl. G64: Torr 4D **28**
Buchanan St. G1: Glas 4F **83** (6D **4**)
G62: Miln 3H **25**
G69: Bail. 1H **107**
G82: Dumb. 5G **17**
ML5: Coat. 5A **90**
ML6: Air. 4A **92**
PA5: John 3E **95**
Buchanan Street Station (Und.)
. . . . 3G 83 (4E 5)
Buchanan Way PA5: John 3E **95**
Buchandyke Rd. G74: E Kil 5B **138**
Buchanen Gdns. G32: Glas 3E **107**
Buchan Ga. G74: E Kil. 6B **138**
Buchan Ho. G67: Cumb 2H **35**
Buchan Rd. ML1: New S 4A **128**
Buchan St. ML2: Wis 3H **145**
ML3: Ham. 3G **153**
Buchan Ter. G72: Camb 4G **121**
Buchlyvie Gdns. G64: B'rig. 2B **64**
Buchlyvie Path G34: Glas 4H **87**
Buchlyvie Rd. PA1: Pais 6G **79**
Buchlyvie St. G34: Glas 4H **87**
Buckie PA8: Ersk. 4E **41**
Buckie Wlk. ML4: Bell. 1C **126**
Buckingham Ct. ML3: Ham 5C **140**
Buckingham Dr. G32: Carm. 5B **106**
G73: Ruth 6F **105**
Buckingham St. G12: Glas 6B **62**
Buckingham Ter. G12: Glas. 6B **62**
Bucklaw Gdns. G52: Glas 1C **100**
Bucklaw Pl. G52: Glas 1C **100**
Bucklaw Ter. G52: Glas. 1C **100**
Buckley St. G22: Glas. 3H **63**
Bucksburn Rd. G21: Glas 5E **65**
Buckthorne Pl. G53: Glas 4B **116**
Buddon St. G40: Glas 1E **105**
Budhill Av. G32: Glas 6B **86**
Budshaw Av. ML6: Chap 3C **112**

Bulldale Ct. G14: Glas 4H **59**
Bulldale St. G14: Glas 3G **59**
Buller Cres. G72: Blan 5A **124**
Bullionslaw Dr. G73: Ruth 1F **121**
Bulloch Av. G46: Giff 5B **118**
Bull Rd. G76: Busby 3D **134**
Bullwood Av. G53: Glas 5H **99**
Bullwood Ct. G53: Glas 5H **99**
Bullwood Dr. G53: Glas 4H **99**
Bullwood Gdns. G53: Glas 4H **99**
Bullwood Pl. G53: Glas 4H **99**
Bunbury Ter. G75: E Kil 3E **149**
Bunessan St. G52: Glas 6F **81**
Bunhouse Rd. G3: Glas 2A **82**
Burch Hall La. G11: Glas 1H **81**
Burghead Dr. G51: Glas 3E **81**
Burghead Pl. G51: Glas 3E **81**
Burgher St. G31: Glas 6E **85**
Burgh Hall St. G11: Glas 1H **81**
Burgh La. *G12: Glas* *6B* ***62***
(off Cresswell St.)
Burleigh Rd. G71: Both 4F **125**
Burleigh St. G51: Glas 3G **81**
ML5: Coat 2D **110**
Burley Pl. G74: E Kil 1B **148**
Burlington Av. G12: Glas 3H **61**
Burmola St. G22: Glas 5F **63**
Burnacre Gdns. G71: Udd 6C **108**
Burnawn Ga. G33: Glas 2F **65**
Burnawn Gro. G33: Glas 2F **65**
Burnawn Pl. G33: Glas 2F **65**
BURNBANK **4E 141**
Burnbank Braes ML8: Carl 4F **165**
Burnbank Cen. ML3: Ham 4E **141**
Burnbank Dr. G78: Barr 6E **115**
Burnbank Gdns. G20: Glas 1D **82**
ML3: Ham *4E* ***141***
(off Burnbank Rd.)
Burnbank La. G20: Glas 1D **82**
Burnbank M. G66: Lenz 3D **50**
Burnbank Pl. G20: Glas 1E **83**
Burnbank Quad. ML6: Air 3H **91**
Burnbank Rd. ML3: Ham 4E **141**
Burnbank St. ML5: Coat 3D **90**
ML6: Air 3H **91**
Burnbank Ter. G20: Glas 1D **82**
G65: Kils 2H **11**
Burnblea Gdns. ML3: Ham 1A **154**
Burnblea St. ML3: Ham 1H **153**
Burnbrae G65: Twe 2D **32**
Burn Brae G81: Dun 1C **42**
Burnbrae Av. G61: Bear 6G **25**
G69: Mood 5D **52**
PA3: Lin 6A **76**
Burnbrae Dr. G73: Ruth 2F **121**
PA3: Lin 2B **96**
Burnbrae Pl. G74: E Kil 1E **149**
Burnbrae Rd. G66: Auch 5E **51**
G66: Kirk 6H **31**
G69: Chry, Lenz 3H **51**
G72: Blan 2A **140**
PA3: Lin 1H **95**
Burnbrae St. G21: Glas 5C **64**
G81: Faif 5F **23**
ML9: Lark 2D **160**
Burncleugh Av. G72: Camb 3A **122**
Burn Cres. ML1: New S 3A **128**
ML6: Chap 3D **112**
Burncrooks Av. G61: Bear 6C **24**
G74: E Kil 1E **149**
Burncrooks Ct. G81: Dun 1B **42**
Burndyke Ct. G51: Glas 4H **81**
Burndyke Sq. G51: Glas 4A **82**
Burnet Rose Ct. G74: E Kil 5E **137**
Burnet Rose Gdns.
G74: E Kil 5E **137**
Burnet Rose Pl. G74: E Kil 5E **137**
Burnett Rd. G33: Glas 4E **87**
Burnfield Av. G46: Giff 3H **117**
Burnfield Cotts. G46: Giff 3H **117**
Burnfield Dr. G43: Glas 3H **117**
Burnfield Gdns. G46: Giff 3A **118**
Burnfield Rd. G43: Glas 2G **117**
G46: Giff 3A **118**
BURNFOOT **2G 91**
Burnfoot Cres. G73: Ruth 2F **121**
PA2: Pais 5G **97**
Burnfoot Dr. G52: Glas 6B **80**
Burnfoot Rd. ML6: Air 3G **91**
Burngill Pl. *PA11: Bri W* *3F* ***73***
(off Kilmalcom Rd.)
Burngreen G65: Kils 3H **11**
Burngreen Ter. G67: Cumb 6B **14**
Burnhall Pl. ML2: Wis 2B **158**
Burnhall Rd. ML2: Wis 1A **158**
Burnhall St. ML2: Wis 2B **158**
Burnham Rd. G14: Glas 5A **60**
Burnhaven PA8: Ersk 5E **41**
BURNHEAD **2G 161**
Burnhead Rd. G43: Glas 2C **118**
G68: Cumb 3E **35**
ML6: Air 1C **92**
ML9: Lark 2F **161**
Burnhead St. G71: View 5F **109**
Burnhill Quad. G73: Ruth 5B **104**
Burnhill Sports Cen. **5B 104**
Burnhill St. G73: Ruth 5B **104**
Burnhouse Brae
G77: Newt M 6G **133**
Burnhouse Cres.
ML3: Ham 2F **153**
Burnhouse Rd. ML3: Ham 2F **153**
Burnhouse St. G20: Glas 3A **62**
(not continuous)
Burniebrae ML6: Air 3G **91**
Burniebrae Rd. ML6: Chap 2E **113**
Burn La. ML1: New S 3A **128**
Burnlea Cres. PA6: Hous 1A **74**
Burnlip Rd. ML5: Glenb 5C **70**
ML6: Glenm 5C **70**
Burnmouth Ct. G33: Glas 5F **87**
Burnmouth Pl. G61: Bear 2G **45**
Burnmouth Rd. G33: Glas 5F **87**
Burnock Pl. G75: E Kil 4A **148**
Burnpark Av. G71: Udd 6B **108**
Burn Pl. G72: Camb 6G **105**
Burn Rd. ML8: Carl 2F **165**
Burns Av. PA7: B'ton 4H **39**
Burns Ct. G66: Kirk 4G **31**
Burn's Cres. ML6: Air 5B **92**
Burns Dr. G66: Kirk 3G **31**
PA5: John 5E **95**
Burns Gdns. G72: Blan 6A **124**
Burns Gro. G46: T'bnk 5G **117**
BURNSIDE **2E 121**
Burnside G61: Bear 6C **24**
Burnside Av. G66: Kirk 6B **30**
G78: Barr 3D **114**
ML4: Bell 3E **127**
ML6: C'bnk 3B **112**
PA5: Brkfld 6C **74**
Burnside Ct. G61: Bear 1C **44**
G73: Ruth 2E **121**
G81: Clyd 3A **42**
ML1: Moth 5B **144**
ML5: Coat *6B* ***90***
(off Kirk St.)
Burnside Cres. G72: Blan 3C **140**
G81: Hard 6D **22**
Burnside Gdns. G76: Clar 2B **134**
PA10: Kilb 3B **94**
Burnside Ga. G73: Ruth 2E **121**
Burnside Gro. PA5: John 3E **95**
Burnside Ind. Est. G65: Kils 3G **11**
Burnside La. ML3: Ham 1A **154**
Burnside Pl. G82: Dumb 5H **17**
ML9: Lark 2F **161**
PA3: Pais 4E **77**
(not continuous)
Burnside Quad. ML1: Holy 2A **128**
Burnside Rd. G46: Giff 3H **133**
G73: Ruth 2E **121**
ML1: N'hill 3C **128**
ML5: Coat 2E **91**
PA5: Eld 4A **96**
Burnside Station (Rail) **2E 121**
Burnside St. G82: Dumb 5H **17**
ML1: Moth 5B **144**
Burnside Ter. *G82: Dumb* *5H* ***17***
(off Burnside Pl.)
PA10: Kilb 3B **94**
Burnside Twr. *ML1: Moth* *5A* ***144***
(off Burnside Ct.)
Burnside Vw. ML5: Coat 6A **90**
Burnside Wlk. ML5: Coat 6A **90**
Burns La. ML6: Chap 2D **112**
Burns Loan *ML9: Lark* *1F* ***161***
(off Carrick Pl.)
Burns Pk. G74: E Kil 1A **150**
Burns Path ML4: Bell 6D **110**
Burns Rd. G66: Kirk 4F **31**
G67: Cumb 3B **36**
ML6: Chap 1D **112**
Burns St. G4: Glas 1F **83**
G81: Clyd 3A **42**
ML3: Ham 1H **153**
Burns Way ML1: N'hill 3C **128**
Burntbroom Dr. G69: Bail 2F **107**
Burntbroom Gdns. G69: Bail 2F **107**
Burntbroom St. G33: Glas 3D **86**
Burn Ter. G72: Camb 6G **105**
Burnthills Ind. Est. *PA5: John* *2F* ***95***
(off High St.)
Burntshields Rd. PA10: Kilb 2A **94**
Burn Vw. G67: Cumb 2C **36**
Burnwood Dr. ML6: Air 5G **93**
Burra Gdns. G64: B'rig 5F **49**
Burrell Collection Mus. **4H 101**
Burrell Ct. G41: Glas 3A **102**
Burrell's La. G4: Glas 4A **84** (5H **5**)
Burrelton Rd. G43: Glas 1D **118**
Burton La. G42: Glas 4E **103**
ML8: Carl 3E **165**
BUSBY **3D 134**
Busby Equitation Cen. **5E 135**
Busby Rd. G76: Clar 1C **134**
G76: Crmck 3G **135**
ML4: Bell 4B **126**
Busby Station (Rail) **4E 135**
Bush Cres. ML2: Wis 1A **158**
Bushelhead Rd. ML8: Carl 6E **165**
Bushes Av. PA2: Pais 4H **97**
Busheyhill St. G72: Camb 2A **122**
Bute G74: E Kil 2C **150**
Bute Av. ML1: Moth 2E **143**
PA4: Renf 2F **79**
Bute Cres. G60: Old K 2G **41**
G61: Bear 5F **45**
PA2: Pais 6H **97**
Bute Dr. G60: Old K 2G **41**
PA5: John 4D **94**
Bute Gdns. G12: Glas 1B **82**
G44: Neth 3D **118**
G60: Old K 1G **41**
Bute La. G12: Glas 1B **82**
PA3: Pais 4F **77**
Bute Pl. G60: Old K 1G **41**
Bute Rd. G66: Kirk 5H **31**
PA3: Glas A 2G **77**
Bute St. ML3: Ham 3F **141**
ML5: Coat 1D **110**
Bute Ter. G71: View 6F **109**
G73: Ruth 2C **120**
Bute Twr. G72: Camb 4G **121**
Butler Wynd ML4: Bell 2B **126**
Butterbiggins Rd. G42: Glas 2E **103**
Butterburn Pk. St.
ML3: Ham 1H **153**
Butterfield Pl. G41: Glas 2E **103**
Buttermere G75: E Kil 6B **148**
Byars Rd. G66: Kirk 5B **30**
Byrebush Rd. G53: Glas 4C **100**
Byres Av. PA3: Pais 5C **78**
Byres Cres. PA3: Pais 5C **78**
Byres Rd. G11: Glas 1A **82**
ML1: N'hill 3E **129**
PA5: Eld 3B **96**
Byrestone Av. G77:
Newt M 5A **134**
Byron Ct. G71: Both 5F **125**
Byron St. G11: Glas 1E **81**
G81: Clyd 3C **42**

Byshot Path—Cambusnethan St.

Byshot Path G22: Glas 5H **63**
Byshot St. G22: Glas. 5H **63**

C

Cable Dpt. Rd. G81: Clyd 5B **42**
CADDER
Bishopbriggs **2D 48**
Gilshochill **2D 62**
Cadder Ct. G64: B'rig 2D **48**
Cadder Gro. *G20: Glas 2C **62***
(off Cadder Rd.)
Cadder Pl. G20: Glas 2C **62**
Cadder Rd. G20: Glas. 1C **62**
G23: Glas 1C **62**
G64: B'rig 2D **48**
Cadder Way G64: B'rig 2D **48**
Cadell Gdns. G74: E Kil 4D **138**
Cadger's Sheuch G65: Kils 3C **12**
Cadoc St. G72: Camb 2B **122**
Cadogan Sq. G2: Glas 4E **83** (6B **4**)
Cadogan St. G2: Glas. 4E **83** (5B **4**)
Cadzow Av. G46: Giff 1H **133**
Cadzow Bri. ML3: Ham. 5A **142**
Cadzow Castle **3C 154**
Cadzow Cres. ML5: Coat. 1A **110**
Cadzow Dr. G72: Camb. 2H **121**
ML4: Bell. 3F **127**
Cadzow Grn. G74: E Kil 1F **149**
Cadzow Ho. ML3: Ham 4A **142**
Cadzow Ind. Est. ML3: Ham 3H **153**
Cadzow La. ML3: Ham 5A **142**
Cadzow Pk. ML3: Ham 5A **142**
Cadzow St. G2: Glas. 4E **83** (6A **4**)
ML1: Moth 3F **143**
ML3: Ham. 5A **142**
ML9: Lark 1E **161**
Caerlaverock Pl. G72: Blan. 3A **140**
Caird Dr. G11: Glas. 1H **81**
Caird Gdns. ML3: Ham. 4G **141**
Caird Pk. ML3: Ham. 4H **141**
Caird St. ML3: Ham 4G **141**
Caird Ter. *G61: Bear. 6D **24***
(off Grampian Way)
Cairhill Trad. Est. ML6: Air. 5A **92**
Cairn Av. PA4: Renf 2G **79**
Cairnbairn Ct. *ML8: Carl 2F **165***
(off Carranbuie Rd.)
Cairnban St. G51: Glas. 5D **80**
Cairnbrook Ind. Est. G34: Glas 2A **88**
Cairnbrook Rd. G34: Glas. 3A **88**
Cairn Ct. G74: E Kil. 5G **137**
ML1: Moth 4H **143**
Cairncraig St. G40: Glas 1E **105**
Cairndow Av. G44: Glas 3D **118**
Cairndow Av. La. G44: Glas 3D **118**
Cairndow Ct. G44: Glas 3D **118**
Cairndow Pl. ML2: Wis. 2H **157**
Cairn Dr. PA3: Lin. 5H **75**
Cairndyke Cres. ML6: Air 5A **92**
Cairneymount Rd. ML8: Carl 3F **165**
Cairney Pl. ML2: Newm 3H **147**
Cairngorm Cres. G61: Bear. 1B **44**
G78: Barr 6E **115**
ML2: Wis. 6F **145**
PA2: Pais 4A **98**
Cairngorm Gdns. G68: Cumb 4D **34**
Cairngorm Rd. G43: Glas 2A **118**
CAIRNHILL **6H 91**
Cairnhill Av. ML6: Air. 6A **92**
Cairnhill Cir. G52: Glas. 2H **99**
Cairnhill Ct. ML8: Carl 3F **165**
Cairnhill Cres. ML5: Coat 2F **111**
Cairnhill Dr. G52: Glas 2H **99**
Cairnhill Pl. G52: Glas 2H **99**
Cairnhill Rd. G61: Bear. 6F **45**
ML6: Air. 6H **91**
Cairnhope Av. ML6: Air 6H **91**
Cairnlea Dr. G51: Glas 5H **81**
Cairnlea Gdns. ML4: Bell 4D **126**
Cairnlea Rd. G62: Miln. 4E **25**
Cairnmuir Rd. G73: Ruth 2H **137**
G74: Roger 3F **137**
Cairnmuir Rd.
G76: Crmck, Roger 4C **136**
Cairnoch Hill G68: Cumb 3E **35**
Cairn Pl. G74: E Kil. 5G **137**
Cairnryan G74: E Kil 6F **137**
CAIRNS **3C 122**
Cairns Av. G72: Camb. 2B **122**
Cairns Dr. G62: Miln. 3G **25**
Cairnsmore Dr. G61: Bear. 6B **24**
Cairnsmore Rd. G15: Glas 5G **43**
Cairns Rd. G72: Camb 3B **122**
PA7: B'ton 3G **39**
Cairns St. ML1: Moth 3G **143**
Cairn St. G21: Glas. 3B **64**
Cairnswell Av. G72: Camb 3C **122**
Cairnswell Pl. G72: Camb. 3C **122**
Cairntoul Ct. G68: Cumb 4D **34**
Cairntoul Dr. G14: Glas. 3A **60**
Cairntoul Pl. G14: Glas. 4A **60**
Cairn Vw. G66: Kirk 6H **31**
ML6: Air. 5H **91**
Cairnview Rd. G66: Milt C 6B **8**
Cairnwood Dr. ML6: Air 6H **91**
Caithness Rd. G74: E Kil. 6C **138**
Caithness St. G20: Glas 5D **62**
G4: Glas 1F **83**
G72: Blan 3A **140**
Cala Sona Ct. ML2: Wis 3E **157**
Calcots Path G34: Glas. 2A **88**
Calcots Pl. G34: Glas 2A **88**
Caldarvan St. G22: Glas 6F **63**
Caldeen Rd. ML5: Coat 6D **90**
Calder Av. G78: Barr. 6E **115**
ML2: Newm. 3E **147**
ML5: Coat. 1D **110**
CALDERBANK **3B 112**
Calderbank Rd. ML6: Air 1A **112**
Calderbank Ter. ML1: Moth 2H **143**
Calderbank Vw. G69: Bail 1A **108**
Calderbankview Cotts.
ML6: C'bnk. 1B **112**
CALDERBRAES. **5C 108**
Calderbraes Av. G71: Tann 4C **108**
Calder Ct. *ML5: Coat 1D **110***
(off Whifflet St.)
Caldercuilt Rd. G20: Glas 1A **62**
G23: Glas 1A **62**
Calder Dr. G72: Camb. 2A **122**
ML4: Bell. 3E **127**
Calder Ga. G64: B'rig 3B **48**
Calderglen Av. G72: Blan 4A **124**
Calderglen Country Pk. **6E 139**
Calderglen Country Pk. Vis. Cen.
. . . . **5D 150**
Calderglen Rd. G74: E Kil. 2C **150**
Caldergrove ML1: Moth 2G **143**
Calderpark Av. G71: Udd 3H **107**
Calderpark Cres. G71: Udd. 3H **107**
Calder Pl. G69: Bail 1H **107**
Calderrigg Pl. ML6: Air. 4E **93**
Calder Rd. G71: View. 4H **109**
G72: Blan 2H **123**
ML4: Moss 2E **127**
PA3: Pais 6E **77**
Calderside Gro. G74: E Kil 5E **139**
Calderside Rd. G72: Blan 3D **150**
Calder St. G42: Glas 3E **103**
G72: Blan 1B **140**
ML5: Coat. 1D **110**
ML6: C'bnk. 3C **112**
Calder Twr. G74: E Kil. 4B **150**
ML1: Moth 4G **143**
Caldervale St. ML6: Gart 1E **113**
Calder Vw. ML1: Moth 2H **143**
ML3: Ham 3F **153**
Calderview Av. ML5: Coat. 1F **111**
CALDERWOOD **6B 138**
Calderwood Av. G69: Bail 2G **107**
Calderwood Dr. G69: Bail 2G **107**
G72: Blan 3B **140**
Calderwood Gdns. G69: Bail. 2G **107**
G74: E Kil 5E **139**
Calderwood Rd. G43: Glas 1B **118**
G73: Ruth 6E **105**
Calderwood Rd. G74: E Kil 2A **150**
Calderwood Sq. *G74: E Kil 6B **138***
(off Pollock Pl.)
Caldwell Av. G13: Glas. 3A **60**
PA3: Lin 6F **75**
Caldwell Gro. ML4: Bell 5C **110**
Caldwell Quad. ML1: Moth 4E **143**
Caldwell Rd. ML8: Carl 5H **165**
Caledonia Av. G5: Glas. 2G **103**
G73: Ruth 5D **104**
Caledonia Ct. PA3: Pais 5H **77**
Caledonia Dr. G69: Bail 2H **107**
ML1: N'hill 3E **129**
Caledonia Gdns. ML8: Carl. 2E **165**
Caledonian Av. ML4: Bell 3B **126**
Caledonian Ct. G74: E Kil 3G **149**
Caledonian Cres. *G12: Glas 1C **82***
(off Otago St.)
Caledonian Pk. ML2: Wis. 6D **144**
Caledonian Rd. ML2: Wis. 2G **157**
ML9: Lark 2E **161**
Caledonia Rd. G5: Glas. 1F **103**
G69: Bail. 2G **107**
Caledonia St. G5: Glas 2G **103**
G81: Clyd 4B **42**
PA3: Pais 6H **77**
Caledonia Ter. G82: Dumb 4C **16**
Caledonia Wlk. *ML3: Ham 2A **154***
(off Chatelherault Cres.)
Caledonia Way PA3: Glas A 2H **77**
Caledonia Way E. PA3: Glas A 2A **78**
Caledonia Way W. PA3: Glas A. 2H **77**
Caledon La. *G12: Glas 1A **82***
(off Highburgh Rd.)
Caledon St. G12: Glas 1A **82**
Caley Brae G71: Udd 1D **124**
Calfhill Rd. G53: Glas. 2B **100**
Calfmuir Rd. G66: Kirk, Lenz 6G **31**
Calgary Pk. G75: E Kil. 3F **149**
Calgary Pl. G75: E Kil 3F **149**
Calgary St. G4: Glas. 2G **83** (2F **5**)
Calico Way G66: Len 2E **7**
Callaghan Wynd G72: Blan. 6H **123**
Callander Ct. G68: Cumb 1H **35**
Callander Rd. G68: Cumb. 1H **35**
ML6: Chap 4D **112**
Callander St. G20: Glas 6E **63**
Callieburn Ct. G64: B'rig. 1C **64**
Callieburn Rd. G64: B'rig 1C **64**
Callon St. ML6: Air. 4A **92**
Cally Av. G15: Glas. 4A **44**
Calside PA2: Pais. 3H **97**
Calside Av. PA2: Pais 2H **97**
Calside Ct. PA2: Pais 3A **98**
CALTON **5A 84**
Calton Entry *G40: Glas 5A **84***
(off Stevenson St.)
Calvay Cres. G33: Glas. 4D **86**
Calvay Pl. G33: Glas. 4E **87**
Calvay Rd. G33: Glas 4D **86**
Cambourne Rd. G69: Mood 4D **52**
Cambridge Av. G81: Clyd 4D **42**
Cambridge Rd. PA4: Renf. 1E **79**
Cambridge St. G2: Glas 3F **83** (3C **4**)
G3: Glas 3F **83** (3C **4**)
Camburn St. G32: Glas. 6H **85**
Cambusdoon Rd. G33: Glas 1C **86**
Cambuskenneth Gdns. G32: Glas . . . 6D **86**
Cambuskenneth Pl. G33: Glas 1C **86**
CAMBUSLANG **1A 122**
Cambuslang Bri. G32: Glas. 6A **106**
Cambuslang Ind. Pk. G32: Glas . . . 5A **106**
Cambuslang Investment Pk.
G32: Glas 5A **106**
Cambuslang Rd. G32: Glas. 5H **105**
G72: Camb 5G **105**
(Bogleshole Rd.)
G72: Camb 6F **105**
(Farmeloan Rd.)
G73: Ruth. 4D **104**
Cambuslang Station (Rail) **1H 121**
Cambusmore Pl. G33: Glas. 1C **86**
CAMBUSNETHAN **6C 146**
Cambusnethan St. ML2: Wis 5C **146**

Cambus Pl. G33: Glas 1C 86
Camden St. G5: Glas 1G 103
Camden Ter. G5: Glas 1G 103
Camellia Dr. ML2: Wis 2E 157
Camelon Cres. G72: Blan 2B 140
Camelon St. G32: Glas 5H 85
Cameron Av. PA7: B'ton 3H 39
Cameron Ct. G52: Hill 4H 79
G73: Ruth 6C 104
G81: Clyd 1E 59
ML6: Air 3E 93
Cameron Cres. G76: Crmck 2A 136
ML3: Ham 6F 141
Cameron Dr. G61: Bear 4G 45
G71: Tann 5E 109
G77: Newt M 2E 133
Cameronian Dr. ML8: Carl 4G 165
Cameronian Pl. ML4: Bell 4B 126
Cameronian Way
ML9: Lark 4G 161
Cameron Path *ML9: Lark 4G 161*
(off Donaldson Rd.)
Cameron Rd. ML8: Carl 5H 165
Cameron Sq. G81: Hard 1E 43
Cameron St. G52: Hill 4G 79
G81: Clyd 1E 59
ML1: Moth 3F 143
ML5: Coat 3D 90
Cameron Way G72: Blan 1B 140
Camie Ct. G66: Kirk 5C 30
CAMLACHIE 6D 84
Camlachie St. G31: Glas 6D 84
(not continuous)
Campbell Av. G62: Miln 4G 25
G82: Dumb 1C 18
PA7: B'ton 3H 39
Campbell Cres. G71: Both 3E 125
G77: Newt M 3E 133
Campbell Dr. G61: Bear 2D 44
G78: Barr 5E 115
G82: Dumb 1C 18
Campbell Ho. G67: Cumb 4G 35
Campbell La. ML3: Ham 6A 142
Campbell Pl. G64: Torr 4D 28
G75: E Kil 4G 149
Campbell St. G20: Glas 2B 62
ML2: Wis 6H 145
ML3: Ham 6A 142
ML4: Bell 2C 126
PA4: Renf 5F 59
PA5: John 3F 95
Campbell Ter. G82: Dumb 1C 18
Camphill PA1: Pais 2H 97
Camphill Av. G41: Glas 5C 102
G66: Kirk 5C 30
Camphill Ct. PA2: Pais 2H 97
Camphill Gdns. PA7: B'ton 4A 40
Camphill Ho. G41: Glas 4D 102
Campion Rd. ML1: Moth 1G 143
Camp Rd. G69: Bail 6H 87
G73: Ruth 3B 104
ML1: Moth 5G 143
Camps Cres. PA4: Renf 1G 79
Campside Gdns. G76: Clar 1A 134
Campsie Av. G78: Barr 6E 115
Campsie Ct. G66: Kirk 1C 50
ML5: Coat 2E 111
ML9: Lark 6H 155
Campsie Cres. ML6: Air 3H 91
Campsie Dr. G61: Bear 6D 24
G62: Miln 3H 25
PA2: Pais 5H 97
PA3: Glas A 1A 78
PA4: Renf 3C 78
Campsie Pl. G69: Chry 1A 68
Campsie Recreation Cen. 3G 7
Campsie Rd. G64: Torr 4E 29
G66: Kirk 4B 30
G66: Len, Milt C 4H 7
ML2: Wis 5E 145
Campsie St. G21: Glas 4B 64
Campsie Vw. G33: Step 5D 66
G66: Kirk 5A 30
G67: Cumb 2B 36
Campsie Vw. G69: Barg 6D 88
G69: Chry 1A 68
G71: Tann 5E 109
G72: Flem 4E 123
ML3: Ham 1D 152
Campston Pl. G33: Glas 2B 86
Camp St. ML1: Moth 4G 143
Camstradden Dr. E. G61: Bear 3C 44
Camstradden Dr. W. G61: Bear 3C 44
Camus Pl. G15: Glas 3H 43
Canal Av. PA5: John 3G 95
Canal Bank *G23: Glas 2E 63*
(off Balmore Rd.)
Canal Gdns. PA5: Eld 2B 96
Canal La. G66: Kirk 4D 30
PA4: Renf 5F 59
Canal Rd. PA5: John 3F 95
Canal St. G4: Glas 2G 83 (1F 5)
G66: Kirk 4D 30
G81: Clyd 1D 58
PA1: Pais 1H 97
PA4: Renf 5F 59
PA5: Eld 2B 96
PA5: John 2G 95
Canal Ter. PA1: Pais 1A 98
Canberra Av. G81: Clyd 3H 41
Canberra Ct. G46: Giff 4C 118
Canberra Dr. G75: E Kil 3E 149
Candermill & Marlage Rd.
ML9: Ashg 6B 162
Cander Rigg G64: B'rig 3C 48
Cander St. ML9: Lark 5F 161
Candimilne Ct. ML8: Carl 4H 165
Candleriggs G1: Glas 4H 83 (6G 5)
Candren Rd. PA3: Lin 6B 76
PA3: Pais 1E 97
(not continuous)
Candren Way PA3: Pais 6E 77
Caneluk Av. ML8: Carl 5H 165
Canmore Pl. G31: Glas 1F 105
Canmore St. G31: Glas 1F 105
Cannerton Cres. G66: Milt C 6B 8
Cannerton Pk. G66: Milt C 6B 8
Cannich Dr. PA2: Pais 4D 98
Cannich Pl. ML2: Newm 3D 146
Canniesburn Rd. G61: Bear 5C 44
Canniesburn Sq. G61: Bear 5F 45
CANNIESBURN TOLL 5F 45
Canniesbury Rd. G61: Bear 4D 44
Canonbie Av. G74: E Kil 5H 137
Canon Ct. ML1: Carf 5D 128
Canongate G74: E Kil 5D 138
Canterbury G75: E Kil 5D 148
Cantieslaw Dr. G74: E Kil 6A 138
Canting Way G51: Glas 4A 82
Canyon Rd. ML2: Wis 1D 156
Capel Av. G77: Newt M 3F 133
Capel Gro. G74: E Kil 6B 138
Capelridge Dr. G74: E Kil 1B 150
Capelrig Dr. G77: Newt M 1D 132
Capelrig La. G77: Newt M 3D 132
Capelrig Rd. G77: Newt M 1D 132
Capelrig St. G46: T'bnk 3F 117
Caper House Play Barn 5D 136
Caplaw Pl. ML2: Wis 3F 157
Caplaw Rd. PA2: Pais 6G 97
Caplaw Twr. ML2: Wis 3F 157
Caplethill Rd. PA2: Pais 6A 98
Caprington Pl. G33: Glas 2A 86
Caprington St. G33: Glas 2A 86
Cara Dr. G51: Glas 3E 81
Caravelle Way PA4: Renf 2F 79
Carbarns ML2: Wis 2D 156
Carbarns E. ML2: Wis 2D 156
Carbarns Rd. ML2: Wis 3C 156
Carbarns W. ML2: Wis 2D 156
Carberry Rd. G41: Glas 3B 102
Carbeth Rd. G62: Miln 4F 25
Carbeth St. G22: Glas 5F 63
Carbisdale St. G22: Glas 4A 64
Carbost St. G23: Glas 6B 46
Carbrach Loan *ML2: Newm 3D 146*
(off Tiree Cres.)
CARBRAIN 4A 36
Carbrain Ind. Est. G67: Cumb 4B 36
Carbrook St. G21: Glas 2C 84
PA1: Pais 1G 97
Cardarrach St. G21: Glas 5C 64
Cardean Rd. ML4: Moss 1G 127
Cardell Av. PA2: Pais 2E 97
Cardell Cres. ML6: Chap 3D 112
Cardell Dr. PA2: Pais 2E 97
Cardell Rd. PA2: Pais 2E 97
CARDONALD 6B 80
Cardonald Dr. G52: Glas 1A 100
Cardonald Gdns. G52: Glas 1B 100
Cardonald Pk. G51: Glas 4B 80
Cardonald Pl. Rd.
G52: Glas 1B 100
Cardonald Station (Rail) 5D 80
Cardowan Dr. G33: Step 4D 66
G68: Cumb 4A 34
Cardowan Pk. G71: Tann 4F 109
Cardowan Rd. G32: Glas 5H 85
G33: Step 3E 67
Cardow Rd. G21: Glas 5E 65
Cardrona St. G33: Glas 6B 66
Cardross Ct. G31: Glas 4B 84
Cardross Rd. G82: Card, Dumb 2A 16
G82: Dumb 3B 16
Cardross St. G31: Glas 4B 84
Cardwell St. G41: Glas 1E 103
Cardyke St. G21: Glas 5C 64
Careston Pl. G64: B'rig 6F 49
Carey Gdns. ML1: Cle 6H 129
CARFIN 5B 128
Carfin Ind. Est. ML1: Carf 5B 128
Carfin Lourdes Grotto 5D 128
Carfin Mill Rd. ML1: Carf 6C 128
Carfin Rd. ML1: N'hill 5D 128
ML2: Wis 5C 144
Carfin Station (Rail) 5D 128
Carfin St. G42: Glas 3F 103
ML1: New S 4A 128
ML5: Coat 1D 110
Carfrae St. G3: Glas 3A 82
Cargill Sq. G64: B'rig 1E 65
Carham Cres. G52: Glas 6C 80
Carham Dr. G52: Glas 6C 80
Caribou Grn. G75: E Kil 3D 148
Carillon Rd. G51: Glas 6A 82
Carinthia Sq. G81: Clyd 5D 42
Carisbrooke Cres. G64: B'rig 3D 48
Carlaverock Rd. G43: Glas 1B 118
Carleith Av. G81: Dun 1B 42
Carleith Quad. G51: Glas 4D 80
Carleith Ter. G81: Dun 1B 42
Carleston St. G21: Glas 5B 64
Carleton Ct. G46: Giff 3A 118
Carleton Dr. G46: Giff 3A 118
Carleton Ga. G46: Giff 3A 118
Carlibar Av. G13: Glas 3H 59
Carlibar Dr. G78: Barr 4E 115
Carlibar Gdns. G78: Barr 4E 115
Carlibar Rd. G78: Barr 4D 114
Carlile Pl. PA3: Pais 5A 78
Carlin La. ML8: Carl 4H 165
Carlisle La. ML6: Air 4C 92
Carlisle Rd. ML1: N'hse 6G 113
ML3: Fern, Ham 6B 142
ML6: Air 5C 92
ML9: Lark 5G 155
(Lanark Rd. End)
ML9: Lark 5F 161
(Strutherhill)
Carlisle St. G21: Glas 6H 63
Carlock Wlk. G32: Glas 5C 86
Carlouk La. ML8: Carl 4H 165
Carloway Ct. G33: Glas 3B 86
Carlowrie Av. G72: Blan 5A 124
CARLSTON 3G 29
Carlton Ct. G5: Glas 5F 83
Carlton Pl. G5: Glas 5F 83
CARLUKE 3F 165
Carluke Leisure Cen. 3G 165
Carluke Station (Rail) 4D 164
Carlyle Av. G52: Hill 3H 79
Carlyle Dr. G74: E Kil 1A 150

Carlyle Ter. G73: Ruth 4D **104**
G74: E Kil 1B **150**
Carmaben Rd. G33: Glas 3D **86**
Carman Vw. G82: Dumb 1G **17**
Carment Dr. G41: Glas 5B **102**
Carmichael Path *ML5: Glenb 3G* ***69***
(off Oval, The)
Carmichael Pl. G42: Glas 6D **102**
Carmichael St. G51: Glas 5H **81**
ML8: Law 6D **158**
Carmichael Way ML8: Law 6D **158**
CARMUNNOCK 2H 135
Carmunnock By-Pass
G76: Crmck 6G **119**
Carmunnock La. G44: Glas 2F **119**
Carmunnock Rd. G44: Glas 6F **103**
G45: Glas 6G **119**
G74: E Kil 1F **149**
G76: Busby 4E **135**
G76: Crmck 6G **119**
(Carmunnock By-Pass)
G76: Crmck 4C **136**
(Kittochside Rd.)
CARMYLE 5C 106
Carmyle Av. G32: Carm, Glas 3B **106**
CARMYLE AV. INTERCHANGE 4B 106
Carmyle Gdns. ML5: Coat 2A **110**
Carmyle Station (Rail) 4B 106
Carna Dr. G44: Glas 2G **119**
Carnarvon St. G3: Glas 2D **82** (1A **4**)
Carnbooth Ct. G45: Glas 5B **120**
CARNBROE 1E 111
Carnbroe Rd. ML4: Bell 6D **110**
ML5: Coat 1F **111**
Carneddans Rd. G62: Miln 1C **24**
Carnegie Hill G75: E Kil 3F **149**
Carnegie Pl. G75: E Kil 3F **149**
Carnegie Rd. G52: Hill 4A **80**
(not continuous)
Carnoch St. G23: Glas 6B **46**
Carnock Cres. G78: Barr 6D **114**
Carnock Gdns. G62: Miln 3E **25**
Carnock Rd. G53: Glas 5C **100**
Carnoustie Ct. G71: Both 5D **124**
Carnoustie Cres. G64: B'rig 6E **49**
G75: E Kil 5C **148**
Carnoustie Pl. G5: Glas 6D **82**
ML4: Bell 6C **110**
Carnoustie St. G5: Glas 6D **82**
Carnoustie Way G68: Cumb 5H **13**
CARNTYNE 4G 85
Carntyne Gdns. G32: Glas 4G **85**
Carntynehall Rd. G32: Glas 4H **85**
Carntyne Ind. Est. G32: Glas 5G **85**
Carntyne Path G32: Glas 4F **85**
Carntyne Pl. G32: Glas 4F **85**
Carntyne Rd. G31: Glas 5E **85**
G32: Glas 4F **85**
Carntyne Station (Rail) 5H 85
CARNWADRIC 3E 117
Carnwadric Rd. G46: T'bnk 3E **117**
Carnwath Av. G43: Glas 1D **118**
Carnwath Rd. ML8: Carl 4F **165**
Caroline St. G31: Glas 6G **85**
Carolside Av. G76: Clar 2C **134**
Carolside Dr. G15: Glas 4B **44**
Carolside Gdns. G76: Clar 2C **134**
Carousel Cres. ML2: Wis 6A **146**
Carradale Cres. G68: Cumb 5B **34**
Carradale Gdns. G64: B'rig 6E **49**
ML8: Carl 5G **165**
Carradale Pl. PA3: Lin 5G **75**
Carradale St. ML5: Coat 4B **90**
(not continuous)
Carranbuie Rd. ML8: Carl 2F **165**
Carrbridge Dr. G20: Glas 3B **62**
Carresbrook Av. G66: Kirk 1G **51**
CARRIAGEHILL 4A 98
Carriagehill Av. PA2: Pais 3A **98**
Carriagehill Dr. PA2: Pais 4A **98**
Carrickarden Rd. G61: Bear 4F **45**
Carrick Ct. G66: Kirk 3G **31**
Carrick Cres. G46: Giff 6A **118**
ML2: Wis 5G **145**
Carrick Dr. G32: Glas 1E **107**
G73: Ruth 2C **120**
ML5: Coat 4H **89**
Carrick Gdns. G72: Blan 3B **140**
ML3: Ham 1C **152**
ML4: Bell 5C **110**
ML8: Carl 5G **165**
Carrick Gro. G32: Glas 1E **107**
Carrick Pl. ML4: Bell 6D **110**
ML5: Coat 4H **89**
ML5: Glenb 3A **70**
ML9: Lark 1F **161**
Carrick Rd. G64: B'rig 6E **49**
G67: Cumb 1A **36**
G73: Ruth 2B **120**
G74: E Kil 6H **137**
PA7: B'ton 5A **40**
CARRICKSTONE 6G 13
Carrickstone Rd. G68: Cumb 6G **13**
CARRICKSTONE RDBT. 6G 13
Carrickstone Vw. G68: Cumb 6H **13**
Carrick St. G2: Glas 4E **83** (6B **4**)
ML9: Lark 3G **161**
Carrick Ter. G82: Dumb 3B **16**
Carrick Vw. ML5: Glenb 3A **70**
Carrick Way G71: Both 4E **125**
Carriden Pl. G33: Glas 4E **87**
Carrington St. G4: Glas 1D **82** (1A **4**)
Carroglen Gdns. G32: Glas 6D **86**
Carroglen Gro. G32: Glas 6D **86**
Carroll Cres. ML1: Carf 5C **128**
Carron Ct. *G72: Camb 2E* ***123***
(off Mill Rd.)
G72: Camb 2D **122**
(Arnhem St.)
ML3: Ham 2F **153**
Carron Cres. G22: Glas 4H **63**
G61: Bear 4C **44**
G64: B'rig 6D **48**
G66: Lenz 3E **51**
Carron Dr. PA7: B'ton 5A **40**
Carron Ho. *G67: Cumb 3H* ***35***
(in Cumbernauld Shop. Cen.)
G67: Cumb 4H ***35***
(off Town Cen.)
Carron Pl. G22: Glas 4A **64**
G75: E Kil 6H **149**
ML5: Coat 2H **89**
Carron St. G22: Glas 4A **64**
ML2: Wis 2H **157**
Carron Way *G67: Cumb 3H* ***35***
(in Cumbernauld Shop. Cen.)
ML1: N'hill 3C **128**
PA3: Pais 4C **78**
Carrour Gdns. G64: B'rig 5B **48**
Carr Quad ML4: Moss 2F **127**
Carruth Rd. PA11: Bri W 3E **73**
Carsaig Dr. G52: Glas 6E **81**
Carsaig Loan ML5: Glenb 3G **69**
Carscallan Rd. ML3: Ham, Quar 5H **153**
Carsegreen Av. PA2: Pais 6F **97**
Carsemeadow PA11: Q'riers 1A **72**
Carse Vw. Dr. G61: Bear 1G **45**
Carstairs St. G40: Glas 3B **104**
Carswell Gdns. G41: Glas 3C **102**
Carswell Rd. G77: Newt M 4B **132**
Cartbank Gdns. G44: Glas 3E **119**
Cartbank Gro. G44: Neth 3D **118**
Cartbank Rd. G44: Glas 3D **118**
Cartcraigs Rd. G43: Glas 1H **117**
Cartha Cres. PA2: Pais 2C **98**
Cartha St. G41: Glas 6C **102**
Cartland Av. ML8: Carl 5F **165**
Cart La. PA3: Pais 5A **78**
Cartsbridge Rd. G76: Busby 3C **134**
CARTSIDE 4D 94
Cartside Av. PA4: Inch 5F **57**
PA5: John 4D **94**
Cartside Dr. G76: Busby 3E **135**
Cartside Pl. G76: Busby 4D **134**
Cartside Quad. G42: Glas 6E **103**
Cartside Rd. G76: Busby 4D **134**
Cartside St. G42: Glas 6D **102**
Cart St. G81: Clyd 1D **58**
Cartvale La. PA3: Pais 5A **78**
Cartvale Rd. G42: Glas 6D **102**
Cartview Ct. G76: Busby 3D **134**
Cart Wlk. PA1: Pais 1B **98**
Cartyne Rd. G32: Glas 4B **86**
Caskie Dr. G72: Blan 6C **124**
Cassells St. ML1: Moth 1G **143**
Cassels Gro. ML1: Moth 6E **127**
Cassels St. ML1: Moth 1G **143**
ML8: Carl 4F **165**
Cassiltoun Gdns. G45: Glas 5H **119**
Cassley Av. PA4: Renf 1H **79**
Castburn Rd. G67: Cumb 5F **15**
Castle Av. G71: Both, Udd 3C **124**
ML1: Holy 1B **128**
PA5: Eld 4H **95**
Castle Bank Ct. G13: Glas 3E **61**
Castlebank Cres. G11: Glas 2G **81**
Castle Bank Gdns. G13: Glas 3E **61**
Castlebank St. G11: Glas 2F **81**
(not continuous)
Castle Bank Vs. G13: Glas 3E **61**
Castlebay Dr. G22: Glas 6G **47**
Castlebay Pl. G22: Glas 1G **63**
Castlebay St. G22: Glas 1G **63**
Castlebrae G82: Dumb 2C **16**
Castlebrae Gdns. G44: Glas 1F **119**
CASTLECARY 3E 15
Castle Cary 4F 15
Castlecary Rd.
G68: C'cry, Cumb 5C **14**
Castle Chimmins Av.
G72: Camb 3D **122**
Castle Chimmins Gdns.
G72: Camb 4D **122**
Castle Chimmins Rd.
G72: Camb 4D **122**
Castle Ct. G66: Kirk 5D **30**
G68: C'cry 3F **15**
Castle Cres. PA7: B'ton 5H **39**
Castlecroft Gdns. G71: Udd 2D **124**
Castle Dr. ML1: Holy 1B **128**
Castlefern Rd. G73: Ruth 4D **120**
Castlefield Ct. G33: Mille 5B **66**
Castlefield Gdns. G75: E Kil 6D **148**
Castle Gait G53: Glas 5A **100**
PA1: Pais 2H **97**
Castle Gdns. G69: Mood 5D **52**
PA2: Pais 2E **97**
Castle Ga. G71: Both 2C **124**
G77: Newt M 6G **133**
Castleglen Rd. G74: E Kil 5B **136**
Castlegreen Cres. G82: Dumb 5H **17**
Castlegreen Gdns.
G82: Dumb 5H **17**
Castlegreen La. G82: Dumb 5G **17**
Castlegreen St. G82: Dumb 5G **17**
Castle Gro. G65: Kils 1G **11**
CASTLEHEAD 2H 97
CASTLEHILL
Carluke 1E 165
Dumbarton 2C 16
Castlehill Cres. FK4: Bank 1E **15**
Castle Hill Cres. ML3: Fern 2E **155**
Castlehill Cres. ML3: Ham 1B **154**
ML6: Chap 4F **113**
ML8: Law 1A **164**
PA4: Renf 5F **59**
Castlehill Dr. G77: Newt M 5F **133**
Castlehill Grn. G74: E Kil 5B **136**
Castlehill Ind. Est. ML8: Carl 1E **165**
Castlehill Quad. G82: Dumb 2C **16**
Castlehill Rd. G61: Bear 1B **44**
G82: Dumb 2C **16**
ML2: Wis 3F **157**
ML8: Carl 1E **165**
Castlehill Vw. G65: Kils 1G **11**
Castlelaw Gdns. G32: Glas 5B **86**
Castlelaw St. G32: Glas 5B **86**
Castle Mains Rd. G62: Miln 3D **24**
CASTLEMILK 4A 120
Castlemilk Arc. G45: Glas 4A **120**
Castlemilk Cres. G44: Glas 2A **120**
Castlemilk Dr. G45: Glas 4A **120**

Castlemilk Rd. G44: Glas 1A **120**
    (Croftend Av.)
  G44: Glas 6A **104**
    (Curtis Av.)
Castlemilk Sports Cen. 4A **120**
Castlemilk Swimming Pool 4A **120**
Castlemount Av. G77: Newt M. . . 6F **133**
Castle Pl. G71: Udd 1C **124**
Castle Quad. ML6: Air 4D **92**
Castle Rd. G77: Newt M 5C **132**
  G82: Dumb 5G **17**
  ML6: Air 4D **92**
  PA11: Bri W 2F **73**
  PA5: Eld 2A **96**
Castle Sq. G81: Clyd 4A **42**
Castle St. G11: Glas 2A **82**
  G4: Glas 3A **84** (5H **5**)
  G69: Bail 2G **107**
  G73: Ruth 5C **104**
  G81: Clyd 4A **42**
  G82: Dumb 4F **17**
  ML3: Ham 5B **142**
  ML6: Chap 3D **112**
  PA1: Pais 1H **97**
Castle Ter. G82: Dumb 4G **17**
  PA11: Bri W *4G **73***
    (off Kilbarchan Rd.)
Castleton Av. G64: B'rig 2A **64**
  G77: Newt M 6F **133**
Castleton Ct. G45: Glas 5B **120**
  G77: Newt M 6F **133**
Castleton Cres. G77: Newt M . . . 6F **133**
Castleton Dr. G77: Newt M 6F **133**
Castleton Gro. G77: Newt M 6F **133**
Castleview G66: Cam G 1B **6**
Castle Vw. G66: Len 2C **6**
Castleview Gdns. G68: Cumb . . . 3E **15**
Castle Vw. G72: Blan 5A **124**
  G81: Clyd 4D **42**
  ML2: Newm 3E **147**
Castleview Av. PA2: Pais 6E **97**
Castleview Dr. PA2: Pais 6E **97**
Castleview Pl. PA2: Pais 6E **97**
Castleview Ter. FK4: Hag 1G **15**
Castle Way G67: Cumb 1C **36**
  G69: Barg 6D **88**
Castle Wynd G71: Both 5F **125**
Cathay St. G22: Glas 1G **63**
Cathburn Rd. ML2: Newm 5F **147**
CATHCART 1E **119**
Cathcart Castle 2F **119**
Cathcart Cres. PA2: Pais 2C **98**
Cathcart Pl. G73: Ruth 6B **104**
Cathcart Rd. G42: Glas 3F **103**
  G73: Ruth 6B **104**
Cathcart Station (Rail) 1E **119**
Cathedral Sq. G4: Glas 4A **84**
  (not continuous)
Cathedral St. G1: Glas 3G **83** (4E **5**)
Catherine St. G66: Kirk 5C **30**
  ML1: Moth 5G **143**
Catherines Wlk. G72: Blan 3B **140**
Catherine Way ML1: New S 4H **127**
CATHKIN 5F **121**
Cathkin Av. G72: Camb 1G **121**
  G73: Ruth 6E **105**
Cathkin Braes Country Pk. 5D **120**
Cathkin By-Pass G73: Ruth 4F **121**
Cathkin Ct. G45: Glas 5B **120**
Cathkin Cres. G68: Cumb 6G **13**
Cathkin Gdns. G71: Tann 4C **108**
Cathkin Pl. G72: Camb 1G **121**
Cathkin Recreation Cen. 5F **103**
Cathkin Rd. G42: Glas 6D **102**
  G71: Tann 4C **108**
  G73: Ruth 1B **136**
  G76: Crmck 1A **136**
Cathkin Vw. G32: Carm 5B **106**
Cathkinview Pl. G42: Glas 6F **103**
Cathkinview Rd. G42: Glas 6E **103**
Catrine G74: E Kil 1F **149**
Catrine Av. G81: Clyd *4F **43***
  (off Kirkoswald Dr.)
Catrine Ct. G53: Glas 5A **100**

Catrine Cres. ML1: Moth 6A **144**
Catrine Gdns. G53: Glas 5A **100**
Catrine Pl. G53: Glas 5A **100**
Catrine Rd. G53: Glas 5A **100**
Catrine St. ML9: Lark 3G **161**
Catriona Way ML1: Holy 2B **128**
Catter Gdns. G62: Miln 2E **25**
Cauldstream Pl. G62: Miln 4E **25**
Causewayside Cres. G32: Glas . . 2A **106**
Causeyside St.
  G32: Glas 3A **106**
Causeyside St. PA1: Pais 1A **98**
    (Forbes Pl.)
  PA1: Pais 2A **98**
    (Thompson Brae)
Causeystanes *G72: Blan* 2B **140**
  (off Winton Cres.)
Cavendish Ct. G5: Glas 1F **103**
Cavendish Dr. G77: Newt M 3F **133**
Cavendish Pl. G5: Glas 1F **103**
Cavendish St. G5: Glas 1F **103**
Cavin Dr. G45: Glas 3A **120**
Cavin Rd. G45: Glas 3A **120**
Cawder Ct. G68: Cumb 6F **13**
Cawder Pl. G68: Cumb 6G **13**
Cawder Rd. G68: Cumb 6G **13**
Cawder Vw. G68: Cumb 6G **13**
Cawder Way G68: Cumb 6G **13**
Cawdor Cres. PA7: B'ton 5H **39**
Cawdor Way G74: E Kil 6F **137**
Cayton Gdns. G69: Bail 1F **107**
Cecil St. G12: Glas 6B **62**
  G76: Clar 2C **134**
  ML5: Coat 6C **90**
Cedar Av. G71: View 5F **109**
  G81: Clyd 3H **41**
  PA5: John 5F **95**
Cedar Ct. G20: Glas 1E **83**
  G72: Flem 3E **123**
  G75: E Kil 6E **149**
  PA10: Kilb 2A **94**
Cedar Cres. ML3: Ham 2A **154**
Cedar Dr. G66: Lenz 2C **50**
  G71: View 5G **109**
  G75: E Kil 6E **149**
Cedar Gdns. G73: Ruth 3E **121**
  ML1: N'hill 3C **128**
  ML8: Law 5D **158**
Cedar La. ML1: Holy 3B **128**
  ML6: Air 4C **92**
Cedar Pl. G72: Blan 6A **124**
  G75: E Kil 6E **149**
  G78: Barr 6F **115**
Cedar Rd. FK4: Bank 1E **15**
  G64: B'rig 1D **64**
  G66: Milt C 6C **8**
  G67: Cumb 2D **36**
Cedar St. G20: Glas 1E **83**
Cedar Wlk. G64: B'rig 1D **64**
Cedarwood Av.
  G77: Newt M 5F **133**
Cedric Pl. G13: Glas 2D **60**
Cedric Rd. G13: Glas 2D **60**
Celtic F.C. 6D **84**
Celtic F.C. Vis. Cen. 1D **104**
Celtic Pk. 6D **84**
Celtic St. G20: Glas 2A **62**
Cemetery Rd. G52: Glas 1D **100**
  G72: Blan 3A **140**
Centenary Av. ML6: Air 4F **91**
Centenary Ct. *G78: Barr* 5D **114**
  (off Cochrane St.)
  G81: Clyd 6D **42**
Centenary Gdns. ML3: Ham 1A **154**
  ML5: Coat 6B **90**
Centenary Quad. ML1: Holy 2A **128**
Central Av. G11: Glas 1F **81**
  G32: Glas 2D **106**
  G71: View 1G **125**
  G72: Blan 4C **140**
  G72: Camb 1H **121**
  G81: Clyd 5C **42**
  ML1: Holy 2H **127**
  ML1: New S 5A **128**

Central Cres. ML9: Ashg 5B **162**
Central Gro. G32: Glas 1D **106**
  G72: Camb 1H **121**
Central Path G32: Glas 2E **107**
Central Rd. PA1: Pais 6A **78**
Central Station (Rail) 4F **83** (6D **4**)
  PA1: Pais 6A **78**
Central Way G67: Cumb 5G **35**
  PA1: Pais 6A **78**
Cen. for Contemporary Arts 3B **4**
Centre Pk. Ct. ML5: Coat 5C **90**
CENTRE RDBT., THE 2H **149**
Centre St. G5: Glas 6E **83**
  ML5: Glenb 3G **69**
Centre, The G78: Barr 5D **114**
Centre Way St. G78: Barr 4D **114**
Ceres Gdns. G64: B'rig 6F **49**
Cessnock Pl. G72: Camb 2D **122**
Cessnock Rd. G33: Mille 4B **66**
Cessnock Station (Und.) 5A **82**
Cessnock St. G51: Glas 5A **82**
Chalmers Ct. *G40: Glas* 5B **84**
  (off Millroad Dr.)
  G71: Udd 1D **124**
Chalmers Cres. G75: E Kil 4H **149**
Chalmers Dr. G75: E Kil 4H **149**
Chalmers Ga. *G40: Glas* 5A **84**
  (off Claythorn St.)
Chalmers Pl. *G40: Glas* 5A **84**
  (off Claythorn St.)
Chalmers St. G40: Glas 5A **84**
  G81: Clyd 6D **42**
Chamberlain La. G13: Glas 4E **61**
Chamberlain Rd. G13: Glas 3E **61**
Chancellor St. G11: Glas 1H **81**
CHANTINGHALL 6F **141**
Chantinghall Rd. ML3: Ham 6F **141**
Chantinghall Ter. ML3: Ham 6F **141**
Chantree Ct. ML1: N'hill 4C **128**
CHAPEL 1G **159**
Chapel Ct. G73: Ruth 5B **104**
Chapelcross Av. ML6: Air 2A **92**
CHAPELHALL 3E **113**
Chapelhall Ind. Est.
  ML6: Chap 1D **112**
CHAPEL HILL 6D **20**
Chapelhill Rd. PA2: Pais 3C **98**
Chapelknowe Rd. ML1: Carf 6C **128**
Chapel Pl. G78: Neil 2D **130**
Chapel Rd. G81: Dun 1C **42**
  ML2: Newm 2F **159**
  PA6: Hous 1B **74**
Chapelside Av. ML6: Air 3A **92**
Chapelside Rd. G74: Ners 3A **138**
Chapel St. G20: Glas 4C **62**
  G66: Len 3F **7**
  G73: Ruth 5B **104**
  ML1: Cle 6H **129**
  ML3: Ham 6A **142**
  (off Leechlee Rd.)
  ML6: Air 3A **92**
  ML8: Carl 3F **165**
Chapel St. Ind. Est. G20: Glas . . 3C **62**
Chapelton Av. G61: Bear 3F **45**
  G82: Dumb 2G **17**
Chapelton Gdns. G61: Bear 3F **45**
  G82: Dumb 2G **17**
Chapelton Rd. G67: Cumb 1E **55**
Chapelton St. G22: Glas 3F **63**
Chaplet Av. G13: Glas 1C **60**
Chapman Av. ML5: Glenb 3G **69**
Chapman St. G42: Glas 3E **103**
Chappell St. G78: Barr 4D **114**
Charing Cross ML9: Lark 2E **161**
Charing Cross La. *G3: Glas* 3D **82**
  (off Granville St.)
Charing Cross Station (Rail)
  . . . . 3E **83** (3A **4**)
Charles Av. PA4: Renf 5F **59**
Charles Cres. G66: Lenz 4D **50**
  ML8: Carl 4H **165**
Charleson Row G65: Croy 2B **34**
Charles Path ML6: Chap 4D **112**
Charles Quad. ML1: Holy 2A **128**

Charles Rennie Mckintosh Society . . . 5E 63
Charles St. G21: Glas . . . 2A **84**
G65: Kils . . . 2H **11**
ML2: Wis . . . 5C **144**
CHARLESTON . . . **3A 98**
Charleston Ga. *PA2: Pais . . . 2A* ***98***
(off Sth. Campbell St.)
Charlotte Av. G64: Torr . . . 5D **28**
Charlotte Path ML9: Lark . . . 3E **161**
Charlotte Pl. PA2: Pais . . . 3A **98**
Charlotte St. G1: Glas . . . 5H **83**
G82: Dumb . . . 3D **16**
Charnwood Av. PA5: John . . . 5D **94**
Chartwell Rd. PA7: B'ton . . . 4H **39**
Chassels St. ML5: Coat . . . 3C **90**
Chateau Gro. ML3: Ham . . . 1C **154**
Chatelherault . . . **3D 154**
Chatelherault Av. G72: Camb . . . 2G **121**
Chatelherault Country Pk. . . . **2C 154**
Chatelherault Country Pk. Vis. Cen. . . . **3D 154**
Chatelherault Cres. ML3: Ham . . . 2A **154**
Chatelherault Wlk. ML3: Ham . . . 2A **154**
Chatham G75: E Kil . . . 4E **149**
Chatton St. G23: Glas . . . 6B **46**
Cheapside St. G3: Glas . . . 4D **82** (6A **4**)
Chelmsford Dr. G12: Glas . . . 4H **61**
Cherry Bank G66: Lenz . . . 2B **50**
Cherrybank Rd. G43: Glas . . . 1D **118**
Cherrybank Wlk. ML6: Air . . . 3F **91**
Cherry Cres. G81: Clyd . . . 3C **42**
Cherryhill Vw. ML9: Lark . . . 2D **160**
Cherry La. FK4: Bank . . . 1E **15**
Cherry Pl. G64: B'rig . . . 1D **64**
G66: Milt C . . . 1B **30**
G71: View . . . 6H **109**
ML1: Holy . . . 2B **128**
PA5: John . . . 4G **95**
Cherrytree Cres. ML9: Lark . . . 6A **156**
Cherrytree Dr. G72: Flem . . . 3E **123**
Cherry Wlk. ML1: Moth . . . 6G **143**
Cherrywood Rd. PA5: Eld . . . 3A **96**
Chesterfield Av. G12: Glas . . . 4G **61**
Chesters Cres. ML1: Moth . . . 1E **143**
Chesters Pl. G73: Ruth . . . 6B **104**
Chesters Rd. G61: Bear . . . 3C **44**
Chester St. G32: Glas . . . 6A **86**
Chestnut Av. G67: Cumb . . . 6E **15**
PA7: B'ton . . . 2F **39**
(not continuous)
Chestnut Ct. G66: Milt C . . . 6B **8**
G67: Cumb . . . 6E **15**
Chestnut Cres. G71: View . . . 6H **109**
G75: E Kil . . . 5E **149**
ML3: Ham . . . 1A **154**
Chestnut Dr. G66: Lenz . . . 1B **50**
G81: Clyd . . . 2B **42**
Chestnut Gro. G69: G'csh . . . 3G **69**
G72: Blan . . . 1A **140**
ML1: Moth . . . 4F **143**
ML8: Carl . . . 4E **165**
ML9: Lark . . . 6A **156**
Chestnut La. G62: Miln . . . 4E **25**
Chestnut Pl. G67: Cumb . . . 6E **15**
PA5: John . . . 5G **95**
Chestnut St. G22: Glas . . . 4H **63**
Chestnut Way G72: Flem . . . 3E **123**
Cheviot Av. G78: Barr . . . 5E **115**
Cheviot Cl. G13: Glas . . . 3B **60**
Cheviot Ct. ML5: Coat . . . 2E **111**
ML6: Air . . . 1B **92**
Cheviot Cres. ML2: Wis . . . 5F **145**
Cheviot Dr. G77: Newt M . . . 6C **132**
Cheviot Gdns. G61: Bear . . . 6D **24**
Cheviot Rd. G43: Glas . . . 2A **118**
ML3: Ham . . . 1B **154**
ML9: Lark . . . 3G **161**
PA2: Pais . . . 4A **98**
Cheviot St. G72: Blan . . . 2A **140**
Chillin Pl. ML9: Lark . . . 2G **161**
Chirmorie Cres. G53: Glas . . . 4A **100**
Chirmorie Pl. G53: Glas . . . 4A **100**
Chirnside Ct. G72: Blan . . . 4D **140**
Chirnside Pl. G52: Glas . . . 5A **80**
Chirnside Rd. G52: Glas . . . 5A **80**
Chirnsyde Sports Cen. . . . **2H 63**
Chisholm Av. PA7: B'ton . . . 4A **40**
Chisholm Dr. G77: Newt M . . . 3E **133**
Chisholm Pl. ML1: Moth . . . 1B **156**
Chisholm St. G1: Glas . . . 5H **83**
ML5: Coat . . . 3D **90**
Chrighton Grn. G71: Tann . . . 5E **109**
Chriss Av. ML3: Ham . . . 4H **153**
Christchurch Pl. G75: E Kil . . . 4D **148**
Christian St. G43: Glas . . . 5A **102**
Christie La. PA3: Pais . . . 6A **78**
Christie Pl. G72: Camb . . . 2A **122**
Christie St. ML4: Bell . . . 2F **127**
PA1: Pais . . . 6B **78**
Christopher St. G21: Glas . . . 2C **84**
CHRYSTON . . . **6B 52**
Chryston Rd. G66: Kirk . . . 1H **51**
G69: Chry . . . 1B **68**
Chryston Valley Bus. Cen.
G69: Chry . . . 1A **68**
Chuckie La. PA5: Brkfld . . . 5C **74**
Church Av. G33: Step . . . 3D **66**
G73: Ruth . . . 2E **121**
ML2: Newm . . . 5D **146**
Church Ct. G82: Dumb . . . 4F **17**
Church Cres. ML3: Ham . . . 5H **153**
ML6: Air . . . 2E **93**
Church Dr. G66: Lenz . . . 1C **50**
Church Hill PA1: Pais . . . 6A **78**
Churchill Av. G74: E Kil . . . 2H **149**
PA5: John . . . 6C **94**
Churchill Cres. G71: Both . . . 4F **125**
Churchill Dr. G11: Glas . . . 5F **61**
PA7: B'ton . . . 4H **39**
Churchill Pl. PA10: Kilb . . . 2A **94**
Churchill Way G64: B'rig . . . 6B **48**
Church La. G65: Kils . . . 3H **11**
(not continuous)
ML2: Newm . . . 5D **146**
ML5: Coat . . . 4C **90**
ML8: Carl . . . 4F **165**
Church Manse La. PA11: Bri W . . . 3F **73**
Church Pl. G60: Old K . . . 1E **41**
G73: Ruth . . . 5D **104**
Church Rd. G69: Muirh . . . 2A **68**
G76: Busby . . . 3D **134**
ML2: Newm . . . 2H **147**
PA11: Bri W . . . 4G **73**
PA11: Q'riers . . . 1A **72**
Church St. G11: Glas . . . 1A **82**
G65: Kils . . . 3H **11**
G69: Bail . . . 1A **108**
G71: Udd . . . 2D **124**
G72: Blan . . . 2C **140**
G81: Clyd . . . 4D **42**
G82: Dumb . . . 4F **17**
ML1: N'hill . . . 3F **129**
ML3: Ham . . . 5A **142**
ML5: Coat . . . 4C **90**
ML9: Lark . . . 2E **161**
PA10: Kilb . . . 2A **94**
PA5: John . . . 2F **95**
Church Street Swimming Pool . . . **1A 82**
Church Vw. G72: Camb . . . 6A **106**
ML5: Coat . . . 4C **90**
Church Vw. Ct. G66: Len . . . 2F **7**
Church Vw. Gdns. ML4: Bell . . . 2C **126**
Circus Dr. G31: Glas . . . 4B **84**
Circus Pl. G31: Glas . . . 4B **84**
Circus Pl. La. G31: Glas . . . 3B **84**
Citadel Pl. ML1: Moth . . . 1E **143**
Citizen La. G2: Glas . . . 4G **83** (5E **5**)
Citizens' Theatre . . . **6G 83**
Citrus Cres. G71: View . . . 5G **109**
Cityford Cres. G73: Ruth . . . 6B **104**
Cityford Dr. G73: Ruth . . . 1B **120**
City Hall . . . **4H 83 (6G 5)**
Civic Sq. *ML1: Moth . . . 4H* ***143***
(off Camp St.)
Civic St. G4: Glas . . . 1F **83** (1C **4**)
Civic Theatre . . . **4F 17**
Civic Way G66: Kirk . . . 6C **30**
Clachan Dr. G51: Glas . . . 3E **81**
Clachan, The ML2: Wis . . . 6H **145**
CLADDENS . . . **3E 51**
Claddens Pl. G66: Lenz . . . 3E **51**
Claddens Quad. G22: Glas . . . 3G **63**
Claddens St. G22: Glas . . . 3F **63**
Claddens Wynd G66: Lenz . . . 3E **51**
Cladence Gro. G75: E Kil . . . 6H **149**
Claire St. ML2: Newm . . . 4E **147**
Clairinish Gdns. PA4: Renf . . . 2E **79**
Clairmont Gdns. G3: Glas . . . 2D **82**
Clair Rd. G64: B'rig . . . 6F **49**
Clamp Rd. ML2: Wis . . . 5C **144**
Clamps Gro. G74: E Kil . . . 3A **150**
Clamps Ter. G74: E Kil . . . 3B **150**
Clamps Wood G74: E Kil . . . 3A **150**
Clanrye Dr. ML5: Coat . . . 1C **110**
Clapperhow Rd. ML1: Carf . . . 6A **128**
Claremont Av. G66: Kirk . . . 5B **30**
Claremont Dr. G62: Miln . . . 4G **25**
Claremont Gdns. G62: Miln . . . 4G **25**
Claremont Ho. G74: E Kil . . . 2C **150**
Claremont Pl. *G3: Glas . . . 2D* ***82***
(off Lynedoch Ter.)
Claremont St. G3: Glas . . . 3C **82**
(not continuous)
Claremont Ter. G3: Glas . . . 2D **82**
Claremont Ter. La. *G3: Glas . . . 2D* ***82***
(off Clifton St.)
Claremount Av. G46: Giff . . . 5A **118**
Clarence Dr. G11: Glas . . . 6G **61**
G12: Glas . . . 6G **61**
PA1: Pais . . . 6C **78**
Clarence Gdns. G11: Glas . . . 6G **61**
Clarence La. *G12: Glas . . . 6H* ***61***
(off Hyndland Rd.)
Clarence St. G81: Clyd . . . 4D **42**
PA1: Pais . . . 6C **78**
Clarendon Pl. G33: Step . . . 4D **66**
G4: Glas . . . 1E **83** (1A **4**)
Clarendon Rd. ML2: Wis . . . 2E **157**
Clarendon St. G20: Glas . . . 1E **83**
Clare St. G21: Glas . . . 2C **84**
Clarinda Ct. G66: Kirk . . . 3G **31**
Clarinda Pl. ML1: N'hill . . . 4C **128**
Clarion Cres. G13: Glas . . . 1A **60**
Clarion Rd. G13: Glas . . . 2A **60**
Clark Pl. G64: Torr . . . 5E **29**
G77: Newt M . . . 5B **132**
CLARKSTON
Airdrie . . . **3D 92**
Glasgow . . . **2C 134**
Clarkston Av. G44: Glas . . . 3D **118**
Clarkston Dr. ML6: Air . . . 4D **92**
Clarkston Rd. G44: Glas . . . 3D **118**
G44: Neth . . . 1C **134**
G76: Clar . . . 1C **134**
Clarkston Station (Rail) . . . **2C 134**
Clark St. G81: Clyd . . . 3B **42**
ML2: Newm . . . 4D **146**
ML6: Air . . . 4B **92**
PA3: Pais . . . 5G **77**
PA4: Renf . . . 6D **58**
PA5: John . . . 2F **95**
Clark Way ML4: Bell . . . 6B **110**
Clarkwell Rd. ML3: Ham . . . 1C **152**
Clarkwell Ter. ML3: Ham . . . 6D **140**
Clathic Av. G61: Bear . . . 3G **45**
Claude Av. G72: Camb . . . 3E **123**
Claude St. ML9: Lark . . . 2E **161**
Claud Rd. PA3: Pais . . . 5C **78**
Clavens Rd. G52: Glas . . . 5G **79**
Claverhouse Pl. PA2: Pais . . . 2C **98**
Claverhouse Rd. G52: Hill . . . 4H **79**
Clavering St. E. PA1: Pais . . . 6G **77**
Clavering St. W. PA1: Pais . . . 6G **77**
Clay Ct. ML1: Moth . . . 5G **143**
Clay Cres. ML4: Bell . . . 6D **110**
Clayhouse Rd. G33: Step . . . 5E **67**
Claymore Dr. PA6: C'lee . . . 3D **74**
Claypotts Pl. G33: Glas . . . 2A **86**
Claypotts Rd. G33: Glas . . . 2A **86**
Clay Rd. ML4: Bell . . . 6D **110**

Clayslaps Rd. G3: Glas	2B **82**	
Claythorn Av. G40: Glas	5A **84**	
Claythorn Ct. *G40: Glas*	5A *84*	
(off Claythorn St.)		
Claythorn Pk. G40: Glas	6A **84**	
Claythorn St. G40: Glas	5A **84**	
Claythorn Ter. G40: Glas	5A **84**	
Clayton Cir. G40: Glas	5A **84**	
Clayton Path ML4: Bell	6D **110**	
Clayton Ter. G31: Glas	4B **84**	
Clearfield Av. ML3: Ham	5F **141**	
CLEDDANS	4F **31**	
Cleddans Cres. G81: Hard	1E **43**	
Cleddans Rd. G66: Kirk	4E **31**	
G81: Hard	2E **43**	
Cleddans Vw. *G81: Clyd*	*4E 43*	
(off Kirkoswald Dr.)		
ML6: Glenm	5G **71**	
Cleddens Ct. G64: B'rig	6C **48**	
ML6: Air	*3F 91*	
(off Monkscourt Av.)		
CLEEKHIMIN	6B **128**	
Cleeves Quad. G53: Glas	2A **116**	
Cleeves Rd. G53: Glas	2A **116**	
Cleghorn St. G22: Glas	6F **63**	
Cleish Av. G61: Bear	6C **24**	
CLELAND	6H **129**	
Cleland La. G5: Glas	6G **83**	
Cleland Pl. G74: E Kil	1A **150**	
Cleland Rd. ML1: Carf	6C **128**	
ML1: Cle	4F **129**	
ML2: Wis	6G **145**	
Cleland St. G5: Glas	6G **83**	
Clelland Av. G64: B'rig	1C **64**	
Clem Attlee Gdns. ML9: Lark	3F **161**	
Clerwood St. G32: Glas	5F **85**	
Cleuch Gdns. G76: Clar	1B **134**	
Clevans Rd. PA11: Bri W	4D **72**	
Cleveden Cres. G12: Glas	4H **61**	
Cleveden Cres. La. G12: Glas	4H **61**	
Cleveden Dr. G12: Glas	4H **61**	
G73: Ruth	1E **121**	
Cleveden Dr. La. G12: Glas	5A **62**	
Cleveden Gdns. G12: Glas	4A **62**	
Cleveden La. *G12: Glas*	*3H 61*	
(off Northampton Dr.)		
Cleveden Pl. G12: Glas	3H **61**	
Cleveden Rd. G12: Glas	2H **61**	
Cleveland La. G3: Glas	3A **4**	
Cleveland St. G3: Glas	3D **82**	
Clifford Gdns. G51: Glas	6H **81**	
Clifford La. G51: Glas	6A **82**	
Clifford Pl. *G51: Glas*	*6B 82*	
(off Clifford La.)		
Clifford St. G51: Glas	6H **81**	
Cliff Rd. G3: Glas	1D **82**	
Cliftonhill Stadium	5E **91**	
Clifton Pl. *G3: Glas*	*2C 82*	
(off Clifton St.)		
ML5: Coat	5E **91**	
Clifton Rd. G46: Giff	4H **117**	
Clifton St. G3: Glas	2C **82**	
Clifton Ter. G72: Camb	4G **121**	
PA5: John	*3G 95*	
(off Auchenlodment Rd.)		
CLIFTONVILLE	4E **91**	
Cliftonville Ct. *ML5: Coat*	*5E 91*	
(off Clifton Pl.)		
CLINCARTHILL	6C **104**	
Clincarthill Rd. G73: Ruth	6C **104**	
Clincart Rd. G42: Glas	5F **103**	
CLIPPENS	5G **75**	
Clippens Rd. PA3: Lin	6H **75**	
PA6: Hous	3E **75**	
Cloan Av. G15: Glas	5B **44**	
Cloan Cres. G64: B'rig	3D **48**	
Clober Farm La. G62: Miln	2E **25**	
Cloberfield G62: Miln	1F **25**	
Cloberfield Gdns. G62: Miln	2F **25**	
Cloberhill Rd. G13: Glas	6C **44**	
Clober Rd. G62: Miln	2F **25**	
Clochan Av. G62: Miln	2F **25**	
Clochbar Gdns. G62: Miln	3F **25**	
Clochoderick Av. PA10: Kilb	3B **94**	

Cloch St. G33: Glas	3A **86**	
Clockerhill Pl. ML1: N'hill	3E **129**	
Clock Sq. *G67: Cumb*	*4H 35*	
(in Cumbernauld Shop. Cen.)		
Cloister Av. ML6: Air	1C **112**	
Clonbeith St. G33: Glas	1E **87**	
Closeburn St. G22: Glas	4G **63**	
Cloth St. G78: Barr	5E **115**	
Clouden Rd. G67: Cumb	3B **36**	
Cloudhowe Ter. G72: Blan	6A **124**	
Clouston Ct. G20: Glas	5C **62**	
Clouston La. G20: Glas	5C **62**	
Clouston St. G20: Glas	5B **62**	
Clova Pl. G71: Udd	1D **124**	
Clova St. G46: T'bnk	3F **117**	
Clove Mill Wynd ML9: Lark	3C **160**	
Clovend Dr. G73: Ruth	4D **120**	
Cloverbank St. G21: Glas	2C **84**	
Clovergate G64: B'rig	6A **48**	
Cloverhill Pl. G69: Chry	1A **68**	
Cloverhill Ter. G74: E Kil	2G **149**	
Cloverhill Vw. G74: E Kil	2F **149**	
Clunie Pl. ML2: Newm	3D **146**	
ML5: Coat	2D **110**	
Clunie Rd. G52: Glas	1E **101**	
Cluny Av. G61: Bear	5G **45**	
G81: Hard	6E **23**	
Cluny Dr. G61: Bear	5G **45**	
G77: Newt M	4B **132**	
PA3: Pais	5C **78**	
Cluny Gdns. G14: Glas	5E **61**	
G69: Bail	1G **107**	
Cluny Vs. G14: Glas	5E **61**	
Clutha Pl. G75: E Kil	4C **148**	
Clutha St. G51: Glas	5B **82**	
Clyde Av. G64: Torr	5D **28**	
G71: Both	6D **124**	
G78: Barr	6F **115**	
ML3: Fern	2E **155**	
CLYDEBANK	6D **42**	
Clydebank Bus. Pk. G81: Clyd	5C **42**	
Clydebank Crematorium		
G81: Dun	1H **41**	
Clydebank District Mus.	6C **42**	
Clydebank Ind. Est. G81: Clyd	5H **41**	
Clydebank Megabowl	6E **43**	
Clydebank Station (Rail)	6D **42**	
Clydebrae Dr. G71: Both	1F **141**	
Clydebrae St. G51: Glas	3H **81**	
Clyde Bri. ML3: Ham	4D **142**	
Clydebuilt	6A **60**	
Clyde Ct. G81: Clyd	2A **42**	
G82: Dumb	3E **17**	
ML5: Coat	*5E 91*	
(off Clifton Pl.)		
Clyde Dr. ML4: Bell	3E **127**	
Clyde F.C.	4B **34**	
Clydeford Dr. G32: Glas	2G **105**	
G71: Udd	6B **108**	
Clydeford Rd. G32: Glas	6A **106**	
G72: Camb	1B **122**	
Clydeholm Rd. G14: Glas	1D **80**	
Clydeholm Ter. G81: Clyd	2F **59**	
Clyde Ho. ML3: Ham	4A **142**	
Clyde La. ML1: New S	3A **128**	
Clydeneuk Dr. G71: Udd	6B **108**	
Clyde Pl. G5: Glas	5E **83**	
G72: Camb	3D **122**	
ML1: New S	3A **128**	
PA5: John	5C **94**	
Clyde Rd. PA3: Pais	4D **78**	
CLYDESDALE	4H **127**	
Clydesdale Av. ML2: Wis	2D **156**	
ML3: Ham	5H **153**	
PA3: Pais	2C **78**	
Clydesdale Pl. ML3: Ham	5H **153**	
Clydesdale St. ML3: Ham	5G **141**	
ML4: Bell	3F **127**	
ML9: Lark	1E **161**	
Clyde Shop. Cen. G81: Clyd	5D **42**	
Clydeshore Rd. G82: Dumb	5E **17**	
Clydeside Expressway G11: Glas	1F **81**	
G14: Glas	6D **60**	
G3: Glas	3B **82**	

Clydeside Ind. Est. G14: Glas	1D **80**	
Clydeside Rd. G73: Ruth	3B **104**	
Clydesmill Dr. G32: Glas	6A **106**	
Clydesmill Gro. G32: Glas	6A **106**	
Clydesmill Pl. G32: Glas	5A **106**	
Clydesmill Rd. G32: Glas	5H **105**	
Clyde Sq. *G67: Cumb*	*4H 35*	
(in Cumbernauld Shop. Cen.)		
Clyde St. G1: Glas	5G **83**	
G81: Clyd	1E **59**	
ML5: Coat	4E **91**	
ML8: Carl	3D **164**	
PA4: Renf	4F **59**	
Clyde Ter. G71: Both	6E **125**	
ML1: Moth	1C **156**	
Clyde Twr. G74: E Kil	4B **150**	
ML1: Moth	*4G 143*	
(off Airbles Rd.)		
Clyde Tunnel G51: Glas	2E **81**	
Clydevale G71: Both	6F **125**	
Clyde Valley Av. ML1: Moth	5G **143**	
Clydeview G71: Both	6G **125**	
Clyde Vw. G82: Dumb	5E **17**	
ML3: Ham	2F **153**	
ML9: Ashg	5C **162**	
PA2: Pais	3D **98**	
Clyde Vw. Ct. G60: Bowl	5A **20**	
Clydeview La. G11: Glas	1F **81**	
Clydeview Shop. Cen. G72: Blan		
	2C **140**	
Clydeview Ter. G32: Carm	5C **106**	
Clyde Wlk. *G67: Cumb*	*4H 35*	
(in Cumbernauld Shop. Cen.)		
ML2: Newm	3E **147**	
Clyde Walkway G3: Glas	6A **4**	
Clyde Way *G67: Cumb*	*4H 35*	
(in Cumbernauld Shop. Cen.)		
PA3: Pais	4D **78**	
Clydeway Ind. Est. *G3: Glas*	*3C 82*	
(off Finnieston Sq.)		
Clyde Workshops G32: Glas	4H **105**	
Clynder St. G51: Glas	5H **81**	
Clyth Dr. G46: Giff	5B **118**	
Coach Cl. G65: Kils	3C **12**	
Coach Pl. G65: Kils	4A **12**	
Coach Rd. G65: Kils	4B **12**	
Coalburn Rd. G71: Both	2F **125**	
Coalhall Av. ML1: Carf	6A **128**	
Coalhill St. G31: Glas	6D **84**	
Coatbank St. ML5: Coat	6D **90**	
Coatbank Way ML5: Coat	5D **90**	
COATBRIDGE	4C **90**	
Coatbridge Central Station (Rail)		
	4B **90**	
Coatbridge College Sports Cen.	4D **90**	
Coatbridge Indoor Bowling Club		
	4F **91**	
Coatbridge Ind. Est.		
ML5: Coat	2C **90**	
Coatbridge Outdoor Sports Complex		
	6B **90**	
Coatbridge Rd. G69: Bail	6B **88**	
G69: Barg	5D **88**	
G69: G'csh	5E **69**	
ML5: Coat	2D **90**	
ML5: Glenb	4B **70**	
ML6: Glenm	2D **90**	
Coatbridge Sunnyside Station (Rail)		
	3C **90**	
COATDYKE	5F **91**	
Coatdyke Station (Rail)	4F **91**	
Coathill St. ML5: Coat	1C **110**	
Coats Cres. G69: Bail	6G **87**	
Coats Dr. PA2: Pais	2F **97**	
COATSHILL	6A **124**	
Coatshill Av. G72: Blan	6A **124**	
Coats Observatory	6H **77**	
Coats St. ML5: Coat	5D **90**	
Cobbett Rd. ML1: Moth	4D **142**	
Cobblerigg Way G71: Udd	2C **124**	
Cobbleton Rd. ML1: New S	5H **127**	
Cobden Rd. G21: Glas	1B **84**	
Cobington Pl. G33: Glas	2B **86**	
Cobinshaw St. G32: Glas	5A **86**	

Coburg St. G5: Glas 6F **83**
(Kilbarchan St.)
G5: Glas 5F **83**
(Norfolk St.)
Cochno Rd. G81: Faif 5F **23**
G81: Hard 6D **22**
Cochno St. G81: Clyd 1E **59**
COCHRANE CASTLE **5E 95**
Cochrane Ct. G62: Miln 5A **26**
Cochranemill Rd. PA5: John 4C **94**
Cochrane Sq. PA3: Lin 5H **75**
Cochrane St. G1: Glas 4G **83** (5F **5**)
G78: Barr 5D **114**
Cochrane St. ML4: Bell 2B **126**
Cochran St. PA1: Pais 1B **98**
Cockburn Pl. ML5: Coat 1B **110**
Cockels Loan PA4: Renf 2D **78**
Cockenzie St. G32: Glas 6A **86**
Cockerhill Rd. G52: Glas 4D **100**
Cockhill Way ML4: Bell 1H **125**
Cockmuir St. G21: Glas 5C **64**
Coddington Cres. ML1: Holy 6H **111**
Cogan Pl. G78: Barr 5D **114**
Cogan Rd. G43: Glas 1A **118**
Cogan St. G43: Glas 6A **102**
G78: Barr 5D **114**
Colbert St. G40: Glas 1B **104**
Colbreggan Ct. G81: Hard 1E **43**
Colbreggan Gdns. G81: Hard 1E **43**
Colbreggan Pl. G81: Hard 1E **43**
Colchester Dr. G12: Glas 3G **61**
Coldingham Av. G14: Glas 3G **59**
Coldstream Cres. ML2: Wis 4A **146**
Coldstream Dr. G73: Ruth 6F **105**
PA2: Pais 4E **97**
Coldstream Pl. G21: Glas 6G **63**
Coldstream Rd. G81: Clyd 6D **42**
Coldstream St. G72: Blan 2B **140**
Cole G74: E Kil 3C **150**
Colebrooke Pl. G12: Glas 6C **62**
Colebrooke St. G12: Glas 6C **62**
Colebrooke Ter. G12: Glas 6C **62**
Colebrook St. G72: Camb 1A **122**
Coleridge G75: E Kil 4C **148**
Coleridge Av. G71: Both 4F **125**
Colfin St. G34: Glas 2A **88**
Colgrain St. G20: Glas 3E **63**
Colgrave Cres. G32: Glas 2H **105**
Colinbar Circ. G78: Barr 6D **114**
Colinslee Av. PA2: Pais 4B **98**
Colinslee Cres. PA2: Pais 4B **98**
Colinslee Dr. PA2: Pais 4B **98**
Colinslie Rd. G53: Glas 5D **100**
Colinton Pl. G32: Glas 4B **86**
Colintraive Av. G33: Glas 6G **65**
Colintraive Cres. G33: Glas 6G **65**
Collace Av. PA11: Bri W 4F **73**
Colla Gdns. G64: B'rig 5F **49**
Coll Av. PA4: Renf 2F **79**
Coll Dr. ML5: Coat 1H **109**
College Ga. G61: Bear 1C **44**
College La. G1: Glas 4H **83** (6H **5**)
COLLEGE MILTON **6D 136**
College St. G1: Glas 4H **83** (6G **5**)
G82: Dumb 3F **17**
Coll. Way Shop. Cen. G82: Dumb 4F **17**
Collessie Dr. G33: Glas 1C **86**
Collier St. PA5: John 2F **95**
Colliertree Rd. ML6: Air 3D **92**
Collina St. G20: Glas 3A **62**
Collins Gallery . . . . **4H 83 (5G 5)**
Collins St. G4: Glas 4A **84** (5H **5**)
G81: Faif 1E **43**
Coll Lea ML3: Ham 2D **152**
Coll Pl. G21: Glas 1D **84**
ML6: Air 6C **92**
Collree Gdns. G34: Glas 4A **88**
Coll St. G21: Glas 1D **84**
ML2: Newm 3D **146**
Collylinn Rd. G61: Bear 3E **45**
Colmonell Av. G13: Glas 2H **59**
Colonsay G74: E Kil 4B **150**
Colonsay Av. PA4: Renf 2E **79**
Colonsay Cres. ML5: Coat 1H **109**
Colonsay Dr. G77: Newt M 4B **132**
Colonsay Rd. G52: Glas 6E **81**
PA2: Pais 6H **97**
Colquhoun Av. G52: Hill 4A **80**
Colquhoun Ct. G41: Glas 1A **102**
Colquhoun Dr. G61: Bear 2D **44**
Colquhoun Pk. *G52: Hill 4B 80*
(off Hepburn Rd.)
Colquhoun Rd. G82: Milt 4E **19**
Colquhoun St. G82: Dumb 3G **17**
Colson Pl. ML4: Bell 4E **127**
COLSTON **2A 64**
Colston Av. G64: B'rig 2B **64**
Colston Dr. G64: B'rig 2B **64**
Colston Gdns. G64: B'rig 2A **64**
ML6: Air 4C **92**
Colston Path G64: B'rig 2A **64**
Colston Pl. G64: B'rig 2A **64**
ML6: Air 4C **92**
Colston Rd. G64: B'rig 2A **64**
ML6: Air 4C **92**
Colston Ter. ML6: Air 4C **92**
Colt Av. ML5: Coat 3A **90**
Coltmuir Cres. G64: B'rig 1A **64**
Coltmuir Dr. G64: B'rig 1A **64**
Coltmuir Gdns. G64: B'rig 1A **64**
Coltmuir St. G22: Glas 3F **63**
COLTNESS **3A 146**
Coltness Dr. ML4: Bell 3D **126**
Coltness La. G33: Glas 4C **86**
Coltness Rd. ML2: Wis 3A **146**
Coltness St. G33: Glas 3C **86**
Coltpark Av. G64: B'rig 1A **64**
Coltpark La. G64: B'rig 1B **64**
Colt Pl. ML5: Coat 3C **90**
Coltsfoot Dr. G53: Glas 4B **116**
Coltswood Ct. ML5: Coat 3C **90**
Coltswood Rd. ML5: Coat 2C **90**
Colt Ter. ML5: Coat 3C **90**
Columba G81: Clyd 5F **43**
Columba Cres. ML1: Moth 5F **127**
Columba Path G72: Blan 1A **140**
Columba Sports Complex
. . . . **1C 110**
Columba St. G51: Glas 4H **81**
Columbia Pl. G75: E Kil 3D **148**
Columbia Way G75: E Kil 3D **148**
Columbine Way ML8: Carl 5F **165**
Colvend La. G40: Glas 2B **104**
Colvend St. G40: Glas 2B **104**
Colville Dr. G73: Ruth 1F **121**
Colvilles Pl. G75: E Kil 5B **150**
Colvilles Rd. G75: E Kil 6A **150**
Colwood Av. G53: Glas 3A **116**
Colwood Gdns. G53: Glas 4A **116**
Colwood Path G53: Glas 3A **116**
Colwood Pl. G53: Glas 4A **116**
Colwood Sq. G53: Glas 4A **116**
Colwyn Ct. ML6: Air 2A **92**
COLZIUM **1C 12**
Colzium Vw. G65: Kils 3A **12**
Combe Quad. ML4: Bell 4A **126**
Comedie Rd. G33: Step 5E **67**
Comely Bank ML3: Ham 6D **140**
Comelybank La. G82: Dumb 3D **16**
Comelybank Rd. G82: Dumb 3D **16**
Comelypark Pl. *G31: Glas 5C 84*
(off Comelypark St.)
Comelypark St. G31: Glas 5B **84**
Commerce St. G5: Glas 6F **83**
Commercial Ct. G5: Glas 6H **83**
Commercial Rd. G5: Glas 1G **103**
G78: Barr 4E **115**
Common Grn. ML3: Ham 5A **142**
Commonhead Av. ML6: Air 2H **91**
Commonhead La. ML6: Air 2H **91**
Commonhead Rd. G34: Glas 3B **88**
Commonhead St. ML6: Air 2H **91**
Commonside St. ML6: Air 2H **91**
Commore Av. G78: Barr 6F **115**
Commore Dr. G13: Glas 2A **60**
Commore Pl. G78: Neil 3C **130**
Community Av. ML4: Bell 5C **126**
Community Pl. ML4: Bell 4D **126**
Community Rd. ML4: Bell 4B **126**
Comrie Cres. ML3: Ham 6B **140**
Comrie Rd. G33: Step 4C **66**
Comrie St. G32: Glas 2B **106**
Conan Ct. G72: Camb 2D **122**
Cona St. G46: T'bnk 3E **117**
Condor Glen ML1: Holy 6G **111**
CONDORRAT **6C 34**
CONDORRAT INTERCHANGE **5D 34**
Condorrat Ring Rd.
G67: Cumb 6D **34**
Condorrat Rd. G67: Cumb 4D **54**
ML6: Glenm 1F **71**
Coneypark Cres. FK4: Bank 1C **14**
Coneypark Pl. FK4: Bank 1C **14**
Congress Rd. G3: Glas 4B **82**
Congress Way G3: Glas 4C **82**
Conifer Pl. G66: Lenz 1B **50**
Conisborough Path G34: Glas 1F **87**
Conisborough Rd. G34: Glas 1F **87**
Coniston G75: E Kil 6B **148**
Coniston Cres. ML3: Ham 5G **153**
Coniston Dr. ML4: Bell 4D **126**
Conistone Cres. G69: Bail 1F **107**
Connal St. G40: Glas 2D **104**
Connell Cres. G62: Miln 4A **26**
Conniston St. G32: Glas 4G **85**
Connor Rd. G78: Barr 4D **114**
Connor St. ML6: Air 2E **93**
Conolly's Land *G81: Hard 1C 42*
(off Dumbarton Rd.)
Conon Av. G61: Bear 4C **44**
Conservation Pl. ML2: Wis 1H **157**
Consett La. G33: Glas 3C **86**
Consett St. G33: Glas 3C **86**
Constarry Rd. G65: Croy 6A **12**
Contin Pl. G20: Glas 4B **62**
Convair Way PA4: Renf 2F **79**
Conval Way PA3: Pais 3H **77**
Cook St. G5: Glas 6E **83**
Coolgardie Grn. G75: E Kil 4E **149**
Coolgardie Pl. G75: E Kil 4E **149**
Cooperage Pl. G3: Glas 3A **82**
Co-operative Ter. PA5: John 2G **95**
Cooper Av. ML8: Carl 2E **165**
Cooper's Well St. G11: Glas 2A **82**
Copenhagen Av. G75: E Kil 5G **149**
Copland Pl. G51: Glas 5H **81**
Copland Quad. G51: Glas 5H **81**
Copland Rd. G51: Glas 6H **81**
Coplaw Ct. G42: Glas 2E **103**
Coplaw St. G42: Glas 2E **103**
Copperfield La. G71: Tann 6E **109**
Coral Mt. Gdns. G66: Kirk 6E **31**
Corbett Ct. G32: Glas 2H **105**
Corbett St. G32: Glas 2H **105**
Corbie Pl. G62: Miln 3D **24**
Corbiston Way G67: Cumb 3B **36**
Cordiner St. G44: Glas 6F **103**
CORKERHILL **3D 100**
Corkerhill Gdns. G52: Glas 1E **101**
Corkerhill Pl. G52: Glas 3D **100**
Corkerhill Rd. G52: Glas 2D **100**
Corkerhill Station (Rail) **3D 100**
Corlaich Av. G42: Glas 6A **104**
Corlaich Dr. G42: Glas 6A **104**
Cormack Av. G64: Torr 4E **29**
Cormorant Av. PA6: C'lee 3D **74**
Cornaig Rd. G53: Glas 5B **100**
Cornalee Gdns. G53: Glas 5A **100**
Cornalee Pl. G53: Glas 5A **100**
(not continuous)
Cornalee Rd. G53: Glas 5B **100**
Cornelian Ter. ML4: Bell 3C **126**
Cornelia St. ML1: Moth 6D **126**
Cornhill Dr. ML5: Coat 3A **90**
Cornhill St. G21: Glas 4C **64**
Cornish Ct. ML5: Coat 3B **90**
Cornock Cres. G81: Clyd 4D **42**
Cornock St. G81: Clyd 4D **42**
Cornsilloch Brae ML9: Lark 2B **162**
Corn St. G4: Glas 1F **83** (1C **4**)
Cornwall Av. G73: Ruth 2F **121**
Cornwall Ct. G74: E Kil 2H **149**

Cornwall St. G41: Glas 6B **82**
G74: E Kil 2F **149**
Cornwall St. Sth. G41: Glas 6B **82**
Cornwall Way G74: E Kil 2H **149**
Coronation Av. ML9: Lark 5E **161**
Coronation Cres. ML9: Lark 5E **161**
Coronation Pl. G69: G'csh 2C **68**
ML9: Lark 5F **161**
Coronation Rd. ML1: New S 3H **127**
Coronation Rd. E. ML1: New S 4H **127**
Coronation St. ML2: Wis 6B **146**
Coronation Way G61: Bear 5F **45**
Corpach Pl. G34: Glas 2B **88**
Corporation Yd. G15: Glas 4H **43**
Corra Linn ML3: Ham 6E **141**
Corran Av. G77: Newt M 3C **132**
Corran St. G33: Glas 3H **85**
Correen Gdns. G61: Bear 6B **24**
Corrie Brae G65: Kils 2G **11**
Corrie Ct. ML3: Ham 1D **152**
Corrie Dr. ML1: Moth 2D **142**
PA1: Pais 1G **99**
Corrie Gro. G44: Neth 3D **118**
Corrie Pl. G66: Lenz 3E **51**
Corrie Rd. G65: Kils 2G **11**
Corrie Vw. G68: Cumb 5B **34**
Corrie Vw. Cotts. G65: Twe 1C **32**
Corrie Way ML9: Lark 3F **161**
Corrour Rd. G43: Glas 6B **102**
G77: Newt M 3C **132**
Corsebar Av. PA2: Pais 3G **97**
Corsebar Cres. PA2: Pais 4G **97**
Corsebar Dr. PA2: Pais 3G **97**
Corsebar La. PA2: Pais 4F **97**
Corsebar Rd. PA2: Pais 4F **97**
Corsebar Way PA2: Pais 2G **97**
CORSEFORD **6B 94**
Corseford Av. PA5: John 5C **94**
Corsehill Path G34: Glas 3A **88**
Corsehill Pl. G34: Glas 3A **88**
Corsehill St. G34: Glas 3A **88**
Corselet Rd. G53: Glas 4A **116**
G78: Barr 1A **132**
Corse Rd. G52: Glas 5G **79**
Corsewall Av. G32: Glas 2E **107**
Corsewall St. ML5: Coat 4A **90**
Corsford Dr. G53: Glas 1C **116**
Corsock Av. ML3: Ham 1C **152**
Corsock St. G31: Glas 4D **84**
Corston St. G33: Glas 3F **85**
Cortachy Pl. G64: B'rig 6F **49**
Coruisk Dr. G76: Clar 1B **134**
Coruisk Way PA2: Pais 5C **96**
Corunna Ct. ML8: Carl 4H **165**
Corunna St. G3: Glas 3C **82**
Coshneuk Rd. G33: Mille 4B **66**
Cosy Neuk ML9: Lark 4G **161**
Cottar St. G20: Glas 2C **62**
Cotton Av. PA3: Lin 6H **75**
Cotton St. G40: Glas 3C **104**
PA1: Pais 1B **98**
Cotton St. Ent. Pk. G40: Glas 3B **104**
Cotton Va. ML1: Cle 1E **145**
Coulin Gdns. G22: Glas 5H **63**
Coulter Av. ML2: Wis 2A **146**
ML5: Coat 3A **90**
Countess Way *G69: Barg 6E* ***89***
(off Princess Dr.)
County Av. G72: Camb 6F **105**
County Pl. PA1: Pais 6A **78**
County Sq. PA1: Pais 6A **78**
Couper Pl. G4: Glas 2H **83** (2G **5**)
Couper St. G4: Glas 2H **83** (2G **5**)
Coursington Cres. ML1: Moth 2A **144**
Coursington Gdns.
ML1: Moth 2H **143**
Coursington Pl. ML1: Moth 2H **143**
Coursington Rd. ML1: Moth 2H **143**
(not continuous)
Coursington Twr. *ML1: Moth 2H* ***143***
(off Coursington Rd.)
Courthill G61: Bear 1D **44**
Court Hill G65: Kils 3A **12**
Courthill Av. G44: Glas 2F **119**
Courthill Cres. G65: Kils 3A **12**
Coustonholm Rd. G43: Glas 6B **102**
Couther Quad. ML6: Air 1A **92**
Covanburn Av. ML3: Ham 2B **154**
Covenant Cres. ML9: Lark 3F **161**
Covenanters Way
ML2: Over 5A **158**
Covenany Pl. ML2: Wis 1C **156**
Coventry Dr. G31: Glas 3D **84**
Cowal Cres. G66: Kirk 4H **31**
Cowal Dr. PA3: Lin 6G **75**
Cowal St. G20: Glas 2A **62**
Cowal Vw. G81: Clyd 4D **42**
Cowan Cres. G78: Barr 4F **115**
Cowan La. *G12: Glas 1C* ***82***
(off Glasgow St.)
Cowan Rd. G68: Cumb 3D **34**
Cowan St. G12: Glas 1C **82**
Cowan Wilson Av. G72: Blan 1B **140**
Cowan Wynd G71: Tann 5E **109**
ML2: Over 4A **158**
COWCADDENS **2F 83 (1E 5)**
Cowcaddens Rd.
G4: Glas 2F **83** (2C **4**)
Cowcaddens Station (Und.)
2F 83 (2C 4)
Cowden Dr. G64: B'rig 4C **48**
Cowdenhill Cir. G13: Glas 1D **60**
Cowdenhill Pl. G13: Glas 1D **60**
Cowdenhill Rd. G13: Glas 1D **60**
Cowden St. G51: Glas 4D **80**
Cowdray Cres. PA4: Renf 6F **59**
Cowgate G66: Kirk 4C **30**
Cowglen Rd. G53: Glas 6C **100**
COWLAIRS **5A 64**
Cowlairs Ind. Est. G21: Glas 5H **63**
Cowlairs Rd. *G21: Glas 5A* ***64***
(off Kemp St.)
G21: Glas 5A **64**
(Millarbank St.)
Coxdale Av. G66: Kirk 5B **30**
Coxhill St. G21: Glas 6H **63**
Coxton Pl. G33: Glas 2D **86**
Coylton Cres. ML3: Ham 2C **152**
Coylton Rd. G43: Glas 2C **118**
Crabb Quad. ML1: Moth 6E **127**
Cragdale G74: E Kil 6E **137**
Craggan Dr. G14: Glas 3H **59**
Crags Av. PA2: Pais 4B **98**
Crags Cres. PA2: Pais 3B **98**
Crags Rd. PA2: Pais 4B **98**
Cragwell Pk. G76: Crmck 2A **136**
Craigallan Av. G72: Camb 3D **122**
Craigallian Av. G62: Miln 1F **25**
Craiganour La. G43: Glas 1A **118**
Craiganour Pl. G43: Glas 1A **118**
Craigard Pl. G73: Ruth 4F **121**
Craigash Quad. G62: Miln 2E **25**
Craigash Rd. G62: Miln 3E **25**
Craigbank Dr. G53: Glas 1A **116**
Craigbank Rd. ML9: Lark 5E **161**
Craigbank St. ML9: Lark 4E **161**
Craigbanzo St. G81: Faif 5F **23**
Craigbarnet Av. G64: Torr 5C **28**
Craigbarnet Cres. G33: Mille 5B **66**
Craigbarnet Rd. G62: Miln 3D **24**
Craigbet Av. PA11: Q'riers 1A **72**
Craigbet Cres. PA11: Q'riers 1A **72**
Craigbet Pl. PA11: Q'riers 1A **72**
Craigbo Av. G23: Glas 6B **46**
Craigbo Ct. G23: Glas 1B **62**
Craigbo Dr. G23: Glas 6B **46**
Craigbog Av. PA5: John 4D **94**
Craigbog Rd. PA5: John 5F **95**
Craigbo Pl. G23: Glas 1B **62**
Craigbo Rd. G23: Glas 1B **62**
Craigbo St. G23: Glas 6B **46**
Craigburn Av. PA6: C'lee 3D **74**
Craigburn Ct. ML9: Ashg 4B **162**
Craigburn Cres. PA6: C'lee 4D **74**
Craigburn Pl. PA6: C'lee 4D **74**
Craigburn St. ML3: Ham 3H **153**
Craig Cres. *G66: Kirk 6H* ***31***
(off Bk. o'Dykes Rd.)
Craigdhu Av. G62: Miln 4F **25**
ML6: Air 4E **93**
Craigdhu Farm Cotts. G62: Miln 4E **25**
Craigdhu Rd. G61: Bear 5D **24**
(not continuous)
Craigdonald Pl. PA5: John 2F **95**
Craigellan Rd. G43: Glas 1B **118**
Craigelvan Av. G67: Cumb 1B **54**
Craigelvan Ct. G67: Cumb 1B **54**
Craigelvan Dr. G67: Cumb 1B **54**
Craigelvan Gdns. G67: Cumb 1B **54**
Craigelvan Gro. G67: Cumb 1B **54**
Craigelvan Pl. G67: Cumb 1B **54**
Craigelvan Vw. G67: Cumb 1B **54**
Craigenbay Cres. G66: Lenz 2E **51**
Craigenbay Rd. G66: Lenz 3D **50**
Craigenbay St. G21: Glas 5D **64**
Craigencart Ct. G81: Dun 1B **42**
CRAIGEND **6C 66**
Craigend Cres. G62: Miln 3F **25**
Craigend Dr. ML5: Coat 1G **109**
Craigend Dr. W. G62: Miln 3E **25**
Craigend Ho. G82: Dumb 3C **16**
CRAIGENDMUIR **5E 67**
Craigendmuir Cvn. Site
G33: Step 5E **67**
Craigendmuir Rd. G33: Step 5E **67**
Craigendmuir St. G33: Glas 1F **85**
Craigendon Oval PA2: Pais 6G **97**
Craigendon Rd. PA2: Pais 6G **97**
Craigend Pl. G13: Glas 3E **61**
Craigend Rd. G67: Cumb 2B **54**
CRAIGENDS **3D 74**
Craigends Av. PA11: Q'riers 1A **72**
Craigends Dr. PA10: Kilb 2A **94**
Craigends Pl. PA11: Q'riers 1A **72**
Craigends Rd. PA6: C'lee, Hous 4D **74**
Craigend St. G13: Glas 3E **61**
Craigend Vw. G67: Cumb 2B **54**
Craigenfeoch Av. PA5: John 4D **94**
Craigens Rd. ML6: Gart 6F **93**
Craigfaulds Av. PA2: Pais 3F **97**
Craigfell Ct. ML3: Ham 1C **152**
Craigflower Av. G53: Glas 3A **116**
Craigflower Gdns. G53: Glas 3A **116**
Craigflower Rd. G53: Glas 4A **116**
Craig Gdns. G77: Newt M 5C **132**
Craighalbert Rd. G68: Cumb 2E **35**
(not continuous)
CRAIGHALBERT RDBT. **1E 35**
Craighalbert Way G68: Cumb 1E **35**
Craighall Quad. G78: Neil 3D **130**
Craighall Rd. G4: Glas 1F **83** (1D **4**)
Craighaw St. G81: Faif 5F **23**
CRAIGHEAD **1E 141**
Craighead Av. G33: Glas 6F **65**
G66: Milt C 5C **8**
Craighead Dr. G62: Miln 3D **24**
Craighead Rd. G66: Milt C 5C **8**
PA7: B'ton 5H **39**
Craighead St. G78: Barr 5D **114**
ML6: Air 3E **93**
Craighead Way G78: Barr 5D **114**
(not continuous)
Craig Hill G75: E Kil 4E **149**
Craighill Dr. G76: Clar 3B **134**
Craighill Gro. G76: Clar 3B **134**
Craigholme PA6: Hous 1D **74**
Craighouse St. G33: Glas 2A **86**
Craighton Gdns. G66: Len 3H **7**
Craighurst Dr. G81: Dun, Hard 6C **22**
Craighurst Rd. G62: Miln 3D **24**
Craigiebar Dr. PA2: Pais 5G **97**
Craigieburn Gdns. G20: Glas 1H **61**
Craigieburn Rd. G67: Cumb 4H **35**
Craigie Dr. G77: Newt M 6E **133**
Craigiehall Av. PA8: Ersk 2E **57**
Craigiehall Cres. PA8: Ersk 2E **57**
Craigiehall Pl. G51: Glas 5B **82**
Craigiehall St. G51: Glas 5C **82**
Craigiehall Way PA8: Ersk 2E **57**
Craigie La. *ML9: Lark 1F* ***161***
(off Duncan Graham St.)
Craigielea Ct. PA4: Renf 5E **59**

Craigielea Cres. G62: Miln . . . 3E **25**
Craigielea Dr. PA3: Pais . . . 5F **77**
Craigielea Pk. PA4: Renf . . . 6E **59**
Craigielea Rd. G81: Dun . . . 6A **22**
PA4: Renf . . . 6E **59**
Craigielea St. G31: Glas . . . 3C **84**
Craigielinn Av. PA2: Pais . . . 6F **97**
Craigie Pk. G66: Lenz . . . 2E **51**
Craigie St. G42: Glas . . . 3E **103**
Craigievar Pl. G77: Newt M . . . 4B **132**
Craigievar St. G33: Glas . . . 1E **87**
Craiglea Pl. ML6: Air . . . 3C **92**
Craiglea Ter. ML6: Plain . . . 1F **93**
Craiglee G75: E Kil . . . 6G **149**
Craigleith St. G32: Glas . . . 5G **85**
CRAIGLINN . . . **4B 34**
Craiglinn Pk. Rd. G68: Cumb . . . 4C **34**
CRAIGLINN RDBT. . . . **4C 34**
Craiglockhart St. G33: Glas . . . 1D **86**
Craigmaddie Gdns. G64: Torr . . . 5C **28**
Craigmaddie Rd.
G62: Balder, Bard . . . 3D **26**
Craigmaddie Ter. La. *G3: Glas . . . 2C **82***
(off Derby St.)
CRAIGMARLOCH . . . **1E 35**
Craigmarloch Av. G64: Torr . . . 5D **28**
CRAIGMARLOCH RDBT. . . . **2E 35**
Craigmillar Av. G62: Miln . . . 3H **25**
Craigmillar Rd. G42: Glas . . . 6E **103**
Craigmochan Av. ML6: Air . . . 1H **91**
Craigmont Dr. G20: Glas . . . 3C **62**
Craigmont St. G20: Glas . . . 3C **62**
Craigmore Pl. ML5: Coat . . . 2A **110**
Craigmore Rd. G61: Bear . . . 6B **24**
Craigmore St. G31: Glas . . . 5E **85**
Craigmore Wynd *ML9: Lark . . . 1F **161***
(off Carrick Pl.)
Craigmount Av. PA2: Pais . . . 6G **97**
Craigmount St. G66: Kirk . . . 6D **30**
Craigmuir Cres. G52: Glas . . . 5H **79**
Craigmuir Gdns. G72: Blan . . . 3H **139**
Craigmuir Pl. G52: Glas . . . 5G **79**
Craigmuir Rd. G52: Glas . . . 5G **79**
G72: Blan . . . 3H **139**
Craigneil St. G33: Glas . . . 1E **87**
Craigneith Castle (Ruins) . . . **6E 139**
Craigneith Ct. G74: E Kil . . . 5E **139**
Craignethan Rd. G46: Giff . . . 2G **133**
ML8: Carl . . . 2E **165**
CRAIGNEUK
Airdrie . . . 4D 92
Wishaw . . . 5D 144
Craigneuk Av. ML6: Air . . . 5C **92**
Craigneuk St. ML1: Moth . . . 4B **144**
ML2: Wis . . . 4B **144**
Craignure Cres. ML6: Air . . . 4E **93**
Craignure Rd. G73: Ruth . . . 4D **120**
Craigpark G31: Glas . . . 4C **84**
Craigpark Dr. G31: Glas . . . 4C **84**
Craigpark St. G81: Faif . . . 6F **23**
Craigpark Ter. G31: Glas . . . 4C **84**
Craigpark Way G71: Tann . . . 6E **109**
Craig Pl. G77: Newt M . . . 4B **132**
Craig Rd. G44: Glas . . . 2E **119**
G78: Neil . . . 3D **130**
PA3: Lin . . . 4F **75**
Craigs Av. G81: Faif, Hard . . . 1E **43**
Craigsheen Av. G76: Crmck . . . 2H **135**
Craigside Ct. G68: Cumb . . . 6B **34**
Craigside Pl. G68: Cumb . . . 6B **34**
Craigside Rd. G68: Cumb . . . 6B **34**
Craigson Pl. ML6: Air . . . 5F **93**
Craigstone Vw. G65: Kils . . . 3B **12**
Craigston Pl. PA5: John . . . 3F **95**
Craigston Rd. PA5: John . . . 3E **95**
Craig St. G72: Blan . . . 3C **140**
ML5: Coat . . . 1B **110**
ML6: Air . . . 4H **91**
Craigthornhill Rd. ML3: Ham . . . 6A **160**
CRAIGTON . . . **6D 80**
Craigton Av. G62: Miln . . . 3F **25**
G78: Barr . . . 6G **115**
Craigton Cl. G77: Newt M . . . 4B **132**
Craigton Cotts. G62: Miln . . . 1C **24**
Craigton Crematorium G52: Glas . . . 6D **80**
Craigton Dr. G51: Glas . . . 5F **81**
G77: Newt M . . . 4C **132**
G78: Barr . . . 6G **115**
Craigton Gdns. G62: Miln . . . 2E **25**
Craigton Ind. Est. G52: Glas . . . 6D **80**
CRAIGTON INTERCHANGE . . . **6B 40**
Craigton Pl. G51: Glas . . . 5E **81**
G72: Blan . . . 6B **124**
Craigton Rd. G51: Glas . . . 5F **81**
G62: Miln . . . 2C **24**
G77: Newt M . . . 6H **131**
Craigton St. G81: Faif . . . 5F **23**
CRAIGTON VILLAGE . . . **2B 24**
Craigvale Cres. ML6: Air . . . 4E **93**
Craigvicar Gdns. G32: Glas . . . 1D **106**
Craigview Av. PA5: John . . . 5D **94**
Craigview Rd. ML1: Moth . . . 1H **143**
Craigview Ter. PA5: John . . . 4D **94**
Craigwell Av. G73: Ruth . . . 1F **121**
Crail St. G31: Glas . . . 1F **105**
Craithie Ct. G11: Glas . . . 1G **81**
Crammond Av. ML5: Coat . . . 1G **109**
Cramond Av. PA4: Renf . . . 1G **79**
Cramond St. G5: Glas . . . 3H **103**
Cramond Ter. G32: Glas . . . 6B **86**
Cranborne Rd. G12: Glas . . . 4G **61**
Cranbrooke Dr. G20: Glas . . . 2B **62**
CRANHILL . . . **3B 86**
Crannog Rd. G82: Milt . . . 4E **19**
CRANSTON HILL . . . **3D 82**
Cranston St. G3: Glas . . . 4D **82**
Cranworth La. *G12: Glas . . . 6B **62***
(off Gt. George St.)
Cranworth St. G12: Glas . . . 6B **62**
Crarae Av. G61: Bear . . . 5E **45**
Crarae Pl. G77: Newt M . . . 4A **132**
Crathes Ct. G44: Glas . . . 3C **118**
Crathie Ct. ML8: Carl . . . 2E **165**
Crathie Dr. G11: Glas . . . 1G **81**
ML6: Glenm . . . 5H **71**
Crathie Pl. G77: Newt M . . . 5H **133**
Crathie Quad. ML2: Wis . . . 4H **145**
Crauchlan Av. PA2: Pais . . . 5A **98**
Crawford Av. G66: Lenz . . . 4D **50**
Crawford Ct. G46: Giff . . . 6H **117**
Crawford Cres. G71: Udd . . . 6C **108**
G72: Blan . . . 6B **124**
Crawford Dr. G15: Glas . . . 6H **43**
G74: E Kil . . . 1B **150**
CRAWFORDDYKE . . . **4G 165**
Crawford Gdns. G72: Blan . . . 2H **139**
Crawford Hill G74: E Kil . . . 1B **150**
Crawford La. *G11: Glas . . . 1G **81***
(off Crawford St.)
Crawford Path *G11: Glas . . . 1G **81***
(off Crawford St.)
Crawford Rd. G62: Miln . . . 1F **25**
G73: Ruth . . . 3D **120**
PA6: C'lee . . . 2D **74**
Crawford St. G11: Glas . . . 1G **81**
ML1: Moth . . . 3E **143**
ML3: Ham . . . 4E **141**
Crawfurd Dr. PA3: Pais . . . 5F **77**
Crawfurd Gdns. G73: Ruth . . . 3E **121**
Crawriggs Av. G66: Kirk . . . 1D **50**
Craw Rd. PA2: Pais . . . 2G **97**
Creamery Rd. ML2: Wis . . . 2B **158**
Crebar Dr. G78: Barr . . . 5E **115**
Crebar St. G46: T'bnk . . . 3E **117**
Credon Dr. ML6: Air . . . 6A **92**
Credon Gdns. G73: Ruth . . . 3E **121**
Cree Av. G64: B'rig . . . 6F **49**
Cree Gdns. G32: Glas . . . 6H **85**
Cree Pl. G75: E Kil . . . 2D **148**
Creighton Gro. G74: E Kil . . . 2G **149**
Creran Ct. ML3: Ham . . . 2E **153**
Creran Dr. PA4: Renf . . . 5D **58**
Creran Path *ML2: Newm . . . 3D **146***
(off Tiree Cres.)
Crescent Ct. *G81: Clyd . . . 4A **42***
(off Crescent, The)
Crescent Rd. G13: Glas . . . 4B **60**
G14: Glas . . . 4B **60**
Crescent, The G62: Miln . . . 5G **25**
G76: Busby . . . 4E **135**
G81: Clyd . . . 4A **42**
Cressdale Av. G45: Glas . . . 5H **119**
Cressdale Ct. G45: Glas . . . 5H **119**
Cressdale Dr. G45: Glas . . . 5H **119**
Cressland Dr. G45: Glas . . . 6H **119**
Cressland Pl. G45: Glas . . . 6H **119**
Cresswell Gro. G77: Newt M . . . 6D **132**
Cresswell La. *G12: Glas . . . 6B **62***
(off Cresswell St.)
Cresswell Pl. G77: Newt M . . . 6E **133**
Cresswell St. G12: Glas . . . 6B **62**
Cressy St. G51: Glas . . . 3E **81**
Crest Av. G13: Glas . . . 1B **60**
Crestlea Av. PA2: Pais . . . 5A **98**
Creswell Ter. G71: Udd . . . 1C **124**
Crichton Ct. G45: Glas . . . 5B **120**
Crichton Pl. G21: Glas . . . 5A **64**
Crichton St. G21: Glas . . . 5A **64**
ML5: Coat . . . 3C **90**
Cricketfield La. PA6: Hous . . . 1B **74**
Crieff Av. ML6: Chap . . . 4D **112**
Criffell Gdns. G32: Glas . . . 2D **106**
Criffell Rd. G32: Glas . . . 1D **106**
Criffel Pl. *ML1: N'hill . . . 4C **128***
(off Clarinda Pl.)
Crighton Wynd ML4: Bell . . . 2H **125**
Crimea St. G2: Glas . . . 4E **83** (6A **4**)
Crimond Pl. G65: Kils . . . 2F **11**
Crinan Cres. ML5: Coat . . . 2H **89**
Crinan Gdns. G64: B'rig . . . 6E **49**
Crinan Pl. ML4: Bell . . . 3D **126**
ML5: Coat . . . 2H **89**
Crinan Rd. G64: B'rig . . . 6E **49**
Crinan St. G31: Glas . . . 3D **84**
CRINDLEDYKE . . . **4G 147**
Crindledyke Cres. ML2: Newm . . . 3F **147**
Cripps Av. G81: Clyd . . . 6F **43**
Croft ML9: Lark . . . 3D **160**
Croftbank Av. G71: Both . . . 6F **125**
Croftbank Cres. G71: Both . . . 6F **125**
G71: Udd . . . 1D **124**
Croftbank Ga. G71: Both . . . 6F **125**
Croftbank St. G21: Glas . . . 5B **64**
Croftburn Dr. G44: Glas . . . 3H **119**
Croftcot Av. ML4: Bell . . . 4B **126**
Croftcroighn Rd. G33: Glas . . . 2B **86**
Croftend Av. G44: Glas . . . 1A **120**
Croftend La. G44: Glas . . . 2B **120**
CROFTFOOT . . . **2A 120**
Croftfoot Cres. G45: Glas . . . 3C **120**
Croftfoot Dr. G45: Glas . . . 3B **120**
Croftfoot Pl. G69: G'csh . . . 3E **69**
Croftfoot Quad. G45: Glas . . . 3A **120**
Croftfoot Rd. G44: Glas . . . 3H **119**
G45: Glas . . . 3B **120**
Croftfoot Station (Rail) . . . **1A 120**
Croftfoot St. G45: Glas . . . 3C **120**
Croftfoot Ter. G45: Glas . . . 3B **120**
Crofthead Cotts. G78: Neil . . . 2C **130**
Crofthead Cres. ML4: Bell . . . 4B **126**
Crofthead Dr. G66: Len . . . 2E **7**
Crofthead La. *G66: Kirk . . . 4C **30***
(off W. High St.)
Crofthead Pl. G77: Newt M . . . 6E **133**
ML4: Bell . . . 4B **126**
Crofthead St. G71: Udd . . . 2D **124**
Crofthill Av. G71: Udd . . . 1D **124**
Crofthill Rd. G44: Glas . . . 1H **119**
Crofthouse Dr. G44: Glas . . . 3A **120**
Croftmont Av. G44: Glas . . . 3A **120**
Croftmoraig Av. G69: Mood . . . 3E **53**
Crofton Av. G44: Glas . . . 3H **119**
Croftpark Av. G44: Glas . . . 3G **119**
Croftpark Cres. G72: Blan . . . 3C **140**
Croftpark Rd. G81: Hard . . . 6D **22**
Croftpark St. ML4: Bell . . . 1C **126**
Croft Pl. ML9: Lark . . . 2D **160**
Croft Rd. G64: Balm . . . 5A **28**
G72: Camb . . . 2B **122**
G75: E Kil . . . 4G **149**
Croftside Av. G44: Glas . . . 3A **120**
Croftspar Av. G32: Glas . . . 5C **86**

Croftspar Ct. G32: Glas . . . 5D **86**
Croftspar Dr. G32: Glas . . . 5C **86**
Croftspar Ga. G32: Glas . . . 5D **86**
Croftspar Gro. G32: Glas . . . 5C **86**
Croftspar Pl. G32: Glas . . . 5C **86**
Croft Way PA4: Renf . . . 2F **79**
Croftwood G64: B'rig . . . 3C **48**
Croftwood Av. G44: Glas . . . 3H **119**
Croftwood Rd. ML3: Ham . . . 2H **153**
Croft Wynd G71: Udd . . . 1E **125**
Crogal Cres. ML6: Chap . . . 3D **112**
Cromalt Cres. G61: Bear . . . 5C **24**
Cromarty Av. G43: Glas . . . 1D **118**
G64: B'rig . . . 5F **49**
Cromarty Cres. G61: Bear . . . 6F **25**
Cromarty Gdns. G76: Clar . . . 6E **119**
Cromarty Pl. G69: Chry . . . 6B **52**
G74: E Kil . . . 6C **138**
Cromarty Rd. ML6: Air . . . 6H **91**
Crombie Gdns. G69: Bail . . . 2F **107**
Cromdale St. G51: Glas . . . 4E **81**
Cromdale Way ML1: New S . . . 5A **128**
Cromer St. G20: Glas . . . 4D **62**
Cromer Way PA3: Pais . . . 4H **77**
Crompton Av. G44: Glas . . . 2F **119**
Crompton Gro. PA1: Pais . . . 2F **97**
Cromwell La. G20: Glas . . . 1E **83**
Cromwell St. G20: Glas . . . 1E **83**
Crona Dr. ML3: Ham . . . 5C **140**
Cronberry Quad. G52: Glas . . . 2H **99**
Cronberry Ter. G52: Glas . . . 2H **99**
Cronin Pl. ML4: Bell . . . 6D **110**
Cronulla Pl. G65: Kils . . . 3B **12**
Crookedshields Rd.
G72: Camb . . . 2B **138**
G74: Ners . . . 2A **138**
CROOKFUR . . . **3C 132**
Crookfur Cott. Homes
G77: Newt M . . . 4D **132**
Crookfur Rd. G77: Newt M . . . 3B **132**
CROOKSTON . . . **1A 100**
Crookston Av. G52: Glas . . . 1A **100**
Crookston Castle (Remains of) . . . **3B 100**
Crookston Ct. G52: Glas . . . 1A **100**
Crookston Dr. PA1: Pais . . . 1H **99**
Crookston Gdns. G52: Glas . . . 1H **99**
Crookston Gro. G52: Glas . . . 1A **100**
Crookstonhill Path *G52: Glas* . . . *1H* ***99***
(off Crookston Quad.)
Crookston Path *G52: Glas* . . . *1H* ***99***
(off Crookston Quad.)
Crookston Pl. G52: Glas . . . 1H **99**
Crookston Quad. G52: Glas . . . 1H **99**
Crookston Rd. G52: Glas . . . 2H **99**
G53: Glas . . . 6A **100**
Crookston Station (Rail) . . . **1H 99**
Crookston Ter. G52: Glas . . . 1A **100**
Crosbie Dr. PA2: Pais . . . 6C **96**
Crosbie La. *G20: Glas* . . . *1A* ***62***
(off Crossbie St.)
Crosbie St. G20: Glas . . . 1A **62**
Crosbie Wood PA2: Pais . . . 4F **97**
Crossan Dr. G66: Len . . . 2C **6**
Cross Arthurlie St. G78: Barr . . . 5D **114**
Crossbank Av. G42: Glas . . . 4A **104**
Crossbank Dr. G42: Glas . . . 4H **103**
Crossbank Rd. G42: Glas . . . 4H **103**
Crossbank Ter. G42: Glas . . . 4H **103**
CROSSBASKET . . . **3F 139**
Crossburn Av. G62: Miln . . . 4F **25**
Cross Ct. G64: B'rig . . . 6B **48**
Crossdykes G66: Kirk . . . 6G **31**
Crossen La. *ML8: Carl* . . . *4H* ***165***
(off Ramage Rd.)
Crossflat Cres. PA1: Pais . . . 6C **78**
Crossford Dr. G23: Glas . . . 6C **46**
Crossgate G66: Kirk . . . 4D **30**
Cross Gates ML4: Bell . . . 3C **126**
Crossgates PA7: B'ton . . . 3F **39**
Crossgates Av. ML1: Cle . . . 4H **129**
Crossgates St. ML9: Lark . . . 1D **160**
CROSSHILL
Baillieston . . . **6B 88**
Glasgow . . . **4F 103**
Crosshill Av. G42: Glas . . . 4F **103**
G66: Kirk . . . 1D **50**
Crosshill Dr. G73: Ruth . . . 1D **120**
ML1: Cle . . . 4H **129**
Crosshill Station (Rail) . . . **4F 103**
Crosshill Rd. G64: B'rig, Lenz . . . 2E **49**
G66: Lenz . . . 3H **49**
Crosshill St. G66: Len . . . 2F **7**
ML1: Moth . . . 3H **143**
ML5: Coat . . . 1F **109**
ML6: Air . . . 4H **91**
Crosshouse Rd. G75: E Kil . . . 6B **148**
Crosslea Gdns. PA6: C'lee . . . 2B **74**
CROSSLEE . . . **3B 74**
Crosslee Cres. PA6: Hous . . . 2C **74**
Crosslee Pk. PA6: C'lee . . . 2C **74**
Crosslee Rd. PA11: Bri W . . . 5H **73**
Crosslees Dr. G46: T'bnk . . . 4F **117**
Crosslees Pk. G46: T'bnk . . . 4F **117**
Crosslees Rd. G46: T'bnk . . . 5F **117**
Crosslee St. G52: Glas . . . 6D **80**
CROSSLET . . . **2C 18**
Crosslet Av. G82: Dumb . . . 1C **18**
Crosslet Ct. G82: Dumb . . . 2C **18**
Crosslet Ho. G82: Dumb . . . 2C **18**
Crosslet Pl. G82: Dumb . . . 4H **17**
Crosslet Rd. G82: Dumb . . . 3G **17**
Crossloan Rd. G51: Glas . . . 4F **81**
Crossloan Ter. G51: Glas . . . 4F **81**
CROSSMILL . . . **3F 115**
Crossmill Av. G78: Barr . . . 3F **115**
Crossmount Ct. ML8: Carl . . . 3E **165**
CROSSMYLOOF . . . **4B 102**
Crossmyloof Gdns. G41: Glas . . . 4B **102**
Crossmyloof Station (Rail) . . . **4B 102**
Cross Orchard Way ML4: Bell . . . 2C **126**
Crosspoint Dr. G23: Glas . . . 6C **46**
Cross Rd. PA2: Pais . . . 3F **97**
CROSS STOBS . . . **2C 114**
Cross Stone Pl. ML1: Moth . . . 3G **143**
Cross St. G32: Carm . . . 4C **106**
PA1: Pais . . . 1G **97**
Cross, The PA1: Pais . . . 6A **78**
PA10: Kilb . . . 2A **94**
Crosstobs Rd. G53: Glas . . . 4A **100**
Crossveggate G62: Miln . . . 4H **25**
Crossveggate Bus. Pk. *G62: Miln* . . . *4H* ***25***
(off Crossveggate)
Crossview Av. G69: Bail . . . 6B **88**
Crossview Pl. G69: Bail . . . 6B **88**
Crossway Gardens . . . **3E 39**
Crossways PA6: Hous . . . 1D **74**
Cross Wynd *G74: E Kil* . . . *1H* ***149***
(off Hunter St.)
Crovie Rd. G53: Glas . . . 6A **100**
Crow Av. ML1: Holy . . . 2B **128**
Crowflats Rd. G71: Udd . . . 1C **124**
Crowfoot Vw. G71: View . . . 4G **109**
Crowford La. *G11: Glas* . . . *1G* ***81***
(off Rosevale St.)
Crowhill Cres. ML6: Air . . . 1H **91**
Crowhill Rd. G64: B'rig . . . 2B **64**
Crowhill St. G22: Glas . . . 3G **63**
Crow La. G13: Glas . . . 4F **61**
Crowlin Cres. G33: Glas . . . 3B **86**
Crown Av. G81: Clyd . . . 4C **42**
Crown Cir. G12: Glas . . . 6A **62**
Crown Gdns. G12: Glas . . . 6A **62**
Crownhall Pl. G32: Glas . . . 6C **86**
Crownhall Rd. G32: Glas . . . 6C **86**
Crownpoint Rd. G40: Glas . . . 6B **84**
Crownpoint Sports Complex . . . **5B 84**
Crown Rd. Nth. G12: Glas . . . 6H **61**
Crown Rd. Sth. G12: Glas . . . 6H **61**
Crown St. G5: Glas . . . 1G **103**
(Alexander Cres.)
G5: Glas . . . 6G **83**
(Ballater St.)
G5: Glas . . . 1F **103**
(Caledonia Rd.)
G69: Bail . . . 2F **107**
ML5: Coat . . . 4E **91**
ML6: C'bnk . . . 2B **112**
Crown Ter. G12: Glas . . . 6H **61**
Crow Rd. G11: Glas . . . 5F **61**
G13: Glas . . . 3F **61**
G66: Len . . . 1F **7**
Crow-Wood Cres. ML6: C'bnk . . . 3B **112**
Crow-Wood Dr. ML6: Air . . . 4D **92**
Crow Wood Rd. G69: Chry . . . 2H **67**
Crow-Wood Rd. ML6: C'bnk . . . 3B **112**
Crow Wood Ter. G69: Chry . . . 2H **67**
CROY . . . **1A 34**
Croy G74: E Kil . . . 6F **137**
Croy Av. G77: Newt M . . . 4G **133**
Croy Pl. G21: Glas . . . 4E **65**
Croy Rd. G21: Glas . . . 4E **65**
ML5: Coat . . . 1A **110**
Croy Station (Rail) . . . **2B 34**
Cruachan Av. PA4: Renf . . . 2E **79**
Cruachan Dr. G77: Newt M . . . 6F **133**
G78: Barr . . . 6E **115**
Cruachan Rd. G61: Bear . . . 6B **24**
G73: Ruth . . . 4F **121**
Cruachan St. G46: T'bnk . . . 3F **117**
Cruachan Way G78: Barr . . . 6E **115**
Cruden St. G51: Glas . . . 5F **81**
Crum Av. G46: T'bnk . . . 4G **117**
Crusader Av. G13: Glas . . . 6D **44**
Cubie St. G40: Glas . . . 6B **84**
Cuckoo Way ML1: Holy . . . 2B **128**
Cuilhill Rd. G69: Barg . . . 3D **88**
Cuillins, The G69: Mood . . . 3E **53**
Cuillin Way G78: Barr . . . 5E **115**
Cuilmuir Ter. G65: Croy . . . 1B **34**
Cuilmuir Vw. G65: Croy . . . 6B **12**
Culbin Dr. G13: Glas . . . 1H **59**
Cullen PA8: Ersk . . . 4E **41**
Cullen La. G75: E Kil . . . 4G **149**
Cullen Pl. G71: Tann . . . 5E **109**
Cullen Rd. G75: E Kil . . . 4F **149**
ML1: Moth . . . 4E **143**
Cullen St. G32: Glas . . . 1A **106**
Cullins Rd. G73: Ruth . . . 4F **121**
Cullins, The G71: Tann . . . 4C **108**
Cullion Way ML1: N'hill . . . 2G **129**
Cullochrig Rd. ML6: Rigg . . . 5G **55**
(not continuous)
Culloch Rd. G61: Bear . . . 5C **24**
Culloden Av. ML4: Bell . . . 3F **127**
Culloden St. G31: Glas . . . 3D **84**
Culrain Gdns. G32: Glas . . . 6A **86**
Culrain St. G32: Glas . . . 6A **86**
Culross Hill G74: E Kil . . . 2F **149**
Culross La. G32: Glas . . . 1C **106**
Culross Pl. G74: E Kil . . . 2F **149**
ML5: Coat . . . 4B **90**
Culross St. G32: Glas . . . 1C **106**
Culross Way G69: Mood . . . 4E **53**
Culterfell Path ML1: Cle . . . 5H **129**
Cult Rd. G66: Lenz . . . 3E **51**
Cults St. G51: Glas . . . 5F **81**
Culvain Av. G61: Bear . . . 6B **24**
Culzean ML6: Glenm . . . 4H **71**
Culzean Av. ML5: Coat . . . 6A **90**
Culzean Ct. *ML5: Coat* . . . *6A* ***90***
(off Torriden St.)
Culzean Cres. G69: Bail . . . 1G **107**
G77: Newt M . . . 4G **133**
Culzean Dr. G32: Glas . . . 1D **106**
G74: E Kil . . . 6F **137**
ML1: Carf . . . 4C **128**
Culzean Pl. G74: E Kil . . . 6F **137**
Cumberland Arc. G5: Glas . . . 1G **103**
Cumberland Pl. G5: Glas . . . 1G **103**
ML5: Coat . . . 6G **89**
Cumberland St. G5: Glas . . . 6F **83**
(not continuous)
CUMBERNAULD . . . **4H 35**
Cumbernauld Mus. . . . **4H 35**
Cumbernauld Rd.
FK4: C'cry, Longc . . . 1F **15**
G31: Glas . . . 4D **84**
G33: Glas . . . 4D **84**
G33: Mille, Step . . . 5A **66**
G33: Step . . . 2G **67**
G67: Mollin . . . 3H **53**
G68: Mollin . . . 1C **68**

Cumbernauld Rd. G69: Chry 2G **67**
G69: Mood 1C **68**
G69: Muirh 2A **68**
CUMBERNAULD RD. INTERCHANGE 1G **85**
Cumbernauld Shop. Cen., The
G67: Cumb 3H **35**
Cumbernauld Station (Rail) **5A 36**
Cumbernauld Theatre **1B 36**
CUMBERNAULD VILLAGE **6B 14**
Cumbrae G74: E Kil 2C **150**
Cumbrae Ct. G81: Clyd 5D **42**
Cumbrae Cres. ML5: Coat 6G **91**
Cumbrae Cres. Nth. G82: Dumb 2C **16**
Cumbrae Cres. Sth. G82: Dumb 2B **16**
Cumbrae Dr. ML1: Moth 1E **143**
Cumbrae Pl. ML5: Coat 1G **111**
Cumbrae Rd. PA2: Pais 6A **98**
PA4: Renf 2F **79**
Cumbrae St. G33: Glas 3A **86**
Cumlodden Dr. G20: Glas 2A **62**
Cumming Dr. G42: Glas 5F **103**
Cummock Dr. G78: Barr 6F **115**
Cumnock Dr. ML3: Ham 2B **152**
ML6: Air 1A **112**
Cumnock Rd. G33: Glas 3G **65**
Cumroch Rd. G66: Len 2E **7**
Cunard Ct. G81: Clyd 1D **58**
Cunard St. G81: Clyd 1D **58**
Cunningair Dr. ML1: Moth 5G **143**
Cunningham Dr. G46: Giff 4C **118**
G81: Dun 1B **42**
Cunninghame Rd. G73: Ruth 5E **105**
G74: E Kil 2G **149**
PA10: Kilb 2B **94**
Cunningham Gdns. PA6: C'lee 2D **74**
Cunningham Rd. G52: Hill 3H **79**
Cunningham St. ML1: Moth 3F **143**
Cuparhead Av. ML5: Coat 1H **109**
Curfew Rd. G13: Glas 6D **44**
Curle St. G14: Glas 1D **80**
(not continuous)
Curlew Pl. PA5: John 6C **94**
Curling Cres. G44: Glas 6G **103**
Curlinghaugh Cres. ML2: Wis 6A **146**
Curlingmire G75: E Kil 5G **149**
Curran Av. ML2: Wis 2E **157**
Currie Ct. *PA5: John* *4E **95***
(off Tannahill Cres.)
Currie St. G20: Glas 3C **62**
Curtis Av. G44: Glas 5G **103**
Curzon St. G20: Glas 3C **62**
Cuthbertson St. G42: Glas 2E **103**
Cuthbert St. G71: View 6F **109**
Cuthelton Dr. G31: Glas 1G **105**
Cuthelton St. G31: Glas 1F **105**
Cuthelton Ter. G31: Glas 1F **105**
Cut, The G71: Udd 2D **124**
Cypress Av. G71: View 5F **109**
G72: Blan 6A **124**
Cypress Ct. G66: Lenz 1B **50**
G75: E Kil 6E **149**
ML3: Ham 1A **154**
Cypress Cres. G75: E Kil 6E **149**
Cypress Pl. G75: E Kil 6E **149**
Cypress St. G22: Glas 4H **63**
Cypress Way G72: Flem 3F **123**
Cyprus Av. PA5: Eld 3H **95**
Cyril St. PA1: Pais 1C **98**

D

Daer Av. PA4: Renf 2G **79**
Daer Wlk. ML9: Lark 5E **161**
Daer Way ML3: Ham 6E **141**
Daffodil Way ML1: Moth 1G **143**
Dairsie Ct. G44: Glas 3D **118**
Dairsie Gdns. G64: B'rig 1F **65**
Dairsie St. G44: Glas 3D **118**
Daisy St. G42: Glas 4F **103**
Dakala Ct. ML2: Wis 1G **157**
Dakota Way PA4: Renf 2F **79**
Dalbeattie Braes ML6: Chap 4E **113**
DALBETH **3G 105**
Dalbeth Pl. G32: Glas 3H **105**
Dalbeth Rd. G32: Glas 3H **105**
Dalcharn Path *G34: Glas* *3G **87***
(off Kildermorie Rd.)
Dalcharn Pl. G34: Glas 3G **87**
Dalcraig Cres. G72: Blan 5A **124**
Dalcross Pass *G11: Glas* *1A **82***
(off Dalcross St.)
Dalcross St. G11: Glas 1A **82**
Dalcruin Gdns. G69: Mood 3E **53**
Daldowie Av. G32: Glas 2D **106**
Daldowie Complex, The (Land Services)
G71: Udd 5G **107**
Daldowie Crematorium
G71: Udd 5H **107**
DALDOWIE INTERCHANGE **4H 107**
Daldowie Rd. G71: Udd 3G **107**
Daldowie St. ML5: Coat 2A **110**
(not continuous)
Dale Av. G75: E Kil 4E **149**
Dale Ct. ML2: Wis 1C **156**
Dale Dr. ML1: New S 3A **128**
Dale Path *G40: Glas* *1B **104***
(off Main St.)
Dale St. G40: Glas 1B **104**
(not continuous)
Daleview Av. G12: Glas 3H **61**
Daleview Dr. G76: Clar 3B **134**
Daleview Gro. G76: Clar 3B **134**
Dale Way G73: Ruth 3D **120**
Dalfoil Ct. PA1: Pais 1H **99**
Dalgarroch Av. G81: Clyd 1G **59**
Dalgleish Av. G81: Dun 1A **42**
Dalhousie Gdns. G64: B'rig 5B **48**
Dalhousie La. G3: Glas 2E **83** (2B **4**)
Dalhousie Rd. PA10: Kilb 3B **94**
Dalhousie St. G3: Glas 3E **83** (3B **4**)
(not continuous)
Dalilea Dr. G34: Glas 2B **88**
(not continuous)
Dalilea Path *G34: Glas* *2B **88***
(off Dalilea Dr.)
Dalilea Pl. G34: Glas 2B **88**
Dalintober St. G5: Glas 5E **83**
Dalkeith Av. G41: Glas 1H **101**
G64: B'rig 4D **48**
Dalkeith Rd. G64: B'rig 3D **48**
Dalmacoulter Rd. ML6: Air 1B **92**
Dalmahoy Cres. PA11: Bri W 5D **72**
Dalmahoy St. G32: Glas 4G **85**
Dalmally St. G20: Glas 6D **62**
DALMARNOCK **2D 104**
Dalmarnock Bri. G73: Ruth 3D **104**
Dalmarnock Ct. G40: Glas 2D **104**
Dalmarnock Rd. G40: Glas 1B **104**
G73: Ruth 3D **104**
Dalmarnock Rd. Ind. Est.
G73: Ruth 4D **104**
Dalmarnock Station (Rail) **2C 104**
Dalmary Dr. PA1: Pais 5D **78**
Dalmellington Ct. *G74: E Kil* *1F **149***
(off Dalmellington Dr.)
ML3: Ham 2B **152**
Dalmellington Dr. G53: Glas 5A **100**
G74: E Kil 1F **149**
Dalmellington Rd. G53: Glas 4A **100**
Dalmeny Av. G46: Giff 4A **118**
Dalmeny Dr. G78: Barr 5C **114**
Dalmeny Rd. ML3: Ham 1H **153**
Dalmeny St. G5: Glas 3A **104**
Dalmoor Dr. ML6: Air 5A **92**
DALMUIR **4A 42**
Dalmuir Ct. G81: Clyd 4A **42**
Dalmuir Station (Rail) **4A 42**
Dalnair Pl. G62: Miln 3D **24**
Dalnair St. G3: Glas 2A **82**
Dalness Pas. *G32: Glas* *1A **106***
(off Ochil St.)
Dalness St. G32: Glas 2A **106**
Dalnottar Av. G60: Old K 1F **41**
Dalnottar Dr. G60: Old K 2F **41**
Dalnottar Gdns. G60: Old K 2F **41**
Dalnottar Hill Rd. G60: Old K 1F **41**
Dalnottar Ter. G60: Old K 1F **41**
DALREOCH **3D 16**
Dalreoch Av. G69: Bail 6A **88**
Dalreoch Ct. G82: Dumb 3D **16**
Dalreoch Ho. *G82: Dumb* *3D **16***
(off School La.)
Dalreoch Path G69: Bail 6A **88**
Dalreoch Station (Rail) **3E 17**
Dalriada Cres. ML1: Moth 5F **127**
Dalriada Dr. G64: Torr 5E **29**
Dalriada St. G40: Glas 1E **105**
Dalry Gdns. ML3: Ham 1B **152**
Dalrymple Ct. G66: Kirk 6D **30**
Dalrymple Dr. G74: E Kil 6G **137**
G77: Newt M 5G **133**
ML5: Coat 6B **90**
Dalry Pl. ML6: Chap 5D **112**
Dalry Rd. G71: View 6F **109**
Dalry St. G32: Glas 1B **106**
DALSERF **3D 162**
Dalserf Ct. G31: Glas 6D **84**
Dalserf Cres. G46: Giff 6H **117**
Dalserf Gdns. G31: Glas 6D **84**
Dalserf Path *ML9: Lark* *4G **161***
(off Bannockburn Dr.)
Dalserf St. G31: Glas 6D **84**
Dalsetter Av. G15: Glas 5H **43**
Dalsetter Pl. G15: Glas 5A **44**
DALSHANNON **1B 54**
Dalshannon Pl. G67: Cumb 6C **34**
Dalshannon Rd. G67: Cumb 6D **34**
Dalshannon Vw. G67: Cumb 6C **34**
Dalshannon Way G67: Cumb 6C **34**
Dalsholm Av. G20: Glas 1H **61**
Dalsholm Ind. Est. G20: Glas 2H **61**
Dalsholm Rd. G20: Glas 2H **61**
Dalskeith Av. PA3: Pais 6E **77**
Dalskeith Cres. PA3: Pais 6E **77**
Dalskeith Rd. PA3: Pais 1E **97**
Dalswinton Path G34: Glas 3B **88**
Dalswinton St. G34: Glas 3A **88**
Dalton Av. G81: Clyd 6G **43**
Dalton Cotts. G72: Flem 5F **123**
Dalton Hill ML3: Ham 1C **152**
Dalton St. G31: Glas 6G **85**
Dalveen Ct. G78: Barr 6E **115**
Dalveen Dr. G71: Tann 5C **108**
Dalveen Quad. ML5: Coat 6F **91**
Dalveen St. G32: Glas 6H **85**
Dalveen Way G73: Ruth 4E **121**
Dalwhinnie Av. G72: Blan 5A **124**
Daly Gdns. G72: Blan 6C **124**
Dalzell Av. ML1: Moth 5A **144**
Dalzell Country Pk. **6H 143**
Dalzell Dr. ML1: Moth 5A **144**
Dalziel Dr. G41: Glas 2A **102**
Dalziel Quad. G41: Glas 2A **102**
Dalziel Rd. G52: Hill 3H **79**
Dalziel St. ML1: Moth 2H **143**
ML3: Ham 4F **141**
Dalziel Twr. ML1: Moth 6B **144**
Damshot Cres. G53: Glas 5D **100**
Damshot Rd. G53: Glas 6D **100**
Danby Rd. G69: Bail 1F **107**
Danes Av. G14: Glas 5C **60**
Danes Cres. G14: Glas 4B **60**
Danes Dr. G14: Glas 4B **60**
Danes La. Nth. G14: Glas 5C **60**
Danes La. Sth. G14: Glas 5C **60**
Daniel McLaughlin Pl. G66: Kirk 4E **31**
Dargarvel Av. G41: Glas 1H **101**
Dargavel Av. PA7: B'ton 4H **39**
Dargavel Path *G41: Glas* *2G **101***
(off Dumbreck Pl.)
Dargavel Rd. PA7: B'ton 6A **40**
(not continuous)
Darkwood Ct. PA3: Pais 5F **77**
Darkwood Cres. PA3: Pais 5F **77**
Darkwood Dr. PA3: Pais 5F **77**
Darleith St. G32: Glas 6H **85**
Darley Pl. ML3: Ham 3F **153**
Darley Rd. G68: Cumb 6G **13**
Darluith Pk. La. PA5: Brkfld 5C **74**
Darluith Rd. PA6: C'lee 5E **75**

Darnaway Av. G33: Glas 1D **86**
Darnaway Dr. G33: Glas 1D **86**
Darnaway St. G33: Glas 1D **86**
Darngavel Ct. *ML6: Air 3F* ***91***
(off Monkscourt Av.)
Darnick St. G21: Glas 6C **64**
Darnley Cres. G64: B'rig 4B **48**
Darnley Gdns. G41: Glas 3C **102**
Darnley Ind. Est. G53: Glas 3B **116**
Darnley Mains Rd. G53: Glas 4C **116**
Darnley Path G46: T'bnk 2E **117**
Darnley Pl. G41: Glas 3C **102**
Darnley Rd. G41: Glas 3C **102**
G78: Barr 4F **115**
Darnley St. G41: Glas 3D **102**
Darragh Grn. ML2: Newm 3E **147**
Darroch Dr. PA8: Ersk 4D **40**
Darroch Way G67: Cumb 2A **36**
Dartford St. G22: Glas 6F **63**
Darvel Cres. PA1: Pais 1F **99**
Darvel Dr. G77: Newt M 4G **133**
Darvel St. G53: Glas 1H **115**
Darwin Pl. G81: Clyd 3H **41**
Darwin Rd. G75: E Kil 3E **149**
Davaar G74: E Kil 2C **150**
Davaar Dr. ML1: Moth 5E **127**
ML5: Coat 4H **89**
PA2: Pais 6A **98**
Davaar Pl. G77: Newt M 3C **132**
Davaar Rd. PA4: Renf 2F **79**
Davaar St. G40: Glas 1D **104**
Davan Loan *ML2: Newm 3D* ***146***
(off Isla Av.)
Dava St. G51: Glas 4G **81**
Dave Barrie Av. ML9: Lark 6H **155**
Daventry Dr. G12: Glas 4G **61**
David Donnely Pl. G66: Kirk 4C **30**
David Gray Dr. G66: Kirk 4G **31**
David Livingstone Cen. **5C 124**
David Lloyd Leisure **2D 78**
David Pl. G69: Bail 1F **107**
PA3: Pais 4D **78**
Davidson Cres. G65: Twe 2D **32**
Davidson Gdns. *G14: Glas 5E* ***61***
(off Westland Dr.)
Davidson La. G14: Glas 5E **61**
ML8: Carl 4H ***165***
(off Ramage Rd.)
Davidson Pl. G32: Glas 5C **86**
Davidson Quad. G81: Dun 1C **42**
Davidson St. G40: Glas 3C **104**
G81: Clyd 1G **59**
ML5: Coat 1D **110**
ML6: Air 3H **91**
Davidston Pl. G66: Lenz 3F **51**
David St. G40: Glas 6C **84**
ML5: Coat 4E **91**
David Way PA3: Pais 4D **78**
Davieland Rd. G46: Giff 6G **117**
Davie's Acre G74: E Kil 5B **136**
Davies Quad. ML1: Moth 5F **127**
Davie's Sq. G81: Dun 1C **42**
Davington Dr. ML3: Ham 1B **152**
Daviot St. G51: Glas 5D **80**
Davlea G51: Glas 4E **81**
Dawson Av. G75: E Kil 2D **148**
Dawson Pl. G4: Glas 6F **63**
Dawson Rd. G4: Glas 6F **63**
Deaconsbank Av. G46: T'bnk 6D **116**
Deaconsbank Cres. G46: T'bnk 6D **116**
Deaconsbank Gdns. G46: T'bnk 6E **117**
Deaconsbank Gro. G46: T'bnk 6D **116**
Deaconsbank Pl. G46: T'bnk 6E **117**
Deacons Rd. G65: Kils 3A **12**
Dealston Rd. G78: Barr 3D **114**
Deanbrae St. G71: Udd 1D **124**
Dean Cres. G69: Chry 6B **52**
ML3: Ham 2G **153**
Deanfield Quad. G52: Glas 5H **79**
DEAN PARK **1G 79**
Dean Pk. Av. G71: Both 5E **125**
Dean Pk. Dr. G72: Camb 3D **122**
Dean Pk. Rd. PA4: Renf 1G **79**
Deans Av. G72: Camb 3D **122**
Deanside Rd. G52: Hill 3A **80**
Deanside Transit Dpt. G52: Hill 2A **80**
Deanston Av. G78: Barr 6D **114**
Deanston Dr. G41: Glas 5B **102**
Deanstone Pl. ML5: Coat 2F **111**
Deanston Gdns G78: Barr 6D **114**
Deanston Gro. ML5: Coat 2A **110**
Deanston Pk. G78: Barr 6D **114**
Dean St. G81: Clyd 6E **43**
ML4: Bell 2D **126**
Deanwood Av. G44: Neth 4D **118**
Deanwood Rd. G44: Neth 4D **118**
Dechmont G75: E Kil 6F **149**
Dechmont Av. G72: Camb 4D **122**
ML1: Moth 2E **143**
Dechmont Cotts. G72: Flem 4F **123**
Dechmont Gdns. G71: Tann 4C **108**
G72: Blan 6A **124**
Dechmont Pl. G72: Camb 4D **122**
Dechmont Rd. G71: Tann 4C **108**
Dechmont St. G31: Glas 1E **105**
ML3: Ham 1G **153**
Dechmont Vw. G71: Tann 6E **109**
ML4: Bell 4B **126**
Dee Av. PA2: Pais 3D **96**
PA4: Renf 6G **59**
Deedes St. ML6: Air 5F **91**
Dee Dr. PA2: Pais 4D **96**
Dee Path ML1: Holy 2B **128**
ML9: Lark 5E **161**
Deep Dale G74: E Kil 6E **137**
Deepdene Rd. G61: Bear 4D **44**
G69: Mood 5D **52**
Dee Pl. G75: E Kil 4A **148**
PA5: John 5C **94**
Deerdykes Ct. Nth. G68: Cumb 1A **54**
Deerdykes Ct. Sth. G68: Cumb 2A **54**
Deerdykes Pl. G68: Cumb 1A **54**
Deerdykes Rd. G68: Cumb 1A **54**
DEERDYKES RDBT. **2H 53**
Deerdykes Vw. G68: Cumb 2H **53**
Deer Pk. Ct. ML3: Ham 4H **153**
Deer Pk. Pl. ML3: Ham 4A **154**
Deeside Dr. ML8: Carl 2G **165**
Deeside Pl. ML5: Coat 1F **111**
Dee St. G33: Glas 2F **85**
ML5: Coat 1H **89**
Dee Ter. ML3: Ham 3F **153**
Delhi Av. G81: Clyd 3G **41**
Dellburn St. ML1: Moth 4A **144**
Dellburn Trad. Est. ML1: Moth 4A **144**
Dell, The G77: Newt M 4H **133**
ML4: Bell 4F **127**
Delny Pl. G33: Glas 4E **87**
Delvin Rd. G44: Glas 1E **119**
Dempsey Rd. ML4: Bell 4B **126**
Denbak Av. ML3: Ham 1E **153**
Denbeck St. G32: Glas 6H **85**
Denbrae St. G32: Glas 6H **85**
Dene Wlk. G64: B'rig 1E **65**
Denewood Av. PA2: Pais 5H **97**
Denham St. G22: Glas 6F **63**
Denholm Cres. G75: E Kil 3G **149**
Denholm Dr. G46: Giff 6A **118**
ML2: Wis 3A **146**
Denholm Grn. G75: E Kil 3H **149**
Denholm Ter. ML3: Ham 6C **140**
Denmark St. G22: Glas 5G **63**
Denmark St. Ind. Cen. G22: Glas 4G **63**
Denmilne Gdns. G34: Glas 4A **88**
Denmilne Path G34: Glas 4A **88**
Denmilne Rd. G69: Barg 4B **88**
Denmilne St. G34: Glas 4A **88**
DENNISTOUN **4C 84**
Dennistoun St. ML4: Bell 2C **126**
Dennystoun Forge G82: Dumb 3E **17**
DENNYSTOWN **3D 16**
Dentdale G74: E Kil 6E **137**
Deramore Av. G46: Giff 2G **133**
Derby St. G3: Glas 3C **82**
Derby Ter. La. *G3: Glas 3C* ***82***
(off Derby St.)
Derby Wynd ML1: Carf 6B **128**
Derrywood Rd. G66: Milt C 5C **8**
Derwent Dr. ML5: Coat 1G **89**
Derwent St. G22: Glas 5F **63**
Derwentwater G75: E Kil 5B **148**
Despard Av. G32: Glas 1D **106**
Despard Gdns. G32: Glas 1E **107**
Deveron Av. G46: Giff 5B **118**
Deveron Cres. ML3: Ham 5B **140**
Deveron Rd. G61: Bear 5C **44**
G74: E Kil 2A **150**
ML1: Holy 1B **128**
Deveron St. G33: Glas 2F **85**
ML5: Coat 2G **89**
Deveron Way *G67: Cumb 4H* ***35***
(in Cumbernauld Shop. Cen.)
PA2: Pais 4D **96**
Devine Ct. ML2: Wis 6H **145**
Devine Gro. ML2: Newm 2E **147**
Devlin Gro. G72: Blan 2C **140**
Devol Cres. G53: Glas 5B **100**
Devondale Av. G72: Blan 6A **124**
Devon Dr. PA7: B'ton 4A **40**
Devon Gdns. G64: B'rig 4B **48**
ML8: Carl 3E **165**
Devonhill Av. ML3: Ham 4H **153**
Devon Pl. G41: Glas 1F **103**
Devonport Pk. G75: E Kil 4C **148**
Devonshire Gdns. G12: Glas 5H **61**
Devonshire Gdns. La. G12: Glas 5H **61**
Devonshire Ter. G12: Glas 5H **61**
Devonshire Ter. La. G12: Glas 5H **61**
Devon St. G5: Glas 1F **103**
Devonview Pl. ML6: Air 5H **91**
Devonview St. ML6: Air 4H **91**
Devon Wlk. G68: Cumb 5A **34**
Devon Way ML1: Moth 3D **142**
Dewar Cl. G71: Tann 4E **109**
Diamond St. ML4: Bell 3C **126**
Diana Av. G13: Glas 1B **60**
Diana Quad. ML1: Holy 2A **128**
Dickens Av. G81: Clyd 3B **42**
Dickens Gro. ML1: Carf 5D **128**
Dickson Sq. ML1: Cle 6H **129**
Dickson St. ML9: Lark 4G **161**
Dicks Pk. G75: E Kil 3F **149**
Dick St. G20: Glas 6D **62**
Differ Av. G65: Twe 3D **32**
Dilwara Av. G14: Glas 1E **81**
Dimity St. PA5: John 3F **95**
DIMSDALE **2A 158**
Dimsdale Cres. ML2: Wis 2A **158**
Dimsdale Rd. ML2: Wis 2A **158**
Dinard Dr. G46: Giff 3A **118**
Dinart St. G33: Glas 2F **85**
Dinduff St. G34: Glas 2A **88**
Dinmont Av. PA2: Pais 4D **96**
Dinmont Cres. ML1: Moth 5E **127**
Dinmont Pl. *G41: Glas 4C* ***102***
(off Dinmont Rd.)
Dinmont Rd. G41: Glas 4B **102**
Dinmont Way PA2: Pais 4C **96**
Dinnet Way *ML2: Newm 3D* ***146***
(off Isla Av.)
Dinwiddie St. G21: Glas 1E **85**
Dinyra Pl. ML5: Glenb 3G **69**
Dipple Pl. G15: Glas 5B **44**
Dirleton Dr. G41: Glas 5C **102**
PA2: Pais 4E **97**
Dirleton Ga. G61: Bear 4D **44**
Dirleton Pl. G41: Glas 5C **102**
Divernia Way G78: Barr 6E **115**
Dixon Av. G42: Glas 3E **103**
G82: Dumb 4E **17**
Dixon Dr. G82: Dumb 5D **16**
Dixon Pl. G74: E Kil 6D **136**
Dixon Rd. G42: Glas 4F **103**
Dixons Blazes Ind. Est. G5: Glas 2G **103**
Dixon St. G1: Glas 5F **83**
ML3: Ham 6H **141**
ML5: Coat 1D **110**
PA1: Pais 1B **98**
Dobbies Ct. ML8: Law 5E **159**
Dobbie's Loan G4: Glas 2F **83** (1D **4**)
DOBBIES LOAN INTERCHANGE
. . . . **2G 83 (1E 5)**

Dobbie's Loan Pl.
G4: Glas 3H **83** (3G **5**)
Dochart Av. PA4: Renf 2G **79**
Dochart Dr. G68: Cumb 6E **13**
ML5: Coat 1G **89**
Dochart St. G33: Glas 1G **85**
Dock St. G81: Clyd 2F **59**
Dodhill Pl. G13: Glas 3B **60**
Dodside Gdns. G32: Glas 1C **106**
Dodside Pl. G32: Glas 1C **106**
Dodside St. G32: Glas 1C **106**
Dolan St. G69: Bail 6H **87**
Dollan Aqua Cen. 2G **149**
Dollar Pk. ML1: Moth 6B **144**
Dollar Ter. *G20: Glas 1A **62***
(off Crosbie St.)
Dolley Rd. ML2: Wis 6G **145**
Dolphin Rd. G41: Glas 3B **102**
Dominica Grn. G75: E Kil 2C **148**
Donaldfield Rd.
PA11: Bri W 4D **72**
Donaldson Av. G65: Kils 4H **11**
Donaldson Cres. G66: Kirk 6C **30**
Donaldson Dr. PA4: Renf 6E **59**
Donaldson Grn. G71: Tann 5E **109**
Donaldson Pl. G66: Kirk 5D **30**
Donaldson Rd. ML9: Lark 4G **161**
Donaldson St. G66: Kirk 6C **30**
ML3: Ham 4E **141**
Donaldswood Pk. PA2: Pais 5G **97**
Donaldswood Rd. PA2: Pais 5G **97**
Donald Ter. ML3: Ham 2G **153**
Donald Way G71: Tann 6E **109**
Don Av. PA4: Renf 1G **79**
Doncaster St. G20: Glas 6E **63**
Don Ct. ML3: Ham 3E **153**
Don Dr. PA2: Pais 4D **96**
Donnelly Way ML2: Wis 5C **144**
Donnies Brae G78: Barr 1F **131**
Donohoe Ct. G64: B'rig 6C **48**
Don Path ML9: Lark 5E **161**
Don Pl. PA5: John 5C **94**
Don St. G33: Glas 3F **85**
Doon Cres. G61: Bear 4D **44**
Doonfoot Ct. G74: E Kil 1F **149**
Doonfoot Gdns. G74: E Kil 1F **149**
Doonfoot Rd. G43: Glas 1B **118**
Doon Pl. G66: Kirk 3F **31**
Doon Rd. G66: Kirk 4F **31**
Doonside G67: Cumb 3B **36**
Doonside Twr. ML1: Moth 5B **144**
Doon St. G81: Clyd 4F **43**
ML1: Moth 5A **144**
ML9: Lark 3G **161**
Doon Way G66: Kirk 4G **31**
Dorain Rd. ML1: N'hill 4D **128**
Dora St. G40: Glas 2C **104**
Dorchester Av. G12: Glas 3G **61**
Dorchester Ct. G12: Glas 3G **61**
Dorchester Pl. G12: Glas 3G **61**
Dorian Dr. G76: Clar 1H **133**
Dorlin Rd. G33: Step 4E **67**
Dormanside Ct. G53: Glas 2B **100**
Dormanside Ga. G53: Glas 2B **100**
Dormanside Gro. G53: Glas 2B **100**
Dormanside Pl. G53: Glas 4C **100**
Dormanside Rd. G53: Glas 2B **100**
(not continuous)
Dornal Av. G13: Glas 2G **59**
Dornford Av. G32: Glas 3D **106**
Dornford Rd. G32: Glas 3D **106**
Dornie Dr. G32: Carm 5B **106**
Dornie Path *ML2: Newm 3D **146***
(off Isla Av.)
Dornoch Av. G46: Giff 6A **118**
Dornoch Ct. ML4: Bell 1C **126**
Dornoch Pl. G64: B'rig 5F **49**
G69: Chry 6B **52**
G74: E Kil 1E **149**
Dornoch Rd. G61: Bear 5D **44**
ML1: Holy 3B **128**
Dornoch St. G40: Glas 6B **84**
Dornoch Way G68: Cumb 6A **14**
ML6: Air 6H **91**
Dorset Sq. *G3: Glas 3D **82***
(off Dorset St.)
Dorset St. G3: Glas 3D **82**
Dosk Av. G13: Glas 1H **59**
Dosk Pl. G13: Glas 1H **59**
Double Hedges Rd. G78: Neil 3D **130**
Dougalston Av. G62: Miln 4H **25**
Dougalston Cres. G62: Miln 4H **25**
Dougalston Gdns. Nth. G62: Miln 4H **25**
Dougalston Gdns. Sth.
G62: Miln 4H **25**
Dougalston Rd. G23: Glas 1C **62**
Douglas Av. G32: Carm 4B **106**
G46: Giff 6A **118**
G66: Lenz 2D **50**
G73: Ruth 2E **121**
PA5: Eld 3H **95**
Douglas Ct. G66: Lenz 2D **50**
Douglas Cres. G71: Tann 5F **109**
ML3: Ham 5H **153**
ML6: Air 5A **92**
PA8: Ersk 4D **40**
Douglasdale G74: E Kil 1F **149**
Douglas Dr. G15: Glas 6H **43**
G69: Bail 6F **87**
G71: Both 6E **125**
G72: Camb 2H **121**
G75: E Kil 4A **148**
G77: Newt M 3E **133**
ML4: Bell 3E **127**
ML9: Ashg 5B **162**
Douglas Dr. La. G45: Glas 4H **119**
Douglas Gdns. G46: Giff 6A **118**
G61: Bear 3F **45**
G66: Lenz 2D **50**
G71: Udd 2D **124**
Douglas Ga. G72: Camb 2H **121**
Douglas Ho. G67: Cumb 3H **35**
G82: Dumb 1H **17**
Douglas La. G2: Glas 4B **4**
Douglas Muir Dr. G62: Miln 2C **24**
Douglas Muir Gdns. G62: Miln 2C **24**
Douglas Muir Pl. G62: Miln 2C **24**
Douglas Muir Rd. G62: Miln 3D **24**
G81: Faif 6F **23**
Douglas Pk. Cres. G61: Bear 1G **45**
Douglas Pk. La. ML3: Ham 5G **141**
Douglas Pl. G61: Bear 2E **45**
G66: Lenz 2D **50**
ML3: Ham 5H **153**
ML5: Coat 5B **90**
Douglas Rd. G82: Dumb 4H **17**
PA4: Renf 3C **78**
Douglas St. G2: Glas 4E **83** (6B **4**)
G62: Miln 4G **25**
G71: Tann 5F **109**
G72: Blan 3A **140**
ML1: Moth 2F **143**
ML2: Over 4B **158**
ML3: Ham 4G **141**
(not continuous)
ML6: Air 5A **92**
ML8: Carl 3E **165**
ML9: Lark 1E **161**
PA1: Pais 6G **77**
Douglas Ter. G41: Glas 3D **102**
Douglas Twr. G71: Both 3B **124**
Douglas Vw. ML5: Coat 2B **110**
Dougray Pl. G78: Barr 5E **115**
Dougrie Dr. G45: Glas 4H **119**
Dougrie Gdns. G45: Glas 5H **119**
Dougrie Pl. G45: Glas 4A **120**
Dougrie Rd. G45: Glas 5G **119**
Dougrie St. G45: Glas 4A **120**
Dougrie Ter. G45: Glas 4H **119**
Doune Cres. G64: B'rig 3D **48**
G77: Newt M 4F **133**
ML6: Chap 4D **112**
Doune Gdns. G20: Glas 6C **62**
Doune Gdns. La. G20: Glas 6C **62**
Doune Pk. Way ML5: Coat 1B **110**
Doune Quad. G20: Glas 6C **62**
Doune Ter. ML5: Coat 2H **89**
Dovecot G43: Glas 5A **102**
Dovecotehall St. G78: Barr 4F **115**
Dovecote Vw. G66: Kirk 6F **31**
DOVECOTHALL 3G **115**
DOVECOTWOOD 2H **11**
Dovecotwood G65: Kils 2H **11**
Doveholm G82: Dumb 2G **17**
Doveholm Av. G82: Dumb 2H **17**
Dove Pl. G75: E Kil 5B **148**
Dover St. G3: Glas 3C **82**
ML5: Coat 1H **89**
G53: Glas 2A **116**
Dove Wynd ML4: Bell 6A **110**
Dowanfield Rd. G67: Cumb 4F **35**
DOWANHILL 6A **62**
Dowanhill St. G11: Glas 1A **82**
Dowan Rd.
G62: Balder, Bard, Miln 6C **26**
Dowanside La. G12: Glas 6B **62**
Dowanside Rd. G12: Glas 6A **62**
Downcraig Dr. G45: Glas 5H **119**
Downcraig Gro. G45: Glas 5G **119**
Downcraig Rd. G45: Glas 6G **119**
Downcraig Ter. G45: Glas 5H **119**
Downfield Dr. ML3: Ham 4F **153**
Downfield Gdns. G71: Both 5D **124**
Downfield St. G32: Glas 2G **105**
Downiebrae Rd. G73: Ruth 3D **104**
Downie Cl. G71: Tann 5F **109**
Downie St. ML3: Ham 2H **153**
Downs St. G21: Glas 4B **64**
Dowrie Cres. G53: Glas 4B **100**
Draffen Ct. ML1: Moth 2H **143**
Draffen St. ML1: Moth 2H **143**
Draffen Twr. ML1: Moth 2H **143**
Drakemire Av. G45: Glas 3G **119**
Drakemire Dr. G45: Glas 5F **119**
Drake St. G40: Glas 6A **84**
Dreghorn St. G31: Glas 4E **85**
Drimmin Rd. G33: Step 4F **67**
Drive Rd. G51: Glas 3E **81**
Drochil St. G34: Glas 2G **87**
Dromore St. G66: Kirk 6D **30**
Drove Hill G68: Cumb 2D **34**
Drumaling Ter. G66: Len 3H **7**
Drumbathie Rd. ML6: Air 3B **92**
Drumbathie Ter. ML6: Air 3C **92**
Drumbeg Dr. G53: Glas 1A **116**
Drumbeg Pl. G53: Glas 1A **116**
Drumbeg Ter. G62: Miln 3D **24**
Drumbottie Rd. G21: Glas 4C **64**
Drumby Cres. G76: Clar 6B **118**
Drumby Dr. G76: Clar 1B **134**
Drumcarn Dr. G62: Miln 4F **25**
Drumcavel Rd. G69: Muirh 2B **68**
Drumchapel Gdns. G15: Glas 5A **44**
Drumchapel Pl. G15: Glas 5B **44**
Drumchapel Rd. G15: Glas 5A **44**
Drumchapel Shop. Cen.
G15: Glas 4H **43**
Drumchapel Sports Cen. 5H **43**
Drumchapel Station (Rail) 6A **44**
Drumchapel Swimming Pool
5H **43**
Drumclair Pl. ML6: Air 4D **92**
Drumclog Av. G62: Miln 1G **25**
Drumclog Gdns. G33: Glas 3H **65**
Drumcross Rd. G53: Glas 4C **100**
PA7: B'ton 4B **40**
Drumduff G75: E Kil 6F **149**
DRUMGELLOCH 3D **92**
Drumgelloch Station (Rail) 4D **92**
Drumgelloch St. ML6: Air 2D **92**
Drumglass Vw. G65: Croy 1B **34**
DRUMGREW 4F **33**
DRUMGREW RDBT. 4F **33**
Drumhead Pl. G32: Glas 4H **105**
Drumhead Rd. G32: Glas 4H **105**
Drumhill G66: Kirk 3H **31**
Drumilaw Cres. G73: Ruth 2C **120**
Drumilaw Rd. G73: Ruth 2C **120**
Drumilaw Way G73: Ruth 2C **120**
Drumlaken Av. *G23: Glas 6A **46***
(off Drumlaken St.)
Drumlaken Ct. G23: Glas 6B **46**

Drumlaken Path—Dundas Ct.

Drumlaken Path *G23: Glas* *6B* ***46***
(off Littleton St.)
Drumlaken Pl. *G23: Glas* *6B* ***46***
(off Drumlaken Ct.)
Drumlaken St. G23: Glas 6A **46**
Drumlanrig Av. G34: Glas 2A **88**
Drumlanrig Pl. G34: Glas 3B **88**
Drumlin Dr. G62: Miln 5F **25**
Drumloch Gdns. G75: E Kil 6G **149**
Drumlochy Rd. G33: Glas 2A **86**
Drum Mains Pk. G68: Cumb 6G **33**
Drummond Av. G73: Ruth 5B **104**
Drummond Dr. ML2: Wis 1H **157**
PA1: Pais 1F **99**
Drummond Hill G74: E Kil 6B **138**
Drummond Ho. G67: Cumb 2A **36**
Drummond Pl. G74: E Kil 6B **138**
Drummond Way G77: Newt M 4A **132**
Drummore Av. ML5: Coat 2F **111**
Drummore Rd. G15: Glas 2A **44**
Drumnessie Ct. G68: Cumb 5B **34**
Drumnessie Rd. G68: Cumb 5B **34**
Drumnessie Vw. G68: Cumb 5B **34**
Drumore Av. ML6: Chap 4D **112**
Drumover Dr. G31: Glas 1G **105**
DRUMOYNE **5E 81**
Drumoyne Av. G51: Glas 4E **81**
Drumoyne Cir. G51: Glas 5E **81**
Drumoyne Dr. G51: Glas 4E **81**
Drumoyne Pl. G51: Glas 5E **81**
Drumoyne Quad. G51: Glas 5E **81**
Drumoyne Rd. G51: Glas 5E **81**
Drumoyne Sq. G51: Glas 4E **81**
Drumpark St. G46: T'bnk 3F **117**
ML5: Coat 1F **109**
DRUMPELLIER **4H 89**
Drumpellier Av. G67: Cumb 1E **55**
G69: Bail 2H **107**
ML5: Coat 4G **89**
Drumpellier Butterfly House **3F 89**
Drumpellier Country Pk. **3F 89**
Drumpellier Country Pk. Vis. Cen. **2E 89**
Drumpellier Ct. G67: Cumb 6E **35**
Drumpellier Cres. ML5: Coat 5H **89**
Drumpellier Gdns.
G67: Cumb 6E **35**
Drumpellier Gro. G67: Cumb 6E **35**
Drumpellier Pl. G67: Cumb 6E **35**
G69: Bail 1H **107**
Drumpellier Rd. G69: Bail 2G **107**
Drumpellier St. G33: Glas 1F **85**
Drumreoch Dr. G42: Glas 5A **104**
Drumreoch Pl. G42: Glas 5A **104**
DRUMRY **4E 43**
Drumry Pl. G15: Glas 5G **43**
Drumry Rd. G81: Clyd 4E **43**
Drumry Rd. E. G15: Glas 5G **43**
Drumry Station (Rail) **5F 43**
Drumsack Av. G69: Chry 1A **68**
Drumsargard Rd. G73: Ruth 2F **121**
Drums Av. PA3: Pais 5G **77**
Drums Cres. PA3: Pais 6G **77**
Drumshangie Pl. ML6: Air 1A **92**
Drumshangie St. ML6: Air 1A **92**
Drumshaw Dr. G32: Carm 5C **106**
Drums Rd. G53: Glas 2A **100**
Drumtrocher St. G65: Kils 3H **11**
Drumvale Dr. G69: Mood 5C **52**
Drury La. Ct. *G74: E Kil* *5C* ***138***
(off Bosworth Rd.)
Drury St. G2: Glas 4F **83** (5D **4**)
Dryad St. G46: T'bnk 2E **117**
Dryburgh Av. G73: Ruth 6D **104**
PA2: Pais 4E **97**
Dryburgh Gdns. G20: Glas 6D **62**
Dryburgh Hill G74: E Kil 2F **149**
Dryburgh La. G74: E Kil 2F **149**
Dryburgh Pl. G66: Kirk 5F **31**
ML5: Coat 4B **90**
Dryburgh Rd. G61: Bear 1C **44**
ML2: Wis 6G **145**
Dryburgh St. ML3: Ham 3F **141**
Dryburgh Wlk. G69: Mood 4E **53**
Dryburgh Way *G72: Blan* *2B* ***140***
(off Winton Cres.)
Dryburn Av. G52: Glas 6A **80**
Dryden St. ML3: Ham 3F **141**
Drygait PA9: How 6A **94**
Drygate G4: Glas 4A **84**
Drygate St. ML9: Lark 1E **161**
Drygrange Rd. G33: Glas 1C **86**
Drymen Pl. G66: Lenz 4D **50**
Drymen Rd. G61: Bear 1D **44**
Drymen St. G52: Glas 6E **81**
Drymen Wynd G61: Bear 4F **45**
Drynoch Pl. G22: Glas 2F **63**
Drysdale St. G14: Glas 4H **59**
(not continuous)
Duart Dr. G74: E Kil 6F **137**
G77: Newt M 4G **133**
PA5: Eld 4H **95**
Duart St. G20: Glas 1A **62**
Dubs Rd. G78: Barr 4G **115**
Dubton Path G34: Glas 2H **87**
Dubton St. G34: Glas 2H **87**
Duchall Pl. G14: Glas 5B **60**
Duchess Ct. ML3: Ham 1C **154**
Duchess Pl. G73: Ruth 5E **105**
Duchess Rd. G73: Ruth 4E **105**
Duchess Way *G69: Barg* *6D* ***88***
(off Park Rd.)
Duchray Dr. PA1: Pais 2G **99**
Duchray La. G33: Glas 2F **85**
Duchray St. G33: Glas 2F **85**
Dudhope St. G33: Glas 1D **86**
Dudley Dr. G12: Glas 6G **61**
ML5: Coat 1G **89**
Dudley La. G12: Glas 6G **61**
Duffus Pl. G32: Carm 5C **106**
Duffus St. G34: Glas 2G **87**
Duffus Ter. G32: Carm 5C **106**
Duich Gdns. G23: Glas 5C **46**
Duisdale Rd. G32: Carm 5C **106**
Duke's Ct. ML9: Lark 1E **161**
Dukes Ga. G71: Both 3C **124**
Dukes Pl. ML3: Ham 5H **153**
Dukes Rd. G69: Barg 6D **88**
Duke's Rd. G72: Camb 1G **121**
G73: Ruth 2E **121**
Duke St. G31: Glas 5D **84**
G4: Glas 4A **84** (5H **5**)
ML1: Moth 1G **143**
ML2: Newm 3D **146**
ML3: Ham 6A **142**
ML9: Lark 1E **161**
PA2: Pais 3A **98**
Duke Street Station (Rail) **4D 84**
DULLATUR **5F 13**
Dullatur Rd. G68: Dull 5F **13**
DULLATUR RDBT. **6H 13**
Dulnain St. G72: Camb 2D **122**
Dulsie Rd. G21: Glas 3E **65**
DUMBARTON **4F 17**
Dumbarton Castle **6G 17**
Dumbarton Central Station (Rail) **3F 17**
Dumbarton East Station (Rail) **4H 17**
Dumbarton Rd. G11: Glas 1F **81**
G14: Glas 3G **59**
G60: Bowl, Old K 5G **19**
G81: Clyd 3G **41**
G81: Dun, Hard 1B **42**
G82: Milt 4E **19**
DUMBRECK **2A 102**
Dumbreck Av. G41: Glas 1G **101**
Dumbreck Ct. G41: Glas 2G **101**
Dumbreck Path *G41: Glas* *2G* ***101***
(off Dumbreck Pl.)
Dumbreck Pl. G41: Glas 2G **101**
G66: Lenz 3E **51**
Dumbreck Rd. G41: Glas 6G **81**
DUMBRECK RD. INTERCHANGE . . . **6H 81**
Dumbreck Sq. G41: Glas 1G **101**
Dumbreck Station (Rail) **1A 102**
Dumbreck Ter. G65: Queen 3D **10**
Dumbrock Rd. G62: Miln 3D **24**
DUMBUCK **4E 19**
Dumbuck Cres. G82: Dumb 5H **17**
Dumbuck Gdns. G82: Dumb 5H **17**
Dumbuck Rd. G82: Dumb 3H **17**
(Overwood Dr., not continuous)
G82: Dumb 2H **17**
(Stirling Rd.)
Dumbuie Av. G82: Dumb 3H **17**
Dumfries Cres. ML6: Air 6H **91**
Dumgoyne Av. G62: Miln 4F **25**
Dumgoyne Ct. *ML6: Air* *1B* ***92***
(off Thrushbush Rd.)
Dumgoyne Dr. G61: Bear 6D **24**
Dumgoyne Gdns. G62: Miln 4F **25**
Dumgoyne Pl. G76: Clar 2A **134**
Dunagoil Gdns. G45: Glas 5A **120**
Dunagoil Pl. G45: Glas 6A **120**
Dunagoil Rd. G45: Glas 5H **119**
Dunagoil St. G45: Glas 5A **120**
Dunalastair Dr. G33: Mille 4B **66**
Dunan Pl. G33: Glas 4E **87**
Dunard Ct. *ML8: Carl* *2F* ***165***
(off Carranbute Rd.)
Dunard Rd. G73: Ruth 6D **104**
Dunard St. G20: Glas 5D **62**
Dunard Way PA3: Pais 4H **77**
Dunaskin St. G11: Glas 2A **82**
Dunavon Pl. ML5: Coat 1F **111**
Dunbar Av. G73: Ruth 6E **105**
ML5: Coat 1H **109**
PA5: John 5E **95**
Dunbar Dr. ML1: Moth 5A **144**
Dunbar Hill G74: E Kil 2E **149**
Dunbar La. ML1: New S 5A **128**
Dunbar Pl. G74: E Kil 2E **149**
Dunbar Rd. PA2: Pais 4E **97**
Dunbar St. ML3: Ham 4F **141**
Dunbeath Av. G77: Newt M 4F **133**
Dunbeith Pl. G20: Glas 4B **62**
DUNBETH **4D 90**
Dunbeth Av. ML5: Coat 4D **90**
Dunbeth Ct. ML5: Coat 4D **90**
Dunbeth Rd. ML5: Coat 3D **90**
Dunblane Dr. G74: E Kil 6H **137**
Dunblane Pl. G74: E Kil 1H **149**
ML5: Coat 1B **110**
Dunblane St. G4: Glas 2F **83** (1D **4**)
(not continuous)
Dunbrach Rd. G68: Cumb 2D **34**
Dunbritton Rd. G82: Dumb 2C **18**
Duncan Av. G14: Glas 6C **60**
Duncan Ct. ML1: Moth 6F **127**
Duncan Graham St. ML9: Lark 1F **161**
Duncan La. *G14: Glas* *6C* ***60***
(off Gleneagles La. Nth.)
Duncan La. Nth. *G14: Glas* *5C* ***60***
(off Norse La. Nth.)
Duncan McIntosh Rd. G68: Cumb . . . 4B **14**
Dun Cann PA8: Ersk 2G **57**
Duncannon La. Nth. *G14: Glas* *5C* ***60***
(off Earlbank Av.)
Duncanrig Sports Cen. **3D 148**
Duncansby Rd. G33: Glas 5D **86**
Duncarnock Av. G78: Neil 2E **131**
Duncarnock Cres. G78: Neil 2E **131**
Dunchattan Pl. G31: Glas 4B **84**
Dunchattan St. G31: Glas 4B **84**
Dunchurch Rd. PA1: Pais 6F **79**
Dunclutha Dr. G71: Both 6E **125**
Dunclutha St. G40: Glas 3D **104**
Duncolm Pl. G62: Miln 3D **24**
Duncombe Av. G81: Hard 6D **22**
Duncombe St. G20: Glas 2B **62**
Duncombe Vw. G81: Clyd 4F **43**
Duncraig Cres. PA5: John 5D **94**
Duncrub Dr. G64: B'rig 6A **48**
Duncruin St. G20: Glas 2A **62**
Duncruin Ter. G20: Glas 2B **62**
Duncryne Av. G32: Glas 1D **106**
Duncryne Gdns. G32: Glas 1E **107**
Duncryne Pl. G64: B'rig 1A **64**
Dundaff Hill G68: Cumb 3E **35**
Dundas Av. G64: Torr 5D **28**
Dundas Cotts. FK4: Alla 1G **15**
Dundas Ct. G74: E Kil 1G **149**

Dundashill G4: Glas 1F **83** (1D **4**)
Dundas La. G1: Glas 3G **83** (4E **5**)
Dundas Pl. G74: E Kil 1G **149**
Dundas St. G1: Glas 3G **83** (4E **5**)
(not continuous)
Dundasvale Ct. G4: Glas. 2F **83** (1D **4**)
Dundee Dr. G52: Glas 1B **100**
Dundee Path G52: Glas. 2C **100**
Dundonald Av. PA5: John 4D **94**
Dundonald Cres. G77: Newt M . . . 5G **133**
Dundonald Dr. ML3: Ham 4H **153**
Dundonald Pl. G78: Neil 2D **130**
Dundonald Rd. G12: Glas 6A **62**
PA3: Pais 4C **78**
Dundonald St. G72: Blan 1A **140**
Dundrennan Rd. G42: Glas . . . 6D **102**
DUNDYVAN 6B **90**
Dundyvan Gdns. ML5: Coat . . . 6C **90**
Dundyvan Ga. ML5: Coat 6C **90**
Dundyvan Ind. Est.
ML5: Coat 6B **90**
Dundyvan La. ML2: Wis 1G **157**
Dundyvan Rd. ML5: Coat 5B **90**
Dundyvan St. ML2: Wis 1G **157**
Dundyvan Way ML5: Coat. 6B **90**
Dunearn Pl. PA2: Pais 2C **98**
Dunearn St. G4: Glas 1D **82**
Duneaton Wynd ML9: Lark . . . 5F **161**
Dunedin Ct. G75: E Kil 3C **148**
Dunedin Dr. G75: E Kil 2C **148**
Dunedin Rd. ML9: Lark 4F **161**
Dunedin Ter. G81: Clyd 1E **59**
Dunellan Av. G69: Mood 5E **53**
Dunellan Ct. G69: Mood 5E **53**
Dunellan Cres. G69: Mood . . . 5E **53**
Dunellan Dr. G81: Hard 6D **22**
Dunellan Gdns. G69: Mood . . . 5E **53**
Dunellan Rd. G62: Miln 3C **24**
Dunellan St. G52: Glas 6E **81**
Dungavel Gdns. ML3: Ham . . . 3A **154**
Dungavel La. *ML8: Carl* *4H **165***
(off Kelso Dr.)
Dungeonhill Rd. G34: Glas . . . 3B **88**
Dunglass Av. G14: Glas 5C **60**
G74: E Kil 6H **137**
Dunglass La. *G14: Glas* *5C **60***
(off Norse La. Sth.)
Dunglass La. Nth. *G14: Glas*. . . *5C **60***
(off Danes La. Sth.)
Dunglass Pl. G62: Miln 2E **25**
G77: Newt M 4A **132**
Dunglass Rd. PA7: B'ton 5A **40**
Dunglass Sq. G74: E Kil 1H **149**
Dungoil Av. G68: Cumb 2D **34**
Dungoil Rd. G66: Lenz 3E **51**
Dungoyne St. G20: Glas 1A **62**
Dunholme Pk. G81: Clyd 4H **41**
Dunira St. G32: Glas 2H **105**
Duniston Rd. ML6: Air 1H **113**
Dunivaig Rd. G33: Glas 4D **86**
Dunkeld Av. G73: Ruth 6D **104**
Dunkeld Dr. G61: Bear 3H **45**
Dunkeld Gdns. G64: B'rig 5D **48**
Dunkeld La. G69: Mood 5E **53**
Dunkeld Pl. G77: Newt M . . . 5H **133**
ML3: Ham 6C **140**
ML5: Coat 1B **110**
Dunkeld St. G31: Glas. 1E **105**
Dunkenny Pl. G15: Glas 3H **43**
Dunkenny Rd. G15: Glas. 4H **43**
Dunkenny Sq. G15: Glas. 4H **43**
Dunlin G12: Glas 3G **61**
G74: E Kil 5G **137**
Dunlin Ct. ML4: Bell 5A **110**
Dunlin Cres. PA6: C'lee 2C **74**
Dunlop Cres. G71: Both 6F **125**
PA4: Renf 5F **59**
Dunlop Gro. G71: Tann 4E **109**
Dunlop Pl. G62: Miln. 2F **25**
ML9: Ashg 5C **162**
Dunlop St. G1: Glas 5G **83**
(not continuous)
G72: Camb 1E **123**

Dunlop St. PA3: Lin 5A **76**
PA4: Renf *5F **59***
(off Dunlop Cres.)
Dunlop Twr. *G75: E Kil* *3G **149***
(off Denholm Cres.)
Dunmore Dr. G62: Miln. 5A **26**
Dunmore St. G81: Clyd 1E **59**
Dunnachie Dr. ML5: Coat . . . 1F **109**
Dunnachie Pl. ML5: Coat . . . 1G **109**
Dunnet Av. ML6: Glenm 4H **71**
Dunnet Dr. PA6: C'lee 2B **74**
Dunnichen Gdns. G64: B'rig . . . 6F **49**
Dunnikier Wlk. G68: Cumb . . . 4A **34**
Dunnolly St. G21: Glas 2C **84**
Dunnotar Wlk. *ML2: Newm* . . . *3D **146***
(off Tiree Cres.)
Dunnottar Ct. G74: E Kil 6E **137**
Dunnottar Cres. G74: E Kil . . . 6E **137**
Dunnottar St. G33: Glas 1B **86**
G64: B'rig 5F **49**
Dunn Sq. PA1: Pais. 1A **98**
Dunn St. G40: Glas 2B **104**
G81: Clyd 4A **42**
G81: Dun 1B **42**
PA1: Pais 6C **78**
Dunns Wood Rd. G67: Cumb . . . 5D **14**
Dunolly Dr. G77: Newt M . . . 4F **133**
Dunottar Av. ML5: Coat 3D **110**
Dunottar St. ML5: Coat 2D **110**
Dun Pk. G66: Kirk 5D **30**
Dunphail Dr. G34: Glas 3B **88**
Dunphail Rd. G34: Glas 3B **88**
Dunragit St. G31: Glas 4E **85**
DUNROBIN 4E **93**
Dunrobin Av. PA5: Eld. 4A **96**
Dunrobin Ct. G74: E Kil 6F **137**
G81: Clyd 5C **42**
Dunrobin Dr. G74: E Kil 6F **137**
Dunrobin Gdns. ML6: Air 5E **93**
Dunrobin Pl. ML5: Coat 4B **90**
Dunrobin Rd. ML6: Air 4E **93**
Dunrobin St. G31: Glas 5D **84**
Dunrod Hill G74: E Kil 6H **137**
Dunrod St. G32: Glas 1B **106**
Dunscore Brae ML3: Ham . . . 1C **152**
Duns Cres. ML2: Wis 3A **146**
Dunside Dr. G53: Glas 1A **116**
Dunskaith Pl. G34: Glas 4B **88**
Dunskaith St. G34: Glas 4B **88**
Dunsmore Rd. PA7: B'ton 3G **39**
Dunsmuir St. G51: Glas 4H **81**
Duns Path ML5: Coat 2F **111**
Dunster Gdns. G64: B'rig 3D **48**
Dunswin Av. G81: Clyd 4A **42**
Dunswin Ct. G81: Clyd 4A **42**
Dunsyre Pl. G23: Glas 6C **46**
Dunsyre St. G33: Glas 3G **85**
Duntarvie Av. G34: Glas 3A **88**
Duntarvie Cl. G34: Glas 3A **88**
Duntarvie Cres. G34: Glas . . . 3A **88**
Duntarvie Dr. G34: Glas 3H **87**
Duntarvie Gdns. G34: Glas . . . 3A **88**
Duntarvie Pl. G34: Glas 3H **87**
Duntarvie Rd. G34: Glas 3H **87**
Dunterlie Av. G13: Glas 3A **60**
Dunterlie Ct. G78: Barr 4E **115**
DUNTIBLAE 6G **31**
Duntiblae Rd. G66: Kirk 6G **31**
Duntiglennan Rd. G81: Dun . . . 1C **42**
DUNTOCHER 1C **42**
Duntocher Rd. G61: Bear . . . 1A **44**
G81: Clyd 4A **42**
G81: Dun 2C **42**
G81: Faif. 6G **23**
Duntreath Av. G13: Glas 1G **59**
G15: Glas 6H **43**
Duntreath Dr. G15: Glas 6H **43**
Duntreath Gdns. G15: Glas . . . 5H **43**
Duntreath Gro. G15: Glas . . . 6H **43**
Duntreath Ter. G65: Kils 3H **11**
Duntroon Pl. *ML4: Bell* *4D **126***
(off Glencalder Cres.)
Duntroon St. G31: Glas. 3D **84**

Dunure Dr. G73: Ruth 2B **120**
G77: Newt M. 4G **133**
ML3: Ham 1B **152**
Dunure Pl. G77: Newt M 5G **133**
ML5: Coat 2A **110**
Dunure St. G20: Glas 2B **62**
ML5: Coat 2A **110**
Dunvegan ML6: Glenm 5G **71**
Dunvegan Av. ML5: Coat 2H **89**
PA5: Eld 4H **95**
Dunvegan Ct. G13: Glas 3B **60**
Dunvegan Dr. G64: B'rig 3C **48**
G77: Newt M. 4G **133**
Dunvegan Pl. G71: Tann 5B **108**
G74: E Kil 6F **137**
Dunvegan Quad. PA4: Renf . . . 5D **58**
Dunwan Av. G13: Glas 2H **59**
Dunwan Pl. G13: Glas 2H **59**
Durban Av. G81: Clyd 3G **41**
Durham St. G41: Glas 6B **82**
Durisdeer Dr. ML3: Ham . . . 2C **152**
Durness Av. G61: Bear 2H **45**
Durno Path G33: Glas 4E **87**
Duror St. G32: Glas 6A **86**
Durris Gdns. G32: Glas. 2D **106**
Durrockstock Cres. PA2: Pais . . 6D **96**
Durrockstock Rd. PA2: Pais . . . 6D **96**
Durrockstock Way PA2: Pais. . . 6D **96**
Durward G74: E Kil 5E **139**
Durward Av. G41: Glas 4B **102**
Durward Ct. G41: Glas 4B **102**
ML1: Moth 5F **127**
Durward Cres. PA2: Pais 4D **96**
Durward Way PA2: Pais 4D **96**
Duthie Pk. Gdns. G13: Glas . . . 3D **60**
Duthie Pk. Pl. G13: Glas. 3D **60**
Duthil St. G51: Glas 5D **80**
Dyce Av. ML6: Air 1G **111**
Dyce La. G11: Glas. 1G **81**
Dyer's La. G1: Glas 5H **83**
Dyer's Wynd PA1: Pais 6A **78**
Dyfrig St. G72: Blan 1A **140**
DYKEBAR 4D **98**
Dykebar Av. G13: Glas 3B **60**
Dykebar Cres. PA2: Pais. 3D **98**
Dykehead Cres. ML6: Air 1H **91**
Dykehead La. G33: Glas 4D **86**
Dykehead Rd. G65: Queen . . . 2C **10**
G68: Dull. 5E **13**
G69: Barg 6D **88**
ML6: Air 1H **91**
Dykehead Sq. ML3: Ham . . . 6D **140**
Dykehead St. G33: Glas 4D **86**
Dykemuir Pl. G21: Glas 5D **64**
Dykemuir Quad. G21: Glas . . . 5C **64**
Dykemuir St. G21: Glas 5C **64**
Dyke Rd. G13: Glas 2A **60**
G14: Glas 4H **59**
Dyke St. G69: Bail. 6A **88**
ML5: Coat 1F **109**
Dysart Ct. G68: Cumb. 4A **34**
Dysart Way ML6: Air 5G **93**

E

Eagle Cres. G61: Bear 1B **44**
Eagle Hgts. G21: Glas 1H **83**
Eaglesham Ct. G51: Glas 5C **82**
Eaglesham Path ML5: Glenb . . . 3G **69**
Eaglesham Pl. G51: Glas 5C **82**
Eaglesham Rd. G75: E Kil . . . 3A **148**
G76: Clar. 6B **134**
G77: Newt M 5D **132**
Eagle St. G4: Glas 1G **83**
Earlbank Av. G14: Glas 5C **60**
Earlbank La. Nth. *G14: Glas* . . . *5C **60***
(off Verona Av.)
G14: Glas *5C **60***
(off Earlbank Av.)
Earlbank La. Sth. G14: Glas . . . 5C **60**
Earl Haig Rd. G52: Hill 4H **79**
Earl La. G14: Glas 6C **60**
(not continuous)

Earl Pl. G14: Glas . . . 5C **60**
PA11: Bri W. . . . 5F **73**
Earlsburn Rd. G66: Lenz . . . 3E **51**
Earlscourt G69: Mood . . . 6D **52**
Earl's Ga. G71: Both . . . 4C **124**
Earlsgate PA6: C'lee . . . 2B **74**
Earl's Hill G68: Cumb . . . 3D **34**
Earlspark Av. G43: Glas . . . 1D **118**
Earlston Cres. ML5: Coat . . . 2F **111**
Earlston St. ML2: Wis . . . 3A **146**
Earl St. G14: Glas . . . 5A **60**
Earl Vw. ML1: New S . . . 4A **128**
Earlybraes Gdns. G33: Glas . . . 5D **86**
Earn Av. G61: Bear . . . 3H **45**
ML4: Bell . . . 1A **126**
PA4: Renf . . . 1G **79**
Earn Cres. ML2: Wis . . . 2H **157**
Earn Gdns. ML9: Lark . . . 5E **161**
Earn La. *ML1: Holy* . . . *2A **128***
(off Howden Pl.)
EARNOCK . . . **1C 152**
Earnock Av. ML1: Moth . . . 3E **143**
Earnock Gdns. ML3: Ham . . . 2D **152**
Earnock Rd. ML3: Ham . . . 1B **152**
Earnock St. G33: Glas . . . 5F **65**
ML3: Ham . . . 5E **141**
Earn Rd. G77: Newt M . . . 2D **132**
Earnside St. G32: Glas . . . 6B **86**
Earn St. G33: Glas . . . 2G **85**
Easdale G74: E Kil . . . 4B **150**
Easdale Dr. G32: Glas . . . 1A **106**
Easdale Path ML5: Coat . . . 1F **111**
ML5: Glenb . . . 3G **69**
Easdale Pl. G77: Newt M . . . 4B **132**
Easdale Ri. ML3: Ham . . . 6C **140**
E. Academy St. ML2: Wis . . . 1H **157**
East Av. G71: View . . . 1G **125**
G72: Blan . . . 4B **140**
ML1: New S . . . 5A **128**
ML6: Plain . . . 1G **93**
ML8: Carl . . . 3D **164**
PA4: Renf . . . 6F **59**
EAST BALGROCHAN . . . **3E 29**
Eastbank Dr. G32: Glas . . . 6C **86**
Eastbank Pl. G32: Glas . . . 6C **86**
Eastbank Ri G32: Glas . . . 6C **86**
E. Barns St. G81: Clyd . . . 1F **59**
E. Bath La. G2: Glas . . . 3G **83** (4E **5**)
E. Buchanan M. *PA1: Pais* . . . *6B **78***
(off E. Buchanan St.)
E. Buchanan St. PA1: Pais . . . 6B **78**
Eastburn Cres. G21: Glas . . . 3D **64**
Eastburn Pl. G21: Glas . . . 3D **64**
Eastburn Rd. G21: Glas . . . 4D **64**
E. Burnside St. G65: Kils . . . 3H **11**
E. Campbell St. G40: Glas . . . 5A **84**
Eastcote Av. G14: Glas . . . 5E **61**
EAST CRAIGEND . . . **6D 40**
EAST CRINDLEDYKE . . . **3E 147**
Eastcroft G73: Ruth . . . 5D **104**
Eastcroft Ter. G21: Glas . . . 5C **64**
E. Dean St. ML4: Bell . . . 2D **126**
Eastend Av. ML1: Carf . . . 6B **128**
Easterbrae ML1: Moth . . . 5F **143**
Easter Cadder Cotts. G66: Kirk . . . 6H **29**
Easter Craigs G31: Glas . . . 3D **84**
Easter Cres. ML2: Wis . . . 5C **146**
Easter Garngaber Rd. G66: Lenz . . . 2E **51**
Eastergreens Av. G66: Kirk . . . 6C **30**
Easterhill Pl. G32: Glas . . . 2H **105**
Easterhill St. G32: Glas . . . 2H **105**
EASTERHOUSE . . . **3G 87**
Easterhouse Pl. G34: Glas . . . 3A **88**
Easterhouse Quad. G34: Glas . . . 3A **88**
Easterhouse Rd. G34: Glas . . . 3A **88**
G69: Bail . . . 6H **87**
EASTERHOUSE ROAD INTERCHANGE . . . **4A 88**
Easterhouse Sports Cen. . . . **2F 87**
Easterhouse Station (Rail) . . . **5A 88**
Easterhouse Swimming Pool . . . **3G 87**
Easterhouse Township Cen.
G34: Glas . . . 2G **87**
Eastermains G66: Kirk . . . 3H **31**
Easter M. G71: Udd . . . 2C **124**
Easter Queenslie Rd. G33: Glas . . . 3E **87**
Easter Rd. G76: Busby . . . 3E **135**
Easterton Av. G76: Busby . . . 4E **135**
Easterton Cotts. G64: Torr . . . 3E **29**
Easter Wood Cres. G71: View . . . 4H **109**
EASTFIELD . . . **6F 105**
Eastfield Av. G72: Camb . . . 1G **121**
Eastfield Cres. G82: Dumb . . . 5H **17**
Eastfield Pl. G82: Dumb . . . 5H **17**
Eastfield Rd. G21: Glas . . . 5A **64**
G68: Cumb . . . 3C **34**
ML8: Carl . . . 4G **165**
Eastfield Ter. ML4: Bell . . . 3F **127**
EAST FULTON . . . **5F 75**
Eastgate G69: G'csh . . . 4E **69**
East Ga. ML2: Wis . . . 6B **146**
ML5: Glenb . . . 2H **69**
E. George St. ML5: Coat . . . 3D **90**
E. Glebe Ter. ML3: Ham . . . 1H **153**
E. Greenlees Av. G72: Camb . . . 4C **122**
E. Greenlees Cres. G72: Camb . . . 4B **122**
E. Greenlees Dr. G72: Camb . . . 4C **122**
East Greenlees Gro. G72: Camb . . . 4H **121**
E. Greenlees Rd. G72: Camb . . . 4A **122**
E. Hallhill Road G69: Bail . . . 5G **87**
Easthall Pl. G33: Glas . . . 4F **87**
E. Hamilton St. ML2: Wis . . . 1H **157**
E. High St. ML6: Air . . . 3A **92**
EAST KILBRIDE . . . **2H 149**
East Kilbride Arts Cen. . . . **6H 137**
East Kilbride Ice Rink . . . **3H 149**
East Kilbride Station (Rail) . . . **1G 149**
E. Kilbride Rd. G73: Ruth . . . 2E **121**
G76: Busby . . . 3E **135**
East Kilbride Rd. G76: Crmck . . . 5G **135**
East Kilbride Sports Cen. . . . **5C 150**
East Kilbride Village Theatre . . . **1H 149**
East La. PA1: Pais . . . 1C **98**
Eastlea Pl. ML6: Air . . . 5B **92**
E. Machan St. ML9: Lark . . . 4F **161**
EAST MAINS . . . **1A 150**
E. Mains Rd. G74: E Kil . . . 1G **149**
E. Milton Gro. G75: E Kil . . . 2D **148**
Eastmuir St. G32: Glas . . . 6B **86**
ML2: Wis . . . 5C **146**
Easton Pl. ML5: Coat . . . 6D **90**
East Rd. ML1: New S . . . 3A **128**
PA10: Kilb . . . 1A **94**
E. Scott Ter. ML3: Ham . . . 2H **153**
EAST SHAWHEAD . . . **3E 111**
Eastside G66: Kirk . . . 4D **30**
Eastside Ind. Est. *G66: Kirk* . . . *4D **30***
(off Kilsyth Rd.)
E. Springfield Ter. G64: B'rig . . . 1D **64**
E. Station Ind. Est. ML9: Lark . . . 1F **161**
E. Stewart Pl. ML5: Coat . . . 4E **91**
E. Stewart St. ML5: Coat . . . 5E **91**
E. Thomson St. G81: Clyd . . . 4D **42**
E. Thornlie St. ML2: Wis . . . 1H **157**
Eastvale Pl. G3: Glas . . . 3A **82**
E. Wellbrae Cres. ML3: Ham . . . 2F **153**
E. Wellington St. G31: Glas . . . 6F **85**
E. Whitby St. G31: Glas . . . 1E **105**
Eastwood Av. G41: Glas . . . 5B **102**
G46: Giff . . . 4A **118**
Eastwood Butterfly Kingdom . . . **5F 117**
Eastwood Cres. G46: T'bnk . . . 3F **117**
Eastwood Dr. ML2: Newm . . . 3E **147**
Eastwoodmains Rd. G46: Giff . . . 6H **117**
G76: Clar . . . 6H **117**
Eastwood Recreation Cen. . . . **5H 117**
Eastwood Rd. G69: Mood . . . 5D **52**
Eastwood Toll G46: Giff . . . 6H **117**
Eastwood Vw. G72: Camb . . . 1E **123**
Eastwood Way *ML9: Lark* . . . *1F **161***
(off Antrim La.)
Easwald Bank PA10: Kilb . . . 3B **94**
Ebroch Dr. G65: Kils . . . 3A **12**
Ebroch Pk. G65: Kils . . . 3A **12**
Eccles St. G22: Glas . . . 4A **64**
Eckford St. G32: Glas . . . 1A **106**
Eck Path *ML1: Holy* . . . *2A **128***
(off Howden Pl.)
Eday St. G22: Glas . . . 3H **63**
Edderton Pl. G34: Glas . . . 4G **87**
Edderton Way G34: Glas . . . 4G **87**
Eddington Dr. G77: Newt M . . . 6C **132**
Eddleston Pl. G72: Camb . . . 2D **122**
EDDLEWOOD . . . **4H 153**
Eddlewood Ct. G33: Glas . . . 4G **87**
Eddlewood Path G33: Glas . . . 4F **87**
Eddlewood Pl. G33: Glas . . . 4F **87**
Eddlewood Rd. G33: Glas . . . 4F **87**
Eddlewood Sports Barn . . . **4H 153**
Eden Dr. G75: E Kil . . . 5B **148**
Eden Gdns. G75: E Kil . . . 4B **148**
Eden Gro. G75: E Kil . . . 4B **148**
Eden La. G33: Glas . . . 2F **85**
Eden Pk. G71: Both . . . 5D **124**
Eden Pl. G72: Camb . . . 2D **122**
PA4: Renf . . . 1G **79**
Edenside G68: Cumb . . . 4B **14**
Eden St. G33: Glas . . . 2F **85**
Edenwood St. G31: Glas . . . 6G **85**
Edgam Dr. G52: Glas . . . 6C **80**
Edgefauld Av. G21: Glas . . . 6B **64**
Edgefauld Dr. G21: Glas . . . 5B **64**
Edgefauld Pl. G21: Glas . . . 4B **64**
Edgefauld Rd. G21: Glas . . . 5B **64**
Edgehill La. G11: Glas . . . 5G **61**
Edgehill Rd. G11: Glas . . . 5F **61**
G61: Bear . . . 1E **45**
Edgemont Pk. ML3: Ham . . . 3G **153**
Edgemont St. G41: Glas . . . 5C **102**
Edinbeg Av. G42: Glas . . . 5A **104**
Edinbeg Pl. G42: Glas . . . 5A **104**
Edinburgh Rd. G33: Glas . . . 4F **85**
G69: Bail . . . 5G **87**
ML1: N'hse . . . 1C **128**
Edington Gdns. G69: Mood . . . 4D **52**
Edington St. G4: Glas . . . 1F **83** (1C **4**)
Edison St. G52: Hill . . . 3G **79**
(not continuous)
Edmiston Dr. G51: Glas . . . 5F **81**
PA3: Lin . . . 5F **75**
Edmonstone Ct. G81: Clyd . . . 2F **59**
Edmonstone Dr. G65: Kils . . . 4H **11**
Edmonton Ter. G75: E Kil . . . 3E **149**
Edmund Kean G74: E Kil . . . 4C **138**
Edrick Ct. *ML5: Coat* . . . *5B **90***
(off Kirk St.)
Edrom Ct. G32: Glas . . . 6H **85**
Edrom Path G32: Glas . . . 6H **85**
Edrom St. G32: Glas . . . 6H **85**
(not continuous)
Edward Av. PA4: Renf . . . 5G **59**
Edward St. G65: Kils . . . 2H **11**
G69: Barg . . . 6D **88**
G81: Clyd . . . 2F **59**
ML1: Moth . . . 4H **143**
ML3: Ham . . . 1H **153**
Edwin St. G51: Glas . . . 6B **82**
Edzell Ct. G14: Glas . . . 1D **80**
Edzell Dr. G77: Newt M . . . 5E **133**
PA5: Eld . . . 3B **96**
Edzell Gdns. G64: B'rig . . . 1E **65**
ML2: Wis . . . 1G **157**
Edzell Pl. G14: Glas . . . 6D **60**
Edzell St. G14: Glas . . . 1D **80**
ML5: Coat . . . 1H **109**
Egidia Av. G46: Giff . . . 5A **118**
Egilsay Cres. G22: Glas . . . 1G **63**
Egilsay Pl. G22: Glas . . . 1G **63**
Egilsay St. G22: Glas . . . 1G **63**
Egilsay Ter. G22: Glas . . . 1G **63**
Eglinton Ct. G5: Glas . . . 6F **83**
Eglinton Dr. G46: Giff . . . 5A **118**
Eglinton St. G41: Glas . . . 1E **103**
ML5: Coat . . . 3D **90**
Egmont Pk. G75: E Kil . . . 4C **148**
Eider G12: Glas . . . 2G **61**
Eider Av. G75: E Kil . . . 6C **148**
Eider Gro. G75: E Kil . . . 6C **148**
Eider Pl. G75: E Kil . . . 6C **148**
Eighth St. G71: Tann . . . 4C **108**

Eildon Cres. ML6: Chap 4F **113**
Eildon Dr. G78: Barr 6E **115**
Eildon Rd. G66: Kirk 5F **31**
Eileen Gdns. G64: B'rig 5D **48**
Eilt Wlk. *ML2: Newm 3D* ***146***
(off Islay Av.)
Elcho St. G40: Glas. 5B **84**
Elderbank G61: Bear 4E **45**
Elder Cres. G72: Flem 3E **123**
Elder Gro. G51: Glas. 4D **80**
G71: View 5F **109**
Elder Gro. Ct. G51: Glas 4D **80**
Elderpark Gdns. G51: Glas 4F **81**
Elderpark Gro. G51: Glas 4F **81**
Elderpark St. G51: Glas. 4F **81**
Elderslea Rd. ML8: Carl 5G **165**
ELDERSLIE 2A **96**
Elderslie Leisure Cen. 2B **96**
Elderslie St. G3: Glas. 2D **82**
Elder St. G51: Glas 4F **81**
(not continuous)
Elders Way ML2: Wis 6B **146**
Eldin Pl. PA11: Bri W 5G **73**
PA5: Eld 3H **95**
Eldon Ct. G11: Glas 1H **81**
Eldon Gdns. G64: B'rig 6A **48**
Eldon St. G3: Glas 1C **82**
Elgin Av. G74: E Kil. 6H **137**
Elgin Gdns. G76: Clar 1D **134**
Elgin Pl. G65: Kils 2H **11**
G74: E Kil 6H **137**
ML5: Coat. 2D **110**
ML6: Air 6G **91**
Elgin Rd. G61: Bear 6F **25**
Elgin Ter. ML3: Ham 5C **140**
Elgin Way ML4: Bell 1C **126**
Elibank St. G33: Glas 2A **86**
Elie Ct. G68: Cumb. 6H **13**
Elie St. G11: Glas 1A **82**
Eliot Cres. ML3: Ham 2H **153**
Eliot Ter. ML3: Ham 1H **153**
Elison Ct. ML1: Moth 5B **144**
Elizabethan Way PA4: Renf. 2E **79**
Elizabeth Av. G66: Milt C 5B **8**
Elizabeth Ct. G74: E Kil. 1H **149**
Elizabeth Cres. G46: T'bnk 4G **117**
Elizabeth Quad. ML1: Holy 2A **128**
Elizabeth St. G51: Glas. 6A **82**
Elizabeth Wynd ML3: Ham 4H **153**
Ella Gdns. ML4: Bell 3E **127**
Ellangowan Rd. G41: Glas 5A **102**
G62: Miln 3G **25**
Ellergreen Rd. G61: Bear 3E **45**
Ellerslie St. PA5: John 2G **95**
Ellesmere St. G22: Glas 6E **63**
Ellinger Ct. G81: Clyd. 3H **41**
Elliot Av. G46: Giff 5A **118**
PA2: Pais 6C **96**
Elliot Ct. ML1: Moth 6F **127**
Elliot Cres. G74: E Kil 1B **150**
Elliot Dr. G46: Giff 4A **118**
Elliot Pl. G3: Glas. 4C **82**
Elliot St. G3: Glas. 4C **82**
(not continuous)
Ellisland G66: Kirk 3H **31**
G74: E Kil 6D **138**
Ellisland Av. G81: Clyd 4E **43**
Ellisland Cres. G73: Ruth 2B **120**
Ellisland Dr. G66: Kirk 3G **31**
G72: Blan 3H **139**
Ellisland Rd. G43: Glas. 1B **118**
G67: Cumb 3B **36**
G76: Busby 4C **134**
Ellisland Wynd ML1: N'hill 4C **128**
Ellismuir Farm Rd. G69: Bail 1B **108**
Ellismuir Pl. G69: Bail 1A **108**
Ellismuir Rd. G69: Bail 1A **108**
Ellismuir St. ML5: Coat 2H **109**
(not continuous)
Ellismuir Way G71: Tann. 4E **109**
Ellis St. ML5: Coat 4C **90**
Elliston Av. G53: Glas 2C **116**
Elliston Cres. G53: Glas 2C **116**
Elliston Dr. G53: Glas 2C **116**
Ellis Way ML1: Moth 4H **143**
Ellon Dr. PA3: Lin. 6G **75**
Ellon Gro. PA3: Pais 4B **78**
Ellon Way PA3: Pais 4B **78**
Ellrig G75: E Kil. 6F **149**
Elm Av. G66: Lenz 1C **50**
PA4: Renf 5E **59**
Elm Bank G64: B'rig 6D **48**
G66: Kirk 4D **30**
Elmbank Av. G71: View 6F **109**
Elmbank Cres. G2: Glas 3E **83** (3A **4**)
ML3: Ham 5E **141**
Elmbank Dr. ML9: Lark. 4G **161**
Elmbank St. G2: Glas 3E **83** (4A **4**)
ML4: Bell 2C **126**
ML8: Carl 5G **165**
Elmbank St. La. G2: Glas 4A **4**
Elm Cres. G71: View. 6H **109**
Elm Dr. G67: Cumb 1F **37**
G72: Camb 2C **122**
PA5: John 5F **95**
Elmfoot St. G5: Glas 3H **103**
Elm Gdns. G61: Bear. 1E **45**
Elmhurst ML1: Moth 5F **143**
Elmira Rd. G69: Muirh 2B **68**
Elm La. W. *G14: Glas. 6D* ***60***
(off Lime St.)
Elm Lea PA5: John. 3H **95**
Elmore Av. G44: Glas 2F **119**
Elmore La. G44: Glas 2F **119**
Elm Pl. G75: E Kil 5E **149**
Elm Quad. ML6: Air 4D **92**
Elm Rd. G73: Ruth 3D **120**
G81: Clyd 2C **42**
G82: Dumb 3F **17**
ML1: Holy. 2B **128**
ML1: New S 5A **128**
PA11: Bri W 2G **73**
PA2: Pais 4C **98**
Elmslie Ct. G69: Bail. 1A **108**
Elms, The G44: Glas 3E **119**
Elm St. G14: Glas. 6D **60**
G66: Len. 3G **7**
G72: Blan 2C **140**
G76: Busby. 3D **134**
ML1: Moth 2F **143**
ML5: Coat 6E **91**
Elm St. E. *G14: Glas. 6D* ***60***
(off Elm St.)
Elmtree Gdns. G45: Glas. 3B **120**
Elmvale Row G21: Glas 4A **64**
Elmvale St. G21: Glas. 4A **64**
Elm Vw. Ct. ML4: Bell 3F **127**
Elm Wlk. G61: Bear 1E **45**
Elm Way G72: Flem. 3E **123**
ML9: Lark 6A **156**
Elmwood ML2: Wis. 2E **157**
Elmwood Av. G11: Glas. 5F **61**
G77: Newt M 3F **133**
Elmwood Ct. G71: Both. 5E **125**
Elmwood Gdns. G66: Lenz 2A **50**
Elmwood La. G11: Glas. 5F **61**
Elphinstone Cres. G75: E Kil. 4H **149**
Elphinstone Pl. G51: Glas. 4A **82**
Elphinstone Rd. G46: Giff. 2G **133**
Elphin St. G23: Glas 6B **46**
Elrig Rd. G44: Glas. 2D **118**
Elsinore Path G75: E Kil 6G **149**
Elspeth Gdns. G64: B'rig. 5E **49**
Eltham St. G22: Glas. 6F **63**
Elvan Ct. ML1: Moth 3F **143**
Elvan Pl. G75: E Kil. 4A **148**
Elvan St. G32: Glas 6H **85**
ML1: Moth 2F **143**
Elvan Twr. ML1: Moth. 4G **143**
Embo Dr. G13: Glas 3B **60**
Emerald Ter. ML4: Bell 3C **126**
Emerson Rd. G64: B'rig 6C **48**
Emerson Rd. W. G64: B'rig. 6C **48**
Emily Dr. ML1: Moth 5G **143**
Emma Jay Rd. ML4: Bell 2D **126**
Empire Way ML1: Moth 6E **127**
Endfield Av. G12: Glas 3H **61**
Endrick Bank G64: B'rig 3C **48**
Endrick Dr. G61: Bear 4F **45**
PA1: Pais 5D **78**
Endrick Gdns. G62: Miln 3E **25**
Endrick Ho. G82: Dumb 1H **17**
Endrick St. G21: Glas 6H **63**
English Row ML6: C'bnk. 3C **112**
English St. ML2: Wis 6D **144**
Ennerdale G75: E Kil. 5B **148**
Ennisfree Rd. G72: Blan 1B **140**
Ensay St. G22: Glas 2H **63**
Enterkin St. G32: Glas 1H **105**
Eriboll Pl. G22: Glas 2F **63**
Eriboll St. G22: Glas 2F **63**
Eribol Wlk. ML1: N'hill 4D **128**
Ericht Rd. G43: Glas 2A **118**
Eriska Av. G14: Glas 4A **60**
Eriskay Av. G77: Newt M. 4B **132**
ML3: Ham. 1D **152**
Eriskay Cres. G77: Newt M 4B **132**
Eriskay Dr. G60: Old K 1G **41**
Eriskay Pl. G60: Old K 1G **41**
Erradale St. G22: Glas 2E **63**
Errogie St. G34: Glas 3H **87**
Errol Gdns. G5: Glas. 1G **103**
ERSKINE. 6F **41**
Erskine Av. G41: Glas 1H **101**
Erskine Bri. G60: Old K. 2E **41**
PA7: B'ton 3D **40**
Erskine Ct. *ML6: Air 3E* ***93***
(off Katherine St.)
Erskine Cres. ML6: Air 6H **91**
Erskinefauld Rd. PA3: Lin. 5G **75**
Erskine Ferry Rd. G60: Old K 2F **41**
Erskine Rd. G46: Giff 3H **133**
Erskine Sq. G52: Hill 4H **79**
Erskine Swimming Pool. 5F **41**
Erskine Vw. G60: Old K. 1E **41**
G81: Clyd 4D **42**
Ervie St. G34: Glas. 4A **88**
Escart Rd. ML8: Carl. 2F **165**
Esdaile Ct. ML1: New S 4A **128**
Esk Av. PA4: Renf. 1G **79**
Eskbank St. G32: Glas 5A **86**
Eskdale G74: E Kil. 6E **137**
G77: Newt M. 4H **133**
Eskdale Dr. G73: Ruth. 6F **105**
Eskdale Rd. G61: Bear 5D **44**
Eskdale St. G42: Glas 4F **103**
Esk Dr. PA2: Pais 4C **96**
Esk St. G14: Glas 4H **59**
Esk Wlk. *G67: Cumb. 4H* ***35***
(in Cumbernauld Shop. Cen.)
Esk Way PA2: Pais 4C **96**
Esmond St. G3: Glas. 2A **82**
Espedair St. PA2: Pais 2A **98**
Espieside Cres. ML5: Coat. 3H **89**
Esporta Health & Fitness Club
Finnieston 3C **82**
Hamilton 4B **142**
Esporta Health & Racquets 2B **26**
Essenside Av. G15: Glas 5B **44**
Essex Dr. G14: Glas 5D **60**
Essex La. G14: Glas 5D **60**
(not continuous)
Esslemont Av. G14: Glas. 4B **60**
Esslemont La. G14: Glas 4C **60**
Estate Quad. G32: Carm 5C **106**
Estate Rd. G32: Carm 5C **106**
Etive Av. G61: Bear. 3H **45**
ML3: Ham. 2E **153**
Etive Ct. G67: Cumb. 1D **54**
G81: Hard 2E **43**
ML5: Coat. 2D **110**
Etive Cres. G64: B'rig 6D **48**
G67: Cumb 1D **54**
ML2: Wis 3H **157**
Etive Dr. G46: Giff. 6B **118**
G67: Cumb 1D **54**
ML6: Air 6C **92**
PA7: B'ton. 5A **40**
Etive Pl. G67: Cumb 1E **55**
Etive St. G32: Glas 6A **86**
ML2: Wis 2H **157**
Etna Ind. Est. ML2: Wis 5C **144**

Etna St. ML2: Wis. 5C **144**
Eton La. *G12:* Glas *1C 82*
(off Gt. George St.)
Etrick Av. ML4: Bell. 6C **110**
Etterick Wynd *G72:* Blan *2A 140*
(off Cheviot St.)
Ettrick Av. PA4: Renf. 1H **79**
Ettrick Ct. G72: Camb 2D **122**
ML5: Coat 2E **111**
Ettrick Cres. G73: Ruth 6E **105**
Ettrick Dr. G61: Bear 6C **24**
PA7: B'ton. 5A **40**
Ettrick Hill G74: E Kil 6A **138**
Ettrick Oval PA2: Pais. 5C **96**
Ettrick Pl. G43: Glas 6B **102**
Ettrick Sq. *G67:* Cumb *4H 35*
(in Cumbernauld Shop. Cen.)
Ettrick St. ML2: Wis. 4G **145**
Ettrick Ter. PA5: John 5C **94**
Ettrick Wlk. *G67:* Cumb *4H 35*
(in Cumbernauld Shop. Cen.)
Ettrick Way *G67:* Cumb. *4H 35*
(in Cumbernauld Shop. Cen.)
PA4: Renf 1H **79**
Eurocentral ML1: Holy 5H **111**
Eurocentral Ind. Est. ML1: Holy . . .6H **111**
Evan Cres. G46: Giff 5B **118**
Evan Dr. G46: Giff 5B **118**
Evanton Dr. G46: T'bnk 4E **117**
Evanton Pl. G46: T'bnk 4E **117**
Everall Dr. ML2: Newm. 4E **147**
Everard Ct. G21: Glas 2A **64**
Everard Dr. G21: Glas 3A **64**
Everard Pl. G21: Glas 2A **64**
Everard Quad. G21: Glas 2A **64**
Everglades, The G69: Chry. 1H **67**
Eversley St. G32: Glas 2A **106**
Everton Rd. G53: Glas. 3C **100**
Ewan Mundy Fine Art Gallery
. . . . .4C **4**
Ewart Cres. ML3: Ham. 1E **153**
Ewart Ter. ML3: Ham. 1F **153**
Ewing Ct. ML3: Ham. 4G **153**
Ewing Pl. G31: Glas 6E **85**
Ewing St. G73: Ruth 6C **104**
PA10: Kilb. 2A **94**
Ewing Wlk. G62: Miln 4A **26**
Excelsior Pk. ML2: Wis 1D **156**
Excelsior St. ML2: Wis 1C **156**
Exchange Pl. G1: Glas. 5E **5**
ML5: Coat 5C **90**
Exeter Dr. G11: Glas 1G **81**
Exeter La. *G11:* Glas *1G 81*
(off Dumbarton Rd.)
Exeter St. ML5: Coat. 6C **90**
Exhibition Centre Station (Rail) . . .3C **82**
Eynort St. G22: Glas 2E **63**
Eyrepoint Ct. G33: Glas. 3A **86**

F

Factory Rd. ML1: Moth. 4G **143**
Fagan Ct. G72: Blan 6C **124**
FAIFLEY 6E **23**
Failley Rd. G81: Faif, Hard 6F **23**
Fairbairn Cres. G46: T'bnk 5G **117**
Fairbairn Path *G40:* Glas. *1C 104*
(off Ruby St.)
Fairbairn St. G40: Glas. 1C **104**
Fairburn St. G32: Glas. 1H **105**
Fairfax Av. G44: Glas 2G **119**
Fairfield Ct. G76: Busby 4C **134**
Fairfield Dr. G76: Busby 4C **134**
PA4: Renf 2F **79**
Fairfield Gdns. G51: Glas 3F **81**
Fairfield Pl. G51: Glas 3F **81**
G71: Both 5F **125**
G74: E Kil 1D **148**
ML3: Ham. 2A **154**
Fairfield St. G51: Glas 3F **81**
Fairford Dr. G67: Cumb. 6F **35**
Fairhaven Av. ML6: Air. 5E **93**
Fairhaven Rd. G23: Glas. 1C **62**

FAIRHILL .3G **153**
Fairhill Av. G53: Glas 6C **100**
ML3: Ham. 2G **153**
Fairhill Cres. ML3: Ham. 2G **153**
ML3: Ham. 4F **153**
Fairholm Av. ML3: Fern 2E **155**
Fairholm St. G32: Glas. 1H **105**
ML9: Lark. 1D **160**
Fairley St. G51: Glas 5H **81**
Fairlie G74: E Kil 6F **137**
Fairlie Pk. Dr. G11: Glas. 1G **81**
Fair Oaks G76: Crmck. 1A **136**
Fairview Ct. *G62:* Miln *4G 25*
(off Main St.)
Fairway G61: Bear 2B **44**
Fairway Av. PA2: Pais. 5H **97**
Fairways ML9: Lark 2G **161**
Fairways, The G44: Neth 5D **118**
PA5: John. 6D **94**
Fairways Vw. G81: Hard 1F **43**
Fairweather Pl.
G77: Newt M. 5C **132**
Fairyknowe Gdns. G71: Both. 5F **125**
Faith Av. PA11: Q'riers 1A **72**
Falconbridge Rd. G74: E Kil 5C **138**
Falcon Cres. PA3: Pais 5F **77**
Falconer Ter. ML3: Ham. 2G **153**
Falcon Ho. G75: Pais 4A **78**
Falcon Rd. PA5: John. 6D **94**
Falcon Ter. G20: Glas 1A **62**
Falcon Ter. La. *G20:* Glas *1A 62*
(off Caldercuilt Rd.)
Falfield St. G5: Glas 1E **103**
Falkland Av. G77: Newt M 4G **133**
Falkland Cres. G64: B'rig 1F **65**
Falkland Dr. G74: E Kil 2E **149**
Falkland La. G12: Glas. 6H **61**
Falkland Pk. G74: E Kil 2F **149**
Falkland Pl. G74: E Kil 2F **149**
ML5: Coat. 2D **110**
Falkland St. G12: Glas 6H **61**
Falloch Rd. G42: Glas 6E **103**
G61: Bear 5C **44**
G62: Miln 3D **24**
FALLSIDE .1G **125**
Fallside Av. G71: View 1G **125**
Fallside Rd. G71: Both 5E **125**
Falside Av. PA2: Pais 4A **98**
Falside Rd. G32: Glas. 3A **106**
PA2: Pais 4H **97**
Falstaff G74: E Kil. 4C **138**
Faraday Av. ML2: Wis. 6A **146**
Faraday Retail Pk. ML5: Coat. 5C **90**
Fara St. G23: Glas 1D **62**
Farie St. G73: Ruth. 5B **104**
Farm Ct. G71: Both 3F **125**
Farm Cres. ML1: N'hill 3F **129**
Farme Castle Ct. G73: Ruth 4E **105**
Farme Castle Est. G73: Ruth. 4E **105**
FARME CROSS 4E **105**
Farme Cross G73: Ruth 4D **104**
Farmeloan Rd. G73: Ruth. 5D **104**
Farmgate Sq. ML4: Bell 3B **126**
Farmington Av. G32: Glas. 6D **86**
Farmington Gdns. G32: Glas. 6D **86**
Farmington Ga. G32: Glas 1D **106**
Farmington Gro. G32: Glas. 6D **86**
Farm La. G71: Udd. 2E **125**
ML4: Bell 4B **126**
Farm Pk. G66: Lenz 3D **50**
Farm Rd. G41: Glas 6H **81**
G72: Blan 6B **124**
G81: Clyd 4H **41**
G81: Dun, Hard. 6C **22**
ML3: Ham. 5D **140**
Farm St. ML1: Moth 2F **143**
Farm Ter. ML3: Ham. 5D **140**
Farndale G74: E Kil 6E **137**
Farne Dr. G44: Glas. 3F **119**
Farnell St. G4: Glas 1F **83**
Farrier Ct. PA5: John 2F **95**
Faskally Av. G64: B'rig 4A **48**
Faskally Wlk. ML2: Newm 3D **146**
Faskin Cres. G53: Glas. 6H **99**

Faskine Av. ML6: Air 5H **91**
ML6: C'bnk 3B **112**
Faskine Cres. ML6: Air. 5H **91**
Faskin Pl. G53: Glas 6H **99**
Faskin Rd. G53: Glas 6H **99**
Fasque Pl. G15: Glas 3G **43**
Fastnet St. G33: Glas 3A **86**
FAULDHEAD 1H **51**
Fauldhouse St. G5: Glas 2H **103**
Faulds G69: Bail. 6A **88**
Faulds Gdns. G69: Bail. 6A **88**
Fauldshead Rd. PA4: Renf 6E **59**
Faulds La. ML5: Coat 2B **110**
Fauldspark Cres. G69: Bail. 5A **88**
Faulds St. ML5: Coat 2A **110**
Fauldswood Cres. PA2: Pais 3F **97**
Fauldswood Dr. PA2: Pais. 3F **97**
Faulkner Gro. ML1: Cle. 1F **145**
Fearnmore Rd. G20: Glas 2B **62**
Fells, The G66: Len 3G **7**
Fellsview Av. G66: Kirk. 4F **31**
Felton Pl. G13: Glas. 2H **59**
Fendoch St. G32: Glas. 1A **106**
Fenella St. G32: Glas 6B **86**
Fennsbank Av. G73: Ruth 4F **121**
Fenwick Dr. G78: Barr. 6E **115**
ML3: Ham. 4A **154**
Fenwick Pl. G46: Giff 6H **117**
Fenwick Rd. G46: Giff. 6H **117**
Ferclay St. G81: Faif 6F **23**
Fereneze Av. G76: Clar 1A **134**
G78: Barr 4D **114**
PA4: Renf 3C **78**
Fereneze Cres. G13: Glas 3A **60**
ML3: Ham. 6D **140**
Fereneze Dr. PA2: Pais 5F **97**
Fereneze Gro. G78: Barr 4D **114**
Fereneze Rd. G78: Neil. 2A **130**
Fergus Av. PA3: Pais. 6E **77**
Fergus Ct. G20: Glas. 5C **62**
Fergus Dr. G20: Glas. 5C **62**
PA3: Pais 6E **77**
Fergus Gdns. ML3: Ham. 1B **154**
Fergus La. G20: Glas 5D **62**
Ferguslie PA1: Pais 2D **96**
FERGUSLIE PARK. 5E **77**
Ferguslie Pk. Av. PA3: Pais. 6E **77**
Ferguslie Pk. Cres. PA3: Pais 1E **97**
Ferguslie Park Sports & Recreation Cen.
. . . . .5E **77**
Ferguslie Wlk. PA1: Pais. 1F **97**
(not continuous)
Ferguson Av. G62: Miln. 3F **25**
PA4: Renf 6F **59**
Ferguson Dr. ML1: Moth. 6G **143**
Ferguson St. PA4: Renf. 5F **59**
PA5: John 2E **95**
Ferguson Way ML6: Air 1B **92**
Fergusson Pl. G74: E Kil. 4D **138**
Fergusson Rd. G67: Cumb 3H **35**
Fergusson Ter. G66: Milt C 5C **8**
Ferguston Rd. G61: Bear. 3F **45**
Fernan St. G32: Glas 6H **85**
Fern Av. G64: B'rig 1D **64**
G66: Lenz 3C **50**
PA8: Ersk 2F **57**
Fernbank Av. G72: Camb 3C **122**
Fernbank St. G21: Glas. 4A **64**
G22: Glas 4A **64**
Fernbrae Av. G73: Ruth 4D **120**
Fernbrae Way G73: Ruth 4D **120**
Fern Cotts. G13: Glas 4F **61**
Ferncroft Dr. G44: Glas. 2H **119**
Ferndale ML9: Lark. 4E **161**
Ferndale Ct. G23: Glas 1B **62**
Ferndale Dr. G23: Glas 1B **62**
Ferndale Gdns. G23: Glas 1B **62**
Ferndale Pl. G23: Glas 1B **62**
Fern Dr. G78: Barr 3D **114**
Ferness Oval G21: Glas. 2E **65**
Ferness Pl. G21: Glas. 2E **65**
Ferness Rd. G21: Glas. 3E **65**
Fern Gro. G69: G'csh 3E **69**
Ferngrove Av. G12: Glas. 3H **61**

FERNHILL 4D 120
Fernhill Grange G71: Both 6E 125
Fernhill Rd. G73: Ruth 2C 120
FERNIEGAIR 2D 154
Fernie Gdns. G20: Glas 2C 62
Fern La. G12: Glas 4F 61
G13: Glas 4F 61
G66: Len 2E 7
Fernlea G61: Bear 4E 45
Fernleigh Pl. G69: Mood 5D 52
Fernleigh Rd. G43: Glas 2B 118
Fernside Wlk. ML3: Ham 2A 154
Fernslea Av. G72: Blan 1A 140
Fern St. ML1: Moth 5A 144
Ferryden Ct. G14: Glas 1E 81
Ferryden St. G11: Glas 1E 81
G14: Glas 1E 81
Ferry Rd. G3: Glas 3H 81
G71: Both 5E 125
G71: Udd 1C 124
Ferry Rd. PA4: Renf 5F 59
PA7: B'ton 4G 39
Fersit Ct. G43: Glas 1A 118
Fersit St. G43: Glas 1A 118
Fetlar Dr. G44: Glas 2G 119
Fetlar Rd. PA11: Bri W 3E 73
Fettercairn Av. G15: Glas 4G 43
Fettercairn Gdns. G64: B'rig 6E 49
Fettes St. G33: Glas 3H 85
Fiddoch Ct. ML2: Newm 2D 146
Fidra St. G33: Glas 3H 85
Fielden Pl. G40: Glas 6C 84
Fielden St. G40: Glas 6C 84
Field Gro. G76: Busby 4D 134
Fieldhead Dr. G43: Glas 2G 117
Fieldhead Sq. G43: Glas 2G 117
Field Rd. G76: Busby 4D 134
G81: Faif 5F 23
ML9: Lark 3F 161
Fields La. PA6: Hous 1B 74
Field St. ML3: Ham 2H 153
Fife Av. G52: Glas 1B 100
ML6: Air 6A 92
Fife Ct. G71: Both 6E 125
Fife Cres. G71: Both 6E 125
Fife Dr. ML1: Moth 5F 127
Fife Way G64: B'rig 1F 65
Fifth Av. G12: Glas 4F 61
G33: Mille 4B 66
G72: Blan 4C 140
ML6: Air 3C 92
PA4: Renf 1E 79
Fifty Pitches Pl. G51: Glas 4B 80
Fifty Pitches Rd. G51: Glas 4B 80
Finart Dr. PA2: Pais 4D 98
Finaven Gdns. G61: Bear 5B 24
Finch Dr. G13: Glas 1H 59
Finch Pl. PA5: John 6D 94
Findhorn PA8: Ersk 4E 41
Findhorn Av. PA2: Pais 4D 96
PA4: Renf 6G 59
Findhorn Ct. G75: E Kil 3A 148
Findhorn Pl. G75: E Kil 3A 148
Findhorn St. G33: Glas 3F 85
Findlay Ct. *ML1: Moth 1F 143*
(off Roman Rd.)
Findlay St. G65: Kils 3H 11
ML1: Moth 4H 143
Findochty PA8: Ersk 4E 41
Findochty St. G33: Glas 2D 86
Fingal La. G20: Glas 2A 62
Fingal St. G20: Glas 2B 62
Fingalton Rd. G77: Newt M 4A 132
Fingask St. G32: Glas 1C 106
Finglas Av. PA2: Pais 4D 98
Finglen Gdns. G62: Miln 3E 25
Finglen Pl. G53: Glas 3B 116
Fingleton Av. G78: Barr 6F 115
Finhaven St. G32: Glas 2G 105
Finlarig St. G34: Glas 4A 88
Finlas St. G22: Glas 5H 63
Finlay Dr. G31: Glas 4C 84
PA3: Lin 6F 75
Finlay Ri. G62: Miln 5H 25
Finlayson Dr. ML6: Air 4E 93
Finlayson Quad. ML6: Air 4E 93
Finlaystone St. ML5: Coat 4A 90
Finnart Sq. G40: Glas 2B 104
Finnart St. G40: Glas 2B 104
FINNIESTON 3C 82
Finnieston Crane 4C 82
Finnieston Sq. G3: Glas 3C 82
Finnieston St. G3: Glas 4C 82
Finnie Wynd ML1: Moth 5B 144
Finsbay St. G51: Glas 5D 80
Fintaig La. ML2: Wis 6C 146
Fintrie Ter. ML3: Ham 5C 140
Fintry Av. PA2: Pais 5A 98
Fintry Ct. ML5: Coat 2E 111
Fintry Cres. G64: B'rig 6E 49
G78: Barr 6E 115
Fintry Dr. G44: Glas 6G 103
Fintry Gdns. G61: Bear 5C 24
Firbank Av. G64: Torr 5D 28
Fir Bank Av. ML9: Lark 3F 161
Firbank Quad. ML6: Chap 2E 113
Firbank Ter. G78: Barr 6G 115
Fir Ct. G72: Flem 3E 123
ML5: Coat 1A 110
Firdon Cres. G15: Glas 6A 44
Fir Dr. G75: E Kil 6D 148
Fir Gro. G71: View 5F 109
ML1: New S 5A 128
FIRHILL 5E 63
Firhill Av. ML6: Air 5H 91
Firhill Pk. 5E 63
Firhill Rd. G20: Glas 5D 62
Firhill St. G20: Glas 5E 63
Firlee G75: E Kil 3B 148
Fir Pk. 5H 143
Firpark Rd. G64: B'rig 1D 64
Firpark St. G31: Glas 3B 84
Fir Pk. St. ML1: Moth 5H 143
Firpark Ter. G31: Glas 4B 84
Fir Pl. G69: Bail 2G 107
G72: Camb 1C 122
ML1: Cle 6H 129
PA5: John 4G 95
First Av. G33: Mille 4B 66
G44: Neth 5D 118
G61: Bear 4G 45
G66: Auch 6D 50
G71: Tann 5C 108
G82: Dumb 3C 18
PA4: Renf 1E 79
First Gdns. G41: Glas 1G 101
Firs, The G44: Glas 2F 119
First Rd. G72: Blan 4C 140
First St. G71: Tann 5D 108
First Ter. G81: Clyd 4C 42
Firthview Ter. G82: Dumb 4C 16
Firtree Pl. ML2: Newm 3F 147
Firtree Rd. ML2: Newm 3F 147
Fir Vw. ML6: C'bnk 3B 112
Firwood Courts G77: Newt M 5E 133
Firwood Dr. G44: Glas 1G 119
Firwood Rd. G77: Newt M 4E 133
Fischer Gdns. PA1: Pais 1D 96
Fisher Av. G65: Kils 3H 11
PA1: Pais 1D 96
Fisher Ct. G31: Glas 4B 84
Fisher Cres. G81: Hard 1D 42
Fisher Dr. PA1: Pais 1D 96
Fishers Rd. PA4: Renf 3E 59
Fisher St. ML9: Lark 4F 161
Fisher Way PA1: Pais 1D 96
Fishescoates Av. G73: Ruth 3E 121
(not continuous)
Fishescoates Gdns. G73: Ruth 2F 121
Fitness First Health Club 3F 103
Fitzalan Dr. PA3: Pais 5C 78
Fitzalan Rd. PA4: Renf 2C 78
Fitzroy La. G3: Glas 3C 82
Fitzroy Pl. *G3: Glas 3C 82*
(off Royal Cres.)
Flakefield G74: E Kil 1D 148
Flanders St. G81: Hard 6E 23
Flaxford Gro. ML1: Moth 5F 127
Flaxmill Av. ML2: Wis 5D 144
Flax Rd. G71: Udd 2E 125
Fleet Av. PA4: Renf 2G 79
Fleet St. G32: Glas 1B 106
Fleming Av. G69: Chry 1A 68
G81: Clyd 1F 59
Fleming Ct. G81: Clyd 5D 42
ML1: Moth 5A 144
ML3: Ham 5C 140
ML8: Carl 4E 165
Fleming Pl. G75: E Kil 3G 149
Fleming Rd. G67: Cumb 3H 35
ML4: Bell 1D 126
PA6: Hous 1A 74
PA7: B'ton 4H 39
Fleming St. G31: Glas 5D 84
PA3: Pais 4A 78
FLEMINGTON
Cambuslang 3E 123
Motherwell 5B 144
Flemington Ind. Est.
G72: Flem 3E 123
Flemington Ind. Pk.
ML1: Moth 4C 144
Flemington Rd. G72: Camb 2E 139
Flemington St. G21: Glas 6A 64
ML1: Moth 4A 144
Fleming Way ML3: Ham 5B 140
Flenders Av. G76: Clar 3A 134
Flenders Rd. G76: Clar 3A 134
Fleurs Av. G41: Glas 1H 101
Fleurs Rd. G41: Glas 1H 101
Flinders Pl. G75: E Kil 3D 148
Flloyd St. ML5: Coat 4B 90
Floorsburn Cres. PA5: John 3E 95
Floors St. PA5: John 3E 95
Floors St. Ind. Est. PA5: John 3F 95
Flora Gdns. G64: B'rig 5E 49
Florence Dr. G46: Giff 5A 118
Florence Gdns. G73: Ruth 3E 121
Florence St. *G5: Glas 1G 103*
(off Caledonia Rd.)
G5: Glas 6G 83
(Ballater St.)
Florida Av. G42: Glas 5F 103
Florida Cres. G42: Glas 5F 103
Florida Dr. G42: Glas 5E 103
Florida Gdns. G69: Bail 6G 87
Florida Sq. G42: Glas 5F 103
Florida St. G42: Glas 5F 103
Florish Rd. PA8: Ersk 1H 57
Flowerdale Pl. G53: Glas 4B 116
Flowerhill Ind. Est.
ML6: Air 3B 92
Flowerhill St. ML6: Air 3B 92
FLUCHTER 3E 27
Fluchter Rd. G62: Balm, Bard 4E 27
G64: Balm 3F 27
Flures Av. PA8: Ersk 1A 58
Flures Cres. PA8: Ersk 1A 58
Flures Dr. PA8: Ersk 1A 58
Flures Pl. PA8: Ersk 1A 58
Fochabers Dr. G52: Glas 5C 80
Fogo Pl. G20: Glas 3B 62
Foinhaven Dr. G46: T'bnk 2F 117
Foinhaven Gdns. G46: T'bnk 1F 117
Foinhaven Way G46: T'bnk 1G 117
Footfield Rd. ML4: Bell 3B 126
Forbes Dr. G40: Glas 6B 84
ML1: Moth 5D 126
Forbes Pl. PA1: Pais 1A 98
Forbes St. G40: Glas 5B 84
Fordneuk St. G40: Glas 6C 84
Fordoun St. G34: Glas 3B 88
Ford Rd. G12: Glas 5B 62
G77: Newt M 6D 132
Fordyce Ct. G77: Newt M 5D 132
Fordyce St. G11: Glas 1H 81
Foremount Ter. La. *G12: Glas 6A 62*
(off Hyndland Rd.)
Fore Row ML3: Ham 5A 142
Forest Av. ML3: Ham 5H 153
Forestburn Ct. *ML6: Air 4F 91*
(off Monkscourt Av.)

Forest Dr. G71: Both 4E **125**
ML4: Bell 4E **127**
Forest Gdns. G66: Lenz 3A **50**
Foresthall Cres. G21: Glas 6C **64**
Foresthall Dr. G21: Glas 6C **64**
(not continuous)
Forest Kirk ML8: Carl 5H **165**
Forest La. ML3: Ham 5H **153**
Forestlea Rd. ML8: Carl 5G **165**
Forest Pk. ML2: Wis 4B **146**
Forest Pl. G66: Lenz 3A **50**
PA2: Pais 3A **98**
Fore St. G14: Glas 6C **60**
Forest Rd. G67: Cumb 5D **14**
ML9: Lark 3F **161**
Forest Vw. G67: Cumb 2C **36**
Forfar Av. G52: Glas 1B **100**
Forfar Cres. G64: B'rig 1E **65**
Forgan Gdns. G64: B'rig 1F **65**
Forge Dr. ML5: Coat 4B **90**
Forge Pl. G21: Glas 1D **84**
Forge Rd. ML6: Air 5F **93**
Forge Row ML6: C'bnk 2C **112**
Forge Shop. Cen., The G31: Glas 6E **85**
Forge St. G21: Glas 1D **84**
Forge, The G46: Giff 4B **118**
FORGEWOOD **6F 127**
Forgewood Path ML6: Air 5F **93**
Forgewood Rd. ML1: Moth 5E **127**
Forglen St. G34: Glas 2H **87**
Formakin Estate Country Pk. **5B 38**
Formby Dr. G23: Glas 6B **46**
Forres Av. G46: Giff 4A **118**
Forres Cres. ML4: Bell 1C **126**
Forres Ga. G46: Giff 5B **118**
Forres Quad. ML2: Wis 4H **145**
Forres St. G23: Glas 6C **46**
G72: Blan 3A **140**
Forrest Dr. G61: Bear 4B **24**
Forrester Ct. G64: B'rig 1B **64**
Forrestfield Cres. G77: Newt M 4E **133**
Forrestfield Gdns. G77: Newt M 4D **132**
Forrestfield St. G21: Glas 2C **84**
Forrest Ga. G71: Tann 4F **109**
ML3: Ham 2F **153**
Forrest St. G40: Glas 6C **84**
G72: Blan 2D **140**
ML6: Air 3C **92**
(not continuous)
Forsyth St. ML6: Air 3B **92**
Fort Antonine Theatre **6B 48**
Forteviot Av. G69: Bail 6A **88**
Forteviot Pl. G69: Bail 6A **88**
Forth Av. PA2: Pais 4D **96**
Forth Ct. G75: E Kil 4A **148**
Forth Cres. G75: E Kil 3A **148**
Forth Gro. G75: E Kil 4A **148**
Forth Pl. ML9: Lark 5F **161**
PA5: John 5C **94**
Forth Rd. G61: Bear 5D **44**
G64: Torr 5D **28**
Forth St. G41: Glas 2D **102**
G81: Clyd 1E **59**
Forth Ter. ML3: Ham 3F **153**
Forth Wlk. *G67: Cumb 4H* ***35***
(in Cumbernauld Shop. Cen.)
Forth Way *G67: Cumb 4H* ***35***
(in Cumbernauld Shop. Cen.)
Forties Ct. G46: T'bnk 2F **117**
Forties Cres. G46: T'bnk 2G **117**
Forties Gdns. G46: T'bnk 2G **117**
Forties Rd. PA6: C'lee 3C **74**
Forties Way G46: T'bnk 2G **117**
Fortieth Av. G75: E Kil 6H **149**
Fortingale Av. G12: Glas 3A **62**
Fortingall Pl. G12: Glas 3A **62**
Fortingall Rd. G72: Blan 4D **140**
Fortrose St. G11: Glas 1H **81**
Fort St. ML1: Moth 1D **142**
Forum Pl. ML1: Moth 6E **127**
Fossil Gro. G66: Kirk 4G **31**
Fossil Ho. **6D 60**
Foswell Pl. G15: Glas 2H **43**
Fotheringay La. G41: Glas 3B **102**
Fotheringay Rd. G41: Glas 3B **102**
Foulis La. G13: Glas 3F **61**
Foulis St. G13: Glas 3F **61**
FOULSYKES **5C 146**
Foulsykes Rd. ML2: Wis 5C **146**
Foundry La. G78: Barr 5E **115**
Foundry Rd. ML1: Cle 5H **129**
Fountain Av. PA4: Inch 5F **57**
Fountain Cres. PA4: Inch 4F **57**
Fountain Dr. PA4: Inch 5G **57**
Fountainwell Av. G21: Glas 1H **83**
Fountainwell Dr. G21: Glas 1H **83**
Fountainwell Path G21: Glas 6H **63**
Fountainwell Pl. G21: Glas 1H **83**
Fountainwell Rd. G21: Glas 1H **83**
Fountainwell Sq. G21: Glas 1A **84**
Fountainwell Ter. G21: Glas 1A **84**
Fourth Av. G33: Mille 4B **66**
G66: Auch 6D **50**
G82: Dumb 3C **18**
PA4: Renf 1E **79**
Fourth Gdns. G41: Glas 1G **101**
Fourth Rd. G72: Blan 4C **140**
Fourth St. G71: Tann 4D **108**
Four Windings PA6: Hous 1B **74**
Fowlis Dr. G77: Newt M 3C **132**
FOXBAR **4D 96**
Foxbar Cres. PA2: Pais 6C **96**
Foxbar Dr. G13: Glas 3B **60**
PA2: Pais 6C **96**
Foxbar Rd. PA2: Pais 6B **96**
PA5: Eld 6B **96**
Foxes Gro. G66: Lenz 2E **51**
Foxglove Pl. G53: Glas 4B **116**
Fox Gro. ML1: Moth 2D **142**
Foxhills Pl. G23: Glas 6C **46**
FOXLEY **3C 106**
Foxley St. G32: Carm 4C **106**
Fox St. G1: Glas 5F **83**
Foyers Ter. G21: Glas 5C **64**
Foyes Ct. G13: Glas 3B **60**
Francis St. G5: Glas 1E **103**
Franconia Sq. G81: Clyd 6D **42**
Frankfield Rd. G33: Step 4E **67**
Frankfield St. G33: Glas 1F **85**
Frankfort St. G41: Glas 4C **102**
Franklin Pl. G75: E Kil 2D **148**
Franklin St. G40: Glas 2B **104**
Fraser Av. G73: Ruth 5E **105**
G77: Newt M 3E **133**
G82: Dumb 1C **18**
PA5: John 3G **95**
PA7: B'ton 3H **39**
Fraser Ct. ML3: Ham 1F **153**
ML6: Air 3E ***93***
(off Katherine St.)
Fraser Cres. ML3: Ham 1F **153**
Fraser Gdns. G66: Kirk 5B **30**
Fraser St. G72: Camb 1G **121**
ML1: Cle 5H **129**
Frazer River Twr. G75: E Kil 3F **149**
Frazer St. G40: Glas 6C **84**
Frederick St. ML5: Coat 3A **90**
FREELAND **2F 57**
Freeland Brae *G75: E Kil 3H* ***149***
(off Telford Rd.)
Freeland Ct. G53: Glas 1C **116**
Freeland Cres. G53: Glas 1B **116**
Freeland Dr. G53: Glas 1B **116**
PA11: Bri W 2F **73**
PA4: Inch 3G **57**
Freeland La. *G75: E Kil 3H* ***149***
(off Telford Rd.)
Freeland Pl. G66: Kirk 5D **30**
Freeland Rd. PA8: Ersk 2F **57**
Freelands Ct. G60: Old K 3G **41**
Freelands Cres. G60: Old K 2G **41**
Freelands Pl. G60: Old K 3G **41**
Freelands Rd. G60: Old K 2G **41**
Freesia Ct. ML1: Moth 4G **143**
French St. G40: Glas 2B **104**
G81: Clyd 4A **42**
ML2: Wis 6H **145**
PA4: Renf 1D **78**
Freuchie St. G34: Glas 4H **87**
Frew St. ML6: Air 3A **92**
Friar Av. G64: B'rig 4D **48**
Friarscourt Av. G13: Glas 6D **44**
Friarscourt La. *G13: Glas 1D* ***60***
(off Knightscliffe Av.)
Friarscourt Rd. G69: Chry 6H **51**
Friars Cft. G66: Kirk 5E **31**
Friars Pl. G13: Glas 1D **60**
Friars Way ML6: Air 1C **112**
Friarton Rd. G43: Glas 2D **118**
Friendship Way PA4: Renf 2F **79**
Frood St. ML1: Moth 6E **127**
Fruin Av. G77: Newt M 3E **133**
Fruin Dr. ML2: Wis 6C **146**
Fruin Ho. G82: Dumb 1H **17**
Fruin Pl. G22: Glas 5G **63**
Fruin Ri. ML3: Ham 1C **152**
Fruin Rd. G15: Glas 6H **43**
Fruin St. G22: Glas 5G **63**
Fulbar Av. PA4: Renf 5E **59**
Fulbar Ct. PA4: Renf 5F **59**
Fulbar Cres. PA2: Pais 3D **96**
Fulbar Gdns. PA2: Pais 3D **96**
Fulbar La. PA4: Renf 5F **59**
Fulbar Path G51: Glas 4C **80**
Fulbar Rd. G51: Glas 4C **80**
PA2: Pais 3D **96**
Fulbar St. PA4: Renf 5F **59**
FULLARTON **3A 106**
Fullarton Av. G32: Glas 3A **106**
Fullarton Dr. G32: Glas 4A **106**
Fullarton La. G32: Glas 3A **106**
Fullarton Pl. ML5: Coat 2H **109**
Fullarton Rd. G32: Glas 5H **105**
G68: Cumb 6G **13**
FULLARTON ROAD INTERCHANGE
4A 106
Fullarton St. ML5: Coat 2A **110**
Fullers Ga. G81: Faif 6E **23**
Fullerton St. PA3: Pais 4H **77**
Fullerton Ter. PA3: Pais 4A **78**
Fullwood Ind. Est. ML3: Ham 5F **141**
Fulmar Ct. G64: B'rig 1B **64**
Fulmar Pk. G74: E Kil 6F **137**
Fulmar Pl. PA5: John 6C **94**
Fulton Cres. PA10: Kilb 2A **94**
Fulton Dr. PA6: C'lee 3E **75**
Fulton Gdns. PA6: C'lee 3E **75**
Fulton Rd. G62: Miln 4H **25**
Fulton St. G13: Glas 2D **60**
Fulwood Av. G13: Glas 2H **59**
PA3: Lin 5H **75**
Fulwood Pl. G13: Glas 2H **59**
Furlongs, The ML3: Ham 4A **142**
Fyneart St. ML2: Wis 5C **146**
Fyne Av. ML4: Bell 6A **110**
Fyne Ct. ML3: Ham 2E **153**
Fyne Cres. ML9: Lark 6H **155**
Fyne Way *ML1: Holy 2A* ***128***
(off Howden Pl.)
Fynloch Pl. G81: Dun 6A **22**
Fyvie Av. G43: Glas 2G **117**
Fyvie Cres. ML6: Air 4F **93**

G

Gadie Av. PA4: Renf 1G **79**
Gadie St. G33: Glas 3F **85**
Gadloch Av. G66: Auch 5D **50**
Gadloch Gdns. G66: Lenz 4D **50**
Gadloch St. G22: Glas 3G **63**
Gadloch Vw. G66: Auch 5D **50**
Gadsburn Ct. G21: Glas 3E **65**
Gadshill St. G21: Glas 2B **84**
Gailes Pk. G71: Both 5D **124**
Gailes Rd. G68: Cumb 6H **13**
Gailes St. G40: Glas 1D **104**
Gain & Shankburn Rd. G67: Cumb
6D **54**
Gainburn Ct. G67: Cumb 1B **54**
Gainburn Cres. G67: Cumb 2B **54**
Gainburn Gdns. G67: Cumb 2B **54**

Gainburn Pl. G67: Cumb. 1B 54
Gainburn Vw. G67: Cumb 1C 54
Gain Rd. G67: Cumb. 6B 54
  ML5: Glenb 6B 54
Gainside Rd. ML5: Glenb 3G 69
Gairbraid Av. G20: Glas 3A 62
Gairbraid Ct. G20: Glas. 3A 62
Gairbraid Pl. G20: Glas. 3B 62
Gairbraid Ter. G69: Barg 6E 89
Gair Cres. ML2: Wis 2H 157
  ML8: Carl 2G 165
Gairloch Gdns. G66: Kirk 4H 31
Gair Rd. ML8: Carl 1G 165
Gala Av. PA4: Renf 1G 79
Gala Cres. ML2: Wis 4G 145
Gala St. G33: Glas 1G 85
Galbraith Cres. ML3: Law 5E 159
Galbraith Dr. G51: Glas 3D 80
  G62: Miln 5F 25
Galdenoch St. G33: Glas. 1B 86
Gallacher Av. PA2: Pais 4E 97
Gallacher Ct. ML1: Moth 6B 144
  PA1: Pais 6G 77
Gallan Av. G23: Glas 6C 46
Gallery of Modern Art 5E 5
Galloway Av. ML3: Ham 4G 153
Galloway Dr. G73: Ruth 4D 120
Galloway Rd. G74: E Kil 6C 138
  ML6: Air 6H 91
Galloway St. G21: Glas 3B 64
GALLOWFLAT. 6E 105
Gallowflat St. G73: Ruth. 5D 104
GALLOWGATE 6C 84
Gallowgate G1: Glas. 5H 83
GALLOWHILL 4D 78
Gallowhill ML9: Lark 3E 161
Gallowhill Av. G66: Lenz 1C 50
Gallowhill Ct. PA3: Pais 3C 78
Gallowhill Gro. G66: Kirk 6C 30
Gallowhill Rd. G66: Kirk, Lenz . . . 1C 50
  G76: Crmck. 1H 135
  PA3: Pais 5B 78
Galston Av. G77: Newt M 4G 133
Galston Ct. ML3: Ham 4A 154
Galston St. G53: Glas 1H 115
Galt Pl. G75: E Kil 4F 149
Gamrie Dr. G53: Glas 6A 100
Gamrie Gdns. G53: Glas 6A 100
Gamrie Rd. G53: Glas. 5A 100
Gannochy Dr. G64: B'rig 6E 49
Gantock Cres. G33: Glas. 4B 86
GARDENHALL 4A 148
Gardenhall G75: E Kil 3A 148
Gardenhall Ct. G75: E Kil 3A 148
Gardenside ML4: Bell 3C 126
Gardenside Av. G32: Carm 5B 106
  G71: Udd 1C 124
Gardenside Cres. G32: Carm 5B 106
Gardenside Gro. G32: Carm 5B 106
Gardenside Pl. G32: Carm 5B 106
Gardenside Rd. ML3: Ham 1H 153
Gardenside St. G71: Udd 1C 124
Garden Sq. Wlk. ML6: Air 3F 91
Gdn. Veteran's Cotts. PA7: B'ton . . 2D 40
Gardner Gro. G71: Tann 5E 109
Gardner St. G11: Glas 1H 81
Gardyne St. G34: Glas 2G 87
Gareloch Av. ML6: Air 1H 91
  PA2: Pais 3E 97
Garfield Av. ML4: Bell 2E 127
Garfield Dr. ML4: Bell 3E 127
Garfield St. G31: Glas 5C 84
Garforth Rd. G69: Bail 1F 107
Gargrave Av. G69: Bail 1F 107
Garion Dr. G13: Glas. 4B 60
Garlieston Rd. G33: Glas 5F 87
Garmouth Ct. G51: Glas 3G 81
Garmouth Gdns. G51: Glas 3G 81
Garmouth St. G51: Glas 3F 81
GARNETHILL 2E 83 (2C 4)
Garnethill St. G3: Glas . . . 2E 83 (2B 4)
Garnet St. G3: Glas 2E 83 (3A 4)
Garngaber Av. G66: Lenz 2D 50
Garngaber Ct. G66: Lenz. 2E 51

Garngrew Rd. FK4: Hag. 1F 15
Garnhall Farm Rd. G68: Cumb . . . 3E 15
Garnie Av. PA8: Ersk 6H 41
Garnie Cres. PA8: Ersk. 6H 41
Garnieland Rd. PA8: Ersk. 6H 41
Garnie La. PA8: Ersk 1H 57
Garnie Oval PA8: Ersk 6H 41
Garnie Pl. PA8: Ersk. 6H 41
GARNKIRK 3G 67
Garnkirk La. G33: Step 4E 67
Garnock Pl. G74: E Kil 2B 150
Garnock St. G21: Glas 2B 84
GARNQUEEN 4H 69
Garrell Av. G65: Kils 2H 11
Garrell Gro. G65: Kils 1H 11
Garrell Pl. G65: Kils 3G 11
Garrell Rd. G65: Kils 4G 11
Garrell Way G65: Kils 3G 11
  G67: Cumb 3G 35
Garrioch Cres. G20: Glas 4B 62
Garrioch Dr. G20: Glas 4B 62
Garrioch Ga. G20: Glas 4B 62
Garriochmill Rd. G20: Glas. 5B 62
                    (not continuous)
Garrioch Quad. G20: Glas. 4B 62
Garrioch Rd. G20: Glas. 5B 62
Garrion Bus. Pk. ML2: Wis. 3H 157
Garrion Pl. ML9: Ashg 4B 162
Garrion St. ML2: Over. 5A 158
Garrochmill Way G20: Glas 6D 62
                    (off Henderson St.)
GARROWHILL 6G 87
Garrowhill Dr. G69: Bail 6F 87
Garrowhill Station (Rail) 6F 87
Garry Av. G61: Bear 5H 45
Garry Dr. PA2: Pais 3E 97
Garry St. G44: Glas. 6E 103
Garscadden Rd. G15: Glas 4H 43
Garscadden Rd. Sth. G13: Glas . . . 1A 60
  G15: Glas 1H 59
                    (off Gt. Western Rd.)
Garscadden Station (Rail) 3A 60
Garscadden Vw. G81: Clyd 4F 43
Garscube Rd. G20: Glas 6E 63
  G4: Glas 2F 83 (1C 4)
Garshake Av. G82: Dumb 3H 17
Garshake Rd. G82: Dumb 3H 17
Garshake Ter. G82: Dumb. 1C 18
Gartartan Rd. PA1: Pais 6H 79
Gartcarron Hill G68: Cumb 2E 35
Gartcloss Rd. ML5: Coat 1G 89
Gartconnell Dr. G61: Bear. 1E 45
Gartconnell Gdns. G61: Bear. 1E 45
Gartconnell Rd. G61: Bear 1E 45
Gartconner Av. G66: Kirk 5H 31
GARTCOSH 4D 68
Gartcosh Rd. G69: Barg 5D 88
                    (Coatbridge Rd.)
  G69: Barg 3E 89
                    (Cuilhill Rd.)
  G69: G'csh 1E 89
Gartcosh Wlk. ML4: Bell 2B 126
Gartcraig Path G33: Glas 2H 85
                    (off Gartcraig Rd.)
Gartcraig Pl. G33: Glas 2H 85
Gartferry Av. G69: Mood 5D 52
Gartferry Rd. G68: Mollin 5C 52
  G69: Chry 5B 52
  G69: Mood 5C 52
Gartferry St. G21: Glas 5C 64
Gartfield St. ML6: Air 5B 92
Gartgill Rd. ML5: Coat 1A 90
GARTHAMLOCK 1E 87
Garthamlock Rd. G33: Glas. 2E 87
Garthland Dr. G31: Glas 4C 84
Garthland La. PA1: Pais 6B 78
Garth St. G1: Glas 4G 83 (6F 5)
GARTLEA 5B 92
Gartlea Av. ML6: Air 4A 92
Gartlea Gdns. ML6: Air 4B 92
Gartleahill ML6: Air 5A 92
Gartlea Rd. ML6: Air 4A 92
Gartliston Rd. ML5: Coat 6B 70
Gartliston Ter. G69: Barg 6E 89

Gartloch Rd. G33: G'csh, Glas. 2C 86
  G33: Glas 1H 85
  G69: G'csh 6H 67
Gartly St. G44: Glas. 3D 118
Gartmore Gdns. G71: Tann 5C 108
Gartmore La. G69: Mood 5E 53
Gartmore Rd. PA1: Pais 1D 98
Gartmore Ter. G72: Camb 4G 121
GARTNESS 6E 93
Gartness Dr. ML6: Gart. 6E 93
Gartness Rd. ML6: Air 2G 113
Gartocher Dr. G32: Glas 6C 86
Gartocher Rd. G32: Glas. 6C 86
Gartocher Ter. G32: Glas 6C 86
Gartons Rd. G21: Glas 4E 65
GARTSHERRIE 2B 90
Gartsherrie Av. ML5: Glenb 4B 70
Gartsherrie Ind. Est. ML5: Coat . . . 2B 90
Gartsherrie Rd. ML5: Coat 3A 90
Gartshore Cres. G65: Twe. 3D 32
Gartshore Gdns. G68: Cumb 4A 34
Garturk St. G42: Glas 3F 103
  ML5: Coat. 1D 110
Garvald Ct. G40: Glas 2D 104
Garvald St. G40: Glas 2D 104
Garve Av. G44: Glas 3E 119
Garvel Cres. G33: Glas 5E 87
Garvel Pl. G62: Miln. 3D 24
Garvel Rd. G33: Glas 5E 87
  G62: Miln 3D 24
Garvin Lea ML4: Bell 5C 110
Garvock Dr. G43: Glas 2H 117
Garwhitter Dr. G62: Miln 3H 25
Gascoyne G75: E Kil 4E 149
Gaskin Path G33: Step 4E 67
Gask Pl. G13: Glas 1H 59
Gas St. PA5: John 2G 95
Gasworks Rd. ML8: Carl 2C 164
Gatehouse St. G32: Glas. 6B 86
GATESIDE 6B 114
Gateside Av. G65: Kils. 3F 11
  G72: Camb 2D 122
Gateside Cres. G78: Barr 6C 114
  ML6: Air 3A 92
Gateside Pk. G65: Kils 2F 11
Gateside Pl. PA10: Kilb 2A 94
Gateside Rd. G78: Barr. 6B 114
  ML2: Wis 5E 145
Gateside St. G31: Glas 5D 84
  ML3: Ham 1A 154
Gateway, The G74: E Kil 5A 138
Gaughan Quad. ML1: Moth 4F 143
Gauldry Av. G52: Glas. 2C 100
Gauze St. PA1: Pais 6A 78
Gavell Rd. G65: Queen 4D 10
Gavinburn Gdns. G60: Old K 6D 20
Gavinburn Pl. G60: Old K 6E 21
Gavinburn St. G60: Old K 6E 21
Gavin's Mill Rd. G62: Miln 4G 25
Gavins Rd. G81: Hard. 2D 42
Gavin St. ML1: Moth 4G 143
Gavinton St. G44: Glas. 2D 118
Gayne Dr. ML5: Glenb 3G 69
Gean Ct. G67: Cumb 1F 37
Gear Ter. G40: Glas 3D 104
Geary St. G23: Glas 6B 46
Geddes Hill G74: E Kil 5B 138
Geddes Rd. G21: Glas 2E 65
Geelong Gdns. G66: Len 2F 7
Geils Av. G82: Dumb 2C 18
Geils Quad. G82: Dumb 2C 18
Gelston St. G32: Glas 1B 106
Gemini Gro. ML1: Holy. 2B 128
Gemmel Pl. G77: Newt M 5B 132
Generals Ga. G71: Udd 1C 124
Gentle Row G81: Dun 1B 42
George Av. G81: Clyd 4E 43
George V Bri. G5: Glas 5H 83
George Cl. ML2: Wis 1E 157
George Ct. ML3: Ham 4E 141
  PA1: Pais 1H 97
George Cres. G81: Clyd 4E 43
George Gray St. G73: Ruth 5E 105
George La. PA1: Pais 1A 98

George Mann Ter. G73: Ruth 3C **120**
George Pl. PA1: Pais 1A **98**
George Reith Av. G12: Glas 4F **61**
George Sq. G2: Glas 4G **83** (5E **5**)
George St. G1: Glas 4G **83** (5F **5**)
G69: Bail 1H **107**
G78: Barr 4D **114**
ML1: Moth 5G **143**
ML1: New S 3B **128**
ML3: Ham 4E **141**
ML4: Bell 2B **126**
ML6: Air 4G **91**
ML6: Chap 2D **112**
PA1: Pais 1G **97**
(Broomlands St.)
PA1: Pais 1H **97**
(George Ct.)
George St. PA5: John 2F **95**
George Way *ML9: Lark 1F **161***
(off Duncan Graham St.)
Gerard Pl. ML4: Bell 6D **110**
GERMISTON **1D 84**
Gertrude Pl. G78: Barr 5C **114**
Ghillies La. ML1: Moth 6E **127**
Gibbon Cres. G74: E Kil 6C **138**
Gibb St. ML1: Cle 6H **129**
ML6: Chap 2D **112**
Gibson Av. G82: Dumb 3H **17**
Gibson Cres. PA5: John 3E **95**
Gibson Hgts. *G4: Glas 4A **84***
(off Drygate)
Gibson Quad. ML1: Moth 6E **127**
Gibson Rd. PA4: Renf 3D **78**
Gibson St. G12: Glas 1B **82**
G40: Glas 5A **84**
G82: Dumb 3G **17**
GIFFNOCK **4A 118**
Giffnock Pk. Av. G46: Giff 3A **118**
Giffnock Station (Rail) **4A 118**
Giffnock Tennis Squash & Hockey Club **6A 118**
Gifford Dr. G52: Glas 6A **80**
Gifford Wynd PA2: Pais 3D **96**
Gigha Gdns. ML8: Carl 5G **165**
Gigha Quad. ML2: Wis 2E **157**
Gilbank La. *ML9: Lark 3G **161***
(off Shawrigg Rd.)
Gilbertfield Path G33: Glas 1B **86**
Gilbertfield Pl. G33: Glas 1B **86**
Gilbertfield Rd. G72: Camb, Flem 4C **122**
Gilbertfield St. G33: Glas 1B **86**
Gilbert St. G3: Glas 3A **82**
Gilchrist Ct. *PA5: John 4E **95***
(off Tannahill Cres.)
Gilchrist Gdns. G71: Both 6F **125**
Gilchrist St. ML5: Coat 3D **90**
Gilchrist Way ML2: Wis 2A **158**
Gilderdale G74: E Kil 1E **149**
Gilfillan Pl. ML2: Over 4A **158**
Gilfillan Way PA2: Pais 5C **96**
Gilhill St. G20: Glas 2B **62**
Gillbank Av. ML8: Carl 3D **164**
Gillburn St. ML2: Over 5A **158**
Gillies Cres. G74: E Kil 4D **138**
Gillies La. G69: Bail 1A **108**
Gill Rd. ML2: Over 4A **158**
(not continuous)
Gilmartin Rd. PA3: Lin 5E **75**
Gilmerton St. G32: Glas 1A **106**
Gilmour Av. G74: T'hall 6F **135**
G81: Hard 2D **42**
Gilmour Cres. G73: Ruth 5B **104**
Gilmour Dr. ML3: Ham 1D **152**
Gilmour Pl. G5: Glas 1G **103**
ML4: Bell 2A **126**
ML5: Coat 3B **90**
Gilmour St. G81: Clyd 3E **43**
PA1: Pais 6A **78**
Gilmourton Cres. G77: Newt M 6D **132**
GILSHOCHILL **2B 62**
Gilshochill Station (Rail) **2C 62**
Gimmerscroft Cres. ML6: Air 5F **93**
Girthon St. G32: Glas 1C **106**
Girvan Cres. ML6: Chap 4D **112**
Girvan St. G33: Glas 2F **85**
Glade, The ML9: Lark 3F **161**
Gladney Av. G13: Glas 1G **59**
Gladsmuir Rd. G52: Glas 5A **80**
GLADSTONE **6H 39**
Gladstone Av. G78: Barr 5D **114**
PA5: John 6D **94**
Gladstone Ct. ML3: Ham 4E **141**
Gladstone St. G4: Glas 1E **83** (1A **4**)
G81: Clyd 5B **42**
ML4: Bell 2D **126**
Glaive Rd. G13: Glas 6D **44**
Glamis Av. G77: Newt M 4F **133**
ML8: Carl 3F **165**
PA5: Eld 4H **95**
Glamis Ct. ML1: Carf 5C **128**
Glamis Dr. G74: E Kil 6H **137**
Glamis Gdns. G64: B'rig 3D **48**
Glamis Rd. G31: Glas 1F **105**
Glanderston Av. G77: Newt M 3B **132**
Glanderston Ct. G13: Glas 1A **60**
Glanderston Dr. G13: Glas 2A **60**
Glanderston Ga. G77: Newt M 3B **132**
Glanderston Rd.
G78: Neil, Newt M 3H **131**
Glandston Av. G78: Barr 5G **115**
GLASGOW **4G 83 (5F 5)**
Glasgow Academical Athletic Ground **3D 60**
Glasgow Airport PA3: Glas A 1H **77**
GLASGOW AIRPORT INTERCHANGE **3H 77**
Glasgow & Edinburgh Rd.
G69: Bail 6B **88**
G69: Barg 1D **108**
ML1: Holy 4A **112**
ML1: N'hse 5E **113**
ML4: Bell 4G **111**
ML5: Coat 1D **108**
Glasgow Botanic Gardens **5B 62**
Glasgow Bri. G5: Glas 5F **83**
Glasgow Bri. Cotts. *G66: Kirk 6G **29***
(off Kirkintilloch Rd.)
Glasgow Crematorium
G23: Glas 1D **62**
Glasgow Film Theatre **3F 83 (3C 4)**
Glasgow Fish Mkt. G21: Glas 2D **84**
Glasgow Fruit Mkt. G21: Glas 2C **84**
Glasgow Golf Course **4A 46**
Glasgow Green Football Cen. **1A 104**
Glasgow Hawks R.U.F.C. **3E 61**
Glasgow Necropolis G31: Glas 4A **84**
Glasgow Rd. G62: Miln 5G **25**
G65: Kils 3E **11**
G66: Kirk 6H **29**
G67: Cumb 5E **35**
(Condorrat Ring Rd.)
G67: Cumb 1B **36**
(Old Glasgow Rd.)
G69: Bail 1F **107**
G69: Barg, Coat 5F **89**
G71: Tann, Udd 4A **108**
G72: Blan 6H **123**
G72: Camb 6G **105**
(Duke's Rd.)
G72: Camb 6H **121**
(E. Kilbride Rd.)
G73: Ruth 5H **121**
(E. Kilbride Rd.)
G73: Ruth 3B **104**
(Shawfield Rd.)
G74: Ners 2A **138**
G76: Water 6B **134**
G78: Barr 3F **115**
G81: Clyd 1D **58**
G81: Hard 1D **42**
G82: Dumb, Milt 3E **17**
ML2: Wis 6D **144**
ML3: Ham 4E **141**
ML5: Barg, Coat 5F **89**
PA1: Pais 6B **78**
PA4: Renf 6G **59**
Glasgow Rowing Club **6A 84**
Glasgow Royal Concert Hall **3G 83 (3E 5)**
Glasgow School of Art **3E 83 (3B 4)**
Glasgow Science Cen. **4B 82**
Glasgow's Grand Ole Opry **5C 82**
Glasgow Ski Cen. **1G 101**
Glasgow St. G12: Glas 6C **62**
Glasgow Zoo **3A 108**
Glassel Rd. G34: Glas 2B **88**
Glasserton Pl. G43: Glas 2D **118**
Glasserton Rd. G43: Glas 2D **118**
Glassford St. G1: Glas 4G **83** (6F **5**)
G62: Miln 3H **25**
ML1: Moth 5A **144**
Glassford Twr. *ML1: Moth 5A **144***
(off Burnside Ct.)
Glaudhall Av. G69: G'csh 2C **68**
Glazert Dr. G66: Len 1C **6**
Glazert Mdw. G66: Len 4G **7**
Glazert Pk. Dr. G66: Len 4G **7**
Glazert Pl. G66: Milt C 6B **8**
Glebe Av. G71: Both 5F **125**
G76: Crmck 2H **135**
ML5: Coat 1H **109**
Glebe Ct. G4: Glas 3H **83** (3H **5**)
Glebe Cres. G74: E Kil 2H **149**
ML3: Ham 1G **153**
ML6: Air 3D **92**
Glebe Gdns. PA6: Hous 1B **74**
Glebe Hollow G71: Both 5F **125**
Glebe La. G77: Newt M 5D **132**
Glebe Pk. G82: Dumb 2H **17**
Glebe Pl. G72: Camb 2B **122**
G73: Ruth 5B **104**
Glebe Rd. G77: Newt M 5D **132**
Glebe St. G4: Glas 2H **83** (2H **5**)
(Kennedy St.)
G4: Glas 3A **84** (3H **5**)
(McAslin St., not continuous)
G74: E Kil 1H **149**
ML3: Ham 1G **153**
ML4: Bell 2B **126**
PA4: Renf 6F **59**
Glebe, The G71: Both 5F **125**
Glebe Wynd G71: Both 5F **125**
Gleddoch Rd. G52: Glas 5G **79**
Gledstane Rd. PA7: B'ton 5H **39**
Glenacre Cres. G71: Tann 5C **108**
Glenacre Dr. G45: Glas 4H **119**
ML6: Air 5D **92**
Glenacre Gro. G45: Glas 3A **120**
Glenacre Quad. G45: Glas 4H **119**
Glenacre Rd. G67: Cumb 5H **35**
Glenacre St. G45: Glas 4H **119**
Glenacre Ter. G45: Glas 4H **119**
Glenafeoch Rd. ML8: Carl 4F **165**
Glen Affric G74: E Kil 2B **150**
Glen Affric Av. G53: Glas 3D **116**
Glen Affric Way *ML6: Chap 4D **112***
(off Glen Avon Dr.)
Glenafton Vw. ML3: Ham 3F **153**
Glen Alby Pl. G53: Glas 3C **116**
Glenallan Ter. ML1: Moth 6F **127**
Glenallan Way PA2: Pais 6B **96**
Glen Almond G74: E Kil 1D **150**
Glenalmond Rd. G73: Ruth 4F **121**
Glenalmond St. G32: Glas 1A **106**
Glenalva Ct. G65: Kils 2H **11**
Glenapp Av. PA2: Pais 4D **98**
Glenapp Pl. G69: Mood 4D **52**
Glenapp Rd. PA2: Pais 4D **98**
Glenapp St. G41: Glas 2D **102**
Glenarklet Dr. PA2: Pais 4C **98**
Glen Arroch G74: E Kil 2B **150**
Glenartney PA6: Hous 1A **74**
Glenartney Rd. G69: Chry 6A **52**
Glenashdale Way PA2: Pais 4C **98**
Glen Av. G32: Glas 5B **86**
G69: Mood 5D **52**
G78: Neil 2E **131**
ML9: Lark 5D **160**
Glenavon Ct. ML3: Ham 2F **153**
Glen Avon Dr. ML6: Chap 4D **112**
Glenavon Rd. G20: Glas 2B **62**

Glenbank Av.—Glenmavis Ct.

Glenbank Av. G66: Lenz 3D **50**
Glenbank Dr. G46: T'bnk 5F **117**
Glenbank Rd. G66: Lenz 3D **50**
Glenbarr St. G21: Glas 2B **84**
Glen Bervie G74: E Kil 1B **150**
Glenbervie Cres. G68: Cumb 1H **35**
Glenbervie Pl. G23: Glas 6B **46**
G77: Newt M 4A **132**
GLENBOIG **3A 70**
Glenboig Farm Rd. ML5: Glenb 3A **70**
Glenboig New Rd. ML5: Glenb 3B **70**
Glenboig Rd. G69: G'csh 1F **69**
Glen Brae PA11: Bri W 3E **73**
Glenbrittle Dr. PA2: Pais 4C **98**
Glenbrittle Way PA2: Pais 4C **98**
Glenbuck Av. G33: Glas 3H **65**
Glenbuck Dr. G33: Glas 3H **65**
GLENBURN **5H 97**
Glenburn Av. G69: Bail 6A **88**
G69: Mood 5D **52**
G72: Camb 2F **121**
ML1: N'hill 3C **128**
Glenburn Ct. *G66: Kirk* *5D* ***30***
(off Willowbank Gdns.)
G74: E Kil 6C **136**
Glenburn Cres. G66: Milt C 6C **8**
G71: View 5G **109**
PA2: Pais 5H **97**
Glenburn Gdns. G64: B'rig 5B **48**
ML5: Glenb 3G **69**
Glenburnie Pl. G34: Glas 4F **87**
Glenburn La. G20: Glas 2C **62**
Glenburn Rd. G46: Giff 6H **117**
G61: Bear 2D **44**
G74: E Kil 6C **136**
ML3: Ham 6F **141**
PA2: Pais 5F **97**
Glenburn St. G20: Glas 2C **62**
Glenburn Ter. ML1: Carf 6C **128**
ML8: Carl 5E **165**
Glenburn Wlk. G69: Bail 6A **88**
Glenburn Way G74: E Kil 6B **136**
Glenburn Wynd *ML9: Lark* *1F* ***161***
(off Muirshot Rd.)
Glencairn Av. ML2: Wis 5D **144**
Glencairn Ct. *PA3: Pais* *3D* ***78***
(off Montgomery Rd.)
Glencairn Dr. G41: Glas 3B **102**
G69: Mood 5C **52**
G73: Ruth 5B **104**
Glencairn Gdns. G41: Glas 3C **102**
G72: Camb 2D **122**
Glencairn La. G41: Glas 3C **102**
Glencairn Path *G32: Glas* *5C* ***86***
(off Mansionhouse Dr.)
Glencairn Rd. G67: Cumb 3C **36**
G82: Dumb 4C **16**
PA3: Pais 4C **78**
Glencairn St. G66: Kirk 6D **30**
ML1: Moth 4G **143**
Glencairn Twr. ML1: Moth 4G **143**
Glen Calder Ct. ML6: Air 6D **92**
Glencalder Cres. ML4: Bell 4D **126**
Glen Cally G74: E Kil 1B **150**
Glencally Av. PA2: Pais 4D **98**
Glen Cannich G74: E Kil 2B **150**
Glen Carron G74: E Kil 2B **150**
Glencart Gro. PA10: John 4C **94**
Glencleland Rd. ML2: Wis 5D **144**
Glenclora Dr. PA2: Pais 4C **98**
Glencloy St. G20: Glas 2A **62**
Glen Clunie G74: E Kil 1D **150**
Glen Clunie Dr. G53: Glas 3C **116**
Glen Clunie Pl. G53: Glas 3C **116**
Glencoats Dr. PA3: Pais 6E **77**
Glencoe Dr. ML1: Holy 2A **128**
Glencoe Pl. G13: Glas 2F **61**
ML3: Ham 3F **153**
Glencoe Rd. G73: Ruth 4F **121**
ML8: Carl 5G **165**
Glencoe St. G13: Glas 2F **61**
Glen Cona Dr. G53: Glas 2C **116**
Glenconner Way G66: Kirk 4G **31**
Glencorse Rd. PA2: Pais 3G **97**
Glencorse St. G32: Glas 4G **85**
Glen Ct. ML1: Moth 5B **144**
ML5: Coat 6H **89**
Glen Cova G74: E Kil 1B **150**
Glen Cova Dr. G68: Cumb 1E **35**
Glencraig St. ML6: Air 4G **91**
Glen Creran Cres. G78: Neil 3C **130**
Glen Cres. G13: Glas 2G **59**
Glencroft Av. G71: Tann 5C **108**
Glencroft Rd. G44: Glas 2H **119**
Glencryan Rd. G67: Cumb 5A **36**
Glendale Av. ML6: Air 5D **92**
Glendale Cres. G64: B'rig 1E **65**
Glendale Dr. G64: B'rig 1E **65**
Glendale Gro. ML5: Coat 2A **110**
Glendale Pl. G31: Glas 5D **84**
G64: B'rig 2E **65**
Glendale St. G31: Glas 5D **84**
Glendaruel Av. G61: Bear 3H **45**
Glendaruel Rd. G73: Ruth 5G **121**
Glendarvel Gdns. G22: Glas 5H **63**
Glendee Gdns. PA4: Renf 1F **79**
Glendee Rd. PA4: Renf 1F **79**
Glen Dene Way G53: Glas 3C **116**
Glendentan Rd. PA11: Bri W 4E **73**
Glendermott Ct. ML8: Carl 2F **165**
Glen Derry G74: E Kil 6D **138**
Glen Dessary G74: E Kil 3B **150**
Glendeveron Way ML1: Carf 5A **128**
Glen Devon G74: E Kil 2D **150**
Glendevon Cotts. G81: Clyd 4B **42**
Glendevon Pl. G81: Clyd 4B **42**
ML3: Ham 3F **153**
Glendevon Sq. G33: Glas 1B **86**
Glen Dewar Pl. G53: Glas 3C **116**
Glendinning Rd. G13: Glas 6E **45**
Glendoick Pl. G77: Newt M 4A **132**
Glen Doll G74: E Kil 1B **150**
Glen Doll Rd. G78: Neil 4B **130**
Glendorch Av. ML2: Wis 2A **146**
Glendore St. G14: Glas 1E **81**
Glen Douglas Dr. G68: Cumb 1E **35**
Glendoune Rd. G76: Clar 4C **134**
Glendower Way PA2: Pais 5C **96**
Glen Dr. ML1: Holy 2B **128**
Glenduffhill Rd. G69: Bail 6F **87**
Glen Dye G74: E Kil 1B **150**
Glen Eagles G74: E Kil 2C **150**
Gleneagles Av. G68: Cumb 6A **14**
Gleneagles Ct. *G64: B'rig* *4C* ***48***
(off Hilton Rd.)
Gleneagles Dr. G64: B'rig 4C **48**
G77: Newt M 5H **133**
Gleneagles Gdns. G64: B'rig 4B **48**
Gleneagles Ga. G77: Newt M 5H **133**
Gleneagles La. Nth. G14: Glas 5C **60**
Gleneagles La. Sth. G14: Glas 6C **60**
Gleneagles Pk. G71: Both 5D **124**
Glenelg Cres. G66: Kirk 4G **31**
Glenelg Path ML5: Glenb 3G **69**
Glenelg Quad. G34: Glas 2B **88**
Glenelm Pl. ML4: Bell 1C **126**
Glen Esk G74: E Kil 1C **150**
Glen Esk Cres. G53: Glas 3C **116**
Glen Esk Dr. G53: Glas 3C **116**
Glen Esk Pl. G53: Glas 3C **116**
Glen Etive Pl. G73: Ruth 5G **121**
Glen Falloch G74: E Kil 2C **150**
Glen Falloch Cres. G78: Neil 4D **130**
Glen Farg G74: E Kil 2D **150**
Glenfarg Ct. ML3: Ham 3F **153**
Glenfarg Cres. G61: Bear 3H **45**
Glenfarg Rd. G73: Ruth 3D **120**
Glenfarg St. G20: Glas 1E **83**
Glenfarm Rd. ML1: N'hill 3E **129**
Glen Farrar G74: E Kil 2B **150**
Glen Feshie G74: E Kil 3B **150**
Glenfield Av. PA2: Pais 6H **97**
Glenfield Cres. PA2: Pais 6H **97**
Glenfield Gdns. PA2: Pais 6H **97**
Glenfield Grange PA2: Pais 1A **114**
Glenfield Gro. PA2: Pais 6H **97**
Glenfield Rd. G75: E Kil 5A **150**
PA2: Pais 6G **97**
Glen Finlet Cres. G78: Neil 4C **130**
Glenfinnan Dr. G20: Glas 3B **62**
G61: Bear 4H **45**
Glenfinnan Gro. ML4: Bell 3F **127**
Glenfinnan Pl. *G20: Glas* *3B* ***62***
(off Glenfinnan Rd.)
Glenfinnan Rd. G20: Glas 3B **62**
Glenfruin Cres. PA2: Pais 4D **98**
Glen Fruin Dr. ML9: Lark 4G **161**
Glen Fruin Pl. *ML6: Chap* *3D* ***112***
(off Glen Rannoch Dr.)
Glenfruin Rd. G72: Blan 1A **140**
Glen Fyne Rd. G68: Cumb 1D **34**
Glen Gairn G74: E Kil 1D **150**
Glen Gairn Cres. G78: Neil 3C **130**
Glen Gdns. PA5: Eld 2A **96**
Glen Garrell Pl. G65: Kils 2F **11**
Glengarriff Rd. ML4: Bell 5D **110**
Glen Garry G74: E Kil 3B **150**
Glengarry Dr. G52: Glas 6C **80**
Glengavel Cres. G33: Glas 3H **65**
Glengavel Gdns. ML2: Wis 2A **146**
Glengonnar St. ML9: Lark 5E **161**
GLENGOWAN **2C 160**
Glengowan Rd. PA11: Bri W 3E **73**
Glen Gro. G65: Kils 1H **11**
G75: E Kil 4F **149**
Glengyre St. G34: Glas 2A **88**
Glenhead Cres. G22: Glas 3G **63**
G81: Dun, Hard 6C **22**
Glenhead Dr. ML1: Moth 5F **143**
Glenhead Rd. G66: Lenz 3D **50**
G81: Clyd 2B **42**
Glenhead St. G22: Glas 3G **63**
Glenholme Av. PA2: Pais 4F **97**
Glenhove Rd. G67: Cumb 3A **36**
Gleniffer Av. G13: Glas 3A **60**
Gleniffer Braes Country Pk. **1A 114**
Gleniffer Ct. PA2: Pais 6F **97**
Gleniffer Cres. PA5: Eld 4A **96**
Gleniffer Dr. G78: Barr 2C **114**
Gleniffer Rd. PA2: Pais 6D **96**
PA4: Renf 3D **78**
Gleniffer Vw. G78: Neil 1D **130**
G81: Clyd 4F **43**
Glen Isla G74: E Kil 1C **150**
Glenisla Av. G69: Mood 3E **53**
Glen Isla Av. G78: Neil 4C **130**
Glenisla St. G31: Glas 2F **105**
Glenkirk Dr. G15: Glas 5B **44**
Glen Kyle Dr. G53: Glas 3C **116**
Glen La. PA3: Pais 6A **78**
Glen Lednock Dr. G68: Cumb 1D **34**
Glen Lee G74: E Kil 1C **150**
Glenlee St. ML3: Ham 4D **140**
Glen Lethnot G74: E Kil 1C **150**
Glen Livet Pl. G53: Glas 3C **116**
Glenlivet Rd. G78: Neil 3C **130**
Glen Lochay Gdns. G68: Cumb 1D **34**
Glenlora Dr. G53: Glas 6A **100**
Glenlora Ter. G53: Glas 6B **100**
Glen Loy Pl. G53: Glas 3C **116**
Glenluce Dr. G32: Glas 2D **106**
Glenluce Gdns. G69: Mood 4E **53**
Glenluce Ter. G74: E Kil 1E **149**
Glenluggie Rd. G66: Kirk 6G **31**
Glenlui Av. G73: Ruth 2D **120**
Glen Luss Gdns. G68: Cumb 1D **34**
Glen Luss Pl. G53: Glas 3C **116**
ML5: Coat 6F **91**
Glen Lyon G74: E Kil 2C **150**
Glen Lyon Ct. G68: Cumb 1D **34**
Glenlyon Ct. ML3: Ham 3F **153**
Glenlyon Pl. G73: Ruth 4E **121**
Glen Lyon Rd. G78: Neil 3C **130**
Glen Mallie G74: E Kil 2C **150**
Glenmalloch Pl. PA5: Eld 2A **96**
Glenmanor Av. G69: Mood 5C **52**
Glenmanor Rd. G69: Mood 5C **52**
Glenmare Av. G66: Kirk 6G **31**
Glen Mark G74: E Kil 1C **150**
Glen Mark Rd. G78: Neil 3C **130**
GLENMAVIS **5G 71**
Glenmavis Ct. ML8: Carl 4G **165**

Glenmavis Cres. ML8: Carl 4G **165**
Glenmavis Rd. ML6: Glenm 6G **71**
Glenmavis St. G4: Glas 2F **83** (1D **4**)
Glen More G74: E Kil 2A **150**
Glenmore Av. G42: Glas 5A **104**
ML4: Bell 4D **126**
Glenmore Rd. ML1: N'hill 4C **128**
Glen Moriston G74: E Kil 2C **150**
Glen Moriston Rd. G53: Glas 4C **116**
G68: Cumb 1D **34**
Glenmoss Av. PA8: Ersk 6D **40**
Glen Moy G74: E Kil 2B **150**
Glenmuir Dr. G53: Glas 2B **116**
Glen Muir Rd. G78: Neil 3C **130**
Glen Nevis G74: E Kil 3B **150**
Glen Nevis Pl. G73: Ruth 5E **121**
Glen Noble ML1: Cle 1G **145**
Glen Ochil Rd. ML6: Chap 4D **112**
Glen Ogilvie G74: E Kil 1C **150**
Glenogle St. G32: Glas 1D **106**
Glenoran La. ML9: Lark 1F **161**
Glenorchard Rd. G64: Balm 3H **27**
Glen Orchy Ct. G68: Cumb 6D **12**
Glen Orchy Dr. G53: Glas 3C **116**
G68: Cumb 1D **34**
Glen Orchy Gro. G53: Glas 3D **116**
Glen Orchy Pl. G53: Glas 4D **116**
G68: Cumb 1D **34**
ML6: Chap 4D 112
(off Glen Rannoch Dr.)
Glen Orchy Way G53: Glas 4C **116**
Glen Orrin Way G78: Neil 3C **130**
Glenpark ML6: Air 5E **93**
Glenpark Av. G46: T'bnk 5F **117**
Glenpark Gdns. G72: Camb 6G **105**
Glenpark Ind. Est. G31: Glas 5D **84**
Glenpark Rd. G31: Glas 5D **84**
Glenpark St. G31: Glas 5D **84**
ML2: Wis 5G **145**
Glenpark Ter. G72: Camb 6G **105**
Glenpath G82: Dumb 2C **18**
Glenpatrick Rd. PA5: Eld 5A **96**
Glen Pl. G76: Clar 2C **134**
Glen Prosen G74: E Kil 1C **150**
Glen Quoich G74: E Kil 6D **138**
Glenraith Path G33: Glas 6B **66**
Glenraith Rd. G33: Glas 6B **66**
Glenraith Sq. G33: Glas 6B **66**
Glenraith Wlk. G33: Glas 6C **66**
Glen Rannoch Dr. ML6: Chap 4D **112**
Glen Rinnes Dr. G78: Neil 4D **130**
Glen Rd. G32: Glas 4B **86**
G60: Old K 1F **41**
G66: Cam G, Len 1C **6**
G68: Dull 4F **13**
G74: E Kil 5B **136**
(not continuous)
ML1: N'hse 6D **112**
ML2: Wis 5G **145**
ML6: Air 5E **93**
PA7: B'ton 3G **39**
Glen Rosa Gdns. G68: Cumb 1D **34**
Glen Roy Dr. G78: Neil 3C **130**
Glen Sannox Vw. G68: Cumb 1D **34**
Glen Sannox Way G68: Cumb 1D **34**
Glen Sannox Wynd G68: Cumb 1E **35**
Glen Sax Dr. PA4: Renf 2G **79**
Glen Shee G74: E Kil 1C **150**
Glen Shee Av. G78: Neil 3C **130**
Glenshee Ct. G31: Glas 1F **105**
Glen Shee Cres. ML6: Chap 4D **112**
Glenshee Gdns. G31: Glas 1G **105**
Glenshee St. G31: Glas 1F **105**
Glenshee Ter. ML3: Ham 3F **153**
Glenshiel Av. PA2: Pais 4C **98**
Glenshira Av. PA2: Pais 4C **98**
Glen Shirva Rd. G65: Twe 1D **32**
Glenside Av. G53: Glas 3B **100**
Glenside Cotts. *PA11: Bri W 3F 73*
(off Mill of Gryffe Rd.)
Glenside Dr. G73: Ruth 1F **121**
Glenside Rd. G82: Dumb 1H **17**
Glen Spean Pl. ML5: Coat 6F **91**
Glenspean St. G43: Glas 1A **118**
Glen St. G72: Camb 3D **122**
G78: Barr 5E **115**
ML1: Moth 6G **127**
ML1: N'hill 3D **128**
PA3: Pais 6H **77**
Glentanar Ct. PA1: Pais 1C **98**
Glentanar Dr. G69: Mood 5E **53**
Glentanar Pl. G22: Glas 2F **63**
Glentanar Rd. G22: Glas 2F **63**
Glen Tanner G74: E Kil 1D **150**
Glentarbert Rd. G73: Ruth 4F **121**
Glen Tarbet Dr. G78: Neil 3C **130**
Glen Tennet G74: E Kil 1C **150**
Glentore Quad. ML6: Air 1A **92**
Glen Twr. *ML1: Moth 5B 144*
(off Glen Ct.)
Glentrool Gdns. G22: Glas 5H **63**
G69: Mood 4E **53**
Glen Turret G74: E Kil 1C **150**
Glenturret St. G32: Glas 1A **106**
Glentyan Av. PA10: Kilb 1A **94**
Glentyan Dr. G53: Glas 6A **100**
Glen Urquhart G74: E Kil 2B **150**
Glenview G66: Kirk 5D **30**
Glen Vw. G67: Cumb 2C **36**
ML3: Ham 5H **153**
Glenview ML6: Air 5D **92**
ML9: Lark 1D **160**
Glenview Av. FK4: Bank 1E **15**
Glenview Cres. G69: Mood 4D **52**
Glenview Pl. G72: Blan 6B **124**
Glenview St. ML6: Glenm 5G **71**
Glenville Av. G46: Giff 4H **117**
Glenville Ga. G76: Busby 4E **135**
Glenville Ter. G76: Busby 4E **135**
Glenward Av. G66: Len 3G **7**
Glenwell St. ML6: Glenm 6G **71**
Glenwood Av. ML6: Air 1C **112**
Glenwood Bus. Cen. G45: Glas 4A **120**
Glenwood Ct. G66: Lenz 2A **50**
Glenwood Dr. G46: T'bnk 5F **117**
Glenwood Gdns. G66: Lenz 2A **50**
Glenwood Path G45: Glas 4A **120**
Glenwood Pl. G45: Glas 4A **120**
G66: Lenz 2A **50**
Glenwood Rd. G66: Lenz 2A **50**
Glidden Ct. ML2: Over 4A **158**
Globe Ct. G74: E Kil 4D **138**
Glorat Av. G66: Len 3G **7**
Gloucester Av. G73: Ruth 2F **121**
G76: Clar 2B **134**
Gloucester St. G5: Glas 6E **83**
Goals (Five a Side Football Cen.)
4F 43
Goals Football Cen. **4D 102**
GOCKSTON **3H 77**
Gockston Rd. PA3: Pais 4H **77**
Goddard Pl. ML2: Newm 4F **147**
Gogar Pl. G33: Glas 3G **85**
Gogar St. G33: Glas 3G **85**
Goil Av. ML4: Bell 1H **125**
Goil Way *ML1: Holy 2A 128*
(off Howden Pl.)
Goldberry Av. G14: Glas 4B **60**
Goldberry La. *G14: Glas 4B 60*
(off Esslemont Av.)
Goldenhill Ct. G81: Hard 1D **42**
Goldenlee Vw. PA6: C'lee 3A **74**
Goldie Rd. G71: Udd 3E **125**
Golf Av. ML4: Bell 4C **126**
Golf Course Rd. G64: Balm 5A **28**
PA11: Bri W 3D **72**
Golf Ct. G44: Neth 5C **118**
Golf Dr. G15: Glas 6H **43**
PA1: Pais 1E **99**
Golf Gdns. ML9: Lark 3G **161**
GOLFHILL **1H 91**
Golfhill Dr. G31: Glas 3C **84**
Golfhill Quad. ML6: Air 1A **92**
Golfhill Rd. ML2: Wis 5D **144**
Golf Pl. ML4: Bell 4D **126**
Golf Rd. G73: Ruth 3D **120**
G76: Clar 2B **134**
Golfview G61: Bear 2B **44**
Golf Vw. G81: Clyd 3B **42**
Golfview Dr. ML5: Coat 4G **89**
Golfview Pl. ML5: Coat 5G **89**
Golspie Av. ML6: Air 1G **111**
Golspie St. G51: Glas 3G **81**
Goodview Gdns.
ML9: Lark 3G **161**
Goosedubs *G1: Glas 5G 83*
(off Bridgegate)
Gooseholm Cres. G82: Dumb 2G **17**
Gooseholm Rd. G82: Dumb 2G **17**
Gopher Av. G71: View 5F **109**
GORBALS **1G 103**
Gorbals Cross G5: Glas 6G **83**
ML9: Lark 2E **161**
Gorbals Leisure Cen. **6G 83**
Gorbals St. G5: Glas 6F **83**
Gordon Av. G44: Neth 5C **118**
G52: Hill 4G **79**
G69: Bail 6F **87**
PA7: B'ton 3G **39**
Gordon Ct. ML6: Air 3E **93**
Gordon Cres. G77: Newt M 3E **133**
Gordon Dr. G44: Neth 5C **118**
G74: E Kil 6B **138**
Gordon La. G1: Glas 4F **83** (5D **4**)
Gordon Pl. ML4: Bell 4B **126**
Gordon Rd. G44: Neth 5C **118**
ML3: Ham 5D **140**
Gordon Sq. PA5: John 3F **95**
Gordon St. G1: Glas 4F **83** (5D **4**)
PA1: Pais 1A **98**
Gordon Ter. G72: Blan 5A **124**
ML3: Ham 6D **140**
Gorebridge St. G32: Glas 4G **85**
Goremire Rd. ML8: Carl 6G **165**
Gorget Av. G13: Glas 6C **44**
Gorget Pl. G13: Glas 6C **44**
Gorget Quad. G13: Glas 6B **44**
Gorse Cres. PA11: Bri W 4G **73**
Gorse Dr. G78: Barr 3D **114**
Gorsehall St. ML1: Cle 5H **129**
Gorse Pl. G71: View 5F **109**
Gorsewood G64: B'rig 6A **48**
Gorstan Path G23: Glas 1B **62**
Gorstan Pl. G20: Glas 4A **62**
Gorstan St. G23: Glas 1B **62**
Gosford La. G14: Glas 5A **60**
Gotter Bank PA11: Q'riers 1A **72**
Goudie St. PA3: Pais 4H **77**
Gough La. *G33: Glas 3F 85*
(off Gough St.)
Gough St. G33: Glas 3F **85**
Gourlay G74: E Kil 4D **138**
Gourlay Dr. ML2: Over 5A **158**
Gourlay St. G21: Glas 6H **63**
(not continuous)
Gourock St. G41: Glas 1E **103**
GOVAN **3G 81**
Govan Fun Pool **4F 81**
GOVANHILL **3F 103**
Govanhill St. G42: Glas 3F **103**
(not continuous)
Govanhill Swimming Pool **3E 103**
Govan Rd. G51: Glas 2D **80**
Govan Station (Und.) **3G 81**
Gowanbank Gdns. PA5: John 3E **95**
Gowanbrae G66: Lenz 1C **50**
Gowanlea Av. G15: Glas 6A **44**
Gowanlea Dr. G46: Giff 3B **118**
Gowanlea Ter. G71: View 6F **109**
Gowanside Pl. ML8: Carl 3D **164**
Gower St. G41: Glas 1A **102**
Gower Ter. G41: Glas 6A **82**
Gowkhall Av. ML1: N'hill 4F **129**
GOWKTHRAPPLE **3G 157**
Goyle Av. G15: Glas 4C **44**
Grace Av. G69: Barg 6D **88**
Grace St. G3: Glas 4D **82**
Graeme Ct. ML1: Moth 5F **127**
Graffham Av. G46: Giff 4B **118**
Grafton Pl. G1: Glas 3G **83** (3F **5**)
Graham Av. G72: Camb 2D **122**
G74: E Kil 1G **149**

Graham Av. G81: Clyd 4D 42
 ML3: Ham. 3H 153
                              (not continuous)
Graham Dr. G62: Miln. 3E 25
Graham Ho. G67: Cumb 3G 35
Graham Pl. G65: Kils 1G 11
 ML9: Ashg 4B 162
Graham Rd. G82: Dumb 3D 16
Grahamsdyke Rd. G66: Kirk 4E 31
Grahamshill Av. ML6: Air 3D 92
Grahamshill St. ML6: Air 3C 92
Graham Sq. G40: Glas 5B 84
Grahamston Ct. PA2: Pais 5E 99
Grahamston Cres. PA2: Pais 5E 99
Grahamston Pk. G78: Barr 2D 114
Grahamston Pl. PA2: Pais 5E 99
Graham St. G78: Barr 4D 114
 ML1: Holy 2A 128
 ML2: Wis 1H 157
 ML3: Ham. 6A 142
 ML6: Air 4A 92
 PA5: John 3E 95
                              (not continuous)
Graham Ter. G64: B'rig. 2D 64
Graignestock Pl. G40: Glas. 6A 84
Graignestock St. G40: Glas. 6A 84
Grainger Rd. G64: B'rig. 6F 49
Grammar School Sq. ML3: Ham. . . 5A 142
Grampian Av. PA2: Pais 5H 97
Grampian Ct. G61: Bear 5C 24
Grampian Cres. G32: Glas 1B 106
 ML6: Chap. 4F 113
Grampian Pl. G32: Glas 1B 106
Grampian Rd. ML2: Wis 5F 145
Grampian St. G32: Glas 1B 106
Grampian Way G61: Bear 6B 24
 G68: Cumb 3C 34
 G78: Barr 6E 115
Granby La. G12: Glas 6B 62
Grandtully Dr. G12: Glas. 3A 62
Grange Av. G62: Miln 3H 25
 ML2: Wis 2E 157
Grange Gdns. G71: Both 6F 125
Grangeneuk Gdns. G68: Cumb . . . 4E 35
Grange Rd. G42: Glas 5E 103
 G61: Bear 2F 45
Grange St. ML1: Moth 5A 144
Grange Twr. ML1: Moth 1B 156
Gran St. G81: Clyd 1G 59
Grant Ct. ML3: Ham 5G 153
 ML6: Air 3E 93
Grantholm Av. ML1: Holy 1B 128
Grantlea Gro. G32: Glas 1D 106
Grantlea Ter. G32: Glas 1D 106
Grantley Gdns. G41: Glas 5B 102
Grantley St. G41: Glas 5B 102
Grantoften Path G75: E Kil. 5F 149
Granton St. G5: Glas. 3A 104
Grantown Av. ML6: Air 5E 93
Grantown Gdns. ML6: Glenm 4H 71
Grants Cres. PA2: Pais 5H 97
Grant St. G3: Glas 2D 82 (1A 4)
Granville St. G3: Glas. 3D 82
 G81: Clyd 4D 42
Grasmere G75: E Kil 6B 148
Grasmere Ct. ML3: Ham. 5H 153
Grathellen Ct. ML1: Moth. 1A 144
Gray Dr. G61: Bear 4F 45
Grayshill Rd. G68: Cumb 6H 33
Gray's Rd. G71: Udd 2F 125
Gray St. G3: Glas 2B 82
 G66: Kirk 6H 31
 ML1: Cle. 6H 129
 ML9: Lark 1E 161
Great Av. ML3: Fern 2C 154
Great Dovehill G1: Glas 5H 83
Gt. George La. G12: Glas 6B 62
Gt. George St. G12: Glas 6B 62
Gt. Hamilton St. PA2: Pais 3A 98
Gt. Kelvin La. G12: Glas. 1C 82
                              (off Glasgow St.)
Gt. Western Retail Pk. G15: Glas . . 5G 43
Gt. Western Rd. G12: Glas 4G 61
 G13: Glas 6H 43

Gt. Western Rd. G15: Glas 6H 43
 G4: Glas 4G 61
 G60: Bowl, Old K. 5H 19
 G81: Clyd, Dun, Hard 1H 41
Gt. Western Ter. G12: Glas 5A 62
Gt. Western Ter. La. G12: Glas 5A 62
Greenacres ML1: Moth 4E 143
Greenacres Ct. G53: Glas 3C 116
Greenacres Vw. ML1: Moth 4E 143
Greenacres Way G53: Glas 3C 116
Greenan Av. G42: Glas 6A 104
Greenbank G72: Blan 2A 140
Greenbank Av. G46: Giff 2G 133
Greenbank Dr. PA2: Pais 6H 97
Greenbank Gardens 4A 134
Green Bank Rd. G68: Cumb 3E 35
Greenbank Rd. ML2: Wis 6A 146
Greenbank St. G73: Ruth 5C 104
Greenbank Ter. ML8: Carl 3F 165
Green Dale ML2: Wis 4B 146
Greendyke St. G1: Glas 5H 83
GREENEND 1F 111
Greenend Av. PA5: John 5D 94
Greenend Pl. G32: Glas 4C 86
Greenend Vw. ML4: Bell 3B 126
Greenfarm Rd. G77: Newt M. 4B 132
Green Farm Rd. PA3: Lin 5H 75
GREENFAULDS 6G 35
Greenfaulds Cres. G67: Cumb . . . 5A 36
Greenfaulds Rd. G67: Cumb 5A 36
                          (Greenfaulds Cres.)
 G67: Cumb 6G 35
                          (Waverley Cres.)
Greenfaulds Station (Rail) 6H 35
GREENFIELD 5B 86
Greenfield Av. G32: Glas 4B 86
Greenfield Cres. ML2: Wis 5B 146
Greenfield Dr. ML2: Wis 5B 146
Greenfield Pl. G32: Glas 5B 86
Greenfield Quad. ML1: N'hill. 3F 129
Greenfield Rd. G32: Glas 4C 86
 G76: Clar. 3C 134
 ML3: Ham 3E 141
 ML8: Carl 2F 165
Greenfield St. G51: Glas 4F 81
 ML2: Wis 5B 146
GREENFOOT 2C 70
Greengairs Av. G51: Glas 3D 80
Green Gdns. ML1: Cle 5H 129
Greenhall Pl. G72: Blan 3A 140
GREENHEAD 1B 158
Greenhead Av. G82: Dumb 4H 17
Greenhead Gdns. G82: Dumb 4H 17
                              (not continuous)
Greenhead Rd. G61: Bear 3F 45
 G66: Len. 3G 7
 G82: Dumb 4H 17
 ML2: Wis 1A 158
 PA4: Inch 2G 57
Greenhead St. G40: Glas 6A 84
GREENHILL 2D 90
Greenhill G64: B'rig 1E 65
Greenhill Av. G46: Giff 6H 117
 G69: G'csh 2C 68
Greenhill Bus. Pk. PA3: Pais 5G 77
Greenhill Ct. G73: Ruth 5C 104
Greenhill Cres. PA3: Lin. 5H 75
 PA5: Eld 3B 96
Greenhill Dr. PA3: Lin. 5A 76
Greenhill Ind. Est. ML5: Coat. 2D 90
Greenhill Rd. G73: Ruth 5C 104
 PA3: Pais 5G 77
GREENHILLS 6D 148
Greenhills Cres. G75: E Kil 6D 148
Greenhills Rd. G75: E Kil 3A 148
Greenhills Sports Cen. 5E 149
Greenhills Sq. G75: E Kil 5C 148
Greenhill St. G73: Ruth 6C 104
Greenhills Way G75: E Kil 5F 149
Greenholm Av. G71: Udd 6C 108
 G76: Clar. 2C 134
Greenholme Ct. G44: Glas. 1F 119
Greenholme St. G44: Glas. 1F 119
Greenknowe Dr. ML8: Law 5D 158

Greenknowe Rd. G43: Glas. 1H 117
Greenknowe St. ML2: Over. 5H 157
Greenlaw Av. ML2: Wis 4A 146
 PA1: Pais 6C 78
Greenlaw Ct. ML2: Wis 1H 157
Greenlaw Cres. PA1: Pais 5C 78
Greenlaw Dr. G77: Newt M 4C 132
 PA1: Pais 6C 78
Greenlaw Ho. PA1: Pais 6C 78
Greenlaw Ind. Est. PA3: Pais 5B 78
Greenlaw Rd. G14: Glas 3F 59
 G77: Newt M. 4C 132
Greenlea Rd. G69: Chry 1H 67
Greenlea St. G13: Glas 3E 61
GREENLEES 4B 122
Greenlees Gdns. G72: Camb 4H 121
Greenlees Gro. ML5: Coat. 6F 91
Greenlees Pk. G72: Camb. 4A 122
Greenlees Rd. G72: Camb 5H 121
Green Loan ML1: New S. 4A 128
Greenloan Av. G51: Glas 3D 80
Greenloan Vw. ML9: Lark 4F 161
                              (off Keir Hardie Rd.)
Greenlodge Ter. G40: Glas 1B 104
Greenmoss Pl. ML4: Bell 2D 126
Greenmount G22: Glas 2E 63
Greenock Av. G44: Glas. 2F 119
Greenock Rd. PA3: Pais 3G 77
                              (not continuous)
 PA7: B'ton. 1A 38
Green Pl. G71: Both 5F 125
 ML6: C'bnk 3B 112
Greenrig G71: Udd 1D 124
Greenrigg Rd. G67: Cumb 4A 36
Greenrig St. G33: Glas 6F 65
 G71: Udd 1D 124
Green Rd. G73: Ruth 5C 104
 PA2: Pais 2D 96
Greens Av. G66: Kirk 6C 30
Greens Cres. G66: Kirk. 6C 30
Greens Health & Fitness 4C 82
Greenshields Rd. G69: Bail 6H 87
Greenside G76: Crmck 1A 136
Greenside Cres. G33: Glas 6G 65
Greenside Pl. G61: Bear 5C 24
Greenside Rd. G81: Hard 6D 22
 ML1: N'hse 6C 112
 ML2: Wis 1A 158
Greenside St. G33: Glas 6G 65
 ML1: N'hill. 3F 129
 ML5: Coat. 2D 90
Greens Rd. G67: Cumb. 1H 55
GREENS, THE 6C 30
Green St. G40: Glas 6A 84
 G71: Both 5F 125
 G81: Clyd 4C 42
Green, The G40: Glas 1A 104
Greentree Dr. G69: Bail. 2F 107
Greenview St. G43: Glas 5A 102
Greenway La. G72: Blan. 3H 139
Greenways Av. PA2: Pais 3E 97
Greenways Ct. PA2: Pais 3E 97
Greenwood Av. G69: Mood 5D 52
 G72: Camb 1E 123
Greenwood Ct. G76: Clar 2C 134
Greenwood Cres. ML5: Coat 6E 91
Greenwood Dr. G61: Bear 3G 45
 PA5: John 5D 94
Greenwood Quad. G81: Clyd 6F 43
Greenwood Rd. G76: Clar. 2B 134
GREENYARDS INTERCHANGE 4B 36
Greer Quad. G81: Clyd 3D 42
Grenada Pl. G75: E Kil 2C 148
Grenadier Gdns. ML1: Moth 6F 143
Grenville Dr. G72: Camb. 3H 121
Gresham Vw. ML1: Moth 1B 156
Greta Meek La. G66: Milt C 5C 8
Gretna St. G40: Glas. 1D 104
Greyfriars Rd. G71: Udd 5A 108
Greyfriars St. G32: Glas 4H 85
Greystone Av. G73: Ruth. 1E 121
Greywood St. G13: Glas 2E 61
Grier Path G31: Glas 6F 85
Grier Pl. ML9: Lark. 3D 160

Grierson La. G33: Glas . . . 3F 85 (off Lomax St.)
Grierson St. G33: Glas . . . 3F 85
Grieve Cft. G71: Both . . . 6D 124
Grieve Rd. G67: Cumb . . . 2A 36
Griffen Av. PA1: Pais . . . 6B 76
Griffin Pl. ML4: Bell . . . 5C 110
Griffiths Way ML8: Law . . . 1H 163
Griqua Ter. G71: Both . . . 5F 125
Grogarry Rd. G15: Glas . . . 3A 44
Grosvenor Cinema . . . 6B 62 (off Ashton La.)
Grosvenor Cres. G12: Glas . . . 6B 62
Grosvenor Cres. La. G12: Glas . . . 6B 62
Grosvenor La. G12: Glas . . . 6B 62
Grosvenor Ter. G12: Glas . . . 6B 62
Groveburn Av. G46: T'bnk . . . 3G 117
Grove Cres. ML9: Lark . . . 3G 161
Grove Pk. G20: Glas . . . 6E 63
G66: Lenz . . . 3D 50
Grovepark Ct. G20: Glas . . . 1E 83
Gro. Park Gdns. G20: Glas . . . 1E 83
Grovepark St. G20: Glas . . . 6E 63
Groves, The G64: B'rig . . . 1E 65
Grove, The G46: Giff . . . 1H 133
G78: Neil . . . 3C 130
PA10: Kilb . . . 1A 94
PA11: Bri W . . . 5G 73
PA7: B'ton . . . 4G 39
Grove Way ML4: Bell . . . 2B 126
Grove Wood G71: View . . . 4H 109
Grovewood Bus. Cen. ML4: Bell . . . 5A 110
Grove Wynd ML1: New S . . . 4A 128
Grudie St. G34: Glas . . . 3G 87
Gryfebank Av. PA6: C'lee . . . 2E 75
Gryfebank Cl. PA6: C'lee . . . 2E 75
Gryfebank Cres. PA6: C'lee . . . 2E 75
Gryfebank Way PA6: C'lee . . . 2E 75
Gryfewood Cres. PA6: C'lee . . . 2E 75
Gryfewood Way PA6: C'lee . . . 2E 75
Gryffe Av. PA11: Bri W . . . 2E 73
PA4: Renf . . . 4D 58
Gryffe Cres. PA2: Pais . . . 4D 96
Gryffe Gro. PA11: Bri W . . . 3F 73
Gryffe Pl. PA11: Bri W . . . 3F 73 (off Main St.)
Gryffe Rd. PA11: Bri W . . . 4F 73
Gryffe St. G44: Glas . . . 6E 103
Guildford St. G33: Glas . . . 2C 86
Gullane Ct. ML3: Ham . . . 3F 153
Gullane Cres. G68: Cumb . . . 5H 13
Gullane St. G11: Glas . . . 2H 81
Gunn Quad. ML4: Bell . . . 4A 126
Guthrie Ct. ML1: Moth . . . 3E 143
Guthrie Dr. G71: Tann . . . 4E 109
Guthrie Pl. G64: Torr . . . 5E 29
G74: E Kil . . . 1H 149
Guthrie St. G20: Glas . . . 3B 62
ML3: Ham . . . 5H 141
Gyle Pl. ML2: Wis . . . 6C 146

H

Haberlea Av. G53: Glas . . . 4C 116
Haberlea Gdns. G53: Glas . . . 5C 116
Haddington Way ML5: Coat . . . 2A 110 (not continuous)
Haddow Gro. G71: Tann . . . 5E 109
Haddow St. ML3: Ham . . . 6A 142
Hadrian Ter. ML1: Moth . . . 1E 143
Hagart Rd. PA6: Hous . . . 1B 74
Hagen Dr. ML1: Cle . . . 6E 129
Hagg Cres. PA5: John . . . 2E 95
Hagg Pl. PA5: John . . . 2E 95
Hagg Rd. PA5: John . . . 3E 95
HAGGS . . . 1G 15
HAGGS CASTLE . . . 3A 102
Haggs La. G41: Glas . . . 3A 102
Haggs Rd. G41: Glas . . . 4A 102
Haggswood Av. G41: Glas . . . 3A 102
HAGHILL . . . 4E 85
Haghill Rd. G31: Glas . . . 5E 85
Hagmill Cres. ML5: Coat . . . 3E 111
Hagmill Rd. ML5: Coat . . . 3C 110
Haig Dr. G69: Bail . . . 1F 107
Haig St. G21: Glas . . . 5B 64
Hailes Av. G32: Glas . . . 6D 86
Haining Rd. PA4: Renf . . . 6F 59
Haining, The PA4: Renf . . . 1F 79
HAIRMYRES . . . 3B 148
Hairmyres Dr. G75: E Kil . . . 3B 148
Hairmyres Pk. G75: E Kil . . . 3B 148
HAIRMYRES RDBT. . . . 2B 148
Hairmyres Station (Rail) . . . 2B 148
Hairmyres St. G42: Glas . . . 3G 103
Hairst St. PA4: Renf . . . 5F 59
Halbeath Av. G15: Glas . . . 4H 43
Halbert St. G41: Glas . . . 4C 102
Haldane La. G14: Glas . . . 6D 60 (off Haldane St.)
Haldane Pl. G75: E Kil . . . 4H 149
Haldane St. G14: Glas . . . 6D 60
Halfmerk Nth. G74: E Kil . . . 1A 150
Halfmerk St. G74: E Kil . . . 1A 150
HALFWAY . . . 3D 122
Halgreen Av. G15: Glas . . . 4G 43
Haliburton Rd. G34: Glas . . . 4F 87
Halifax Way PA4: Renf . . . 2E 79 (off Tiree Av.)
Hallbrae St. G33: Glas . . . 1G 85
Hallburton Ter. G34: Glas . . . 4G 87
Hallcraig Pl. ML8: Carl . . . 3D 164
Hallcraig St. ML6: Air . . . 3A 92
Halley Dr. G13: Glas . . . 2G 59
Halley Pl. G13: Glas . . . 2G 59
Halley Sq. G13: Glas . . . 2H 59
Halley St. G13: Glas . . . 2G 59
Hallforest St. G33: Glas . . . 1B 86
Hallhill Cres. G33: Glas . . . 5E 87
Hallhill Rd. G32: Glas . . . 6B 86
G33: Glas . . . 5D 86
G69: Bail . . . 5G 87
PA5: John . . . 6C 94
Hallidale Cres. PA4: Renf . . . 1H 79
Hallinan Gdns. ML2: Wis . . . 2F 157
Hall Pl. G33: Step . . . 4F 67
Hallrule Dr. G52: Glas . . . 6C 80
HALLSIDE . . . 3F 123
Hallside Av. G72: Camb . . . 2E 123
Hallside Blvd. G72: Flem . . . 4F 123
Hallside Cres. G72: Camb . . . 2E 123
Hallside Dr. G72: Camb . . . 2E 123
Hallside Gdns. ML2: Wis . . . 5C 146
Hallside Pl. G5: Glas . . . 1G 103
Hallside Rd. G72: Flem . . . 3F 123 (Hallside Blvd.)
G72: Flem . . . 3E 123 (Newton Sta. Rd.)
Hall St. G81: Clyd . . . 6C 42
ML1: New S . . . 3A 128
ML3: Ham . . . 2H 153
Hallydown Dr. G13: Glas . . . 4C 60
Halpin Cl. ML4: Bell . . . 2H 125
Halton Gdns. G69: Bail . . . 1F 107
Hamersley Pl. G75: E Kil . . . 4D 148
Hamilcomb Rd. ML4: Bell . . . 4C 126
Hamill Dr. G65: Kils . . . 3B 12
HAMILTON . . . 6A 142
Hamilton Academical F.C. . . . 5E 91
Hamilton Av. G41: Glas . . . 2H 101
Hamilton Bus. Pk. ML3: Ham . . . 4H 141
Hamilton Central Station (Rail) . . . 6A 142
Hamilton Ct. PA2: Pais . . . 3A 98
Hamilton Cres. G61: Bear . . . 6E 25
G72: Camb . . . 3C 122
ML5: Coat . . . 6C 90
PA4: Renf . . . 4F 59
PA7: B'ton . . . 4F 39
Hamilton Dr. G12: Glas . . . 6C 62
G46: Giff . . . 5B 118
G71: Both . . . 6F 125
G72: Blan . . . 4H 139
G72: Camb . . . 2A 122
ML1: Moth . . . 5H 143
ML6: Air . . . 2B 92
PA8: Ersk . . . 4D 40
Hamilton Farm G73: Ruth . . . 5G 105
HAMILTONHILL . . . 5F 63
Hamiltonhill Cres. G22: Glas . . . 5F 63
Hamiltonhill Rd. G22: Glas . . . 6F 63
HAMILTON INTERCHANGE . . . 5C 142
Hamilton Intl. Tech. Pk. (Technology Av.)
G72: Blan . . . 4A 140
Hamilton Intl. Tech. Pk. (Watt Pl.)
G72: Blan . . . 5A 140
Hamilton Mausoleum . . . 4B 142
Hamilton Pk. Av. G12: Glas . . . 6C 62
Hamilton Pk. Nth. ML3: Ham . . . 3H 141
Hamilton Pk. Racecourse . . . 3H 141
Hamilton Pk. Sth. ML3: Ham . . . 3H 141
Hamilton Pl. G75: E Kil . . . 4G 149
G78: Neil . . . 2F 131
ML1: N'hill . . . 3C 128
ML1: New S . . . 3B 128
ML3: Ham . . . 5H 153
Hamilton Retail Pk. ML3: Ham . . . 4G 141
Hamilton Rd. G32: Glas . . . 2B 106
G71: Both . . . 6F 125
G71: Udd . . . 3F 107
G72: Blan . . . 4F 139
G72: Camb, Flem . . . 1A 122
G73: Ruth . . . 5D 104
G74: E Kil . . . 4C 138
ML1: Moth . . . 4D 142
ML4: Bell . . . 4B 126
ML9: Lark . . . 6H 155
Hamilton St. G42: Glas . . . 4G 103
G81: Clyd . . . 2F 59
G82: Dumb . . . 3G 17
ML8: Carl . . . 4F 165
ML9: Lark . . . 1E 161
PA3: Pais . . . 6B 78
Hamilton Ter. G81: Clyd . . . 2F 59
Hamilton Twr. G71: Both . . . 3B 124
Hamilton Vw. G71: Tann . . . 6E 109
Hamilton Water Palace . . . 5H 141 (off Almada St.)
Hamilton West Station (Rail) . . . 5G 141
Hamlet G74: E Kil . . . 4C 138
Hampden Dr. G42: Glas . . . 6F 103
Hampden La. G42: Glas . . . 5F 103
Hampden Pk. . . . 6F 103
Hampden Ter. G42: Glas . . . 5F 103
Hampden Way PA4: Renf . . . 2F 79
Handel Pl. G5: Glas . . . 1G 103
HANGINGSHAW . . . 5G 103
Hangingshaw Pl. G42: Glas . . . 5G 103
Hannay St. PA1: Pais . . . 6G 77 (off Well St.)
Hanover Cl. G42: Glas . . . 5E 103
Hanover Ct. G1: Glas . . . 3G 83 (4F 5)
G11: Glas . . . 1G 81
PA1: Pais . . . 6C 78
PA5: John . . . 2F 95
Hanover Gdns. G64: B'rig . . . 6C 48
PA1: Pais . . . 1G 97 (off Wilson St.)
Hanover Pl. G11: Glas . . . 1G 81
Hanover St. G1: Glas . . . 4G 83 (5E 5)
Hanson St. G31: Glas . . . 4B 84
Hapland Av. G53: Glas . . . 3C 100
Hapland Rd. G53: Glas . . . 3C 100
Harbour La. PA3: Pais . . . 6A 78
Harbour Rd. PA3: Pais . . . 4A 78
Harburn Pl. G23: Glas . . . 6C 46
Harbury Pl. G14: Glas . . . 3H 59
Harcourt Dr. G31: Glas . . . 3D 84
HARDGATE . . . 1E 43
Hardgate Dr. G51: Glas . . . 3C 80
Hardgate Gdns. G51: Glas . . . 3C 80
Hardgate Path G51: Glas . . . 3C 80
Hardgate Pl. G51: Glas . . . 3C 80
Hardgate Rd. G51: Glas . . . 3C 80
Hardie Av. G73: Ruth . . . 5E 105
Hardie St. G72: Blan . . . 2B 140
ML1: Moth . . . 1G 143
ML3: Ham . . . 1F 153
Hardmoor Gdns. G66: Kirk . . . 4E 31
Hardmoor Rd. G66: Kirk . . . 4E 31
Hardridge Av. G52: Glas . . . 3E 101
Hardridge Pl. G52: Glas . . . 3E 101

Hardridge Rd.—Helenslee Rd.

Hardridge Rd. G52: Glas. 3D **100**
Harefield Dr. G14: Glas. 4B **60**
Harelaw Av. G44: Glas 3C **118**
G78: Barr. 6F **115**
G78: Neil. 3D **130**
Harelaw Cres. PA2: Pais. 6G **97**
HARELEESHILL 3F **161**
Hareleeshill Rd. ML9: Lark 3F **161**
Hareleeshill Sports Barn 4G **161**
HARESTANES 4H **31**
Harestanes Gdns. G66: Kirk 4G **31**
Harestone Cres. ML2: Wis 1A **158**
Harestone Rd. ML2: Wis. 1A **158**
Harhill St. G51: Glas. 4F **81**
Harkins Av. G72: Blan 2A **140**
Harkness Av. G66: Milt C 6B **8**
Harland Cotts. G14: Glas 6C **60**
Harland St. G14: Glas. 6C **60**
Harlaw Gdns. G64: B'rig 5F **49**
Harley St. G51: Glas. 5A **82**
Harmetray St. G22: Glas. 3H **63**
Harmony Pl. G51: Glas. 4G **81**
Harmony Row G51: Glas. 4G **81** (not continuous)
Harmony Sq. G51: Glas 4G **81**
Harmsworth St. G11: Glas. 1E **81**
Harper Cres. ML2: Wis. 5C **146**
Harport St. G46: T'bnk 2E **117**
Harriet Pl. G43: Glas 1H **117**
Harriet St. G73: Ruth 6C **104**
Harrington Rd. G74: E Kil 2G **149**
Harris Cl. G77: Newt M. 3B **132**
Harris Cres. G60: Old K. 2F **41**
Harris Dr. G60: Old K 2F **41**
Harris Gdns. G60: Old K 2G **41**
Harrison Dr. G51: Glas 5H **81**
Harrison Quad. ML2: Wis 4C **146**
Harris Rd. G23: Glas. 6C **46**
G60: Old K. 2F **41**
Harrow Ct. G15: Glas 4H **43**
Harrow Pl. G15: Glas 4H **43**
Hartfield Ct. G82: Dumb 3G **17**
Hartfield Cres. G78: Neil. 2E **131**
Hartfield Gdns. G82: Dumb 3G **17**
Hartfield Ter. PA2: Pais. 3B **98**
Hartlaw Cres. G52: Glas 5A **80**
Hartree Av. G13: Glas. 1G **59**
Hartstone Pl. G53: Glas 6B **100**
Hartstone Rd. G53: Glas 6B **100**
Hartstone Ter. G53: Glas. 6B **100**
Hart St. G31: Glas 6G **85**
G81: Faif 6F **23**
PA3: Lin 6H **75**
Harvest Dr. ML1: Moth 5F **143**
Harvey St. G4: Glas 1G **83**
Harvey Way ML4: Bell. 6E **111**
Harvie Av. G77: Newt M 4C **132**
Harvie St. G51: Glas. 5B **82**
Harwood Gdns. G69: Mood. 4E **53**
Harwood St. G32: Glas. 4G **85**
Hastie St. G3: Glas. 2B **82**
Hastings G75: E Kil. 4D **148**
Hatfield Dr. G12: Glas. 4F **61**
Hathaway Dr. G46: Giff. 5H **117**
Hathaway La. G20: Glas 4C **62**
Hathaway St. G20: Glas 4C **62**
Hathersage Av. G69: Bail 6H **87**
Hathersage Dr. G69: Bail 6H **87**
Hathersage Gdns. G69: Bail 6H **87**
Hatton Gdns. G52: Glas 1A **100**
Hattonhill ML1: Carf. 5C **128**
Hatton Path *G52: Glas.* *1A* ***100*** *(off Hatton Gdns.)*
Hatton Pl. ML1: Carf. 5C **128**
Hattonrigg ML4: Bell. 1D **126**
Hattonrigg Rd. ML4: Bell 1D **126**
Hatton Ter. ML1: Carf 5C **128**
Haughburn Pl. G53: Glas 6B **100**
Haughburn Rd. G53: Glas. 6B **100**
Haughburn Ter. G53: Glas. 6C **100**
HAUGHHEAD 1C **6**
Haughhead Bri. G71: Udd. 5A **108**
Haugh Pl. ML3: Ham 2A **154**
Haugh Rd. G3: Glas 3B **82**
G65: Kils. 3G **11**
Haughton Av. G65: Kils. 3A **12**
Haughview Rd. ML1: Moth. 3D **142**
Havelock La. G11: Glas 1A **82**
Havelock Pk. G75: E Kil 2C **148**
Havelock St. G11: Glas. 1A **82**
Haven Pl. G75: E Kil 5B **148**
Havoc Rd. G82: Dumb 4B **16**
Hawbank Rd. G74: E Kil 6C **136**
HAWBANK RDBT. 1D **148**
Hawick Av. PA2: Pais 4F **97**
Hawick Cres. ML9: Lark 3E **161**
Hawick Dr. ML5: Coat 2F **111**
Hawick St. G13: Glas 3G **59**
ML2: Wis 4A **146**
HAWKHEAD 3E **99**
Hawkhead Av. PA2: Pais. 3D **98**
Hawkhead Rd. PA1: Pais 1D **98**
Hawkhead Station (Rail) 1D **98**
Hawksland Wlk. ML3: Ham. 2A **154**
Hawkwood G75: E Kil 6F **149**
Hawkwood Rd. ML6: Glenm 5H **71**
Hawthorn Av. G61: Bear 6G **25**
G64: B'rig 1D **64**
G66: Lenz 2C **50**
G82: Dumb 2B **16**
ML2: Newm 3G **147**
PA5: John. 4G **95**
PA8: Ersk 1A **58**
Hawthorn Ct. G22: Glas 4G **63**
G76: Busby 3C **134**
Hawthorn Cres. PA8: Ersk. 1A **58**
Hawthornden Gdns. G23: Glas 5C **46**
Hawthorn Dr. FK4: Bank 1E **15**
G78: Barr. 6F **115**
ML1: New S 4B **128**
ML2: Wis 1A **158**
ML5: Coat 6F **91**
ML6: Air 4D **92**
Hawthorn Gdns. G72: Flem 3E **123**
G76: Busby 3C **134**
ML4: Bell. 3E **127**
ML9: Lark. 3G **161**
Hawthorn Gro. ML8: Law 5D **158**
Hawthorn Hill ML3: Ham 2A **154**
Hawthornhill Rd. G82: Dumb 2B **16**
Hawthorn Pl. G72: Blan 2C **140**
Hawthorn Quad. G22: Glas. 4G **63**
Hawthorn Rd. G67: Cumb 1F **37**
G76: Busby 3C **134**
PA8: Ersk 1A **58**
Hawthorn St. G22: Glas 4G **63**
G64: Torr. 4E **29**
G81: Clyd 3C **42**
Hawthorn Ter. G71: View. 6F **109**
G75: E Kil 5D **148**
Hawthorn Wlk. G72: Camb 2F **121**
Hawthorn Way G66: Milt C 6C **8**
G82: Dumb 3B **16**
PA8: Ersk 1A **58**
Hay Av. PA7: B'ton 4A **40**
Hayburn Cres. G11: Glas 6G **61**
Hayburn Ga. G11: Glas. 1H **81**
Hayburn La. G12: Glas 6G **61**
Hayburn St. G11: Glas 2G **81**
Hay Dr. PA5: John 2H **95**
Hayfield Ct. G5: Glas 1H **103**
Hayfield St. G5: Glas 1H **103**
Hayle Gdns. G69: Mood. 4D **52**
Haylynn St. G14: Glas. 1E **81**
Haymarket St. G32: Glas 4G **85**
Haystack Pl. G66: Lenz. 3D **50**
HAYSTON 5A **30**
Hayston Cres. G22: Glas. 4F **63**
Hayston Rd. G66: Kirk 5A **30**
G68: Cumb 1G **35**
Hayston St. G22: Glas. 4F **63**
Haywood St. G22: Glas 3F **63**
Hazel Av. G44: Glas 3D **118**
G61: Bear 6G **25**
G66: Lenz. 1D **50**
G82: Dumb 2B **16**
Hazel Av. PA5: John. 4G **95**
Hazel Bank G66: Milt C. 1B **30**
Hazelbank ML1: Holy 2B **128**
Hazelbank Wlk. ML6: Air 3F **91**
Hazeldean Cres. ML2: Wis 4A **146**
Hazel Dene G64: B'rig 6D **48**
Hazeldene La. *ML9: Lark* *4G* ***161*** *(off Keir Hardie Rd.)*
Hazelden Gdns. G44: Glas 3C **118**
Hazelden Pk. G44: Glas 3C **118**
Hazelfield Gro. ML6: Chap 4E **113**
Hazel Gdns. ML1: Moth 6G **143**
Hazel Gro. G66: Lenz 1D **50**
ML8: Law 5D **158**
Hazelhead G74: E Kil 1B **150**
Hazellea Dr. G46: Giff. 3C **118**
Hazel Pk. ML3: Ham. 1A **154**
Hazel Path ML1: Cle. 6H **129**
Hazel Rd. FK4: Bank 1E **15**
G67: Cumb 2D **36**
Hazel Ter. G71: View. 6F **109**
Hazelton ML1: Moth 4F **143**
Hazel Wood ML2: Wis 4B **146**
Hazelwood Av. G77: Newt M 5E **133**
PA11: Bri W. 4F **73**
PA2: Pais 6C **96**
Hazelwood Dr. G72: Blan 1A **140**
Hazelwood Gdns. G73: Ruth 3E **121**
Hazelwood La. PA11: Bri W 4F **73**
Hazelwood Rd. G41: Glas 1A **102**
PA11: Bri W. 4F **73**
Hazlitt Gdns. G20: Glas. 3E **63**
Hazlitt Pl. G20: Glas 3E **63**
Hazlitt St. G20: Glas 3F **63**
Headhouse Ct. G75: E Kil 3F **149**
Headhouse Grn. G75: E Kil 3G **149**
Headsmuir Av. ML8: Carl 3D **164**
Heath Av. G64: B'rig 1D **64**
G66: Lenz 3C **50**
Heathcliffe Av. G72: Blan 6A **124**
Heathcot Av. G15: Glas. 5G **43**
Heathcot Pl. G15: Glas 5F **43**
Heather Av. G61: Bear 5D **24**
G78: Barr 2C **114**
G81: Hard 6C **22**
ML1: Holy 2A **128**
Heatherbank Mus. of Social Work 1C **82**
Heatherbank Wlk. ML6: Air. 3F **91**
HEATHERBELL 6H **69**
Heatherbrae G64: B'rig 6A **48**
Heather Dr. G66: Lenz 3A **50**
Heather Gdns. G66: Lenz 3A **50**
Heather Gro. *G75: E Kil* *4G* ***149*** *(off Heathery Knowe)*
Heatherlea Pl. ML5: Coat 2F **111**
Heather Pl. G66: Lenz 2A **50**
PA5: John. 3G **95**
Heather Row ML8: Carl. 1E **165**
Heather Vw. G66: Len 2G **7**
Heather Way ML1: New S. 3A **128**
Heathery Knowe G75: E Kil. 4G **149**
Heatheryknowe Rd. G69: Barg 4C **88** (not continuous)
Heathery Rd. ML2: Wis. 6F **145**
Heathfield ML2: Wis. 4G **157**
Heathfield Av. G69: Mood 5D **52**
Heathfield Dr. G62: Miln. 2H **25**
Heathfield St. G33: Glas. 3C **86**
Heath Rd. ML9: Lark. 2F **161**
Heathside Rd. G46: Giff 4B **118**
Heathwood Dr. G46: T'bnk 4G **117**
Hecla Av. G15: Glas 4H **43**
Hecla Pl. G15: Glas 4H **43**
Hecla Sq. G15: Glas. 5H **43**
Hector Rd. G41: Glas 5B **102**
Helena Pl. G76: Clar. 1C **134**
Helena Ter. G81: Dun 1C **42**
Helensburgh Dr. G13: Glas. 3D **60**
Helenslea G72: Camb. 3D **122**
Helenslea Pl. ML4: Bell 3B **126**
Helenslee Ct. G82: Dumb. 4D **16**
Helenslee Cres. G82: Dumb. 4D **16**
Helenslee Rd. G82: Dumb 4D **16**

Helen St. G51: Glas 6F **81**
G52: Glas 6F **81**
HELEN ST. INTERCHANGE **6F 81**
Helenvale Ct. G31: Glas 6F **85**
Helenvale St. G31: Glas 1E **105**
Helen Wynd ML9: Lark 3E **161**
Helmsdale Av. G72: Blan 4A **124**
Helmsdale Ct. G72: Camb 2D **122**
Helmsdale Dr. PA2: Pais 3D **96**
Hemlock St. G13: Glas 2F **61**
Henderland Dr. G61: Bear 5E **45**
Henderland Rd. G61: Bear 5E **45**
Henderson Av. G72: Camb 1D **122**
Henderson St. G20: Glas 6D **62**
G81: Clyd 1G **59**
ML5: Coat 5B **90**
ML6: Air 3B **92**
PA1: Pais 6H **77**
Henrietta St. G14: Glas 6C **60**
Henry Bell Grn. *G75: E Kil* *3H* ***149***
(off Muirhouse La.)
Henry St. G78: Barr 4D **114**
Henry Wood Hall, The **3C** 82
Hepburn Hill ML3: Ham 3F **153**
Hepburn Rd. G52: Hill 4B **80**
Herald Av. G13: Glas 6D **44**
Herald Gro. ML1: Moth 5F **143**
Herald Way PA4: Renf 2E **79**
Herbertson Gro. G72: Blan 6A **124**
Herbertson St. G5: Glas 6F **83**
G72: Blan 2C **140**
Herbert St. G20: Glas 6D **62**
Herbison Ct. ML9: Lark 1F **161**
Hercules Way PA4: Renf 2F **79**
Heriot Av. PA2: Pais 5C **96**
Heriot Ct. PA2: Pais 5D **96**
Heriot Cres. G64: B'rig 4C **48**
Heriot Rd. G66: Lenz 4C **50**
Heritage Ct. G77: Newt M 4E **133**
Heritage Vw. ML5: Coat 3B **90**
Heritage Way ML5: Coat 4B **90**
Herma St. G23: Glas 1C **62**
Hermes Way ML4: Moss 2H **127**
Hermiston Av. G32: Glas 5C **86**
Hermiston Pl. G32: Glas 5C **86**
ML1: Holy *2A* ***128***
(off Windsor Rd.)
Hermiston Rd. G32: Glas 4B **86**
Hermitage Av. G13: Glas 2C **60**
Hermitage Cres. ML5: Coat 2D **110**
Herndon Ct. G77: Newt M 3G **133**
Heron Ct. G81: Hard 2D **42**
Heron Pl. PA5: John 6D **94**
Heron St. G40: Glas 1B **104**
Heron Way PA4: Renf 2E **79**
Herries Rd. G41: Glas 4A **102**
Herriet St. G41: Glas 2D **102**
Herriot St. ML5: Coat 3A **90**
Herschell St. G13: Glas 3F **61**
Hertford Av. G12: Glas 3H **61**
Hewett Cres. PA6: C'lee 2C **74**
Hexham Gdns. G41: Glas 4B **102**
Heys St. G78: Barr 5E **115**
Hickman St. G42: Glas 4F **103**
Hickman Ter. G42: Glas 3G **103**
Hickory Cres. G71: View 4G **109**
Hickory St. G22: Glas 4A **64**
High Avon St. ML9: Lark 1D **160**
HIGH BALMALLOCH **2G** 11
High Barholm PA10: Kilb 2A **94**
High Barrwood Rd. G65: Kils 3A **12**
High Beeches G76: Crmck 1A **136**
HIGH BLANTYRE **4A** 140
High Blantyre Rd. ML3: Ham 4D **140**
Highburgh Dr. G73: Ruth 2D **120**
Highburgh Rd. G12: Glas 6A **62**
HIGH BURNSIDE **3E** 121
High Burnside Av. ML5: Coat 6A **90**
High Calside PA2: Pais 2H **97**
High Coats ML5: Coat 4D **90**
High Comn. Rd. G75: E Kil 4B **150**
Highcraig Av. PA5: John 4D **94**
High Craigends G65: Kils 3H **11**
High Craighall Rd. G4: Glas 1F **83**
Highcroft Av. G44: Glas 2H **119**
Highcross Av. ML5: Coat 1H **109**
HIGH CROSSHILL **2D 120**
Higherness Way ML5: Coat 2A **110**
Highfield Av. G66: Kirk 4E **31**
PA2: Pais 6H **97**
Highfield Ct. G66: Kirk 5F **31**
Highfield Cres. ML1: Moth 1A **144**
PA2: Pais 6H **97**
Highfield Dr. G12: Glas 3H **61**
G73: Ruth 4E **121**
G76: Clar 2B **134**
Highfield Gro. G66: Kirk 4E **31**
Highfield Pl. G12: Glas 3H **61**
G74: E Kil 6H **137**
Highfield Rd. G66: Kirk 4E **31**
ML9: Lark 2F **161**
High Flender Rd. G76: Clar 3A **134**
HIGH GALLOWHILL **2B** 50
High Kirk Vw. PA5: John 3F **95**
HIGH KNIGHTSWOOD **1D** 60
Highland Av. G72: Blan 1A **140**
Highland La. G51: Glas 3A **82**
HIGHLAND PARK **1G** 11
Highland Pk. G65: Kils 2G **11**
Highland Pl. G65: Kils 1G **11**
Highland Rd. G62: Miln 3G **25**
High Mains Av. G82: Dumb 2C **18**
High Mair PA4: Renf 1E **79**
High Mdw. ML8: Carl 5H **165**
(not continuous)
High Mill Rd. ML8: Carl 3G **165**
High Murray Gro.
G72: Camb 2C **122**
High Parksail PA8: Ersk 1G **57**
High Parks Cres. ML3: Ham 5H **153**
High Patrick St. ML3: Ham 1A **154**
High Pleasance ML9: Lark 2E **161**
High Rd. ML1: Moth 2F **143**
PA2: Pais 2G **97**
High Row Cotts. G64: B'rig 2D **48**
Highstonehall Rd.
ML3: Ham 4C **152**
High St. G1: Glas 5H **83** (6G **5**)
G66: Kirk 4C **30**
G73: Ruth 5C **104**
G78: Neil 2D **130**
G82: Dumb 4E **17**
ML1: N'hill 3E **129**
ML6: Air 3H **91**
ML8: Carl 3F **165**
PA1: Pais 1H **97**
PA4: Renf 5F **59**
PA5: John 2E **95**
High Street Station (Rail) **4H 83 (6H 5)**
High Whitehills Rd.
G75: E Kil 6F **149**
Hilary Dr. G69: Bail 6F **87**
Hilda Cres. G33: Glas 5G **65**
Hillary Av. G73: Ruth 1F **121**
Hill Av. G77: Newt M 5C **132**
Hill Cres. G76: Busby 3C **134**
Hillcrest G69: Chry 1B **68**
G76: Crmck 1H **135**
Hillcrest Av. G32: Carm 5B **106**
G44: Glas 3C **118**
G67: Cumb 5G **35**
G81: Dun 6C **22**
ML2: Wis 6E **145**
ML5: Coat 5E **91**
PA2: Pais 6G **97**
Hillcrest Ct. G67: Cumb 4H **35**
Hillcrest Dr. G77: Newt M 4G **133**
Hillcrest Rd. G32: Carm 4C **106**
G61: Bear 3F **45**
G65: Queen 3C **10**
G71: Tann 6E **109**
Hillcrest St. G62: Miln 3G **25**
Hillcrest Ter. G71: Both 4F **125**
Hillcrest Vw. ML9: Lark 3F **161**
Hillcroft Ter. G64: B'rig 1B **64**
Hillend Cotts. G66: Lenz 1C **50**
Hillend Cres. G76: Clar 3A **134**
G81: Dun 1B **42**
Hillend Rd. G22: Glas 2E **63**
G73: Ruth 2D **120**
G76: Clar 3A **134**
Hillfoot PA6: C'lee 3D **74**
Hillfoot Av. G61: Bear 2F **45**
G73: Ruth 6C **104**
G82: Dumb 1C **18**
ML2: Wis 2B **146**
Hillfoot Cres. ML2: Wis 2B **146**
Hillfoot Dr. G61: Bear 2F **45**
ML2: Wis 2B **146**
ML5: Coat 5H **89**
Hillfoot Gdns. G71: Tann 5C **108**
ML2: Wis 2B **146**
Hillfoot Rd. ML6: Air 5A **92**
Hillfoot Station (Rail) **2G** 45
Hillfoot St. G31: Glas 4C **84**
Hillfoot Ter. ML8: Carl 4G **165**
HILLHEAD
Glasgow **6B** 62
Kirkintilloch **4D** 30
Hillhead Av. FK4: Bank 1E **15**
G69: Mood 5D **52**
G73: Ruth 3D **120**
ML1: Carf 5A **128**
ML8: Carl 3G **165**
Hillhead Cres. ML1: Carf 5A **128**
ML3: Ham 6C **140**
Hillhead Dr. ML1: Carf 6A **128**
ML6: Air 5A **92**
Hillhead Pl. G73: Ruth 3D **120**
Hillhead Rd. G21: Glas 2F **65**
G66: Kirk 4D **30**
Hillhead Station (Und.) **6B** 62
Hillhead St. G12: Glas 1B **82**
G62: Miln 3G **25**
Hillhead Ter. ML3: Ham 6C **140**
HILLHOUSE **6D** 140
Hillhouse Cres. ML3: Ham 6D **140**
Hillhouse Ga. ML8: Carl 5H **165**
Hillhouse Pk. Ind. Est.
ML3: Ham 5E **141**
Hillhouse Rd. G72: Blan 4H **139**
ML3: Ham 5C **140**
Hillhouse St. G21: Glas 5C **64**
Hillhouse Ter. ML3: Ham 6D **140**
HILLINGTON **6A** 80
Hillington East Station (Rail)
5B 80
Hillington Gdns. G52: Glas 1C **100**
HILLINGTON INDUSTRIAL ESTATE
3H 79
HILLINGTON INTERCHANGE **2H** 79
Hillington Pk. Cir. G52: Glas 6C **80**
Hillington Quad. G52: Glas 6A **80**
Hillington Rd. G52: Hill 2H **79**
(not continuous)
Hillington Rd. Sth. G52: Glas 5A **80**
Hillington Shop. Cen.
G52: Hill 3H **79**
Hillington Ter. G52: Glas 6A **80**
Hillington West Station (Rail)
4H 79
Hillkirk Pl. G21: Glas 5B **64**
Hillkirk St. G21: Glas 5B **64**
Hillkirk St. La. *G21: Glas* *5B* ***64***
(off Hillkirk St.)
Hillneuk Av. G61: Bear 2F **45**
Hillneuk Dr. G61: Bear 2G **45**
Hillpark Av. PA2: Pais 4H **97**
Hillpark Dr. G43: Glas 1H **117**
Hill Pl. ML1: Carf 5C **128**
ML4: Bell 4B **126**
Hillrigg Av. ML6: Air 3C **92**
Hill Rd. G65: Kils 1H **11**
G67: Cumb 3G **35**
Hillsborough Rd. G69: Bail 6F **87**
HILLSIDE **5B** 114
Hillside G65: Croy 6B **12**
PA6: C'lee 3D **74**
Hillside Av. G61: Bear 2F **45**
G76: Clar 2B **134**
Hillside Cotts. ML5: Glenb 3A **70**
Hillside Ct. G46: T'bnk 4F **117**

Hillside Cres. G78: Neil 2D **130**
ML1: N'hill 3D **128**
ML3: Ham. 1H **153**
ML5: Coat. 1B **110**
Hillside Dr. G61: Bear. 2G **45**
G64: B'rig 5C **48**
G78: Barr 4C **114**
Hillside Gdns. La. *G11: Glas 6H 61*
(off Nth. Gardner St.)
Hillside Gro. G78: Barr 5C **114**
Hillside La. ML3: Ham 1G **153**
Hillside Pk. G81: Hard 1D **42**
Hillside Pl. ML1: N'hill 4D **128**
Hillside Quad. G43: Glas 2H **117**
Hillside Rd. G43: Glas 2H **117**
G78: Barr 5B **114**
G78: Neil. 2D **130**
PA2: Pais 3C **98**
Hillside Ter. G60: Old K 1F **41**
G66: Milt C 6B **8**
ML3: Ham. 1G **153**
Hill St. G3: Glas 2E **83** (2A **4**)
G82: Dumb 4D **16**
ML2: Wis 1G **157**
ML3: Ham. 6D **140**
ML6: Chap 3D **112**
ML9: Lark 3E **161**
Hillsview G69: Chry 1H **67**
Hillswick Cres. G22: Glas 1F **63**
Hill Ter. ML1: Carf 5C **128**
Hilltop Av. ML4: Bell. 6C **110**
Hilltop Ter. G69: Mood 5D **52**
Hill Vw. G75: E Kil 3G **149**
G82: Milt 4F **19**
Hillview Av. G65: Kils. 4H **11**
G66: Len. 3G **7**
Hillview Cotts. G65: Twe 1D **32**
Hillview Cres. G71: Tann 5C **108**
ML4: Bell 5C **110**
ML9: Lark 3F **161**
Hillview Dr. G72: Blan 5A **124**
G76: Clar. 2B **134**
Hill Vw. Gdns. G64: B'rig 1F **65**
Hillview Pl. G76: Clar 2C **134**
G77: Newt M. 5D **132**
Hillview Rd. PA11: Bri W 4G **73**
PA5: Eld 3H **95**
Hillview St. G32: Glas 6H **85**
Hillview Ter. G60: Old K 2F **41**
Hiltonbank St. ML3: Ham 5F **141**
Hilton Ct. G64: B'rig 4C **48**
Hilton Gdns. G13: Glas 2F **61**
Hilton Gdns. La. G13: Glas 2F **61**
Hilton Pk. G64: B'rig. 3B **48**
Hilton Rd. G62: Miln. 3E **25**
G64: B'rig 4B **48**
Hilton Ter. G13: Glas. 2E **61**
G64: B'rig 3B **48**
G72: Camb 4G **121**
Hindsland Rd. ML9: Lark 4F **161**
Hinshaw St. G20: Glas 6E **63**
Hinshelwood Dr. G51: Glas. 5G **81**
Hinshelwood Pl. G51: Glas. 6H **81**
Hirsel Pl. G71: Both 5F **125**
Hobart Cres. G81: Clyd. 2H **41**
Hobart Quad. ML2: Wis 6C **146**
Hobart Rd. G75: E Kil 4E **149**
Hobart St. G22: Glas 5F **63**
Hobden St. G21: Glas 6C **64**
Hoddam Av. G45: Glas 4B **120**
Hoddam Ter. G45: Glas. 4C **120**
Hodge Ct. G22: Glas 3F **63**
Hoey Dr. ML2: Over 4A **158**
Hogan Ct. G81: Dun 1B **42**
Hogan Way ML1: Cle. 6E **129**
Hogarth Av. G32: Glas. 4F **85**
Hogarth Cres. G32: Glas 4F **85**
Hogarth Dr. G32: Glas. 4F **85**
Hogarth Gdns. G32: Glas. 4F **85**
HOGGANFIELD **1A 86**
Hogganfield St. G33: Glas. 1F **85**
Hogg Av. PA5: John 4E **95**
Hogg Rd. ML6: Chap 1D **112**
Hogg St. ML6: Air. 4A **92**
Holeburn La. G43: Glas 1A **118**
Holeburn Rd. G43: Glas 1A **118**
HOLEHILLS **2B 92**
Holehills Dr. ML6: Air. 1B **92**
Holehills Pl. ML6: Air. 1B **92**
HOLEHOUSE **2C 130**
Holehouse Brae G78: Neil. 2C **130**
Holehouse Dr. G13: Glas. 3A **60**
Holehouse Ter. G78: Neil 2C **130**
Hollandbush Av. FK4: Bank. 1E **15**
Hollandbush Cres. FK4: Bank 1F **15**
Hollandbush Gro. ML3: Ham 3H **153**
Hollandhurst Rd. ML5: Coat 2B **90**
Holland St. G2: Glas. 3E **83** (4A **4**)
Hollinwell Rd. G23: Glas 1B **62**
Hollowglen Rd. G32: Glas. 5B **86**
Hollows Av. PA2: Pais 6D **96**
Hollows Cres. PA2: Pais. 6D **96**
Hollows, The *G46: Giff. 6H 117*
(off Ayr Rd.)
Holly Av. G66: Milt C 6B **8**
Hollybank Pl. G72: Camb 3B **122**
Hollybank St. G21: Glas 2C **84**
Hollybrook Pl. *G42: Glas. 3F 103*
(off Jamieson St.)
Hollybrook St. G42: Glas. 3F **103**
(not continuous)
Hollybush Av. PA2: Pais 6F **97**
Hollybush Rd. G52: Glas 6H **79**
Holly Dr. G21: Glas. 6C **64**
G82: Dumb 2B **16**
Holly Gro. FK4: Bank. 1F **15**
ML4: Moss 2H **127**
Hollymount G61: Bear 5F **45**
Holly Pl. PA5: John 5G **95**
Holly St. G81: Clyd 3C **42**
ML6: Air 4C **92**
Hollytree Gdns. G66: Len 3E **7**
Hollywood Bowl **1F 109**
Holm Av. G71: Udd 6C **108**
PA2: Pais 3B **98**
Holmbank Av. G41: Glas 6B **102**
Holmbrae Av. G71: Tann. 6D **108**
Holmbrae Rd. G71: Tann 6D **108**
Holmbyre Ct. G45: Glas. 6F **119**
Holmbyre Rd. G45: Glas 6F **119**
Holmbyre Ter. G45: Glas. 5G **119**
Holmes Av. PA4: Renf. 2E **79**
Holmes Quad. ML4: Bell. 4C **126**
Holmfauldhead Pl. G51: Glas 3E **81**
Holmfauld Rd. G51: Glas 3E **81**
Holmfield G66: Kirk 6E **31**
Holm Gdns. ML4: Bell. 3E **127**
Holmhead Cres. G44: Glas 1E **119**
Holmhead Pl. G44: Glas 1E **119**
Holmhead Rd. G44: Glas. 2E **119**
Holmhill Av. G72: Camb 3A **122**
Holmhills Dr. G72: Camb 4H **121**
Holmhills Gdns. G72: Camb 3H **121**
Holmhills Gro. G72: Camb 3H **121**
Holmhills Pl. G72: Camb 3H **121**
Holmhills Rd. G72: Camb. 3H **121**
Holmhills Ter. G72: Camb. 3H **121**
Holm La. G74: E Kil 2G **149**
Holmlea Rd. G42: Glas 6E **103**
G44: Glas 1E **119**
HOLMPARK. **4H 39**
Holmpark PA7: B'ton 4G **39**
Holm Pl. ML9: Lark 3C **160**
PA3: Lin 4H **75**
Holms Cres. PA8: Ersk 5D **40**
Holms Pl. G69: G'csh 2C **68**
Holm St. G2: Glas 4E **83** (6B **4**)
ML1: New S 4A **128**
ML8: Carl 3E **165**
Holmswood Av. G72: Blan. 1B **140**
Holmwood Av. G71: Udd. 6D **108**
Holmwood Gdns. G71: Udd 6D **108**
Holyknowe Cres. G66: Len. 3G **7**
Holyknowe Rd. G66: Len 4G **7**
Holyrood Cres. G4: Glas. 1D **82**
Holyrood Quad. *G20: Glas 1D 82*
(off Holyrood Cres.)
Holyrood Sports Cen. **4G 103**
Holyrood St. ML3: Ham 4E **141**
HOLYTOWN **2A 128**
Holytown Rd. ML4: Moss. 2G **127**
Holytown Station (Rail) **4A 128**
Holywell St. G31: Glas. 6D **84**
Homeblair Ho. G46: Giff. 2A **118**
Homefield Pl. G51: Glas 3E **81**
Homer Pl. ML4: Moss 2G **127**
Homeston Av. G71: Both. 4E **125**
Honeybank Cres. ML8: Carl. 2F **165**
Honeybog Rd. G52: Glas 5G **79**
Honeywell Cres. ML6: Chap 4E **113**
Hood St. G81: Clyd 5E **43**
Hope Av. PA11: Q'riers 1A **72**
Hope Cres. ML9: Lark. 2F **161**
Hopefield Av. G12: Glas 4A **62**
Hopehill Gdns. G20: Glas 6E **63**
Hopehill Rd. G20: Glas. 6E **63**
(not continuous)
Hopeman PA8: Ersk 4E **41**
Hopeman Av. G46: T'bnk. 3E **117**
Hopeman Dr. G46: T'bnk. 3E **117**
Hopeman Path G46: T'bnk 2E **117**
Hopeman Rd. G46: T'bnk 3E **117**
Hopeman St. G46: T'bnk. 3E **117**
Hope St. G2: Glas. 4F **83** (6C **4**)
ML1: Moth 2G **143**
ML2: Newm. 5E **147**
ML3: Ham. 6A **142**
ML4: Moss 2E **127**
ML8: Carl 3G **165**
Hopetoun Pl. G23: Glas 6C **46**
Hopetoun Ter. G21: Glas. 6C **64**
Hopkins Brae G66: Kirk 4D **30**
Horatius St. ML1: Moth 6D **126**
Hornal Rd. G71: Udd 3D **124**
Hornbeam Dr. G81: Clyd. 3C **42**
Hornbeam Rd. G67: Cumb 6E **15**
G71: View 5F **109**
Horndean Ct. G64: B'rig 3C **48**
Horne St. G22: Glas 4A **64**
Hornock Rd. ML5: Coat. 2B **90**
Hornshill Dr. ML1: Cle 5H **129**
Hornshill Farm Rd. G33: Step. 3E **67**
HORNSHILL INTERCHANGE **1E 67**
Hornshill St. G21: Glas. 5C **64**
Horsbrugh Av. G65: Kils 2H **11**
Horsburgh St. G33: Glas. 1D **86**
Horse Shoe Rd. G61: Bear 2E **45**
Horsewood Rd. PA11: Bri W. 4E **73**
Horslethill Rd. G12: Glas 5A **62**
Horslet St. ML5: Coat. 1G **109**
Horsley Brae ML2: Over 2C **162**
Hospital Rd. ML2: Wis 3H **157**
Hospital St. ML5: Coat 1C **110**
Hotspur St. G20: Glas. 4C **62**
Houldsworth Ct. ML2: Wis 1A **158**
Houldsworth La. *G3: Glas. 3C 82*
(off Elliot St.)
Houldsworth St. G3: Glas 3C **82**
House for an Art Lover **1G 101**
Househillmuir Cres.
G53: Glas 1C **116**
Househillmuir La. *G53: Glas. 6C 100*
(off Househillmuir Rd.)
Househillmuir Pl. G53: Glas 6C **100**
Househillmuir Rd. G53: Glas 2A **116**
HOUSEHILLWOOD. **6B 100**
Househillwood Cres.
G53: Glas 6B **100**
Househillwood Rd. G53: Glas. 1A **116**
Housel Av. G13: Glas 2B **60**
HOUSTON. **1A 74**
Houston Ct. *PA5: John 2F 95*
(off Houston Sq.)
Houstonfield Quad. PA6: Hous 1A **74**
Houstonfield Rd. PA6: Hous 1A **74**
Houston Pl. G5: Glas 5D **82**
PA5: Eld 3A **96**
Houston Rd. PA11: Bri W 3F **73**
PA4: Inch 5D **56**
PA6: Hous. 1B **74**
(not continuous)
PA7: B'ton. 5C **38**

Houston St. G5: Glas 6D **82**
  ML2: Wis 2B **158**
  ML3: Ham 2H **153**
  PA4: Renf 5F **59**
Houston Ter. G74: E Kil 1F **149**
Houstoun Sq. PA5: John 2F **95**
Howard Av. G72: Blan 4A **138**
Howard Ct. G74: E Kil 4A **138**
Howard St. G1: Glas 5F **83** (6D **4**)
  ML9: Lark 4G **161**
  PA1: Pais 6C **78**
Howatshaws Rd. G82: Dumb . . . 1H **17**
Howat St. G51: Glas 3G **81**
Howcraigs St. G81: Clyd 2F **59**
                (off Clydeholm Ter.)
Howden Av. ML1: N'hse 5D **112**
Howden Dr. PA3: Lin 6G **75**
Howden Pl. ML1: Holy 2A **128**
Howe Gdns. G71: Tann 6E **109**
Howe Rd. G65: Kils 4H **11**
Howes St. ML5: Coat 1D **110**
Howe St. PA3: Pais 1D **96**
Howford Rd. G52: Glas 1B **100**
Howgate Av. G15: Glas 4H **43**
Howgate Rd. ML3: Ham 3F **153**
Howie Bldgs. G76: Clar 1C **134**
Howieshill Av. G72: Camb 2B **122**
Howieshill Rd. G72: Camb 3B **122**
Howie St. ML9: Lark 4F **161**
Howletnest Rd. ML6: Air 5C **92**
Howlet Pl. ML3: Ham 5A **154**
Howson Lea ML1: Moth 5B **144**
Howson Vw. ML1: Moth 2D **142**
Howth Dr. G13: Glas 1F **61**
Howth Ter. G13: Glas 1F **61**
HOWWOOD ROAD 4E **95**
Hoylake Pk. G71: Both 5D **124**
Hoylake Pl. G23: Glas 6C **46**
Hozier Cres. G71: Tann 5D **108**
Hozier Loan ML9: Lark 1F **161**
          (off Duncan Graham St.)
Hozier Pl. G71: Both 4F **125**
Hozier St. ML5: Coat 6C **90**
  ML8: Carl 3F **165**
Hub Leisure Cen 4D **42**
             (off Kilbowie Rd.)
Hudson Ter. G75: E Kil 3D **148**
Hudson Way G75: E Kil 3E **149**
Hughenden Dr. G12: Glas 5H **61**
Hughenden Gdns. G12: Glas 5G **61**
Hughenden La. G12: Glas 5H **61**
Hughenden Rd. G12: Glas 5H **61**
Hughenden Ter. G12: Glas 5H **61**
Hugh Fraser Ct. G77: Newt M . . . 4D **132**
Hugo St. G20: Glas 4D **62**
Humbie Ct. G77: Newt M 6E **133**
Humbie Ga. G77: Newt M 6E **133**
Humbie Gro. G77: Newt M 6E **133**
Humbie Rd. G77: Newt M 6E **133**
Hume Dr. G71: Both 4E **125**
  G71: Udd 6C **108**
Hume Pl. G75: E Kil 3F **149**
Hume Rd. G67: Cumb 2A **36**
Hume St. G81: Clyd 6D **42**
Hunterfield Dr. G72: Camb 2G **121**
HUNTERHILL 3C **98**
Hunterhill Av. PA2: Pais 2B **98**
Hunterhill Rd. PA2: Pais 2B **98**
Hunter Ho. Mus. 5C **138**
Hunterian Gallery 1B **82**
Hunterian Mus. 1B **82**
Hunter Pl. G62: Miln 4E **25**
  PA10: Kilb 3A **94**
Hunter Rd. G62: Miln 3E **25**
  G73: Ruth 4E **105**
  ML3: Ham 3F **141**
Hunter's Av. G82: Dumb 2D **18**
Hunters Dr. G77: Newt M 6B **132**
Huntersfield Rd. PA5: John 4C **94**
Hunters Hill Ct. G21: Glas 3B **64**
Huntershill Ho. G64: B'rig 1B **64**
Huntershill Rd. G64: B'rig 1B **64**
Huntershill Village G64: B'rig 1B **64**
Huntershill Way G64: B'rig 2B **64**

Hunter St. G4: Glas 5A **84**
  G74: E Kil 1H **149**
  ML4: Bell 2C **126**
  ML6: Air 2H **91**
  PA1: Pais 6A **78**
Hunt Hill G68: Cumb 4G **33**
Hunthill La. G72: Blan 3H **139**
Hunthill Pl. G76: Busby 4E **135**
Hunthill Rd. G72: Blan 2H **139**
HUNT HILL RDBT. 4G **33**
Huntingdon Rd. G21: Glas 1A **84**
Huntingdon Sq. G21: Glas 1A **84**
Hunting Lodge Gdns. ML3: Ham . . 1C **154**
Huntingtower Rd. G69: Bail 1F **107**
Huntly Av. G46: Giff 5B **118**
  ML4: Bell 1C **126**
Huntly Ct. G64: B'rig 1C **64**
Huntly Dr. G61: Bear 6E **25**
  G72: Camb 3B **122**
  ML5: Coat 1H **109**
Huntly Gdns. G12: Glas 6B **62**
Huntly Ga. G46: Giff 4B **118**
Huntly Path G69: Mood 5E **53**
Huntly Quad. ML2: Wis 4H **145**
Huntly Rd. G12: Glas 6A **62**
  G52: Hill 3H **79**
Huntly Ter. PA2: Pais 4C **98**
Huntshill St. G21: Glas 3A **64**
Hurlawcrook Rd. G75: E Kil 6A **150**
HURLET 6H **99**
Hurlet Rd. PA2: Pais 4E **99**
Hurlford Av. G13: Glas 2H **59**
Hurly Hawkin G64: B'rig 1F **65**
Hutcheson Rd. G46: Giff, T'bnk . . 5G **117**
Hutchesons' Hall 5F **5**
Hutcheson St. G1: Glas 4G **83** (6E **5**)
HUTCHESONTOWN 1H **103**
Hutcheson Town Ct. G5: Glas . . . 1G **103**
Hutchinson Pl. G72: Flem 4E **123**
Hutchison Ct. G46: Giff 6A **118**
Hutchison Dr. G61: Bear 5G **45**
Hutchison Pl. ML5: Coat 5B **90**
Hutchison St. ML2: Over 4B **158**
  ML3: Ham 3H **153**
Hutton G12: Glas 3G **61**
Hutton Av. PA6: C'lee 3C **74**
Hutton Dr. G51: Glas 3E **81**
  G74: E Kil 5H **137**
Huxley St. G20: Glas 3D **62**
Hyacinth Way ML8: Carl 5F **165**
Hydepark St. G3: Glas 4D **82**
Hyndal Av. G53: Glas 4C **100**
HYNDLAND 6H **61**
Hyndland Av. G11: Glas 1H **81**
Hyndland Rd. G12: Glas 6H **61**
Hyndland Station (Rail) 5G **61**
Hyndland St. G11: Glas 1A **82**
  G12: Glas 1A **82**
Hyndlee Dr. G52: Glas 6C **80**
Hyndshaw Rd. ML8: Carl 2F **165**
Hyndshaw Vw. ML8: Law 1A **164**
Hyslop Pl. G81: Clyd 4C **42**
Hyslop St. ML6: Air 3G **91**

I

Iain Dr. G61: Bear 1C **44**
Iain Nicholson Recreation Cen. . . . 1C **68**
Iain Rd. G61: Bear 2C **44**
Ian Smith Ct. G81: Clyd 1F **59**
IBROX 6H **81**
Ibroxholm Av. G51: Glas 6H **81**
Ibroxholm Oval G51: Glas 5H **81**
Ibroxholm Pl. G51: Glas 6H **81**
Ibrox Ind. Est. G51: Glas 5H **81**
Ibrox Stadium 5G **81**
Ibrox St. G51: Glas 5A **82**
Ibrox Ter. G51: Glas 5H **81**
Ibrox Ter. La. G51: Glas 5H **81**
Ibrox Station (Und.) 5H **81**
Ida Quad. ML4: Bell 2B **126**
Iddesleigh Av. G62: Miln 3G **25**
Ilay Av. G61: Bear 1F **61**

Ilay Ct. G61: Bear 1G **61**
Ilay Rd. G61: Bear 1G **61**
Imlach Pl. ML1: Moth 4F **143**
Imperial Dr. ML6: Air 6H **91**
Inchbrae Rd. G52: Glas 1C **100**
Inchcolm Gdns. G69: Mood 4E **53**
Inchcolm Pl. G74: E Kil 1E **149**
Inchcruin Pl. G15: Glas 3G **43**
Inchfad Dr. G15: Glas 4G **43**
Inchfad Pl. G15: Glas 4G **43**
Inch Garvie G74: E Kil 2D **150**
INCHINNAN 2H **57**
Inchinnan Dr. PA4: Inch 6F **57**
Inchinnan Ind. Est. PA4: Inch 5G **57**
Inchinnan Rd. ML4: Bell 6B **110**
  PA3: Pais 4A **78**
  PA4: Renf 5D **58**
Inch Keith G74: E Kil 2D **150**
Inchkeith Pl. G32: Glas 4B **86**
Inchlaggan Pl. G15: Glas 3G **43**
Inchlee St. G14: Glas 1E **81**
Inch Marnock G74: E Kil 3C **150**
Inchmoan Pl. G15: Glas 3G **43**
Inch Murrin G74: E Kil 2D **150**
Inchmurrin Av. G66: Kirk 5H **31**
Inchmurrin Dr. G73: Ruth 5F **121**
Inchmurrin Gdns. G73: Ruth 5F **121**
Inchmurrin Pl. G73: Ruth 5F **121**
Inchneuk Path ML5: Glenb 3H **69**
Inchneuk Rd. ML5: Glenb 3A **70**
Inchnock Av. G69: G'csh 3D **68**
Inchoch St. G33: Glas 1E **87**
Incholm La. G11: Glas 1E **81**
             (off Incholm St.)
Incholm St. G11: Glas 1E **81**
Inchrory Pl. G15: Glas 3G **43**
Inchwood Ct. G68: Cumb 6B **34**
Inchwood Pl. G68: Cumb 6B **34**
Inchwood Rd. G68: Cumb 6B **34**
Incle St. PA1: Pais 6B **78**
India Dr. PA4: Inch 3G **57**
India St. G2: Glas 3E **83** (3A **4**)
Industry St. G66: Kirk 6D **30**
           (not continuous)
Inga St. G20: Glas 2C **62**
Ingerbreck Av. G73: Ruth 3F **121**
Ingleby Dr. G31: Glas 4D **84**
         (Cumbernauld Rd.)
  G31: Glas 4C **84**
           (Whitehill St.)
Ingleby Pl. G78: Neil 2E **131**
Inglefield Ct. ML6: Air 4A **92**
Inglefield St. G42: Glas 3F **103**
Ingleneuk Av. G33: Mille 4B **66**
Ingleside G66: Lenz 1C **50**
Inglestone Av. G46: T'bnk 5G **117**
Inglewood Cres. G75: E Kil 3C **148**
  PA2: Pais 3D **96**
Inglis Pl. G75: E Kil 4H **149**
Inglis St. G31: Glas 5C **84**
  ML2: Wis 1D **156**
Ingliston Dr. PA7: B'ton 4F **39**
Ingram St. G1: Glas 4G **83** (5E **5**)
Inishail Rd. G33: Glas 2C **86**
Inkerman Rd. G52: Glas 6H **79**
Inner City Trad. Est. G4: Glas 2G **5**
Innerleithen Dr. ML2: Wis 3A **146**
Innermanse Quad. ML1: N'hill . . . 2F **129**
Innerwick Dr. G52: Glas 6B **80**
Innes Ct. G74: E Kil 5G **137**
  ML6: Air 3E **93**
Innspark G65: Kils 2H **11**
International Av. G72: Blan 5B **140**
Inveraray Dr. G64: B'rig 3D **48**
Inveraray Gdns. ML1: Carf 5C **128**
Inverarish PA8: Ersk 2G **57**
Inveravon Dr. ML1: Moth 4D **142**
Inverbervie PA8: Ersk 5E **41**
Invercanny Dr. G15: Glas 3H **43**
Invercanny Pl. G15: Glas 3A **44**
Invercargill G75: E Kil 4C **148**
Inverclyde Gdns. G73: Ruth 4F **121**
Invercree Wlk. ML5: Glenb 3G **69**
             (off Dinyra Pl.)

Inveresk Pl. ML5: Coat 3C 90
Inveresk Quad. G32: Glas 5A 86
Inveresk St. G32: Glas 5H 85
Inverewe Av. G46: T'bnk 5D 116
Inverewe Dr. G46: T'bnk 5D 116
Inverewe Gdns. G46: T'bnk 5D 116
Inverewe Pl. G46: T'bnk 4D 116
Inverewe Way G77: Newt M 4A 132
Invergarry Av. G46: T'bnk 6D 116
Invergarry Ct. G46: T'bnk 5E 117
Invergarry Dr. G46: T'bnk 5D 116
Invergarry Gdns. G46: T'bnk 6D 116
Invergarry Gro. G46: T'bnk 5D 116
Invergarry Pl. G46: T'bnk 5E 117
Invergarry Quad. G46: T'bnk 5E 117
Invergarry Vw. G46: T'bnk 5E 117
Inverglas Av. PA4: Renf 2H 79
Invergordon Av. G43: Glas 6D 102
Invergordon Pl. ML6: Air 5A 92
Invergyle Dr. G52: Glas 6B 80
Inverkar Dr. PA2: Pais 3E 97
Inverlair Av. G43: Glas 1D 118
G44: Glas 1D 118
Inverleith St. G32: Glas 5F 85
Inverlochy St. G33: Glas 2D 86
Inverness St. G51: Glas 5D 80
Invernia Sq. G81: Clyd 5D 42
Inveroran Dr. G61: Bear 3H 45
Inver Rd. G33: Glas 4E 87
Invershiel Rd. G23: Glas 6B 46
Invershin Dr. G20: Glas 4B 62
Inverurie St. G21: Glas 6H 63
Invervale Av. ML6: Air 5F 93
Inzievar Ter. G32: Carm 4B 106
Iona ML6: Air 6D 92
Iona Av. G74: E Kil 5A 138
Iona Ct. G51: Glas 4H 81
Iona Cres. G60: Old K 2G 41
Iona Dr. PA2: Pais 6H 97
Iona Gdns. G60: Old K 2G 41
Iona La. G69: Mood 5E 53
Iona Path G72: Blan 2A 140
Iona Pl. G60: Old K 2G 41
ML5: Coat 2H 89
Iona Quad. ML2: Wis 4C 146
Iona Ridge ML3: Ham 2C 152
Iona Rd. G73: Ruth 4G 121
ML2: Newm 3D 146
PA4: Renf 2E 79
Iona St. G51: Glas 4H 81
ML1: Moth 6F 127
Iona Wlk. ML5: Coat 1A 110
Iona Way G33: Step 5E 67
G66: Kirk 5G 31
Iris Av. G45: Glas 4C 120
Irongray St. G31: Glas 4E 85
Irvine Cres. ML5: Coat 4E 91
Irvine Dr. PA3: Lin 4F 75
Irvine Gdns. G66: Milt C 6B 8
Irvine Pl. G65: Kils 2F 11
Irvine St. G40: Glas 2D 104
ML6: Glenm 5H 71
Irvine Ter. ML3: Ham 3H 153
Irving Av. G81: Hard 1D 42
Irving Ct. G81: Hard 1D 42
Irving Quad. G81: Hard 1D 42
Isabella Gdns. ML3: Fern 2D 154
Iser La. G41: Glas 5C 102
Isla Av. ML2: Newm 3D 146
Island Rd. G67: Cumb 5F 35
Islay ML6: Air 5E 93
Islay Av. G73: Ruth 4G 121
Islay Ct. ML3: Ham 1D 152
Islay Cres. G60: Old K 2G 41
PA2: Pais 6H 97
Islay Dr. G60: Old K 2G 41
G77: Newt M 4B 132
Islay Gdns. ML8: Carl 5F 165
ML9: Lark 2F 161
Islay Quad. ML2: Wis 2E 157
Islay Rd. G66: Kirk 5G 31
Islay Way ML5: Coat 1H 109
Ivanhoe G74: E Kil 5D 138
Ivanhoe Ct. ML8: Carl 4D 164
Ivanhoe Cres. ML2: Wis 6H 145
Ivanhoe Dr. G66: Kirk 5E 31
Ivanhoe Pl. ML1: Holy 2B 128
Ivanhoe Rd. G13: Glas 1D 60
G67: Cumb 5G 35
PA2: Pais 4D 96
Ivanhoe Way PA2: Pais 5D 96
Ivybank Av. G72: Camb 3C 122
Ivy Gro. ML5: Coat 5D 90
Ivy Pl. G72: Blan 1A 140
ML1: New S 4A 128
Ivy Rd. G71: View 5G 109
Ivy Ter. ML1: Holy 2A 128
Ivy Way ML6: Chap 2E 113

J

Jackson Ct. ML5: Coat 5D 90
Jackson Dr. G33: Step 4F 67
Jackson Pl. ML8: Carl 2E 165
Jackson St. ML5: Coat 4D 90
Jack's Rd. G71: Udd 2E 125
Jack St. ML1: Moth 5B 144
ML3: Ham 3H 153
Jackton Rd. G75: E Kil 6A 148
Jacob's Ladder ML2: Over 5B 158
Jacob's Ladder Way ML2: Over . . . 4A 158
Jade Ter. ML4: Bell 3C 126
Jagger Gdns. G69: Bail 1F 107
Jamaica Dr. G75: E Kil 2C 148
Jamaica St. G1: Glas 5F 83 (6D 4)
James Dempsey Ct. ML5: Coat 5B 90
James Dempsey Gdns.
ML5: Coat 5B 90
James Dunlop Gdns. G64: B'rig 2D 64
James Gray St. G41: Glas 5C 102
James Hamilton Dr. ML4: Bell 2D 126
James Hamilton Heritage Cen., The
. . . . 5F 137
James Hamilton Heritage Pk. 5F 137
James Healy Dr. ML3: Ham 4G 153
James Hemphill Ct. G66: Len 3G 7
James Leeson Ct. G66: Milt C 5C 8
James Morrison St. G1: Glas 5H 83
James Nisbet St. G21: Glas 2B 84
James St. FK4: Hag 1G 15
G40: Glas 1A 104
ML1: Moth 2F 143
ML4: Bell 1A 126
ML8: Carl 4F 165
James Vw. ML1: New S 4H 127
James Watt Av. G75: E Kil 3H 149
James Watt La. G2: Glas 6B 4
James Watt Pl. G74: E Kil 6D 136
James Watt Rd. G62: Miln 2F 25
James Watt St. G2: Glas 4E 83 (6B 4)
Jamieson Ct. G42: Glas 3F 103
G81: Hard 6D 22
Jamieson Dr. G74: E Kil 1A 150
Jamieson St. G42: Glas 3F 103
(Batson St.)
G42: Glas 3F 103
(Cathcart Rd.)
Janebank Av. G72: Camb 3C 122
Jane Ct. ML9: Lark 3E 161
Janefield Av. PA5: John 3E 95
Janefield Pl. G66: Len 2F 7
G72: Blan 3A 140
Janefield St. G31: Glas 6D 84
Jane Rae Gdns. G81: Clyd 1F 59
Jane's Brae G67: Cumb 5H 35
JANE'S BRAE INTERCHANGE 5H 35
Janesmith St. ML2: Wis 5C 144
Janetta St. G81: Clyd 4C 42
Jardine St. G20: Glas 6D 62
Jardine Ter. G69: G'csh 4D 68
Jarvie Av. ML6: Plain 1G 93
Jarvie Cres. G65: Kils 4H 11
Jarvie Way PA2: Pais 5C 96
Jasmine Pl. G67: Cumb 6D 34
Jasmine Way ML8: Carl 5E 165
Java St. ML1: Moth 6E 127
Jean Armour Dr. G81: Clyd 4E 43
Jeanette Av. ML3: Ham 4H 153
Jean Maclean Pl. G64: B'rig 3D 48
Jedburgh Av. G73: Ruth 6D 104
Jedburgh Dr. PA2: Pais 4E 97
Jedburgh Gdns. G20: Glas 6D 62
Jedburgh Pl. G74: E Kil 1H 149
ML5: Coat 2B 110
Jedburgh St. G72: Blan 2B 140
ML2: Wis 4A 146
Jedworth Av. G15: Glas 4B 44
Jedworth Ct. G61: Bear 2E 45
(off Manse Rd.)
Jedworth Pl. G15: Glas 4C 44
Jedworth Rd. G15: Glas 4B 44
Jeffrey Pl. G65: Kils 2G 11
Jellicoe St. G81: Clyd 4A 42
JELLYHILL 3C 48
Jennie Lee Dr. ML2: Over 4H 157
JENNY LIND 5D 116
Jennys Well Ct. PA2: Pais 3E 99
Jennys Well Rd. PA2: Pais 3D 98
Jervis Ter. G75: E Kil 4D 148
Jerviston Ct. ML1: Carf 6A 128
Jerviston Rd. G33: Glas 1C 86
ML1: Carf 5A 128
Jerviston St. ML1: Moth 1H 143
ML1: New S 4A 128
(not continuous)
Jerviswood ML1: Carf 6A 128
Jessie St. G42: Glas 3H 103
Jessiman Sq. PA4: Renf 2D 78
Jimmy Sneddon Way
ML1: Moth 5F 127
Joanna Ter. G72: Blan 1B 140
Jocelyn Sq. G1: Glas 5G 83
Jock Stein Sports Barn 5C 140
John Bassy Dr. FK4: Bank 1D 14
John Bownman Gdns. ML4: Bell . . . 1D 126
John Brannan Way ML4: Bell 1H 125
John Brown Pl. G69: Chry 1A 68
John Burnside Dr. G81: Faif 6E 23
John Ewing Gdns. ML9: Lark 1E 161
John Hendry Rd. G71: Udd 3E 125
John Jarvie Sq. G65: Kils 2H 11
John Knox La. ML3: Ham 5B 140
John Knox St. G4: Glas 4A 84
G81: Clyd 1E 59
John Lang St. PA5: John 2G 95
John Marshall Dr. G64: B'rig 1A 64
John McEwan Way G64: Torr 5D 28
John Murray Ct. ML1: Moth 6G 143
John Pl. ML9: Lark 6F 161
Johnsburn Dr. G53: Glas 1B 116
Johnsburn Rd. G53: Glas 1B 116
Johnshaven PA8: Ersk 5E 41
Johnshaven St. G43: Glas 6A 102
John Smith Ct. ML3: Ham 3H 153
(off Hollandbush Gro.)
ML6: Air 3H 91
John Smith Gdns. ML5: Coat 6F 91
John Smith Ga. G78: Barr 3E 115
John Smith Swimming Pool 4H 91
Johnson Dr. G72: Camb 2A 122
Johnston Av. G65: Kils 4H 11
G81: Clyd 1F 59
JOHNSTONE 2F 95
Johnstone Av. G52: Hill 3B 80
Johnstone By-Pass PA5: John 3D 94
PA9: How 6A 94
JOHNSTONE CASTLE 4G 95
Johnstone Dr. G73: Ruth 6C 104
Johnstone La. ML8: Carl 4H 165
(off Ramage Rd.)
Johnstone Rd. ML3: Ham 1A 154
Johnstone Station (Rail) 3G 95
Johnstone St. ML4: Moss 2E 127
Johnstone Swimming Pool 2F 95
Johnstone Ter. G65: Twe 2D 32
Johnston Rd. G69: G'csh 3D 68
Johnston St. ML6: Air 3B 92
PA1: Pais 1A 98
John St. G1: Glas 4G 83 (5F 5)
G66: Kirk 4D 30
G72: Blan 2C 140

John St.—Kenmuirhill Ga.

John St. G78: Barr 4D **114**
ML2: Wis 5C **144**
ML3: Ham 6A **142**
ML4: Bell 2C **126**
ML8: Carl 4F **165**
ML9: Lark 3E **161**
John Wilson Dr. G65: Kils 2F **11**
John Wright Sports Cen. **1A 150**
Jones Wynd ML1: Cle 6E **129**
Jonquil Way ML8: Carl 5F **165**
Joppa St. G33: Glas 4G **85**
JORDANHILL **4E 61**
Jordanhill Cres. G13: Glas 4D **60**
Jordanhill Dr. G13: Glas 4C **60**
Jordanhill La. *G13: Glas* *4E* ***61***
(off Munro Rd.)
Jordanhill Station (Rail) **5F 61**
Jordan St. G14: Glas 1D **80**
Jordanvale Av. G14: Glas 1D **80**
Jowitt Av. G81: Clyd 6F **43**
Jubilee Bank G66: Lenz 4C **50**
Jubilee Ct. G52: Hill 4H **79**
Jubilee Gdns. G61: Bear 3E **45**
Jubilee Ter. PA5: John 3D **94**
Julian Av. G12: Glas 5A **62**
Julian Ct. *G12: Glas* *5A* ***62***
(off Julian Av.)
Julian La. G12: Glas 5A **62**
Juniper Av. G75: E Kil 5F **149**
Juniper Ct. G66: Lenz 2B **50**
Juniper Dr. G66: Milt C 1B **30**
Juniper Gro. ML3: Ham 1B **154**
Juniper Pl. G32: Glas 1E **107**
G71: View 5H **109**
PA5: John 5G **95**
Juniper Rd. G71: View 6H **109**
Juniper Ter. G32: Glas 1E **107**
Juniper Wynd *ML1: Holy* *2B* ***128***
(off Dornoch Rd.)
Juno St. ML1: Moth 6F **127**
Jupiter St. ML1: Moth 6F **127**
Jura G74: E Kil 4B **150**
Jura Av. PA4: Renf 2F **79**
Jura Ct. G52: Glas 6E **81**
Jura Dr. G60: Old K 2G **41**
G66: Kirk 5G **31**
G72: Blan 4A **124**
G77: Newt M 3B **132**
Jura Gdns. G60: Old K 2G **41**
ML3: Ham 1E **153**
ML8: Carl 5G **165**
ML9: Lark 2G **161**
Jura Pl. G60: Old K 2G **41**
Jura Quad. ML2: Wis 2E **157**
Jura Rd. G60: Old K 2G **41**
PA2: Pais 6H **97**
Jura St. G52: Glas 6F **81**
Jura Wynd ML5: Glenb 3G **69**
Justice Cres. ML1: N'hill 3C **128**

K

Kaim Dr. G53: Glas 1C **116**
Karadale Gdns. ML9: Lark 3E **161**
Karol Path G4: Glas 1E **83**
Katewell Av. G15: Glas 3G **43**
Katewell Pl. G15: Glas 3G **43**
Katherine St. ML6: Air 3E **93**
Kathkin Dr. G76: Clar 1A **134**
Katrine Av. G64: B'rig 6D **48**
ML4: Bell 1H **125**
Katrine Ct. *G20: Glas* *1E* ***83***
(off Cedar St.)
Katrine Cres. ML6: Air 2H **91**
Katrine Dr. G77: Newt M 5H **133**
PA2: Pais 3D **96**
Katrine Pl. G72: Camb 1A **122**
ML5: Coat 1H **89**
Katrine Way G71: Both 4E **125**
Katrine Wynd *ML1: Holy* *2A* ***128***
(off Glencoe Dr.)
Katriona Path *ML9: Lark* *4G* ***161***
(off Trinity Way)
Kay Gdns. ML1: Moth 3D **142**
Kaystone Rd. G15: Glas 6A **44**
Kay St. G21: Glas 5B **64**
Keal Av. G15: Glas 1A **60**
Keal Cres. G15: Glas 1A **60**
Keal Dr. G15: Glas 1A **60**
Keal Pl. G15: Glas 1A **60**
Kearn Av. G15: Glas 6B **44**
Kearn Pl. G15: Glas 6B **44**
Keats Pk. G71: Both 4F **125**
Keil Cres. G82: Dumb 4D **16**
Keir Cres. ML2: Wis 5H **145**
Keir Dr. G64: B'rig 5B **48**
Keir Hardie Av. ML1: Holy 2B **128**
Keir Hardie Ct. G64: B'rig 6C **48**
Keir Hardie Dr. G65: Kils 4H **11**
ML4: Bell 3B **126**
Keir Hardie Pl. ML4: Bell 3B **126**
Keir Hardie Rd. ML9: Lark 4F **161**
Keir Hardie Sports Cen. **1A 128**
Keir St. G41: Glas 2D **102**
Keir's Wlk. G72: Camb 1A **122**
Keith Av. G46: Giff 4B **118**
Keith Ct. G11: Glas 2A **82**
Keith Quad. ML2: Wis 4H **145**
Keith St. G11: Glas 1A **82**
ML3: Ham 5B **142**
ML4: Bell 1C **126**
Kelbourne Cres. ML4: Bell 2B **126**
Kelbourne St. G20: Glas 5C **62**
Kelburne Ct. PA1: Pais 6C **78**
Kelburne Dr. PA1: Pais 6D **78**
Kelburne Gdns. G69: Bail 2G **107**
PA1: Pais 6C **78**
Kelburne Oval PA1: Pais 6C **78**
Kelburn St. G78: Barr 6C **114**
Kelhead Av. G52: Glas 6H **79**
(not continuous)
Kelhead Dr. G52: Glas 6H **79**
Kelhead Path G52: Glas 6H **79**
Kelhead Pl. G52: Glas 6H **79**
Kellas St. G51: Glas 4G **81**
Kellie Gro. G74: E Kil 6F **137**
Kells Pl. G15: Glas 3G **43**
Kelly's La. *ML8: Carl* *4H* ***165***
(off Kelso Dr.)
Kelso Av. G73: Ruth 6D **104**
PA11: Bri W 4F **73**
PA2: Pais 4E **97**
Kelso Cres. ML2: Wis 3H **145**
Kelso Dr. G74: E Kil 6A **138**
ML8: Carl 4H **165**
Kelso Gdns. G69: Mood 4D **52**
Kelso Pl. G14: Glas 3G **59**
Kelso Quad. ML5: Coat 3B **90**
Kelso St. G13: Glas 2H **59**
G14: Glas 3G **59**
Kelton St. G32: Glas 1B **106**
KELVIN **6A 150**
Kelvin Av. G52: Hill 2H **79**
KELVINBRIDGE RDBT. **5D 28**
Kelvinbridge Station (Rail) **1C** 82
Kelvin Ct. G12: Glas 4G **61**
G66: Kirk 4C **30**
Kelvin Cres. G61: Bear 5F **45**
KELVINDALE **3H 61**
Kelvindale G64: Torr 4E **29**
Kelvindale Bldgs. G12: Glas 4A **62**
Kelvindale Gdns. G20: Glas 3A **62**
Kelvindale Pl. G20: Glas 3B **62**
Kelvindale Rd. G12: Glas 4H **61**
G20: Glas 4H **61**
Kelvin Dr. G20: Glas 5B **62**
G64: B'rig 5C **48**
G66: Kirk 5A **30**
G69: Mood 5C **52**
G75: E Kil 4H **149**
G78: Barr 6F **115**
ML6: Air 2B **92**
Kelvin Gdns. G65: Kils 4H **11**
ML3: Ham 5C **140**
KELVINGROVE **2C 82**
Kelvingrove Art Gallery & Mus.
2B 82
Kelvingrove St. G3: Glas 3C **82**
Kelvin Hall International Sports Arena
2B 82
Kelvin Hall Transport Mus. **2A** 82
Kelvinhall Station (Und.) **1A** 82
KELVINHAUGH **3B 82**
Kelvinhaugh Ga. G3: Glas 3B **82**
Kelvinhaugh Pl. G3: Glas 3B **82**
Kelvinhaugh St. G3: Glas 3A **82**
KELVINHEAD **1H 13**
Kelvinhead Rd. G65: Bant 1G **13**
Kelvin Pk. Sth. G75: E Kil 6A **150**
Kelvin Pl. G75: E Kil 4A **150**
Kelvin Rd. G62: Miln 2E **25**
G67: Cumb 5A **36**
G71: Tann 6C **108**
G75: E Kil 4H **149**
ML4: Bell 6D **110**
Kelvin Rd. Nth. G67: Cumb 5A **36**
KELVINSIDE **4H 61**
Kelvinside Av. G20: Glas 5C **62**
Kelvinside Dr. G20: Glas 5D **62**
Kelvinside Gdns. G20: Glas 5C **62**
Kelvinside Gdns. E. G20: Glas 6D **62**
Kelvinside Gdns. La. G20: Glas 6C **62**
Kelvinside Ter. Sth. G20: Glas 6C **62**
Kelvinside Ter. W. G20: Glas 6C **62**
Kelvin Sth. Bus. Pk. G75: E Kil 6A **150**
Kelvin St. ML5: Coat 6E **91**
Kelvin Ter. G65: Twe 3D **32**
Kelvinvale G66: Kirk 4D **30**
Kelvin Vw. G64: Torr 5E **29**
G65: Twe 3D **32**
Kelvinview Av. FK4: Bank 1E **15**
Kelvin Way G12: Glas 2B **82**
G3: Glas 2B **82**
G65: Kils 2G **11**
G66: Kirk 5A **30**
G71: Both 4E **125**
Kemp Av. PA3: Pais 2C **78**
Kemp Ct. ML3: Ham 6A **142**
Kempock St. G40: Glas 1E **105**
Kempsthorn Cres. G53: Glas 4B **100**
Kempsthorn Path *G53: Glas* *4B* ***100***
(off Kempsthorn Cres.)
Kempsthorn Rd. G53: Glas 4A **100**
Kemp St. G21: Glas 5A **64**
ML3: Ham 6H **141**
Kenbank Cres. PA11: Bri W 3F **73**
Kenbank Rd. PA11: Bri W 3F **73**
Kendal Av. G12: Glas 3G **61**
G46: Giff 4A **118**
Kendal Dr. G12: Glas 3G **61**
Kendal Rd. G75: E Kil 5B **148**
Kendoon Av. G15: Glas 4G **43**
Kenhill Quad. ML6: Air 2A **92**
Kenilburn Av. ML6: Air 1B **92**
Kenilburn Cres. ML6: Air 1B **92**
Kenilworth G74: E Kil 5D **138**
Kenilworth Av. G41: Glas 5B **102**
ML2: Wis 6H **145**
PA2: Pais 5D **96**
Kenilworth Ct. G67: Cumb 5G **35**
ML1: Holy *2B* ***128***
(off Rowantree Ter.)
ML8: Carl 4E **165**
Kenilworth Cres. G61: Bear 1C **44**
ML3: Ham 5D **140**
ML4: Bell 1C **126**
Kenilworth Dr. ML6: Air 3C **92**
Kenilworth Rd. G66: Kirk 5E **31**
Kenilworth Way PA2: Pais 4D **96**
Kenmar Gdns. G71: Tann 5C **108**
Kenmar Rd. ML3: Ham 4F **141**
Kenmar Ter. ML3: Ham 4F **141**
Kenmore Gdns. G61: Bear 2H **45**
Kenmore Rd. G67: Cumb 3B **36**
Kenmore St. G32: Glas 6A **86**
Kenmore Way ML5: Coat 2E **111**
ML8: Carl 2F **165**
Kenmuiraid Pl. ML4: Bell 4B **126**
Kenmuir Av. G32: Glas 2E **107**
Kenmuirhill Gdns. G32: Glas 3D **106**
Kenmuirhill Ga. G32: Glas 3D **106**

Kenmuirhill Rd. G32: Glas 3D **106**
Kenmuir Rd. G32: Carm, Glas 5C **106**
(not continuous)
G71: Udd. 3E **107**
Kenmuir St. ML5: Coat 1F **109**
Kenmure Av. G64: B'rig. 6A **48**
Kenmure Cres. G64: B'rig. 6B **48**
Kenmure Dr. G64: B'rig. 6B **48**
Kenmure Gdns. G61: B'rig 6A **48**
Kenmure La. G64: B'rig 6B **48**
Kenmure Rd. G46: Giff 3H **133**
Kenmure St. G41: Glas 2D **102**
Kenmure Way G73: Ruth 4D **120**
Kennedar Dr. G51: Glas 3E **81**
Kennedy Av. G65: Twe 2E **33**
Kennedy Ct. G46: Giff 3A **118**
Kennedy Dr. ML6: Air 4G **91**
Kennedy Gdns. ML2: Over 4H **157**
Kennedy Path G4: Glas 3H **83** (3G **5**)
Kennedy St. G4: Glas 3G **83** (3F **5**)
ML2: Wis 6A **146**
Kennelburn Rd. ML6: Chap 4D **112**
Kenneth Rd. ML1: Moth 4E **143**
Kennihill ML6: Air 1A **92**
KENNISHEAD 2E **117**
Kennishead Av. G46: T'bnk 2E **117**
Kennishead Path *G46: T'bnk 2E 117*
(off Kennisholme Av.)
Kennishead Pl. G46: T'bnk 3E **117**
Kennishead Rd. G43: Glas 2E **117**
G46: T'bnk. 3F **117**
G53: Glas 3B **116**
Kennishead Station (Rail) 2E **117**
Kennisholm Av. G46: T'bnk. 2E **117**
Kennisholm Path *G46: T'bnk 2E 117*
(off Kennisholme Av.)
Kennisholm Pl. G46: T'bnk 2E **117**
Kennoway Dr. G11: Glas 1F **81**
Kennoway La. *G11: Glas. 1F 81*
(off Thornwood Av.)
Kennyhill Sq. G31: Glas 3D **84**
Kenshaw Av. ML9: Lark 5E **161**
Kenshaw Pl. ML9: Lark 5E **161**
Kensington Ct. *G12: Glas 5A 62*
(off Kingsborough Gdns.)
Kensington Dr. G46: Giff 6B **118**
Kensington Ga. G12: Glas. 5A **62**
Kensington Ga. La. G12: Glas. 5A **62**
Kensington Rd. G12: Glas. 5A **62**
Kentallen Rd. G33: Glas 5E **87**
Kent Dr. G73: Ruth 2F **121**
Kentigern Ter. G64: B'rig 1D **64**
Kentmere Cl. G75: E Kil 5C **148**
Kentmere Dr. G75: E Kil 5C **148**
Kentmere Pl. G75: E Kil 5C **148**
Kent Pl. G75: E Kil 5B **148**
Kent Rd. G3: Glas 3C **82** (3A **4**)
Kent St. G40: Glas 5A **84**
Keppel Dr. G44: Glas 6A **104**
Keppochhill Dr. G21: Glas 6H **63**
Keppochhill Pl. G21: Glas 1H **83**
Keppochhill Rd. G21: Glas 6G **63**
Keppochhill Way G21: Glas 1H **83**
Keppoch St. G21: Glas 6H **63**
Kerfield La. *G15: Glas 3G 43*
(off Kerfield Pl.)
Kerfield Pl. G15: Glas. 3G **43**
Kerr Cres. ML3: Ham 2G **153**
Kerr Dr. G40: Glas 6B **84**
ML1: Moth 3E **143**
Kerrera Pl. G33: Glas 5D **86**
Kerrera Rd. G33: Glas 5D **86**
Kerr Gdns. G71: Tann 5E **109**
Ker Rd. G62: Miln 2E **25**
Kerr Pl. G40: Glas. 6B **84**
Kerr St. G40: Glas. 6B **84**
G66: Kirk 5C **30**
G72: Blan 1C **140**
G78: Barr 5C **114**
PA3: Pais 6H **77**
Kerrycroy Av. G42: Glas 6H **103**
Kerrycroy Pl. G42: Glas 5H **103**
Kerrycroy St. G42: Glas 5H **103**
Kerrydale St. G40: Glas 1D **104**

Kerrylamont Av. G42: Glas 6A **104**
Kerry Pl. G15: Glas. 4G **43**
Kershaw St. ML2: Over. 4A **158**
Kersland Dr. G62: Miln 3H **25**
Kersland La. *G12: Glas. 6B 62*
(off Kersland St.)
G62: Miln 3H **25**
Kersland St. G12: Glas. 6B **62**
Kessington Dr. G61: Bear 3G **45**
Kessington Rd. G61: Bear. 4G **45**
Kessington Sq. G61: Bear. 4H **45**
Kessock Dr. G22: Glas. 6F **63**
Kessock Pl. G22: Glas. 6F **63**
Kestrel Ct. G81: Hard 2C **42**
Kestrel Pl. PA5: John 6D **94**
Kestrel Rd. G13: Glas. 3C **60**
Kestrel Vw. ML4: Bell 4A **110**
Keswick Dr. ML3: Ham 5G **153**
Keswick Rd. G75: E Kil 5B **148**
Kethers La. ML1: Moth 2E **143**
Kethers St. ML1: Moth 2E **143**
Kew Gdns. G71: Tann 6F **109**
Kew La. G12: Glas 6B **62**
Kew Ter. G12: Glas 6B **62**
Keynes Sq. ML4: Bell 3F **127**
Keystone Av. G62: Miln 5G **25**
Keystone Quad. G62: Miln. 5F **25**
Keystone Rd. G62: Miln 5G **25**
Kibbleston Rd. PA10: Kilb. 2A **94**
Kidston Pl. G5: Glas 1G **103**
Kidston Ter. G5: Glas 1G **103**
Kierhill G68: Cumb 3E **35**
Kilallan Av. PA11: Bri W 2F **73**
KILBARCHAN. 2A **94**
Kilbarchan Rd. PA10: John. 3C **94**
PA10: Kilb. 3C **94**
PA11: Bri W 4G **73**
PA5: John. 4D **94**
Kilbarchan St. G5: Glas 6F **83**
Kilbeg Ter. G46: T'bnk 4D **116**
Kilberry St. G21: Glas 2C **84**
Kilbirnie Pl. G5: Glas 1E **103**
Kilbirnie St. G5: Glas 1E **103**
KILBOWIE. 4D **42**
Kilbowie Ct. G81: Clyd 4D **42**
Kilbowie Pl. ML6: Air 5D **92**
Kilbowie Rd. G67: Cumb 4A **36**
G81: Hard 2D **42**
Kilbreck Gdns. G61: Bear 5C **24**
Kilbreck La. ML1: N'hill 3C **128**
Kilbrennan Dr. ML1: Moth 2D **142**
Kilbrennan Rd. PA3: Lin 5H **75**
Kilbride St. G5: Glas 3H **103**
Kilbride Vw. G71: Tann 6E **109**
Kilburn Gro. G22: Blan 6B **124**
Kilburn Pl. G13: Glas 3B **60**
Kilcadzow Rd. ML8: Carl 4H **165**
Kilchattan Dr. G44: Glas 6G **103**
Kilchoan Rd. G33: Glas 1C **86**
Kilcloy Av. G15: Glas 3A **44**
Kildale Way G73: Ruth 5B **104**
Kildary Av. G44: Glas 2E **119**
Kildary Rd. G44: Glas 2E **119**
Kildermorie Path G34: Glas 3G **87**
Kildermorie Rd. G34: Glas 3F **87**
Kildonan Ct. ML2: Newm 2D **146**
Kildonan Dr. G11: Glas 1G **81**
Kildonan Pl. ML1: Moth 2E **143**
Kildonan St. ML5: Coat 4D **90**
Kildrostan St. G41: Glas 3D **102**
KILDRUM 2B **36**
Kildrummy Pl. G74: E Kil. 6F **137**
Kildrum Rd. G67: Cumb 2B **36**
KILDRUM SOUTH RDBT. 4B **36**
Kilearn Rd. PA3: Pais. 4D **78**
Kilearn Sq. PA3: Pais. 4D **78**
Kilearn Way PA3: Pais 4D **78**
(not continuous)
Kilfinan St. G22: Glas 2F **63**
Kilgarth St. ML5: Coat. 1F **109**
Kilgraston Rd. PA11: Bri W 5E **73**
Kilkerran Ct. G77: Newt M 5B **132**
Kilkerran Dr. G33: Glas 3H **65**
Kilkerran Pk. G77: Newt M 5B **132**

Kilkerran Way G77: Newt M 5B **132**
Killearn Dr. PA1: Pais. 1H **99**
Killearn St. G22: Glas 5F **63**
Killermont Av. G61: Bear 5G **45**
Killermont Ct. G61: Bear 4H **45**
Killermont Mdws. G71: Both. 5C **124**
Killermont Rd. G61: Bear 4F **45**
Killermont St. G2: Glas 3G **83** (3E **5**)
Killermont Vw. G20: Glas. 5G **45**
Killiegrew Rd. G41: Glas 3B **102**
Killin Ct. ML5: Coat 2D **110**
Killin Dr. PA3: Lin 6F **75**
Killin St. G32: Glas 2B **106**
Killoch Av. PA3: Pais. 6E **77**
Killoch Dr. G13: Glas 2A **60**
G78: Barr. 6F **115**
Killoch La. PA3: Pais 6E **77**
Killoch Rd. PA3: Pais 6E **77**
Killoch Way PA3: Pais. 6E **77**
Kilmacolm Rd. PA11: Bri W 1C **72**
PA6: Hous. 1B **74**
Kilmailing Rd. G44: Glas 2F **119**
Kilmair Pl. G20: Glas 4B **62**
Kilmaluag Ter. G46: T'bnk 4D **116**
Kilmannan Gdns. G62: Miln 2D **24**
Kilmany Dr. G32: Glas 6H **85**
Kilmany Gdns. G32: Glas 6H **85**
Kilmardinny Art Cen. 1G **45**
Kilmardinny Av. G61: Bear 2F **45**
Kilmardinny Cres. G61: Bear. 1F **45**
Kilmardinny Dr. G61: Bear 1F **45**
Kilmardinny Ga. G61: Bear 2F **45**
Kilmardinny Gro. G61: Bear 1F **45**
Kilmari Gdns. G15: Glas. 3G **43**
Kilmarnock Rd. G43: Glas. 2B **118**
Kilmartin La. ML8: Carl. 2F **165**
Kilmartin Pl. G46: T'bnk 3E **117**
G71: Tann 4E **109**
ML6: Air 5D **92**
Kilmaurs Dr. G46: Giff 4C **118**
Kilmaurs St. G51: Glas. 5F **81**
Kilmeny Cres. ML2: Wis 4A **146**
Kilmichael Av. ML2: Newm 3E **147**
Kilmore Cres. G15: Glas 3G **43**
Kilmorie Dr. G73: Ruth. 6A **104**
Kilmory Av. G71: Tann 6E **109**
Kilmory Dr. G77: Newt M 3E **133**
Kilmory Gdns. ML8: Carl. 2F **165**
Kilmory Rd. ML8: Carl 5H **165**
Kilmuir Cres. G46: T'bnk 3D **116**
Kilmuir Dr. G46: T'bnk 3E **117**
(not continuous)
Kilmuir Rd. G46: T'bnk. 4D **116**
G71: Tann 4D **108**
Kilmun St. G20: Glas 2A **62**
Kilnburn Rd. ML1: Moth 2E **143**
Kilncroft La. PA2: Pais 4A **98**
Kilnside Rd. PA1: Pais. 6B **78**
Kilnwell Quad. ML1: Moth 2F **143**
Kiloran Gro. G77: Newt M. 5A **132**
Kiloran Pl. G77: Newt M 4A **132**
Kiloran St. G46: T'bnk 3F **117**
Kilpatrick Av. PA2: Pais. 3F **97**
Kilpatrick Ct. G60: Old K 1E **41**
Kilpatrick Cres. PA2: Pais. 4H **97**
Kilpatrick Dr. G61: Bear 5C **24**
PA4: Renf. 3D **78**
PA8: Ersk 4F **41**
Kilpatrick Gdns. G76: Clar 1H **133**
Kilpatrick Station (Rail) 1F **41**
Kilpatrick Vw. G82: Dumb 3H **17**
Kilpatrick Way G71: Tann 5E **109**
KILSYTH 3H **11**
Kilsyth Heritage Mus. 3A **12**
Kilsyth Rd. FK4: Bank 1C **14**
G65: Queen. 5B **10**
G66: Kirk 4D **30**
Kilsyth Swimming Pool 2G **11**
Kiltarie Cres. ML6: Air 4F **93**
Kiltearn Rd. G33: Glas 4F **87**
Kiltongue Cotts. *ML6: Air 3F 91*
(off Monkscourt Av.)
Kilvaxter Dr. G46: T'bnk 3E **117**
Kilwinning Cres. ML3: Ham 2C **152**

Kilwynet Way PA3: Pais 4C 78
Kimberley Gdns. G75: E Kil. 3E 149
Kimberley St. G81: Clyd 2H 41
   ML2: Wis 5C 144
Kinalty Rd. G44: Glas 2E 119
Kinarvie Cres. G53: Glas 6H 99
Kinarvie Gdns. G53: Glas 6H 99
Kinarvie Pl. G53: Glas 6H 99
Kinarvie Rd. G53: Glas 6H 99
Kinarvie Ter. G53: Glas 6H 99
Kinbuck Pas. G22: Glas 5G 63
Kinbuck St. G22: Glas 5H 63
Kincaid Dr. G66: Len. 2E 7
Kincaid Fld. G66: Milt C 6C 8
Kincaid Gdns. G72: Camb. 1A 122
Kincaid Way G66: Milt C 6B 8
Kincardine Dr. G64: B'rig 1D 64
Kincardine Pl. G64: B'rig 2E 65
   G74: E Kil 6C 138
Kincardine Sq. G33: Glas 2D 86
Kincath Av. G73: Ruth 4F 121
Kinclaven Av. G15: Glas 4A 44
Kincraig St. G51: Glas 5D 80
Kinellan Rd. G61: Bear 6F 45
Kinellar Dr. G14: Glas. 3A 60
Kinfauns Dr. G15: Glas. 3H 43
   G77: Newt M 4F 133
Kingarth St. G42: Glas 3E 103
   ML3: Ham. 3H 153
King Edward La. *G13: Glas* *4E 61*
   (off Woodend Dr.)
King Edward Rd. G13: Glas. 4F 61
Kingfisher Dr. G13: Glas. 2H 59
Kingfisher Gdns. G13: Glas. 2A 60
King George Ct. PA4: Renf 2G 79
King George Gdns. PA4: Renf. 1G 79
King George Pk. Av. PA4: Renf. . . . 2G 79
King George Pl. PA4: Renf 2G 79
King George Way PA4: Renf 2G 79
Kinghorn Dr. G44: Glas. 1G 119
Kinghorn La. G44: Glas 6G 103
Kinglas Ho. G82: Dumb 1H 17
Kinglas Rd. G61: Bear 5C 44
King Pl. G69: Barg 6E 89
Kingsacre Rd. G44: Glas. 6G 103
   G73: Ruth 1A 120
Kingsbarns Dr. G44: Glas 6F 103
Kingsborough Gdns. G12: Glas. . . . 6H 61
Kingsborough Ga. G12: Glas. 6H 61
Kingsborough La. G12: Glas. 6H 61
Kingsborough La. E. G12: Glas. . . . 6H 61
Kingsbrae Av. G44: Glas. 6G 103
King's Bri. G5: Glas 1H 103
Kingsbridge Cres. G44: Glas 1H 119
Kingsbridge Dr. G44: Glas 1H 119
   G73: Ruth 1A 120
Kingsburgh Dr. PA1: Pais 6D 78
Kingsburn Dr. G73: Ruth. 1C 120
Kingsburn Gro. G73: Ruth. 1B 120
Kingscliffe Av. G44: Glas 1G 119
Kings Ct. *ML3: Ham* *5B 142*
   (off Castle St.)
Kingscourt Av. G44: Glas 6H 103
Kings Cres. G72: Camb. 2B 122
King's Cres. ML8: Carl 3G 165
Kingsdale Av. G44: Glas 6G 103
King's Dr. G40: Glas 1A 104
   G68: Cumb 5H 13
Kings Dr. G77: Newt M 6F 133
   ML1: New S 4H 127
Kingsdyke Av. G44: Glas. 6G 103
Kingsford Av. G44: Glas 3C 118
Kingsford Ct. G77: Newt M 3B 132
King's Gdns. G77: Newt M 6G 133
Kingsgate Retail Pk. G74: Ners . . . 3H 137
Kingsheath Av. G73: Ruth 1A 120
Kingshill Av. G68: Cumb. 4A 34
Kingshill Dr. G44: Glas. 1G 119
Kingshill Vw. ML8: Law 1A 164
Kingshouse Av. G44: Glas. 6G 103
Kingshurst Av. G44: Glas 6G 103
Kings Inch Dr. G51: Glas. 1A 80
King's Inch Rd. PA4: Renf. 4F 59

Kingsknowe Dr. G73: Ruth 1A 120
Kingsland Cres. G52: Glas 5B 80
Kingsland Dr. G52: Glas. 5B 80
Kingsland La. G52: Glas. 5C 80
Kingslea Rd. PA6: Hous 1B 74
Kingsley Av. G42: Glas 4F 103
Kingsley Ct. G71: Tann 6E 109
Kingslynn Dr. G44: Glas 1H 119
Kingslynn La. G44: Glas 1H 119
Kingsmuir Dr. G73: Ruth. 1A 120
KING'S PARK 1A 120
King's Pk. G64: Torr 4E 29
King's Pk. Av. G44: Glas 1F 119
King's Pk. La. G44: Glas 1F 119
King's Park Station (Rail) 1G 119
King's Pl. G22: Glas 3F 63
King's Rd. PA5: Eld 3H 95
King's Theatre 3A 4
KINGSTON
   Bishopton 4A 40
   Glasgow 6E 83
Kingston Av. G71: Tann. 5E 109
   G78: Neil. 3D 130
   ML6: Air 4C 92
Kingston Bri. G5: Glas 5D 82
Kingston Flats G65: Kils. 2H 11
Kingston Gro. PA7: B'ton 4H 39
Kingston Ind. Est. G5: Glas. 6D 82
Kingston Pl. G81: Clyd 3H 41
Kingston Rd. G65: Kils 2H 11
   G78: Neil. 5C 130
   PA7: B'ton 5H 39
   (not continuous)
Kingston St. G5: Glas 5E 83
King St. G1: Glas 5G 83
   G65: Kils 3H 11
   G73: Ruth 5C 104
   G81: Clyd 1H 109
   ML2: Newm 4D 146
   ML2: Wis 1H 157
   ML3: Ham 4D 140
   ML5: Coat 5A 90
   ML9: Lark 2E 161
   PA3: Pais 6G 77
King St. La. G65: Kils 3H 11
   G73: Ruth 5C 104
King's Vw. G68: Cumb 5H 13
Kings Vw. G73: Ruth. 6B 104
Kingsway G14: Glas 4A 60
   G65: Kils. 2H 11
   G66: Kirk 3H 31
   G74: E Kil 4A 138
Kingsway Ct. G14: Glas 4A 60
Kingswood Dr. G44: Glas 1G 119
Kingswood Rd. PA7: B'ton 3F 39
Kingussie Dr. G44: Glas 1G 119
Kiniver Dr. G15: Glas 6A 44
Kinkell Gdns. G66: Kirk 4H 31
Kinloch Av. G72: Camb 3B 122
   PA3: Lin 6G 75
Kinloch Rd. ML1: Moth 5F 127
Kinloch Rd. G77: Newt M 3C 132
   PA4: Renf 3D 78
Kinloch St. G40: Glas 1E 105
Kinloss Pl. G74: E Kil 1H 149
Kinmount Av. G44: Glas 6F 103
Kinmount La. G44: Glas 6G 103
Kinnaird Av. G77: Newt M 4G 133
Kinnaird Cres. G61: Bear 3H 45
Kinnaird Dr. PA3: Lin 5H 75
Kinnaird Pl. G64: B'rig 2D 64
Kinnear Rd. G40: Glas 2C 104
Kinneil Ho. ML3: Ham 4A 142
Kinneil Pl. ML3: Ham 1D 152
Kinnell Av. G52: Glas 2C 100
Kinnell Cres. G52: Glas 2C 100
Kinnell Path G52: Glas 2C 100
Kinnell Pl. G52: Glas. 2D 100
Kinnell Sq. G52: Glas. 2C 100
KINNING PARK 1C 102
Kinning Pk. Ind. Est.
   G5: Glas 6D 82

Kinning Park Station (Und.) 6B 82
Kinning St. G5: Glas 6E 83
Kinnoul Gdns. G61: Bear 6D 24
Kinnoul La. G12: Glas. 6A 62
Kinnoull Pl. G72: Blan 2B 140
Kinpurnie Rd. PA1: Pais 6F 79
Kinross Av. G52: Glas 1B 100
Kinross Pk. G74: E Kil. 6D 138
Kinsail Dr. G52: Glas 5H 79
Kinstone Av. G14: Glas 4A 60
Kintail Gdns. G66: Kirk. 4H 31
Kintessack Pl. G64: B'rig 5F 49
Kintillo Dr. G13: Glas 3B 60
Kintore Pk. ML3: Ham. 4F 153
Kintore Rd. G43: Glas. 1D 118
Kintore Twr. G72: Camb 4G 121
Kintra St. G51: Glas 5H 81
   (not continuous)
Kintyre Av. PA3: Lin 1G 95
Kintyre Cres. G77: Newt M 3C 132
   ML6: Plain 1F 93
Kintyre Gdns. G66: Kirk 4H 31
Kintyre Rd. G72: Blan 1A 140
Kintyre St. G21: Glas 2C 84
Kintyre Wynd ML8: Carl 2F 165
Kipland Wlk. ML5: Coat 6F 91
Kippen Dr. G76: Busby 4E 135
Kippen St. G22: Glas 3H 63
   ML6: Air 5F 91
Kipperoch Rd. G82: Dumb 1B 16
Kippford Pl. ML6: Chap. 4F 113
Kippford St. G32: Glas 1C 106
Kipps Av. ML6: Air 3G 91
Kippsbyre Ct. *ML6: Air* *4F 91*
   (off Monkscourt Av.)
Kirkaig Av. PA4: Renf 1H 79
Kirk Bean Av. G73: Ruth 3C 120
Kirkburn Av. G72: Camb 3A 122
Kirkcaldy Rd. G41: Glas 3B 102
Kirkconnel Av. G13: Glas 3H 59
   G68: Cumb 4A 34
Kirkconnel Dr. G73: Ruth 2B 120
Kirk Cres. G60: Old K 6E 21
Kirkcudbright Pl. G74: E Kil 6D 138
Kirkdale Dr. G52: Glas 1E 101
Kirkdene Av. G77: Newt M 4H 133
Kirkdene Bank G77: Newt M 4H 133
Kirkdene Cres. G77: Newt M 4H 133
Kirkdene Gro. G77: Newt M 5H 133
Kirkdene Pl. G77: Newt M 4H 133
Kirkfieldbank Way ML3: Ham 6E 141
Kirkfield Rd. G71: Both. 4E 125
Kirkford Rd. G69: Mood 5C 52
Kirk Glebe G78: Neil 2E 131
Kirkgate ML2: Newm 5D 146
Kirkhall Rd. ML1: N'hill 3D 128
KIRKHILL
   Cambuslang 2B 122
   Newton Mearns. 4G 133
Kirkhill Av. G72: Camb 4A 122
Kirkhill Bowling Club 3H 121
Kirkhill Cres. G78: Neil 1E 131
Kirkhill Dr. G20: Glas 4B 62
Kirkhill Gdns. G72: Camb 4A 122
Kirkhill Ga. G77: Newt M 5H 133
Kirkhill Gro. G72: Camb 4A 122
Kirkhill Pl. G20: Glas 4B 62
   ML2: Wis 1C 156
Kirkhill Rd. G69: G'csh. 4D 68
   G71: Tann 5C 108
   G77: Newt M. 4G 133
   ML2: Wis 2B 156
Kirkhill Station (Rail) 2A 122
Kirkhill St. ML2: Wis 2D 156
Kirkhill Ter. G72: Camb 4A 122
Kirkhope Dr. G15: Glas 6B 44
Kirkinner Pl. *PA11: Bri W* *3F 73*
   (off Main Rd.)
Kirkinner Rd. G32: Glas 2D 106
KIRKINTILLOCH 4C 30
Kirkintilloch Ind. Est.
   G66: Kirk 3C 30
Kirkintilloch Rd. G64: B'rig. 2B 64
   G64: B'rig, Kirk 1F 49

Kirkintilloch Rd. G66: Kirk 2H **29**
(Campsie Rd.)
G66: Kirk 1G **49**
(Torrence Rd.)
G66: Lenz 2C **50**
Kirkland Gro. PA5: John 2F **95**
KIRKLANDNEUK **5D 58**
Kirklandneuk Cres. PA4: Renf. 5C **58**
Kirklandneuk Rd. PA4: Renf 5C **58**
Kirklands Cres. G65: Kils 4H **11**
G71: Both 4E **125**
Kirklands Dr. G77: Newt M 6D **132**
Kirklands Pl. G77: Newt M 6D **132**
Kirkland St. G20: Glas 6D **62**
ML1: Moth 2F **143**
Kirk La. G43: Glas 6A **102**
G61: Bear 2E **45**
Kirklea Gdns. PA3: Pais 6E **77**
Kirkle Dr. G77: Newt M. 4H **133**
Kirklee Cir. G12: Glas 5A **62**
Kirklee Gdns. G12: Glas 4B **62**
Kirklee Gdns. La. G12: Glas 4B **62**
Kirklee Ga. G12: Glas. 4B **62**
Kirklee Pl. G12: Glas 5B **62**
Kirklee Quad. G12: Glas 5B **62**
Kirklee Quad. La. G12: Glas 5B **62**
Kirklee Rd. G12: Glas. 5A **62**
ML1: New S 6G **127**
ML4: Bell. 3F **127**
Kirklee Ter. G12: Glas. 5A **62**
Kirklee Ter. La. G12: Glas. 5B **62**
Kirklee Ter. Rd. G12: Glas 5A **62**
Kirkliston St. G32: Glas 5H **85**
Kirk M. *G72: Camb 2A* ***122***
(off Greenlees Rd.)
Kirkmichael Av. G11: Glas 6G **61**
Kirkmichael Gdns.
G11: Glas 6G **61**
Kirkmuir Dr. G73: Ruth. 4D **120**
Kirkness St. ML6: Air 3A **92**
Kirknethan ML2: Wis 2C **156**
Kirknewton St. G32: Glas 5B **86**
Kirkoswald G74: E Kil. 6D **138**
Kirkoswald Dr. G81: Clyd 4E **43**
Kirkoswald Rd. G43: Glas. 1B **118**
ML1: N'hill 3E **129**
Kirkpatrick Dr. G33: Step 4E **67**
Kirkpatrick St. G40: Glas 6C **84**
Kirk Pl. G61: Bear. 2E **45**
G67: Cumb 6C **34**
G71: Udd 2C **124**
Kirkriggs Av. G73: Ruth 2D **120**
Kirkriggs Gdns. G73: Ruth 2D **120**
Kirkriggs Vw. G73: Ruth. 2D **120**
Kirkriggs Way *G73: Ruth 2D* ***120***
(off Kirkriggs Gdns.)
Kirk Rd. G61: Bear 2E **45**
G76: Crmck. 2H **135**
ML1: N'hse. 6D **112**
ML2: Wis 6H **145**
ML8: Carl 3E **165**
ML9: Dals. 3D **162**
PA6: Hous. 1B **74**
Kirkshaw Ct. *PA5: John. 2F* ***95***
(off Walkinshaw St.)
KIRKSHAWS **2A 110**
Kirkshaws Av. ML5: Coat 2A **110**
Kirkshaws Pl. ML5: Coat. 2B **110**
Kirkshaws Rd. ML5: Coat 2H **109**
Kirkstall Gdns. G64: B'rig. 3D **48**
Kirkstone G77: Newt M. 4H **133**
Kirkstone Cl. G75: E Kil 5B **148**
Kirk St. G62: Miln. 3E **25**
ML1: Moth 2G **143**
ML5: Coat. 5B **90**
(not continuous)
ML8: Carl 3E **165**
Kirkstyle Av. ML8: Carl 4E **165**
Kirkstyle Cres. G78: Neil. 2D **130**
ML6: Air 1H **91**
Kirkstyle La. G78: Neil 2E **131**
Kirkstyle Pl. ML6: Glenm 5F **71**
Kirksyde Av. G66: Kirk 6D **30**
KIRKTON **3E 131**
Kirkton G60: Old K 6E **21**
PA8: Ersk 4E **41**
Kirkton Av. G13: Glas 3A **60**
G72: Blan 4A **140**
G78: Barr 5D **114**
ML8: Carl 3E **165**
Kirkton Ct. ML8: Carl 4E **165**
Kirkton Cres. G13: Glas 3A **60**
G66: Milt C 6C **8**
ML5: Coat 2F **111**
Kirktonfield Dr. G78: Neil 2F **131**
Kirktonfield Rd. G78: Neil 2E **131**
Kirkton Ga. G74: E Kil. 1G **149**
KIRKTONHILL **4D 16**
Kirktonholme Cres. G74: E Kil. 1F **149**
Kirktonholme Rd. G74: E Kil. 1D **148**
Kirkton Ho. G72: Blan. 3B **140**
Kirkton Pk. G74: E Kil. 1H **149**
Kirkton Pl. G72: Blan 3B **140**
G74: E Kil 1H **149**
(not continuous)
ML5: Coat 1F **111**
Kirkton Rd. G72: Camb 2B **122**
G78: Neil. 3D **130**
G82: Dumb. 4D **16**
Kirkton Side G78: Barr 6D **114**
Kirkton St. ML8: Carl. 4F **165**
Kirkton Ter. G66: Cam G. 1B **6**
Kirkvale Ct. G77: Newt M 4H **133**
Kirkvale Cres. G77: Newt M 4H **133**
Kirkvale Dr. G77: Newt M. 4H **133**
Kirkview G67: Cumb. 1C **54**
Kirkview Ct. G67: Cumb 1C **54**
Kirkview Cres. G77: Newt M 6E **133**
Kirkview Gdns. G71: Tann 5D **108**
Kirkville Pl. G15: Glas 6B **44**
Kirkwall G67: Cumb 6A **14**
Kirkwall Av. G72: Blan 5A **124**
Kirkwell Rd. G44: Glas 2F **119**
KIRKWOOD **1G 109**
Kirkwood Av. G33: Step 4G **67**
G81: Clyd 6F **43**
Kirkwood Pl. ML5: Coat 6A **90**
Kirkwood Quad. G81: Clyd 6F **43**
Kirkwood Rd. G71: Tann. 5D **108**
Kirkwood Sports Barn **1F 109**
Kirkwood Station (Rail). **6H 89**
Kirkwood St. G51: Glas. 6A **82**
G73: Ruth 5C **104**
ML5: Coat. 5A **90**
Kirn St. G20: Glas. 1A **62**
Kirriemuir G74: E Kil 4D **138**
Kirriemuir Av. G52: Glas. 2C **100**
Kirriemuir Gdns. G64: B'rig 5E **49**
Kirriemuir Pl. *G52: Glas 1C* ***100***
(off Bucklaw Gdns.)
Kirriemuir Rd. G64: B'rig 6E **49**
Kirtle Dr. PA4: Renf 1G **79**
Kirtle Pl. G75: E Kil. 4A **148**
Kishorn Pl. G33: Glas 2C **86**
Kitchener St. ML2: Wis 6G **145**
Kittoch Pl. G74: E Kil 1H **149**
KITTOCHSIDE. **5C 136**
Kittochside Rd. G76: Crmck 2A **136**
Kittoch St. G74: E Kil 1G **149**
Klondike Ct. ML1: New S 4B **128**
Knapdale St. G22: Glas. 2E **63**
Knightsbridge St. G13: Glas 2D **60**
Knightscliffe Av. G13: Glas. 1D **60**
Knights Ga. G71: Both 2C **124**
KNIGHTSWOOD **2D 60**
Knightswood Ct. G13: Glas. 3D **60**
Knightswood Cross G13: Glas. 2D **60**
Knightswood Rd. G13: Glas 6C **44**
Knightswood Swimming Pool **3B 60**
Knightswood Ter. G72: Blan 6C **124**
Knivysbridge Pl. ML4: Bell 4B **126**
Knockburnie Rd. G71: Both. 3E **125**
Knockhall St. G33: Glas 1D **86**
Knockhill Dr. G44: Glas 6F **103**
Knockhill La. G44: Glas. 6F **103**
Knockhill Rd. PA4: Renf 2D **78**
Knockside Av. PA2: Pais. 6H **97**
Knock Way PA3: Pais 4C **78**
Knollpark Dr. G76: Clar. 2B **134**
Knowe Cres. ML1: N'hill. 3D **128**
Knowehead Dr. G71: Udd 1C **124**
Knowehead Gdns. G41: Glas. 2C **102**
G71: Udd 1C **124**
Knowehead Rd. ML2: Wis 1A **158**
Knowehead Ter. G41: Glas 2C **102**
Knowenoble St. ML1: Cle. 5H **129**
Knowe Rd. G69: Chry. 1A **68**
PA3: Pais 4D **78**
Knowes Av. G77: Newt M 4E **133**
Knowes Rd. G77: Newt M 4F **133**
Knowe St. G62: Miln. 3F **25**
Knowetap St. G20: Glas 2C **62**
KNOWETOP. **5H 143**
Knowetop Av. ML1: Moth 4H **143**
Knowetop Cres. G82: Dumb 2C **16**
KNOWNOBLE. **5H 129**
Knox Av. PA11: Bri W 4E **73**
Knoxland Sq. G82: Dumb 5G **17**
Knoxland St. G82: Dumb 5G **17**
Knox Pl. G77: Newt M. 5B **132**
Knox St. ML6: Air. 3B **92**
PA1: Pais. 1F **97**
Koko's **4C 90**
Kronberg Way G75: E Kil. 6F **149**
Kyleakin Dr. G72: Blan 5H **123**
Kyleakin Rd. G46: T'bnk. 4D **116**
Kyleakin Ter. G46: T'bnk. 4D **116**
Kyle Ct. G72: Camb 1A **122**
Kyle Dr. G46: Giff 4C **118**
Kyle Gro. ML1: New S 4A **128**
Kylemore Cres. ML1: Moth. 5F **127**
KYLEPARK. **6B 108**
Kylepark Av. G71: Udd 1B **124**
Kylepark Cres. G71: Udd 6B **108**
Kylepark Dr. G71: Udd 6B **108**
Kyle Quad. ML1: N'hill 3C **128**
ML2: Wis 2E **157**
Kylerhea Rd. G46: T'bnk. 4D **116**
Kyle Rd. G67: Cumb. 2B **36**
Kyle Sq. G73: Ruth. 2B **120**
Kyle St. G4: Glas 2G **83** (2F **5**)
ML1: Moth 2D **142**
Kyle Ter. G82: Dumb 2B **16**

L

La Belle Allee *G3: Glas. 2C* ***82***
(off Claremont St.)
La Belle Pl. G3: Glas 2C **82**
Laberge Gdns. ML1: New S 4B **128**
Laburnum Av. G75: E Kil. 5E **149**
Laburnum Ct. G75: E Kil 5E **149**
Laburnum Cres. ML2: Wis 4H **145**
Laburnum Dr. G66: Milt C. 6B **8**
Laburnum Gdns. G66: Lenz 2B **50**
Laburnum Gro. G66: Lenz. 2B **50**
ML5: Coat. 6D **90**
Laburnum Lea ML3: Ham 2A **154**
Laburnum Pl. PA5: John. 5G **95**
Laburnum Rd. FK4: Bank 1E **15**
G41: Glas 1A **102**
G67: Cumb 3D **36**
G71: View. 4G **109**
Lachlan Cres. PA8: Ersk 6C **40**
La Crusse Ter. G12: Glas 6C **62**
Lacy St. PA1: Pais 6C **78**
Ladeside Cl. G77: Newt M 3C **132**
Ladeside Dr. G65: Kils 2B **12**
PA5: John. 3D **94**
Lade Ter. G52: Glas 1A **100**
Ladhope Pl. G13: Glas 1G **59**
Ladyacres PA4: Inch. 3H **57**
Ladyacres Way PA4: Inch. 3H **57**
Lady Ann Cres. ML6: Air. 5C **92**
Lady Anne St. G14: Glas. 4H **59**
Ladybank G68: Cumb 5H **13**
Ladybank Ct. G74: E Kil 1G **149**
Ladybank Dr. G52: Glas. 1E **101**
Ladybank Gdns. G74: E Kil 1G **149**
Ladybank Pl. G74: E Kil 1G **149**
Ladyburn St. PA1: Pais. 1C **98**

Ladyhill Dr. G69: Bail 1G 107
Lady Isle Cres. G71: Udd 1C 124
Lady Jane Ga. G71: Both 3B 124
Ladykirk Cres. G52: Glas 5B 80
   PA2: Pais 2B 98
Ladykirk Dr. G52: Glas 5B 80
Lady La. PA1: Pais 1H 97
Ladyloan Av. G15: Glas 3G 43
Ladyloan Ct. G15: Glas. 3H 43
Ladyloan Gdns. G15: Glas 3H 43
Ladyloan Pl. G15: Glas. 3G 43
Lady Mary Wlk. ML3: Ham 2A 154
Ladymuir Circ. PA8: Ersk 6D 40
Ladymuir Cres. G53: Glas 3C 100
Ladysmith Av. PA10: Kilb 3B 94
Ladysmith St. ML2: Wis 5C 144
Lady Watson Gdns. ML3: Ham . . . 1E 153
Ladywell Rd. ML12: Moth 3D 142
Ladywell St. G4: Glas 4A 84
Lady Wilson St. ML6: Air 5B 92
Ladywood G62: Miln. 3H 25
Lagan Rd. ML8: Carl 4F 165
Laggan Quad. ML6: Air 2G 91
Laggan Rd. G43: Glas. 2C 118
   G64: B'rig 6D 48
   G77: Newt M. 2D 132
   ML6: Air 2H 91
Laggan Ter. PA4: Renf 5D 58
Laggan Way ML2: Newm 2D 146
Lagholm Dr. PA3: Lin 6A 76
Lagoon Leisure Cen. 1B 98
Laidlaw Av. ML1: New S. 4H 127
Laidlaw Gdns. G71: Tann 4D 108
Laidlaw St. G5: Glas. 6E 83
       (not continuous)
Laidon Rd. ML6: Air. 2H 91
Laidon Wlk. ML2: Newm 3D 146
      (off Murdostoun Vw.)
Laighcartside St. PA5: John 2G 95
Laighlands Rd. G71: Both 5F 125
Laighmuir St. G71: Udd 2D 124
LAIGH PARK 5A 78
Laighpark Av. PA7: B'ton 4H 39
Laighpark Vw. PA3: Pais 4A 78
Laigh Rd. G77: Newt M 4H 133
LAIGHSTONEHALL 1F 153
Laighstonehall Rd. ML3: Ham . . . 1F 153
Laightoun Ct. G67: Cumb 1C 54
Laightoun Dr. G67: Cumb 1C 54
Laightoun Gdns. G67: Cumb. 1C 54
Lainshaw Dr. G45: Glas. 5E 119
Laird Gro. G71: Tann. 5E 109
Laird Pl. G40: Glas 1B 104
Lairds Ga. G71: Both 2B 124
Lairds Hill G67: Cumb 3G 35
Laird's Hill Ct. G65: Kils 3E 11
Laird's Hill Pl. G65: Kils 3E 11
Lairdsland Rd. G66: Kirk 5D 30
Laird St. ML5: Coat 4D 90
Lairg Dr. G72: Blan 5A 124
Lairhills Rd. G75: E Kil 4G 149
Lamberton Dr. G52: Glas 5B 80
LAMBHILL 2E 63
Lambhill Quad. G41: Glas. 6C 82
Lambhill St. G41: Glas 6B 82
Lambie Cres. G77: Newt M. 4C 132
Lamb St. G22: Glas 3F 63
   ML3: Ham 6A 142
Lamerton Rd. G67: Cumb 3C 36
Lamington Rd. G52: Glas 1B 100
Lamlash Cres. G33: Glas 3B 86
Lamlash Pl. G33: Glas 3B 86
   ML1: Moth 2E 143
Lamlash Sq. G33: Glas 3C 86
Lammermoor G74: E Kil 5E 139
Lammermoor Av. G52: Glas 1C 100
Lammermoor Cres. G66: Kirk 5F 31
Lammermoor Ct. G67: Cumb 6G 35
Lammermoor Gdns.
   G66: Kirk. 5F 31
Lammermoor Rd. G66: Kirk 5F 31
Lammermoor Ter. ML2: Wis. 6H 145
Lammermuir Ct. PA2: Pais 5A 98
Lammermuir Dr. PA2: Pais 5H 97

Lammermuir Gdns. G61: Bear 6C 24
Lammermuir Pl. ML1: Holy 3B 128
      (off Cherry Pl.)
Lammermuir Way ML6: Chap 4F 113
Lammermuir Wynd ML1: Lark . . . 6H 155
Lammer Wynd ML9: Lark 4G 161
      (off Pitlochry Dr.)
Lamont Av. PA7: B'ton 4A 40
Lamont Rd. G21: Glas 3D 64
Lanark Av. ML6: Air 1H 111
Lanark Rd. ML8: Carl 4F 165
   ML8: Crsfd, Rose 4E 163
   ML9: Dals, Lark. 4G 155
Lanark Rd. End ML9: Lark 4G 155
Lanarkshire Ice Rink 4A 142
Lancaster Av. ML6: Chap 4D 112
Lancaster Cres. G12: Glas 5A 62
Lancaster Cres. La. G12: Glas . . . 5A 62
Lancaster Rd. G64: B'rig 3D 48
Lancaster Ter. G12: Glas. 5A 62
Lancaster Ter. La. G12: Glas 5A 62
Lancaster Way PA4: Renf 2E 79
Lancefield Quay G3: Glas 4C 82
Lancefield St. G3: Glas. 4D 82
Landemer Ct. G73: Ruth 1C 120
Landemer Dr. G73: Ruth. 1B 120
Landressy Pl. G40: Glas 1B 104
Landressy St. G40: Glas 6B 84
Landsdowne Gdns. ML3: Ham . . . 6B 142
Landsdowne Rd. ML9: Lark 3G 161
Lane, The G68: Dull 5F 13
Lanfine Rd. PA1: Pais. 1D 98
Langa Gro. G20: Glas 2C 62
      (off Lochburn Cres.)
Langa St. G20: Glas 2C 62
Lang Av. PA4: Renf 1E 79
   PA7: B'ton. 4A 40
Langbank St. G5: Glas 6F 83
Langbar Cres. G33: Glas 4E 87
Langbar Gdns. G33: Glas 4F 87
Langbar Path G33: Glas 4D 86
      (off Langbar Cres.)
Langcraigs G82: Dumb 2G 17
Langcraigs Ct. PA2: Pais 5G 97
Langcraigs Dr. PA2: Pais 6G 97
Langcraigs Ter. PA2: Pais. 6G 97
Langcroft Dr. G72: Camb 3C 122
Langcroft Pl. G51: Glas. 4C 80
Langcroft Rd. G51: Glas 4C 80
Langcroft Ter. G51: Glas. 4D 80
Langdale G74: E Kil 6E 137
   G77: Newt M. 4H 133
Langdale Av. G33: Glas 6G 65
Langdale Rd. G69: Mood 5D 52
Langdales Av. G68: Cumb. 3F 35
Langdale St. G33: Glas. 6G 65
Langfaulds Cres. G81: Faif 6F 23
Langford Dr. G53: Glas 4A 116
Langford Pl. G53: Glas. 4B 116
Langhaul Rd. G53: Glas 4H 99
Langhill Dr. G68: Cumb 2F 35
Langholm G75: E Kil 5B 148
Langholm Ct. G69: Mood 5D 52
Langholm Cres. ML2: Wis 3H 145
Langholm Path G72: Blan 2A 140
Langlands Av. G51: Glas 4D 80
   G75: E Kil 6H 149
Langlands Ct. G51: Glas 3F 81
Langlands Dr. G51: Glas. 3C 80
   G75: E Kil 6H 149
Langlands Path G51: Glas. 4E 81
      (off Langlands Rd.)
Langlands Rd. G51: Glas 4D 80
LANGLANDS-SEAFAR INTERCHANGE
   . . . . 5G 35
Langlands Ter. G82: Dumb 1H 17
Langlea Av. G72: Camb 3F 121
Langlea Ct. G72: Camb 3G 121
Langlea Dr. G72: Camb 2G 121
Langlea Gdns. G72: Camb 2G 121
Langlea Rd. G72: Camb 3G 121
Langlea Way G72: Camb 2G 121
Langlees Av. G77: Newt M 4H 133

Langley Av. G13: Glas. 1B 60
Langley Gro. G72: Camb 3G 121
LANGLOAN 6A 90
Langloan Cres. ML5: Coat 6A 90
Langloan Pl. ML5: Coat 5A 90
Langloan St. ML5: Coat 6A 90
LANGMUIR 4H 31
Langmuir Av. G66: Kirk. 4E 31
Langmuirhead Rd. G66: Auch . . . 1H 65
Langmuir Rd. G66: Kirk 4G 31
   G69: Barg 6E 89
Langmuir Way G69: Barg 6E 89
Langness Rd. G33: Glas 3B 86
Langoreth Av. ML3: Ham 1D 152
Lang Pl. PA5: John 2F 95
Langrig Rd. G21: Glas 4C 64
   G77: Newt M. 6C 132
Langshaw Cres. ML8: Carl 3F 165
Langshot St. G51: Glas 6B 82
LANGSIDE. 5D 102
Langside Av. G41: Glas. 4C 102
   G71: View. 1G 125
Langside Ct. G71: Both 6F 125
Langside Dr. G43: Glas 3C 118
   PA10: Kilb. 3A 94
Langside Gdns. G42: Glas. 6E 103
Langside La. G42: Glas. 4E 103
Langside Pk. PA10: Kilb 3A 94
Langside Pl. G41: Glas. 5D 102
Langside Rd. G42: Glas 5D 102
   G71: Both 6F 125
Langside Station (Rail) 1C 118
Langside St. G81: Faif 1G 43
Langstile Pl. G52: Glas. 6H 79
Langstile Rd. G52: Glas 6H 79
Lang St. PA1: Pais 1C 98
Langton Cres. G53: Glas 4C 100
   G78: Barr. 6F 115
Langton Gdns. G69: Bail 1F 107
Langton Ga. G77: Newt M. 4C 132
Langton Pl. G77: Newt M 4C 132
Langton Rd. G53: Glas 4C 100
Langtree Av. G46: Giff 6G 117
LANRIGG 6A 52
Lanrig Pl. G69: Chry. 1A 68
Lanrig Rd. G69: Chry 6A 52
Lansbury Gdns. PA3: Pais 4H 77
Lansbury Ter. ML9: Lark. 4G 161
Lansdowne Cres. G20: Glas 1D 82
Lansdowne Cres. La.
   G20: Glas 1D 82
      (off Holyrood Cres.)
Lansdowne Dr. G68: Cumb. 6H 13
Lantana Gro. ML1: Moth. 1F 143
Lanton Dr. G52: Glas 6B 80
Lanton Rd. G43: Glas 2C 118
Lappin St. G81: Clyd. 1F 59
Larbert St. G4: Glas 2F 83 (2D 4)
Larch Av. G64: B'rig 1D 64
   G66: Lenz 1C 50
Larch Ct. G67: Cumb 1D 36
   G72: Blan 1A 140
   G75: E Kil 6D 148
Larch Cres. G66: Lenz 1C 50
Larch Dr. FK4: Bank 1E 15
   G75: E Kil 6D 148
Larches, The G69: Mood 3E 53
Larchfield Av. G14: Glas. 5B 60
   G77: Newt M. 5E 133
Larchfield Ct. G77: Newt M 5D 132
Larchfield Cres. ML2: Wis 3A 146
Larchfield Dr. G73: Ruth. 3D 120
Larchfield Gdns. ML2: Wis 3A 146
Larchfield Gro. ML2: Wis 2B 146
Larchfield Pl. G14: Glas. 5B 60
   ML2: Wis 3B 146
Larchfield Rd. G61: Bear. 6F 45
Larch Gro. G66: Milt C 6B 8
   G67: Cumb 1D 36
   ML1: Holy 2B 128
   ML3: Ham. 1A 154
Larchgrove Av. G32: Glas 5C 86
Larchgrove Pl. G32: Glas 4C 86
Larchgrove Rd. G32: Glas. 4C 86

Larch Pl.—Lenzie Way

Larch Pl. G71: View 5H **109**
G75: E Kil 6D **148**
PA5: John 5G **95**
Larch Rd. G41: Glas 1H **101**
G67: Cumb 1D **36**
Larchwood Ter. G78: Barr 6F **115**
Largie Rd. G43: Glas 2D **118**
Largo Pl. G51: Glas 4E **81**
Larkfield Ct. G72: Blan 3A **140**
Larkfield Dr. G72: Blan 3B **140**
Larkfield Rd. G66: Lenz 1E **51**
Larkfield St. G42: Glas 2F **103**
LARKHALL. **2E 161**
Larkhall Ind. Est. ML9: Lark 5G **161**
LARKHALL INTERCHANGE **5A 156**
Larkhall Leisure Cen. **3E 161**
Larkin Gdns. PA3: Pais 4H **77**
Larkin Way ML4: Bell 6B **110**
Larksfield Dr. ML8: Carl 5G **165**
Larkspur Dr. G74: E Kil 5E **137**
Larkspur Way ML8: Carl 5F **165**
Lark Way ML4: Bell. 5B **110**
Lashley Gro. ML2: Over 4A **158**
Lasswade St. G14: Glas 3G **59**
Latherton Dr. G20: Glas 4B **62**
Latimer Gdns. G52: Glas. 1A **100**
Latimer Path *G52: Glas*. *1A* ***100***
(off Hatton Gdns.)
Latta St. G82: Dumb. 3G **17**
Lauchlin Pl. G66: Kirk 6H **31**
Lauchope Rd. ML1: N'hse 6D **112**
Lauchope St. ML6: Chap. 3E **113**
Lauder Cres. ML2: Wis. 3H **145**
Lauderdale Dr. G77: Newt M 6C **132**
Lauderdale Gdns. G12: Glas. 6H **61**
Lauderdale La. G12: Glas. 6H **61**
Lauder Dr. G73: Ruth 1F **121**
PA3: Lin 6H **75**
Lauder Gdns. G72: Blan 5A **124**
ML5: Coat 2F **111**
Lauder Grn. G74: E Kil 5B **138**
Lauder La. ML3: Ham. 6C **140**
Lauder St. G5: Glas. 1E **103**
Laughland Dr. ML1: N'hill. 4D **128**
Laundry La. G33: Step 4C **66**
Lauranne Pl. ML4: Bell. 2A **126**
Laurel Av. G66: Lenz 1D **50**
G81: Clyd 3H **41**
Laurel Bank ML3: Ham. 3G **153**
Laurelbank ML5: Coat 3C **90**
Laurelbank Rd. G32: Carm 5C **106**
G69: Chry. 2H **67**
Laurel Cl. G75: E Kil 6F **149**
Laurel Dr. G75: E Kil. 6E **149**
ML2: Wis 5D **144**
ML9: Lark. 3G **161**
Laurel Gdns. G71: Tann 5D **108**
ML6: Chap 3E **113**
Laurel La. *ML9: Lark* *4G* ***161***
(off Donaldson Rd.)
Laurel Pk. Gdns. G13: Glas 3C **60**
Laurel Pk. Sports Club **3D 60**
Laurel Pl. G11: Glas. 1G **81**
G75: E Kil 6F **149**
Laurel Sq. FK4: Bank 1E **15**
Laurels, The G77: Newt M 4D **132**
ML1: Carf 5B **128**
Laurel St. G11: Glas. 1G **81**
Laurel Wlk. G73: Ruth 4E **121**
Laurel Way G78: Barr. 4D **114**
Laurence Ct. G15: Glas. 4G **43**
Laurence Dr. G15: Glas 4G **43**
G61: Bear 1D **44**
Laurence Gdns. G15: Glas 4G **43**
Laurenstone Ter. *G74: E Kil* *1B* ***150***
(off Capelrig Dr.)
Lauren Vw. ML6: Air 4H **91**
Lauren Way PA2: Pais 4D **96**
Laurie Ct. G71: Tann. 6E **109**
LAURIESTON. **6F 83**
Laurieston Rd. G5: Glas 1F **103**
Laurieston Way G73: Ruth 3D **120**
Lauriston Gro. G77: Newt M 4B **132**
Lavelle Dr. ML5: Coat. 4E **91**
Lavender Dr. G75: E Kil. 6F **149**
Lavender La. ML8: Carl 5E **165**
Laverock Av. ML3: Ham 1C **154**
Laverockhall St. G21: Glas 6B **64**
Laverock Rd. ML6: Air 1B **92**
Laverock Ter. G69: Mood 6D **52**
LAW **6D 158**
Law Dr. ML1: N'hill. 3C **128**
Lawers Dr. G61: Bear 1C **44**
Lawers La. ML1: N'hill 3C **128**
Lawers Rd. G43: Glas. 2H **117**
PA4: Renf 2E **79**
Lawfield Av. G77: Newt M 4H **133**
LAW HILL **1A 164**
Lawhill Av. G45: Glas 3H **119**
Lawhill Rd. ML8: Carl, Law 6D **158**
Lawhope Mill Rd. ML6: Chap 2F **113**
Lawmarnock Cres. PA11: Bri W 4E **73**
Lawmarnock Rd. PA11: Bri W. 5E **73**
Lawmoor Av. G5: Glas 3G **103**
Lawmoor Pl. G5: Glas. 3G **103**
Lawmoor Rd. G5: Glas 2G **103**
Lawmoor St. G5: Glas. 2G **103**
Lawmuir Cres. G81: Faif. 6G **23**
Lawmuir Pl. ML4: Bell 5C **126**
Lawmuir Rd. ML4: Bell. 4C **126**
ML8: Law 6D **158**
LAWN PARK **4A 26**
Lawn Pk. G62: Miln 4A **26**
Lawn St. PA1: Pais 6B **78**
LAW OF MAULDSLIE. **1H 163**
Law Pl. G74: E Kil 5G **137**
Lawrence Av. G46: Giff. 6A **118**
Lawrence St. G11: Glas 1A **82**
Lawrie St. G11: Glas 1H **81**
ML2: Newm 4D **146**
Lawrie Way ML9: Lark 4G **161**
LAW RDBT. **5G 137**
Lawson Av. ML1: Moth 6G **143**
Law St. G40: Glas. 6C **84**
Law Vw. ML2: Over 5A **158**
Laxford Av. G44: Glas 3E **119**
Laxford Pl. ML5: Coat. 6F **91**
Laxford Rd. PA8: Ersk. 6C **40**
Laxford Way ML1: N'hill 3C **128**
Laxton Dr. G66: Lenz 3E **51**
Lea Av. G78: Neil 2D **130**
Leabank Av. PA2: Pais 5A **98**
Leadburn Rd. G21: Glas 5E **65**
Leadburn St. G32: Glas 4G **85**
Leader St. G33: Glas. 2F **85**
Leaend Rd. ML6: Air 2G **91**
Leander Cres. ML4: Moss 2G **127**
PA4: Renf. 1G **79**
Learigg Rd. ML6: Plain. 1H **93**
Learmouth Pl. G62: Miln. 3F **25**
Leathem Pl. ML2: Wis 2C **156**
Leathen Pl. PA8: Ersk. 6C **40**
Leckethill Av. G68: Cumb 6B **34**
Leckethill Ct. G68: Cumb 6B **34**
Leckethill Pl. G68: Cumb 6A **34**
Leckethill Vw. G68: Cumb 6B **34**
Leckie Ct. *ML3: Ham* *5G* ***141***
(off Leckie Dr.)
Leckie Dr. ML3: Ham 5G **141**
Leckie St. G43: Glas. 5A **102**
Ledaig St. G31: Glas. 4E **85**
Ledard Rd. G42: Glas. 5D **102**
Ledcameroch Cres. G61: Bear 3D **44**
Ledcameroch Pk. G61: Bear. 3D **44**
Ledcameroch Rd. G61: Bear. 3D **44**
Ledgate G66: Kirk. 4D **30**
Ledgowan Pl. G20: Glas. 1B **62**
Ledi Dr. G61: Bear 6B **24**
Ledi Path ML1: N'hill 4C **128**
Ledi Rd. G43: Glas 2A **118**
Ledmore Dr. G15: Glas. 3H **43**
Lednock Rd. G33: Step. 4C **66**
G52: Glas 6A **80**
Lee Av. G33: Glas. 2G **85**
Leebank Dr. G44: Neth 6D **118**
Leeburn Av. PA6: Hous. 2C **74**
Leeburn Gdns. PA6: Hous. 2C **74**
Leechlee Rd. ML3: Ham. 6A **142**
Lee Cres. G64: B'rig 1C **64**
Leefield Dr. G44: Neth 5D **118**
Leehill Rd. G21: Glas 2A **64**
Lee Pl. ML4: Bell 3F **127**
Leesburn Pl. G74: E Kil 5H **137**
Lee's Ct. ML5: Coat 6C **90**
Leeside Rd. G21: Glas 2A **64**
Leesland G71: Tann 5E **109**
Leeward Circ. G75: E Kil. 2C **148**
Leewood Dr. G44: Neth. 5E **119**
Le Froy Gdns. G75: E Kil. 3E **149**
Le Froy La. G75: E Kil. 3E **149**
Lefroy St. ML5: Coat. 4A **90**
Legbrannock Av. ML1: N'hse 6D **112**
Legbrannock Cres. ML1: N'hill 3D **128**
Legbrannock Rd. ML1: N'hse 1E **129**
Leggatson Rd. G53: Glas 4C **116**
Leglen Wood Cres. G21: Glas 3F **65**
Leglen Wood Dr. G21: Glas. 3F **65**
Leglen Wood Gdns. G21: Glas 3F **65**
Leglen Wood Pl. G21: Glas 3G **65**
Leglen Wood Rd. G21: Glas 3F **65**
Leicester Av. G12: Glas 4H **61**
Leighton St. G20: Glas 3C **62**
ML2: Wis 1H **157**
Leisuredome Bishopbriggs Sports Cen.
. . . . **3A 48**
Leitchland Rd. PA2: Pais 5B **96**
PA5: Eld 5B **96**
Leithington Rd. G46: Giff 2G **133**
Leithland Av. G53: Glas 4B **100**
Leithland Rd. G53: Glas 4B **100**
Leith St. G33: Glas 3F **85**
Leman Dr. PA6: C'lee 3D **74**
Leman Gro. PA6: C'lee 3D **74**
Lembert Dr. G76: Clar. 1B **134**
Lendale La. G64: B'rig 3C **48**
Lendalfoot Gdns. ML3: Ham. 1B **152**
Lendal Pl. G75: E Kil 5A **148**
Lendel Pl. G51: Glas. 5B **82**
Lenihall Dr. G45: Glas 5A **120**
Lenihall Ter. G45: Glas 5A **120**
Lennox Av. G14: Glas 6C **60**
G62: Miln 4G **25**
ML5: Coat. 4A **90**
PA7: B'ton 4H **39**
Lennox Ct. *G66: Kirk*. *5E* ***31***
(off Highfield Rd.)
Lennox Cres. G64: B'rig 1B **64**
Lennox Dr. G61: Bear 1F **45**
G81: Faif. 6E **23**
Lennox Gdns. G14: Glas. 5D **60**
Lennox Ho. G67: Cumb 3H **35**
Lennox La. E. G14: Glas. 6D **60**
Lennox La. W. *G14: Glas* *6C* ***60***
(off Earlbank Av.)
G14: Glas *5D* ***60***
(off Norse La. Nth.)
Lennox Pl. G66: Len 3F **7**
G81: Clyd 4A **42**
Lennox Rd. G66: Len 2E **7**
G67: Cumb 3H **35**
G82: Dumb. 4H **17**
G82: Milt. 4E **19**
Lennox Sq. *G66: Len* *3F* ***7***
(off Service St.)
Lennox St. G20: Glas 2A **62**
G82: Dumb. 4G **17**
ML2: Wis 5C **146**
Lennox Ter. PA3: Pais. 3C **78**
LENNOXTOWN. **3F 7**
Lennox Vw. G81: Clyd 4D **42**
Lentran St. G34: Glas 4A **88**
Leny St. G20: Glas 5D **62**
LENZIE. **2C 50**
LENZIEMILL **5A 36**
Lenziemill Rd. G67: Cumb 6H **35**
Lenzie Pl. G21: Glas. 3B **64**
Lenzie Rd. G33: Step 2D **66**
G66: Kirk 6D **30**
Lenzie Station (Rail). **3C 50**
Lenzie St. G21: Glas. 4B **64**
Lenzie Ter. G21: Glas 3A **64**
Lenzie Way G21: Glas. 3A **64**

Lesley Quad. ML4: Bell 5B **126**
Leslie Av. G77: Newt M. 2E **133**
PA7: B'ton 4H **39**
Leslie Rd. G41: Glas. 3C **102**
Leslie St. G41: Glas 2D **102**
ML1: Moth 2H **143**
Lesmuir Dr. G14: Glas 4H **59**
Lesmuir Pl. G14: Glas 4H **59**
Letham Ct. G43: Glas 2C **118**
Letham Dr. G43: Glas 2C **118**
G64: B'rig 1E **65**
Letham Grange G68: Cumb 1H **35**
Lethamhill Cres. G33: Glas 2H **85**
Lethamhill Pl. G33: Glas 2G **85**
Lethamhill Rd. G33: Glas 2G **85**
Letham Oval G64: B'rig. 1F **65**
Lethbridge Pl. G75: E Kil. 3E **149**
Letherby Dr. G44: Glas 6F **103**
Letheron Dr. ML2: Wis 4H **145**
Lethington Av. G41: Glas 5C **102**
Lethington Pl. G41: Glas. 5D **102**
Letterfearn Dr. G23: Glas 6C **46**
Letterickhills Cres. G72: Flem. 4E **123**
Lettoch St. G51: Glas 4G **81**
Leven Av. G64: B'rig. 6D **48**
Leven Ct. G78: Barr 2D **114**
G82: Dumb 3E **17**
Leven Dr. G61: Bear 3F **45**
ML3: Ham 3F **153**
Levenford Ter. G82: Dumb 4E **17**
Levengrove Ct. G82: Dumb. 4E **17**
Levengrove Ter. G82: Dumb 4E **17**
Leven Path *ML1: Holy. 2A 128*
(off Graham St.)
Leven Pl. PA8: Ersk 6C **40**
Leven Quad. ML6: Air 1H **91**
Leven Rd. ML5: Coat 2G **89**
Leven Sq. PA4: Renf 5D **58**
Leven St. G41: Glas 2D **102**
G82: Dumb 4G **17**
ML1: Moth 4G **143**
Leven Ter. ML1: Carf 5C **128**
Leven Valley Ent. Cen.
G82: Dumb. 3D **16**
Leven Vw. G81: Clyd 4D **42**
Leven Way *G67: Cumb. 4H 35*
(in Cumbernauld Shop. Cen.)
G75: E Kil 5B **148**
PA2: Pais 4C **96**
Levern Cres. G78: Barr. 5D **114**
Leverndale Ct. G53: Glas 4H **99**
Leverndale Ind. Cen. G53: Glas 5H **99**
Levern Gdns. G78: Barr 4D **114**
Levern Rd. G53: Glas 1G **115**
Levernside Av. G53: Glas 5C **100**
G78: Barr 5C **114**
Levernside Cres. G53: Glas 4B **100**
Levernside Rd. G53: Glas. 4C **100**
Lewis Av. ML2: Wis 4C **146**
PA4: Renf 2F **79**
Lewis Cres. G60: Old K 2G **41**
PA10: Kilb. 3C **94**
Lewis Dr. G60: Old K. 2F **41**
Lewis Gdns. G60: Old K 2G **41**
G61: Bear 1B **44**
Lewis Gro. G60: Old K 2G **41**
Lewis Pl. G60: Old K 2G **41**
G77: Newt M. 3B **132**
ML6: Air. 5D **92**
Lewiston Dr. *G23: Glas. 6B 46*
(off Lewiston Rd.)
Lewiston Pl. *G23: Glas 6B 46*
(off Lewiston Rd.)
Lewiston Rd. G23: Glas 6B **46**
Lexwell Av. PA5: Eld. 2B **96**
Leyden Ct. G20: Glas 4C **62**
Leyden Gdns. G20: Glas. 4D **62**
Leyden St. G20: Glas 4C **62**
Leys Pk. ML3: Ham. 5E **141**
Leys, The G64: B'rig. 6C **48**
Libberton Way ML3: Ham 6E **141**
Liberton St. G33: Glas. 3F **85**
Liberty Av. G69: Barg 6E **89**
Liberty Path G72: Blan 2B **140**
Liberty Rd. ML4: Bell 3C **126**
Libo Av. G53: Glas 4D **100**
Libo Pl. PA8: Ersk. 5C **40**
Library Gdns. G72: Camb 1H **121**
Library La. G46: T'bnk 4F **117**
Library Rd. ML2: Wis. 6H **145**
Lickprivick Rd. G75: E Kil. 6D **148**
Liddell Gro. G75: E Kil 4F **149**
Liddells Ct. G64: B'rig 2C **64**
Liddell St. G32: Carm. 4C **106**
Liddel Rd. G67: Cumb 4G **35**
(Seafar Rd.)
G67: Cumb 4A **36**
(Torbrex Rd.)
Liddesdale Pl. G22: Glas 2A **64**
Liddesdale Rd. G22: Glas 2F **63**
Liddesdale Sq. G22: Glas 2H **63**
Liddesdale Ter. G22: Glas. 2A **64**
Liddlesdale Pas. G22: Glas 2G **63**
Liddoch Way G73: Ruth 5B **104**
Liff Gdns. G64: B'rig 1F **65**
Liff Pl. G34: Glas 2A **88**
LIGHTBURN
Cambuslang 4E 123
Glasgow 4A 86
Lightburn Pl. G32: Glas 4B **86**
Lightburn Rd. G31: Glas 5E **85**
G72: Camb, Flem 3D **122**
Lighthouse, The 6D 4
Lilac Av. G67: Cumb. 6E **15**
G81: Clyd 2H **41**
Lilac Ct. G67: Cumb 6E **15**
Lilac Cres. G71: View 5F **109**
Lilac Gdns. G64: B'rig 1D **64**
Lilac Hill G67: Cumb. 6F **15**
ML3: Ham. 1B **154**
Lilac Pl. G67: Cumb 6F **15**
Lilac Way ML1: Holy. 2B **128**
Lilac Wynd G72: Flem. 3E **123**
Lillie Art Gallery 3H 25
Lillyburn Pl. G15: Glas. 3G **43**
Lilybank Av. G69: Muirh 2A **68**
G72: Camb 3B **122**
ML6: Air. 1B **92**
Lilybank Gdns. G12: Glas 1B **82**
Lilybank Gdns. La.
G12: Glas 1B 82
(off Lilybank Gdns.)
Lilybank La. *G12: Glas. 1B 82*
(off Lilybank Gdns.)
Lilybank St. ML3: Ham. 5G **141**
Lilybank Ter. G12: Glas. 1B **82**
Lilybank Ter. La. *G12: Glas. 1B 82*
(off Gt. George St.)
Lily St. G40: Glas 2D **104**
Limecraigs Av. PA2: Pais 6G **97**
Limecraigs Cres. PA2: Pais 6G **97**
Limecraigs Rd. PA2: Pais 6F **97**
Lime Cres. G67: Cumb 2E **37**
ML6: Air 4C **92**
Lime Gro. G66: Lenz 2D **50**
G72: Blan 6A **124**
ML1: Moth 5G **143**
Limegrove St. ML4: Bell 6C **110**
Limekilns Rd. G67: Cumb 1H **55**
Limekilns St. G81: Faif 6F **23**
Lime La. G14: Glas 6D **60**
Lime Loan ML1: Holy 3B **128**
Lime Rd. G82: Dumb 3F **17**
Limeside Av. G73: Ruth 6D **104**
Limeside Gdns. G73: Ruth 6E **105**
Limes, The G44: Glas 3F **119**
Lime St. G14: Glas. 6D **60**
Limetree Av. G71: View. 5F **109**
Limetree Ct. ML3: Ham 4E **141**
Limetree Cres. G77: Newt M 5D **132**
Limetree Dr. G81: Clyd. 3C **42**
Limetree Quad. G71: View 5G **109**
Limetree Wlk. G66: Milt C 1B **30**
Limeview Av. PA2: Pais. 6F **97**
Limeview Cres. PA2: Pais 6F **97**
Limeview Rd. PA2: Pais 6F **97**
Limeview Way PA2: Pais. 6F **97**
Linacre Dr. G32: Glas 6C **86**
Linacre Gdns. G32: Glas. 6D **86**
LINBURN 6D 40
Linburn Pl. G52: Glas 5A **80**
Linburn Rd. G52: Glas 4G **79**
PA8: Ersk 6C **40**
LINCLIVE INTERCHANGE 6B 76
Linclive Spur PA3: Lin 6B **76**
Linclive Ter. PA3: Lin 6B **76**
Lincluden Path G41: Glas 1D **102**
Lincoln Av. G13: Glas 2C **60**
G71: Tann. 4D **108**
Lincuan Av. G46: Giff 6A **118**
Lindams G71: Udd 2D **124**
Lindcres Av. G73: Ruth. 6D **104**
Linden Av. ML2: Wis. 3A **146**
Linden Ct. G81: Hard 1C **42**
Linden Dr. FK4: Bank 1E **15**
G81: Hard. 1C **42**
Linden Lea G66: Milt C. 6B **8**
ML3: Ham 5F **141**
Linden Pl. G13: Glas. 2F **61**
Linden St. G13: Glas. 2F **61**
Linden Way G13: Glas. 2F **61**
Lindores Dr. G74: E Kil 2E **149**
Lindores Pl. G74: E Kil 2E **149**
Lindores St. G42: Glas 5F **103**
Lindrick Dr. G23: Glas. 6C **46**
Lindsaybeg Ct. G69: Chry. 1A **68**
Lindsaybeg Rd. G66: Lenz 3D **50**
G69: Chry. 5H **51**
G69: Lenz. 4G **51**
Lindsay Dr. G12: Glas. 3H **61**
Lindsayfield Av. G75: E Kil 6D **148**
Lindsayfield Rd. G75: E Kil. 6D **148**
Lindsay Gro. G74: E Kil 1H **149**
Lindsay Pl. G12: Glas. 3H **61**
G66: Lenz. 4D **50**
G74: E Kil 2A **150**
PA5: John. 2G 95
(off John Lang St.)
Lindsay Rd. G74: E Kil 2H **149**
Lindsay Ter. G66: Len 3G **7**
Lindum Cres. ML1: Moth 1D **142**
Lindum St. ML1: Moth 1D **142**
Linfern Rd. G12: Glas. 6A **62**
Linghope Pl. ML2: Wis 3F **157**
Lingley Av. ML6: Air. 5A **92**
Linhope Pl. G75: E Kil. 4A **148**
Links Rd. G32: Glas 2D **106**
G44: Glas 3G **119**
Links, The G68: Cumb 5B **14**
Links Vw. ML9: Lark. 3G **161**
Linksview Rd. ML1: Carf 6B **128**
Linkwood Av. G15: Glas 4H **43**
Linkwood Cres. G15: Glas. 4A **44**
Linkwood Dr. G15: Glas 4H **43**
Linkwood Gdns. G15: Glas 4B **44**
Linkwood Pl. G15: Glas 4H **43**
Linlithgow Gdns. G32: Glas 6D **86**
Linn Crematorium G45: Glas. 5E **119**
Linn Cres. PA2: Pais. 6G **97**
Linn Dr. G44: Neth 4D **118**
Linnet Av. PA5: John 6C **94**
Linnet Pl. G13: Glas 2H **59**
Linnet Rd. ML4: Bell. 3D **126**
Linnet Way ML4: Bell 5B **110**
Linn Gdns. G68: Cumb 3B **34**
Linn Glen G66: Len 3H **7**
Linnhead Dr. G53: Glas. 1B **116**
Linnhead Pl. G14: Glas. 5B **60**
Linnhe Av. G44: Glas. 3E **119**
G64: B'rig 6D **48**
ML3: Ham. 2E **153**
Linnhe Ct. ML9: Lark 6H **155**
Linnhe Cres. ML2: Wis. 2H **157**
Linnhe Dr. G78: Barr. 2D **114**
Linnhe Pl. G72: Blan. 5A **124**
PA8: Ersk 6C **40**
Linnpark Av. G44: Neth. 5D **118**
Linnpark Ct. G44: Neth 4D **118**
Linn Pk. Gdns. PA5: John. 3G **95**
Linnpark Ind. Est. G45: Glas. 4G **119**
Linnvale Way G68: Dull 5E **13**
Linn Valley Dr. G45: Glas 4H **119**

Linside Av. PA1: Pais 1C **98**
Lint Butts G72: Blan 2A **140**
Lintfield Loan *G71: Udd 2E 125*
(off Bellshill Rd.)
Linthaugh Rd. G53: Glas. 3A **100**
Linthaugh Ter. G53: Glas 4D **100**
LINTHOUSE **3E 81**
Linthouse Bldgs. G51: Glas. 3E **81**
Linthouse Rd. G51: Glas. 2E **81**
Lintie Rd. ML1: N'hill 3C **128**
Lintlaw G72: Blan 5B **124**
Lintlaw Dr. G52: Glas 5B **80**
Lintmill Ter. G78: Neil. 3C **130**
Linton Pl. ML5: Coat. 2A **110**
Linton St. G33: Glas. 3G **85**
Lintwhite Ct. *PA11: Bri W. 4G 73*
(off Lintwhite Cres.)
Lintwhite Cres. PA11: Bri W. 3G **73**
LINVALE **6G 43**
Linwell Cres. PA2: Pais 6H **97**
LINWOOD **6A 76**
Linwood Av. G74: E Kil 1B **148**
G76: Busby. 2D **134**
Linwood Ct. G44: Glas 2E **119**
Linwood Ind. Est. PA3: Lin 1H **95**
Linwood Rd. PA1: Pais 6B **76**
PA3: Pais 6B **76**
Linwood Sports Complex **4G 75**
Linwood Ter. ML3: Ham 5F **141**
Lion Bank G66: Kirk 4D **30**
Lismore G74: E Kil 3C **150**
Lismore Av. ML1: Moth 1D **142**
PA4: Renf 2F **79**
Lismore Dr. ML5: Coat 1H **109**
PA2: Pais 6H **97**
PA3: Lin 6F **75**
Lismore Gdns. PA10: Kilb. 3C **94**
Lismore Hill ML3: Ham 6B **140**
Lismore Pl. G69: Mood. 4E **53**
G77: Newt M. 4B **132**
Lismore Rd. G12: Glas. 4H **61**
Lister Gdns. G76: Busby 4E **135**
Lister Hgts. *G4: Glas 4A 84*
(off Drygate)
Lister Pl. G52: Hill 4A **80**
Lister Rd. G52: Hill. 4H **79**
(not continuous)
Lister St. G4: Glas 2H **83** (2H **5**)
Lister Twr. *G75: E Kil 3H 149*
(off Sinclair Pl.)
Lister Wlk. ML4: Bell 6E **111**
Lithgow Av. G66: Kirk 6E **31**
Lithgow Cres. PA2: Pais 3C **98**
Lithgow Dr. ML1: Cle 6H **129**
Lithgow Pl. G74: E Kil. 1D **148**
Lit. Dovehill G1: Glas. 5H **83**
Lit. Drum Rd. G68: Cumb 5F **33**
LITTLE EARNOCK **2E 153**
Littlehill St. G21: Glas 5C **64**
Littleholm Pl. G81: Clyd 3A **42**
Lit. John Gdns. ML2: Newm 5D **146**
Littlemill Av. G68: Cumb 4A **34**
Littlemill Cres. G53: Glas 5A **100**
Littlemill Dr. G53: Glas. 5A **100**
Littlemill Gdns. G53: Glas 5A **100**
Littlemill La. G60: Bowl 5A **20**
Lit. Mill Way ML1: Carf 6B **128**
Littlesdale Av. PA2: Pais. 6B **96**
Littleston Gdns. PA8: Ersk 6D **40**
Little St. G3: Glas. 4D **82**
Littleton Dr. *G23: Glas 6B 46*
(off Littleton St.)
Littleton St. G23: Glas 6B **46**
Lively Pl. *G72: Blan 2A 140*
(off Burnbrae Rd.)
Livery Wlk. *PA11: Bri W. 3F 73*
(off Main St.)
Livingston Dr. ML6: Plain 1G **93**
Livingstone Av. G52: Hill 3A **80**
Livingstone Blvd. G72: Blan 4A **140**
Livingstone Cl. G75: E Kil 4F **149**
Livingstone Cres. G72: Blan 6B **124**
Livingstone Dr. G75: E Kil 3F **149**
Livingstone Gdns. ML9: Lark 2F **161**
Livingstone La. G71: Both 4E **125**
Livingstone Pk. G65: Kils 1F **11**
Livingstone Pl. ML6: Air. 4B **92**
Livingstone St. G81: Clyd 6E **43**
ML3: Ham. 5D **140**
Lloyd Av. G32: Glas 3A **106**
Lloyd Dr. ML1: Carf 6A **128**
Lloyds St. ML5: Coat 6C **90**
Lloyd St. G31: Glas. 3C **84**
G73: Ruth. 4D **104**
ML1: Carf 6A **128**
Loanbank Pl. G51: Glas 4G **81**
Loanbank Quad. G51: Glas 4F **81**
Loancroft Av. G69: Bail 2A **108**
Loancroft Gdns. G71: Udd 2C **124**
Loancroft Ga. G71: Udd 2C **124**
Loancroft Ho. G69: Bail 2H **107**
Loancroft Pl. G69: Bail 2H **107**
Loanend Cotts. G72: Flem. 6F **123**
Loanfoot Av. G13: Glas. 2A **60**
G78: Neil. 3D **130**
Loanfoot Rd. G72: Blan. 4B **140**
LOANHEAD **1E 79**
Loanhead Av. ML1: N'hill 4D **128**
PA3: Lin 5G **75**
PA4: Renf 6F **59**
Loanhead Cres. ML1: N'hill 4D **128**
Loanhead La. PA3: Lin. 5G **75**
Loanhead Rd. ML1: N'hill. 4C **128**
PA3: Lin 5G **75**
Loanhead St. G32: Glas 4H **85**
ML5: Coat. 2A **110**
Loaning *ML9: Lark 3G 161*
(off Hareleeshill Rd.)
Loaninghead Dr.
G82: Dumb. 1H **17**
Loaning, The G46: Giff 1G **133**
G61: Bear 2E **45**
G66: Kirk 6C **30**
ML1: Moth 2E **143**
Loan Lea Cres. ML9: Lark. 4F **161**
Loan, The G62: Miln. 1C **24**
Lobnitz Av. PA4: Renf 6F **59**
Lochaber Dr. G73: Ruth. 3F **121**
Lochaber Path G72: Blan 2B **140**
Lochaber Pl. G74: E Kil 6H **137**
Lochaber Rd. G61: Bear. 5G **45**
Lochaber Wlk. G66: Milt C 4C **8**
Lochachray Gdns. G32: Glas. 1C **106**
Lochachray St. G32: Glas 1C **106**
Lochaline Av. PA2: Pais 3E **97**
Lochaline Dr. G44: Glas 3E **119**
Lochalsh Cres. G66: Milt C. 5C **8**
Lochalsh Dr. PA2: Pais 3E **97**
Lochalsh Pl. G72: Blan. 5H **123**
Lochar Cres. G53: Glas. 3D **100**
Lochard Dr. PA2: Pais. 4E **97**
Lochar Pl. G75: E Kil 4A **148**
Loch Assynt G74: E Kil 3B **150**
Loch Awe G74: E Kil 3A **150**
Loch Awe Pl. ML5: Coat 5B **90**
Lochay St. G32: Glas 1C **106**
Lochbrae Dr. G73: Ruth 3E **121**
Lochbridge Rd. G34: Glas. 4G **87**
Lochbroom Dr. G77: Newt M 3F **133**
PA2: Pais 3E **97**
Loch Brora Cres. ML5: Coat 5A **90**
Lochbrown Ct. G77: Newt M 3F **133**
Lochbuie La. ML6: Glenm 5G **71**
Lochburn Cres. G20: Glas 2C **62**
Lochburn Gro. *G20: Glas 2C 62*
(off Lochburn Cres.)
Lochburn Pas. G20: Glas 2C **62**
Lochburn Rd. G20: Glas 3B **62**
Lochdochart Path *G34: Glas 4B 88*
(off Lentran St.)
Lochdochart Rd. G34: Glas. 3A **88**
Lochearn Cres. ML6: Air 1H **91**
PA2: Pais 3E **97**
Lochearnhead Rd. G33: Step 4B **66**
Lochend Av. G69: G'csh 2C **68**
Lochend Cres. G61: Bear 4D **44**
Lochend Dr. G61: Bear 4D **44**
Lochend Path G34: Glas. 2H **87**
Lochend Rd. G34: Glas. 2H **87**
G61: Bear 4E **45**
G69: G'csh 2B **88**
(Easterhouse)
G69: G'csh 2D **68**
(Mount Ellen)
Lochend St. ML1: Moth 3H **143**
Locher Av. PA6: C'lee 2E **75**
Locherburn Av. PA6: C'lee. 3D **74**
Locherburn Gro. PA6: C'lee. 3D **74**
Locherburn Pl. PA6: C'lee 3D **74**
Locher Cres. PA6: C'lee 3E **75**
Locher Gait PA6: C'lee 3E **75**
Locher Gdns. PA6: C'lee 3E **75**
Locher Pl. ML5: Coat 2F **111**
Locher Rd. PA11: Bri W 6H **73**
Locher Way PA6: C'lee 3E **75**
Lochfauld Rd. G23: Glas. 5E **47**
LOCHFIELD **4B 98**
Lochfield Cres. PA2: Pais 4B **98**
Lochfield Dr. PA2: Pais. 4C **98**
Lochfield Gdns. G34: Glas 2B **88**
Lochfield Rd. PA2: Pais 4A **98**
Lochgarry Way ML5: Coat 1H **109**
Lochgilp St. G20: Glas 2A **62**
Loch Goil G74: E Kil 2A **150**
Lochgoin Av. G15: Glas 3G **43**
Lochgoin Gdns. G15: Glas 3G **43**
Lochgreen Pl. ML3: Ham 3F **153**
ML5: Coat. 1G **89**
Lochgreen St. G33: Glas 6F **65**
Lochhead Av. PA3: Lin 6H **75**
Lochiel Ct. *ML6: Air 4F 91*
(off Monkscourt Av.)
Lochiel Dr. G66: Milt C 5C **8**
Lochiel La. G73: Ruth 3F **121**
Lochiel Rd. G46: T'bnk 3F **117**
Lochinch Pl. G77: Newt M 4A **132**
Lochinvar Rd. G67: Cumb 6F **35**
Lochinver Cres. PA2: Pais. 3E **97**
Lochinver Dr. G44: Glas 3E **119**
Lochinver Gro. G72: Camb 2B **122**
Loch Laidon Ct. G32: Glas 1C **106**
Loch Laidon St. G32: Glas 1D **106**
Loch Laxford G74: E Kil 3B **150**
Loch Lea G66: Kirk 3F **31**
Lochlea G74: E Kil 5D **138**
Lochlea Av. G81: Clyd. 4E **43**
Lochlea Loan *ML9: Lark. 3G 161*
(off Catrine St.)
Lochlea Rd. G43: Glas 1B **118**
G67: Cumb 2B **36**
G73: Ruth. 2G **121**
(Burnside)
G73: Ruth 2B **120**
(Spittal)
G76: Busby. 4C **134**
Lochlea Way ML1: N'hill. 3E **129**
Lochleven La. G42: Glas. 6E **103**
Lochleven Rd. G42: Glas. 6E **103**
LOCHLIBO **6C 114**
Lochlibo Av. G13: Glas 3H **59**
Lochlibo Cres. G78: Barr 6C **114**
Lochlibo Rd. G78: Neil 3A **130**
Lochlibo Ter. G78: Barr. 6C **114**
Loch Long G74: E Kil 3A **150**
Loch Loyal G74: E Kil 3B **150**
Lochmaben Rd. G52: Glas 1H **99**
Lochmaddy Av. G44: Glas 3E **119**
Loch Maree G74: E Kil 3B **150**
Loch Meadie G74: E Kil 3B **150**
Lochnagar Dr. G61: Bear. 6B **24**
Lochnagar Way *ML9: Lark 3G 161*
(off Keir Hardie Way)
Loch Naver G74: E Kil. 3B **150**
Lochore Av. PA3: Pais. 4B **78**
Loch Pk. ML2: Wis 6A **146**
Loch Pk. Av. ML8: Carl 5E **165**
Loch Pk. Pl. ML9: Lark 4E **161**
Lochpark Stadium **5F 165**
Loch Pl. PA11: Bri W. 3F **73**
Lochranza Ct. ML1: Carf. 5B **128**
Lochranza Dr. G75: E Kil. 6D **148**
Lochranza La. G75: E Kil. 6E **149**

Loch Rd. G33: Step 4D **66**
G62: Miln 2H **25**
G66: Kirk 6D **30**
ML6: Chap 3D **112**
PA11: Bri W 3F **73**
Loch Shin G74: E Kil 3B **150**
Lochside G61: Bear 4F **45**
G69: G'csh 3D **68**
Lochside St. G41: Glas 4C **102**
Loch St. ML6: C'bnk 3B **112**
Loch Striven G74: E Kil 2A **150**
Loch Torridon G74: E Kil 3B **150**
Loch Vw. ML6: C'bnk 3B **112**
Lochview Cres. G33: Glas 6H **65**
Lochview Dr. G33: Glas 6H **65**
Lochview Gdns. G33: Glas 6H **65**
Lochview Pl. G33: Glas 6H **65**
Lochview Quad. ML4: Bell 4B **126**
Lochview Rd. G61: Bear 4E **45**
ML5: Coat 2G **89**
Lochview Ter. G69: G'csh 4D **68**
Loch Voil St. G32: Glas 1D **106**
Lochwood Loan G69: Mood 4E **53**
Lochwood St. G33: Glas 1G **85**
Lochy Av. PA4: Renf 2H **79**
Lochy Gdns. G64: B'rig 6D **48**
Lochy Pl. PA8: Ersk 6C **40**
Lochy St. ML2: Wis 2G **157**
Locke Gro. ML1: Cle 6F **129**
Lockerbie Av. G43: Glas 1D **118**
Locket Yett Vw. ML4: Bell 2A **126**
Lockhart Av. G72: Camb 1D **122**
Lockhart Dr. G72: Camb 1D **122**
G77: Newt M 6D **132**
Lockhart Pl. ML2: Wis 5C **146**
Lockhart St. G21: Glas 1D **84**
ML3: Ham 5G **153**
ML8: Carl 3F **165**
Lockhart Ter. G74: E Kil 1B **150**
Locksley Av. G13: Glas 1C **60**
G67: Cumb 1G **55**
Locksley Ct. G67: Cumb 1G **55**
Locksley Cres. G67: Cumb 1G **55**
Locksley Pl. G67: Cumb 1G **55**
Locksley Rd. G67: Cumb 1G **55**
PA2: Pais 4D **96**
Locksley Way PA2: Pais 4D **96**
Locks St. ML5: Coat 5F **91**
Lodge Twr. *ML1: Moth* *5A* ***144***
(off Glassford St.)
Logan Av. G77: Newt M 3C **132**
Logandale Av. ML2: Newm 3D **146**
Logan Dr. G68: Cumb 2F **35**
PA3: Pais 5G **77**
Logan Gdns. ML1: Cle 1H **145**
Loganlea Dr. ML1: Carf 6A **128**
Logans Rd. ML1: Moth 2D **142**
Logan St. G5: Glas 3H **103**
G72: Blan 2C **140**
Loganswell Dr. G46: T'bnk 5E **117**
Loganswell Gdns.
G46: T'bnk 5E **117**
Loganswell Pl. G46: T'bnk 5E **117**
Loganswell Rd. G46: T'bnk 5E **117**
Logan Twr. G72: Camb 3E **123**
Logie Pk. G74: E Kil 6A **138**
Logie Sq. G74: E Kil 6A **138**
Lomax St. G33: Glas 3F **85**
Lomond G75: E Kil 6G **149**
Lomond Av. PA4: Renf 2D **78**
Lomond Ct. G67: Cumb 6E **35**
G78: Barr 5E **115**
G82: Dumb 3E **17**
Lomond Cres. G67: Cumb 6E **35**
PA11: Bri W 3E **73**
PA2: Pais 5H **97**
Lomond Dr. G64: B'rig 4B **48**
G67: Cumb 6D **34**
G71: Both 4F **125**
G77: Newt M 2D **132**
G78: Barr 3D **114**
G82: Dumb 1H **17**
ML2: Wis 1G **157**
ML6: Air 2G **91**
Lomond Gdns. PA5: Eld 3A **96**
Lomond Gro. G67: Cumb 6E **35**
Lomond Pl. G33: Step 5D **66**
G67: Cumb 6D **34**
ML5: Coat 2A **90**
PA8: Ersk 6C **40**
(not continuous)
Lomond Rd. G61: Bear 5E **45**
G66: Lenz 2D **50**
G71: Tann 4D **108**
ML5: Coat 1G **89**
Lomondside Av. G76: Clar 1A **134**
Lomond St. G22: Glas 4F **63**
Lomondveiw Ind. Est.
PA5: John *2F* ***95***
(off High St.)
Lomond Vw. G67: Cumb 6E **35**
G81: Clyd *4D* ***42***
(off Church St.)
ML3: Ham 1D **152**
Lomond Wlk. ML1: N'hill 3C **128**
Lomond Wlk. *ML9: Lark* *1F* ***161***
(off Ashburn Loan)
Lomond Way *ML1: Holy* *2A* ***128***
(off Graham St.)
London La. *G1: Glas* *5H* ***83***
(off St Andrews St.)
London Rd. G1: Glas 5H **83**
G32: Glas 4A **106**
G40: Glas 1D **104**
London St. ML9: Lark 1E **161**
PA4: Renf 4F **59**
Lonend PA1: Pais 1B **98**
Longay Pl. G22: Glas 1G **63**
Longay St. G22: Glas 1G **63**
Long Calderwood Cotts.
G74: E Kil *5C* ***138***
(off Maxwellton Rd.)
Long Crags Vw. G82: Dumb 1H **17**
LONGCROFT 1G **15**
Longcroft Dr. PA4: Renf 5E **59**
Longden St. G81: Clyd 1F **59**
Long Dr. G75: E Kil 4A **150**
Longford St. G33: Glas 3F **85**
Longlee G69: Bail 1H **107**
Longmeadow PA5: John 4D **94**
Longmorn Pl. ML1: Carf 6B **128**
Long Row G66: Kirk 6H **31**
G69: Bail 5A **88**
Longstone Pl. G33: Glas 3B **86**
Longstone Rd. G33: Glas 3B **86**
Longwill Ter. G67: Cumb 1B **36**
Lonsdale Av. G46: Giff 4A **118**
Loom Wlk. PA10: Kilb 2A **94**
(not continuous)
Lora Dr. G52: Glas 1E **101**
Lord Way G69: Barg 6D **88**
Loretto Pl. G33: Glas 3H **85**
Loretto St. G33: Glas 3H **85**
Lorimer Cres. G75: E Kil 4F **149**
Lorn Av. G69: Chry 1B **68**
Lorne Ct. *G20: Glas* *1E* ***83***
(off Cedar St.)
Lorne Cres. G64: B'rig 5F **49**
Lorne Dr. ML1: Moth 5F **127**
PA3: Lin 6G **75**
Lorne Pl. ML5: Coat 6F **91**
Lorne Rd. G52: Hill 3H **79**
Lorne St. G51: Glas 5B **82**
ML3: Ham 5G **141**
Lorne Ter. G72: Camb 4H **121**
Lorn Pl. G66: Kirk 4A **32**
Lorraine Gdns. G12: Glas 5A **62**
Lorraine Gdns. La. *G12: Glas* *5A* ***62***
(off Lorraine Gdns.)
Lorraine Rd. G12: Glas 5A **62**
Loskin Dr. G22: Glas 2F **63**
Lossie Cres. PA4: Renf 1H **79**
Lossie St. G33: Glas 2F **85**
Lothian Cres. PA2: Pais 4H **97**
Lothian Dr. G76: Clar 1B **134**
Lothian Gdns. G20: Glas 6C **62**
Lothian St. G52: Hill 3G **79**
(not continuous)
Lothian Way G74: E Kil 6C **138**
Louden Hill Dr. G33: Glas 3G **65**
Louden Hill Gdns. G33: Glas 3G **65**
Louden Hill Pl. G33: Glas 3G **65**
Louden Hill Rd. G33: Glas 3G **65**
Louden Hill Way G33: Glas 3G **65**
Louden St. ML6: Air 4A **92**
Loudon G75: E Kil 6G **149**
Loudon Gdns. PA5: John 2G **95**
Loudonhill Av. ML3: Ham 3A **154**
Loudon Rd. G33: Mille 5B **66**
Loudon St. ML2: Wis 3H **145**
Loudon Ter. *G61: Bear* *6D* ***24***
(off Grampian Way)
Louise Gdns. ML1: Holy 2H **127**
Louisville Av. ML2: Wis 4B **146**
LOUNSDALE 3E **97**
Lounsdale Av. PA2: Pais 2F **97**
Lounsdale Cres. PA2: Pais 3E **97**
Lounsdale Dr. PA2: Pais 3F **97**
Lounsdale Gro. PA2: Pais 2F **97**
Lounsdale Ho. PA2: Pais 4D **96**
Lounsdale Pl. G14: Glas 5B **60**
Lounsdale Rd. PA2: Pais 3F **97**
Lounsdale Way PA2: Pais 2F **97**
Lourdes Av. G52: Glas 1D **100**
Lourdes Ct. G52: Glas 1D **100**
Lovat Av. G61: Bear 6E **25**
Lovat Dr. G66: Kirk 5B **30**
Lovat Path *ML9: Lark* *3G* ***161***
(off Shawrigg Rd.)
Lovat Pl. G52: Hill 4G **79**
G73: Ruth 3F **121**
Love Av. PA11: Q'riers 1A **72**
Love St. PA3: Pais 5A **78**
Low Barholm PA10: Kilb 3B **94**
LOW BLANTYRE 6C **124**
Low Broadlie Rd. G78: Neil 1D **130**
Low Craigends G65: Kils 3A **12**
Low Cres. G81: Clyd 1G **59**
Lwr. Admiralty Rd. G60: Old K 2F **41**
Lwr. Auchingramont Rd.
ML3: Ham 5A **142**
Lwr. Bourtree Dr. G73: Ruth 3E **121**
Lower Millgate G71: Udd 1D **124**
Lwr. Mill Rd. G76: Busby 3D **134**
Low Flender Rd. G76: Clar 4B **134**
Low Moss Ind. Est. G64: B'rig 3E **49**
Lowndes St. G78: Barr 5E **115**
Low Parksail PA8: Ersk 1G **57**
Low Parks Mus. 5A **142**
Low Patrick St. ML3: Ham 6B **142**
Low Pleasance ML9: Lark 2F **161**
Low Quarry Gdns. ML3: Ham 1H **153**
Low Rd. PA2: Pais 2G **97**
Lowther Av. G61: Bear 6C **24**
Lowther Ter. G12: Glas 5A **62**
LOW WATERS 2A **154**
Low Waters Rd. ML3: Ham 3H **153**
Loyal Av. PA8: Ersk 6D **40**
Loyal Gdns. G61: Bear 6B **24**
Loyal Pl. PA8: Ersk 6D **40**
Loyne Dr. PA4: Renf 1H **79**
Luath St. G51: Glas 3G **81**
Lubas Av. G42: Glas 6H **103**
Lubas Pl. G42: Glas 6H **103**
Lubnaig Dr. PA8: Ersk 6D **40**
Lubnaig Gdns. G61: Bear 6C **24**
Lubnaig Pl. ML6: Air 1G **91**
Lubnaig Rd. G43: Glas 2C **118**
Lubnaig Wlk. ML1: Holy 2A **128**
Luckiesfauld G78: Neil 3D **130**
Luckingsford Av. PA4: Inch 2H **57**
Luckingsford Dr. PA4: Inch 2G **57**
Luckingsford Rd. PA4: Inch 2G **57**
Lucy Brae G71: Tann 5C **108**
Ludovic Sq. PA5: John 2F **95**
Luffness Gdns. G32: Glas 3B **106**
Lugar Dr. G52: Glas 1E **101**
Lugar Pl. G44: Glas 2B **120**
Lugar St. ML5: Coat 3D **90**
Luggiebank Pl. G69: Barg 1E **109**
Luggiebank Rd. G66: Kirk 5D **30**
(not continuous)

Luggie Rd. ML8: Carl 3D 164
Luggie Vw. G67: Cumb 6C 34
Luing ML6: Air 5E 93
Luing Rd. G52: Glas 6E 81
Luma Gdns. G51: Glas 4C 80
LUMLOCH 1G 65
Lumloch St. G21: Glas 5C 64
Lumsden La. G3: Glas 2B 82
(off Lumsden St.)
Lumsden St. G3: Glas 3B 82
Lunan Av. G64: B'rig 1E 65
Lunan Dr. G64: B'rig 1E 65
Lunan Pl. G51: Glas 4E 81
Lunar Path ML6: Chap 4D 112
Luncarty Pl. G32: Glas 2A 106
Luncarty St. G32: Glas 2A 106
Lunderston Cl. G53: Glas 1B 116
Lunderston Dr. G53: Glas 6A 100
Lunderston Gdns. G53: Glas 1B 116
Lundie Gdns. G64: B'rig 1F 65
Lundie St. G32: Glas 2G 105
Luss Brae ML3: Ham 1C 152
Lusset Glen G60: Old K 1F 41
Lussett Rd. G60: Old K 1F 41
Lusset Vw. G81: Clyd 4D 42
Lusshill Ter. G71: Udd 3H 107
Luss Rd. G51: Glas 4F 81
Lybster Cres. G73: Ruth 4F 121
Lye Brae G67: Cumb 3B 36
Lyell Gro. G74: E Kil 6G 137
Lyell Pl. G74: E Kil 6G 137
Lyle Cres. PA7: B'ton 3F 39
Lyle Pl. PA2: Pais 3B 98
Lyle Rd. ML6: Air 4F 93
Lyle's Land PA6: Hous 1B 74
Lylesland Ct. PA2: Pais 3A 98
Lyle Sq. ML2: Miln 3E 25
(Hilton Rd.)
G62: Miln 3E 25
(Kelvin Rd.)
Lyman Dr. ML2: Wis 2A 146
Lymburn St. G3: Glas 3B 82
Lymekilns Rd. G74: E Kil 1F 149
Lyndale Pl. G20: Glas 1B 62
Lyndale Rd. G20: Glas 1B 62
Lyndhurst Gdns. G20: Glas 6D 62
Lyndhurst Gdns. La. G20: Glas 6C 62
(off Lothian Gdns.)
Lyne Cft. G64: B'rig 3C 48
Lynedoch Cres. G3: Glas 2D 82
Lynedoch Cres. La. G3: Glas 2D 82
(off Woodlands Rd.)
Lynedoch Pl. G3: Glas 2D 82
Lynedoch St. G3: Glas 2D 82
Lynedoch Ter. G3: Glas 2D 82
Lyne St. ML2: Wis 4G 145
Lynnburn Av. ML4: Bell 1C 126
Lynn Ct. ML9: Lark 3E 161
Lynn Dr. G62: Miln 3A 26
Lynne Dr. G23: Glas 6C 46
Lynnhurst G71: Tann 6D 108
Lynn Wlk. G71: Udd 2E 125
(off Bellshill Rd.)
Lynton Av. G46: Giff 6G 117
Lynwood Rd. ML2: Newm 3G 147
Lyoncross Av. G78: Barr 5F 115
Lyoncross Cres. G78: Barr 4F 115
Lyoncross Rd. G53: Glas 2B 100
Lyon Rd. PA2: Pais 4D 96
PA3: Lin 1H 95
PA8: Ersk 6C 40
Lyons Quad. ML2: Wis 5D 144
Lysander Way PA4: Renf 2F 79
Lysa Va. Pl. ML3: Ham 2A 126
Lytham Dr. G23: Glas 6C 46
Lytham Mdws. G71: Both 5C 124
Lyttelton G75: E Kil 5D 148

M

Mabel St. ML1: Moth 4G 143
Macadam Gdns. ML4: Bell 1C 126
Macadam Pl. G75: E Kil 3G 149
McAllister Av. ML6: Air 3D 92

McAlpine St. G2: Glas 4E 83 (6A 4)
ML2: Wis 1H 157
McArdle Av. ML1: Moth 2D 142
McArron Way G67: Cumb 4H 35
(in Cumbernauld Shop. Cen.)
Macarthur Av. ML6: Glenm 6F 71
Macarthur Ct. G74: E Kil 6E 137
Macarthur Cres. G74: E Kil 5E 137
(not continuous)
Macarthur Dr. G74: E Kil 6E 137
Macarthur Gdns. G74: E Kil 6E 137
McArthur Pk. G66: Kirk 6C 30
McArthur St. G43: Glas 6A 102
Macarthur Wynd G72: Camb 2C 122
McAslin Ct. G4: Glas 3H 83 (3H 5)
McAslin St. G4: Glas 3A 84 (3H 5)
Macbeth G74: E Kil 4B 138
Macbeth Pl. G31: Glas 1F 105
Macbeth St. G31: Glas 1F 105
McBride Av. G66: Kirk 6C 30
MacCabe Gdns. G66: Len 4H 7
McCallum Av. G73: Ruth 6D 104
McCallum Ct. G74: E Kil 5D 136
Maccallum Dr. G72: Camb 2C 122
McCallum Gdns. ML4: Bell 5B 126
McCallum Gro. G74: E Kil 5D 136
McCallum Rd. ML9: Lark 4F 161
McCarrison Rd. ML2: Newm 3E 147
McCash Pl. G66: Kirk 6C 30
McClue Av. PA4: Renf 6D 58
McClue Rd. PA4: Renf 5E 59
McClurg Ct. ML1: Moth 4G 143
McCormack Gdns. ML1: N'hill 3E 128
McCourt Gdns. ML4: Moss 2E 127
(off Main St.)
McCracken Av. PA4: Renf 1D 78
McCracken Dr. G71: View 5G 109
McCreery St. G81: Clyd 1F 59
Maccrimmon Pk. G74: E Kil 5D 136
McCrorie Pl. PA10: Kilb 2A 94
McCulloch Av. G71: View 1G 125
McCulloch St. G41: Glas 1D 102
McCulloghs Wlk. G66: Len 3F 7
Macdairmid Dr. ML3: Ham 4F 153
Macdonald Av. G74: E Kil 5C 136
McDonald Av. PA5: John 4E 95
Macdonald Cres. G65: Twe 2D 32
McDonald Cres. G81: Clyd 1F 59
MacDonald Gro. ML4: Bell 5B 126
McDonald Pl. G78: Neil 2E 131
ML1: Holy 2A 128
Macdonald St. G73: Ruth 6C 104
ML1: Moth 4H 143
Macdougal Dr. G72: Camb 2C 122
Macdougall St. G43: Glas 6A 102
Macdougal Quad. ML4: Bell 5B 126
Macdowall St. PA3: Pais 5H 77
PA5: John 2F 95
Macduff PA8: Ersk 5E 41
Macduff Pl. G31: Glas 1F 105
Macduff St. G31: Glas 1F 105
Macedonian Gro. ML1: N'hill 3C 128
Mace Rd. G13: Glas 6C 44
McEwan Gdns. G74: E Kil 5C 136
Macfarlane Cres. G72: Camb 2C 122
Macfarlane Rd. G61: Bear 4G 45
McFarlane St. G40: Glas 5A 84
PA3: Pais 4G 77
Macfie Pl. G74: E Kil 5D 136
McGhee St. G81: Clyd 3D 42
McGowan Pl. ML3: Ham 4E 141
McGown St. PA3: Pais 5H 77
McGregor Av. ML6: Air 3D 92
PA4: Renf 1D 78
Macgregor Ct. G72: Camb 2C 122
McGregor Dr. G82: Dumb 1C 18
McGregor Path ML5: Glenb 3G 69
McGregor Rd. G67: Cumb 4G 35
McGregor St. G51: Glas 5F 81
G81: Clyd 1F 59
ML2: Wis 5D 144
McGrigor Rd. G62: Miln 2F 25
MACHAN 4F 161

Machan Av. ML9: Lark 2E 161
Machanhill ML9: Lark 2F 161
Machanhill Vw. ML9: Lark 3F 161
Machan Rd. ML9: Lark 3E 161
Machrie Dr. G45: Glas 3B 120
G77: Newt M 3E 133
Machrie Rd. G45: Glas 3A 120
Machrie St. G45: Glas 4A 120
ML1: Moth 2D 142
McInnes Ct. ML2: Wis 1H 157
McInnes Pl. ML2: Over 4H 157
McIntosh Ct. G31: Glas 4B 84
(off McIntosh St.)
McIntosh Pl. G31: Glas 4B 84
Macintosh Pl. G75: E Kil 4E 149
McIntosh Quad. ML4: Bell 5B 126
McIntosh St. G31: Glas 4B 84
McIntosh Way ML1: Moth 4E 143
McIntyre Pl. PA2: Pais 3A 98
McIntyre St. G3: Glas 4D 82
McIntyre Ter. G72: Camb 1A 122
Macintyre Ter. G72: Camb 1A 122
McIver St. G72: Camb 1D 122
Macivor Cres. G74: E Kil 5C 136
McKay Ct. G77: Newt M 5C 132
McKay Cres. PA5: John 3G 95
McKay Gro. ML4: Bell 2B 126
McKay Pl. G74: E Kil 5C 136
G77: Newt M 5C 132
MacKean St. PA3: Pais 5G 77
McKechnie St. G51: Glas 3G 81
MacKeith St. G40: Glas 1B 104
McKenna Dr. ML6: Air 4G 91
McKenzie Av. G81: Clyd 3D 42
Mackenzie Dr. PA10: Kilb 4B 94
Mackenzie Gdns. G74: E Kil 5C 136
McKenzie St. PA3: Pais 6G 77
Mackenzie Ter. ML4: Bell 6C 110
McKeown Gdns. ML4: Bell 3F 127
McKerrell St. PA1: Pais 6C 78
Mackie's Mill Rd. PA5: Eld 5B 96
MacKinlay Pl. G77: Newt M 5D 132
Mackinlay St. G5: Glas 1F 103
MacKinnon Mills ML5: Coat 2C 110
Mack St. ML6: Air 3A 92
McLaren Ct. G46: Giff 6H 117
McLaren Cres. G20: Glas 2C 62
McLaren Dr. ML4: Bell 3F 127
McLaren Gro. G74: E Kil 5C 136
McLaren Pl. G44: Neth 5D 118
McLaurin Cres. PA5: John 4D 94
Maclay Av. PA10: Kilb 3A 94
McLean Av. PA4: Renf 2E 79
Maclean Ct. G74: E Kil 5D 136
McLean Dr. ML4: Bell 5B 126
Maclean Gro. G74: E Kil 5D 136
Maclean Pl. G67: Cumb 6C 34
(off Airdrie Rd.)
McLean Pl. PA3: Pais 4H 77
Maclean Rd. G74: E Kil 5D 136
G78: Neil 3E 131
Maclean Sq. G51: Glas 5B 82
Maclean St. G51: Glas 5B 82
Mclean St. G81: Clyd 1G 59
(off Wood Quad.)
McLees La. ML1: Moth 2D 142
Maclehose Rd. G67: Cumb 2C 36
McLelland Dr. ML6: Plain 1H 93
Maclellan St. G41: Glas 6B 82
Mclennan Galleries 3F 83 (3C 4)
McLennan St. G42: Glas 5F 103
Macleod Pl. G74: E Kil 6B 138
McLeod Rd. G82: Dumb 1C 18
Macleod St. G4: Glas 4A 84 (5H 5)
Macleod Way G72: Camb 2C 122
McMahon Dr. ML2: Newm 3E 147
McMahon Gro. ML4: Bell 1D 126
Macmillan Gdns. G71: Tann 5E 109
McMillan Rd. ML2: Wis 1D 156
Macmillan St. ML9: Lark 3D 160
McMillan Way ML8: Law 6D 158
McNair St. G32: Glas 6A 86
McNeil Av. G81: Clyd 6G 43
McNeil Dr. ML1: Holy 6G 111
McNeil Gdns. G5: Glas 1H 103

Macneill Dr. G74: E Kil 5D **136**
Macneill Gdns. G74: E Kil. 5D **136**
Macneill St. ML9: Lark 2D **160**
McNeil Pl. ML2: Over 4A **158**
McNeil St. G5: Glas 1H **103**
Macneish Way G74: E Kil 5D **136**
Macnicol Ct. G74: E Kil. 5C **136**
Macnicol Pk. G74: E Kil 5C **136**
Macnicol Pl. G74: E Kil. 5C **136**
McPhail St. G40: Glas. 1A **104**
McPhater St. G4: Glas 2F **83** (2D **4**)
McPherson Cres. ML6: Chap. 4E **113**
McPherson Dr. G71: Both 4F **125**
Macpherson Pk. G74: E Kil 6E **137**
McPherson St. G1: Glas. 5H **83** (6G **5**)
ML4: Moss 2F **127**
Macphie Rd. G82: Dumb 1C **18**
Macquisten Bri. G41: Glas 6B **102**
Macrae Ct. *PA5: John. 4E **95***
(off Tannahill Cres.)
Macrae Gdns. G74: E Kil. 6E **137**
Macrimmon Pl. G75: E Kil 3G **149**
McShannon Gro. ML4: Bell 4C **126**
McSparran Rd. G65: Croy. 1B **34**
MacTaggart Rd. G67: Cumb 5G **35**
Madison Av. G44: Glas 2F **119**
Madison La. G44: Glas 2F **119**
Madison Pl. G72: Blan 2B **140**
Madras Pl. G40: Glas 2B **104**
G78: Neil. 2E **131**
Madras St. G40: Glas 2B **104**
Mafeking St. G51: Glas. 5H **81**
ML2: Wis 5D **144**
Mafeking Ter. G78: Neil 2C **130**
Magdalen Way PA2: Pais 6B **96**
Magna St. ML1: Moth. 1D **142**
Magnolia Dr. G72: Flem 4F **123**
Magnolia Gdns. ML1: N'hill 4C **128**
Magnolia Pl. G71: View 5G **109**
Magnolia St. ML2: Wis. 4H **145**
Magnus Cres. G44: Glas 3F **119**
Magnus Rd. PA6: C'lee 3C **74**
Mahon Ct. G69: Mood 6D **52**
Maidens G74: E Kil 6F **137**
Maidens Av. G77: Newt M 4G **133**
Maidland Rd. G53: Glas 5C **100**
Mailerbeg Gdns. G69: Mood 4D **52**
Mailie Wlk. ML1: N'hill. 4C **128**
Mailing Av. G64: B'rig 5D **48**
Mainhead Ter. G67: Cumb 6B **14**
Mainhill Av. G69: Bail 6B **88**
Mainhill Dr. G69: Bail 6A **88**
Mainhill Pl. G69: Bail 5B **88**
Mainhill Rd. G69: Barg. 6C **88**
Main Rd. G67: Cumb 2B **54**
PA2: Pais 1H **97**
PA5: Eld 3H **95**
Mains Av. G46: Giff 6H **117**
Mains Castle **4F 137**
Mainscroft PA8: Ersk 6G **41**
Mains Dr. PA8: Ersk 6G **41**
Mains Hill PA8: Ersk 6F **41**
Mainshill Av. PA8: Ersk. 6F **41**
Mainshill Gdns. PA8: Ersk 6F **41**
Mains Pl. ML4: Bell 4C **126**
Mains River PA8: Ersk 6G **41**
Mains Rd. G74: E Kil 6G **137**
G74: E Kil, Ners. 4G **137**
Main St. G40: Glas 2B **104**
G46: T'bnk. 4F **117**
G62: Miln 4G **25**
(not continuous)
G64: Torr 5D **28**
G65: Kils. 2H **11**
G65: Twe 1D **32**
G66: Len. 3F **7**
G67: Cumb 6B **14**
G69: Bail. 1H **107**
G69: Chry 1A **68**
G71: Both 5E **125**
G71: Udd 1D **124**
G72: Blan 3H **139**
G72: Camb 1A **122**
G73: Ruth 5C **104**
Main St. G74: E Kil. 1H **149**
G76: Busby. 3D **134**
G78: Barr 5D **114**
G78: Neil. 2D **130**
ML1: Cle. 1H **145**
ML1: Holy. 2A **128**
ML2: Newm. 6E **147**
ML2: Over. 5A **158**
ML2: Wis. 5F **145**
ML4: Bell 2B **126**
ML5: Coat. 4C **90**
(not continuous)
ML5: Glenb. 3H **69**
ML6: C'bnk 2C **112**
ML6: Chap 2E **113**
ML6: Plain 1G **93**
PA11: Bri W. 3F **73**
PA6: Hous. 1A **74**
Mains Wood PA8: Ersk 6H **41**
Mair St. G51: Glas 5C **82**
Maitland Bank ML9: Lark 2G **161**
Maitland Dr. G64: Torr 4D **28**
Maitland Pl. PA4: Renf. 1D **78**
Maitland St. G4: Glas. 2F **83** (1D **4**)
Malcolm Gdns. G74: E Kil. 1E **149**
Malcolm St. ML1: Moth 3E **143**
Mal Fleming's Brae G65: Kils 4B **12**
Malin Pl. G33: Glas 3H **85**
Mallaig Path *G51: Glas. 4D **80***
(off Mallaig Rd.)
Mallaig Pl. G51: Glas. 4D **80**
Mallaig Rd. G51: Glas 4D **80**
Mallard Cres. G75: E Kil. 6C **148**
Mallard La. G71: Both 4E **125**
Mallard Pl. G75: E Kil. 6C **148**
Mallard Rd. G81: Hard 2D **42**
Mallard Ter. G75: E Kil 6C **148**
Mallard Way ML4: Bell 4B **110**
Malleable Gdns. ML1: Moth 5E **127**
MALLETSHEUGH **5B 132**
Malletsheugh Rd. G77: Newt M . . . 6A **132**
(not continuous)
Malloch Cres. PA5: Eld. 3H **95**
Malloch Pl. G74: E Kil. 1B **150**
Malloch St. G20: Glas. 4C **62**
Mallotts Vw. G77: Newt M 6B **132**
Malov Ct. G75: E Kil 6G **149**
Malplaquet Ct. ML8: Carl 4H **165**
Malta Ter. G5: Glas 1F **103**
Maltbarns St. G20: Glas 6E **63**
Malvaig La. G72: Blan 3A **140**
Malvern Ct. G31: Glas 5C **84**
Malvern Way PA3: Pais 3H **77**
Mambeg Dr. G51: Glas 3E **81**
Mamore Pl. G43: Glas 1A **118**
Mamore St. G43: Glas 1A **118**
Manchester Dr. G12: Glas. 3G **61**
M & D's Theme Pk. **6A 126**
Mandora Ct. ML8: Carl 4H **165**
Manitoba Cres. G75: E Kil 2D **148**
Mannering G74: E Kil 5D **138**
Mannering Ct. G41: Glas. 5A **102**
Mannering Rd. G41: Glas 5A **102**
PA2: Pais 6C **96**
Mannering Way PA2: Pais. 5C **96**
Mannoch Pl. ML5: Coat. 2F **111**
Mannofield G61: Bear. 3D **44**
Manor Dr. ML6: Air. 3G **91**
Manor Ga. G77: Newt M 6F **133**
Manor Pk. ML3: Ham 1H **153**
Manor Pk. Av. PA2: Pais 4F **97**
Manor Rd. G14: Glas 5E **61**
G15: Glas 6H **43**
G69: G'csh 4D **68**
PA2: Pais 4D **96**
Manor Vw. ML6: C'bnk 3B **112**
ML9: Lark. 3G **161**
Manor Way G73: Ruth. 3E **121**
Manresa Pl. G4: Glas 1F **83**
Manse Av. G61: Bear. 2F **45**
G71: Both 5E **125**
ML5: Coat. 1H **109**
Manse Brae G44: Glas. 1F **119**
G72: Flem 5F **123**
Manse Brae ML9: Ashg, Dals 6D **162**
Manse Bri. ML8: Carl 4G **165**
Manse Ct. G65: Kils 4H **11**
G78: Barr. 4F **115**
ML8: Law 1A **164**
Manse Cres. PA6: Hous 1B **74**
Mansefield Av. G72: Camb 3A **122**
Mansefield Cres. G60: Old K. 6E **21**
G76: Clar. 3B **134**
Mansefield Dr. G71: Udd 1D **124**
Mansefield Rd. G76: Clar 3C **134**
ML3: Ham. 5H **153**
Manse Gdns. G32: Glas 1D **106**
Manse La. G74: E Kil 6H **137**
Mansel St. G21: Glas 4B **64**
Manse Pl. ML6: Air 4A **92**
Manse Rd. G32: Glas 1D **106**
G60: Bowl. 5B **20**
G61: Bear 2E **45**
G65: Kils. 4H **11**
G69: Barg 5C **88**
G76: Crmck. 2H **135**
G78: Neil. 2D **130**
ML1: Moth 1G **155**
ML2: Newm 5D **146**
Manse St. ML5: Coat 5B **90**
PA4: Renf 5F **59**
Manse Vw. ML1: N'hill 3F **129**
ML9: Lark 3F **161**
MANSEWOOD **2A 118**
Mansewood Dr. G82: Dumb 2H **17**
Mansewood Rd. G43: Glas 1H **117**
Mansfield Rd. G52: Hill 4H **79**
ML4: Bell 3B **126**
Mansfield St. G11: Glas 1A **82**
Mansion Ct. G72: Camb 1A **122**
Mansionhouse Av. G32: Carm. 5C **106**
Mansionhouse Dr. G32: Glas 5C **86**
Mansionhouse Gdns. G41: Glas . . . 6C **102**
Mansionhouse Gro. G32: Glas 2E **107**
Mansionhouse Rd. G32: Glas 1E **107**
G41: Glas 6C **102**
PA1: Pais 6C **78**
Mansion St. G22: Glas 4G **63**
G72: Camb 1A **122**
Manson Pl. G75: E Kil. 6B **150**
Manus Duddy Ct. G72: Blan 1B **140**
Maple Av. G66: Milt C. 6B **8**
G77: Newt M. 5D **132**
G82: Dumb 2B **16**
Maple Bank ML3: Ham 1B **154**
Maple Ct. G67: Cumb 6F **15**
*ML5: Coat. 1B **110***
(off Ailsa Rd.)
Maple Cres. G72: Flem 4F **123**
Maple Dr. G66: Lenz. 2A **50**
G78: Barr. 6F **115**
G81: Clyd 2B **42**
ML9: Lark. 6A **156**
PA5: John 5F **95**
Maple Gro. G75: E Kil. 6D **148**
Maple Pl. FK4: Bank 1E **15**
G71: View 5H **109**
G75: E Kil 5D **148**
PA5: John. 5G **95**
Maple Quad. ML6: Air 5D **92**
Maple Rd. G41: Glas 1H **101**
G67: Cumb 6F **15**
ML1: Holy. 2B **128**
Maple Ter. G75: E Kil 5D **148**
Maple Wlk. G66: Milt C 6B **8**
Maple Way G72: Blan 2A **140**
Maplewood ML2: Wis. 2D **156**
Mar Av. PA7: B'ton 4H **39**
Marchbank Gdns. PA1: Pais 1F **99**
Marchfield G64: B'rig 4A **48**
Marchfield Av. PA3: Pais 3H **77**
Marchglen Pl. G51: Glas 4D **80**
Marchmont Gdns. G64: B'rig. 4B **48**
Marchmont Ter. *G12: Glas 6A **62***
(off Observatory Rd.)
March St. G41: Glas. 3D **102**
Mardale G74: E Kil 6E **137**
Mar Dr. G61: Bear 6F **25**

Maree Dr. G52: Glas 1E **101**
G67: Cumb 6D **34**
Maree Gdns. G64: B'rig 6D **48**
Maree Rd. PA2: Pais. 3E **97**
Maree Wlk. *ML2: Newm. 3D 146*
(off Banavie Rd.)
Maree Way G72: Blan 1B **140**
Marfield St. G32: Glas 4G **85**
Mar Gdns. G73: Ruth 3F **121**
Margaret Av. FK4: Hag 1G **15**
Margaret Pl. ML4: Bell 2A **126**
Margaret Rd. ML3: Ham 3F **141**
Margaret's Pl. ML9: Lark 2E **161**
Margaret St. ML5: Coat 1C **110**
Margaretta Bldgs. G44: Glas. 1E **119**
Margaretvale Dr. ML9: Lark 3E **161**
Marguerite Av. G66: Lenz 1C **50**
Marguerite Dr. G66: Lenz 1C **50**
Marguerite Gdns. G66: Lenz. 1C **50**
G71: Both 5F **125**
Marguerite Gro. G66: Lenz 1C **50**
Marguerite Pl. G66: Milt C 5B **8**
Marian Dr. ML1: Carf 5C **128**
Maric La. ML6: Plain 1G **93**
Marigold Av. ML1: Moth. 1G **143**
Marigold Way ML8: Carl 5F **165**
Marina Ct. ML4: Bell. 4B **126**
Marine Cres. G51: Glas 5C **82**
Marine Gdns. G51: Glas 5C **82**
Mariner Ct. G81: Clyd. 5C **42**
Marion St. ML4: Moss 2F **127**
Mariscat Rd. G41: Glas. 3C **102**
Marjory Dr. PA3: Pais. 4C **78**
Marjory Rd. PA4: Renf 2C **78**
Markdow Av. G53: Glas. 4A **100**
Market Cl. G65: Kils 3H **11**
Market Ct. *G65: Kils 3H 11*
(off Market St.)
Markethill Rd. G74: E Kil, Roger . . . 3F **137**
(not continuous)
MARKETHILL RDBT. **6G 137**
Market Pl. G65: Kils 3H **11**
G71: View 6G **109**
ML8: Carl 3F **165**
Market Rd. G66: Kirk 6G **31**
G71: View 6G **109**
ML8: Carl 3F **165**
Market Sq. G65: Kils 3H **11**
Market St. G65: Kils 3H **11**
G71: View 6G **109**
ML6: Air 4A **92**
Marlach Pl. G53: Glas. 5A **100**
Marlborough Av. G11: Glas 6F **61**
Marlborough La. Nth. G11: Glas 6F **61**
Marlborough La. Sth. *G11: Glas 6F 61*
(off Broomhill Dr.)
G52: Hill 4B 80
(off Nasmyth Rd. Nth.)
Marlborough Pk. G75: E Kil. 4C **148**
Marldon La. G11: Glas 6F **61**
Marley Way G66: Milt C 5B **8**
Marlfield Gdns. ML4: Bell. 6C **110**
Marlow St. G41: Glas 1C **102**
Marlow Ter. G41: Glas 1C **102**
Marmion Ct. PA2: Pais 5D **96**
Marmion Cres. ML1: Moth 5F **127**
Marmion Dr. G66: Kirk 5F **31**
Marmion Pl. G67: Cumb. 6G **35**
Marmion Rd. G67: Cumb 6G **35**
PA2: Pais 5C **96**
Marne St. G31: Glas. 4D **84**
Marnoch Dr. ML5: Glenb. 2H **69**
Marnoch Way G69: Mood 5D **52**
MARNOCK **3G 69**
Marnock Ter. PA2: Pais. 2C **98**
Marquis Ga. G71: Both 2C **124**
Marrswood Grn. ML3: Ham. 5E **141**
Marshall Gro. ML3: Ham. 6F **141**
Marshall La. ML2: Wis. 6G **145**
Marshall's La. PA1: Pais. 1A **98**
Marshall St. ML2: Wis 1F **157**
ML9: Lark 2E **161**
Martha Pl. ML9: Lark 3F **161**
Martha St. G1: Glas 3G **83** (4F **5**)
Martin Ct. ML3: Ham 6G **141**
Martin Cres. G69: Bail 6A **88**
Martin Pl. ML1: N'hill 4C **128**
Martinside G75: E Kil 6G **149**
Martin St. G40: Glas 2B **104**
ML5: Coat 4F **91**
Martlet Dr. PA5: John 6C **94**
Mart St. G1: Glas 5G **83**
(not continuous)
Martyn St. ML6: Air 4G **91**
Martyrs Pl. G64: B'rig 1C **64**
Marwick St. G31: Glas 4D **84**
Mary Dr. ML4: Bell 4A **126**
Mary Fisher Cres. G82: Dumb 3C **18**
Mary Glen ML2: Wis. 4B **146**
MARYHILL **1A 62**
Maryhill Rd. G20: Glas. 3B **62** (1A **4**)
G61: Bear 5F **45**
Maryhill Shop. Cen. G20: Glas 4C **62**
Maryhill Station (Rail) **1A 62**
Maryknowe Rd. ML1: Carf 5C **128**
Maryland Dr. G52: Glas. 6E **81**
Maryland Gdns. G52: Glas 6E **81**
Maryland Rd. G82: Dumb. 1H **17**
Mary Rae Rd. ML4: Bell 4A **126**
Mary Sq. G69: Barg 6D **88**
Maryston St. G33: Glas 1F **85**
Mary St. ML3: Ham 1G **153**
PA2: Pais 3A **98**
PA5: John. 2G **95**
Maryville Av. G46: Giff 5A **118**
Maryville Gdns. G46: Giff 5A **118**
MARYVILLE INTERCHANGE
. . . . **5A 108**
Maryville La. G71: Tann 5B **108**
Maryville Vw. G71: Tann. 4B **108**
Marywood Sq. G41: Glas 3D **102**
Mary Young Pl. G76: Busby 3D **134**
Masonfield Av. G68: Cumb 3F **35**
Mason La. ML1: Moth 3G **143**
(not continuous)
Mason St. ML1: Moth. 3G **143**
ML9: Lark 4G **161**
Masterton Pl. G21: Glas 6G **63**
Masterton Way G71: Tann 4F **109**
Matherton Av. G77: Newt M 4H **133**
Mathieson Rd. G73: Ruth 4E **105**
Mathieson St. PA1: Pais. 6D **78**
Matilda Rd. G41: Glas 2C **102**
Matthew McWhirter Pl.
ML9: Lark 1F **161**
Mauchline G74: E Kil 6D **138**
Mauchline Av. G66: Kirk. 3G **31**
Mauchline Ct. G66: Kirk 3G **31**
ML3: Ham. 1B **152**
Mauchline St. G5: Glas. 1E **103**
Maukinfauld Ct. G32: Glas 2F **105**
Maukinfauld Gdns. G31: Glas. 1G **105**
Maukinfauld Rd. G32: Glas. 2G **105**
Mauldslie Dr. ML8: Law. 5D **158**
Mauldslie Pl. ML9: Ashg 5B **162**
Mauldslie Rd. ML8: Carl 2F **163**
Mauldslie St. G40: Glas 1D **104**
ML4: Bell 3C **126**
ML5: Coat. 6C **90**
Maule Dr. G11: Glas. 1G **81**
Mausoleum Dr. ML3: Ham 4A **142**
Mavis Bank G64: B'rig 1B **64**
G72: Blan 2A **140**
Mavisbank Gdns. G51: Glas 5C **82**
ML4: Bell 1C **126**
Mavisbank Rd. G51: Glas 4B **82**
Mavisbank St. ML2: Newm. 4G **147**
ML6: Air. 3G **91**
Mavisbank Ter. PA1: Pais 2B **98**
PA5: John 3F **95**
Mavis Valley Rd.
G64: B'rig 3A **48**
Mavor Av. G74: E Kil. 5H **137**
MAVOR RDBT. **5H 137**
Maxton Av. G78: Barr 4C **114**
Maxton Cres. ML2: Wis 3A **146**
Maxton Gro. G78: Barr 5C **114**
Maxton Ter. G72: Camb 4H **121**
Maxwell Av. G41: Glas 1C **102**
G61: Bear 4E **45**
G69: Bail. 1G **107**
Maxwell Ct. G41: Glas 1C **102**
Maxwell Cres. G72: Blan 3B **140**
Maxwell Dr. G41: Glas 1A **102**
G69: Bail 6F **87**
G74: E Kil 1H **149**
PA8: Ersk 4D **40**
Maxwell Gdns. G41: Glas 1B **102**
Maxwell Gro. G41: Glas 1B **102**
Maxwell La. G41: Glas 1C **102**
Maxwell Oval G41: Glas 1D **102**
Maxwell Park Station (Rail)
. . . . **3B 102**
Maxwell Path *ML9: Lark. 3G 161*
(off Keir Hardie Rd.)
Maxwell Pl. G41: Glas 2E **103**
G65: Kils. 2H **11**
G71: Udd. 1E **125**
ML5: Coat. 6B **90**
PA11: Bri W. 3F **73**
Maxwell Rd. G41: Glas. 1D **102**
PA7: B'ton 4H **39**
Maxwell St. G1: Glas 4G **83** (6E **5**)
(Argyle St.)
G1: Glas 5G **83**
(Broomielaw)
G69: Bail. 1H **107**
G81: Clyd 3B **42**
PA3: Pais 6A **78**
Maxwell Ter. G41: Glas. 1C **102**
Maxwellton Av. G74: E Kil. 1A **150**
Maxwellton Ct. PA1: Pais 1G **97**
Maxwellton Pl. G74: E Kil 6B **138**
Maxwellton Rd. G74: E Kil 6B **138**
PA1: Pais. 1F **97**
Maxwellton St. PA1: Pais 1G **97**
Maxwelton Rd. G33: Glas 1F **85**
Maybank La. G42: Glas. 4E **103**
Maybank St. G42: Glas 4E **103**
Mayberry Cres. G32: Glas 6D **86**
Mayberry Gdns. G32: Glas 6D **86**
Mayberry Gro. G32: Glas 6D **86**
Mayberry Pl. G72: Blan. 1B **140**
Maybole Cres. G77: Newt M. 5G **133**
Maybole Gdns. ML3: Ham 1B **152**
Maybole Gro. G77: Newt M 5G **133**
Maybole Pl. ML5: Coat 2F **111**
Maybole St. G53: Glas 1H **115**
Mayfield Av. G76: Clar 2C **134**
Mayfield Gdns. ML8: Carl. 6G **165**
Mayfield Pl. ML5: Coat. 2C **110**
ML8: Carl 6G **165**
Mayfield Rd. ML3: Ham 5D **140**
Mayfield St. G20: Glas 4D **62**
May Gdns. ML3: Ham. 4G **141**
May Rd. PA2: Pais 6A **98**
May St. ML3: Ham 4H **141**
May Ter. G42: Glas 5F **103**
G46: Giff. 4A **118**
Meadow Av. G72: Blan 3B **140**
Meadowbank La. G71: Udd 1C **124**
Meadowbank Pl. G77: Newt M 4D **132**
Meadowbank St. G82: Dumb 3E **17**
(not continuous)
Meadowburn G64: B'rig 3C **48**
Meadowburn Av. G66: Lenz 2E **51**
G77: Newt M. 4D **132**
Meadowburn Rd. ML2: Wis 6A **146**
Meadow Ct. G82: Dumb 2F **17**
Meadowfield Pl. ML2: Newm 3G **147**
Meadowhead Av. G69: Mood 5D **52**
Meadowhead Rd. ML2: Wis 5C **144**
(not continuous)
Meadowhead Rd. ML6: Plain 1F **93**
MEADOWHILL **2F 161**
Meadowhill G77: Newt M 4D **132**
Meadowhill St. ML9: Lark. 2F **161**
Meadow La. G71: Both 5F **125**
PA4: Renf 4F **59**
Meadowpark St. G31: Glas. 4D **84**
(not continuous)
Meadow Path ML6: Chap 4D **112**

Meadow Rd. G11: Glas 1G **81**
G82: Dumb 3F **17**
ML1: Moth 4H **143**
Meadows Av. ML9: Lark 2F **161**
PA8: Ersk 6G **41**
Meadows Dr. PA8: Ersk 6G **41**
Meadow Side ML3: Ham 5H **153**
Meadowside Av. PA5: Eld 3B **96**
Meadowside Gdns. ML6: Air 4D **92**
Meadowside Ind. Est. PA4: Renf 3F **59**
Meadowside Pl. ML6: Air 4D **92**
Meadowside Rd. G65: Queen 3C **10**
Meadowside St. G11: Glas 2G **81**
PA4: Renf 4F **59**
Meadow Sports Cen. 3F **17**
Meadows., The PA6: Hous 2D **74**
Meadow St. ML5: Coat 1D **110**
Meadow Vw. G67: Cumb 1C **36**
ML6: Plain 1G **93**
Meadow Wlk. ML5: Coat 5D **90**
Meadow Way G77: Newt M 4D **132**
Meadowwell St. G32: Glas 6B **86**
Meadside Av. PA10: Kilb 1A **94**
Meadside Rd. PA10: Kilb 1A **94**
Mealkirk St. G81: Faif 6E **23**
MEARNS 6E **133**
MEARNS CASTLE 6G **133**
Mearns Castle 6G **133**
Mearns Ct. ML3: Ham 4A **154**
Mearnscroft Gdns. G77: Newt M 6F **133**
Mearnscroft Rd. G77: Newt M 6F **133**
Mearnskirk Rd. G77: Newt M 6D **132**
Mearns Rd. G76: Clar 3H **133**
Mearns Rd. G77: Newt M 6E **133**
ML1: Moth 1E **143**
Mearns Way G64: B'rig 5F **49**
Medlar Ct. G72: Flem 4F **123**
Medlar Rd. G67: Cumb 3D **36**
Medrox Gdns. G67: Cumb 2B **54**
Medwin Ct. G75: E Kil 4A **148**
Medwin Gdns. G75: E Kil 4A **148**
Medwin St. G72: Camb 2D **122**
Medwyn St. G14: Glas 6D **60**
(not continuous)
Meek Pl. G72: Camb 2B **122**
Meetinghouse La. PA1: Pais 6A **78**
Megan Ga. G40: Glas 1B **104**
Megan St. G40: Glas 1B **104**
Meigle Rd. ML6: Air 1H **111**
Meikle Av. PA4: Renf 1E **79**
Meikle Bin Brae G66: Len 3G **7**
Meikle Cres. ML3: Ham 4G **153**
MEIKLE EARNOCK 4G **153**
Meikle Earnock Rd. ML3: Ham 5D **152**
Meiklehill Ct. G66: Kirk 4E **31**
(not continuous)
Meiklehill Rd. G66: Kirk 4E **31**
Meiklem St. ML4: Moss 2E **127**
Meiklerig Cres. G53: Glas 3C **100**
MEIKLERIGGS 3F **97**
Meikleriggs Ct. PA2: Pais 3F **97**
Meikleriggs Dr. PA2: Pais 4E **97**
Meikle Rd. G53: Glas 5C **100**
Meiklewood Rd. G51: Glas 5D **80**
(not continuous)
Melbourne Av. G75: E Kil 4E **149**
G81: Clyd 2H **41**
Melbourne Ct. G46: Giff 4B **118**
Melbourne Grn. G75: E Kil 3E **149**
Melbourne St. G31: Glas 5B **84**
Meldon Pl. G51: Glas 4D **80**
Meldrum Gdns. G41: Glas 3B **102**
Meldrum Mains ML6: Glenm 5G **71**
Meldrum St. G81: Clyd 1F **59**
Melford Av. G46: Giff 5B **118**
G66: Kirk 5B **30**
Melford Ct. G81: Clyd 5E **43**
Melford Rd. ML4: Bell 1H **125**
Melford Way PA3: Pais 3D **78**
Melfort Av. G41: Glas 1H **101**
G81: Clyd 4D **42**
Melfort Gdns. PA10: John 4C **94**
Melfort Path *ML2: Newm 2D 146*
(off Kildonan Ct.)
Melfort Quad. *ML1: N'hill 4D 128*
(off Glenmore Rd.)
Melfort Rd. ML3: Ham 6C **140**
Mellerstain Dr. G14: Glas 3G **59**
Mellerstain Gro. G14: Glas 3H **59**
Melness Pl. G51: Glas 4D **80**
Melrose Av. G69: Barg 6D **88**
G73: Ruth 6D **104**
ML1: Holy 1B **128**
ML6: Chap 3D **112**
PA2: Pais 4E **97**
PA3: Lin 6H **75**
Melrose Ct. *G73: Ruth 6D 104*
(off Dunard Rd.)
Melrose Cres. ML2: Wis 4G **145**
Melrose Gdns. G20: Glas 6D **62**
G65: Twe 1C 32
(off Glen Shirva Rd.)
G71: Tann 4D **108**
Melrose Pl. G72: Blan 6A **124**
ML5: Coat 4B **90**
ML9: Lark 4E **161**
Melrose Rd. G67: Cumb 6G **35**
Melrose St. G4: Glas 1A **4**
ML3: Ham 4F **141**
Melrose Ter. G74: E Kil 6H **137**
ML3: Ham 3F **141**
Melvaig Pl. G20: Glas 4B **62**
Melvick Pl. G51: Glas 4D **80**
Melville Ct. G1: Glas 6F **5**
Melville Cres. ML1: Moth 3H **143**
Melville Dr. ML1: Moth 3G **143**
Melville Gdns. G64: B'rig 5C **48**
Melville Pk. G74: E Kil 6B **138**
Melville Pl. ML8: Carl 3E **165**
Melville St. G41: Glas 2D **102**
Memel St. G21: Glas 4A **64**
Memus Av. G52: Glas 1C **100**
Mennock Ct. ML3: Ham 1C **152**
Mennock Dr. G64: B'rig 3C **48**
Mennock St. ML1: Cle 5H **129**
Menock Rd. G44: Glas 1F **119**
Menteith Av. G64: B'rig 6D **48**
Menteith Dr. G73: Ruth 5F **121**
Menteith Gdns. G61: Bear 5C **24**
Menteith Loan ML1: Holy 2A **128**
Menteith Pl. G73: Ruth 5F **121**
Menteith Rd. ML1: Moth 2G **143**
Menzies Dr. G21: Glas 4C **64**
Menzies Pl. G21: Glas 4C **64**
Menzies Rd. G21: Glas 3D **64**
Merchant La. G1: Glas 5G **83**
Merchants Cl. PA10: Kilb 2A **94**
Merchants Ho. 5E **5**
Merchiston Av. PA3: Lin 6F **75**
Merchiston Dr. PA5: Brkfld 6D **74**
Merchiston St. G32: Glas 4G **85**
Merkins Av. G82: Dumb 1H **17**
MERKLAND 4G **31**
Merkland Ct. G11: Glas 2H **81**
G66: Kirk 4F **31**
Merkland Dr. G66: Kirk 4G **31**
Merkland Pl. G66: Kirk 4F **31**
Merkland Rd. ML5: Coat 1G **89**
Merkland St. G11: Glas 1H **81**
Merksworth Way *PA3: Pais 4A 78*
(off Mosslands Rd.)
Merlewood Av. G71: Both 3F **125**
Merlin Av. ML4: Bell 6C **110**
Merlinford Av. PA4: Renf 6G **59**
Merlinford Cres.
PA4: Renf 6G **59**
Merlinford Dr. PA4: Renf 6G **59**
Merlinford Way PA4: Renf 6G **59**
Merlin Way PA3: Pais 4D **78**
Merrick Ct. ML6: Air 1B **92**
Merrick Gdns. G51: Glas 6H **81**
G61: Bear 6C **24**
Merrick Path *G51: Glas 6H 81*
(off Merrick Gdns.)
Merrick Ter. G71: View 6F **109**
Merrick Way G73: Ruth 4D **120**
Merryburn Av. G46: Giff 2B **118**
Merrycrest Av. G46: Giff 3A **118**
Merrycroft Av. G46: Giff 3B **118**
Merryflats G65: Twe 1D **32**
Merryland Pl. G51: Glas 4H **81**
Merryland St. G51: Glas 4H **81**
(not continuous)
MERRYLEE 3B **118**
Merrylee Cres. G46: Giff 2A **118**
Merrylee Pk. Av. G46: Giff 3A **118**
Merrylee Pk. M. G46: Giff 2A **118**
Merrylee Rd. G43: Glas 2B **118**
G44: Glas 2D **118**
Merrylees Rd. G72: Blan 2A **140**
Merryston Ct. ML5: Coat 5A **90**
Merrystone St. ML5: Coat 4B **90**
Merry St. ML1: Carf 6B **128**
ML1: Moth 2G **143**
(not continuous)
Merryton Av. G15: Glas 4B **44**
G46: Giff 3A **118**
Merryton Pl. G15: Glas 4B **44**
Merryton Rd. ML1: Moth 1B **156**
ML9: Lark 5H **155**
Merryton St. ML9: Lark 6H **155**
Merryton Twr. ML1: Moth 1B **156**
Merryvale Av. G46: Giff 2B **118**
Merryvale Pl. G46: Giff 2A **118**
Merton Dr. G52: Glas 6A **80**
Meryon Gdns. G32: Glas 3D **106**
Meryon Rd. G32: Glas 2D **106**
Methil St. G14: Glas 6C **60**
Methlan Pk. G82: Dumb 5E **17**
Methlick Av. ML6: Air 1G **111**
Methuen Rd. PA3: Pais 2B **78**
Methven Av. G61: Bear 2H **45**
Methven Pl. G74: E Kil 1E **149**
Methven Rd. G46: Giff 3G **133**
Methven St. G31: Glas 2F **105**
G81: Clyd 3B **42**
Methven Ter. ML5: Coat 2D **90**
Metropole La. G1: Glas 5G **83**
Mews La. PA3: Pais 4B **78**
Mey Ct. G77: Newt M 5A **132**
Mey Pl. G77: Newt M 5A **132**
M8 Food Pk. G21: Glas 1H **83**
Michael McParland Dr. G64: Torr 5D **28**
Michael Ter. ML6: Chap 4D **112**
Micklehouse Oval G69: Bail 5H **87**
Micklehouse Pl. G69: Bail 5H **87**
Micklehouse Rd. G69: Bail 5H **87**
Micklehouse Wynd G69: Bail 5H **87**
Midas Pl. ML4: Moss 2G **127**
Mid Barrwood Rd. G65: Kils 4A **12**
Mid Carbarns ML2: Wis 2D **156**
Midcroft G64: B'rig 4A **48**
Midcroft Av. G44: Glas 2H **119**
Middlefield G75: E Kil 6G **149**
Middlehouse Ct. ML8: Carl 3D **164**
Middlemuir Av. G66: Lenz 2D **50**
Middlemuir Rd. G66: Lenz 1D **50**
Middlerigg Rd. G68: Cumb 3F **35**
Middlesex Gdns G41: Glas 5C **82**
Middlesex St. G41: Glas 6C **82**
Middleton Av. ML9: Lark 5F **161**
Middleton Dr. G62: Miln 3H **25**
Middleton Rd. PA3: Lin 5A **76**
PA3: Pais 5F **77**
Middleton St. G51: Glas 5A **82**
Middleward St. G81: Faif 6F **23**
Midfaulds Av. PA4: Renf 1G **79**
Midland St. G1: Glas 4F **83** (6C **4**)
Midlem Dr. G52: Glas 6C **80**
Midlem Oval G52: Glas 6C **80**
Midlock St. G51: Glas 6A **82**
Midlothian Dr. G41: Glas 4B **102**
Mid Park G75: E Kil 3G **149**
Mid Rd. G67: Cumb 1H **55**
Midton Rd. PA9: How 6B **94**
Midton St. G21: Glas 6B **64**
Mid Wharf St. G4: Glas 1G **83** (1F **5**)
Migvie Pl. G20: Glas 4B **62**
Milford G75: E Kil 4D **148**
Milford St. G33: Glas 3A **86**
Millands Av. G72: Blan 6A **124**
Millarbank St. G21: Glas 5A **64**

Millar Gro.—Moat Av.

Millar Gro. ML3: Ham 5E **141**
Millar Pk. ML3: Ham 5F **141**
Millars Pl. G66: Lenz 3D **50**
MILLARSTON **1E 97**
Millarston Av. PA1: Pais 1E **97**
Millarston Ct. PA1: Pais 1F **97**
Millarston Dr. PA1: Pais 1E **97**
Millarston Ind. Est. PA1: Pais 2E **97**
Millar St. PA1: Pais 6B **78**
Millar Ter. G73: Ruth 4D **104**
Millbank Av. ML4: Bell 4D **126**
Millbank Rd. ML2: Wis 1F **157**
Millbeg Cres. G33: Glas 5E **87**
Millbeg Pl. G33: Glas 6E **87**
Mill Brae PA11: Bri W 3F **73**
Millbrae Av. G69: Chry 1B **68**
Millbrae Ct. G42: Glas 6D **102**
ML5: Coat 6H **89**
Millbrae Cres. G42: Glas 6C **102**
G81: Clyd 2F **59**
Millbrae Gdns. G42: Glas 6D **102**
Millbrae Rd. G43: Glas 6C **102**
Millbrix Av. G14: Glas 4A **60**
Millbrook G74: E Kil 1D **148**
Millburn Av. G73: Ruth 1C **120**
G81: Clyd 1G **59**
PA4: Renf 6F **59**
Millburn Ct. G75: E Kil 4A **148**
Millburn Cres. G82: Dumb 4H **17**
Millburn Dr. PA4: Renf 6G **59**
Millburn Gdns. G75: E Kil 4A **148**
Millburn La. ML9: Lark 3G **161**
Millburn Pl. ML9: Lark 5F **161**
Millburn Rd. G82: Dumb 4H **17**
ML9: Ashg 4B **162**
PA4: Renf 6F **59**
Millburn St. G21: Glas 2C **84**
G66: Len 3F **7**
ML1: Moth 2G **143**
Millburn Way G75: E Kil 4A **148**
PA4: Renf 6G **59**
Mill Ct. G73: Ruth 5C **104**
ML3: Ham 1G **153**
Mill Cres. G40: Glas 2B **104**
G64: Torr 4E **29**
Millcroft Rd. G67: Cumb 4B **36**
(Sth. Carbrain Rd.)
G67: Cumb 3G **55**
(Summerhill & Garngibbock Rd)
G73: Ruth 3B **104**
Milldam Rd. G81: Faif 6E **23**
Millennium Ct. G34: Glas 3A **88**
Millennium Gdns. G34: Glas 4A **88**
Millennium Pk. ***2D 82***
(off Ashley St.)
Miller Ct. G82: Dumb 3H **17**
Millerfield Pl. G40: Glas 2D **104**
ML3: Ham 6B **142**
Millerfield Rd. G40: Glas 2D **104**
Millerslea *G82: Milt 4F* ***19***
(off Colquhoun Rd.)
MILLERSNEUK **3E 51**
Millersneuk Av. G66: Lenz 3D **50**
Millersneuk Ct. G66: Lenz 3D **50**
Millersneuk Cres. G33: Mille 4A **66**
Millersneuk Dr. G66: Lenz 3D **50**
Millersneuk Rd. G66: Lenz 3D **50**
(not continuous)
Miller's Pl. ML6: Air 4B **92**
MILLERSTON **5C 134**
Millerston St. G40: Glas 5C **84**
Miller St. G1: Glas 4G **83** (6E **5**)
G69: Bail 1H **107**
G81: Clyd 6D **42**
G82: Dumb 3H **17**
ML2: Wis 6G **145**
ML3: Ham 6B **142**
ML5: Coat 6D **90**
ML8: Carl 3F **165**
ML9: Lark 2E **161**
PA5: John 2H **95**
Millfield Av. ML1: Moth 1H **143**
PA8: Ersk 6D **40**
Millfield Cres. PA8: Ersk 6E **41**
Millfield Dr. PA8: Ersk 1E **57**
Millfield Gdns. PA8: Ersk 6E **41**
Millfield Hill PA8: Ersk 6D **40**
Millfield La. PA8: Ersk 6D **40**
Millfield Mdw. PA8: Ersk 6D **40**
Millfield Pl. PA8: Ersk 6D **40**
Millfield Vw. PA8: Ersk 6D **40**
Millfield Wlk. PA8: Ersk 1E **57**
Millfield Wynd PA8: Ersk 6D **40**
Millford Dr. PA3: Lin 6H **75**
Millgate G71: Tann 5D **108**
Millgate Av. G71: Tann 5D **108**
Millgate Ct. G71: Udd 6D **108**
Millgate Rd. ML3: Ham 2G **153**
Mill Gro. ML3: Ham 1G **153**
MILLHEUGH **3C 160**
Millheugh Brae ML9: Lark 3C **160**
Millheugh Pl. G72: Blan 3A **140**
Millheugh Rd. ML3: Ham 6C **160**
ML9: Lark 3C **160**
Millholm Rd. G44: Glas 3F **119**
Millhouse Cres. G20: Glas 2A **62**
Millhouse Dr. G20: Glas 2H **61**
Millichen Rd. G23: Glas 3B **46**
Milliken Dr. PA10: Kilb 3C **94**
MILLIKENPARK **4C 94**
Millikenpark Station (Rail) **5C 94**
Milliken Pk. Rd. PA10: Kilb 4C **94**
Milliken Pl. *PA10: Kilb 3C 94*
(off Easwald Bank)
Milliken Rd. PA10: Kilb 3C **94**
Mill Loan ML6: Air 3A **92**
Mill of Gryffe Rd.
PA11: Bri W 3F **73**
Mill Pk. ML3: Ham 1G **153**
Mill Pl. PA3: Lin 5G **75**
Millport Av. G44: Glas 6G **103**
Millrig G75: E Kil 6F **149**
Mill Ri. G66: Lenz 3D **50**
Mill Rd. G65: Queen 4C **10**
G71: Both 6E **125**
G72: Camb 3D **122**
(Hamilton Rd.)
G72: Camb 1C **122**
(Westburn Rd.)
G78: Barr 4D **114**
G81: Clyd 2F **59**
ML1: Moth 2H **143**
ML2: Newm 6G **147**
ML6: Air 2A **92**
ML8: Carl 4E **165**
Millroad Dr. G40: Glas 5A **84**
Millroad Gdns. *G40: Glas 5B* ***84***
(off Millroad Dr.)
Millroad St. G40: Glas 5A **84**
(not continuous)
Millstream Ct. PA1: Pais 1B **98**
Mill St. G40: Glas 2B **104**
G73: Ruth 6C **104**
(not continuous)
PA1: Pais 1B **98**
Mill St. Ind. Est. ML6: Air 3A **92**
Mill Vennel PA4: Renf 6F **59**
Millview G78: Barr 4F **115**
Millview Mdws. G78: Neil 2C **130**
Millview Pl. G53: Glas 3B **116**
Millview Ter. G78: Neil 2C **130**
Mill Way G66: Kirk 6G **31**
Millwood St. G41: Glas 5C **102**
MILNBANK **3C 84**
Milnbank St. G31: Glas 3C **84**
Milncroft Pl. G33: Glas 2A **86**
Milncroft Rd. G33: Glas 2A **86**
Milner La. G13: Glas 4E **61**
Milner Rd. G13: Glas 4E **61**
MILNGAVIE **3H 25**
Milngavie Station (Rail) **4H 25**
Milngavie Rd. G61: Bear 4F **45**
Milnpark Gdns. G41: Glas 6B **82**
Milnpark St. G41: Glas 6C **82**
MILNWOOD **3E 127**
Milnwood Dr. ML1: Moth 5E **127**
ML4: Bell 3E **127**
Milovaig Av. G23: Glas 6B **46**
Milovaig St. G23: Glas 6B **46**
Milrig Rd. G73: Ruth 6B **104**
Milroy Gdns. ML4: Bell 5C **110**
MILTON
Dumbarton **4F 19**
Glasgow **1G 63**
Milton Av. G72: Camb 2G **121**
Milton Brae G82: Milt 1F **19**
Milton Ct. *G66: Kirk 5E* ***31***
(off Highfield Rd.)
G82: Milt 3F **19**
ML6: Air 3A **92**
Milton Cres. ML8: Carl 4F **165**
Milton Douglas Rd.
G81: Dun, Hard 2C **42**
Milton Dr. G64: B'rig 2B **64**
Milton Gdns. G71: Tann 5C **108**
Milton Hill G82: Milt 4F **19**
Milton Mains Rd. G81: Clyd 2C **42**
MILTON OF CAMPSIE **5C 8**
Milton Rd. G66: Kirk 3C **30**
G66: Len 4G **7**
G74: E Kil 1C **148**
ML8: Carl 5B **164**
Milton St. G4: Glas 2F **83** (2D **4**)
ML1: Moth 1G **143**
ML3: Ham 5E **141**
ML6: Air 3A **92**
ML8: Carl 3E **165**
Milton Ter. ML3: Ham 4E **141**
Milverton Av. G61: Bear 1C **44**
Milverton Rd. G46: Giff 6G **117**
Mimosa Rd. PA11: Bri W 3F **73**
Mimosas, The *PA11: Bri W 3F* ***73***
(off Mimosa Rd.)
Minard Rd. G41: Glas 4C **102**
Minard Way G71: Tann 6E **109**
Mincher Cres. ML1: Moth 5G **143**
Minch Way ML6: Air 6C **92**
Minella Gdns. ML4: Bell 5C **110**
Minerva Ct. *G3: Glas 3C* ***82***
(off Houldsworth St.)
Minerva St. G3: Glas 3C **82**
Minerva Way G3: Glas 3B **82**
Mingarry La. G20: Glas 5C **62**
Mingarry St. G20: Glas 5C **62**
Mingulay Cres. G22: Glas 1H **63**
Mingulay Pl. G22: Glas 1A **64**
Mingulay St. G22: Glas 1H **63**
Minister's Pk. G74: E Kil 5B **136**
Minmoir Rd. G53: Glas 6H **99**
Minster Wlk. G69: Barg 6D **88**
Minstrel Rd. G13: Glas 6D **44**
Minto Av. G73: Ruth 3F **121**
Minto Cres. G52: Glas 6F **81**
Minto Pk. ML2: Wis 3A **146**
Minto St. G52: Glas 6F **81**
Mireton St. G22: Glas 4F **63**
Mirren Ct. PA3: Pais 4B **78**
Mirren Dr. G81: Dun 6B **22**
Mirrlees Dr. G12: Glas 5A **62**
Mirrlees La. G12: Glas 5A **62**
Mitchell Arc. G73: Ruth 5D **104**
Mitchell Av. G72: Camb 1E **123**
PA4: Renf 1D **78**
Mitchell Ct. G74: E Kil 1E **149**
Mitchell Dr. G62: Miln 4A **26**
G73: Ruth 1D **120**
Mitchell Gro. G74: E Kil 1E **149**
Mitchell Hill Rd. G45: Glas 5B **120**
Mitchell La. G1: Glas 4F **83** (5D **4**)
Mitchell Rd. G67: Cumb 3A **36**
Mitchell St. G1: Glas 4F **83** (6D **4**)
ML5: Coat 1F **109**
ML6: Air 3H **91**
Mitchell Theatre, The **3D 82**
Mitchison Rd. G67: Cumb 2A **36**
Mitre Ct. G11: Glas 5F **61**
Mitre Ga. G11: Glas 6F **61**
Mitre La. G14: Glas 5E **61**
Mitre La. W. G14: Glas 5D **60**
Mitre Rd. G11: Glas 5F **61**
G14: Glas 5D **60**
Moat Av. G13: Glas 2C **60**

A-Z Glasgow 225

Mochrum Rd. G43: Glas 1C **118**
Moffat Ct. G75: E Kil 4A **148**
Moffat Gdns. G75: E Kil 4A **148**
Moffathill ML6: Gart 6E **93**
MOFFAT MILLS 5F 93
Moffat Pl. G72: Blan 6B **124**
G75: E Kil 4A **148**
ML5: Coat 1F **111**
ML6: Air 3F **93**
Moffat Rd. ML6: Air 4F **93**
Moffat St. G5: Glas 1H **103**
Moffat Vw. ML6: Plain 1G **93**
Mogarth Av. PA2: Pais 5D **96**
Moidart Av. PA4: Renf 5D **58**
Moidart Ct. G78: Barr 3D **114**
Moidart Cres. G52: Glas 6F **81**
Moidart Gdns. G66: Kirk 4H **31**
G77: Newt M 3E **133**
Moidart Pl. G52: Glas 6F **81**
Moidart Rd. G52: Glas 6E **81**
Moir St. G1: Glas 5H **83**
Molendinar St. G1: Glas 5H **83**
Molendinar Ter. G78: Neil 3C **130**
MOLLINSBURN 3H 53
MOLLINSBURN JUNC. 4G **53**
Mollinsburn Rd. G67: Cumb 3A **54**
ML5: Anna 6B **54**
Mollinsburn St. G21: Glas 6A **64**
Mollins Ct. G68: Cumb 2H **53**
Mollins Rd. G68: Cumb 1G **53**
MOLLINS RDBT. 3H **53**
Monach Rd. G33: Glas 3C **86**
Monar Dr. G22: Glas 6F **63**
Monar Pl. G22: Glas 6F **63**
Monar St. G22: Glas 6F **63**
Monart Pl. G20: Glas 4D **62**
Monar Way *ML2: Newm 3D* ***146***
(off Murdostoun Vw.)
Moncrieff Av. G66: Lenz 2C **50**
Moncrieffe Rd. ML6: Chap 1D **112**
Moncrieff Gdns. G66: Lenz 2D **50**
Moncrieff St. PA3: Pais 6A **78**
Moncur St. G40: Glas 5A **84**
(not continuous)
Moness Dr. G52: Glas 1E **101**
Money Gro. ML1: Moth 5B **144**
Monieburgh Cres. G65: Kils 2A **12**
Monieburgh Rd. G65: Kils 2A **12**
Monifieth Av. G52: Glas 2D **100**
Monikie Gdns. G64: B'rig 6F **49**
Monkcastle Dr. G72: Camb 1A **122**
Monkdyke Ho. PA4: Renf 6F **59**
Monkland Av. G66: Kirk, Lenz 6D **30**
Monkland La. ML5: Coat 1A **110**
Monklands Ind. Est. ML5: Coat 3B **110**
Monkland St. ML6: Air 4B **92**
Monkland Ter. ML5: Glenb 3H **69**
Monkland Vw. G71: Tann 4E **109**
ML6: C'bnk 3B **112**
Monkland Vw. Cres. G69: Barg 1D **108**
Monksbridge Av. G13: Glas 6C **44**
Monkscourt Av. ML6: Air 3G **91**
Monkscroft Av. G11: Glas 6G **61**
Monkscroft Ct. G11: Glas 1G **81**
Monkscroft Gdns. G11: Glas 6G **61**
Monks Rd. ML6: Air 6C **92**
Monkton Dr. G15: Glas 5B **44**
Monkton Gdns. G77: Newt M 5G **133**
Monmouth Av. G12: Glas 3G **61**
Monreith Av. G61: Bear 5D **44**
Monreith Rd. G43: Glas 1B **118**
Monreith Rd. E. G44: Glas 2E **119**
Monroe Dr. G71: Tann 4D **108**
Monroe Pl. G71: Tann 4D **108**
Montague La. G12: Glas 5H **61**
Montague St. G4: Glas 1D **82**
Montalto Av. ML1: Carf 6A **128**
Montclair Pl. PA3: Lin 5H **75**
Montego Grn. G75: E Kil 2C **148**
Monteith Dr. G76: Clar 1D **134**
Monteith Gdns. G76: Clar 1D **134**
Monteith Pl. G40: Glas 6A **84**
G72: Blan 1C **140**
Monteith Row G40: Glas 5H **83**
Montford Av. G44: Glas 6H **103**
G73: Ruth 6A **104**
Montgomery Av. ML5: Coat 4B **90**
PA3: Pais 4D **78**
Montgomery Ct. PA3: Pais 4D **78**
Montgomery Cres. ML2: Wis 2E **157**
Montgomery Dr. G46: Giff 6A **118**
PA10: Kilb 1A **94**
Montgomery Pl. G74: E Kil 1H **149**
ML9: Lark 3F **161**
Montgomery Rd. PA3: Pais 3C **78**
Montgomery St. G72: Camb 2D **122**
G74: E Kil 1H **149**
ML9: Lark 1E **161**
Montgomery Ter. G40: Glas 1C **104**
G66: Milt C 6B **8**
Montgomery Wynd *G74: E Kil 1H* ***149***
(off Montgomery St.)
Montraive St. G73: Ruth 4E **105**
Montrave Path G52: Glas 1D **100**
Montrave St. G52: Glas 1D **100**
Montreal Ho. G81: Clyd 1H **41**
Montreal Pk. G75: E Kil 2E **149**
Montrose Av. G32: Carm 4B **106**
G52: Hill 3G **79**
Montrose Ct. PA2: Pais 5D **96**
Montrose Cres. ML3: Ham 5H **141**
Montrose Dr. G61: Bear 6E **25**
Montrose Gdns. G62: Miln 2H **25**
G65: Kils 2G **11**
G72: Blan 5A **124**
Montrose La. ML3: Ham 5G **141**
Montrose Pl. PA3: Lin 5G **75**
Montrose Rd. PA2: Pais 5D **96**
Montrose St. G1: Glas 4H **83** (5G **5**)
G81: Clyd 5D **42**
ML1: Moth 6F **127**
Montrose Ter. G64: B'rig 2E **65**
PA11: Bri W 4F **73**
Montrose Way PA2: Pais 5D **96**
Monument Dr. G33: Glas 4G **65**
Monymusk Gdns. G64: B'rig 5F **49**
Monymusk Pl. G15: Glas 2G **43**
MOODIESBURN 5D 52
Moodiesburn St. G33: Glas 1F **85**
Moorburn Av. G46: Giff 4H **117**
Moorburn Pl. PA3: Lin 5E **75**
Moorcroft Dr. ML6: Air 4E **93**
Moorcroft Rd. G77: Newt M 6C **132**
Moore Dr. G61: Bear 4F **45**
Moore Gdns. ML3: Ham 4A **154**
Moore St. G31: Glas 5B **84**
ML1: New S 4A **128**
Moorfield Cres. ML6: Air 4F **93**
Moorfield Rd. G72: Blan 3A **140**
Moorfoot G64: B'rig 5E **49**
Moorfoot Av. G46: T'bnk 4G **117**
PA2: Pais 4H **97**
Moorfoot Dr. ML2: Wis 6F **145**
Moorfoot Path PA2: Pais 5H **97**
Moorfoot St. G32: Glas 5G **85**
Moorfoot Way G61: Bear 5B **24**
Moorhill Cres. G77: Newt M 6C **132**
Moorhill Rd. G77: Newt M 5C **132**
Moorhouse Av. G13: Glas 3H **59**
PA2: Pais 3F **97**
Moorhouse St. G78: Barr 5E **115**
Moorings, The PA2: Pais 2F **97**
Moorland Dr. ML6: Air 4F **93**
MOORPARK 1D 78
Moorpark Av. G52: Glas 5H **79**
G69: Muirh 2A **68**
ML6: Air 4E **93**
Moorpark Ct. PA4: Renf 1D **78**
Moorpark Pl. G52: Glas 5H **79**
Moorpark Sq. PA4: Renf 1D **78**
Moor Rd. G62: Miln 3H **25**
Moorside St. ML8: Carl 3G **165**
Morag Av. G72: Blan 6A **124**
Moraine Av. G15: Glas 6A **44**
Moraine Cir. G15: Glas 6A **44**
Moraine Dr. G15: Glas 6A **44**
G76: Clar 1B **134**
Moraine Pl. G15: Glas 6B **44**
Morar Av. G81: Clyd 3D **42**
Morar Ct. G67: Cumb 5D **34**
G81: Clyd 3D **42**
ML3: Ham 2E **153**
ML9: Lark 6H **155**
Morar Cres. G64: B'rig 5B **48**
G81: Clyd 3D **42**
ML5: Coat 2H **89**
ML6: Air 1G **91**
PA7: B'ton 5A **40**
Morar Dr. G61: Bear 4H **45**
G67: Cumb 6D **34**
G73: Ruth 4D **120**
G81: Clyd 3D **42**
PA2: Pais 3D **96**
PA3: Lin 6G **75**
Morar Pl. G74: E Kil 6H **137**
G77: Newt M 2D **132**
G81: Clyd 3D **42**
PA4: Renf 5D **58**
Morar Rd. G52: Glas 6E **81**
G81: Clyd 3D **42**
Morar St. ML2: Wis 2G **157**
Morar Ter. G71: View 6F **109**
G73: Ruth 4F **121**
Morar Way ML1: N'hill 4C **128**
Moravia Av. G71: Both 4E **125**
Moray Av. ML6: Air 6A **92**
Moray Ct. G73: Ruth 5C **104**
Moray Dr. G64: Torr 4D **28**
G76: Clar 2D **134**
Moray Gdns. G68: Cumb 6H **13**
G71: Tann 5D **108**
G76: Clar 1D **134**
Moray Ga. G71: Both 3C **124**
Moray Pl. G41: Glas 3C **102**
G64: B'rig 6E **49**
G66: Kirk 4G **31**
G69: Chry 1B **68**
G72: Blan 3A **140**
PA3: Lin 5G **75**
Moray Quad. ML4: Bell 2C **126**
Moray Way ML1: Holy 2A **128**
Mordaunt St. G40: Glas 2C **104**
Moredun Cres. G32: Glas 4C **86**
Moredun Dr. PA2: Pais 4F **97**
Moredun Rd. PA2: Pais 4F **97**
Moredun St. G32: Glas 4C **86**
Morefield Rd. G51: Glas 4D **80**
Morgan M. G42: Glas 2F **103**
Morgan St. ML3: Ham 1H **153**
ML9: Lark 2D **160**
Morina Gdns. G53: Glas 4C **116**
Morion Rd. G13: Glas 1D **60**
Morison Ho. *G67: Cumb 3A* ***36***
(off Burns Rd.)
Moriston Ct. ML2: Newm 3D **146**
Morland G74: E Kil 4D **138**
Morley St. G42: Glas 6E **103**
Morna La. *G14: Glas 1E* ***81***
(off Glendore St.)
MORNINGSIDE 6G 147
Morningside Rd.
ML2: Newm 4E **147**
Morningside St. G33: Glas 3F **85**
Morrin Path G21: Glas 6A **64**
Morrin St. G21: Glas 5A **64**
Morris Cres. G72: Blan 2B **140**
ML1: Cle 6E **129**
Morrishall Rd. G74: E Kil 5C **138**
Morrison Dr. G66: Len 4G **7**
Morrison Gdns. G64: Torr 5E **29**
Morrison Pl. *PA11: Bri W 3F* ***73***
(off Main St.)
Morrison Quad. G81: Clyd 6G **43**
Morrison St. G5: Glas 5E **83**
G81: Dun 1B **42**
Morris St. ML3: Ham 2H **153**
ML9: Lark 4G **161**
Morriston Cres. PA4: Renf 2H **79**
Morriston Pk. Dr. G72: Camb 1A **122**
Morriston St. G72: Camb 1A **122**
Morton Gdns. G41: Glas 4A **102**
Morton St. ML1: Moth 1G **143**

Morton Ter. *PA11: Bri W* *3E 73*
(off Horsewood Rd.)
Morvan St. G52: Glas 6E 81
Morven Av. G64: B'rig 6E 49
G72: Blan 6A 124
PA2: Pais 5H 97
Morven Dr. G76: Clar 1B 134
PA3: Lin 6G 75
Morven Gait PA8: Ersk 1A 58
Morven Gdns. G71: Tann 5D 108
Morven La. G72: Blan 6A 124
Morven Rd. G61: Bear 1E 45
G72: Camb 4H 121
Morven St. ML5: Coat. 3C 90
Morven Way G66: Kirk 5H 31
G71: Both 4F 125
Mosesfield St. G21: Glas 4B 64
Mosque Av. G5: Glas 6G 83
Mossacre Rd. ML2: Wis 5A 146
Moss Av. PA3: Lin 5H 75
Mossbank G72: Blan 3B 140
G75: E Kil 3B 148
Mossbank Av. G33: Glas 5H 65
Mossbank Cres. ML1: N'hill. 3F 129
Mossbank Dr. G33: Glas 5H 65
Mossbank Rd. ML2: Wis. 5A 146
Mossbell Rd. ML4: Bell 1A 126
Mossblown St. ML9: Lark. 2D 160
Mossburn Rd. ML2: Wis 6B 146
Mossburn St. ML2: Wis 2B 158
Mosscastle Rd. G33: Glas. 1C 86
Mossdale G74: E Kil 6E 137
Mossdale Ct. ML4: Bell 2F 127
Mossdale Gdns. ML3: Ham. 1C 152
Moss Dr. G78: Barr 2C 114
PA8: Ersk 2F 57
Mossedge Ind. Est. PA3: Lin. 5A 76
MOSSEND 2E 127
Mossend La. G33: Glas 3D 86
Mossend St. G33: Glas 3D 86
Mossgiel G75: E Kil 4D 148
Mossgiel Av. G73: Ruth 2C 120
Mossgiel Cres. G76: Busby 4D 134
Mossgiel Dr. G81: Clyd. 4E 43
Mossgiel Gdns. G66: Kirk 4F 31
G71: Tann 5C 108
Mossgiel La. *ML9: Lark* *4G 161*
(off Keir Hardie La.)
Mossgiel Pl. G73: Ruth 2C 120
Mossgiel Rd. G43: Glas 1B 118
(Doonfoot Rd., not continuous)
G43: Glas 6B 102
(Newlands Rd.)
G67: Cumb 2B 36
(not continuous)
Mossgiel Ter. G72: Blan 5A 124
Mossgiel Way ML1: N'hill. 3C 128
Mosshall Gro. ML1: N'hill 3F 129
Mosshall Rd. ML1: N'hse 6D 112
Mosshall St. ML1: N'hill 3F 129
Mosshead Rd. G61: Bear 6F 25
Moss Hgts. Av. G52: Glas 6D 80
Mosshill Rd. ML4: Bell 5D 110
Moss Knowe G67: Cumb. 3C 36
Mossland Dr. ML2: Wis 5A 146
Mossland Rd. G52: Hill 3F 79
PA4: Renf 2H 79
Mosslands Rd. PA3: Pais 3H 77
Mosslingal G75: E Kil 6G 149
Mossmulloch G75: E Kil 6G 149
MOSSNEUK 4B 148
Mossneuk Av. G75: E Kil. 3A 148
Mossneuk Cres. ML2: Wis 5B 146
Mossneuk Dr. G75: E Kil 4B 148
ML2: Wis 5A 146
PA2: Pais 5G 97
Mossneuk Pk. ML2: Wis. 5A 146
Mossneuk Rd. G75: E Kil 3B 148
Mossneuk St. ML5: Coat. 2B 110
MOSSPARK 2E 101
Mosspark Av. G52: Glas 2F 101
G62: Miln 2G 25
Mosspark Blvd. G52: Glas. 1E 101
Mosspark Dr. G52: Glas 1C 100

Mosspark La. G52: Glas 2E 101
Mosspark Oval G52: Glas 2E 101
Mosspark Rd. G62: Miln. 2G 25
ML5: Coat. 3H 89
Mosspark Sq. G52: Glas 2E 101
Mosspark Station (Rail) 2C 100
Moss Path G69: Bail 2F 107
Moss Rd. G51: Glas 3D 80
G66: Kirk 6H 31
G66: Lenz 1B 50
G67: Cumb 2E 37
G69: Muirh 2A 68
ML2: Wis 6C 146
ML6: Air 5A 92
PA11: Bri W 3G 73
PA6: Hous 1H 75
Moss Side Av. ML6: Air 3G 91
ML8: Carl 3D 164
Mossside Rd. G41: Glas 4B 102
Moss St. PA1: Pais 6A 78
Mossvale Cres. G33: Glas. 1C 86
Mossvale La. PA3: Pais 5H 77
Mossvale Path G33: Glas 6C 66
Mossvale Rd. G33: Glas 6B 66
Mossvale Sq. G33: Glas 1B 86
PA3: Pais 5H 77
Mossvale St. PA3: Pais 4H 77
Mossvale Ter. G69: Mood 4E 53
Mossvale Wlk. G33: Glas 1C 86
Mossvale Way G33: Glas 1C 86
Mossview Cres. ML6: Air 5A 92
Mossview La. G52: Glas 6C 80
Mossview Quad. G52: Glas. 6D 80
Mossview Rd. G33: Step. 4E 67
Mosswell Rd. G62: Miln 2H 25
Mossywood Ct. G68: Cumb 6B 34
Mossywood Pl. G68: Cumb 6B 34
Mossywood Rd. G68: Cumb 6B 34
Mote Hill ML3: Ham 5A 142
Motehill Rd. PA3: Pais 5C 78
MOTHERWELL 3G 143
Motherwell Bus. Cen. ML1: Moth. . 2H 143
Motherwell Concert Hall & Theatre
Complex 4H 143
Motherwell F.C. 5H 143
Motherwell Heritage Cen. *3F 143*
(off High Rd.)
Motherwell Rd. ML1: Carf 6C 128
ML1: N'hse 2G 129
ML3: Ham 5C 142
ML4: Bell 2C 126
Motherwell Station (Rail) 2G 143
Motherwell St. ML6: Air 2C 92
Moulin Cir. G52: Glas 1A 100
Moulin Pl. G52: Glas 1A 100
Moulin Rd. G52: Glas 1A 100
Moulin Ter. G52: Glas 1A 100
Mountainblue St. G31: Glas 6D 84
Mt. Annan Dr. G44: Glas. 6F 103
MOUNTBLOW 2G 41
Mountblow Rd. G81: Clyd, Dun. . . . 1H 41
Mt. Cameron Dr. Nth. G74: E Kil . . 3A 150
Mt. Cameron Dr. Sth. G74: E Kil . . 3A 150
MOUNT ELLEN 2C 68
MOUNT FLORIDA 5F 103
Mount Florida Station (Rail) 5E 103
Mountgarrie Path G51: Glas 4D 80
Mountgarrie Rd. G51: Glas. 4D 80
Mt. Harriet Av. G33: Step 3E 67
Mt. Harriet Dr. G33: Step 3D 66
Mountherrick G75: E Kil 6G 149
Mt. Lockhart G71: Udd 3H 107
Mt. Lockhart Gdns. G71: Udd 3H 107
Mt. Lockhart Pl. G71: Udd 3H 107
Mt. Pleasant Cres. G66: Milt C 5B 8
Mt. Pleasant Ho. G60: Old K 1E 41
Mt. Pleasant Pl. *G60: Old K* *1F 41*
(off Station Rd.)
G60: Old K *1F 41*
(off Mt. Pleasant Rd.)
Mt. Pleasant Rd. G60: Old K. 6F 21
Mt. Stewart St. ML8: Carl 3E 165
Mount St. G20: Glas 6D 62
Mt. Stuart St. G41: Glas 5C 102

Mount, The ML1: Moth 3F 143
MOUNT VERNON 3D 106
Mt. Vernon Av. G32: Glas 3E 107
ML5: Coat. 4A 90
Mount Vernon Station (Rail) 3F 107
Mournian Way ML3: Ham. 2H 153
Mowbray G74: E Kil 5C 138
Mowbray Av. G69: G'csh 4D 68
Moyne Rd. G53: Glas 3A 100
Moy Path *ML2: Newm* *3D 146*
(off Murdostoun Vw.)
Muckcroft Rd. G66: Kirk, Lenz 3H 51
G69: Chry, Lenz 3H 51
Mugdock Rd. G62: Miln 3G 25
Mugdock Rd. S. G62: Miln 3G 25
Muirbank Av. G73: Ruth 6B 104
Muirbank Gdns. G73: Ruth 6B 104
Muirbrae Rd. G73: Ruth. 3D 120
Muirbrae Way G73: Ruth 3D 120
Muirburn Av. G44: Glas. 3C 118
Muir Ct. G44: Neth 5C 118
(not continuous)
Muircroft Dr. ML1: Cle 5H 129
Muirdrum Av. G52: Glas 2D 100
Muirdyke Rd. ML5: Coat. 3H 89
ML5: Glenb 5B 70
Muirdykes Av. G52: Glas. 6A 80
Muirdykes Rd. G52: Glas 6A 80
PA3: Pais 4F 77
Muiredge Ct. G71: Udd 1D 124
Muiredge Ter. G69: Bail 1H 107
MUIREND 3D 118
Muirend Av. G44: Glas 3D 118
Muirend Rd. G44: Glas 3C 118
Muirend Station (Rail). 3D 118
Muirfield Ct. G44: Glas. 3D 118
Muirfield Cres. G23: Glas 6C 46
Muirfield Mdws. G71: Both. 5C 124
Muirfield Rd. G68: Cumb 6A 14
MUIRHEAD
Glasgow 1H 107
North Lanarkshire 2A 68
MUIRHEAD-BRAEHEAD INTERCHANGE
. . . . 3A 36
Muirhead Cotts. G66: Kirk 6H 31
Muirhead Ct. G69: Bail 1A 108
Muirhead Dr. ML1: N'hill 3F 129
ML8: Law 5E 159
PA3: Lin 6G 75
Muirhead Gdns. G69: Bail. 1A 108
Muirhead Ga. G71: Tann 5F 109
Muirhead Gro. G69: Bail 1A 108
Muirhead Rd. G69: Bail 2H 107
G78: Neil. 4A 130
MUIRHEAD RDBT. 2B 36
Muirhead St. G66: Kirk. 6C 30
Muirhead Ter. ML1: Moth. 5G 143
Muirhead Way G64: B'rig 6F 49
Muirhill Av. G44: Glas. 3C 118
Muirhill Cres. G13: Glas. 2A 60
MUIRHOUSE 1B 156
Muirhouse Av. ML1: Moth 6B 144
ML2: Newm. 3F 147
Muirhouse Dr. ML1: Moth 1B 156
Muirhouse La. G75: E Kil 3H 149
Muirhouse Pk. G61: Bear 5D 24
Muirhouse Rd. ML1: Moth 1B 156
Muirhouse St. G41: Glas 2E 103
Muirhouse Twr. ML1: Moth. 6B 144
Muirhouse Works G41: Glas 2E 103
Muirkirk Dr. G13: Glas. 2F 61
ML3: Ham 1B 152
Muirlee Rd. ML8: Carl 4H 165
Muirlees Cres. G62: Miln 3E 25
Muirmadkin Rd. ML4: Bell 2D 126
Muirpark Av. PA4: Renf. 1E 79
Muirpark Dr. G52: Glas 5A 80
G64: B'rig 1C 64
Muirpark St. G11: Glas 1H 81
Muirpark Ter. G64: B'rig 1B 64
Muir Rd. G82: Dumb 1H 17
Muirshiel Av. G53: Glas 1C 116
Muirshiel Cres. G53: Glas. 1C 116
Muirshot Rd. ML9: Lark 1F 161

Muirside Av. G32: Glas 2E 107
G66: Kirk 5G 31
Muirside Pl. ML2: Newm 3D 146
Muirside Rd. G69: Bail 1H 107
PA3: Pais 4F 77
Muirside St. G69: Bail 1H 107
Muirskeith Cres. G43: Glas 1D 118
Muirskeith Pl. G43: Glas 1D 118
Muirskeith Rd. G43: Glas 1D 118
Muir St. G64: B'rig 6C 48
G72: Blan 3B 140
ML1: Moth 1F 143
ML3: Ham 5H 141
ML5: Coat 4A 90
ML8: Law 5D 158
ML9: Lark 2E 161
PA4: Renf 5F 59
Muir Ter. PA3: Pais 4C 78
Muirton Dr. G64: B'rig 4B 48
Muiryfauld Dr. G31: Glas 1G 105
Muiryhall St. ML5: Coat 4C 90
Muiryhall St. E. ML5: Coat 4D 90
Mulben Cres. G53: Glas 6H 99
Mulben Pl. G53: Glas 6H 99
Mulben Ter. G53: Glas 5H 99
Mulberry Cres. ML6: Chap 2E 113
Mulberry Dr. G75: E Kil 6E 149
Mulberry Rd. G43: Glas 2B 118
G71: View 4G 109
Mulberry Way G75: E Kil 6E 149
Mulberry Wynd G72: Flem 4F 123
Mull G74: E Kil 3C 150
ML6: Air 6D 92
Mullardoch St. *G23: Glas* *6B 46*
(off Rothes Dr.)
Mull Av. PA2: Pais 6A 98
PA4: Renf 2E 79
Mull Ct. ML3: Ham 2D 152
Mullen Ct. G33: Step 4F 67
Mull Quad. ML2: Wis 4C 146
Mull St. G21: Glas 1D 84
Mulvey Cres. ML6: Air 4G 91
Mungo Pk. G75: E Kil 3F 149
Mungo Pl. G71: Tann 4E 109
Munlochy Rd. G51: Glas 4D 80
Munro Ct. G81: Dun 1B 42
Munro Dr. G66: Milt C 6B 8
Munro La. G13: Glas 4E 61
Munro La. E. G13: Glas 4E 61
Munro Pl. G13: Glas 2E 61
G74: E Kil 6B 138
Munro Rd. G13: Glas 4E 61
Murano St. G20: Glas 4D 62
Murchison G12: Glas 3G 61
Murchison Dr. G75: E Kil 4D 148
Murchison Rd. PA6: C'lee 2C 74
Murdoch Ct. *PA5: John* *4E 95*
(off Tannahill Cres.)
Murdoch Dr. G62: Miln 5B 26
Murdoch Pl. ML1: New S 4H 127
Murdoch Sq. ML4: Bell 6E 111
Murdock Rd. G75: E Kil 3G 149
Murdostoun Gdns. ML2: Wis 4H 145
Murdostoun Rd. ML2: Newm 1G 147
Murdostoun Vw. ML2: Newm 3D 146
Muriel La. G78: Barr 4E 115
Muriel St. G78: Barr 4E 115
Murray Av. G65: Kils 4H 11
Murray Business Area PA3: Pais 5G 77
Murray Bus. Area PA3: Pais 5H 77
Murray Cres. ML2: Newm 2E 147
Murrayfield G64: B'rig 4C 48
Murrayfield Dr. G61: Bear 6E 45
Murrayfield St. G32: Glas 4G 85
Murray Gdns. G66: Milt C 5C 8
Murray Gro. G61: Bear 5B 24
Murrayhill G75: E Kil 3F 149
Murray Path G71: Udd 1C 124
Murray Pl. G78: Barr 3F 115
G82: Dumb 1C 18
ML4: Bell 6A 110
Murray Rd. G71: Both 4E 125
ML8: Law 1H 163
Murray Rd., The G75: E Kil 3E 149
MURRAY RDBT., THE 3H 149
Murray Sq., The G75: E Kil 4G 149
Murray St. PA3: Pais 5G 77
PA4: Renf 6E 59
Murray Ter. ML1: Moth 2D 142
MURRAY, THE 4G 149
Murrin Av. G64: B'rig 6F 49
Murroch Av. G82: Dumb 1H 17
Murroes Rd. G51: Glas 4D 80
Mus. of 602 (City of Glasgow) Squadron 4G 79
Mus. of Piping 2D 4
Mus. of Scottish Country Life 5B 136
Musgrove Pl. G75: E Kil 3E 149
Muslin St. G40: Glas 1B 104
Muttonhole Rd.
ML3: Ham 3H 151
M.V. Gipsy Princess 5H 11
Mybole Dr. ML6: Air 1A 112
Mybster Pl. G51: Glas 4D 80
Myers Cres. G71: Udd 2E 125
Myreside Pl. G32: Glas 5F 85
Myreside St. G32: Glas 5F 85
Myres Rd. G53: Glas 5D 100
Myrie Gdns. G64: B'rig 5D 48
Myroch Pl. G34: Glas 2A 88
Myrtle Av. G66: Lenz 2C 50
Myrtle Dr. ML1: Holy 2B 128
ML2: Wis 5D 144
Myrtle Hill La. G42: Glas 5G 103
Myrtle La. ML9: Lark 4F 161
Myrtle Pk. G42: Glas 4F 103
Myrtle Pl. G42: Glas 4G 103
Myrtle Rd. G71: View 5F 109
G81: Clyd 3H 41
Myrtle Sq. G64: B'rig 1C 64
Myrtle St. G72: Blan 6B 124
Myrtle Vw. Rd. G42: Glas 5G 103
Myrtle Wlk. G72: Camb 1H 121
Myvot Av. G67: Cumb 1D 54
Myvot Rd. G67: Cumb 1D 54
(Condorrat)
G67: Cumb 3A 54
(Mollinsburn)

N

Naburn Ga. G5: Glas 1G 103
Nagle Gdns. ML1: Cle 1F 145
Nairn Av. G72: Blan 5A 124
ML4: Bell 1C 126
Nairn Cres. ML6: Air 6A 92
Nairn Pl. G74: E Kil 6C 138
G81: Clyd 4B 42
Nairn Quad. ML2: Wis 4H 145
Nairnside Rd. G21: Glas 2E 65
Nairn St. G3: Glas 2B 82
G72: Blan 3A 140
G81: Clyd 4B 42
ML9: Lark 3D 160
Nairn Way G68: Cumb 6A 14
Naismith St. G32: Carm 5C 106
Naismith Wlk. ML4: Bell 6E 111
Nansen St. G20: Glas 6E 63
Napier Ct. G60: Old K 2G 41
G68: Cumb 3D 14
Napier Cres. G82: Dumb 4C 16
Napier Dr. G51: Glas 3H 81
Napier Gdns. PA3: Lin 5A 76
Napier Hill G75: E Kil 3G 149
Napier La. G75: E Kil 3G 149
Napier Pk. G68: Cumb 4C 14
Napier Pl. G51: Glas 3H 81
G60: Old K 2G 41
G68: Cumb 3C 14
Napier Rd. G51: Glas 3H 81
G52: Hill 2H 79
G68: Cumb 4C 14
Napiershall La. *G20: Glas* *1D 82*
(off Napiershall St.)
Napiershall Pl. G20: Glas 1D 82
Napiershall St. G20: Glas 1D 82
Napier Sq. ML4: Bell 6D 110
Napier St. G51: Glas 3H 81
G81: Clyd 2E 59
PA3: Lin 5A 76
PA5: John 2E 95
Napier Ter. G51: Glas 3H 81
Napier Way G68: Cumb 4C 14
Naproch Pl. G77: Newt M 4A 134
Naseby Av. G11: Glas 6F 61
Naseby La. G11: Glas 6F 61
Nasmyth Av. G61: Bear 5B 24
G75: E Kil 4H 149
Nasmyth Bank G75: E Kil 4H 149
Nasmyth Rd. G52: Hill 4A 80
Nasmyth Rd. Nth. G52: Hill 4A 80
(not continuous)
Nasmyth Rd. Sth. G52: Hill 4A 80
Nassau Pl. G75: E Kil 2C 148
National Bank La.
G1: Glas 4F 83 (5D 4)
Navar Pl. PA2: Pais 3C 98
Naver St. G33: Glas 2G 85
Naylor La. ML6: Air 3B 92
Needle Grn. ML8: Carl 3F 165
Neidpath G69: Bail 1G 107
Neidpath Av. ML5: Coat 2D 110
Neidpath E. G74: E Kil 1F 149
Neidpath Pl. ML5: Coat 2C 110
Neidpath Rd. ML8: Carl 2E 165
Neidpath Rd. E. G46: Giff 3G 133
Neidpath Rd. W. G46: Giff 2G 133
Neidpath W. G74: E Kil 1F 149
Neilsland Dr. ML1: Moth 3D 142
ML3: Ham 4G 153
Neilsland Oval G53: Glas 5D 100
Neilsland Rd. ML3: Ham 2F 153
Neilsland Sq. G53: Glas 4D 100
ML3: Ham 2G 153
Neilsland St. ML3: Ham 2G 153
Neilson Ct. ML3: Ham 1A 154
Neilson St. ML4: Bell 2C 126
NEILSTON 2E 131
Neilston Av. G53: Glas 2C 116
(not continuous)
Neilston Leisure Cen. 2E 131
Neilston Pl. G65: Kils 2F 11
Neilston Rd. G78: Neil 1E 131
PA2: Pais 2A 98
Neilston Station (Rail) 2D 130
Neilston Wlk G65: Kils 2F 11
(not continuous)
Neil St. PA4: Renf 4F 59
Neilvaig Dr. G73: Ruth 4D 120
Neistpoint Dr. G33: Glas 3A 86
Nelson Av. ML5: Coat 1A 110
Nelson Cres. ML1: Moth 5B 144
Nelson Mandela Pl.
G2: Glas 3G 83 (4E 5)
Nelson Pl. G69: Bail 1H 107
Nelson St. G5: Glas 5E 83
G69: Bail 1H 107
Nelson Ter. G74: E Kil 3A 150
Neptune St. G51: Glas 4H 81
Neptune Way ML4: Moss 2G 127
NERSTON 3A 138
Nerston Rd. G74: Ners, Roger 3G 137
Ness Av. PA5: John 5C 94
Ness Dr. G72: Blan 6C 124
G74: E Kil 2B 150
Ness Gdns. G64: B'rig 6D 48
ML9: Lark 5E 161
Ness Rd. PA4: Renf 5D 58
Ness St. G33: Glas 2G 85
ML2: Wis 3H 157
Ness Ter. ML3: Ham 2E 153
Ness Way ML1: Holy 2A 128
Nethan Av. ML2: Wis 1C 156
Nethan Ga. ML3: Ham 6G 141
Nethan Path ML9: Lark 5E 161
Nethan Pl. ML3: Ham 5H 153
Nethan St. G51: Glas 3G 81
ML1: Moth 5E 127
Nether Auldhouse Rd.
G43: Glas 1H 117

Netherbank Rd. ML2: Wis 1D **156**
Netherbog Av. G82: Dumb 3H **17**
Netherbog Rd. G82: Dumb 3H **17**
Netherburn Av. G44: Neth 5D **118**
PA6: C'lee 3E **75**
Netherburn Gdns. PA6: C'lee 3E **75**
Netherburn Rd. ML9: Ashg 5C **162**
Netherby Dr. G41: Glas 1B **102**
Nethercairn Pl. G77: Newt M 4A **134**
Nethercairn Rd. G43: Glas 3A **118**
Nethercliffe Av. G44: Neth 5D **118**
Nethercommon Ind. Est.
PA3: Pais 3A **78**
(not continuous)
Nethercraigs Ct. PA2: Pais 6F **97**
Nethercraigs Dr. PA2: Pais 5G **97**
Nethercraigs Rd. PA2: Pais 6F **97**
Nethercroy Rd. G65: Croy 6A **12**
Netherdale G77: Newt M 4H **133**
Netherdale Cres. ML2: Wis 1C **156**
Netherdale Dr. PA1: Pais 1H **99**
Netherdale Rd. ML2: Wis 1E **157**
Nethergreen Cres. PA4: Renf 6D **58**
Nethergreen Wynd PA4: Renf 6D **58**
Netherhall Rd. ML2: Wis 1D **156**
Netherhill Av. G44: Neth 6D **118**
Netherhill Cotts. *PA3: Pais 4C **78***
(off Netherhill Rd.)
Netherhill Cres. PA3: Pais 5C **78**
Netherhill Rd. G69: Mood 6D **52**
PA3: Pais 5B **78**
Netherhill Way PA3: Pais 4D **78**
Netherhouse Av. G66: Lenz 3E **51**
ML5: Coat 2B **110**
Netherhouse Pl. G34: Glas 3C **88**
Netherhouse Rd. G34: Glas 4B **88**
G69: Barg 4B **88**
NETHER KIRKTON **1F 131**
NETHERLEE **5D 118**
Netherlee Pl. G44: Glas 3E **119**
Netherlee Rd. G44: Glas 2E **119**
Nethermains Rd. G62: Miln 5G **25**
Netherpark Av. G44: Neth 6D **118**
Netherplace **5A 132**
Netherplace Cres. G77: Newt M . . . 5C **132**
Netherplace Rd. G53: Glas 5B **100**
G77: Newt M 5A **132**
Netherpool Cres. G53: Glas 5B **100**
NETHERTON
Glasgow **1E 61**
Wishaw **2E 157**
Netherton Av. G13: Glas 2E **61**
Netherton Ct. G45: Glas 5B **120**
G77: Newt M 3F **133**
Netherton Dr. G78: Barr 5F **115**
Netherton Hill G66: Len 3C **6**
Netherton Ind. Est. ML2: Wis 1E **157**
Netherton Oval G66: Len 3D **6**
Netherton Rd. G13: Glas 1E **61**
G75: E Kil 6C **148**
(Mallard Cres.)
G75: E Kil 5E **149**
(Owen Av.)
G77: Newt M 3F **133**
ML2: Wis 1C **156**
Netherton St. ML2: Wis 1F **157**
Nethervale Av. G44: Neth 6D **118**
Netherview Rd. G44: Neth 6E **119**
Netherway G44: Neth 6D **118**
Netherwood Av. G68: Cumb 5C **34**
Netherwood Ct. G68: Cumb 5C **34**
*ML1: Moth 1B **156***
(off Muirhouse Rd.)
Netherwood Gro. G68: Cumb 5C **34**
Netherwood Pl. G68: Cumb 5B **34**
Netherwood Rd. G68: Cumb 5B **34**
ML1: Moth 6B **144**
Netherwood Twr. ML1: Moth 1B **156**
Netherwood Way G68: Cumb 5C **34**
Nethy Way PA4: Renf 2H **79**
Neuk Av. G69: Muirh 2A **68**
PA6: Hous 2C **74**
Neuk Cres. PA6: Hous 1C **74**
Neuk, The ML2: Wis 6E **145**
Neuk Way G32: Carm 5C **106**
PA6: Hous 2C **74**
Neva Pl. *PA11: Bri W 3F **73***
(off Main St.)
Neville G74: E Kil 4C **138**
Nevis Av. ML3: Ham 1E **153**
Nevis Ct. G78: Barr 6E **115**
ML1: Moth 5G **143**
ML5: Coat 2E **111**
Nevis Dr. G64: Torr 4D **28**
Nevison St. ML9: Lark 3F **161**
Nevis Rd. G43: Glas 2H **117**
G61: Bear 6B **24**
PA4: Renf 2D **78**
Nevis Way PA3: Glas A 2A **78**
Newark Dr. G41: Glas 2B **102**
ML2: Wis 3A **146**
PA2: Pais 5G **97**
Newark Pl. ML2: Wis 3B **146**
NEWARTHILL **3F 129**
Newarthill Rd. ML1: Carf 5C **128**
New Ashtree St. ML2: Wis 6E **145**
Newbank Ct. G31: Glas 1G **105**
Newbank Gdns. G31: Glas 1F **105**
Newbank Rd. G31: Glas 1G **105**
Newbarns St. ML8: Carl 2F **165**
Newbattle Av. ML6: C'bnk 3B **112**
Newbattle Ct. G32: Glas 3B **106**
Newbattle Gdns. G32: Glas 3B **106**
Newbattle Pl. G32: Glas 3B **106**
Newbattle Rd. G32: Glas 3A **106**
Newbold Av. G21: Glas 2A **64**
NEWBRIDGE END **5F 165**
New Broomfield Stadium **5C 92**
Newburgh PA8: Ersk 4E **41**
Newburgh St. G43: Glas 6B **102**
Newcastleton Dr. G23: Glas 6C **46**
New City Rd. G4: Glas 1E **83** (1B **4**)
(not continuous)
Newcraigs Dr. G76: Crmck 2H **135**
Newcroft Dr. G44: Glas 2H **119**
New Cross *ML6: Air 4A **92***
(off Stirling St.)
New Cross Cen. ML3: Ham 6A **142**
Newdyke Av. G66: Kirk 5E **31**
Newdyke Rd. G66: Kirk 5E **31**
New Edinburgh Rd.
G71: Tann, View 6C **108**
ML4: Bell 2A **126**
Newfield Cres. ML3: Ham 5F **141**
Newfield La. G71: Both 4F **125**
Newfield Pl. G46: T'bnk 5F **117**
G73: Ruth 6A **104**
Newfield Sq. G53: Glas 1A **116**
Newford Gro. G76: Busby 4D **134**
Newgrove Gdns. G72: Camb 1A **122**
Newhall St. G40: Glas 2B **104**
Newhaven Rd. G33: Glas 3B **86**
Newhaven St. G32: Glas 4A **86**
Newhills Rd. G33: Glas 4E **87**
NEWHOUSE **5H 113**
Newhouse Ind. Est. ML1: N'hse . . . 6C **112**
(Greenside Rd.)
ML1: N'hse 5D **112**
(York Rd.)
NEWHOUSE INTERCHANGE **5G 113**
Newhousemill Rd.
G72: Blan 4F **151**
Newhousemill Rd. G74: E Kil 4C **150**
ML3: Ham 3H **151**
Newhut Rd. ML1: Moth 1F **143**
New Inchinnan Rd. PA3: Pais 4A **78**
Newington St. G32: Glas 5H **85**
New Kirk Rd. G61: Bear 2E **45**
New Lairdsland Rd. G66: Kirk 4C **30**
NEWLANDS **2C 118**
Newlands Dr. ML3: Ham 3H **153**
Newlandsfield Rd.
G43: Glas 6B **102**
Newlands Gdns. PA5: Eld 4A **96**
NEWLANDSMUIR **6B 148**
Newlandsmuir Rd.
G75: E Kil 5B **148**
Newlands Pl. G74: E Kil 2G **149**
Newlands Rd. G43: Glas 6B **102**
G71: Tann 5D **108**
G75: E Kil 6A **148**
(Newlandsmuir)
G75: E Kil 4C **148**
(Westwood)
Newlands Squash & Tennis Club
G43: Glas **1D 118**
Newlands St. ML5: Coat 1C **110**
Newlands Ter. G66: Milt C 5C **8**
ML8: Carl 3F **165**
New La. ML6: C'bnk 3B **112**
New Line Pend *G74: E Kil 1H **149***
(off Kittoch Pl.)
New Luce Dr. G32: Glas 2D **106**
NEWMAINS
Renfrew **2E 79**
Wishaw **5E 147**
Newmains Av. PA4: Inch 4F **57**
Newmains Rd. PA4: Renf 1D **78**
Newmill Rd. G21: Glas 4E **65**
NEW MONKLAND **5G 71**
Newnham Rd. PA1: Pais 1G **99**
Newpark Cres. G72: Camb 6A **106**
New Pk. St. ML3: Ham 4G **141**
New Plymouth G75: E Kil 4C **148**
New Rd. G72: Camb 3E **123**
Newrose Av. ML4: Bell 6D **110**
Newshot Ct. *G81: Clyd 2F **59***
(off Clydeholm Ter.)
Newshot Dr. PA8: Ersk 5F **41**
New Sneddon St. PA3: Pais 5A **78**
(not continuous)
Newstead Gdns. G23: Glas 6C **46**
NEW STEVENSTON **3A 128**
New Stevenston Rd. ML1: Carf 5B **128**
(not continuous)
New St. G72: Blan 2A **140**
G81: Dun 1C **42**
PA1: Pais 1A **98**
PA10: Kilb 2A **94**
NEWTON **1G 123**
Newton Av. G72: Camb 1D **122**
G78: Barr 6F **115**
PA3: Pais 4D **78**
PA5: Eld 2C **96**
Newton Brae G72: Newt 1F **123**
Newton Ct. G77: Newt M 6D **132**
Newton Dr. G71: Tann 6E **109**
ML2: Newm 4E **147**
PA5: Eld 2C **96**
Newton Farm Rd. G72: Newt 6F **107**
Newtongrange Av. G32: Glas 2B **106**
Newtongrange Gdns.
G32: Glas 3B **106**
Newton Gro. G77: Newt M 6D **132**
Newtonlea Av. G77: Newt M 5E **133**
NEWTON MEARNS **5D 132**
Newton Pl. G3: Glas 2D **82**
G77: Newt M 6E **133**
Newton Rd. G66: Lenz 3E **51**
PA7: B'ton 4F **39**
Newton Station (Rail) **2E 123**
Newton Sta. Rd.
G72: Flem, Newt 3E **123**
Newton St. G3: Glas 3E **83** (3A **4**)
ML5: Coat 1A **110**
PA1: Pais 1G **97**
Newton Ter. *G3: Glas 3D **82***
(off Sauchiehall St.)
PA1: Pais 2D **96**
Newton Ter. La. *G3: Glas 3D **82***
(off Elderslie St.)
Newton Way PA3: Pais 4D **78**
Newtown St. G65: Kils 3H **11**
Newtyle Dr. G53: Glas 4H **99**
Newtyle Pl. G53: Glas 4H **99**
G64: B'rig 6F **49**
Newtyle Rd. PA1: Pais 1D **98**
New Vw. Cres. ML4: Bell 4C **126**
New Vw. Dr. ML4: Bell 4C **126**
New Vw. Pl. ML4: Bell 4C **126**
New Wynd G1: Glas 5G **83** (6F **5**)
Next Generation Health Club **1F 61**

Niamh Ct. PA4: Inch 2G **57**
Nicholas St. G1: Glas 4H **83** (5H **5**)
Nicholson St. G5: Glas 6F **83**
Nicklaus Way ML1: N'hse 6E **113**
Nicolson Ct. G33: Step 4D **66**
Nicol St. ML6: Air 2C **92**
Niddrie Rd. G42: Glas 3D **102**
Niddrie Sq. G42: Glas 3D **102**
Niddry St. PA3: Pais 6B **78**
Nigel Gdns. G41: Glas 4B **102**
Nigel St. ML1: Moth 3F **143**
Nigg Pl. G34: Glas 3G **87**
Nightingale Pl. PA5: John 6D **94**
Nikitas Av. ML9: Lark 6F **161**
Nimmo Dr. G51: Glas 4E **81**
Nimmo Pl. ML2: Wis 6A **146**
ML8: Carl 2E **165**
Ninian Av. PA6: C'lee 3C **74**
Ninian Rd. ML6: Air 6B **92**
Ninian's Ri. G66: Kirk 6F **31**
Nisbet St. G31: Glas 6F **85**
Nisbett Pl. ML6: Chap 2E **113**
Nisbett St. ML6: Chap 3E **113**
Nissen Pl. G53: Glas 4H **99**
Nith Dr. ML3: Ham 3E **153**
PA4: Renf 1G **79**
Nith La. *ML2: Newm 3D 146*
(off King St.)
Nith Path ML1: Cle 5H **129**
Nith Pl. PA5: John 5C **94**
Nith Quad. ML1: N'hill 4C **128**
Nithsdale G74: E Kil 6D **138**
Nithsdale Cres. G61: Bear 1C **44**
Nithsdale Dr. G41: Glas 3D **102**
Nithsdale Pl. G41: Glas 2D **102**
Nithsdale Rd. G41: Glas 1H **101**
(Dumbreck Rd.)
G41: Glas 3D **102**
(Pollokshaws Rd.)
Nithsdale St. G41: Glas 3D **102**
Nith St. G33: Glas 2F **85**
Nith Way PA4: Renf 1G **79**
NITSHILL **2A 116**
Nitshill Rd. G53: Glas, T'bnk 1H **115**
Nitshill Station (Rail) **2A 116**
Niven St. G20: Glas 3A **62**
Noble Rd. ML4: Bell 2C **126**
Nobles Pl. ML4: Bell 3B **126**
Nobles Vw. ML4: Bell 3B **126**
Noldrum Av. G32: Carm 5C **106**
Noldrum Gdns. G32: Carm 5C **106**
Norbreck Dr. G46: Giff 3A **118**
Norby Rd. G11: Glas 6F **61**
Noremac Way ML4: Bell 6B **110**
Norfield Dr. G44: Glas 6F **103**
Norfolk Ct. G5: Glas 6F **83**
Norfolk Cres. G64: B'rig 4A **48**
Norfolk St. G5: Glas 6F **83**
Norham St. G41: Glas 4C **102**
Norman St. G40: Glas 2B **104**
Norse La. Nth. G14: Glas 5C **60**
Norse La. Sth. G14: Glas 5C **60**
Norse Pl. G14: Glas 5C **60**
Norse Rd. G14: Glas 5C **60**
Northall Quad. ML1: Carf 6A **128**
Northampton Dr. G12: Glas 3H **61**
Northampton La. *G12: Glas 3H 61*
(off Northampton Dr.)
North & South Rd. ML1: Cle 1C **146**
North Av. G72: Camb 1H **121**
G81: Clyd 4C **42**
ML1: New S 5A **128**
ML8: Carl 3D **164**
North Bank *PA6: Hous 1B 74*
(off North St.)
Northbank Av. G66: Kirk 5C **30**
G72: Camb 1D **122**
Nth. Bank Pl. G81: Clyd 1E **59**
Northbank Rd. G66: Kirk 5C **30**
Northbank St. G72: Camb 1D **122**
Nth. Bank St. G81: Clyd 1E **59**
NORTH BARR **4E 41**
Nth. Barr Av. PA8: Ersk 4E **41**
NORTH BARRWOOD **3A 12**
Nth. Berwick Av. G68: Cumb 6H **13**
Nth. Berwick Cres. G75: E Kil 5C **148**
Nth. Berwick Gdns. G68: Cumb 6H **13**
Nth. Biggar Rd. ML6: Air 3B **92**
Nth. Birbiston Rd. G66: Len 3F **7**
Northbrae Pl. G13: Glas 3B **60**
North Bri. St. ML6: Air 3H **91**
Nth. British Rd. G71: Udd 1D **124**
Northburn Av. ML6: Air 2B **92**
Northburn Pl. ML6: Air 1B **92**
Northburn Rd. ML5: Coat 2E **91**
Northburn St. ML6: Plain 1H **93**
Nth. Bute St. ML5: Coat 1D **110**
Nth. Caldeen Rd. ML5: Coat 6E **91**
Nth. Calder Dr. ML6: Air 5D **92**
Nth. Calder Gro. G71: Udd 3H **107**
Nth. Calder Pl. G71: Udd 3H **107**
Nth. Calder Rd. G71: View 4G **109**
Nth. Campbell Av. G62: Miln 4F **25**
Nth. Canal Bank G4: Glas 1G **83**
Nth. Canal Bank St.
G4: Glas 1G **83** (1E **5**)
Nth. Carbrain Rd. G67: Cumb 5G **35**
NORTH CARDONALD **4B 80**
Nth. Claremont La. G62: Miln 3G **25**
Nth. Claremont St. G3: Glas 2C **82**
Nth. Corsebar Rd. PA2: Pais 3G **97**
North Ct. G1: Glas 4G **83** (5E **5**)
North Ct. La. G1: Glas 4G **83** (5E **5**)
Northcroft Rd. G69: Mood 5C **52**
Nth. Croft St. PA3: Pais 6B **78**
Nth. Dean Pk. Av. G71: Both 4E **125**
Nth. Douglas St. G81: Clyd 1E **59**
North Dr. G1: Glas 4F **83** (6D **4**)
PA3: Lin 5H **75**
Nth. Dryburgh Rd. ML2: Wis 4G **145**
Nth. Dumgoyne Av. G62: Miln 2F **25**
Nth. Elgin Pl. G81: Clyd 2E **59**
Nth. Elgin St. G81: Clyd 2E **59**
Nth. Erskine Pk. G61: Bear 2D **44**
NORTHFIELD **2F 11**
Northfield G75: E Kil 4B **148**
Northfield Rd. G65: Kils 2F **11**
Northfield St. ML1: Moth 1G **143**
Nth. Frederick St. G1: Glas 4G **83** (5F **5**)
Nth. Gardinar St. G11: Glas 1H **81**
Northgate Quad. G21: Glas 2E **65**
Northgate Rd. G21: Glas 2E **65**
Nth. Gower St. G51: Glas 6A **82**
Nth. Grange Rd. G61: Bear 1E **45**
Nth. Hanover St. G1: Glas 3G **83** (5F **5**)
Northinch Ct. G14: Glas 1D **80**
Northinch St. G14: Glas 1D **80**
Nth. Iverton Pk. Rd. PA5: John 2G **95**
NORTH KELVIN **6C 62**
Nth. Kilmeny Cres. ML2: Wis 3A **146**
Northland Av. G14: Glas 4C **60**
Northland Dr. G14: Glas 4C **60**
Northland Gdns. G14: Glas 4C **60**
Northland La. G14: Glas 5C **60**
North La. PA3: Lin 5A **76**
NORTH LODGE **5F 143**
Nth. Lodge Av. ML1: Moth 5G **143**
Nth. Lodge Rd. PA4: Renf 5E **59**
Nth. Moraine La. G15: Glas 5C **44**
NORTH MOTHERWELL **2D 142**
Northmuir Dr. ML2: Wis 5B **146**
Northmuir Rd. G15: Glas 3B **44**
Nth. Orchard St. ML1: Moth 2F **143**
Nth. Park Av. G46: T'bnk 3F **117**
G78: Barr 4D **114**
Northpark St. G20: Glas 5D **62**
North Pk. Vs. G46: T'bnk 4F **117**
Nth. Portland St. G1: Glas 4H **83** (5G **5**)
North Rd. G68: Cumb 5C **34**
ML4: Bell 2C **126**
PA5: John 3E **95**
North Sq. ML5: Coat 3A **90**
North St. G3: Glas 2D **82** (2A **4**)
ML1: Moth 1H **143**
ML9: Lark 1E **161**
PA3: Pais 5A **78**
PA6: Hous 1A **74**
Northumberland St. G20: Glas 5C **62**
North Vw. G61: Bear 5D **44**
North Vw. Rd. PA11: Bri W 5H **73**
Nth. Wallace St. G4: Glas 2H **83** (2G **5**)
Northway G72: Blan 6A **124**
Northwood Dr. ML2: Newm 3E **147**
Nth. Woodside Leisure Cen. **1E 83**
Nth. Woodside Rd. G20: Glas 6D **62**
(not continuous)
Norval St. G11: Glas 1G **81**
Norwich Dr. G12: Glas 4H **61**
Norwood Av. G66: Kirk 5B **30**
Norwood Dr. G46: Giff 6G **117**
Norwood Pk. G61: Bear 4F **45**
Norwood Ter. G71: Tann 6E **109**
Nottingham Av. G12: Glas 3H **61**
Nottingham La. *G12: Glas 3H 61*
(off Northampton Dr.)
Novar Dr. G12: Glas 5G **61**
Novar Gdns. G64: B'rig 5A **48**
Novar St. ML3: Ham 1H **153**
Nuneaton St. G40: Glas 2C **104**
Nuneaton St. Ind. Est.
G40: Glas 2C **104**
Nurseries Rd. G69: Bail 5F **87**
Nursery Av. PA7: B'ton 3C **40**
Nursery Ct. ML8: Carl 2E **165**
Nursery Dr. ML9: Ashg 5C **162**
Nursery La. G41: Glas 3D **102**
Nursery Pk. ML8: Carl 3E **165**
Nursery Pl. G72: Blan 3B **140**
Nursery St. G41: Glas 2E **103**
Nutberry Ct. G42: Glas 4F **103**

O

Oak Av. G61: Bear 6F **25**
G75: E Kil 5D **148**
Oakbank Av. ML2: Wis 2E **157**
Oakbank Dr. G78: Barr 6F **115**
Oakbank Ind. Est. G20: Glas 6F **63**
Oakbank St. ML6: Air 4D **92**
Oakburn Av. G62: Miln 4F **25**
Oakburn Cres. G62: Miln 3F **25**
Oak Cres. G69: Bail 1G **107**
Oakdene Av. G71: Tann 6F **109**
ML4: Bell 6C **110**
Oakdene Cres. ML1: N'hill 4C **128**
Oak Dr. G66: Lenz 2B **50**
G72: Camb 3C **122**
Oak Fern Dr. G74: E Kil 5F **137**
Oak Fern Gro. G74: E Kil 5F **137**
Oakfield Av. G12: Glas 1C **82**
Oakfield Dr. ML1: Moth 3G **143**
Oakfield La. *G12: Glas 1C 82*
(off Gibson St.)
Oakfield Rd. ML1: Moth 3G **143**
Oakfield Twr. ML1: Moth 4G **143**
Oak Gro. ML6: Chap 2E **113**
Oakhill Av. G69: Bail 2F **107**
Oak Lea ML3: Ham 1B **154**
Oaklea Cres. G72: Blan 1A **140**
Oakley Dr. G44: Neth 4D **118**
Oakley Ter. G31: Glas 4B **84**
Oak Pk. G64: B'rig 6D **48**
ML1: Moth 5F **143**
Oak Pl. G71: View 6G **109**
G75: E Kil 5D **148**
ML5: Coat 6E **91**
Oakridge Cres. PA3: Pais 6F **77**
Oak Rd. G67: Cumb 1E **37**
G81: Clyd 2B **42**
PA2: Pais 4C **98**
Oakshaw Brae PA1: Pais 6H **77**
Oakshawhead PA1: Pais 6H **77**
Oakshaw St. E. PA1: Pais 6H **77**
Oakshaw St. W. PA1: Pais 6H **77**
Oakside Pl. ML3: Ham 4H **153**
Oaks, The G44: Glas 3F **119**
PA5: John 3E **95**
Oak St. G2: Glas 4E **83** (5A **4**)
Oaktree Gdns. G45: Glas 3B **120**
G82: Dumb 3C **18**
Oakwood Av. PA2: Pais 4F **97**

Oakwood Cres. G34: Glas 2B **88**
Oakwood Dr. G34: Glas 2B **88**
  G77: Newt M 5F **133**
  ML5: Coat. 6H **89**
Oakwood Vw. ML1: Holy 2B **128**
Oak Wynd G72: Flem. 4F **123**
Oates Gdns. ML1: Moth 5B **144**
Oatfield St. G21: Glas. 5D **64**
OATLANDS 3H **103**
Oban Ct. G20: Glas 5C **62**
Oban Dr. G20: Glas 5C **62**
Oban La. G20: Glas 5C **62**
Oban Pass G20: Glas 5C **62**
Observatory La. G12: Glas 6B **62**
Observatory Rd. G12: Glas. 6A **62**
Ochel Path ML6: Chap. 4F **113**
Ochil Dr. G72: Barr 6D **114**
  PA2: Pais 5H **97**
Ochil Pl. G32: Glas 1A **106**
Ochil Rd. G61: Bear 6B **24**
  G64: B'rig 6E **49**
  PA4: Renf 2D **78**
Ochil St. G32: Glas 1A **106**
  ML2: Wis. 5F **145**
Ochiltree Av. G13: Glas. 2F **61**
Ochiltree Dr. ML3: Ham 2C **152**
Ochil Vw. G71: Tann 5E **109**
Odense Ct. G75: E Kil 5G **149**
Odeon Cinema. 5D **82**
Ogilvie Athletic Ground 5A **66**
Ogilvie Ct. *ML6: Air 3E **93**
  (off Katherine St.)
Ogilvie Pl. G31: Glas 1F **105**
Ogilvie St. G31: Glas. 1F **105**
Old Aisle Rd. G66: Kirk 6F **31**
Old Albert St. ML5: Coat. 4C **90**
Old Avon Rd. ML3: Ham 1C **154**
OLD BALORNOCK 4D **64**
Old Bore Rd. ML6: Air 3E **93**
Old Bothwell Rd. G71: Both 6F **125**
Old Bridgend ML8: Carl. 4F **165**
Old Bridge of Weir Rd.
  PA6: Hous. 1A **74**
Old Castle Rd. G44: Glas 1E **119**
Old Chu. Gdns. G69: Barg. 6E **89**
Old Coach Rd. G74: E Kil 6H **137**
Old Cross ML6: Air 3A **92**
Old Dalmarnock Rd.
  G40: Glas 1B **104**
Old Dalnottar Rd. G60: Old K 2F **41**
Old Dullatur Rd. G68: Dull 5F **13**
Old Dumbarton Rd. G3: Glas. 2A **82**
Old Edinburgh Rd. G71: Tann 4B **108**
  ML4: Bell 1A **126**
Old Farm Rd. PA2: Pais 4F **99**
Old Ferry Rd. PA8: Ersk 3D **40**
Old Gartloch Rd. G69: G'csh. 5D **68**
Old Glasgow Rd. G67: Cumb 1H **35**
  G71: Udd 6B **108**
  (not continuous)
Old Govan Rd. PA4: Renf 6H **59**
Old Greenock Rd. PA4: Inch 6C **40**
  (East Craigend)
  PA4: Inch 2G **57**
  (Inchinnan)
  PA7: B'ton. 2A **38**
  PA8: Ersk 6C **40**
Oldhall Rd. PA1: Pais 6E **79**
OLDHILL 6G **79**
Old Howwood Rd. PA9: How. 6C **94**
Old Humbie Rd. G77: Newt M 6E **133**
OLD INNS INTERCHANGE. 5B **14**
OLD INNS RDBT. 5B **14**
OLD KILPATRICK 1E **41**
Old Lanark Rd. ML8: Carl 4F **165**
  (not continuous)
Old Manse Rd. G32: Glas 1D **106**
  ML2: Wis 3E **157**
Old Mill Ga. *G73: Ruth 1C **120**
  (off Mill St.)
Old Mill Pk. Ind. Est. G66: Kirk. 4C **30**
Old Mill Rd. G71: Both 6E **125**
  G71: Udd 2D **124**
  (Bellshill Rd.)

Old Mill Rd. G71: Udd 1D **124**
  (Lwr. Millgate)
  G72: Camb 2D **122**
  G74: E Kil 1H **149**
  G81: Dun, Hard. 1C **42**
  PA2: Pais. 2F **97**
Old Mill Vw. G65: Croy. 1B **34**
OLD MONKLAND 1A **110**
Old Monkland Rd. ML5: Coat 2H **109**
Old Playfield Rd. G76: Crmck. 1H **135**
Old Quarry Rd. G68: Cumb. 2H **53**
Old Rd. PA5: Eld. 2H **95**
Old Rutherglen Rd. G5: Glas. 6G **83**
Old School Ct. ML5: Coat. 1C **110**
Old Schoolhouse La.
  PA6: Hous. 1B **74**
Old Shettleston Rd. G32: Glas 6H **85**
Old Sneddon St. PA3: Pais 6A **78**
Old Stable Row ML5: Coat. 4D **90**
Old St. G81: Dun 1B **42**
Old Union St. ML6: Air 4B **92**
Old Vic Ct. *G74: E Kil 5B **138**
  (off Bosworth Rd.)
Old Wishaw Rd. ML8: Carl 2E **165**
  ML8: Law 6G **159**
Old Wood Rd. G69: Bail 2G **107**
Old Wynd G1: Glas 5G **83** (6F **5**)
Olifard Av. G71: Both 4F **125**
Oliphant Ct. PA2: Pais 5D **96**
Oliphant Cres. G76: Busby 4C **134**
  PA2: Pais 5C **96**
Oliphant Oval PA2: Pais 5C **96**
Olive Bank G71: View. 4G **109**
Olive Ct. *ML1: Holy 2B **128**
  (off Elm Rd.)
Olive St. G33: Glas 5F **65**
Ollach PA8: Ersk. 2G **57**
Olympia G74: E Kil 2H **149**
Olympia Arc. *G74: E Kil 3H **149**
  (off Olympia Ct.)
Olympia Ct. G74: E Kil 2H **149**
Olympia St. G40: Glas 6B **84**
Olympia, The *G74: E Kil 3H **149**
  (off Olympia Ct.)
Olympia Way G74: E Kil 2H **149**
Omoa Rd. ML1: Cle 6G **129**
O'Neill Av. G64: B'rig 1D **64**
Onslow G75: E Kil 4E **149**
Onslow Dr. G31: Glas 4C **84**
Onslow Rd. G81: Clyd 5E **43**
Onslow Sq. G31: Glas 4C **84**
Ontario Pk. G75: E Kil 2D **148**
Ontario Pl. G75: E Kil 2D **148**
Onyx St. ML4: Bell 3C **126**
Oran Gdns. G20: Glas 4C **62**
Oran La. G20: Glas. 4C **62**
Oran Pl. G20: Glas 4C **62**
Oran St. G20: Glas 4C **62**
ORBISTON. 3C **126**
Orbiston Ct. ML1: Moth 4A **144**
Orbiston Dr. G81: Faif 6F **23**
  ML4: Bell 4D **126**
Orbiston Gdns. G32: Glas 6A **86**
Orbiston Pl. G81: Faif 6F **23**
Orbiston Pl. ML4: Bell 5D **126**
  (Community Rd.)
  ML4: Bell 3B **126**
  (Crofthead Cres.)
Orbiston Sq. ML4: Bell 4B **126**
Orbiston St. ML1: Moth 3H **143**
Orcades Dr. G44: Glas. 3F **119**
Orchard Av. G71: Both. 6F **125**
Orchard Brae G66: Lenz 3E **51**
Orchard Ct. G32: Carm 5B **106**
  G46: T'bnk 4G **117**
Orchard Dr. G46: Giff 4H **117**
  (not continuous)
  G72: Blan 1A **140**
  G73: Ruth 5B **104**
Orchard Fld. G66: Lenz. 3E **51**
Orchard Ga. ML9: Lark 3E **161**
Orchard Grn. G74: E Kil 5B **138**
Orchard Gro. G46: Giff 3H **117**
  ML5: Coat. 5D **90**

ORCHARD PARK
  Lenzie 4E **51**
  Thornliebank 4H **117**
Orchard Pk. G46: Giff 4A **118**
Orchard Pk. Av. G46: T'bnk. 3G **117**
Orchard Pl. G66: Kirk 6G **31**
  ML3: Ham. 6H **141**
  ML4: Bell 4B **126**
Orchard St. G69: Bail 2F **107**
  ML1: Moth 2F **143**
  ML2: Over. 5H **157**
  ML3: Ham 6H **141**
  ML8: Carl 4F **165**
  PA1: Pais 1A **98**
  PA4: Renf 5F **59**
Orchardton Rd. G68: Cumb 1G **53**
  (Mollins Rd.)
  G68: Cumb 2H **53**
  (Old Quarry Rd.)
Orchardton Woods Ind. Pk.
  G68: Cumb 5G **33**
Orchid Pl. G66: Len 3E **7**
Orchy Av. G76: Clar 6D **118**
Orchy Ct. G81: Hard 2E **43**
Orchy Cres. G61: Bear 5D **44**
  ML6: Air 6C **92**
  PA2: Pais 4D **96**
Orchy Dr. G76: Clar. 6D **118**
Orchy Gdns. G76: Clar. 6D **118**
Orchy St. G44: Glas. 1E **119**
Orchy Ter. G74: E Kil 2B **150**
Orefield Pl. G74: E Kil 6G **137**
Oregon Pl. G5: Glas 1G **103**
Orion Pl. ML4: Moss 2G **127**
Orion Way G72: Camb 1A **122**
  ML8: Carl 3D **164**
Orkney Pl. G51: Glas 4H **81**
Orkney Quad. ML2: Wis 5B **146**
Orkney St. G51: Glas 4H **81**
Orlando G74: E Kil 4C **138**
Orleans Av. G14: Glas. 6E **61**
Orleans La. *G14: Glas. 6E **61**
  (off Victoria Pk. Dr. Nth.)
Orlington Ct. ML5: Coat 3B **90**
Ormiston Av. G14: Glas. 5C **60**
Ormiston Dr. ML3: Ham 3G **153**
Ormiston La. *G14: Glas 5C **60**
  (off Norse La. Sth.)
Ormiston La. Nth. *G14: Glas. 5C **60**
  (off Norse La. Nth.)
Ormonde Av. G44: Neth 4D **118**
Ormonde Ct. G44: Neth. 4D **118**
Ormonde Cres. G44: Neth. 4D **118**
Ormonde Dr. G44: Neth 4D **118**
Ornsay St. G22: Glas 2H **63**
Oronsay Ct. G60: Old K. 1G **41**
Oronsay Cres. G60: Old K 1G **41**
  G61: Bear 4H **45**
Oronsay Gdns. G60: Old K 1G **41**
Oronsay Pl. G60: Old K 1G **41**
Oronsay Sq. G60: Old K 1G **41**
Orr Church Sq. PA1: Pais 6H **77**
Orr Sq. PA1: Pais 6A **78**
Orr St. G40: Glas 6B **84**
  (not continuous)
  PA1: Pais 6A **78**
  PA2: Pais 2A **98**
Orr Ter. G78: Neil 3C **130**
Orton Pl. G51: Glas 5G **81**
Osborne Cres. G74: T'hall 6F **135**
Osborne St. G1: Glas 5G **83** (6E **5**)
  G81: Clyd 4C **42**
Oskaig PA8: Ersk 2G **57**
Osprey Cres. ML2: Wis. 5G **145**
Osprey Dr. G71: Tann 6E **109**
Osprey Ho. PA3: Pais 3A **78**
Ossian Av. PA1: Pais 6H **79**
Ossian Rd. G43: Glas 1C **118**
Oswald St. G1: Glas 5F **83** (6C **4**)
Oswald Wlk. G62: Miln. 5A **26**
Otago La. G12: Glas 1C **82**
Otago La. Nth. *G12: Glas 1C **82**
  (off Otago St.)
Otago Pk. G75: E Kil 2C **148**

Otago St. G12: Glas 1C **82**
Othello G74: E Kil 5B **138**
Ottawa Cres. G81: Clyd 3H **41**
Otterburn Dr. G46: Giff 6A **118**
Otterswick Pl. G33: Glas 1C **86**
Oudenarde Ct. ML8: Carl 4H **165**
Our Lady of Good Aid R.C. Cathedral
. . . . 2G **143**
Oval Path G52: Glas 2E **101**
Oval, The G76: Clar 6D **118**
ML5: Glenb 3G **69**
Overbrae Pl. G15: Glas. 2H **43**
Overburn Av. G82: Dumb 3F **17**
Overburn Cres. G82: Dumb 2F **17**
Overburn Ter. G82: Dumb. 2G **17**
Overcroy Rd. G65: Croy 1B **34**
Overdale Av. G42: Glas. 5D **102**
Overdale Gdns. G42: Glas 5D **102**
Overdale Pl. ML2: Over 5A **158**
Overdale St. G42: Glas 5D **102**
Overjohnstone Dr. ML2: Wis. 5D **144**
Overlea Av. G73: Ruth. 1F **121**
Overlee Rd. G76: Busby 2D **134**
Overnewton Pl. G3: Glas. 3B **82**
Overnewton Sq. G3: Glas 2B **82**
Overnewton St. G3: Glas 2B **82**
Overton Cres. PA5: John 2H **95**
Overton Rd.
G72: Camb, Flem 3D **122**
PA5: John. 3G **95**
Overton St. G72: Camb. 3D **122**
Overtoun Av. G82: Dumb 4H **17**
Overtoun Dr. G73: Ruth. 6C **104**
G81: Clyd 3B **42**
Overtoun Rd. G81: Clyd 3A **42**
OVERTOWN 5A **158**
Overtown Av. G53: Glas 1A **116**
Overtown Ct. G81: Clyd. 4A **42**
Overtown Rd. ML2: Wis 4B **158**
Overtown St. G40: Glas. 6C **84**
Overwood Dr. G44: Glas 1G **119**
G82: Dumb 3H **17**
Overwood Gro. G82: Dumb 3H **17**
Owen Av. G75: E Kil 4E **149**
Owendale Av. ML4: Bell 6D **110**
Owen Pk. G75: E Kil 4F **149**
Owen St. ML1: Moth 1G **143**
O'Wood Av. ML1: Holy 1B **128**
Oxford Dr. PA3: Lin. 5H **75**
Oxford La. G5: Glas. 6F **83**
PA4: Renf 6E **59**
Oxford Rd. PA4: Renf 6E **59**
Oxford St. G5: Glas 5F **83**
G66: Kirk 5C **30**
ML5: Coat. 5B **90**
OXGANG 6F **31**
Oxgang Pl. G66: Kirk 6E **31**
Oxhill Pl. G82: Dumb 4D **16**
Oxhill Rd. G82: Dumb 3D **16**
Oxton Dr. G52: Glas 6B **80**

P

Pacific Dr. G51: Glas 5A **82**
Paddock St. ML5: Coat 1F **111**
Paddock, The G76: Busby 4E **135**
Paidmyre Cres. G77: Newt M 6D **132**
Paidmyre Gdns. G77: Newt M 6D **132**
Paidmyre Rd. G77: Newt M 6C **132**
PAISLEY 1H **97**
Paisley Arts Cen. 1A **98**
Paisley Canal Station (Rail) 2A **98**
Paisley Cen., The PA1: Pais 1A **98**
Paisley Gilmour Street Station (Rail)
. . . . 6A **78**
Paisley Mus. & Art Gallery 6H **77**
Paisley Rd. G5: Glas 5D **82**
G78: Barr 2D **114**
PA4: Renf 3C **78**
Paisley Rd. W. G51: Glas 6A **82**
(not continuous)
G52: Glas 1H **99**
Paisley St James Station (Rail) . . . 5G **77**

Palacecraig St. ML5: Coat 2C **110**
Palace Gdns. Retail Pk.
ML3: Ham. 5B **142**
Palace Grounds Rd. ML3: Ham. . . 5B **142**
Palace of Art 6G **81**
Palace of Paisley, The 1B **98**
Palacerigg Country Pk. 6E **37**
Paladin Av. G13: Glas. 1B **60**
Palermo St. G21: Glas. 5A **64**
Palladium Pl. G14: Glas. 6D **60**
Palmer Av. G13: Glas. 6C **44**
Palmerston G75: E Kil. 4C **148**
Palmerston Pl. G3: Glas. 3B **82**
PA5: John. 5C **94**
Palm Pl. G71: View. 4F **109**
Pandora Way G71: Tann. 6E **109**
Pankhurst Pl. G74: E Kil 1H **149**
Panmure St. G20: Glas. 5E **63**
Parkandarroch Cres. ML8: Carl. . . 4G **165**
Park Av. G3: Glas 1D **82**
G62: Miln 4G **25**
G64: B'rig 4C **48**
G65: Twe 1D **32**
G66: Kirk 5C **30**
G78: Barr 6D **114**
G82: Dumb 4H **17**
ML1: Holy 2A **128**
ML8: Carl 2F **165**
PA2: Pais 4G **97**
PA5: Eld 3A **96**
Park Bank PA8: Ersk 6F **41**
Park Brae PA8: Ersk. 1G **57**
Parkbrae Av. G20: Glas 3E **63**
Parkbrae Dr. G20: Glas 3E **63**
Parkbrae Gdns. G20: Glas. 3E **63**
Parkbrae Ga. G20: Glas 3E **63**
Parkbrae La. G20: Glas 3E **63**
Parkburn Av. G66: Kirk 1C **50**
Park Burn Ct. ML3: Ham 3D **140**
Park Burn Ind. Est.
ML3: Ham. 3E **141**
Parkburn Rd. G65: Kils 2H **11**
Park Cir. G3: Glas 2C **82**
ML8: Carl 2F **165**
Park Cir. La. G3: Glas. 2C **82**
Park Cir. Pl. G3: Glas 2D **82**
Park Ct. G46: Giff 4H **117**
G64: B'rig 4D **48**
G81: Clyd 3A **42**
Park Cres. G61: Bear 2B **44**
G64: B'rig 5C **48**
G64: Torr. 4E **29**
G72: Blan 3A **140**
G82: Dumb 2F **17**
ML6: Air 3G **91**
PA4: Inch 2G **57**
Park Dr. G3: Glas 1D **82**
G73: Ruth 6C **104**
G74: T'hall 6G **135**
ML2: Newm. 4E **147**
ML3: Fern 2E **155**
PA8: Ersk 1F **57**
ML9: Lark 2F **161**
Parker Pl. G65: Kils 3H **11**
Parkfield G75: E Kil 6G **149**
Parkfoot St. G65: Kils. 2H **11**
Park Gdns. G3: Glas 2C **82**
PA10: Kilb 1B **94**
Park Gdns. La. G3: Glas 2C **82**
(off Clifton St.)
Park Ga. G3: Glas. 2C **82**
PA8: Ersk 1F **57**
Park Ga. Pl. ML4: Bell 2B **126**
Park Glade PA8: Ersk 1F **57**
Park Grn. PA8: Ersk 1F **57**
Park Gro. PA8: Ersk 1G **57**
Parkgrove Av. G46: Giff 3B **118**
Parkgrove Ter. G3: Glas 2C **82**
Parkgrove Ter. La. G3: Glas 2C **82**
(off Derby St.)
PARKHALL 2B **42**
Parkhall Rd. G81: Clyd 3B **42**
Parkhall St. G74: E Kil 1H **149**
Parkhall Ter. G81: Clyd. 2B **42**

PARKHEAD 6F **85**
Parkhead Cross G31: Glas. 6F **85**
Parkhead La. ML6: Air 3A **92**
Parkhead St. ML1: Moth. 4H **143**
ML6: Air 3A **92**
Park Hill PA8: Ersk 6F **41**
Parkhill Dr. G73: Ruth 6C **104**
Parkhill Rd. G43: Glas 5B **102**
Parkholm La. G5: Glas. 5D **82**
PARKHOUSE 3H **115**
Park Ho. ML3: Ham 4H **141**
Parkhouse Path G53: Glas 3B **116**
Parkhouse Rd. G53: Glas 3H **115**
G78: Barr 3H **115**
Parkinch PA8: Ersk 1G **57**
Parklands Rd. G44: Neth 4D **118**
Parklands Vw. G53: Glas 4H **99**
Park La. G40: Glas 6B **84**
G65: Kils. 3H **11**
G72: Blan 1B **140**
ML8: Carl 4E **165**
Parklea G64: B'rig 4A **48**
Parklee Dr. G76: Crmck 2A **136**
PARK MAINS 2G **57**
Park Moor PA8: Ersk. 1F **57**
PARKNEUK 1G **151**
Parkneuk Rd. G43: Glas 3H **117**
G72: Blan 1G **151**
Parkneuk St. ML1: Moth 1F **143**
Parknook Way ML9: Lark 2F **161**
(off Muirshot Rd.)
Park Pl. G74: T'hall. 6G **135**
ML4: Bell 4A **126**
ML5: Coat 1F **111**
PA3: Lin 5A **76**
PA5: John 3F **95**
Park Quad. G3: Glas 2C **82**
ML2: Wis 2E **157**
Park Rd G4: Glas 1C **82**
Park Ridge PA8: Ersk 1F **57**
Park Rd. G32: Carm 5C **106**
G46: Giff 5A **118**
G62: Miln 4G **25**
G64: B'rig 5C **48**
G69: Barg 6D **88**
G69: Chry 1A **68**
G81: Clyd 4B **42**
ML1: New S 4A **128**
ML3: Ham. 6H **141**
ML4: Bell 3C **126**
ML6: C'bnk 3B **112**
PA11: Bri W. 2F **73**
PA2: Pais 5H **97**
PA4: Inch 2H **57**
PA5: John 3F **95**
Parksail PA8: Ersk 2G **57**
Parksail Dr. PA8: Ersk 1G **57**
Parkside Gdns. G20: Glas 3E **63**
Parkside Pl. G20: Glas 3E **63**
Parkside Rd. ML1: Moth. 3D **142**
Park St. G66: Kirk. 6H **31**
G82: Dumb 4G **17**
ML1: Cle. 4H **129**
ML1: Moth 2G **143**
ML1: New S 4A **128**
ML5: Coat. 3D **90**
ML6: Air 3G **91**
ML8: Carl 4F **165**
Park St. Sth. G3: Glas. 2C **82**
Parks Vw. ML3: Ham 5H **153**
Park Ter. G3: Glas 2C **82**
G46: Giff 5A **118**
G74: E Kil 2G **149**
Park Ter. E. La. G3: Glas 2D **82**
Park Ter. La. G3: Glas. 2C **82**
Park Top PA8: Ersk. 6G **41**
Parkvale Cres. PA8: Ersk 1H **57**
Parkvale Dr. PA8: Ersk 1H **57**
Parkvale Gdns. PA8: Ersk 1H **57**
Parkvale Pl. PA8: Ersk 1H **57**
Parkvale Way PA8: Ersk 1H **57**
Parkview G82: Milt 3F **19**
Park Vw. ML9: Lark. 3F **161**
PA10: Kilb. 1A **94**

Park Vw. PA2: Pais. 3H 97
Parkview Av. G66: Kirk 6D 30
Parkview Ct. G66: Kirk 6D 30
Parkview Cres. ML2: Newm 5E 147
Parkview Dr. G33: Step. 3E 67
   ML5: Coat. 4A 90
Parkville Dr. G72: Blan 3C 140
                 (not continuous)
Parkville Rd. ML4: Bell 6E 111
Parkway G32: Carm 5C 106
Park Way G67: Cumb 1B 36
Parkway PA8: Ersk 1F 57
Parkway Ct. G69: Bail. 4H 87
   ML5: Coat. 5A 90
Parkway Pl. ML5: Coat. 6A 90
Park Winding PA8: Ersk 1G 57
Park Wood PA8: Ersk 6G 41
Parlbrae G20: Glas 3E 63
Parnell St. ML6: Air 6H 91
Parnie St. G1: Glas. 5G 83
Parry Ter. G75: E Kil 2D 148
Parsonage Row G1: Glas 4H 83 (6H 5)
Parsonage Sq. G1: Glas. . . . 4H 83 (6H 5)
                 (not continuous)
Parson St. G4: Glas 3A 84 (3H 5)
PARTICK. 1H 81
Partick Bri. St. G11: Glas 2A 82
PARTICKHILL 1H 81
Partickhill Av. G11: Glas. 6H 61
Partickhill Ct. G11: Glas. 6H 61
Partickhill Rd. G11: Glas. 6H 61
Partick Station (Rail, Und.) 1H 81
Partick St. ML5: Coat 6E 91
Partick Thistle F.C. 5E 63
Patchy Pk. ML9: Lark 5E 161
Paterson Pl. G61: Bear 5C 24
Paterson's Laun G64: Balm. 6A 28
Paterson St. G5: Glas 6E 83
                 (not continuous)
   ML1: Moth 2G 143
Paterson Ter. G75: E Kil 4F 149
Pathead Gdns. G33: Glas 3H 65
Pather St. ML2: Wis. 1H 157
Pathhead Rd. G76: Crmck 2H 135
Patna Ct. ML3: Ham 2C 152
Patna St. G40: Glas 2D 104
PATNER 2H 157
Paton St. G31: Glas 4D 84
Patrick St. PA2: Pais. 2B 98
Patterson Dr. ML8: Law 5E 159
PATTERTON. 1D 132
Patterton Dr. G78: Barr 6F 115
Patterton Station (Rail) 1D 132
Pattison St. G81: Clyd 4A 42
Pavilion Theatre 3D 4
Paxton Ct. G74: E Kil 5H 137
           (off Paxton Cres.)
Paxton Cres. G74: E Kil 5H 137
Payne St. G4: Glas. 1G 83 (1E 5)
Peace Av. PA11: Q'riers 1B 72
Peacock Av. PA2: Pais 3D 96
Peacock Cross ML3: Ham. 5G 141
Peacock Cross Ind. Est.
   ML3: Ham. 5G 141
Peacock Dr. ML3: Ham. 5G 141
   PA2: Pais. 3D 96
Peacock Loan ML8: Carl 2F 165
        (off Carranbute Rd.)
Pearce La. G51: Glas 3G 81
Pearce St. G51: Glas 3G 81
Pearl St. ML4: Bell 4D 126
Pearson Dr. PA4: Renf 1F 79
Pearson Pl. PA3: Lin 6H 75
Peathill Av. G69: Chry 6H 51
Peathill St. G21: Glas. 6G 63
Peat Pl. G53: Glas 2A 116
Peat Rd. G53: Glas 2A 116
   PA11: Bri W 4G 73
Pedmyre La. G76: Crmck 2G 135
Peebles Dr. G73: Ruth 6F 105
Peebles Path ML5: Coat 2F 111
Peel Av. ML1: Moth 5G 143
Peel Brae G66: Kirk 4C 30
Peel Ct. G72: Camb 1A 122

Peel Glen Gdns. G15: Glas 2A 44
Peel Glen Rd. G15: Glas 3A 44
Peel La. G11: Glas 1H 81
PEEL PARK 1A 148
Peel Pk. Ind. Est. G74: E Kil 1A 148
Peel Pk. Pl. G74: E Kil 2B 148
Peel Pl. G71: Both 4E 125
   ML5: Coat. 6H 89
Peel Rd. G74: T'hall 6F 135
Peel St. G11: Glas 1H 81
Peel Vw. G81: Clyd 4F 43
Pegasus Av. ML8: Carl 3E 165
   PA1: Pais 6B 76
Pegasus Rd. ML4: Moss. 2G 127
Peinchorran PA8: Ersk 2G 57
Peiter Pl. G72: Blan 2A 140
        (off Burnbrae Rd.)
Pembroke G74: E Kil. 5D 138
Pembroke St. G3: Glas 3D 82
Pencaitland Dr. G32: Glas. 2A 106
Pencaitland Gro. G32: Glas. 3A 106
Pencaitland Pl. G23: Glas. 6C 46
Pendale Ri. G45: Glas 4H 119
Pend Cl. PA5: John. 4F 95
Pendeen Cres. G33: Glas 6E 87
Pendeen Pl. G33: Glas. 5F 87
Pendeen Rd. G33: Glas. 6E 87
Pendicle Cres. G61: Bear 4D 44
Pendicle Rd. G61: Bear 4D 44
Pendle Ct. G69: G'csh 3D 68
Penfold Cres. G75: E Kil 3F 149
Penicuik St. G32: Glas. 5F 85
PENILEE. 5G 79
Penilee Rd. G52: Hill 3F 79
Penilee Ter. G52: Glas 4G 79
Peninver Dr. G51: Glas 3E 81
Penman Av. G73: Ruth 5B 104
Pennan PA8: Ersk 5E 41
Pennan Pl. G14: Glas 4A 60
Penneld Rd. G52: Glas. 6H 79
Penniecroft Av. G82: Dumb 2H 17
Pennine Gro. ML6: Chap. 4F 113
Pennyroyal Ct. G74: E Kil 5F 137
Penrith Av. G46: Giff. 4A 118
Penrith Dr. G12: Glas 3G 61
Penrith Pl. G75: E Kil 5B 148
Penryn Gdns. G32: Glas 2D 106
Penston Rd. G33: Glas 3D 86
Pentland Av. PA3: Lin 6G 75
Pentland Ct. G78: Barr 6D 114
   ML5: Coat. 2E 111
   ML6: Air 1B 92
Pentland Cres. ML9: Lark. 6G 155
   PA2: Pais 5H 97
Pentland Dr. G64: B'rig. 5F 49
   G78: Barr 6D 114
   PA4: Renf 3D 78
Pentland Pl. G61: Bear 6B 24
   G69: Chry 1B 68
   ML2: Wis 5E 145
Penzance Way G69: Mood 4C 52
Peockland Gdns. PA5: John. 2G 95
Peockland Pl. PA5: John 2G 95
People's Palace (Museum) 6A 84
Peploe Dr. G74: E Kil 4D 138
Perchy Vw. ML2: Wis 2A 158
Percy Dr. G46: Giff 6A 118
Percy Rd. PA4: Renf 3C 78
Percy St. G51: Glas 6B 82
   ML9: Lark 1E 161
Perran Gdns. G69: Mood 5C 52
Perray Av. G82: Dumb 2B 16
Perrays Cres. G82: Dumb 2A 16
Perrays Dr. G82: Dumb. 3A 16
Perrays Way G82: Dumb 2A 16
Perth Av. ML6: Air 1A 112
Perth Cres. G81: Clyd 2H 41
Perth St. G3: Glas. 4D 82
                 (not continuous)
Peter Coats Bldg. PA2: Pais 2A 98
Peter Dr. G66: Kirk 4D 30
PETERSBURN 5E 93
Petersburn Pl. ML6: Air 5D 92

Petersburn Rd. ML6: Air. 6C 92
PETERSHILL 6D 64
Petershill Ct. G21: Glas 6D 64
Petershill Dr. G21: Glas 5D 64
Petershill Pl. G21: Glas 5D 64
Petershill Rd. G21: Glas. 6B 64
Peterson Dr. G13: Glas. 1G 59
Peterson Gdns. G13: Glas. 1G 59
Petition Pl. G71: Udd 2E 125
Pettigrew St. G32: Glas 6A 86
Peveril Av. G41: Glas 4B 102
   G73: Ruth 2E 121
Peveril Ct. G73: Ruth 3E 121
Pharonhill St. G31: Glas 6G 85
Philip Murray Rd. ML4: Bell 1H 125
PHILIPSHILL 5A 136
Philipshill Ga. G74: E Kil 5A 136
Philipshill Rd. G76: Crmck 6A 136
Phoenix Bus. Pk., The PA1: Pais . . . 6C 76
Phoenix Ct. G74: E Kil 4D 138
        (off Bosworth Rd.)
Phoenix Cres. ML4: Bell 5A 110
Phoenix Ind. Est. PA3: Glas A 3A 98
Phoenix Pl. ML1: New S 4A 128
   PA5: Eld 2B 96
Phoenix Retail Pk., The
   PA1: Pais 1D 96
Phoenix Rd. G4: Glas 1E 83 (1A 4)
   ML4: Moss 2G 127
Phyliss Jane Ct. ML2: Wis 2H 157
Piazza Shop. Cen. PA1: Pais 6A 78
Picadilly St. G3: Glas. 4D 82 (6A 4)
PICKERSTONHILL 2F 129
Pickerstonhill ML1: N'hill 3E 129
Picketlaw Dr. G76: Crmck. 2H 135
Picketlaw Farm Rd. G76: Crmck. . . 2G 135
Piershill St. G32: Glas 4H 85
Pikeman Rd. G13: Glas. 3C 60
Pillans Ct. ML3: Ham 3E 141
Pilmuir Av. G44: Glas 3D 118
Pilrig St. G32: Glas 4G 85
Pilton Rd. G15: Glas 3A 44
Pine Av. G72: Flem 4F 123
Pine Cl. G67: Cumb 1E 37
Pine Ct. G67: Cumb 1E 37
   G75: E Kil 6D 148
   ML5: Coat 1A 110
                 (off Ailsa Rd.)
Pine Cres. G67: Cumb 1E 37
   G75: E Kil 6D 148
   PA5: John. 4G 95
Pine Gro. G67: Cumb 1E 37
   G71: View 5F 109
   ML1: Holy 2B 128
   ML6: C'bnk 3B 112
Pinelands G64: B'rig. 3C 48
Pine Lawn ML2: Wis. 4B 146
Pine Pk. ML3: Ham. 2A 154
Pine Pl. G5: Glas 1G 103
   G67: Cumb 1E 37
Pine Quad. ML6: Chap 2E 113
Pine Rd. G67: Cumb 6E 15
   G81: Clyd 3H 41
   G82: Dumb 3F 17
Pines, The G44: Glas 3F 119
Pine St. G66: Len 3G 7
   ML6: Air 4D 92
   PA2: Pais 3C 98
Pinewood Av. G66: Lenz 2A 50
Pinewood Ct. G66: Lenz 2A 50
   G82: Dumb 2H 17
Pinewood Pl. G66: Lenz 2A 50
Pinewood Sq. G15: Glas 4B 44
Pinkerton Av. G73: Ruth 5A 104
Pinkston Dr. G21: Glas. 1H 83 (1H 5)
Pinkston Rd. G21: Glas 6H 63 (1H 5)
   G4: Glas 1H 83
Pinmore Pl. G53: Glas 2H 115
Pinmore St. G53: Glas 2H 115
Pinwherry Dr. G33: Glas. 3H 65
Pinwherry Pl. G71: Both 4E 125
Piper Av. PA6: C'lee 3C 74
Piper Rd. ML6: Air 6C 92
   PA6: C'lee 3C 74

Pirnie Pl. G65: Kils. 3H 11
Pirnmill Av. ML1: Moth 2D 142
Pitcairn Cres. G75: E Kil. 3B 148
Pitcairn Gro. G75: E Kil. 3C 148
Pitcairn Pl. G75: E Kil. 3B 148
Pitcairn St. G31: Glas. 1G 105
Pitcairn Ter. ML3: Ham. 5E 141
Pitcaple Dr. G43: Glas 1H 117
Pitlochry Dr. G52: Glas. 1B 100
  ML9: Lark. 4G 161
Pitmedden Rd. G64: B'rig 5F 49
Pitmilly Rd. G15: Glas 3C 44
Pitreavie Ct. ML3: Ham. 3F 153
Pitreavie Pl. G33: Glas. 2C 86
Pit Rd. G66: Kirk 6A 32
  ML4: Bell 1B 126
Pitt St. G2: Glas 4E 83 (5B 4)
Pladda Rd. PA4: Renf 2F 79
Pladda St. ML1: Moth 2D 142
PLAINS 1G 93
Plaintrees Ct. PA2: Pais 4A 98
Plane Pl. G71: View 4G 109
Planetree Pl. PA5: John 4G 95
Planetree Rd. G81: Clyd. 2C 42
PLANTATION 5B 82
Plantation Av. ML1: Holy 1B 128
Plantation Pk. Gdns. G51: Glas . . 6B 82
(not continuous)
PLANTATION RD. INTERCHANGE . . . 6B 82
Plantation Sq. G51: Glas 5C 82
Plant St. G31: Glas 5E 85
Platthorn Dr. G74: E Kil. 2H 149
Platthorn Rd. G74: E Kil. 2H 149
Play Drome, The 6D 42
Playfair St. G40: Glas 2C 104
Plaza, The G74: E Kil 2G 149
Pleaknowe Cres. G69: Mood 5C 52
Pleamuir Pl. G68: Cumb. 4E 35
Plean St. G14: Glas. 4A 60
Pleasance La. G43: Glas. 6A 102
Pleasance St. G43: Glas 5A 102
Plotcock Castle (Remains of) . . . 4A 160
Plotcock Rd. ML3: Ham 4A 160
Plover Dr. G75: E Kil 6C 148
Plover Pl. PA5: John 6C 94
Plusgarten Loan ML2: Newm 2D 146
Pochard Way ML4: Bell 5B 126
Poet's Vw. G66: Kirk 6F 31
Poindfauld Ter. G82: Dumb 3G 17
Pointhouse Rd. G3: Glas. 3A 82
Pollock Av. ML3: Ham 6A 140
Pollock Rd. G61: Bear 4G 45
  G77: Newt M 5C 132
Pollock St. ML1: Moth 2G 143
  ML4: Bell 2E 127
POLLOK 6C 100
Pollok Av. G43: Glas 5H 101
Pollok Country Pk 4G 101
Pollok Dr. G64: B'rig 5A 48
Pollok Ho 5F 101
Pollok La. G74: E Kil 6B 138
Pollok Leisure Pool 6C 100
Pollok Pl. G74: E Kil 6B 138
POLLOKSHAWS 6A 102
Pollokshaws East Station (Rail)
. . . . 6B 102
Pollokshaws Rd. G41: Glas. 4C 102
  G43: Glas 6H 101
Pollokshaws Sports Cen. 5A 102
(off Ashtree Rd.)
Pollokshaws West Station (Rail)
. . . . 6H 101
POLLOKSHIELDS 2C 102
Pollokshields East Station (Rail)
. . . . 2E 103
Pollokshields Sq. G41: Glas 3C 102
Pollokshields West Station (Rail)
. . . . 3D 102
Pollok Township Cen. G53: Glas . . 6C 100
POLMADIE 3H 103
Polmadie Av. G5: Glas 3H 103
Polmadie Ind. Est. G5: Glas 3A 104
Polmadie Rd. G42: Glas 4G 103
Polmadie St. G42: Glas 4G 103

Poinoon Av. G13: Glas 3A 60
Polquhap Cl. G53: Glas. 5A 100
Polquhap Gdns. G53: Glas 5A 100
Polquhap Pl. G53: Glas. 5A 100
Polquhap Rd. G53: Glas 5A 100
Polson Dr. PA5: John 3E 95
Polsons Cres. PA2: Pais 3H 97
Polwarth La. G12: Glas. 6H 61
Polwarth St. G12: Glas. 6H 61
Pomona Pl. ML3: Ham 1D 152
Poplar Av. G11: Glas. 5F 61
  G77: Newt M 6D 132
  PA5: John 4G 95
  PA7: B'ton 5H 39
Poplar Ct. ML5: Coat 1A 110
Poplar Cres. PA7: B'ton 5H 39
Poplar Dr. G66: Lenz 2A 50
  G81: Milt C 6C 8
  G81: Clyd 2B 42
Poplar Gdns. G75: E Kil 6E 149
  G72: Blan 6A 124
  ML1: Holy. 3B 128
Poplar Rd. G82: Dumb 3F 17
Poplars, The G61: Bear 5D 24
Poplar St. ML6: Air 4D 92
Poplar Way G72: Flem. 4F 123
Poplin St. G40: Glas 2B 104
Porchester St. G33: Glas 1D 86
Portal Rd. G13: Glas 1C 60
PORT DUNDAS 1G 83
Port Dundas Ind. Est. G4: Glas . . 1G 83
Port Dundas Pl. G2: Glas . . . 3G 83 (3E 5)
Port Dundas Rd. G4: Glas . . . 2F 83 (1D 4)
PORT EGLINGTON 1E 103
PORTERFIELD 1D 78
Porterfield Rd. PA4: Renf 6D 58
Porters La. ML6: Chap 3D 112
Porter St. G51: Glas 6A 82
Porters Well G71: Udd 2C 124
Portessie PA8: Ersk 5E 41
Portland Pk. ML3: Ham 1A 154
Portland Pl. ML3: Ham 1A 154
Portland Rd. G68: Cumb 6H 13
  PA2: Pais 2D 98
Portland Sq. ML3: Ham 1A 154
Portland St. ML5: Coat 3D 90
Portland Wynd ML9: Lark 1F 161
(off Muirshot Rd.)
Portlethen PA8: Ersk. 5E 41
Portman St. G41: Glas 6C 82
Portmarnock Dr. G23: Glas 1C 62
Porton Pl. PA7: B'ton 4G 39
Portpatrick Rd. G60: Old K 6D 20
Portreath Rd. ML6: Mood 4D 52
Portree Av. ML5: Coat 1A 110
Portree Pl. G15: Glas 3G 43
Portsoy PA8: Ersk 5E 41
Portsoy Av. G13: Glas. 1H 59
Portsoy Pl. G13: Glas 1G 59
Port St. G3: Glas 4D 82
Portugal St. G5: Glas 6F 83
Portwell ML3: Ham. 5A 142
POSSIL PARK 4G 63
Possilpark & Parkhouse Station (Rail)
. . . . 3F 63
Possil Pk. Millennium Cen. 5F 63
Possil Pk. Trad. Cen. G22: Glas . . 4G 63
Possil Rd. G4: Glas. 1F 83
Postgate ML3: Ham 5A 142
Potassels Rd. G69: Muirh. 2A 68
Potrail Pl. ML3: Ham 6E 141
Potter Cl. G32: Glas 2G 105
Potter Gro. G32: Glas. 2G 105
POTTERHILL 4H 97
Potterhill Av. PA2: Pais 5A 98
Potterhill Rd. G53: Glas 3A 100
Potter Path G32: Glas 2G 105
Potter Pl. G32: Glas 2G 105
Potter St. G32: Glas 2G 105
Potts Way ML1: Moth 6E 127
Powbrone G75: E Kil. 6G 149
POWBURN 5C 108
Powburn Cres. G71: Udd 6B 108

Powerdrome Bowl 5E 91
Powerleague Soccer Cen.
  Glasgow. 3A 84 (2H 5)
  Hamilton 3G 141
  Paisley 2C 98
Powfoot St. G31: Glas 6F 85
Powforth Cl. ML9: Lark 2C 160
Powrie St. G33: Glas 6C 66
Prentice La. G71: Tann 5E 109
Prentice Rd. ML1: Moth 4D 142
Prestonfield G62: Miln 4E 25
Preston Pl. G42: Glas 3F 103
Preston St. G42: Glas 3F 103
Prestwick Ct. G68: Cumb 1H 35
Prestwick Pl. G77: Newt M 5G 133
Prestwick St. G53: Glas 1A 116
Priestfield Ind. Est. G72: Blan . . . 4B 140
Priestfield St. G72: Blan 3A 140
PRIESTHILL 1A 116
Priesthill & Darnley Station (Rail)
. . . . 2C 116
Priesthill Av. G53: Glas. 1C 116
Priesthill Cres. G53: Glas 1C 116
Priesthill Rd. G53: Glas 1B 116
PRIESTKNOWE RDBT. 2H 149
Prieston Rd. PA11: Bri W 4E 73
Primrose Av. ML4: Bell 6C 110
  ML9: Lark 5E 161
Primrose Ct. G14: Glas 6D 60
Primrose Cres. ML1: Moth 4G 143
Primrose Pl. G67: Cumb 6D 34
  G71: View 5G 109
Primrose St. G14: Glas. 6C 60
Primrose Way ML8: Carl 5E 165
Prince Albert Rd. G12: Glas 6H 61
Prince Edward St. G42: Glas 3E 103
Prince of Wales Gdns. G20: Glas . . 1A 62
Prince Pl. ML2: Newm 3E 147
Prince's Gdns. G12: Glas 6H 61
Prince's Gdns. La. G12: Glas 6H 61
Princes Ga. G71: Both 3C 124
  G73: Ruth 5C 104
Princes Mall G74: E Kil 2G 149
(off Olympia)
Princes Pk. PA7: B'ton 3C 40
Prince's Pl. G12: Glas 6A 62
Princess Anne Quad. ML1: Holy. . 2H 127
(off Sherry Av.)
Princess Cres. PA1: Pais 6D 78
Princess Dr. G69: Barg 6E 89
Princess Sq. G74: E Kil 2G 149
Princess Sq. Shop. Cen.
  G1: Glas 6E 5
Princess Rd. ML1: New S 3H 127
Princess Sq. G78: Barr 4F 115
  ML2: Newm 4D 146
Princes St. G73: Ruth 5C 104
  ML1: Moth 1G 143
Prince's Ter. G12: Glas 6A 62
Prince's Ter. La. G12: Glas 6A 62
Printers Land G76: Busby 3E 135
Printers Lea G66: Len. 3E 7
Priorscroft Bowling Club 1B 98
(off Cochran St.)
Priorwood Ct. G13: Glas. 3D 60
Priorwood Gdns. G13: Glas 3D 60
Priorwood Ga. G77: Newt M 5A 132
Priorwood Pl. G13: Glas. 3D 60
Priorwood Rd. G77: Newt M 5A 132
Priorwood Way G77: Newt M 5A 132
Priory Av. PA3: Pais 4C 78
Priory Dr. G71: Udd 6B 108
Priory Ga. ML2: Over 4H 157
Priory Pl. G13: Glas. 2D 60
  G68: Cumb 4A 34
Priory Rd. G13: Glas. 2D 60
Priory St. G72: Blan 1B 140
Priory Ter. ML2: Wis. 1C 156
Pro Bowl 4D 30
Procession Rd. PA2: Pais 1A 114
Professors Sq. G12: Glas 1B 82
Pro Lane Bowl 5A 150
Pro Life Fitness Cen. 5A 78
Prosen St. G32: Glas 2G 105

Prospect Av. G71: Udd	1C **124**
G72: Camb	1H **121**
Prospect Ct. G72: Blan	4B **140**
Prospect Dr. ML9: Ashg	5B **162**
Prospecthill Cir. G42: Glas	4H **103**
Prospecthill Cres. G42: Glas	5A **104**
Prospect Hill Dr. G42: Glas	5G **103**
Prospecthill Pl. G42: Glas	5A **104**
Prospecthill Rd. G42: Glas	5E **103**
Prospecthill Sq. G42: Glas	4H **103**
Prospect Rd. G43: Glas	5B **102**
G68: Dull.	5E **13**
Provandhall Cres. G69: Bail	2H **107**
Provand's Lordship	4H **5**
Provan Hall	2F **87**
Provanhill St. G21: Glas	2B **84**
PROVAN INTERCHANGE.	2E **85**
PROVANMILL	6G **65**
Provanmill Pl. G33: Glas.	6F **65**
(off Provanmill Rd.)	
Provanmill Rd. G33: Glas	6F **65**
Provan Rd. G33: Glas	2E **85**
Provost Cl. PA5: John	2F **95**
Provost Dr. Ct. PA4: Renf	1F **79**
Provost Ga. ML9: Lark	2E **161**
P.S. Waverley	5D **82**
Purdie G74: E Kil	4D **138**
Purdie St. ML3: Ham	4E **141**
Purdon St. G11: Glas	1H **81**
Pyatshaw Rd. ML9: Lark	4F **161**

Q

Quadrant Rd. G43: Glas	1C **118**
Quadrant Shop. Cen. ML5: Coat	4C **90**
Quadrant, The G76: Clar	1C **134**
QUARRELTON	3E **95**
Quarrelton Gro. PA5: John	4F **95**
Quarrelton Rd. PA5: John	3E **95**
QUARRIER'S VILLAGE.	1A **72**
Quarry Av. G72: Camb	4D **122**
Quarrybank PA10: Kilb	3C **94**
Quarrybrae Av. G76: Clar	2B **134**
Quarrybrae Gdns. G71: View	1G **125**
Quarrybrae St. G31: Glas	6F **85**
Quarry Dr. G66: Kirk	5F **31**
Quarryknowe G73: Ruth	6B **104**
Quarry Knowe G82: Dumb	2D **16**
Quarry Knowe Pl. ML4: Bell	4B **126**
Quarryknowe St. G31: Glas.	6G **85**
G81: Faif	6F **23**
Quarry La. G66: Len	2F **7**
G82: Dumb	4E **17**
Quarry Pk. G75: E Kil	3G **149**
G82: Dumb	2D **16**
ML3: Ham	6A **142**
Quarry Pl. G72: Camb	1G **121**
G82: Dumb	2D **16**
ML3: Ham	6A **142**
Quarry Rd. G75: E Kil	6F **149**
G78: Barr	3D **114**
ML6: Air	2H **91**
ML8: Carl	3H **163**
ML9: Lark	3E **161**
PA2: Pais	4B **98**
Quarryside St. ML6: Glenm	5G **71**
Quarry St. ML1: New S	3A **128**
ML2: Wis	6G **145**
ML3: Ham	6A **142**
ML5: Coat	5F **91**
ML9: Lark	4F **161**
PA5: John	2F **95**
Quarrywood Av. G21: Glas	5E **65**
Quarrywood Rd. G21: Glas	5E **65**
Quay Pend G82: Dumb	4E **17**
Quay Rd. G73: Ruth	4C **104**
Quay Rd. Nth. G73: Ruth	4C **104**
Quay St. G82: Dumb	4F **17**
Quay, The G5: Glas	5D **82**
Quebec Dr. G75: E Kil	3E **149**
Quebec Grn. G75: E Kil	2E **149**
Quebec Ho. G81: Clyd	1H **41**
Quebec Wynd G32: Carm	5C **106**
Queen Elizabeth Av.	
G52: Hill	4G **79**

Queen Elizabeth Ct. G81: Clyd	4C **42**
ML1: Moth	2F **143**
Queen Margaret Ct. *G20: Glas*	*5C **62***
(off Fergus Dr.)	
Queen Margaret Dr. G12: Glas	6B **62**
Queen Margaret Rd. G20: Glas	5C **62**
Queen Mary Av. G42: Glas	4E **103**
G81: Clyd	5F **43**
Queen Mary Gdns. G81: Clyd	4C **42**
Queen Mary St. G40: Glas	1C **104**
Queen's Av. G72: Camb	1B **122**
Queensbank Av. G69: G'csh	2C **68**
Queensberry Av. G61: Bear	6E **25**
G76: Clar.	2C **134**
Queensborough Gdns. G12: Glas	5G **61**
Queensby Av. G69: Bail	6H **87**
Queensby Dr. G69: Bail	5H **87**
Queensby Pl. G69: Bail	5A **88**
Queensby Rd. G69: Bail	5H **87**
Queen's Ct. G62: Miln	5G **25**
Queen's Cres. G4: Glas	1D **82** (1A **4**)
G69: Barg	6D **88**
Queens Cres. ML1: New S	4H **127**
Queen's Cres. ML4: Bell	3B **126**
ML6: Chap	2D **112**
ML8: Carl	3G **165**
Queensdale Av. ML9: Lark	5F **161**
Queensdale Rd. ML9: Lark	5F **161**
Queen's Dr. G42: Glas	3D **102**
G68: Cumb	5H **13**
Queens Dr. ML3: Ham	5H **153**
PA7: B'ton	4H **39**
Queensferry St. G5: Glas	3A **104**
Queen's Gdns. G12: Glas	6A **62**
Queen's Ga. La. G12: Glas	6A **62**
Queenside Cres. PA8: Ersk.	6D **40**
Queensland Ct. G52: Glas	5C **80**
Queensland Dr. G52: Glas	5C **80**
Queensland Gdns. G52: Glas	5C **80**
Queensland La. E. G52: Glas	5C **80**
Queensland La. W. G52: Glas	5C **80**
Queenslie Ind. Est. G33: Glas.	3D **86**
Queenslie St. G33: Glas	1F **85**
Queen's Pk. Av. G42: Glas	4F **103**
Queen's Pk. F.C.	6F **103**
Queen's Park Station (Rail)	3E **103**
Queens Pl. G12: Glas	6A **62**
Queen Sq. G41: Glas	3D **102**
Queen's Rd. PA5: Eld	3A **96**
Queen's St. ML1: Cle	5H **129**
Queen St. G1: Glas	4G **83** (6E **5**)
G66: Kirk	5C **30**
G73: Ruth	5C **104**
ML1: Moth	2G **143**
ML2: Newm	3D **146**
ML3: Ham	4E **141**
PA1: Pais	1G **97**
PA4: Renf	6F **59**
Queen Street Station (Rail)	
	3G **83** (4E **5**)
Queens Way G64: Torr	5D **28**
Queensway G74: E Kil.	6B **136**
Queen Victoria Ct. G14: Glas	5C **60**
Queen Victoria Dr. G13: Glas	5C **60**
G14: Glas	5C **60**
Queen Victoria Ga. G13: Glas	4C **60**
Queen Victoria St. ML6: Air	4H **91**
QUEENZIEBURN	3C **10**
Queenzieburn Ind. Est.	
G65: Queen.	4D **10**
Quendale Dr. G32: Glas	2H **105**
Quentin St. G41: Glas	4C **102**
Quinton Gdns. G69: Bail	6G **87**

R

Raasay Cres. ML6: Air	5E **93**
Raasay Dr. PA2: Pais	6H **97**
Raasay Gdns. G77: Newt M	4B **132**
Raasay Pl. G22: Glas	1G **63**
Raasay St. G22: Glas	1G **63**

Racecourse Vw. ML3: Ham.	4A **142**
RADNOR PARK	3C **42**
Radnor St. G3: Glas	2B **82**
G81: Clyd	4C **42**
(not continuous)	
Raeberry St. G20: Glas	6D **62**
Raebog Cres. ML6: Air	1H **91**
Raebog Rd. ML6: Glenm	5G **71**
Raeburn Av. G74: E Kil	5B **138**
PA1: Pais	1B **98**
Raeburn Cres. ML3: Ham	6C **140**
Raeburn Pl. G74: E Kil	5B **138**
Raeburn Wlk. ML4: Bell	6D **110**
Raeside Av. G77: Newt M.	6D **132**
Raes Rd. ML8: Carl	5B **164**
Raeswood Dr. G53: Glas	5H **99**
Raeswood Gdns. G53: Glas	5H **99**
Raeswood Pl. G53: Glas	5H **99**
Raeswood Rd. G53: Glas	5H **99**
Raewell Cres. ML4: Bell	4B **126**
Rafford St. G51: Glas	4G **81**
Raglan St. G4: Glas	1E **83**
Railway Rd. ML6: Air	4F **91**
Raith Av. G45: Glas	3H **119**
Raithburn Av. G45: Glas	3G **119**
Raithburn Rd. G45: Glas	4G **119**
Raith Cottage Vis. Cen.	6H **125**
Raith Dr. G68: Cumb	4H **33**
ML4: Bell	3D **126**
RAITH INTERCHANGE	5G **125**
RALSTON	1F **99**
Ralston Av. PA1: Pais	2H **99**
Ralston Cotts. PA1: Pais	1F **99**
Ralston Ct. G52: Glas	1H **99**
Ralston Dr. G52: Glas	1H **99**
Ralston Path G52: Glas	1H **99**
Ralston Pl. G52: Glas	1H **99**
Ralston Rd. G61: Bear	2E **45**
G78: Barr	5E **115**
Ralston St. ML6: Air	4G **91**
PA1: Pais	1C **98**
Ramage Rd. ML8: Carl	5H **165**
Ramillies Ct. G81: Clyd	5E **43**
ML8: Carl	4G **165**
Rampart Av. G13: Glas	1A **60**
Ramsay Av. PA5: John	4E **95**
Ramsay Ct. G77: Newt M	6E **133**
Ramsay Cres. PA10: Kilb	3B **94**
Ramsay Hill G74: E Kil	6A **138**
Ramsay Ind. Est. G66: Kirk.	4B **30**
Ramsay Pl. ML5: Coat	6G **89**
PA5: John	4E **95**
Ramsay St. G81: Clyd.	4B **42**
Ramsey Wynd ML4: Bell.	6D **110**
Ram St. G32: Glas	6H **85**
Ranaldard Gdns. G73: Ruth	4F **121**
Randolph Av. G76: Clar.	6E **119**
Randolph Dr. G76: Clar.	6D **118**
Randolph Gdns. G76: Clar	6D **118**
Randolph La. G11: Glas	6F **61**
Randolph Rd. G11: Glas	6F **61**
RANFURLY	5G **73**
Ranfurly Ct. PA11: Bri W.	4F **73**
Ranfurly Dr. G68: Cumb	1G **35**
Ranfurly Pl. PA11: Bri W.	4F **73**
Ranfurly Rd. G52: Glas	6H **79**
PA11: Bri W.	5F **73**
Range Av. ML1: Moth	5C **144**
Range Pl. ML3: Ham	2A **154**
Rangers F.C.	5G **81**
Rangers F.C. Training Cen. &	
Youth Academy.	5A **26**
Rangerhouse Rd. G75: E Kil	6B **149**
Range Rd. ML1: Moth	5B **144**
Range Rd. Ind. Est. ML1: Moth	6C **144**
(Range Av.)	
ML1: Moth	5B **144**
(Range Rd.)	
Range St. ML1: Moth	5B **144**
Rankin Dr. G77: Newt M	3C **132**
Rankine Av. G75: E Kil	4A **150**
Rankine Pl. G75: E Kil	4A **150**
PA5: John	2F **95**
Rankine St. PA5: John	2F **95**

Rankin Gait Cen. *ML8: Carl* *3F 165*
(off High St.)
Rankin Rd. ML2: Wis 5C **146**
Rankin St. ML8: Carl 3F **165**
Rankin Way G78: Barr 4G **115**
Rannoch Av. G64: B'rig 6D **48**
G77: Newt M 2D **132**
ML3: Ham 2E **153**
ML5: Coat 2H **89**
Rannoch Ct. G67: Cumb 1D **54**
G72: Blan 4D **140**
Rannoch Dr. G61: Bear 2H **45**
G66: Kirk 4H **31**
G67: Cumb 1D **54**
ML2: Wis 2H **157**
PA4: Renf 5E **59**
Rannoch Gdns. G64: B'rig 6E **49**
Rannoch Grn. G74: E Kil 6H **137**
Rannoch La. G69: Mood 5E **53**
Rannoch Pl. PA2: Pais 2C **98**
Rannoch Rd. G71: Tann 4C **108**
ML6: Air 2H **91**
PA5: John 4E **95**
Rannoch St. G44: Glas 1E **119**
Rannoch Ter. ML9: Lark 4G **161**
Rannoch Way G71: Both 4E **125**
RAPLOCH **2D 160**
Raploch Av. G14: Glas 5B **60**
Raploch Cres. G81: Faif 6F **23**
Raploch La. G14: Glas 5B **60**
Raploch Rd. ML9: Lark 2D **160**
Raploch St. ML9: Lark 2D **160**
RASHIEBURN **5E 41**
Rashieburn PA8: Ersk 5E **41**
Rashieglen PA8: Ersk 5E **41**
Rashiehill PA8: Ersk 5E **41**
Rashielee Rd. PA8: Ersk 5E **41**
Rashiewood PA8: Ersk 5F **41**
Rashilee Av. PA8: Ersk 5F **41**
Rathlin St. G51: Glas 3G **81**
Rathlin Ter. G82: Dumb 2C **16**
Ratho Dr. G21: Glas 5A **64**
G68: Cumb 6F **13**
Ratho Pk. ML3: Ham 4F **153**
Rattray PA8: Ersk 4E **41**
Rattray St. G32: Glas 2G **105**
Ravel Row G31: Glas 6F **85**
Ravelston Rd. G61: Bear 5E **45**
(not continuous)
Ravelston St. G32: Glas 5F **85**
Ravel Wynd G71: Tann 5F **109**
Ravenscliffe Dr. G46: Giff 4H **117**
Ravens Ct. G64: B'rig 1B **64**
Ravenscourt G74: T'hall 6G **135**
Ravenscraig Av. PA2: Pais 4G **97**
Ravenscraig Ct. ML4: Bell 2D **126**
Ravenscraig Dr. G53: Glas 1B **116**
Ravenscraig Ter. G53: Glas 2C **116**
Ravenshall ML1: Cle 1H **145**
Ravenshall Rd. G41: Glas 5A **102**
Ravenshill Dr. ML1: Cle 6H **129**
Ravenstone Dr. G46: Giff 2A **118**
Ravenswood Av. PA2: Pais 6C **96**
Ravenswood Dr. G41: Glas 4B **102**
Ravenswood Rd. G69: Bail 6A **88**
Raven Wynd ML2: Wis 5H **145**
RAWYARDS **2C 92**
Rawyards Av. ML6: Air 1B **92**
Raymond Pl. G75: E Kil 2E **149**
Rayne Pl. G15: Glas 3B **44**
Ream Av. ML6: Air 5F **93**
Reay Av. G74: E Kil 1D **148**
Reay Gdns. G74: E Kil 1D **148**
Rebrae Pl. G66: Kirk 4E **31**
Redan St. G40: Glas 6B **84**
Redbrae Rd. G66: Kirk 4D **30**
Red Bri. Ct. ML5: Coat 3C **90**
Redburn Av. G46: Giff 1H **133**
Redburn Ct. G67: Cumb 5F **15**
Redburn Pl. G67: Cumb 6F **15**
Redburn Rd. G67: Cumb 5F **15**
Redcastle Sq. G33: Glas 2E **87**
Redcliffe Dr. G75: E Kil 3D **148**
Red Deer Rd. G75: E Kil 3E **149**
Rederech Cres. ML3: Ham 1D **152**
Redford St. G33: Glas 3F **85**
Redgate Pl. G14: Glas 5B **60**
Redgrave G74: E Kil 4C **138**
Redhill Rd. G68: Cumb 2F **35**
Redhills Vw. G66: Len 4G **7**
Redholme *ML9: Lark* *4F 161*
(off Keir Hardie Rd.)
Redhouse La. ML8: Carl 2F **165**
Redhurst Cres. PA2: Pais 6F **97**
Redhurst La. PA2: Pais 6G **97**
Redhurst Way PA2: Pais 6F **97**
Redlands La. G12: Glas 5A **62**
Redlands Rd. G12: Glas 5A **62**
Redlands Ter. G12: Glas 5A **62**
Redlands Ter. La. G12: Glas 5A **62**
Redlawood Pl. G72: Newt 1G **123**
Redlawood Rd. G72: Newt 1G **123**
Redmoss Rd. G66: Milt C 6B **8**
G81: Dun 1B **42**
Redmoss St. G22: Glas 4F **63**
Rednock St. G22: Glas 5G **63**
Redpath Dr. G52: Glas 5B **80**
Red Rd. G21: Glas 5D **64**
Red Rd. Ct. G21: Glas 6D **64**
Red Road Recreation Cen. **6E 65**
Redwing Gdns. ML2: Wis 2F **157**
Redwood Av. G74: E Kil 2A **148**
Redwood Ct. G74: E Kil 2A **148**
Redwood Cres. G71: View 5G **109**
G72: Flem 3F **123**
G74: E Kil 6A **136**
PA7: B'ton 4A **40**
Redwood Dr. G21: Glas 6C **64**
G74: E Kil 3A **148**
Redwood Gro. ML5: Coat 5D **90**
Redwood Pl. G66: Lenz 2B **50**
G71: View 5G **109**
G74: E Kil 1A **148**
Redwood Rd. G67: Cumb 3D **36**
ML1: Holy 2C **128**
Redwood Way G72: Flem 4F **123**
Reelick Av. G13: Glas 1G **59**
Reelick Quad. G13: Glas 1G **59**
Reema Rd. ML4: Bell 1D **126**
Reen Pl. G71: Both 3F **125**
Regency Ct. ML3: Ham 1C **154**
Regency M. G69: Bail 1A **108**
Regency Way ML1: New S 3H **127**
Regent Dr. G73: Ruth 5C **104**
Regent Moray St. G3: Glas 2B **82**
Regent Pk. Sq. G41: Glas 3D **102**
Regent Pl. G81: Clyd 3A **42**
Regents Ga. G71: Both 3B **124**
Regent Shop. Cen. G66: Kirk 5C **30**
Regent Sq. G66: Lenz 3C **50**
Regent St. G66: Kirk 5C **30**
G81: Clyd 3A **42**
PA1: Pais 6D **78**
Regent Way ML3: Ham 6A **142**
Register Av. ML4: Bell 4C **126**
Register Rd. G65: Kils 3A **12**
Regwood St. G41: Glas 5B **102**
Reid Av. G61: Bear 1G **45**
PA3: Lin 6H **75**
Reid Gro. ML1: Moth 5B **144**
Reid Pl. G40: Glas 1B **104**
Reid St. G40: Glas 2B **104**
G73: Ruth 5D **104**
ML3: Ham 4D **140**
ML5: Coat 3C **90**
ML6: Air 2B **92**
Reidvale St. G31: Glas 5B **84**
Reilly Rd. PA6: Hous 6B **38**
Reith Dr. G75: E Kil 4F **149**
Remus Pl. ML4: Moss 2G **127**
Renfield La. G2: Glas 4F **83** (5D **4**)
Renfield St. G2: Glas 4F **83** (5D **4**)
PA4: Renf 5F **59**
RENFREW **5F 59**
Renfrew Community Mus. **5F 59**
Renfrew Ct. *G1: Glas* *3G 5*
(off St Mungo Av.)
G2: Glas 3G **83** (3E **5**)
Renfrew La. G2: Glas 3F **83** (3D **4**)
Renfrew Pl. ML5: Coat 1G **109**
Renfrew Rd. G51: Glas 3B **80**
PA3: Pais 5B **78**
PA4: Renf 1A **80**
Renfrew St. G3: Glas 2E **83** (2A **4**)
ML5: Coat 1G **109**
Rennie Pl. G74: E Kil 6C **136**
Rennie Rd. G65: Kils 2F **11**
Renshaw Dr. G52: Glas 5B **80**
Renshaw Rd. PA5: Eld 4A **96**
PA7: B'ton 4H **39**
Renton Rd. G82: Dumb 1D **16**
Renton St. G4: Glas 2G **83** (1E **5**)
Resipol Rd. G33: Step 4E **67**
Reston Dr. G52: Glas 5B **80**
Reuther Av. G73: Ruth 6D **104**
Revoch Dr. G13: Glas 2A **60**
Reynolds Av. G75: E Kil 4A **150**
Reynolds Dr. G33: Step 4F **67**
Reynolds Path ML2: Wis 2B **158**
Rhannan Rd. G44: Glas 2E **119**
Rhannan Ter. G44: Glas 2E **119**
Rhindhouse Pl. G69: Bail 6B **88**
Rhindhouse Rd. G69: Bail 6B **88**
Rhindmuir Av. G69: Bail 6A **88**
Rhindmuir Ct. G69: Bail 5A **88**
Rhindmuir Cres. G69: Bail 5B **88**
Rhindmuir Dr. G69: Bail 5A **88**
Rhindmuir Gdns. G69: Bail 5A **88**
Rhindmuir Gro. G69: Bail 5B **88**
Rhindmuir Path G69: Bail 5B **88**
Rhindmuir Pl. G69: Bail 5A **88**
Rhindmuir Rd. G69: Bail 5A **88**
Rhindmuir Vw. G69: Bail 5B **88**
Rhindmuir Wynd G69: Bail 5B **88**
Rhinds St. ML5: Coat 1F **109**
Rhinsdale Cres. G69: Bail 6A **88**
Rhumhor Gdns. PA10: Kilb 3C **94**
Rhu Quad. ML2: Over 5A **158**
Rhymer St. G21: Glas 2A **84**
Rhymie Rd. G32: Glas 2D **106**
Rhynie Dr. G51: Glas 6H **81**
Riach Gdns. ML1: Moth 6E **127**
Ribblesdale G74: E Kil 6E **137**
Riccarton G75: E Kil 4D **148**
Riccarton St. G42: Glas 3G **103**
Riccartsbar Av. PA2: Pais 2G **97**
Rice Way ML1: Moth 5B **144**
Richmond Av. G76: Clar 2C **134**
Richmond Ct. G73: Ruth 5E **105**
Richmond Dr. G64: B'rig 3D **48**
G72: Camb 2G **121**
G73: Ruth 6E **105**
PA3: Lin 4G **75**
Richmond Gdns. G69: Chry 1H **67**
Richmond Gro. G73: Ruth 6E **105**
Richmond Pl. G73: Ruth 5E **105**
Richmond Rd. G73: Ruth 6F **105**
Richmond St. G1: Glas 4H **83** (5G **5**)
G81: Clyd 6E **43**
Riddell St. G81: Clyd 4D **42**
ML5: Coat 4E **91**
Riddon Av. G13: Glas 1G **59**
Riddon Pl. G13: Glas 1G **59**
RIDDRIE **2F 85**
Riddrie Cres. G33: Glas 3G **85**
RIDDRIE KNOWES **3G 85**
Riddrie Knowes G33: Glas 3G **85**
Riddrievale Ct. G33: Glas 2G **85**
Riddrievale St. G33: Glas 2G **85**
Rigby St. G31: Glas 6G **85**
Rigghead Av. G67: Cumb 6B **14**
Rigg Pl. G33: Glas 4E **87**
Riggside Rd. G33: Glas 1C **86**
Riggs, The G62: Miln 2G **25**
Righead Ga. *G74: E Kil* *2G 149*
(off Princess Sq.)
Righead Ind. Est. ML4: Bell 6A **110**
RIGHEAD RDBT. **2F 149**
Riglands Way PA4: Renf 6E **59**
Riglaw Pl. G13: Glas 2A **60**
Rigmuir Rd. G51: Glas 4C **80**
Rimsdale St. G40: Glas 6C **84**

Ringford St. G21: Glas 6B **64**
Ripon Dr. G12: Glas 3G **61**
Risk St. G81: Clyd 3B **42**
G82: Dumb 4E **17**
Ristol Rd. G13: Glas 4B **60**
Ritchie Cres. PA5: Eld 2A **96**
Ritchie Pk. PA5: John 2H **95**
Ritchie Pl. G77: Newt M 5C **132**
Ritchie St. G5: Glas 1E **103**
ML2: Wis 6D **144**
Riverbank Dr. ML4: Bell 4E **127**
Riverbank St. G43: Glas 6A **102**
River Ct. G76: Busby 3D **134**
Riverdale Gdns. ML3: Ham. 2A **154**
Riverford Rd. G43: Glas 6A **102**
G73: Ruth 4E **105**
River Rd. G32: Carm 6B **106**
Riversdale La. G14: Glas 4A **60**
Riverside G62: Miln 3G **25**
G66: Len. 1C **6**
PA6: Hous 2D **74**
Riverside Ct. G44: Neth 4D **118**
Riverside Gdns. G76: Busby. 4D **134**
Riverside La. G82: Dumb 4E **17**
Riverside Pk. G44: Neth 5E **119**
Riverside Pl. G72: Camb. 1E **123**
Riverside Rd. G43: Glas 6C **102**
ML9: Lark 5E **161**
Riverside Ter. G76: Busby 4D **134**
Riverside Wlk. ML1: Moth 1H **143**
Riverton Dr. G75: E Kil 3D **148**
Riverview Dr. G5: Glas 5E **83**
Riverview Gdns. G5: Glas 5E **83**
Riverview Pl. G5: Glas 5E **83**
R.N.I.B. Springfield Cen.
G64: B'rig 6D **48**
Roaden Av. PA2: Pais 6D **96**
Roaden Rd. PA2: Pais 6D **96**
Roadside G67: Cumb 6A **14**
Robb Ter. G66: Kirk 1G **51**
Robert Burns Av. G81: Clyd. 4E **43**
ML1: N'hill 3E **129**
Robert Burns Quad. ML4: Bell 2B **126**
Robert Dr. G51: Glas 4G **81**
Roberton St. ML6: Chap 2E **113**
Robert Smillie Cres. ML9: Lark . . . 4E **161**
Robertson Av. G41: Glas. 3A **102**
PA4: Renf 6D **58**
Robertson Cl. PA4: Renf 6E **59**
Robertson Cres. G78: Neil 2D **130**
Robertson Dr. G74: E Kil. 1B **150**
ML4: Bell 3C **126**
Robertson La. G2: Glas 6B **4**
Robertson St. G1: Glas 5F **83** (6C **4**)
G78: Barr 5D **114**
ML3: Ham. 4D **140**
ML6: Air 4G **91**
Robertson Ter. G69: Bail 6A **88**
Roberts Quad. ML4: Bell. 4D **126**
Roberts St. G81: Clyd. 4A **42**
ML2: Wis 6G **145**
Robert St. G51: Glas. 4G **81**
Robert Templeton Dr.
G72: Camb 2B **122**
Robert Wynd ML2: Newm 3E **147**
Robet Gilson Gdns. ML5: Coat 6D **90**
Robin Pl. ML2: Wis 6H **145**
Robin Way G32: Carm 5C **106**
ROBROYSTON **3G 65**
Robroyston Av. G33: Glas. 6G **65**
ROBROYSTON INTERCHANGE
. . . . **4H 65**
Robroyston Rd. G33: Glas. 4F **65**
G64: B'rig 6H **49**
G66: Auch. 6H **49**
Robshill Ct. G77: Newt M. 5D **132**
Robslee Dr. G46: Giff 4H **117**
Robslee Rd. G46: Giff, T'bnk 5G **117**
Robson Gro. G42: Glas 2F **103**
Rochdale Pl. G66: Kirk. 5C **30**
Rochsoles Cres. ML6: Air. 1A **92**
Rochsoles Dr. ML6: Air 1H **91**
Rochsolloch Farm Cotts.
ML6: Air. 4G **91**
Rochsolloch Rd. ML6: Air. 5F **91**
Rockall Dr. G44: Glas 3F **119**
Rockbank Pl. G40: Glas 6C **84**
G81: Hard 1E **43**
Rockbank St. G40: Glas 6C **84**
Rockburn Cres. ML4: Bell 6C **110**
Rockburn Dr. G76: Clar. 1A **134**
Rockcliffe St. G40: Glas 2B **104**
Rock Dr. PA10: Kilb 3B **94**
Rockfield Pl. G21: Glas. 4E **65**
Rockfield Rd. G21: Glas 4E **65**
Rockhampton Av. G75: E Kil 4D **148**
Rockmount Av. G46: T'bnk 3G **117**
G78: Barr. 6F **115**
Rock St. G4: Glas 6F **63**
Rockwell Av. PA2: Pais. 5G **97**
Roddinghead Rd. G46: Giff. 3G **133**
Rodger Av. G77: Newt M. 4C **132**
Rodger Dr. G73: Ruth 1C **120**
Rodger Pl. G73: Ruth 1C **120**
Rodil Av. G44: Glas 3G **119**
Rodney St. G4: Glas 1F **83**
Roebank Dr. G78: Barr 6E **115**
Roebank St. G31: Glas 3D **84**
(not continuous)
Roffey Pk. Rd. PA1: Pais. 6F **79**
Rogart St. G40: Glas. 6B **84**
(not continuous)
Rogerfield Rd. G69: Barg 4A **88**
ROGERTON **3F 137**
Roland Cres. G77: Newt M 6F **133**
Roman Av. G15: Glas 6A **44**
G61: Bear 2F **45**
Roman Bath House **2F 45**
Roman Ct. G61: Bear 2F **45**
Roman Cres. G60: Old K 6D **20**
Roman Dr. G61: Bear 2F **45**
ML4: Bell 3D **126**
Roman Gdns. G61: Bear 2F **45**
Roman Hill Rd. G81: Hard 6D **22**
Roman Pl. ML4: Bell. 4A **126**
Roman Rd. G61: Bear. 2E **45**
G66: Kirk 5B **30**
G81: Hard 1C **42**
ML1: Moth 1F **143**
(not continuous)
Roman Way G71: View. 1G **125**
Romney Av. G44: Glas 2G **119**
Romulus Ct. ML1: Moth 6E **127**
Ronaldsay Dr. G64: B'rig. 5F **49**
Ronaldsay Pas. G22: Glas 2H **63**
Ronaldsay Pl. G67: Cumb. 5F **35**
Ronaldsay St. G22: Glas. 2G **63**
Ronald St. ML5: Coat 3C **90**
Rona St. G21: Glas. 1D **84**
Rona Ter. G72: Camb 4H **121**
Ronay St. G22: Glas. 2H **63**
ML2: Wis 4C **146**
Rooksdell Av. PA2: Pais 4G **97**
Ropework La. G1: Glas. 5G **83**
Rorison Pl. ML9: Ashg 4B **162**
Rosa Burn Av. G75: E Kil 6D **148**
ROSEBANK
Carluke **5E 163**
Glasgow **5G 31**
Rosebank PA5: John. 3F **95**
Rosebank Av. G66: Kirk 4E **31**
G72: Blan 6C **124**
Rosebank Dr. G71: View. 6G **109**
G72: Camb 3C **122**
Rosebank Gdns. G71: Udd 3H **107**
Rosebank La. G71: Both 4F **125**
Rosebank Pl. G68: Dull. 5E **13**
G71: Udd 3H **107**
ML3: Ham. 6E **141**
Rosebank Rd. ML2: Over 5A **158**
ML4: Bell 5D **110**
Rosebank St. ML6: Air 3E **93**
Rosebank Ter. G69: Barg 1D **108**
Rosebank Twr. *G72: Camb 1A 122*
(off Main St.)
Roseberry La. ML6: Chap 2E **113**
Roseberry Pl. ML3: Ham 5E **141**
Roseberry Rd. ML6: Chap 1D **112**
Roseberry St. G5: Glas. 2A **104**
Roseburn Ct. G67: Cumb 5F **15**
Rose Cres. ML3: Ham 5D **140**
Rose Dale G64: B'rig 1D **64**
Rosedale G74: E Kil 6E **137**
Rosedale Av. PA2: Pais. 6B **96**
Rosedale Dr. G69: Bail 1G **107**
Rosedale Gdns. G20: Glas 1A **62**
Rosedene Ter. ML4: Bell. 1C **126**
Rosefield Gdns. G71: Udd 6C **108**
Rosegreen Cres. ML4: Bell. 5C **110**
ROSEHALL **2D 110**
Rosehall Av. ML5: Coat 1D **110**
Rosehall Ind. Est. ML5: Coat 2C **110**
Rosehall Rd. ML4: Bell. 1B **126**
Rosehall Ter. ML2: Wis. 2E **157**
Rosehill Dr. G67: Cumb 1C **54**
Rosehill Pl. G67: Cumb 1C **54**
Rosehill Rd. G64: Torr 5D **28**
Rose Knowe Rd. G42: Glas. 5H **103**
Roselea Dr. G62: Miln 2H **25**
Roselea Gdns. G13: Glas 2F **61**
Roselea Pl. G72: Blan. 6A **124**
Roselea Rd. G71: Tann. 5C **108**
Roselea St. ML9: Lark 1F **161**
Rosemary Cres. G74: E Kil 5F **137**
Rosemary Pl. G74: E Kil 5F **137**
Rosemount G68: Cumb. 6H **13**
Rose Mt. Ct. ML6: Air. 3C **92**
Rosemount Gdns. ML6: Air. 4A **92**
Rosemount La. *ML9: Lark 4G 161*
(off Dickson St.)
PA11: Bri W 5D **72**
Rosemount Mdws. G71: Both 5D **124**
Rosemount St. G21: Glas 2B **84**
Rosendale Way G72: Blan 2C **140**
Roseneath Ga. G74: E Kil 1E **149**
Roseness Pl. G33: Glas 3A **86**
Rosepark Av. G71: View 1G **125**
Rosepark Cotts. ML5: Coat. 2B **110**
Rose St. G3: Glas. 3F **83** (3C **4**)
G66: Kirk 5D **30**
G67: Cumb 6D **34**
ML1: Moth 4A **144**
Rosevale Cres. ML4: Bell 3E **127**
Rosevale Gdns. ML3: Ham 1F **153**
Rosevale Rd. G61: Bear 3E **45**
Rosevale St. G11: Glas. 1G **81**
Rosewood Av. ML4: Bell. 6D **110**
PA2: Pais. 4F **97**
Rosewood Path ML4: Bell. 2A **126**
Rosewood St. G13: Glas 2E **61**
Roslea Dr. G31: Glas 4C **84**
Roslin Twr. G72: Camb. 4G **121**
Roslyn Dr. G69: Barg 6D **88**
Rosneath St. G51: Glas 3G **81**
Ross Av. G66: Kirk 5F **31**
PA4: Renf 2C **78**
Ross Cres. ML1: Moth 4E **143**
Ross Dr. G71: View. 4G **109**
ML1: Moth 4E **143**
ML6: Air 1G **111**
Rossendale Ct. G43: Glas. 5A **102**
Rossendale Rd. G43: Glas 5A **102**
Ross Gdns. ML1: Moth 4E **143**
ROSSHALL **2A 100**
Rosshall Av. PA1: Pais 1E **99**
Ross Hall Pl. PA4: Renf 6F **59**
Rosshill Av. G52: Glas 6H **79**
Rosshill Rd. G52: Glas. 6H **79**
Rossie Cres. G64: B'rig. 1E **65**
Rossie Gro. G77: Newt M. 4B **132**
ROSSLAND **5H 39**
Rossland Cres. PA7: B'ton 4G **39**
Rossland Gdns. PA7: B'ton. 4G **39**
Rossland Pl. PA7: B'ton 5H **39**
Rossland Vw. PA7: B'ton 4G **39**
Rosslea Dr. G46: Giff 5A **118**
Rosslee Cres. G46: Giff 4G **117**
Rosslyn Av. G73: Ruth 6D **104**
G74: E Kil 6H **137**
Rosslyn Ct. ML3: Ham 5E **141**
Rosslyn Rd. G61: Bear 1B **44**
ML9: Ashg 5B **162**

Rosslyn Ter. G12: Glas 5A **62**
Ross Pl. G73: Ruth 3F **121**
G74: E Kil 6C **138**
Ross St. G40: Glas 5H **83**
ML5: Coat 4C **90**
PA1: Pais 2C **98**
Ross Ter. ML3: Fern 2E **155**
Rostan Rd. G43: Glas 2A **118**
Rosyth Rd. G5: Glas 3A **104**
Rosyth St. G5: Glas 3A **104**
Rotherwick Dr. PA1: Pais 1G **99**
Rotherwood Av. G13: Glas 6C **44**
PA2: Pais 5D **96**
Rotherwood Pl. G13: Glas 1D **60**
Rotherwood Way PA2: Pais 5D **96**
Rothesay Cres. ML5: Coat 1D **110**
Rothesay Pl. G74: E Kil 2G **149**
ML5: Coat 1D **110**
Rothesay St. G74: E Kil 2G **149**
Rothes Dr. G23: Glas 6A **46**
Rothes Pl. G23: Glas 6A **46**
Rottenrow G1: Glas 3H **83** (4G **5**)
G4: Glas 4A **84** (5H **5**)
Rottenrow E. G4: Glas 4H **83** (5H **5**)
Roughcraig St. ML6: Air 1A **92**
Roughrigg Rd. ML6: Air 5F **93**
Roukenburn St. G46: T'bnk 3E **117**
Rouken Glen Pk. **6F 117**
Rouken Glen Rd. G46: T'bnk 5F **117**
Roundel, The ML2: Wis 1A **158**
Roundhill Dr. PA5: Eld 2C **96**
Roundknowe Rd. G71: Udd 4A **108**
Round Riding Rd.
G82: Dumb 3G **17**
Rowallan Gdns. G11: Glas 6G **61**
Rowallan La. G11: Glas 6F **61**
G76: Clar 2C **134**
Rowallan Rd. G46: T'bnk 5F **117**
Rowallan Ter. G33: Mille 5B **66**
Rowallen La. E. G11: Glas 6G **61**
Rowan Av. G66: Milt C 6B **8**
PA4: Renf 5E **59**
Rowanbank Pl. ML6: Air 3E **91**
Rowan Ct. G72: Flem 3F **123**
ML2: Wis 1D **156**
PA2: Pais 3A **98**
Rowan Cres. G66: Lenz 2C **50**
ML6: Chap 2E **113**
Rowandale Av. G69: Bail 1G **107**
Rowand Av. G46: Giff 5A **118**
Rowanden Av. ML4: Bell 1C **126**
Rowan Dr. FK4: Bank 1E **15**
G61: Bear 6F **25**
G81: Clyd 3B **42**
G82: Dumb 3A **16**
Rowan Gdns. G41: Glas 1H **101**
Rowan Ga. PA2: Pais 3B **98**
Rowan La. ML1: New S 4A **128**
Rowanlea PA5: John 3E **95**
Rowanlea Av. PA2: Pais 6B **96**
Rowanlea Dr. G46: Giff 3B **118**
Rowanpark Dr. G78: Barr 2C **114**
Rowan Pl. G72: Blan 1B **140**
G72: Camb 1C **122**
ML5: Coat 1A **110**
Rowan Ri. ML3: Ham 1A **154**
Rowan Rd. G41: Glas 1H **101**
G67: Cumb 2D **36**
PA3: Lin 4F **75**
Rowans Gdns. G71: Both 3F **125**
Rowans, The G64: B'rig 5B **48**
Rowan St. ML2: Wis 4H **145**
PA2: Pais 3A **98**
Rowantree Av. G71: View 6G **109**
G73: Ruth 2D **120**
ML1: N'hse 6C **112**
Rowantree Gdns. G73: Ruth 2D **120**
Rowantree Pl. G66: Len 4G **7**
Rowan Tree Pl. ML9: Lark 3H **161**
Rowantree Pl. *PA5: John 4F **95***
(off Rowantree Rd.)
Rowantree Rd. PA5: John 4F **95**
Rowantree Ter. ML1: Holy 2B **128**
Rowanwood Cres. ML5: Coat 6H **89**
Rowena Av. G13: Glas 6D **44**
Rownlea *ML6: Plain 1F **93***
(off Craiglea Ter.)
Roxburgh Dr. G61: Bear 6E **25**
ML5: Coat 1F **111**
Roxburgh Pk. G74: E Kil 2H **149**
Roxburgh Pl. *G72: Blan 2B **140***
(off Jedburgh St.)
Roxburgh Rd. PA2: Pais 6B **96**
Roxburgh St. G12: Glas 6B **62**
Royal Bank Pl. G1: Glas 5E **5**
Royal Cres. G3: Glas 3C **82**
Royal Dr. ML3: Ham 1C **154**
Royal Exchange Ct. G1: Glas 6E **5**
Royal Exchange Sq.
G1: Glas 4G **83** (5E **5**)
Royal Highland Fusiliers Mus.
2E 83 (2A 4)
Royal Inch Cres. PA4: Renf 4F **59**
Royal Scottish Academy of Music & Drama **3F 83 (3D 4)**
Royal Ter. G3: Glas 2C **82**
ML2: Wis 2A **146**
Royal Ter. La. G3: Glas 2C **82**
Royellen Av. ML3: Ham 1D **152**
ROYSTON **2B 84**
Roystonhill G21: Glas 2B **84**
Royston Rd. G21: Glas 2A **84**
G33: Glas 6G **65**
Royston Sq. G21: Glas 2A **84**
Roy St. G21: Glas 6H **63**
Rozelle Av. G15: Glas 4B **44**
G77: Newt M 5B **132**
Rozelle Dr. G77: Newt M 5B **132**
Rozelle Pl. G77: Newt M 5B **132**
Rubislaw Dr. G61: Bear 4E **45**
Ruby St. G40: Glas 1C **104**
Ruby Ter. ML4: Bell 3C **126**
RUCHAZIE **2B 86**
Ruchazie Pl. G33: Glas 3H **85**
Ruchazie Rd. G33: Glas 3H **85**
RUCHILL **4D 62**
Ruchill Pl. G20: Glas 4D **62**
Ruchill Sports Cen. **3D 62**
Ruchill St. G20: Glas 4C **62**
Ruel St. G44: Glas 6E **103**
Rufflees Av. G78: Barr 3F **115**
Rugby Av. G13: Glas 1B **60**
Rullion Pl. G33: Glas 3H **85**
Rumford St. G40: Glas 2B **104**
Runciman Pl. G74: E Kil 5B **138**
Rundell Dr. G66: Milt C 6C **8**
Rupert St. G4: Glas 1D **82**
Rushyhill St. G21: Glas 5C **64**
Ruskin La. G12: Glas 6C **62**
Ruskin Pl. G12: Glas 6C **62**
G65: Kils 3H **11**
Ruskin Sq. G64: B'rig 6C **48**
Ruskin Ter. G12: Glas 6C **62**
G73: Ruth 4D **104**
Russell Colt St. ML5: Coat 3C **90**
Russell Dr. G61: Bear 1E **45**
Russell Gdns. G71: Tann 5E **109**
G77: Newt M 5C **132**
Russell La. ML2: Wis 1G **157**
Russell Pl. G75: E Kil 4E **149**
G76: Busby 4E **135**
PA3: Lin 5F **75**
Russell Rd. G81: Dun 6A **22**
Russell St. ML2: Wis 1G **157**
ML3: Ham 4D **140**
ML4: Moss 2F **127**
ML6: Chap 3E **113**
PA3: Pais 4H **77**
PA5: John 2G **95**
Rutherford Av. G61: Bear 5B **24**
G66: Kirk 1H **51**
Rutherford Ct. G81: Clyd 5C **42**
Rutherford Grange G66: Lenz 1C **50**
Rutherford La. G75: E Kil 3H **149**
Rutherford Sq. G75: E Kil 3G **149**
RUTHERGLEN **5C 104**
Rutherglen Ind. Est. (Glasgow Rd.)
G73: Ruth 4B **104**
Rutherglen Ind. Est. (Quay Rd.)
G73: Ruth 4C **104**
Rutherglen Mus. **5D 104**
Rutherglen Rd. G5: Glas 2H **103**
G73: Ruth 3A **104**
Rutherglen Station (Rail) **5D 104**
Rutherglen Swimming Pool **6C 104**
Ruthven Av. G46: Giff 6B **118**
Ruthven La. G12: Glas 6A **62**
ML5: Glenb 3G **69**
Ruthven Pl. G64: B'rig 1E **65**
Ruthven St. G12: Glas 6B **62**
Rutland Ct. *G51: Glas 5C **82***
(off Rutland Cres.)
Rutland Cres. G51: Glas 5C **82**
Rutland Pl. G51: Glas 5C **82**
Ryan Rd. G64: B'rig 6D **48**
Ryan Way G73: Ruth 4E **121**
Ryat Dr. G77: Newt M 3C **132**
Ryat Grn. G77: Newt M 3C **132**
(not continuous)
Ryatt Linn PA8: Ersk 6D **40**
Rydal Gro. G75: E Kil 5B **148**
Rydal Pl. G75: E Kil 5B **148**
Ryden Mains Rd. ML6: Glenm 5F **71**
Ryde Rd. ML2: Wis 6A **146**
Ryebank Rd. G21: Glas 4E **65**
Rye Cres. G21: Glas 4D **64**
Ryecroft Dr. G69: Bail 6H **87**
Ryedale Pl. G15: Glas 3A **44**
Ryefield Av. ML5: Coat 4H **89**
PA5: John 4D **94**
Ryefield Pl. PA5: John 4D **94**
Ryefield Rd. G21: Glas 4D **64**
Ryehill Pl. G21: Glas 4E **65**
Ryehill Rd. G21: Glas 4E **65**
Ryemount Rd. G21: Glas 4E **65**
Rye Rd. G21: Glas 4D **64**
Ryeside Rd. G21: Glas 4D **64**
Rye Way PA2: Pais 4C **96**
Rylands Dr. G32: Glas 1D **106**
Rylands Gdns. G32: Glas 1E **107**
Rylees Cres. G52: Glas 5G **79**
Rylees Pl. G52: Glas 5G **79**
Rylees Rd. G52: Glas 5G **79**
Rysland Av. G77: Newt M 4E **133**
Rysland Cres. G77: Newt M 4E **133**
Ryvra Rd. G13: Glas 3D **60**

S

Sachelcourt Av. PA7: B'ton 5H **39**
Sackville Av. G13: Glas 4F **61**
Sackville La. G13: Glas 4F **61**
Saddell Rd. G15: Glas 3B **44**
Sadlers Wells Ct. *G74: E Kil 5B **138***
(off Bosworth Rd.)
Saffron Cres. ML2: Wis 2D **156**
Saffronhall Cres. ML3: Ham 5H **141**
Saffronhall La. ML3: Ham 5H **141**
St Abb's Dr. PA2: Pais 4E **97**
St Aidan's Path ML2: Wis 3A **146**
St Andrew's Av. G64: B'rig 5A **48**
St Andrews Av. G71: Both 6E **125**
St Andrew's Brae G82: Dumb 1H **17**
St Andrew's Ct. G75: E Kil 5E **149**
St Andrews Ct. ML1: Holy 1A **128**
*ML4: Bell 2D **126***
(off Anderson Ct.)
ML8: Carl 3E **165**
St Andrew's Cres. G41: Glas 1C **102**
G82: Dumb 2H **17**
PA3: Glas A 2G **77**
St Andrew's Dr. G41: Glas 3A **102**
St Andrews Dr. G61: Bear 6D **24**
St Andrew's Dr. G68: Cumb 5B **14**
ML3: Ham 5B **140**
St Andrews Dr. ML5: Coat 5A **90**
St Andrew's Dr. PA11: Bri W 4E **73**
PA3: Glas A 3H **77**
St Andrew's Dr. W. PA3: Glas A 2G **77**
St Andrew's Gdns. ML6: Air 3B **92**
St Andrew's Ga. ML4: Bell 2B **126**

St Andrew's La. *G1: Glas* *5H 83*
(off Gallowgate)
St Andrew's Path *ML9: Lark* *4G 161*
(off Glen Fruin Dr.)
St Andrews Pl. G65: Kils 2G **11**
St Andrew's Rd. G41: Glas 1D **102**
PA4: Renf 6E **59**
St Andrew's Sports Cen. 5G **149**
St Andrew's Sq. G1: Glas 5H **83**
St Andrew's St. G1: Glas 5H **83**
St Andrews St. ML1: Holy 2A **128**
St Andrew's Wlk. ML2: Wis 3A **146**
St Andrew's Way *ML1: Moth* *5A 144*
(off Glassford St.)
St Anne's Av. PA8: Ersk 1H **57**
St Anne's Wynd PA8: Ersk 1H **57**
St Ann's Dr. G46: Giff 5A **118**
St Blanes Dr. G73: Ruth 1A **120**
St Boswell's Cres. PA2: Pais 4E **97**
St Boswells Dr. ML5: Coat 1F **111**
St Bride's Av. G71: View 6G **109**
St Bride's Rd. G43: Glas 6B **102**
St Brides Way G71: Both 3E **125**
St Bryde St. G74: E Kil 1H **149**
St Catherine's Rd. G46: Giff 5A **118**
St Clair Av. G46: Giff 4A **118**
St Clair St. G20: Glas 1D **82**
St Columba Dr. G66: Kirk 6E **31**
St Cyrus Gdns. G64: B'rig 6E **49**
St Cyrus Rd. G64: B'rig 6E **49**
St Davids Dr. ML6: Air 1C **112**
St David's Pl. ML9: Lark 2E **161**
St Denis Way ML5: Coat 3B **90**
St Edmunds Gro. G62: Miln 2G **25**
St Enoch Av. G71: View 5G **109**
St Enoch Pl. G1: Glas 4F **83** (6D **4**)
St Enoch Shop. Cen.
G1: Glas 5G **83** (6E **5**)
St Enoch Sq. G1: Glas 5F **83** (6D **4**)
St Enoch Station (Und.) 5F **83** (6D **4**)
St Fillans Dr. PA6: Hous 1A **74**
St Fillans Rd. G33: Step 4C **66**
St Flanan Rd. G66: Kirk 4B **32**
ST GEORGE'S CROSS INTERCHANGE
. . . . **1A 4**
St Georges Cross Station (Und.)
. . . . 1E **83** (1A **4**)
St George's Pl. G4: Glas 1A **4**
St George's Rd. G3: Glas 2D **82** (2A **4**)
G4: Glas 1E **83** (1A **4**)
St George's Ter. *PA11: Bri W* *3E 73*
(off Horsewood Rd.)
St Germains G61: Bear 3E **45**
St Giles Pk. ML3: Ham 1F **153**
St Giles Way ML3: Ham 1F **153**
St Helena Cres. G81: Hard 1E **43**
St Ives Rd. G69: Mood 4D **52**
St James Av. PA3: Pais 4F **77**
St James Bus. Cen. PA1: Pais 1B **96**
St James Ct. ML5: Coat 1A **110**
ST JAMES E. INTERCHANGE **3G 77**
St James Rd. G4: Glas 3H **83** (3G **5**)
St James' St. PA3: Pais 6A **78**
St James Way ML5: Coat 2A **110**
ST JAMES W. INTERCHANGE **3F 77**
St John's Ct. G41: Glas 1C **102**
St John's Quad. G41: Glas 1C **102**
St John's Rd. G41: Glas 2C **102**
St John St. ML5: Coat 4C **90**
St Joseph's Ct. G21: Glas 2B **84**
St Joseph's Pl. G21: Glas 2B **84**
St Joseph's Vw. G21: Glas 2B **84**
St Kenneth Dr. G51: Glas 3D **80**
St Kilda Dr. G14: Glas 5E **61**
St Kilda Way ML2: Wis 4C **146**
St Lawrence Pk. G75: E Kil 2E **149**
ST LEONARDS **2C 150**
St Leonard's Dr. G46: Giff 4A **118**
St Leonards Rd. G74: E Kil 1B **150**
St Leonards Sq. G74: E Kil 2C **150**
St Leonards Wlk. ML5: Coat 2E **111**
St Lukes Bus. Cen. *G5: Glas* *6G 83*
(off St Lukes Pl.)
St Lukes Pl. G5: Glas 6G **83**
St Lukes's Av. ML8: Carl 5E **165**
St Lukes Ter. G5: Glas 6G **83**
St Machan's Way G66: Len 2F **7**
St Machars Rd. PA11: Bri W 4G **73**
St Margaret's Av. G65: Bant 1G **13**
St Margaret's Ct. *ML4: Bell* *2D 126*
(off Dean St.)
St Margarets Ct. *PA3: Pais* *4B 78*
(off Renfrew Rd.)
St Margarets Dr. ML2: Wis 2E **157**
St Margaret's Pl. *G1: Glas* *5G 83*
(off Bridgegate)
St Mark Gdns. G32: Glas 6H **85**
St Mark's Ct. ML2: Wis 3A **146**
St Mark St. G32: Glas 6G **85**
(not continuous)
St Marnock St. G40: Glas 6C **84**
St Martins Ga. ML5: Coat 1C **110**
St Mary's Ct. G2: Glas 5D **4**
ML2: Wis 1H **157**
St Mary's Cres. G78: Barr 5E **115**
St Mary's Gdns. G78: Barr 5F **115**
St Mary's La. G2: Glas 5D **4**
St Mary's Rd. G64: B'rig 5A **48**
ML4: Bell 2A **126**
St Mary's Way G82: Dumb 4F **17**
ST MAURICE'S RDBT. **4C 34**
St Michael Rd. ML2: Wis 2C **156**
St Michaels Ct. G31: Glas 6E **85**
St Michaels La. G31: Glas 6E **85**
St Mirren F.C. 5A **78**
St Mirren Pk.. . . . . 5A **78**
St Mirren R.C. Cathedral 6B **78**
St Mirren Sports & Leisure Complex
. . . . 5A **78**
St Mirren's Rd. G65: Kils 3A **12**
St Mirren St. PA1: Pais 1A **98**
St Monance St. G21: Glas 4B **64**
St Monicas Way ML5: Coat 1H **109**
St Mungo Av. G4: Glas 3G **83** (3F **5**)
St Mungo Ct. PA11: Bri W 3G **73**
St Mungo Mus. of Religious Life & Art
. . . . 3A **84**
St Mungo Pl. G4: Glas 3H **83** (3H **5**)
ML3: Ham 5B **140**
St Mungo's Cathedral 3A **84**
St Mungo's Cres. ML1: Carf 5B **128**
St Mungo's Rd. G67: Cumb 4H **35**
St Mungo St. G64: B'rig 1B **64**
St Mungo's Wlk. *G67: Cumb* *3H 35*
(in Cumbernauld Shop. Cen.)
St Ninian's Cres. PA2: Pais 3B **98**
St Ninians Gro. ML2: Wis 3B **146**
St Ninian's Pl. ML3: Ham 6D **140**
St Ninian's Rd. ML3: Ham 6D **140**
PA2: Pais 3B **98**
St Ninian Ter. G5: Glas 6G **83**
St Peters La. G2: Glas 4E **83** (5B **4**)
St Peter's Path *G4: Glas* *1E 83*
(off St Peter's St.)
St Peter's St. G4: Glas 1E **83** (1B **4**)
St Rollox Brae G21: Glas 1A **84**
St Rollox Bus. & Retail Pk.
G21: Glas 1B **84**
St Ronan's Dr. G41: Glas 4B **102**
St Ronans Dr. G73: Ruth 1E **121**
St Ronan's Dr. ML3: Ham 3G **153**
St Stephen's Av. G73: Ruth 4F **121**
St Stephen's Cres. G73: Ruth 4G **121**
St Vigean's Av. G77: Newt M 6B **132**
St Vigeans Pl. G77: Newt M 6C **132**
St Vincent Cres. G3: Glas 3B **82**
St Vincent Cres. La.
G3: Glas 3B **82**
St Vincent La. G2: Glas 3E **83** (4B **4**)
St Vincent Pl. G1: Glas 4G **83** (5E **5**)
G75: E Kil 3C **148**
ML1: Moth 2G **143**
St Vincent St. G2: Glas 3E **83** (4A **4**)
G3: Glas 3D **82** (4A **4**)
St Vincent Ter. G3: Glas 3D **82** (4A **4**)
St Winifred's Way ML2: Wis 5G **145**
Salamanca St. G31: Glas 6F **85**
(not continuous)
Salasaig Ct. G33: Glas 4A **86**
Salen St. G52: Glas 6F **81**
Salford Pl. *G66: Kirk* *4C 30*
(off Glasgow Rd.)
Saline St. ML6: Air 5F **91**
Salisbury G74: E Kil 5D **138**
Salisbury Cres. ML1: Moth 1D **142**
Salisbury Pl. G81: Clyd 2H **41**
Salisbury St. G5: Glas 1F **103**
Salkeld St. G5: Glas 1E **103**
Salmona St. G22: Glas 5F **63**
Saltaire Av. G71: Udd 2E **125**
Salterland Rd. G53: Glas 2G **115**
Saltire Cres. ML9: Lark 3G **161**
Saltmarket G1: Glas 5G **83**
Saltmarket Pl. G1: Glas 5G **83**
Saltoun La. G12: Glas 6B **62**
Saltoun St. G12: Glas 6A **62**
Salvia St. G72: Camb 1H **121**
Samson Cres. ML8: Carl 5H **165**
Sandaig Rd. G33: Glas 6E **87**
Sandale Path G72: Blan 3A **140**
Sandalwood Av. G74: E Kil 5F **137**
Sandalwood Ct. G74: E Kil 5F **137**
Sanda St. G20: Glas 5C **62**
Sandbank Av. G20: Glas 2B **62**
Sandbank Cres. G20: Glas 3B **62**
Sandbank Dr. G20: Glas 2B **62**
Sandbank St. G20: Glas 1B **62**
Sandbank Ter. G20: Glas. 2B **62**
Sandend PA8: Ersk 4E **41**
Sandend Rd. G53: Glas 6A **100**
Sanderling Pl. G75: E Kil 6C **148**
PA5: John 6D **94**
Sanderling Rd. PA3: Glas A 3H **77**
Sanderson Av. G71: View 1H **125**
Sandfield Av. G62: Miln 2G **25**
Sandfield St. G20: Glas 4C **62**
Sandford Gdns. G69: Bail 6H **87**
Sandgate Av. G32: Glas 2D **106**
Sandhaven Pl. G53: Glas 6A **100**
Sandhaven Rd. G53: Glas 6A **100**
Sandhead Cres. ML6: Chap 4E **113**
Sandholes Rd. PA5: Brkfld 6C **74**
Sandholes St. PA1: Pais 1G **97**
Sandholm Pl. G14: Glas 4H **59**
Sandholm Ter. G14: Glas 4H **59**
Sandiefield Rd. G5: Glas 1G **103**
Sandielands Av. PA8: Ersk 2H **57**
Sandilands Cres. ML1: Moth 4D **142**
Sandilands St. G32: Glas 6B **86**
Sandmill St. G21: Glas 2C **84**
Sandpiper Dr. G75: E Kil 6C **148**
Sandpiper Pl. G75: E Kil 6C **148**
Sandpiper Way ML4: Bell 5A **110**
Sandra Rd. G64: B'rig 5E **49**
Sandringham Av. G77: Newt M 3G **133**
Sandringham Ct. G77: Newt M 4G **133**
Sandringham Dr. PA5: Eld 4H **95**
Sandwood G52: Glas 6A **80**
Sandwood Cres. G52: Glas 6A **80**
Sandwood Path G52: Glas. 6A **80**
Sandwood Rd. G52: Glas 1A **100**
Sandyfaulds Sq. G5: Glas 1G **103**
Sandyfaulds St. G5: Glas 1H **103**
Sandyford Av. ML1: N'hse 5D **112**
Sandyford Pl. *G3: Glas* *3C 82*
(off Claremont St.)
ML1: N'hse 6D **112**
Sandyford Pl. La. G3: Glas 3C **82**
Sandyford Rd. G3: Glas 3A **82**
ML1: N'hse 6D **112**
PA3: Pais 3C **78**
SANDYHILLS **1D 106**
Sandyhills Cres. G32: Glas 2B **106**
Sandyhills Dr. G32: Glas 2B **106**
Sandyhills Gro. G32: Glas 3B **106**
Sandyhills Pl. G32: Glas 2B **106**
Sandyhills Rd. G32: Glas 2B **106**
Sandyknowes Rd. G67: Cumb 5A **36**
Sandy La. G11: Glas 1G **81**
Sandy Rd. G11: Glas 1G **81**
ML8: Carl 3F **165**
PA4: Renf 2E **79**

Sannox Dr. ML1: Moth 2D **142**
Sannox Gdns. G31: Glas 3D **84**
Sanquhar Dr. G53: Glas 5A **100**
Sanquhar Gdns. G53: Glas 5A **100**
  G72: Blan 5H **123**
Sanquhar Pl. G53: Glas 5A **100**
Sanquhar Rd. G53: Glas 5A **100**
Sanson La. ML8: Carl. 5H **165**
Sapphire Rd. ML4: Bell. 4C **126**
Saracen Head La. G1: Glas. 5A **84**
Saracen St. G22: Glas 6G **63**
Sarazen Ct. ML1: Cle 1E **145**
Sardinia La. G12: Glas 6B **62**
Saskatoon Pl. G75: E Kil 2D **148**
Saucel Hill Ter. PA2: Pais 2A **98**
Saucel St. PA1: Pais. 1A **98**
Sauchiehall Cen. G2: Glas 3C **4**
Sauchiehall La. G2: Glas . . . 3E **83** (3A **4**)
  (not continuous)
Sauchiehall St. G3: Glas . . . 2B **82** (2A **4**)
Sauchiesmoor Rd. ML8: Carl . . . 5G **165**
Saughs Av. G33: Glas 3H **65**
Saughs Dr. G33: Glas 3H **65**
Saughs Ga. G33: Glas 3H **65**
Saughs Pl. G33: Glas 3H **65**
Saughs Rd. G33: Glas 3H **65**
  G33: Mille 3A **66**
Saughton St. G32: Glas 4G **85**
Saunders Ct. G78: Barr. 4D **114**
Savoy Cen. G2: Glas 3F **83** (3C **4**)
Savoy St. G40: Glas 1B **104**
Sawmillfield St. G4: Glas 1F **83**
Sawmill Rd. G11: Glas 1F **81**
Saxon Rd. G13: Glas 2D **60**
Scadlock Rd. PA3: Pais 5F **77**
Scalpay G74: E Kil 2C **150**
Scalpay Pas. G22: Glas 2H **63**
Scalpay Pl. G22: Glas 2H **63**
Scalpay St. G22: Glas 2G **63**
Scapa St. G23: Glas 1C **62**
Scapesland Ter. G82: Dumb 3G **17**
Scaraway Dr. G22: Glas 1H **63**
Scaraway Pl. G22: Glas 1H **63**
Scaraway St. G22: Glas 1G **63**
Scaraway Ter. G22: Glas 1H **63**
Scarba Dr. G43: Glas 2H **117**
Scarba Quad. ML2: Wis 2E **157**
Scarffe Av. PA3: Lin 6F **75**
Scarhill Av. ML6: Air 6H **91**
Scarhill La. ML6: Air 6A **92**
Scarhill St. ML1: Cle 5H **129**
  ML5: Coat. 2B **110**
Scarrel Dr. G45: Glas 3C **120**
Scarrel Gdns. G45: Glas 3C **120**
Scarrel Rd. G45: Glas 3C **120**
Scarrel Ter. G45: Glas 3C **120**
Scavaig Cres. G15: Glas 3G **43**
Schaw Ct. G61: Bear 1E **45**
Schaw Dr. G61: Bear 1D **44**
  G81: Faif 6G **23**
Schaw Rd. PA3: Pais 5C **78**
Scholar's Ga. G75: E Kil 5F **149**
Schoolhouse La. G72: Blan. 3A **140**
School La. G66: Len 3F **7**
  G66: Milt C 5C **8**
  G82: Dumb 3D **16**
  ML8: Carl 4E **165**
School Quad. ML6: Air 1H **91**
School Rd. G33: Step 3E **67**
  G64: Torr. 4E **29**
  G77: Newt M. 5D **132**
  ML2: Newm. 5F **147**
    (Morningside)
  ML2: Newm. 5E **147**
    (Newmains)
  PA1: Pais 6G **79**
School St. ML3: Ham 2H **153**
  ML5: Coat 1C **110**
  ML6: Chap 3D **112**
School Wynd PA1: Pais. 1A **98**
Scioncroft Av. G73: Ruth. 6E **105**
Scone Pl. G74: E Kil 6F **137**
  G77: Newt M. 5H **133**

Scone St. G21: Glas 6G **63**
Scone Wlk. G69: Bail. 2G **107**
Sconser PA8: Ersk 2G **57**
Sconser St. G23: Glas. 6C **46**
Scorton Gdns. G69: Bail 1F **107**
Scotcart Indoor Kart Racing
. . . . 1C **122**
Scotia Cres. ML9: Lark 4E **161**
Scotia Gdns. ML3: Ham 4G **153**
Scotia St. ML1: Moth 2E **143**
Scotland St. G5: Glas 6D **82**
Scotland Street School Mus. 6D **82**
Scotland St. W. G41: Glas 6B **82**
Scotsblair Av. G66: Kirk 1C **50**
Scotsburn Rd. G21: Glas. 5E **65**
SCOTSTOUN 5B **60**
Scotstoun Athletic Track 5C **60**
SCOTSTOUNHILL 3B **60**
Scotstounhill Station (Rail) 4B **60**
Scotstoun Leisure Cen. 5D **60**
Scotstoun St. G14: Glas 6C **60**
Scott Av. G60: Bowl 5B **20**
  G66: Milt C 5C **8**
  PA5: John 5E **95**
Scott Cres. G67: Cumb 6F **35**
Scott Dr. G61: Bear 1C **44**
  G67: Cumb 6F **35**
Scott Gro. ML3: Ham 1H **153**
Scott Hill G74: E Kil 6A **138**
Scott Ho. G67: Cumb 2A **36**
Scottish Enterprise Technology Pk.
  G75: E Kil 4A **150**
Scottish Exhibition & Conference Cen.
. . . . 4B **82**
Scottish Maritime Mus.
  Dumbarton 4F **17**
  Renfrew 6A **60**
Scottish National Football Mus.
. . . . 6F **103**
Scott Pl. ML4: Bell 6D **110**
  PA5: John 5E **95**
Scott Rd. G52: Hill 3H **79**
Scott's Pl. ML6: Air 3B **92**
Scott's Rd. PA2: Pais 2D **98**
Scott St. G3: Glas. 3E **83** (3B **4**)
  G69: Bail. 1H **107**
  G81: Clyd 3A **42**
  ML1: Moth 2G **143**
  ML3: Ham. 2H **153**
  ML9: Lark 3F **161**
SEAFAR 3G **35**
Seafar Rd. G67: Cumb 5G **35**
SEAFAR RDBT. 5G **35**
Seafield Av. G61: Bear 6F **25**
Seafield Cres. G68: Cumb 4A **34**
Seafield Dr. G73: Ruth 4F **121**
Seaforth Cres. G78: Barr 2D **114**
Seaforth La. G69: Mood 5E **53**
Seaforth Pl. ML4: Bell. 4B **126**
Seaforth Rd. G52: Hill. 4A **80**
  G81: Clyd 6D **42**
Seaforth Rd. Nth. G52: Hill 4A **80**
Seaforth Rd. Sth. G52: Hill 4A **80**
Seagrove St. G32: Glas 5F **85**
Seamill Gdns. G74: E Kil 1F **149**
Seamill Path G53: Glas 2H **115**
Seamill St. G53: Glas 2H **115**
Seamore St. G20: Glas 1D **82**
Seath Av. ML6: Air 4G **91**
Seath Rd. G73: Ruth. 4C **104**
Seath St. G42: Glas 3G **103**
Seaton Ter. ML3: Ham 5E **141**
Seaward Pl. G41: Glas 6D **82**
Seaward St. G41: Glas 6C **82**
  (not continuous)
SEAWARD ST. INTERCHANGE 6C **82**
Second Av. G33: Mille. 4B **66**
  G44: Glas 1F **119**
  G61: Bear 4F **45**
  G66: Auch. 6C **50**
  G71: Tann 4C **108**
  G81: Clyd 4B **42**
  G82: Dumb 3C **18**
  PA4: Renf 2E **79**

Second Av. La. G44: Glas 6F **103**
Second Gdns. G41: Glas. 1G **101**
Second Rd. G72: Blan. 4C **140**
Second St. G71: Tann 5D **108**
SEEDHILL 1C **98**
Seedhill PA1: Pais 1B **98**
Seedhill Rd. PA1: Pais 1B **98**
Seggielea La. G13: Glas. 3D **60**
  (off Helensburgh Dr.)
Seggielea Rd. G13: Glas 3D **60**
Seil Dr. G44: Glas 3F **119**
Selborne Pl. G13: Glas 4E **61**
Selborne Pl. La. G13: Glas 4E **61**
Selborne Rd. G13: Glas 4E **61**
Selby Gdns. G32: Glas 6D **86**
Selby Pl. ML5: Coat 1H **89**
Selby St. ML5: Coat 1H **89**
Selkirk Av. G52: Glas 1C **100**
  PA2: Pais 4E **97**
Selkirk Dr. G73: Ruth 6E **105**
Selkirk Pl. G74: E Kil 6D **138**
  ML3: Ham. 1A **154**
Selkirk St. G72: Blan 2B **140**
  ML2: Wis 4A **146**
  ML3: Ham. 1A **154**
Selkirk Way ML4: Bell 6D **110**
  ML5: Coat. 2G **111**
Sella Rd. G64: B'rig 5F **49**
Selvieland Rd. G52: Glas 6H **79**
Semphill Gdns. G74: E Kil 1B **150**
Sempie St. ML3: Ham 5D **140**
Sempill Av. PA8: Ersk. 5D **40**
Semple Av. PA7: B'ton 4H **39**
Semple Pl. PA3: Lin. 4H **75**
Senga Cres. ML4: Bell 6C **110**
Seres Rd. G76: Clar 1B **134**
Sergeantlaw Rd. PA2: Pais 6E **97**
Service St. G66: Len. 2E **7**
Seton Ter. G31: Glas. 4B **84**
Settle Gdns. G69: Bail. 1F **107**
Seven Sisters G66: Lenz 2E **51**
Seventh Av. G71: Tann 5D **108**
Seventh Rd. G72: Blan 4C **140**
Severn Rd. G75: E Kil 4B **148**
Seymour Grn. G75: E Kil. 3D **148**
Seyton Av. G46: Giff 6A **118**
Seyton Ct. G46: Giff 6A **118**
Seyton La. G74: E Kil 6G **137**
Shaftesbury Av. G81: Clyd 5B **42**
Shaftesbury Ct. G74: E Kil. 4C **138**
Shaftesbury Cres. ML1: N'hill 4D **128**
Shafton Pl. G13: Glas 1E **61**
Shafton Rd. G13: Glas 1E **61**
Shaftesbury St. G3: Glas 3D **82** (4A **4**)
  (not continuous)
Shakespeare Av. G81: Clyd. 3B **42**
Shakespeare St. G20: Glas 4C **62**
Shamrock St. G4: Glas 2E **83** (1B **4**)
  G66: Kirk 5D **30**
Shandon Cres. ML4: Bell 6C **110**
Shandon Ter. ML3: Ham 6D **140**
Shand Pl. ML8: Carl 2F **165**
Shand St. ML2: Wis 6H **145**
Shandwick Sq. G34: Glas 3G **87**
Shandwick St. G34: Glas 3G **87**
Shanks Av. G78: Barr 5E **115**
Shanks Cres. PA5: John 3E **95**
Shanks Pk. Ind. Est. G78: Barr . . . 3E **115**
Shanks St. G20: Glas 4C **62**
  ML6: Air 2A **92**
Shanks Way G78: Barr 2E **115**
Shannon St. G20: Glas 4D **62**
Shapinsay St. G22: Glas 1H **63**
Sharmanka Kinetic Gallery & Theatre
. . . . 5G **83**
  (off Trongate)
Sharp Av. ML5: Coat. 1G **109**
Sharp St. ML1: Moth 2D **142**
Shaw Av. PA7: B'ton 4A **40**
Shawbridge Arc. G43: Glas 5A **102**
Shawbridge Ind. Est.
  G43: Glas 6A **102**
Shawbridge St. G43: Glas. 6H **101**
Shawburn Cres. ML3: Ham 5F **141**

Shawburn St. ML3: Ham 5F **141**
Shaw Ct. G77: Newt M 5F **133**
PA8: Ersk 4D **40**
Shaw Cres. ML2: Wis. 2D **156**
SHAWFIELD **3B 104**
Shawfield Cres. ML8: Law 6D **158**
Shawfield Dr. G5: Glas 3A **104**
Shawfield Ind. Est. G73: Ruth 3B **104**
Shawfield Rd. G73: Ruth 3B **104**
Shawfield Stadium **3B 104**
Shawgill Ct. ML8: Law 1H **163**
SHAWHEAD **2B 110**
Shawhead Av. ML5: Coat 1D **110**
Shawhead Cotts. ML5: Coat 3D **110**
Shawhead Ind. Est. ML5: Coat 2E **111**
Shawhill Cres. G77: Newt M 6E **133**
Shawhill Rd. G41: Glas. 5A **102**
G43: Glas 5A **102**
Shawholm Cres. G43: Glas. 6H **101**
(not continuous)
SHAWLANDS **5C 102**
Shawlands Arc. G41: Glas 5B **102**
Shawlands Station (Rail) **5B 102**
Shawmoss Rd. G41: Glas 4A **102**
Shawpark St. G20: Glas 3C **62**
Shaw Pl. PA3: Lin. 6H **75**
Shawrigg Rd. ML9: Lark. 3G **161**
Shaw Rd. G62: Miln 5G **25**
G77: Newt M. 5E **133**
SHAWSBURN **3A 162**
Shaws Rd. ML9: Lark 6F **161**
Shaw St. G51: Glas 3G **81**
ML9: Lark 5F **161**
Shawwood Cres. G77: Newt M 6E **133**
Shearer Dr. ML3: Ham 4G **153**
Shears La. PA4: Renf 6F **59**
Sheddens Pl. G32: Glas 6G **85**
Sheepburn Rd. G71: Udd 6C **108**
Sheila St. G33: Glas. 5G **65**
Sheiling Hill ML3: Ham 5A **142**
Sheldaig Rd. G22: Glas. 1F **63**
Sheldrake Pl. PA5: John. 6D **94**
Shelley Ct. G12: Glas. 4G **61**
Shelley Dr. G71: Both 4F **125**
G81: Clyd 3C **42**
Shelley Rd. G12: Glas. 4F **61**
Shells Rd. G66: Kirk. 4E **31**
Sherbrooke Av. G41: Glas. 2A **102**
Sherbrooke Dr. G41: Glas 1A **102**
Sherbrooke Gdns. G41: Glas. 2A **102**
Sherbrooke Pl. G75: E Kil 2E **149**
Sherburn Gdns. G69: Bail 2F **107**
Sherdale Av. ML6: Chap. 3D **112**
Sheriff Pk. Av. G73: Ruth 6C **104**
Sherry Av. ML1: Holy 2H **127**
Sherry Dr. ML3: Ham 2E **153**
Sherry Hgts. G72: Camb. 1A **122**
Sherwood Av. G71: Udd 2E **125**
PA1: Pais 5C **78**
Sherwood Dr. G46: T'bnk 4G **117**
Sherwood Pl. G15: Glas 4B **44**
Shetland Dr. G44: Glas 3F **119**
SHETTLESTON **6B 86**
Shettleston Rd. G31: Glas. 5E **85**
Shettleston Station (Rail) **6B 86**
Shiel Av. G74: E Kil 6H **137**
Shielbridge Gdns. G23: Glas. 6C **46**
Shiel Ct. G78: Barr 2D **114**
Shieldaig Dr. G73: Ruth 3D **120**
Shieldburn Rd. G51: Glas. 4C **80**
SHIELDHALL **3C 80**
Shieldhall Gdns. G51: Glas. 4C **80**
Shieldhall Rd. G51: Glas 3B **80**
Shieldhill G75: E Kil 4H **149**
Shieldhill Rd. ML8: Carl 5E **165**
Shieldmuir Station (Rail) **5C 144**
Shieldmuir St. ML2: Wis 5C **144**
Shiel Dr. ML9: Lark 6H **155**
Shields Ct. ML1: Moth 6B **144**
Shields Dr. ML1: Moth 6B **144**
Shields Rd. G41: Glas. 3C **102**
G75: E Kil 6E **149**
ML1: Moth 5A **144**
Shields Rd. Station (Und.). **6D 82**
Shields Twr. ML1: Moth 6B **144**
Shiel Pl. G74: E Kil. 6H **137**
ML5: Coat 6F **91**
Shiel Rd. G64: B'rig 6D **48**
Shiel Ter. ML2: Newm 3D **146**
Shilford Av. G13: Glas. 2A **60**
Shillay St. G22: Glas 1A **64**
Shillingworth Pl. PA11: Bri W 5F **73**
Shilton Dr. G53: Glas 2C **116**
Shilton La. PA7: B'ton 3C **40**
Shinwell Av. G81: Clyd 6F **43**
Shipbank La. *G1: Glas 5G 83*
(off Clyde St.)
Shira Ter. G74: E Kil 2B **150**
Shirley Quad. ML1: Moth 6F **143**
SHIRREL **6C 110**
Shirrel Av. ML4: Bell. 6C **110**
Shirrel Rd. ML1: Holy. 3A **128**
Shirva Lea G65: Twe 1D **32**
Shiskine Pl. G20: Glas 1A **62**
Shiskine St. G20: Glas 1A **62**
Sholto Cres. ML4: Bell 6H **109**
Shore St. G40: Glas 3B **104**
Shortridge St. G20: Glas. 4C **62**
SHORTROODS **4A 78**
Shortroods Av. PA3: Pais 4H **77**
Shortroods Cres. PA3: Pais. 4H **77**
Shortroods Rd. PA3: Pais 4H **77**
Shotts St. G33: Glas. 3D **86**
Showcase Cinema (Kirkwood) . . . **1F 109**
Showcase Cinema (Paisley) **6C 76**
Shuna Pl. G20: Glas 4C **62**
G77: Newt M. 3B **132**
Shuna St. G20: Glas 3C **62**
Shuttle St. G1: Glas. 4H **83** (6G **5**)
G65: Kils. 3H **11**
PA1: Pais 1A **98**
PA10: Kilb. 1A **94**
Sidland Rd. G21: Glas 4E **65**
Sidlaw Av. G78: Barr. 6E **115**
ML3: Ham. 1D **152**
Sidlaw Ct. ML5: Coat 2E **111**
Sidlaw Dr. ML2: Wis. 6F **145**
Sidlaw Rd. G61: Bear 1B **44**
Sidlaw Way ML6: Chap 4F **113**
ML9: Lark. 6H **155**
Sielga Pl. G34: Glas. 3G **87**
Siemens Pl. G21: Glas 1D **84**
Siemens St. G21: Glas 1D **84**
Sievewright St. G73: Ruth 4E **105**
SIGHTHILL **1A 84**
Sighthill Loan *ML9: Lark. 1F 161*
(off Muirshot Rd.)
SIKESIDE **6F 91**
Sikeside Pl. ML5: Coat 6F **91**
Sikeside St. ML5: Coat 6F **91**
Silkin Av. G81: Clyd 6F **43**
Silk St. PA1: Pais 6B **78**
Silvan Pl. G76: Busby. 4E **135**
SILVERBANK **1G 121**
Silverburn Cres. ML1: N'hill 4D **128**
Silverburn St. G33: Glas. 3G **85**
Silverdale G74: E Kil. 6E **137**
Silverdale St. G40: Glas 1E **105**
Silverfir Ct. G5: Glas 1H **103**
Silver Firs ML1: N'hill. 4C **128**
Silverfir St. G5: Glas 2H **103**
Silver Glade G52: Glas 1B **100**
Silvergrove St. G40: Glas 1A **104**
SILVERTON **4H 17**
Silverton Av. G82: Dumb 4H **17**
SILVERTONHILL **1B 154**
Silvertonhill Av. ML3: Ham. 3A **154**
Silvertonhill La. G82: Dumb. 4H **17**
Silvertonhill Pl. ML3: Ham. 4H **153**
SILVERWELLS **6E 125**
Silverwells G71: Both 6F **125**
Silverwells Ct. G71: Both 6E **125**
Silverwells Cres. G71: Both 6E **125**
Silverwood Ct. G71: Both 6F **125**
Simons Cres. PA4: Renf 4F **59**
Simpson Ct. G71: Udd 1D **124**
G81: Clyd 5C **42**
Simpson Dr. G75: E Kil 4F **149**
Simpson Gdns. G78: Barr. 5D **114**
Simpson Hgts. *G4: Glas 4A 84*
(off John Knox St.)
Simpson Pl. G75: E Kil 4F **149**
Simpson St. G20: Glas 6D **62**
Simpson Way ML4: Bell 6E **111**
Simshill Rd. G44: Glas 4F **119**
Sinclair Av. G61: Bear. 1E **45**
Sinclair Dr. G42: Glas. 6D **102**
ML5: Coat. 4H **89**
Sinclair Gdns. G64: B'rig 1D **64**
Sinclair Gro. ML4: Bell 5B **126**
Sinclair Pk. G75: E Kil 3H **149**
Sinclair Pl. G75: E Kil. 3H **149**
Sinclair St. G62: Miln. 3G **25**
G81: Clyd 1F **59**
Singer Rd. G75: E Kil 5H **149**
G81: Clyd 4B **42**
Singer Station (Rail). **5D 42**
Singer St. G81: Clyd. 4D **42**
Sir Matt Busby Sports Complex . . . **2B 126**
Sir Michael Pl. PA1: Pais 1H **97**
Sixth Av. PA4: Renf. 2E **79**
Sixth St. G71: Tann. 4C **108**
Skaethorn Rd. G20: Glas 2H **61**
Skara Wlk. *ML2: Newm 2D 146*
(off Kildonan Ct.)
Skaterigg Dr. G13: Glas. 4F **61**
Skaterigg Gdns. G13: Glas 4F **61**
Skaterigg La. *G13: Glas 4E 61*
(off Chamberlain Rd.)
Skelbo Path G34: Glas 2B **88**
Skelbo Pl. G34: Glas. 2B **88**
Skellyton Cres. ML9: Lark. 3F **161**
Skene Rd. G51: Glas 6H **81**
Skerne Gro. G75: E Kil 5B **148**
Skerray Quad. G22: Glas 1G **63**
Skerray St. G22: Glas. 1G **63**
Skerryvore Pl. G33: Glas 3B **86**
Skerryvore Rd. G33: Glas 3B **86**
Skibo La. G46: T'bnk 4E **117**
Skipness Av. ML8: Carl. 5G **165**
Skipness Dr. G51: Glas. 4D **80**
Skirsa Ct. G23: Glas 1E **63**
Skirsa Pl. G23: Glas. 2D **62**
Skirsa Sq. G23: Glas. 2E **63**
Skirsa St. G23: Glas. 1D **62**
Skirving St. G41: Glas 5C **102**
Skovlunde Way G75: E Kil 5G **149**
Skye G74: E Kil. 2C **150**
Skye Av. PA4: Renf. 2E **79**
Skye Ct. G67: Cumb 5F **35**
Skye Cres. G60: Old K 2G **41**
PA2: Pais 6H **97**
Skye Dr. G60: Old K 2G **41**
G67: Cumb 5F **35**
Skye Gdns. G61: Bear. 1B **44**
Skye Pl. G67: Cumb 5F **35**
Skye Quad. ML2: Wis 4C **146**
Skye Rd. G67: Cumb. 5F **35**
G73: Ruth 4F **121**
Skye Wynd ML3: Ham 2D **152**
Slakiewood Av. G69: G'csh. 2C **68**
Slatefield G66: Len. 3F **7**
Slatefield Ct. *G31: Glas 5C 84*
(off Slatefield St.)
Slatefield St. G31: Glas 5C **84**
Sleaford Av. ML1: Moth 5F **143**
Slenavon Av. G73: Ruth 4F **121**
Slessor Dr. G75: E Kil. 4G **149**
Slioch Sq. ML1: N'hill. 3C **128**
Sloy St. G22: Glas 5H **63**
ML2: Wis 2G **157**
Small Cres. G72: Blan 2B **140**
Sma'Shot Cottages. **1A 98**
Smeaton Av. G64: Torr 5D **28**
Smeaton Dr. G64: B'rig. 3C **48**
Smeaton St. G20: Glas. 3D **62**
Smith Av. ML2: Wis 4G **157**
Smith Cres. G81: Hard 2D **42**
Smithhills St. PA1: Pais 6A **78**
Smith Pk. Pl. G76: Busby. 4D **134**
Smith Quad. ML5: Coat. 4E **91**
Smith's La. PA3: Pais 5A **78**

SMITHSTONE 2B 34
Smithstone Cres. G65: Croy 6A 12
Smithstone Rd. G68: Cumb 3B 34
Smith St. G14: Glas 1E 81
(not continuous)
Smith Ter. G73: Ruth 4D 104
Smithview ML2: Over 4A 158
Smithycroft ML3: Ham 1C 154
Smithycroft Rd. G33: Glas 3F 85
Smithyends G67: Cumb 6B 14
Smollett Rd. G82: Dumb 4H 17
Snaefell Av. G73: Ruth 3E 121
Snaefell Cres. G73: Ruth 2E 121
Snead Vw. ML1: Cle 6E 129
Sneddon Av. ML2: Wis 2A 158
Sneddon St. ML3: Ham 3D 140
Sneddon Ter. ML3: Ham 3D 140
Snowdon Pl. G5: Glas 1H 103
Snowdon St. G5: Glas 1H 103
Snuff Mill Rd. G44: Glas 2E 119
Society St. G31: Glas 6D 84
Solar Ct. ML9: Lark 5F 161
Sollas Pl. G13: Glas 1G 59
Solsgirth Gdns. G66: Kirk 4H 31
Solway Ct. ML3: Ham 3F 153
Solway Pl. G69: Chry 6B 52
Solway Rd. G64: B'rig 5F 49
Solway St. G40: Glas 3B 104
Somerford Rd. G61: Bear 6F 45
Somerled Av. PA3: Pais 2B 78
Somerset Av. ML3: Ham 5F 141
Somerset Pl. G3: Glas 2D 82
Somerset Pl. M. *G3: Glas 2D 82*
(off Somerset Pl.)
Somervell St. G72: Camb 1H 121
Somerville Dr. G42: Glas 5F 103
G75: E Kil 4G 149
Somerville La. G75: E Kil 4H 149
Somerville Ter. G75: E Kil 4G 149
Sorby St. G31: Glas 6F 85
Sorley St. G11: Glas 1F 81
Sorn St. G40: Glas 2D 104
Souterhouse Path ML5: Coat 6B 90
Souterhouse Rd. ML5: Coat 6B 90
Southampton Dr. G12: Glas 3H 61
Southampton La. *G12: Glas 3H 61*
(off Burlington Av.)
Sth. Annandale St. G42: Glas 3F 103
South Av. G72: Blan 4B 140
G81: Clyd 5C 42
ML8: Carl 4E 165
PA2: Pais 5B 98
PA4: Renf 6F 59
Southbank Bus. Pk. G66: Kirk 6C 30
Southbank Dr. G66: Kirk 6C 30
Southbank Rd. G66: Kirk 6B 30
Southbank St. G31: Glas 6F 85
Sth. Bank St. G81: Clyd 2E 59
SOUTHBAR 1E 57
Southbar Av. G13: Glas 2A 60
Southbar Rd. PA4: Inch 3E 57
SOUTH BARRWOOD 4A 12
Sth. Barrwood Rd. G65: Kils 4A 12
Sth. Biggar Rd. ML6: Air 4B 92
South Brae G66: Len 5E 7
Southbrae Av. PA11: Bri W 4D 72
Southbrae Dr. G13: Glas 4C 60
Southbrae La. *G13: Glas 4E 61*
(off Selborne Rd.)
Sth. Bridge St. ML6: Air 3A 92
Sth. Burn Rd. ML6: Air 4F 91
Sth. Caldeen Rd. ML5: Coat 6D 90
Sth. Calder ML1: Moth 1H 143
Sth. Campbell St. PA2: Pais 2A 98
Sth. Carbrain Rd. G67: Cumb 5H 35
SOUTH CARDONALD 1C 100
Sth. Chester St. G32: Glas 6A 86
Sth. Circular Rd. ML5: Coat 4C 90
Sth. Claremont La. G62: Miln 4G 25
Sth. Commonhead Av. ML6: Air 2H 91
Southcroft Rd. G73: Ruth 4A 104
Southcroft St. G51: Glas 4H 81
Sth. Crosshill Rd. G64: B'rig 6C 48
Sth. Dean Pk. Av. G71: Both 5E 125
Southdeen Av. G15: Glas 4A 44
Southdeen Rd. G15: Glas 4A 44
Sth. Douglas St. G81: Clyd 1E 59
South Dr. PA3: Lin 5H 75
Sth. Dumbreck Rd. G65: Kils 3F 11
Sth. Elgin Pl. G81: Clyd 2E 59
Sth. Elgin St. G81: Clyd 2E 59
Southend Pl. ML4: Bell 3B 126
Southend Rd. G81: Hard 2D 42
Southern Av. G73: Ruth 2D 120
Southerness Dr. G68: Cumb 6A 14
Sth. Erskine Pk. G61: Bear 2D 44
Southesk Av. G64: B'rig 4B 48
Southesk Gdns. G64: B'rig 4B 48
Sth. Exchange Ct. G1: Glas 6E 5
Southfield Av. PA2: Pais 5A 98
Southfield Cres. G53: Glas 5C 100
ML5: Coat 6E 91
Southfield Rd. G68: Cumb 4E 35
Sth. Frederick St. G1: Glas 4G 83 (5F 5)
Southgate G62: Miln 4G 25
G74: E Kil 2G 149
(off Olympia Ct.)
Sth. Glassford St. G62: Miln 4H 25
Southhill Av. G73: Ruth 1E 121
Southinch Av. G14: Glas 3G 59
Southlea Av. G46: T'bnk 4G 117
South Loan G69: Chry 1B 68
Southloch Gdns. G21: Glas 6B 64
Southloch St. G21: Glas 6B 64
Sth. Mains Rd. G62: Miln 4F 25
Sth. Medrox St. ML5: Glenb 2G 69
Sth. Moraine La. G15: Glas 5C 44
South Mound PA6: Hous 1A 74
Sth. Muirhead Rd. G67: Cumb 3A 36
Southmuir Pl. G20: Glas 4B 62
Sth. Nimmo St. ML6: Air 4B 92
SOUTH NITSHILL 3A 116
South Pk. ML3: Ham 1H 153
Southpark Av. G12: Glas 1B 82
Sth. Park Av. G78: Barr 4D 114
Sth. Park Dr. PA2: Pais 3A 98
Sth. Park Gro. ML3: Ham 6H 141
Sth. Park La. G12: Glas 1C 82
Sth. Park Ter. G12: Glas 1C 82
South Pl. ML4: Bell 3B 126
South Portland St. G5: Glas 5F 83
Sth. Portland St. G5: Glas 6F 83
(not continuous)
South Rd. G76: Busby 4E 135
Sth. Robertson Pl. ML6: Air 4G 91
Sth. Scott St. G69: Bail 1H 107
Southside Cres. G5: Glas 1G 103
Sth. Spiers Wharf G4: Glas 1F 83 (1D 4)
South St. G14: Glas 5A 60
PA4: Inch 5F 57
PA6: Hous 1A 74
Sth. Vesalius St. G32: Glas 6A 86
South Vw. G72: Blan 6A 124
G81: Clyd 4B 42
ML4: Bell 3A 126
Southview Av. G76: Busby 4D 134
Southview Ct. G64: B'rig 2B 64
Southview Cres. PA11: Bri W 2F 73
Southview Dr. G61: Bear 2C 44
Southview Pl. G69: G'csh 3C 68
Southview Ter. G64: B'rig 2B 64
Sth. William St. PA5: John 3F 95
Southwold Rd. PA1: Pais 6G 79
Southwood Dr. G44: Glas 2G 119
Sth. Woodside Rd. G20: Glas 6D 62
G4: Glas 1C 82
Soutra Pl. G33: Glas 3B 86
Sovereigns Ga. G71: Both 5C 124
Spalehall Dr. ML1: N'hill 4F 129
SPATESTON 6C 94
Spateston Rd. PA5: John 6C 94
Spean Av. G74: E Kil 2B 150
Spean St. G44: Glas 6E 103
Spectrum Ho. G81: Clyd 5D 42
Speirsfield Ct. PA1: Pais 2H 97
Speirsfield Gdns. PA2: Pais 2A 98
Speirshall Cl. G14: Glas 4H 59
Speirshall Ter. G14: Glas 3G 59
Speirs Rd. G61: Bear 4G 45
PA5: John 2H 95
Spencer Dr. PA2: Pais 5B 96
Spencerfield Gdns. ML3: Ham 6B 142
Spencer St. G13: Glas 2F 61
G81: Clyd 4C 42
Spence St. G20: Glas 1A 62
Spey Av. PA2: Pais 5C 96
Spey Ct. ML2: Newm 3D 146
ML6: Air 6C 92
Spey Dr. ML5: Coat 1A 110
PA4: Renf 1G 79
Spey Gdns. ML3: Ham 3F 153
Spey Gro. G75: E Kil 4A 148
Spey Pl. PA5: John 5C 94
Spey Rd. G61: Bear 5C 44
Spey St. G33: Glas 3H 85
Spey Ter. G75: E Kil 4B 148
Spey Wlk. *G67: Cumb 4H 35*
(in Cumbernauld Shop. Cen.)
ML1: Holy 1C 128
Spey Wynd ML9: Lark 5E 161
Spiersbridge Av. G46: T'bnk 5E 117
(Nitshill Rd.)
G46: T'bnk 4F 117
(Spiersbridge Rd.)
Spiersbridge Bus. Pk.
G46: T'bnk 4E 117
Spiersbridge La. G46: T'bnk 4E 117
Spiersbridge Rd. G46: T'bnk 5F 117
Spiersbridge Ter. G46: T'bnk 4E 117
Spiers Gro. G46: T'bnk 4F 117
Spiers Pl. PA3: Lin 4A 76
Spiers Rd. G61: Bear 4H 45
PA6: Hous 1B 74
Spiers Wharf G4: Glas 1F 83 (1D 4)
Spindlehowe Rd. G71: Tann 1E 125
G71: Udd 2D 124
Spinners Gdns. PA2: Pais 2F 97
Spinners La. G81: Hard 6D 22
SPITTAL 2B 120
Spittal Rd. G73: Ruth 3B 120
Spittal Ter. G72: Flem 5H 123
Spoolers Rd. PA1: Pais 2F 97
Spoutmouth G1: Glas 5H 83
Springbank Rd. PA3: Pais 4H 77
Springbank St. G20: Glas 5D 62
Springbank Ter. PA3: Pais 4H 77
SPRINGBOIG 5C 86
Springboig Av. G32: Glas 5C 86
Springboig Rd. G32: Glas 4C 86
SPRINGBURN 5B 64
Springburn Leisure Cen. 5B 64
Springburn Mus. *5B 64*
(off Ayr St.)
Springburn Pl. G74: E Kil 6C 136
Springburn Rd. G21: Glas 2A 84
Springburn Shop. Cen. G21: Glas 5B 64
Springburn Station (Rail) 5B 64
Springburn Way G21: Glas 5A 64
Springcroft Av. G69: Bail 5H 87
Springcroft Cres. G69: Bail 5H 87
Springcroft Dr. G69: Bail 5G 87
Springcroft Gdns. G69: Bail 5A 88
Springcroft Gro. G69: Bail 5H 87
Springcroft Wynd G69: Bail 5H 87
Springfield Av. G64: B'rig 1C 64
G71: Udd 2D 124
PA1: Pais 1D 98
Springfield Ct. G1: Glas 4G 83 (6E 5)
G64: B'rig 6D 48
Springfield Cres. G64: B'rig 1C 64
G71: Udd 2D 124
G72: Blan 2A 140
ML8: Carl 5F 165
Springfield Dr. G78: Barr 6G 115
Springfield Gro. G78: Barr 6F 115
Springfield Pk. PA5: John 3G 95
Springfield Pk. Rd. G73: Ruth 1E 121
Springfield Quay G5: Glas 5D 82
Springfield Rd. G31: Glas 1E 105
G40: Glas 2C 104
G64: B'rig 6C 48
G67: Cumb 1A 36

Springfield Rd. G78: Barr, Neil 2F **131**
  ML6: Air 3E **93**
Springfield Sq. G64: B'rig. 1C **64**
Springfield Woods PA5: John 3G **95**
SPRINGHALL 3F **121**
Springhall Ct. G73: Ruth. 4F **121**
  (off Slenavon Av.)
SPRINGHILL 1G **131**
Springhill Av. ML5: Coat. 1G **109**
  ML6: Air 3B **92**
Springhill Dr. Sth. G68: Bail 5G **87**
Springhill Farm Gro. G69: Bail 5G **87**
Springhill Farm Pl. G69: Bail 5G **87**
Springhill Farm Rd. G69: Bail. 5G **87**
Springhill Farm Way
  G69: Bail. 5G **87**
Springhill Gdns. G41: Glas 4C **102**
Springhill Parkway G69: Bail 5G **87**
Springhill Pl. ML5: Coat. 1G **109**
Springhill Rd. G69: Bail 6F **87**
  G76: Busby 2D **134**
  G78: Barr 5D **114**
  G78: Neil. 4G **131**
Springholm Dr. ML6: Air 1H **91**
Springkell Av. G41: Glas. 2H **101**
Springkell Dr. G41: Glas. 3H **101**
Springkell Gdns. G41: Glas 3B **102**
Springkell Ga. G41: Glas 3B **102**
Springside Gdns. G15: Glas 3A **44**
Springside Pl. G15: Glas 3A **44**
Springvale Dr. PA2: Pais 3D **96**
Springvale Ter. G21: Glas 5A **64**
SPRINGWELL 4D **122**
Springwell Cres. G72: Blan. 2D **140**
SPRINGWELLS 3D **140**
Springwells Av. ML6: Air. 3C **92**
Springwells Cres. ML6: Air. 3C **92**
Spruce Av. G72: Blan 1A **140**
  ML3: Ham. 1A **154**
  PA5: John 4G **95**
Spruce Ct. ML3: Ham 2A **154**
  ML5: Coat. 1B **110**
Spruce Dr. G66: Lenz 2A **50**
  G72: Flem 3F **123**
Spruce Rd. G67: Cumb. 1D **36**
Spruce St. G22: Glas 4H **63**
Spruce Way G72: Flem 3F **123**
  ML1: Holy 3B **128**
Spynie Pl. G64: B'rig. 5F **49**
Spynie Way ML2: Newm. 3D **146**
  (off Iona Rd.)
Squire St. G14: Glas. 1D **80**
Sraehouse Wynd ML8: Carl 4H **165**
Stabcross Bus. Pk. G3: Glas 3C **82**
  (off St Vincent Cres.)
Stable Gro. PA1: Pais 2F **97**
Stable Pl. G62: Miln 2F **25**
Stable Rd. G62: Miln. 2F **25**
Staffa G74: E Kil 3C **150**
Staffa Av. PA4: Renf 2E **79**
Staffa Dr. G66: Kirk 5H **31**
  ML6: Air 4F **93**
  PA2: Pais 6A **98**
Staffa Rd. G72: Camb. 4H **121**
Staffa St. G31: Glas 3D **84**
Staffin Dr. G23: Glas. 6B **46**
Staffin Path G23: Glas 6C **46**
  (off Staffin St.)
Staffin St. G23: Glas. 6C **46**
Stafford St. G4: Glas 2G **83** (2G **5**)
  ML4: Bell 3B **126**
Stag Ct. G71: View 1G **125**
Stag St. G51: Glas 4H **81**
Staig Wynd ML1: Moth 5A **144**
Staineybraes Pl. ML6: Air 1H **91**
Stalker St. ML2: Wis 5C **144**
Stamford St. G31: Glas. 6D **84**
  G40: Glas 6D **84**
STAMPERLAND 6D **118**
Stamperland Av. G76: Clar 2D **134**
Stamperland Cres. G76: Clar 1C **134**
Stamperland Dr. G76: Clar 2D **134**
Stamperland Gdns. G76: Clar 6D **118**

Stamperland Hill G76: Clar. 1C **134**
Stanalane St. G46: T'bnk 3F **117**
Standburn Rd. G21: Glas. 2F **65**
Stand Comedy Club, The 1C **82**
Standford Hall G72: Camb 1A **122**
  (off Main St.)
Staneacre Pk. ML3: Ham 6B **142**

Stanecraigs Pl.
  ML2: Newm 3D **146**
Stanefield Dr. ML1: N'hill 3E **129**
Stanely Av. PA2: Pais. 5F **97**
Stanely Cres. PA2: Pais 5F **97**
Stanely Dr. PA2: Pais. 4G **97**
Stanely Rd. PA2: Pais. 4G **97**
Stanford St. G81: Clyd 6E **43**
Stanhope Dr. G73: Ruth 2F **121**
Stanhope Pl. ML2: Wis. 4G **157**
Stanistone Rd. ML8: Carl 3G **165**
Stanka Av. PA2: Pais 2G **97**
STANLEY 4G **97**
Stanley Blvd. G72: Blan 5B **140**
Stanley Dr. G64: B'rig. 5D **48**
  ML4: Bell 1C **126**
  PA5: Brkfld 6C **74**
Stanley Gro. PA2: Pais 5F **97**
Stanley La. PA5: Brkfld. 6C **74**
Stanley Pk. ML6: Air. 3B **92**
Stanley Pl. G72: Blan 6B **124**
Stanley Rd. PA2: Pais. 3H **97**
Stanley St. G41: Glas 6C **82**
  ML3: Ham. 5D **140**
Stanley St. La. G41: Glas 6C **82**
Stanmore Rd. G42: Glas 5F **103**
Stanrigg St. ML6: Plain 1G **93**
Stark Av. G81: Dun 1A **42**
Starling Way ML4: Bell 5A **110**
Startpoint St. G33: Glas 3A **86**
Station Brae G78: Neil 1C **130**
Station Bldgs. G67: Cumb 5A **36**
Station Cres. PA4: Renf 5G **59**
Station Pk. G69: Bail. 1A **108**
Station Pl. ML8: Law 5E **159**
Station Rd. G20: Glas 1A **62**
  G33: Mille 4A **66**
  G33: Step 4D **66**
  G46: Giff 4A **118**
  G60: Old K 1F **41**
  G61: Bear 3C **44**
  G62: Bard 6E **27**
  G62: Miln 3G **25**
  G65: Kils. 2H **11**
  G66: Len 3F **7**
  G69: Bail. 1A **108**
  G69: Muirh. 2A **68**
  G71: Both 5E **125**
  G71: Udd 1C **124**
  G72: Blan 1C **140**
  G76: Busby 4E **135**
  G78: Neil. 2D **130**
  G82: Dumb 3E **17**
  ML1: Cle. 6H **129**
  ML1: New S 4B **128**
  ML2: Wis 1G **157**
  ML6: Air 3E **93**
  ML6: Plain 1H **93**
  ML8: Carl 4E **165**
  ML8: Law 6D **158**
  ML9: Lark 1F **161**
  PA1: Pais 2E **97**
  PA10: Kilb. 3A **94**
  PA11: Bri W 4G **73**
  PA4: Renf 5F **59**
  PA7: B'ton 5H **39**
Station Row ML8: Law 5E **159**
Station Way G71: Udd 1D **124**
Station Wynd PA10: Kilb. 3B **94**
Staybrae Dr. G53: Glas. 4H **99**
Staybrae Gro. G53: Glas 4H **99**
Steading, The ML2: Wis 4H **145**
Steel St. G1: Glas 5H **83**
  ML2: Wis 1H **157**
Steeple Sq. PA10: Kilb 2A **94**
Steeple St. PA10: Kilb 2A **94**
Stemac La. ML6: Plain 1G **93**

Stenhouse Av. G69: Muirh 2A **68**
Stenton Cres. ML2: Wis 2D **156**
Stenton Pl. ML2: Wis 2D **156**
Stenton St. G32: Glas 4G **85**
Stepends Rd. ML6: Air 5H **93**
Stepford Path G33: Glas 4G **87**
Stepford Pl. G33: Glas 4F **87**
Stepford Rd. G33: Glas 4F **87**
Stepford Sports Pk. 5G **87**
Stephen Cres. G69: Bail 6F **87**
Stephenson Pl. G75: E Kil 3F **149**
Stephenson Sq. G75: E Kil 3F **149**
Stephenson St. G52: Hill 3G **79**
Stephenson Ter. G75: E Kil 3F **149**
STEPPS 4C **66**
Steppshill Ter. G33: Step 4C **66**
Stepps Rd. G33: Glas 2C **86**
  G66: Auch. 5E **51**
STEPPS RD. INTERCHANGE 2C **86**
Stepps Station (Rail). 4E **67**
Stevens La. ML1: New S 4A **128**
Stevenson Pl. ML4: Bell 6D **110**
Stevenson St. G40: Glas 5A **84**
  (not continuous)
  G81: Clyd 3B **42**
  ML8: Carl 3E **165**
  PA2: Pais 2A **98**
Stevenston Ct. ML1: New S 3A **128**
Stevenston St. ML1: New S 3A **128**
Stewart Av. G72: Blan 2A **140**
  G77: Newt M 3E **133**
  PA4: Renf 2D **78**
Stewart Ct. G73: Ruth 6E **105**
  G78: Barr 3E **115**
  ML5: Coat. 5E **91**
  (off Clifton Pl.)
Stewart Cres. G78: Barr 3F **115**
  ML2: Newm. 3E **147**
Stewart Dr. G69: Barg 5F **89**
  G76: Clar. 1B **134**
  G81: Hard 1D **42**
STEWARTFIELD 5E **137**
Stewartfield Dr. G74: E Kil 5F **137**
Stewartfield Rd. G74: E Kil 6E **137**
Stewartfield Way G74: E Kil 6A **136**
Stewart Gdns. ML5: Coat 4E **91**
Stewart Gill Pl. ML9: Ashg. 4B **162**
Stewarton Dr. G72: Camb 2G **121**
Stewarton Ho. ML2: Wis. 1H **157**
  (off Stewarton St.)
Stewarton Rd. G46: T'bnk. 6D **116**
  G77: Newt M 4A **132**
Stewarton St. ML2: Wis 1H **157**
Stewarton Ter. ML2: Wis 1H **157**
Stewart Pl. G78: Barr 3F **115**
  ML8: Carl 3F **165**
Stewart Quad. ML1: Holy 1B **128**
Stewart Rd. PA2: Pais. 5B **98**
Stewarts La. ML2: Wis 6A **146**
Stewart St. G4: Glas. 2F **83** (1D **4**)
  G62: Miln 4G **25**
  G78: Barr. 3F **115**
  G81: Clyd 4A **42**
  ML3: Ham. 4E **141**
  (not continuous)
  ML4: Moss 2E **127**
  ML5: Coat. 3C **90**
  ML8: Carl 2E **165**
Stewartville St. G11: Glas 1H **81**
Stirling Av. G61: Bear 5E **45**
Stirling Dr. G61: Bear 1D **44**
  G64: B'rig 4A **48**
  G73: Ruth 2D **120**
  G74: E Kil 6A **138**
  ML3: Ham. 5C **140**
  PA3: Lin 6F **75**
  PA5: John 3D **94**
Stirlingfauld Pl. G5: Glas 6F **83**
Stirling Gdns. G64: B'rig 4A **48**
Stirling Ho. G81: Clyd 5D **42**
Stirling Pl. G66: Len 3G **7**
Stirling Rd. G4: Glas 3H **83** (4H **5**)
  G65: Kils. 2A **12**
  G66: Kirk 4D **30**

Stirling Rd. G82: Dumb, Milt 1G **17**
ML6: Air, Rigg. 1B **92**
ML6: Chap 1D **112**
ML8: Carl 1E **165**
Stirling Rd. Ind. Est.
ML6: Air 1B **92**
Stirling St. G67: Cumb 1B **36**
ML1: Moth 5B **144**
ML5: Coat. 1H **109**
ML6: Air 4H **91**
Stirling Way G69: Bail 1G **107**
PA4: Renf 2F **79**
Stirrat St. G20: Glas 3A **62**
PA3: Pais. 4F **77**
Stobcross Rd. G3: Glas. 3A **82**
Stobcross St. G3: Glas 4C **82** (5A **4**)
ML5: Coat. 5C **90**
Stobcross Wynd G3: Glas 4B **82**
Stobhill Cotts. G21: Glas 2C **64**
Stobhill Rd. G21: Glas 2B **64**
Stobo G74: E Kil 5C **138**
Stobo Ct. G74: E Kil 5C **138**
Stobo St. ML2: Wis. 4A **146**
Stobs Dr. G78: Barr 2D **114**
Stobs Pl. G34: Glas 2A **88**
Stock Av. PA2: Pais. 2A **98**
Stock Exchange G2: Glas 5E **5**
Stockholm Cres. PA2: Pais 2A **98**
Stockiemuir Av. G61: Bear 6D **24**
Stockiemuir Ct. G61: Bear. 6E **25**
Stockiemuir Rd. G61: Bear 1D **44**
G62: Miln 3C **24**
Stocks Rd. ML1: Cle 1D **146**
Stock St. PA2: Pais 3A **98**
Stockwell Pl. G1: Glas 5G **83**
Stockwell St. G1: Glas 5G **83** (6F **5**)
Stoddard Sq. PA5: Eld 2B **96**
Stonebyres Ct. ML3: Ham 6E **141**
Stonecraig Rd. ML2: Wis 1H **157**
Stonedyke Cres. ML8: Carl 2G **165**
Stonedyke Gro. G15: Glas. 5B **44**
Stonedyke Rd. ML8: Carl 2G **165**
STONEFIELD **1C 140**
Stonefield Av. G12: Glas. 3A **62**
PA2: Pais 4B **98**
Stonefield Cres. G72: Blan 3A **140**
G76: Clar. 1A **134**
PA2: Pais 4B **98**
Stonefield Dr. PA2: Pais 4B **98**
Stonefield Gdns. ML8: Carl 2F **165**
PA2: Pais 4B **98**
Stonefield Grn. PA2: Pais 4A **98**
Stonefield Gro. PA2: Pais 4A **98**
Stonefield Pk. PA2: Pais 5A **98**
Stonefield Pk. Gdns.
G72: Blan 1C **140**
Stonefield Pl. G72: Blan 3H **139**
Stonefield Rd. G72: Blan 2A **140**
Stonefield St. ML6: Air 2A **92**
Stonehall Av. ML3: Ham 1F **153**
Stonehaven Cres. ML6: Air. 6G **91**
Stonelaw Dr. G73: Ruth 6D **104**
Stonelaw Rd. G73: Ruth. 6D **104**
Stonelaw Towers G73: Ruth 1E **121**
Stoneside Dr. G43: Glas 1G **117**
Stoneside Sq. G43: Glas. 1G **117**
Stoney Brae PA2: Pais 5A **98**
(not continuous)
Stoneyetts Rd. G69: Mood 4D **52**
Stoneymeadow Rd. G72: Blan. 3E **139**
G74: E Kil 5B **138**
Stony Brae PA1: Pais 6A **78**
PA3: Pais 6A **78**
Stonyflatt Av. G82: Dumb 2H **17**
Stonyflatt Rd. G82: Dumb. 2H **17**
Stonyhurst St. G22: Glas 5F **63**
(not continuous)
Stonylee Rd. G67: Cumb 4A **36**
Storie St. PA1: Pais 1A **98**
(not continuous)
Stormyland Way G78: Barr 5E **115**
Stornoway Cres. ML2: Wis 4C **146**
Stornoway St. G22: Glas. 1G **63**
Stow Brae PA1: Pais 1A **98**
Stow St. PA1: Pais 1A **98**
Strachan St. ML4: Bell 3C **126**
Strachur St. G22: Glas 2E **63**
Strain Cres. ML6: Air 5B **92**
Straiton Dr. ML3: Ham 1B **152**
Straiton Pl. G72: Blan. 1B **140**
Straiton St. G32: Glas. 4G **85**
Stranraer Dr. G15: Glas 5C **44**
Stratford G74: E Kil. 4D **138**
Stratford St. G20: Glas 4B **62**
Strathallan Gdns. *G66: Kirk 5D* ***30***
(off Willowbank Gdns.)
Strathallon Pl. *G73: Ruth 4F* ***121***
(off St Stephen's Av.)
Strathaven Rd. G75: E Kil 3A **150**
ML3: Ham. 6G **153**
Strathavon Cres. ML6: Air 1A **92**
Strathblane Cres. ML6: Air. 6H **71**
Strathblane Dr. G75: E Kil. 3A **148**
Strathblane Rd. G62: Miln 3H **25**
G66: Cam G 1A **6**
Strathbran St. G31: Glas 1F **105**
STRATHBUNGO **3D 102**
Strathcairn Cres. ML6: Air 6H **71**
Strath Carron ML8: Law 6E **159**
Strathcarron Cres. PA2: Pais 5D **98**
Strathcarron Dr. PA2: Pais 4D **98**
Strathcarron Pl. G20: Glas 3B **62**
PA2: Pais 5D **98**
Strathcarron Rd. PA2: Pais. 5D **98**
Strathcarron Way PA2: Pais 4D **98**
Strathclyde Arts Cen. **6A 4**
Strathclyde Bus. Cen.
G72: Flem 4E **123**
Strathclyde Bus. Pk. ML4: Bell 5A **110**
Strathclyde Country Pk. **1A 142**
Strathclyde Dr. G73: Ruth. 6C **104**
Strathclyde Homes Stadium **5G 17**
Strathclyde Path G71: Udd 1C **124**
Strathclyde Rd. G82: Dumb 2G **17**
ML1: Moth 3D **142**
Strathclyde St. G40: Glas 3C **104**
Strathclyde Vw. G71: Both 6F **125**
Strathcona Dr. G13: Glas. 2F **61**
Strathcona Gdns. G13: Glas 2G **61**
Strathcona La. G75: E Kil 4G **149**
Strathcona Pl. G73: Ruth 3F **121**
G75: E Kil 4G **149**
Strathcona St. G13: Glas. 3F **61**
Strathconon Gdns. *G75: E Kil 2A* ***148***
(off Strathnairn Dr.)
Strath Dearn ML8: Law. 6E **159**
Strathdearn Gro. G75: E Kil. 3A **148**
Strathdee Av. G81: Hard 2D **42**
Strathdee Rd. G44: Neth. 5C **118**
Strathdon Av. G44: Neth 5C **118**
PA2: Pais 3G **97**
Strathdon Dr. G44: Neth 5D **118**
Strathdon Pl. *G75: E Kil 3A* ***148***
(off Strathnairn Dr.)
Strathearn Gro. G66: Kirk. 4H **31**
Strathearn Rd. G76: Clar. 3C **134**
Strath Elgin ML8: Law 6D **158**
Strathendrick Dr. G44: Glas 3C **118**
Strathfillan Rd. G74: E Kil. 1F **149**
Strath Halladale ML8: Law 6E **159**
Strathhalladale Ct. *G75: E Kil. 3A* ***148***
(off Strathmore Gro.)
Strathkelvin Av. G64: B'rig 2B **64**
Strathkelvin La. G75: E Kil 3A **148**
Strathkelvin Retail Pk. G64: B'rig . . . 3E **49**
Strathlachan Av. ML8: Carl 4G **165**
Strathleven Pl. G82: Dumb 4F **17**
Strathmore Av. G72: Blan 6A **124**
PA1: Pais. 1F **99**
Strathmore Cres. ML6: Air 1A **92**
Strathmore Gdns. G73: Ruth. 3F **121**
Strathmore Gro. G75: E Kil 3A **148**
Strathmore Ho. *G74: E Kil 2G* ***149***
(off Princess Sq.)
Strathmore Pl. ML5: Coat 6F **91**
Strathmore Rd. G22: Glas 2F **63**
ML3: Ham. 6A **142**
Strathmore Wlk. ML5: Coat. 6F **91**
Strathmungo Cres. ML6: Air. 1H **91**
Strath Nairn ML8: Law 6E **159**
Strathnairn Av. G75: E Kil 3A **148**
Strathnairn Ct. G75: E Kil 3A **148**
Strathnairn Dr. G75: E Kil 3A **148**
Strathnairn Way G75: E Kil 3A **148**
Strath Naver ML8: Law 6E **159**
Strathnaver Gdns. G75: E Kil 3A **148**
Strathord Pl. G69: Mood 3E **53**
Strathord St. G32: Glas. 2A **106**
Strath Peffer ML8: Law. 6D **158**
Strathpeffer Cres. ML6: Air. 1A **92**
Strathpeffer Dr. *G75: E Kil 3A* ***148***
(off Strathnairn Dr.)
Strathspey Av. G75: E Kil 3A **148**
Strathspey Cres. ML6: Air 6H **71**
Strathtay Av. G44: Neth 5C **118**
G75: E Kil 3A **148**
Strathtummel Cres. ML6: Air 6H **71**
Strathview Gro. G44: Neth 5C **118**
Strathview Pk. G44: Neth 5C **118**
Strathview Rd. ML4: Bell 4A **126**
Strathy Pl. G20: Glas 3B **62**
Strathyre Gdns. G61: Bear 2H **45**
G69: Mood 4E **53**
G75: E Kil 3A **148**
ML6: Glenm 4H **71**
Strathyre Rd. G72: Blan 3D **140**
Strathyre St. G41: Glas. 5C **102**
Stratton Dr. G46: Giff 5H **117**
Strauss Av. G81: Clyd. 6G **43**
Stravaig Path PA2: Pais 6E **97**
Stravaig Wlk. PA2: Pais 6E **97**
Stravanan Ct. G45: Glas 5A **120**
Stravanan Gdns. G45: Glas. 5H **119**
Stravanan Rd. G45: Glas 6H **119**
Stravanan St. G45: Glas 5H **119**
Stravanan Ter. G45: Glas 5H **119**
Stravenhouse Rd. ML8: Law. 1G **163**
Strawberry Fld. Rd. PA6: C'lee 2B **74**
Strawhill Ct. G76: Busby 2D **134**
Strawhill Rd. G76: Clar. 2C **134**
Strayhgryffe Cres. PA11: Bri W. 2E **73**
Streamfield Gdns. G33: Glas 2G **65**
Streamfield Ga. G33: Glas 2F **65**
Streamfield Lea G33: Glas 1G **65**
Streamfield Pl. G33: Glas. 2G **65**
Strenabey Av. G73: Ruth. 3F **121**
Striven Ct. ML5: Coat. 2D **110**
Striven Cres. ML2: Wis 2G **157**
Striven Gdns. G20: Glas 6D **62**
Striven Ter. ML3: Ham 2E **153**
Stroma St. G21: Glas 1D **84**
Stromness St. G5: Glas. 1E **103**
Strone Gdns. G65: Kils 3F **11**
Stronend St. G22: Glas 4F **63**
Strone Path ML5: Glenb 3G **69**
Strone Pl. ML6: Air. 6C **92**
Strone Rd. G33: Glas 4B **86**
Stronsay Pl. G64: B'rig 5F **49**
Stronsay St. G21: Glas 1D **84**
Stronvar Dr. G14: Glas 5B **60**
Stronvar La. G14: Glas 5B **60**
Stroud Rd. G75: E Kil 6E **149**
Strowan Cres. G32: Glas. 1B **106**
Strowan's Rd. G82: Dumb 2C **18**
Strowan St. G32: Glas. 1B **106**
Strowan's Well Rd. G82: Dumb 2C **18**
Struan Av. G46: Giff 4A **118**
Struan Gdns. G44: Glas. 2E **119**
Struan Rd. G44: Glas 2E **119**
Struie St. G34: Glas 3G **87**
Struma Dr. G76: Clar. 1A **134**
Struther & Swinhill Rd.
ML9: Lark. 6G **161**
STRUTHERHILL **5F 161**
Strutherhill ML9: Lark. 4F **161**
Strutherhill Ind. Est. ML9: Lark . . . 5G **161**
Struthers Cres. G74: E Kil. 5B **138**
Struther St. ML9: Lark. 5F **161**
Stuart Av. G60: Old K 2F **41**
G73: Ruth 2D **120**
Stuart Dr. G64: B'rig 1A **64**
ML9: Lark 4G **161**

Stuart Ho. G67: Cumb 2B **36**
Stuarton Pk. G74: E Kil 1G **149**
Stuart Quad. ML2: Wis 2E **157**
Stuart Rd. G76: Crmck 1H **135**
   G82: Dumb 1C **18**
   PA7: B'ton 3H **39**
Stuart St. G60: Old K. 2F **41**
   G74: E Kil 1H **149**
Stuartville ML5: Coat 4D **90**
Succoth St. G13: Glas 2F **61**
Sudbury Cres. G75: E Kil 2D **148**
Suffolk St. G40: Glas 5H **83**
Sugworth Av. G69: Bail 6H **87**
Suisnish PA8: Ersk 2G **57**
Sumburgh St. G33: Glas 4H **85**
Summerfield Cotts. G14: Glas. . . . 1E **81**
Summerfield Rd. G67: Cumb 1C **54**
Summerfield St. G40: Glas. 2D **104**
Summerhill & Garngibbock Rd.
   G67: Cumb 5E **55**
Summerhill Av. ML9: Lark 3E **161**
Summerhill Dr. G15: Glas. 3B **44**
Summerhill Gdns. G15: Glas 3B **44**
Summerhill Pl. G15: Glas 3B **44**
Summerhill Rd. G15: Glas 3A **44**
   G76: Busby. 2D **134**
Summerhill Way ML4: Bell 3B **126**
Summerlea Rd. G46: T'bnk 3F **117**
SUMMERLEE 3B **90**
Summerlee Cotts. ML5: Coat 4B **90**
Summerlee Heritage Trust 3B **90**
Summerlee Rd. ML2: Wis 5C **144**
   ML9: Lark 6H **155**
Summerlee St. G33: Glas 3C **86**
   ML5: Coat 4B **90**
SUMMERSTON 6B **46**
Summerston Station (Rail). 1B **62**
Summer St. G40: Glas 6B **84**
Summertown Path G51: Glas 4H **81**
Summertown Rd. G51: Glas 4H **81**
Summyside Oval PA2: Pais. 4A **98**
Sunart Av. PA4: Renf 5D **58**
Sunart Ct. ML3: Ham 2E **153**
Sunart Gdns. G64: B'rig 6E **49**
Sunart Rd. G52: Glas 6E **81**
   G64: B'rig 6E **49**
Sunart St. ML2: Wis 2G **157**
Sunbury Av. G76: Clar. 2A **134**
Sundale Av. G76: Clar. 3B **134**
Sunderland Av. G82: Dumb 3C **16**
Sunflower Gdns. ML1: Moth 1F **143**
Sunningdale Av.
   G77: Newt M 4F **133**
Sunningdale Dr. PA11: Bri W 5E **73**
Sunningdale Rd. G23: Glas. 1B **62**
Sunningdale Wynd G71: Both . . . 4C **124**
Sunnybank Dr. G76: Clar. 3B **134**
Sunnybank Gro. G76: Clar. 3B **134**
Sunnybank St. G40: Glas 2D **104**
Sunnyhill G65: Twe. 2D **32**
Sunnylaw Dr. PA2: Pais. 3F **97**
Sunnylaw St. G22: Glas 5F **63**
SUNNYSIDE 3C **90**
Sunnyside Av. G71: Udd 2D **124**
   ML1: Holy. 2B **128**
Sunnyside Cres. ML1: Holy. 2A **128**
Sunnyside Dr. G15: Glas. 6A **44**
   G69: Barg 6D **88**
   G76: Clar. 1B **134**
Sunnyside Pl. G15: Glas. 6A **44**
   G78: Barr 5D **114**
   ML1: Holy. 2A **128**
Sunnyside Rd. ML1: Cle 1H **145**
   ML3: Ham, Quar 3A **160**
   ML5: Coat 4C **90**
   ML9: Lark 2B **160**
   PA2: Pais 4H **97**
Sunnyside St. ML9: Lark 1D **160**
Sunnyside Ter. ML1: Holy 2A **128**
Surrey La. G5: Glas. 1F **103**
Surrey St. G5: Glas 1F **103**
Sussex St. G41: Glas 6C **82**
Sutcliffe Ct. G13: Glas 2E **61**
Sutcliffe Rd. G13: Glas 2E **61**

Sutherland Av. G41: Glas 2H **101**
   G61: Bear 6E **25**
Sutherland Ct. G41: Glas 1C **102**
Sutherland Cres. ML3: Ham 5E **141**
Sutherland Dr. G46: Giff 6B **118**
   G82: Dumb 2C **18**
   ML6: Air 6G **91**
Sutherland La. G12: Glas 1B **82**
Sutherland Pl. ML4: Bell. 5B **126**
Sutherland Rd. G81: Clyd 5D **42**
Sutherland St. G72: Blan 4A **140**
   PA1: Pais 6H **77**
Sutherness Dr. G33: Glas 4A **86**
Swaledale G74: E Kil 6E **137**
Swallow Dr. PA5: John 6C **94**
Swallow Gdns. G13: Glas 2H **59**
Swallow Rd. G81: Faif. 6F **23**
   ML2: Wis 5H **145**
Swan Pl. PA5: John 6C **94**
Swanston St. G40: Glas 3C **104**
Swan St. G4: Glas 2G **83** (1F **5**)
   G81: Clyd 4B **42**
Swan Way ML8: Law 1H **163**
Sween Av. G44: Glas 3E **119**
Sween Dr. ML3: Ham 2E **153**
Sween Path ML4: Bell. 4E **127**
                       (off Millbank Av.)
Sweethill Ter. ML5: Coat. 2F **111**
Sweethill Wlk. ML4: Bell. 6E **111**
Sweethope Gdns. G71: Both 5F **125**
Sweethope Pl. G71: Both 4E **125**
Swift Bank ML3: Ham 2C **152**
Swift Cres. G13: Glas 1H **59**
Swift Pl. G75: E Kil 5A **148**
   PA5: John 6D **94**
Swindon St. G81: Clyd 4A **42**
SWINHILL. 6G **161**
Swinstie Rd. ML1: Cle 1A **146**
SWINTON 5G **87**
Swinton Av. G69: Bail 6A **88**
Swinton Cres. G69: Bail 6A **88**
   ML5: Coat 1F **109**
Swinton Dr. G52: Glas 6B **80**
Swinton Gdns. G69: Bail 6B **88**
Swinton Path G69: Bail. 6B **88**
Swinton Pl. G52: Glas. 6B **80**
   ML5: Coat 1F **109**
                     (off Swinton Cres.)
Swinton Rd. G69: Bail 6A **88**
Swinton Vw. G69: Bail 6B **88**
Swisscot Av. ML3: Ham 3F **153**
Swisscot Wlk. ML3: Ham 3F **153**
Switchback Rd. G61: Bear. 5F **45**
Swordale Path G34: Glas 3G **87**
                 (off Kildermorie Rd.)
Swordale Pl. G34: Glas 3G **87**
Sword St. G31: Glas 5B **84**
   ML6: Air 4H **91**
Sycamore Av. G66: Lenz. 2D **50**
   G71: View. 6G **109**
   PA5: John. 4G **95**
Sycamore Ct. G75: E Kil 5F **149**
   ML5: Coat. 1B **110**
                         (off Ailsa Rd.)
Sycamore Cres. G75: E Kil 5E **149**
   ML6: Air 5D **92**
Sycamore Dr. G81: Clyd 3C **42**
   ML3: Ham 1B **154**
   ML6: Air 5D **92**
Sycamore Gro. G72: Blan 1A **140**
Sycamore Pl. G75: E Kil 5F **149**
   ML1: N'hill 4C **128**
Sycamore Way G66: Milt C 6C **8**
   G72: Flem 3F **123**
   G76: Crmck. 2H **135**
Sydenham Ct. G12: Glas. 5H **61**
             (off Westbourne Gdns. La.)
Sydenham La. G12: Glas. 6A **62**
Sydenham Rd. G12: Glas 6A **62**
Sydes Brae G72: Blan. 5H **139**
Sydney Dr. G75: E Kil 4E **149**
Sydney Pl. G75: E Kil 3E **149**

Sydney St. G31: Glas 5A **84**
   G81: Clyd 3H **41**
Sykehead Av. ML4: Bell. 2D **126**
Sykeside Rd. ML6: Air 1G **111**
Sykes Ter. G78: Neil 2F **131**
Sylvania Way G81: Clyd 5D **42**
Sylvania Way Sth.
   G81: Clyd 6D **42**
Symington Dr. G81: Clyd 5C **42**
Symington Sq. G75: E Kil 3H **149**
Syriam Pl. G21: Glas 5B **64**
Syriam St. G21: Glas 4B **64**

T

Tabard Pl. G13: Glas. 1C **60**
Tabard Rd. G13: Glas. 1C **60**
Tabernacle La. G72: Camb 2A **122**
Tabernacle St. G72: Camb 2A **122**
Taggart Rd. G65: Croy 2B **34**
Taig Rd. G66: Kirk 6H **31**
Tait Av. G78: Barr 3F **115**
Takmadoon Rd. G65: Kils 2A **12**
Talbot G74: E Kil 5C **138**
Talbot Ct. G13: Glas 4B **60**
Talbot Dr. G13: Glas 4B **60**
Talbot Pl. G13: Glas. 4B **60**
Talbot Ter. G13: Glas. 4B **60**
   G71: Tann 5C **108**
Talisman Av. G82: Dumb 3C **16**
Talisman Cres. ML1: Moth 5F **127**
Talisman Rd. G13: Glas 3C **60**
   PA2: Pais 6C **96**
Tallant Ho. G15: Glas 4B **44**
Tallant Ter. G15: Glas 4B **44**
Talla Rd. G52: Glas 5A **80**
Tall Ship at Glasgow Harbour, The
   . . . . 3A **82**
Tamarack Cres. G71: View 4G **109**
Tamar Dr. G75: E Kil 5B **148**
Tambowie Av. G62: Miln 3F **25**
Tambowie Cres. G62: Miln 3F **25**
Tambowie St. G13: Glas 1E **61**
Tamshill St. G20: Glas 3D **62**
Tanar Av. PA4: Renf 2G **79**
Tanar Way PA4: Renf 1G **79**
TANDLEHILL 3B **94**
Tanera Av. G44: Glas 2G **119**
Tanfield Pl. G32: Glas. 4C **86**
Tanfield St. G32: Glas. 4C **86**
Tankerland Rd. G44: Glas 1E **119**
Tannadice Av. G52: Glas 2C **100**
Tannadice Path G52: Glas 1C **100**
                   (off Tannadice Av.)
Tanna Dr. G52: Glas 2F **101**
Tannahill Cen. PA3: Pais. 5E **77**
Tannahill Cres. PA5: John. 4E **95**
                  (not continuous)
Tannahill Dr. G74: E Kil. 6C **138**
Tannahill Rd. G43: Glas 1D **118**
   PA3: Pais. 5F **77**
Tannahill's Cottage. 1G **97**
Tannahill Ter. PA3: Pais 5F **77**
Tannoch Dr. G62: Miln 2G **25**
   G67: Cumb 6H **35**
Tannoch Pl. G67: Cumb 6H **35**
TANNOCHSIDE 4F **109**
Tannochside Dr. G71: Tann 4E **109**
Tannochside Pk. G71: Tann 4F **109**
Tannock St. G22: Glas 5F **63**
Tantallon Ct. ML8: Carl 2E **165**
Tantallon Dr. ML5: Coat 2G **89**
   PA2: Pais. 4E **97**
Tantallon Pk. G74: E Kil. 1F **149**
Tantallon Rd. G41: Glas 5C **102**
   G69: Bail. 2G **107**
   G71: Both 4F **125**
Tanzieknowe Av. G72: Camb . . . 4B **122**
Tanzieknowe Dr. G72: Camb . . . 4B **122**
Tanzieknowe Pl. G72: Camb . . . 4A **122**
Tanzieknowe Rd. G72: Camb . . . 4A **122**
Taransay St. G51: Glas 3G **81**

Tarbert Av. G72: Blan 5A **124**
  ML2: Wis 2G **157**
Tarbert Ct. ML3: Ham 2E **153**
Tarbert Pl. ML8: Carl 4G **165**
Tarbert Way ML5: Coat 1A **110**
Tarbolton Cres. ML6: Chap 5D **112**
Tarbolton Dr. G81: Clyd 4E **43**
Tarbolton Path ML9: Lark 2D **160**
Tarbolton Rd. G43: Glas 1B **118**
  G67: Cumb 3B **36**
Tarbolton Sq. G81: Clyd 4F **43**
Tarbrax Way ML3: Ham 6E **141**
Tarfside Av. G52: Glas 1C **100**
Tarfside Gdns. G52: Glas 1D **100**
Tarfside Oval G52: Glas 1D **100**
Target Rd. ML6: Air 5B **92**
Tarland St. G51: Glas 5F **81**
Tarn Gro. G33: Glas 1G **65**
Tarras Dr. PA4: Renf 2G **79**
Tarras Pl. G72: Camb 2D **122**
Tasman Dr. G75: E Kil 4D **148**
Tasmania Quad. ML2: Wis 6C **146**
Tassie Pl. G74: E Kil 1A **150**
Tassie St. G41: Glas 5B **102**
Tattershall Rd. G33: Glas 1C **86**
Tavistock Dr. G43: Glas 2B **118**
Tay Av. PA4: Renf 6G **59**
Tay Ct. G75: E Kil 4A **148**
Tay Cres. G33: Glas 2G **85**
  G64: B'rig 6D **48**
Tay Gdns. ML3: Ham 3F **153**
Tay Gro. G75: E Kil 4A **148**
Tayinloan Dr. ML8: Carl 5H **165**
Tay La. ML2: Newm 4E **147**
Tay Loan *ML1: Holy* *2A **128***
  (off Windsor Rd.)
Taylor Av. ML1: Carf 5D **128**
  PA10: Kilb 2A **94**
Taylor Pl. G4: Glas 3H **83** (3H **5**)
Taylor St. G4: Glas 3H **83** (4H **5**)
                     (not continuous)
  G81: Clyd 1E **59**
Taymouth St. G32: Glas 2B **106**
Taynish Dr. G44: Glas 3F **119**
Tay Pl. G75: E Kil 4A **148**
  G82: Dumb 1H **17**
  ML9: Lark 5E **161**
  PA5: John 5C **94**
Tay Rd. G61: Bear 5D **44**
  G64: B'rig 6D **48**
Tayside ML6: Air 2H **91**
Tay St. ML5: Coat 2G **89**
Tay Ter. G75: E Kil 3A **148**
Tay Wlk. *G67: Cumb.* *4H **35***
  (in Cumbernauld Shop. Cen.)
Teak Pl. G71: View 4H **109**
Teal Ct. ML4: Bell 5A **110**
Teal Cres. G75: E Kil 6B **148**
Teal Dr. G13: Glas 2A **60**
Tealing Av. G52: Glas 1C **100**
Tealing Cres. G52: Glas 1C **100**
Teasel Av. G53: Glas 4B **116**
Teawell Rd. G77: Newt M 4D **132**
Technology Av. G72: Blan 5A **140**
Teesdale G74: E Kil 6E **137**
Teign Gro. G75: E Kil 5B **148**
Teith Av. PA4: Renf 1H **79**
Teith Dr. G61: Bear 4D **44**
Teith Pl. G72: Camb 2D **122**
Teith St. G33: Glas 2G **85**
Telephone La. *G12: Glas* *1A **82***
  (off Highburgh Rd.)
Telford Av. ML9: Lark 5G **161**
Telford Ct. G81: Clyd 5C **42**
Telford Pl. G67: Cumb 5A **36**
Telford Rd. G67: Cumb 5A **36**
  G75: E Kil 3F **149**
Telford St. ML4: Bell 1C **126**
Telford Ter. *G75: E Kil.* *3H **149***
  (off Telford Rd.)
Teme Pl. G75: E Kil. 4B **148**
Templar Av. G13: Glas 6D **44**
TEMPLE 2F **61**

Temple Gdns. G13: Glas 2F **61**
Templeland Rd. G53: Glas. 3C **100**
Templeland Rd. G53: Glas. 3C **100**
Temple Locks Ct. G13: Glas 2F **61**
Temple Locks Pl. G13: Glas 2F **61**
Temple Rd. G13: Glas 2G **61**
Templeton Bus. Cen.
  G40: Glas. 6A **84**
Templeton St. G40: Glas 6A **84**
Tenement Ho. G3: Glas 2E **83** (2A **4**)
Tennant Av. G74: E Kil 1C **148**
Tennant Complex, The G74: E Kil
                    . . . . 1C **148**
Tennant St. PA4: Renf 5F **59**
Tennent St. ML5: Coat 6D **90**
Tennyson Dr. G31: Glas 1G **105**
Tenters Way PA2: Pais 2F **97**
Tern Pl. PA5: John 6D **94**
Terregles Av. G41: Glas 3H **101**
Terregles Cres. G41: Glas 3A **102**
Terregles Dr. G41: Glas 3A **102**
Teviot Av. G64: B'rig. 4C **48**
  PA2: Pais 5C **96**
Teviot Cres. G61: Bear 5D **44**
Teviotdale *G74: E Kil.* *1F **149***
  (off Strathfillan Rd.)
  G77: Newt M 4H **133**
Teviot Dr. PA7: B'ton 5A **40**
Teviot Path G72: Blan 2A **140**
Teviot Pl. G72: Camb 2E **123**
Teviot Sq. *G67: Cumb.* *4H **35***
  (in Cumbernauld Shop. Cen.)
Teviot St. G3: Glas 3A **82**
  ML5: Coat. 1H **89**
Teviot Ter. PA5: John 5C **94**
Teviot Wlk. *G67: Cumb.* *4H **35***
  (in Cumbernauld Shop. Cen.)
Teviot Way *G67: Cumb.* *4H **35***
  (in Cumbernauld Shop. Cen.)
Tewkesbury Rd. G74: E Kil 4D **138**
Thane Rd. G13: Glas. 3C **60**
Thanes Ga. G71: Both. 2C **124**
Thankerton Av. ML1: Holy 2H **127**
Thankerton Rd. ML9: Lark. 4F **161**
Tharsis St. G21: Glas 2B **84**
Theatre Royal. 3F **83** (3D **4**)
Third Av. G33: Mille 4B **66**
  G44: Glas 6F **103**
  G66: Auch. 5D **50**
  G82: Dumb 3C **18**
  PA4: Renf 1E **79**
Third Av. La. G44: Glas 6F **103**
Third Gdns. G41: Glas 1G **101**
Thirdpart Cres. G13: Glas 2G **59**
Third Rd. G72: Blan 4C **140**
Third St. G71: Tann 5D **108**
Thirlmere G75: E Kil 6B **148**
Thistle Bank G66: Lenz. 3D **50**
Thistlebank PA11: Bri W 2E **73**
Thistlebank Gdns.
  ML5: Coat 2A **110**
Thistle Cres. ML9: Lark 3F **161**
Thistledown Gro.
  ML5: Coat 5E **91**
Thistle Gdns. ML1: Holy 2A **128**
Thistleneuk G60: Old K 6E **21**
Thistle Pl. G74: E Kil 6G **137**
Thistle Quad. ML6: Air 2B **92**
Thistle Rd. ML1: New S 4A **128**
Thistle St. G5: Glas 6G **83**
  G66: Kirk 5D **30**
  ML1: Cle. 6H **129**
  ML6: Air 2B **92**
  PA2: Pais 3G **97**
Thistle Ter. G5: Glas. 1G **103**
Thomas Muir Av. G64: B'rig 1C **64**
Thomas Muir Mus.. . . . . 6C **48**
Thomas St. PA1: Pais 1F **97**
Thompson Av. G66: Kirk 5E **31**
Thompson Brae PA1: Pais. 2A **98**
Thompson Pl. G81: Hard. 1E **43**
Thompson St. PA4: Renf 1E **79**
Thomson Av. ML2: Wis. 2D **156**
  PA5: John 2E **95**

Thomson Dr. G61: Bear. 1F **45**
  ML1: Moth 4F **143**
  ML4: Bell 2H **125**
  ML6: Air 5H **91**
Thomson Gro. G72: Camb. 6A **106**
Thomson St. G31: Glas 5C **84**
  ML8: Carl 3F **165**
  PA5: John 3E **95**
Thorn Av. G74: T'hall 6G **135**
Thornbank St. G3: Glas 3A **82**
Thornbridge Av. G12: Glas 4A **62**
  G69: Bail. 6H **87**
Thornbridge Gdns. G69: Bail. 6G **87**
Thornbridge Rd. G69: Bail 6G **87**
Thorncliffe Gdns. G41: Glas 3C **102**
Thorncroft Dr. G44: Glas 3H **119**
Thorndale Gdns. FK4: Alla 1H **15**
Thorndean Av. ML4: Bell. 3D **126**
Thorndean Cres. ML4: Bell 3D **126**
Thorndene PA5: Eld 2H **95**
Thorndene Av. ML1: Carf 5C **128**
Thornden La. G14: Glas 5A **60**
Thorn Dr. G61: Bear 1D **44**
  G73: Ruth 3E **121**
Thorndyke G74: E Kil 4C **138**
Thorne Brae PA5: John. 2G **95**
Thornhill PA5: John 3H **95**
Thornhill Av. G72: Blan 1B **140**
  PA5: Eld 3H **95**
Thornhill Dr. PA5: Eld 3H **95**
Thornhill Gdns. G77: Newt M 6D **132**
  PA5: John 2G **95**
Thornhill La. G71: Both. 4F **125**
Thornhill Path G31: Glas 6F **85**
Thornhill Rd. ML3: Ham 5C **140**
Thornhill Way ML5: Coat. 2F **111**
Thorniecroft Dr. G67: Cumb 1E **55**
Thorniecroft Pl. G67: Cumb 1E **55**
Thornielee G74: E Kil 1B **150**
Thorniewood Gdns. G71: Tann . . . 6E **109**
Thorniewood Rd. G71: Tann 5D **108**
Thornkip Pl. ML5: Coat 6E **91**
Thornlea Dr. G46: Giff. 3B **118**
Thornlea St. ML8: Carl 5G **165**
Thornley Av. G13: Glas 3B **60**
THORNLIEBANK 4F **117**
Thornliebank Ind. Est.
  G46: T'bnk 4E **117**
Thornliebank Rd. G43: Glas 1H **117**
Thornliebank Station (Rail) 3G **117**
Thornlie Gill ML2: Wis 1H **157**
THORNLY PARK 5B **98**
Thornly Pk. Av. PA2: Pais 5B **98**
Thornly Pk. Dr. PA2: Pais 5B **98**
Thornly Pk. Gdns. PA2: Pais 4B **98**
Thornly Pk. Rd. PA2: Pais. 4A **98**
Thorn Rd. G61: Bear. 2C **44**
  ML4: Bell 2D **126**
Thornside Rd. PA5: John 2G **95**
THORNTONHALL 6G **135**
Thorntonhall Station (Rail) 6F **135**
Thornton La. G20: Glas. 2C **62**
Thornton Pl. ML3: Ham 5H **153**
Thornton Rd. G74: T'hall. 6G **135**
Thornton St. G20: Glas 2B **62**
  ML5: Coat. 1H **89**
Thorntree Av. ML3: Ham. 4D **140**
Thorntree Way G71: Both 4F **125**
Thornwood Av. G11: Glas. 1G **81**
  G66: Lenz 2A **50**
Thornwood Cres. G11: Glas. 6F **61**
Thornwood Dr. G11: Glas 1F **81**
                     (not continuous)
  PA11: Bri W 4D **72**
  PA2: Pais. 3F **97**
Thornwood Gdns. G11: Glas 1F **81**
Thornwood Pl. G11: Glas 6F **61**
                     (not continuous)
Thornwood Quad. G11: Glas 6F **61**
Thornwood Rd. G11: Glas 1F **81**
Thornwood Ter. G11: Glas 1F **81**
Thornyburn Dr. G69: Bail. 1B **108**
Thornyburn Pl. G69: Bail. 1A **108**
Thorny Pk. Ct. PA2: Pais 5A **98**

Thorp Ct. PA5: John 3G **95**
THRASHBUSH 1A 92
Thrashbush Av. ML2: Wis 5B **146**
Thrashbush Cres. ML2: Wis 5B **146**
Thrashbush Rd. ML2: Wis 5B **146**
Threave Ct. ML8: Carl 2E **165**
Threave Pl. G77: Newt M 4B **132**
Three Queens Sq. G81: Clyd 6D **42**
Three Rivers Wlk. G75: E Kil 3D **148**
Threestonehill Av. G32: Glas 5B **86**
Threshold Pk. G74: E Kil 1A **150**
Threshold Rd. G74: E Kil 1A **150**
Thriplee Rd. PA11: Bri W 3E **73**
Thrnyland Way PA8: Ersk 2F **57**
Thrums G74: E Kil 4D **138**
Thrums Av. G64: B'rig 6E **49**
Thrums Gdns. G64: B'rig 6E **49**
Thrushbush La. ML6: Air 1B **92**
Thrushbush Quad. ML6: Air 1A **92**
Thrushbush Rd. ML6: Air 1A **92**
Thrushcraig Cres. PA2: Pais 3B **98**
Thrush Pl. PA5: John 6D **94**
Thurso St. G11: Glas 2A **82**
Thurston Rd. G52: Glas 6A **80**
Thyme Sq. ML1: Moth 1G **143**
Tianavaig PA8: Ersk 2G **57**
Tibbermore Rd. G11: Glas 6G **61**
Tiber Av. ML1: Moth 6E **127**
Tighnasheen Way G72: Blan 1B **140**
Tillanburn Rd. ML1: N'hill 4F **129**
Tillet Oval PA3: Pais 4H **77**
Tillie St. G20: Glas 6D **62**
Till St. ML2: Wis 3H **145**
Tillycairn Av. G33: Glas 1D **86**
Tillycairn Dr. G33: Glas 1D **86**
Tillycairn Pl. G33: Glas 1E **87**
Tillycairn Rd. G33: Glas 1E **87**
Tillycairn St. G33: Glas 1E **87**
Tilt Rd. ML2: Newm 3D **146**
Tilt St. G33: Glas 1G **85**
Time Capsule, The 5B 90
Timmons Gro. ML4: Moss 2F **127**
Timmons Ter. ML6: Chap 4D **112**
Tinker's La. ML1: Moth 3E **143**
Tintagel Gdns. G69: Mood 4D **52**
TINTOCK 3A 32
Tintock Dr. G66: Kirk 4F **31**
Tintock Pl. G68: Dull 5F **13**
Tintock Rd. G66: Kirk 3H **31**
Tinto Ct. ML5: Coat 2E **111**
Tinto Cres. ML2: Wis 1A **158**
Tinto Dr. G78: Barr 6D **114**
Tinto Rd. G43: Glas 2A **118**
G61: Bear 1B **44**
G64: B'rig 6F **49**
ML6: Air 5B **92**
Tinto Sq. PA4: Renf 2D **78**
Tinto St. ML2: Wis 1A **158**
Tinto Vw. ML3: Ham 3A **154**
Tinto Vw. Rd. ML9: Shaw 6H **161**
Tinto Way G75: E Kil 6D **148**
ML1: Cle 5H **129**
Tinwald Path G52: Glas 6A **80**
Tiree G74: E Kil 4C **150**
Tiree Av. PA2: Pais 6H **97**
PA4: Renf 3E **79**
Tiree Ct. G67: Cumb 5F **35**
Tiree Cres. ML2: Newm 2D **146**
Tiree Dr. G67: Cumb 5F **35**
Tiree Gdns. G60: Old K 1G **41**
G61: Bear 1B **44**
ML6: Glenm 4H **71**
Tiree Grange ML3: Ham 2D **152**
Tiree Pl. G60: Old K 1G **41**
G77: Newt M 4B **132**
ML5: Coat 1H **109**
Tiree Rd. G67: Cumb 5F **35**
Tiree St. G21: Glas 1E **85**
Tirry Av. PA4: Renf 1H **79**
Tirry Way PA4: Renf 1H **79**
Titwood Rd. G41: Glas 3A **102**
(not continuous)
Tiverton Av. G32: Glas 2D **106**
Tivoli Ct. G75: E Kil 5G **149**
Tobago Pl. G40: Glas 6B **84**
G75: E Kil 2C **148**
Tobago St. G40: Glas 6A **84**
Tobermory Rd. G73: Ruth 4F **121**
Todburn Dr. PA2: Pais 6B **98**
Todd St. G31: Glas 4E **85**
Todhills *G75: E Kil 3H 149*
(off Todhills Nth.)
Todhills Nth. G75: E Kil 3H **149**
Todhills Sth. G75: E Kil 3H **149**
Todholm Cres. PA2: Pais 3D **98**
Todholm Rd. PA2: Pais 3D **98**
Todholm Ter. PA2: Pais 3D **98**
Tofthill Av. G64: B'rig 5B **48**
Tofthill Gdns. G64: B'rig 5B **48**
Tolbooth Steeple *5H 83*
(off Saltmarket)
Tollbrae Av. ML6: Air 4B **92**
TOLLCROSS 2A 106
Tollcross Leisure Cen. 2H 105
Tollcross Pk. Gdns. G32: Glas 2G **105**
Tollcross Pk. Gro. G32: Glas 2H **105**
Tollcross Pk. Vw. G32: Glas 2G **105**
Tollcross Rd. G31: Glas 6F **85**
Tollhouse Gdns. ML4: Bell 4E **127**
Toll La. G51: Glas 5C **82**
Tollpark Cres. ML2: Newm 4E **147**
Tollpark Pl. G68: Cumb 3E **15**
Tollpark Rd. G68: Cumb 3D **14**
TOLL PLAZA INTERCHANGE
. . . . **4D 40**
Toll St. ML1: Moth 4H **143**
Toll, The G76: Clar 1C **134**
Toll Wynd ML3: Ham 4G **153**
Tolsta St. G23: Glas 6C **46**
Tomtain Brae G68: Cumb 6B **34**
Tomtain Ct. G68: Cumb 6B **34**
Toner Gdns. ML2: Over 4H **157**
Tontine La. G1: Glas 5H **83** (6G **5**)
Tontine Pl. G73: Ruth 3G **121**
Topaz Ter. ML4: Bell 4C **126**
Toppersfield PA10: Kilb 3C **94**
Torbreck St. G52: Glas 6F **81**
Torbrex Rd. G67: Cumb 4A **36**
Torburn Av. G46: Giff 3H **117**
TORBUSH 5F 147
Tordene Path G68: Cumb 2F **35**
Torgyle St. G23: Glas 6B **46**
Tormeadow Rd. G77: Newt M 4D **132**
Tormore St. G51: Glas 5D **80**
Tormusk Dr. G45: Glas 3C **120**
Tormusk Gdns. G45: Glas 3C **120**
Tormusk Gro. G45: Glas 3C **120**
Tormusk Rd. G45: Glas 3B **120**
Torness St. G11: Glas 1A **82**
Torogay Pl. G22: Glas 1A **64**
Torogay St. G22: Glas 2G **63**
Torogay Ter. G22: Glas 1G **63**
Toronto Wlk. G32: Carm 5C **106**
Torphin Cres. G32: Glas 5A **86**
Torphin Wlk. G32: Glas 5B **86**
TORRANCE 5D 28
Torrance Av. ML6: Air 4D **92**
Torrance Rd. G74: E Kil 1G **149**
TORRANCE RDBT. **6B 150**
Torran Dr. PA8: Ersk 2A **58**
Torran Rd. G33: Glas 4F **87**
Torranyard Ter. ML3: Ham 2C **152**
Torr Av. PA11: Q'riers 1A **72**
Torrence Rd. G64: B'rig, Torr 5D **28**
Torriden Pl. ML5: Coat 6A **90**
Torriden St. ML5: Coat 6A **90**
Torridon Av. G41: Glas 2G **101**
ML1: N'hill 4D **128**
Torridon Ct. *G20: Glas 1E 83*
(off Cedar St.)
Torridon Gdns. G77: Newt M 5H **133**
Torridon Path *G41: Glas 2G 101*
(off Dumbreck Pl.)
Torrindon Gdns. G61: Bear 6D **24**
Torrington Av. G46: Giff 1G **133**
Torrington Cres. G32: Glas 2D **106**
Torrin Rd. G23: Glas 6B **46**
Torrisdale Pl. ML5: Coat 4A **90**
Torrisdale St. G42: Glas 3D **102**
ML5: Coat 4A **90**
Torr La. PA11: Q'riers 1A **72**
Torr Rd. G64: B'rig 6F **49**
PA11: Bri W 2C **72**
Torr St. G22: Glas 5H **63**
Torryburn Rd. G21: Glas 5E **65**
Torwood Brae ML3: Ham 1D **152**
Torwood La. G69: Mood 5E **53**
TORYGLEN 5A 104
Toryglen Rd. G73: Ruth 5B **104**
Toryglen St. G5: Glas 3H **103**
Tourmaline Ter. ML4: Bell 4D **126**
Tournai Path G72: Blan 2B **140**
Toward Ct. G72: Blan 6C **124**
Toward Rd. G33: Glas 4C **86**
Tower Av. G78: Barr 3F **115**
Tower Castle *4G 95*
(off Tower Pl.)
Tower Cres. PA4: Renf 1D **78**
Tower Dr. PA4: Renf 1D **78**
Towerhill Rd. G13: Glas 6C **44**
Tower Pl. G20: Glas 3B **62**
G62: Miln 3H **25**
PA5: John 4G **95**
Tower Rd. G64: Balm, Torr 2G **27**
G67: Cumb 1H **55**
PA5: John 4F **95**
Towerside Cres. G53: Glas 3A **100**
Towerside Rd. G53: Glas 3A **100**
Towers Pl. ML6: Air 4F **93**
Towers Rd. ML6: Air 3E **93**
Tower St. G41: Glas 6C **82**
Tower Ter. PA1: Pais 1H **97**
Towerview Dr. G69: G'csh 6A **68**
Towie Pl. G71: Udd 1D **124**
TOWNEND 2F 17
Townend Rd. G82: Dumb 3F **17**
TOWNHEAD
Coatbridge 2H 89
Glasgow 4G 83 (6F 5)
Kirkintilloch 5D 30
Townhead G66: Kirk 5D **30**
Townhead Av. ML1: Holy 5G **111**
Townhead Dr. ML1: N'hill 4F **129**
TOWNHEAD INTERCHANGE ***3A 84***
(M8, JUNCTION 15)
Townhead Pl. G71: Tann 5E **109**
Townhead Rd. G77: Newt M 5C **132**
ML5: Coat 1E **89**
Townhead St. G65: Kils 3H **11**
ML3: Ham 6B **142**
Townhead Ter. PA1: Pais 1H **97**
Townhill Rd. ML3: Ham 6B **140**
Townhill Ter. ML3: Ham 6C **140**
Townmill Rd. G31: Glas 3B **84**
Townsend St. G4: Glas 1G **83** (1E **5**)
Traction Bus. Pk. ML1: Moth 4E **143**
TRADESTON 6E 83
Tradeston Ind. Est. G5: Glas 1D **102**
Tradeston St. G5: Glas 6E **83**
Trafalgar Ct. G68: Dull 5F **13**
Trafalgar St. G40: Glas 2B **104**
G81: Clyd 4B **42**
Trainard Av. G32: Glas 1H **105**
Tramway 2E 103
Tranent Path ML1: Cle 5H **129**
Tranent Pl. G33: Glas 3G **85**
ML1: Cle 5H **129**
Traquair Av. ML2: Wis 4A **146**
PA2: Pais 5C **96**
Traquair Dr. G52: Glas 1B **100**
Traquair Wynd *G72: Blan 2A 140*
(off Winton Cres.)
Treeburn Av. G46: Giff 4H **117**
Treemain Rd. G46: Giff 1G **133**
Trees Pk. Av. G78: Barr 3D **114**
Trefoil Av. G41: Glas 5B **102**
Trefoil Pl. *PA6: Hous 1B 74*
(off North St.)
Trent Pl. G75: E Kil 5A **148**
Trent St. ML5: Coat 1H **89**
Tresta Rd. G23: Glas 1C **62**
Triangle, The G64: B'rig 6C **48**

Tribboch St. ML9: Lark . . . 2D **160**
Trident Way PA4: Renf . . . 2E **79**
Trigg St. PA2: Pais . . . 2E **97**
Trinidad Grn. G75: E Kil . . . 2C **148**
Trinidad Way G75: E Kil . . . 2C **148**
Trinity Av. G52: Glas . . . 1C **100**
Trinity Dr. G72: Camb . . . 4C **122**
Trinity Way ML9: Lark . . . 4G **161**
Trinley Rd. G13: Glas . . . 6D **44**
Triton Pl. ML4: Moss . . . 2H **127**
Tronda Path G34: Glas. . . . 3F **87**
Trondra Pl. G34: Glas . . . 3F **87**
Trongate G1: Glas. . . . 5G **83** (6F **5**)
Tron Theatre . . . ***5H 83***
(off Trongate)
Troon Av. G75: E Kil . . . 5C **148**
Troon Ct. G75: E Kil . . . 5D **148**
Troon Dr. PA11: Bri W. . . . 4E **73**
Troon Gdns. G68: Cumb . . . 5H **13**
Troon Pl. G77: Newt M . . . 5G **133**
Troon St. G40: Glas . . . 2D **104**
Trossachs Av. ML1: Holy. . . . 2A **128**
Trossachs Ct. G20: Glas . . . 6E **63**
Trossachs Rd. G73: Ruth. . . . 5F **121**
Trossachs St. G20: Glas . . . 6E **63**
Troubridge Av. PA10: Kilb . . . 4B **94**
Troubridge Cres. PA10: Kilb . . . 3B **94**
Trovaig PA8: Ersk . . . 2G **57**
Trows Rd. ML2: Over . . . 5H **157**
Truce Rd. G13: Glas . . . 1B **60**
Truro Av. G69: Mood . . . 4D **52**
Tryst Rd. G67: Cumb . . . 4H **35**
(not continuous)
Tryst Sports Cen. . . . **3A 36**
Tryst Wlk. G67: Cumb. . . . 3A **36**
Tudor La. Sth. G14: Glas. . . . 6E **61**
Tudor St. G69: Bail . . . 2F **107**
Tulley Wynd ML1: Moth . . . 5F **127**
Tulliallan Pl. G74: E Kil. . . . 3A **150**
Tullis Ct. G40: Glas. . . . 1A **104**
Tullis St. G40: Glas. . . . 1A **104**
Tulloch-Ard Pl. G73: Ruth . . . 4F **121**
Tulloch Gdns. ML1: Moth . . . 5B **144**
Tulloch St. G44: Glas . . . 1E **119**
Tullymet Rd. ML3: Ham . . . 3H **153**
Tummel Dr. ML6: Air . . . 1H **91**
Tummel Grn. G74: E Kil . . . 6G **137**
Tummell Way PA2: Pais . . . 4D **96**
Tummel St. G33: Glas. . . . 1G **85**
Tummel Wlk. *G67: Cumb* . . . *4H 35*
(in Cumbernauld Shop. Cen.)
Tummel Way *G67: Cumb* . . . *3H 35*
(in Cumbernauld Shop. Cen.)
Tunnel St. G3: Glas. . . . 4C **82**
Tuphall Rd. ML3: Ham . . . 1H **153**
Tureen St. *G40: Glas.* . . . *5A 84*
(off Millroad Dr.)
Turnberry Av. G11: Glas . . . 6H **61**
Turnberry Cres. ML5: Coat . . . 1A **110**
ML6: Chap . . . 4E **113**
Turnberry Dr. G73: Ruth . . . 2B **120**
G77: Newt M. . . . 5G **133**
ML3: Ham. . . . 1B **152**
PA11: Bri W . . . 5E **73**
Turnberry Gdns. G68: Cumb . . . 6H **13**
Turnberry Pl. G75: E Kil . . . 5D **148**
G82: Dumb . . . 3C **16**
Turnberry Rd. G11: Glas. . . . 6G **61**
Turnberry Wynd G71: Both . . . 4C **124**
Turnbull St. G1: Glas . . . 5H **83**
Turner Rd. G21: Glas . . . 1B **84**
PA3: Pais . . . 3B **78**
Turners Av. PA1: Pais . . . 2F **97**
Turner St. ML5: Coat . . . 5B **90**
Turnhill Av. PA8: Ersk . . . 2F **57**
Turnhill Cres. PA8: Ersk . . . 2F **57**
Turnhill Dr. PA8: Ersk . . . 1F **57**
Turnhill Gdns. PA8: Ersk . . . 2F **57**
Turnlaw G75: E Kil. . . . 6F **149**
Turnlaw Rd. G72: Camb . . . 6A **122**
Turnlaw St. G5: Glas. . . . 1H **103**
Turnyland Mdws. PA8: Ersk. . . . 2F **57**
Turquoise Ter. ML4: Bell. . . . 4D **126**
Turret Cres. G13: Glas . . . 1C **60**
Turret Rd. G13: Glas. . . . 6C **44**
Turriff St. G5: Glas . . . 1F **103**
Twechar Recreation Cen. . . . **2D 32**
Tweed Av. PA2: Pais. . . . 3D **96**
Tweed Ct. ML6: Air. . . . 6C **92**
Tweed Cres. G33: Glas . . . 2F **85**
ML2: Wis . . . 4A **146**
PA4: Renf . . . 6G **59**
Tweed Dr. G61: Bear. . . . 4D **44**
Tweed La. ML1: Holy . . . 2B **128**
Tweedmuir Pl. ML5: Coat . . . 2F **111**
Tweed Pl. PA5: John. . . . 5C **94**
Tweedsmuir G64: B'rig . . . 5E **49**
Tweedsmuir Cres. G61: Bear. . . . 6E **25**
Tweedsmuir Pk. ML3: Ham. . . . 3G **153**
Tweedsmuir Rd. G52: Glas . . . 1B **100**
Tweed St. G75: E Kil. . . . 4B **148**
ML5: Coat. . . . 2D **110**
ML9: Lark . . . 4E **161**
Tweedvale Av. G14: Glas . . . 3G **59**
Tweedvale Pl. G14: Glas . . . 3G **59**
Tweed Wlk. *G67: Cumb* . . . *4H 35*
(in Cumbernauld Shop. Cen.)
Twinlaw St. G34: Glas. . . . 2B **88**
Tylney Rd. PA1: Pais. . . . 6F **79**
Tyndrum Rd. G61: Bear . . . 2H **45**
Tyndrum St. G4: Glas . . . 2G **83** (1E **5**)
Tynecastle Cres. G32: Glas. . . . 4B **86**
Tynecastle Path G32: Glas . . . 4B **86**
Tynecastle Pl. G32: Glas. . . . 4B **86**
Tynecastle St. G32: Glas. . . . 4B **86**
Tyne Pl. G75: E Kil . . . 5A **148**
Tynron Ct. ML3: Ham . . . 2C **152**
Tynwald Av. G73: Ruth . . . 3F **121**

U

UCI Cinema
Clydebank . . . **6D 42**
East Kilbride. . . . **3H 149**
UDDINGSTON . . . **2D 124**
Uddingston Rd. G71: Both . . . 4D **124**
Uddingston Station (Rail)
. . . 1C **124**
UDSTON . . . **5E 141**
Udston Rd. ML3: Ham . . . 5C **140**
Udston Ter. ML3: Ham . . . 4D **140**
UGC Cinema . . . **6E 85**
Uig Pl. G33: Glas . . . 6E **87**
Uist Cres. G33: Step . . . 5E **67**
Uist Dr. G66: Kirk . . . 5G **31**
Uist Pl. ML6: Air . . . 5D **92**
Uist St. G51: Glas . . . 4F **81**
Uist Way ML2: Wis. . . . 4C **146**
Ullswater G75: E Kil . . . 6B **148**
Ulundi Rd. PA5: John. . . . 3D **94**
Ulva St. G52: Glas. . . . 6F **81**
Ulverston Ter. ML3: Ham . . . 5H **153**
Umachan PA8: Ersk . . . 2G **57**
Underwood Dr. ML2: Newm . . . 2E **147**
Underwood La. PA1: Pais. . . . 6H **77**
Underwood Rd. G73: Ruth . . . 1E **121**
PA3: Pais . . . 6G **77**
Underwood St. G41: Glas . . . 5C **102**
Union Ct. PA2: Pais . . . 3A **98**
Union Pl. G1: Glas . . . 4F **83** (5D **4**)
Union St. G1: Glas . . . 4F **83** (5D **4**)
G66: Kirk . . . 5C **30**
ML1: New S . . . 3A **128**
ML3: Ham. . . . 5G **141**
ML8: Carl . . . 4F **165**
ML9: Lark . . . 2E **161**
PA2: Pais . . . 3A **98**
Unitas Cres. ML8: Carl . . . 4E **165**
Unitas Rd. ML4: Moss . . . 2E **127**
Unity Pl. G4: Glas . . . 1E **83**
University Av. G12: Glas. . . . 1B **82**
University Gdns. G12: Glas. . . . 1B **82**
University of Glasgow Vis. Cen. . . . **1B 82**
University Pl. G12: Glas . . . 1A **82**
Unsted Pl. PA1: Pais. . . . 1C **98**
Unthank Rd. ML4: Moss . . . 2E **127**
Uphall Pl. G33: Glas. . . . 4G **85**
Upland La. *G14: Glas* . . . *5C 60*
(off Danes La. Nth.)
Upland Rd. G14: Glas . . . 5C **60**
U.P. La. G65: Kils. . . . 3H **11**
Uplawmoor Rd. G78: Neil . . . 4A **130**
Up. Bourtree Ct. G73: Ruth . . . 3E **121**
Up. Bourtree Dr. G73: Ruth . . . 3D **120**
Up. Glenburn Rd. G61: Bear . . . 2C **44**
Up. Mill St. ML6: Air . . . 3A **92**
U.P. Rd. G65: Kils . . . 3H **11**
Urquhart Cres. PA4: Renf . . . 1E **79**
Urquhart Dr. G74: E Kil . . . 6A **138**
Urrdale Rd. G41: Glas . . . 6H **81**
Usmore Pl. G33: Glas . . . 6E **87**

V

Vaila Pl. G23: Glas . . . 2E **63**
Vaila St. G23: Glas. . . . 1D **62**
Valence Twr. G71: Both . . . 3B **124**
Valerio Ct. G72: Blan . . . 1B **140**
Valetta Pl. G81: Clyd . . . 4H **41**
Valeview Ter. G42: Glas . . . 5E **103**
G82: Dumb . . . 1G **17**
Vale Wlk. G64: B'rig . . . 1E **65**
Vallantine Cres. G71: Tann . . . 5E **109**
Vallay St. G22: Glas . . . 1H **63**
Valleybank G65: Bant . . . 1F **13**
Valley Ct. ML3: Ham . . . 1G **153**
Valleyfield G66: Milt C . . . 5A **8**
G75: E Kil . . . 2F **149**
Valleyfield Dr. G68: Cumb . . . 4A **34**
Valleyfield St. G21: Glas . . . 6A **64**
Valley Vw. G72: Camb . . . 1C **122**
ML1: Moth . . . 6B **144**
Vancouver Ct. G75: E Kil. . . . 2D **148**
Vancouver Dr. G75: E Kil . . . 2D **148**
Vancouver La. *G14: Glas* . . . *5D 60*
(off Norse La. Nth., not continuous)
Vancouver Pl. G81: Clyd. . . . 4H **41**
Vancouver Rd. G14: Glas . . . 5C **60**
Vanguard St. G81: Clyd. . . . 5E **43**
Vanguard Way PA4: Renf . . . 2E **79**
Vardar Av. G76: Clar . . . 1A **134**
Vardon Lea ML1: Cle. . . . 6E **129**
Varna La. G14: Glas . . . 6E **61**
Varna Rd. G14: Glas . . . 5E **61**
Varnsdorf Way ML6: Air . . . 5D **92**
Vasart Pl. G20: Glas. . . . 5D **62**
Veir Ter. G82: Dumb . . . 4E **17**
Veitches Ct. G81: Dun . . . 1C **42**
Veitch Pl. G66: Len. . . . 3F **7**
Vennacher Rd. PA4: Renf . . . 5C **58**
Vennard Gdns. G41: Glas . . . 3C **102**
Vermont Av. G73: Ruth . . . 6C **104**
Vermont St. G41: Glas . . . 6B **82**
Vernon Bank G74: E Kil. . . . 6G **137**
Vernon Dr. PA3: Lin . . . 5G **75**
Verona Av. G14: Glas . . . 5C **60**
Verona Gdns. G14: Glas . . . 5C **60**
Verona La. G14: Glas . . . 5C **60**
Vesalius St. G32: Glas . . . 6A **86**
Viaduct Rd. G76: Busby . . . 2D **134**
Vicarfield St. G51: Glas . . . 4H **81**
VICARLAND . . . **2A 122**
Vicarland Pl. G72: Camb . . . 3A **122**
Vicarland Rd. G72: Camb . . . 2A **122**
Vicars Wlk. G72: Camb. . . . 2B **122**
Vickers St. ML1: Moth . . . 1D **142**
Victoria Av. G78: Barr. . . . 3D **114**
ML8: Carl . . . 4E **165**
Victoria Baths . . . **5F 59**
Victoria Bri. G5: Glas . . . 5G **83**
Victoria Cir. G12: Glas . . . 6A **62**
Victoria Ct. ML9: Lark. . . . 1E **161**
Victoria Cres. G65: Kils. . . . 3F **11**
G76: Busby. . . . 2D **134**
G78: Barr . . . 3D **114**
ML2: Wis . . . 5D **144**
ML6: Air. . . . 5G **91**
Victoria Cres. La. G12: Glas . . . 6A **62**
Victoria Cres. Pl. G12: Glas . . . 6A **62**
Victoria Cres. Rd. G12: Glas. . . . 6A **62**

Victoria Cross—Waterfoot Ter.

Victoria Cross G42: Glas . . . 3E **103**
Victoria Dr. G78: Barr . . . 3D **114**
Victoria Dr. E. PA4: Renf . . . 1E **79**
Victoria Dr. W. PA4: Renf . . . 6D **58**
Victoria Gdns. G78: Barr . . . 3D **114**
ML6: Air . . . 4H **91**
PA2: Pais . . . 3G **97**
Victoria Glade G68: Dull . . . 5F **13**
Victoria Gro. G78: Barr . . . 3D **114**
Victoria Mans. G44: Glas . . . 1F **119**
Victoria Pk. G65: Kils . . . 3F **11**
Victoria Pk. Cnr. G14: Glas . . . 6D **60**
Victoria Pk. Dr. Nth. G14: Glas . . . 5D **60**
Victoria Pk. Dr. Sth. G14: Glas . . . 6D **60**
(not continuous)
Victoria Pk. Gdns. Nth. G11: Glas . . . 6F **61**
Victoria Pk. Gdns. Sth. G11: Glas . . . 6F **61**
Victoria Pk. La. Nth. G14: Glas . . . 6D **60**
Victoria Pk. La. Sth. *G14: Glas . . . 6D* ***60***
(off Westland Dr.)
Victoria Pk. St. G14: Glas . . . 6D **60**
Victoria Pl. G62: Miln . . . 4H **25**
G65: Kils . . . 3G **11**
G73: Ruth . . . 5C ***104***
(off King St.)
G78: Barr . . . 3E **115**
G81: Hard . . . 1D **42**
ML4: Bell . . . 3B **126**
ML6: Air . . . 5G **91**
Victoria Quad. ML1: Holy . . . 2H **127**
Victoria Rd. G33: Step . . . 4C **66**
G42: Glas . . . 4E **103**
G66: Lenz . . . 3C **50**
G68: Dull . . . 5F **13**
G73: Ruth . . . 1D **120**
G78: Barr . . . 3D **114**
PA2: Pais . . . 3G **97**
PA5: Brkfld . . . 6D **74**
Victoria St. G66: Kirk . . . 5C **30**
G72: Blan . . . 3B **140**
G73: Ruth . . . 5C **104**
G82: Dumb . . . 5G **17**
ML2: Newm . . . 5E **147**
ML3: Ham . . . 3F **141**
ML9: Lark . . . 2E **161**
Victoria Ter. G68: Dull . . . 5F **13**
Victor St. ML6: Plain . . . 1G **93**
Victory Dr. PA10: Kilb . . . 1A **94**
VICTORY GARDENS . . . **1E 79**
Victory Way G69: Bail . . . 1H **107**
Viewbank G46: T'bnk . . . 4G **117**
Viewbank Av. ML6: C'bnk . . . 3B **112**
Viewbank St. ML5: Glenb . . . 4B **70**
VIEWFIELD . . . **4B 126**
Viewfield G69: Mood . . . 3C **52**
ML6: Air . . . 5G **91**
Viewfield Av. G64: B'rig . . . 1A **64**
G66: Lenz . . . 2C **50**
G66: Milt C . . . 6B **8**
G69: Bail . . . 6F **87**
G72: Blan . . . 6C **124**
Viewfield Dr. G64: B'rig . . . 1A **64**
G69: Bail . . . 6F **87**
Viewfield La. G12: Glas . . . 1C **82**
Viewfield Rd. FK4: Bank . . . 1D **14**
G64: B'rig . . . 1A **64**
ML4: Bell . . . 4B **126**
ML5: Coat . . . 1F **109**
Viewglen Ct. G45: Glas . . . 6H **119**
Viewmount Dr. G20: Glas . . . 2B **62**
VIEWPARK . . . **6G 109**
Viewpark G62: Miln . . . 4H **25**
Viewpark Av. G31: Glas . . . 3D **84**
Viewpark Ct. G73: Ruth . . . 1E **121**
Viewpark Dr. G73: Ruth . . . 1D **120**
Viewpark Gardens . . . **1F 125**
Viewpark Gdns. PA4: Renf . . . 1D **78**
Viewpark Pl. ML1: Moth . . . 3E **143**
Viewpark Rd. ML1: Moth . . . 3E **143**
Viewpark Shop. Cen.
G71: View . . . 1H **125**
Viewpoint Pl. G21: Glas . . . 3B **64**
Viewpoint Rd. G21: Glas . . . 3B **64**
Vigilant Ho. PA3: Pais . . . 4A **78**
Viking Cres. PA6: C'lee . . . 3D **74**
Viking Rd. ML6: Air . . . 6B **92**
Viking Ter. G75: E Kil . . . 5G **149**
Viking Way G46: T'bnk . . . 2F **117**
PA4: Renf . . . 2E **79**
Villafield Av. G64: B'rig . . . 4C **48**
Villafield Dr. G64: B'rig . . . 4C **48**
Villafield Loan G64: B'rig . . . 4C **48**
Village Gdns. G72: Blan . . . 6C **124**
Village Rd. G72: Flem . . . 2E **123**
Vincent Ct. *ML4: Bell . . . 3C* ***126***
(off Gardenside)
Vine St. G11: Glas . . . 1H **81**
Vinicombe La. *G12: Glas . . . 6B* ***62***
(off Vinicombe St.)
Vinicombe St. G12: Glas . . . 6B **62**
Vintner St. G4: Glas . . . 1G **83**
Viola Pl. G64: Torr . . . 5E **29**
Violet Gdns. ML8: Carl . . . 5E **165**
Violet Pl. ML1: Holy . . . 1B **128**
Violet St. PA1: Pais . . . 1C **98**
Virginia Ct. G1: Glas . . . 4G **83** (6E **5**)
Virginia Gdns. G62: Miln . . . 5A **26**
Virginia Pl. G1: Glas . . . 4G **83** (6F **5**)
Virginia St. G1: Glas . . . 4G **83** (6F **5**)
Viscount Av. PA4: Renf . . . 2E **79**
Viscount Ga. G71: Both . . . 2C **124**
Vivian Av. G62: Miln . . . 4F **25**
Voil Dr. G44: Glas . . . 3E **119**
Vorlich Ct. G78: Barr . . . 6E **115**
Vorlich Gdns. G61: Bear . . . 6C **24**
Vorlich Wynd ML1: N'hill . . . 3C **128**
Vulcan St. G21: Glas . . . 5A **64**
(not continuous)
ML1: Moth . . . 1G **143**

W

Waddell Av. ML6: Glenm . . . 5F **71**
Waddell Ct. G5: Glas . . . 6H **83**
Waddell St. G5: Glas . . . 1H **103**
ML6: Air . . . 2A **92**
Waid Av. G77: Newt M . . . 3C **132**
Waldemar Rd. G13: Glas . . . 2C **60**
Waldo St. G13: Glas . . . 2F **61**
Walkerburn Dr. ML2: Wis . . . 3A **146**
Walkerburn Rd. G52: Glas . . . 1B **100**
Walker Ct. G11: Glas . . . 2H **81**
Walker Dr. PA5: Eld . . . 3H **95**
Walker Path G71: Tann . . . 5E **109**
Walker St. G11: Glas . . . 2H **81**
PA1: Pais . . . 1H **97**
Walkinshaw Rd. PA4: Inch . . . 6F **57**
Walkinshaw St. G40: Glas . . . 1C **104**
PA5: John . . . 2F **95**
(Collier St.)
PA5: John . . . 2F **95**
(High St.)
Walkinshaw Way PA3: Pais . . . 4A **78**
Wallace Av. PA5: Eld . . . 2A **96**
PA7: B'ton . . . 4H **39**
Wallace Dr. ML9: Lark . . . 3G **161**
Wallacegait PA4: Renf . . . 6D **58**
Wallace Gdns. G64: Torr . . . 4D **28**
Wallace Ho. G67: Cumb . . . 3G **35**
Wallace Pl. G72: Blan . . . 6C **124**
ML3: Ham . . . 1C **154**
Wallace Rd. ML1: New S . . . 5B **128**
PA4: Renf . . . 2C **78**
Wallace St. G5: Glas . . . 5E **83**
G73: Ruth . . . 6C **104**
G81: Clyd . . . 1D **58**
G82: Dumb . . . 5G **17**
ML1: Moth . . . 2F **143**
ML5: Coat . . . 6C **90**
ML6: Plain . . . 1G **93**
PA3: Pais . . . 5A **78**
Wallacewell Cres. G21: Glas . . . 4D **64**
Wallacewell Pl. G21: Glas . . . 4D **64**
Wallacewell Quad. G21: Glas . . . 3E **65**
Wallacewell Rd. G21: Glas . . . 4C **64**
Wallace Wynd ML8: Law . . . 5E **159**
Wallbrae Rd. G67: Cumb . . . 5A **36**
Waller Gdns. G41: Glas . . . 4B **102**
Wallneuk PA3: Pais . . . 6B **78**
Wallneuk Rd. PA3: Pais . . . 6B **78**
Walls St. G1: Glas . . . 4H **83** (6G **5**)
Walmer Cres. G51: Glas . . . 5A **82**
Walnut Ct. G66: Milt C . . . 6B **8**
Walnut Cres. G22: Glas . . . 4H **63**
PA5: John . . . 4H **95**
Walnut Dr. G66: Lenz . . . 1B **50**
Walnut Ga. G72: Flem . . . 3F **123**
Walnut Pl. G22: Glas . . . 4G **63**
G71: View . . . 4G **109**
Walnut Rd. G22: Glas . . . 4G **63**
Walpole Pl. PA5: John . . . 6D **94**
Walter St. G31: Glas . . . 4D **84**
ML2: Wis . . . 6B **146**
Walton Av. G77: Newt M . . . 3C **132**
Walton Ct. G46: Giff . . . 5A **118**
Walton St. G41: Glas . . . 5C **102**
G78: Barr . . . 4E **115**
Wamba Av. G13: Glas . . . 1E **61**
Wamba Pl. G13: Glas . . . 1E **61**
Wamphray Pl. G75: E Kil . . . 4A **148**
Wandilla Av. G81: Clyd . . . 5F **43**
Wanlock St. G51: Glas . . . 3G **81**
Wardend Rd. G64: Torr . . . 4D **28**
Warden Rd. G13: Glas . . . 2D **60**
Wardhill Rd. G21: Glas . . . 4D **64**
Wardhouse Rd. PA2: Pais . . . 6G **97**
Wardie Path G33: Glas . . . 4F **87**
Wardie Pl. G33: Glas . . . 4F **87**
Wardie Rd. G33: Glas . . . 4F **87**
Wardlaw Av. G73: Ruth . . . 6D **104**
Wardlaw Cres. G75: E Kil . . . 4H **149**
Wardlaw Dr. G73: Ruth . . . 5D **104**
Wardlaw Rd. G61: Bear . . . 6F **45**
WARDPARK . . . **4C 14**
Wardpark Ct. G67: Cumb . . . 5D **14**
Wardpark E. Ind. Est. G68: Cumb . . . 3E **15**
Wardpark Nth. Ind. Est.
G68: Cumb . . . 4C **14**
Wardpark Pl. G67: Cumb . . . 5D **14**
Wardpark Rd. G67: Cumb . . . 5C **14**
WARDPARK RDBT. . . . **4D 14**
Wardpark Sth. Ind. Est.
G67: Cumb . . . 5D **14**
Wardrop Pl. G74: E Kil . . . 6H **137**
Wardrop St. G51: Glas . . . 3G **81**
PA1: Pais . . . 1A **98**
Wards Cres. ML5: Coat . . . 6A **90**
Ware Rd. G34: Glas . . . 4F **87**
Warilda Av. G81: Clyd . . . 5E **43**
Warlock Dr. PA11: Bri W . . . 2F **73**
Warlock Rd. PA11: Bri W . . . 2F **73**
Warnock Cres. ML4: Bell . . . 3D **126**
Warnock Rd. G77: Newt M . . . 3C **132**
Warnock St. G31: Glas . . . 3A **84**
Warren Rd. ML3: Ham . . . 3H **153**
Warren St. G42: Glas . . . 4F **103**
Warren Wlk. G66: Len . . . 4G **7**
Warrington Ct. G33: Glas . . . 3H **85**
Warriston Cres. G33: Glas . . . 3F **85**
Warriston Pl. G32: Glas . . . 4B **86**
Warriston St. G33: Glas . . . 3F **85**
Warriston Way *G73: Ruth . . . 3F* ***121***
(off Kilbride Rd.)
Warroch St. G3: Glas . . . 4D **82**
Warwick G74: E Kil . . . 5C **138**
Warwick Gro. ML3: Ham . . . 4C **140**
Warwick Vs. *G81: Clyd . . . 2G* ***59***
(off Edward St.)
Washington Rd. G66: Kirk . . . 5B **30**
PA3: Pais . . . 3B **78**
Washington St. G3: Glas . . . 4E **83** (6A **4**)
Watchmeal Cres. G81: Faif . . . 6E **23**
Waterbank Rd. G76: Crmck . . . 3H **135**
WATERFOOT . . . **6B 134**
Waterfoot Av. G53: Glas . . . 5C **100**
Waterfoot Bank G74: T'hall . . . 6C **134**
Waterfoot Rd. G74: T'hall . . . 6C **134**
Waterfoot Rd. G77: Newt M . . . 6F **133**
Waterfoot Row G76: Water . . . 6B **134**
Waterfoot Ter. *G53: Glas . . . 5C* ***100***
(off Waterfoot Av.)

Waterford Rd. G46: Giff 4H **117**
Waterhaughs Gdns. G33: Glas 2F **65**
Waterhaughs Gro. G33: Glas. 2F **65**
Waterhaughs Pl. G33: Glas 2F **65**
Waterlands Gdns. ML8: Carl. 2G **165**
Waterlands Pl. ML8: Law 1A **164**
Waterlands Rd. ML8: Law. 5F **159**
WATERLOO **2B 158**
Waterloo Cl. G66: Kirk 4D **30**
Waterloo Gdns. *G66: Kirk. 4D* ***30***
(off John St.)
Waterloo La. G2: Glas 4F **83** (5C **4**)
Waterloo St. G2: Glas. 4E **83** (5B **4**)
G66: Kirk 4D **30**
Watermill Av. G66: Lenz. 3D **50**
Water Rd. G78: Barr 4E **115**
Water Row G51: Glas 3G **81**
Watershaugh Dr. ML1: Cle 5H **129**
WATERSIDE
Barrhead **2G 115**
Kirkintilloch **6H 31**
Waterside Av. G77: Newt M 5C **132**
Waterside Cotts. G66: Kirk 6H **31**
Waterside Ct. G76: Crmck 2H **135**
Waterside Dr. G77: Newt M 5C **132**
Waterside Gdns. G72: Flem 4E **123**
G76: Crmck. 2H **135**
ML3: Ham. 2A **154**
Waterside La. PA10: John 3C **94**
Waterside Rd. G66: Kirk 6E **31**
(not continuous)
G76: Crmck. 4H **135**
Waterside St. G5: Glas 1H **103**
Waterside Ter. *PA10: Kilb 3C* ***94***
(off Kilbarchan Rd.)
Waterside Way PA10: Kilb 3C **94**
Water Sports Cen. **3C 142**
Watling Pl. G75: E Kil. 2C **148**
Watling St. G71: Tann. 4C **108**
ML1: Moth 6D **126**
Watson Av. G73: Ruth. 6B **104**
PA3: Lin 5H **75**
Watson Cres. G65: Kils. 3A **12**
Watson Pl. G72: Blan 2H **139**
Watson St. G1: Glas. 5H **83** (6H **5**)
G71: Udd 2D **124**
G72: Blan 2H **139**
ML1: Moth 4G **143**
ML9: Lark. 2D **160**
Watsonville Pk. ML1: Moth 3G **143**
Watt Cres. ML4: Bell. 6D **110**
Watt La. PA11: Bri W 4G **73**
Watt Low Av. G73: Ruth 1B **120**
Watt Pl. G62: Miln 2F **25**
G72: Blan 5A **140**
Watt Rd. G52: Hill 4H **79**
PA11: Bri W. 4F **73**
Watt St. G5: Glas 5D **82**
ML6: Air 2C **92**
Waukglen Av. G53: Glas 5B **116**
Waukglen Cres. G53: Glas 4C **116**
Waukglen Dr. G53: Glas 4B **116**
Waukglen Gdns. G53: Glas 5B **116**
Waukglen Path G53: Glas 4B **116**
Waukglen Pl. G53: Glas 4B **116**
Waukglen Rd. G53: Glas 4B **116**
Waulking Mill Rd. G81: Faif, Hard. . . 6E **23**
Waulkmill Av. G78: Barr 3F **115**
Waulkmill St. G46: T'bnk 3E **117**
Waulkmill Way G78: Barr 3F **115**
Waverley G74: E Kil 5D **138**
G81: Clyd 5E **43**
Waverley Ct. G71: Both 5E **125**
PA2: Pais 5D **96**
Waverley Cres. G66: Kirk 5E **31**
G67: Cumb 6F **35**
ML3: Ham. 5D **140**
Waverley Dr. G73: Ruth 6E **105**
ML2: Wis 5H **145**
ML6: Air 2B **92**
Waverley Gdns. G41: Glas 4C **102**
PA5: Eld 3B **96**
WAVERLEY PARK **4B 102**
Waverley Pk. G66: Kirk 5D **30**
Waverley Rd. PA2: Pais 6D **96**
Waverley St. G41: Glas. 4C **102**
ML3: Ham. 5D **140**
ML5: Coat. 2D **90**
ML9: Lark 5E **161**
Waverley Ter. G72: Blan 4A **140**
G82: Dumb 3B **16**
Waverley Way PA2: Pais 6D **96**
Weardale La. G33: Glas 3C **86**
Weardale St. G33: Glas 3C **86**
Weaver Av. G77: Newt M 2C **132**
Weaver Cres. ML6: Air 6A **92**
Weaver La. PA10: Kilb 1A **94**
Weaver Pl. G75: E Kil. 4A **148**
Weavers Av. PA2: Pais 2F **97**
Weaver's Cottage *. 2A* ***94***
(off Weavers Ct.)
Weaver's Cottage Mus., The
. . . . **3A 92**
Weavers Ct. *G74: E Kil. 1H* ***149***
(off Parkhall St.)
PA10: Kilb. 2A **94**
Weaver's Ga. PA1: Pais 2E **97**
Weavers Rd. PA2: Pais 2F **97**
Weaver St. G4: Glas 4H **83** (5H **5**)
Weaver Ter. PA2: Pais 2C **98**
Webster Groves ML2: Wis 4B **146**
Webster St. G40: Glas 2C **104**
G81: Clyd 1G **59**
Wedderlea Dr. G52: Glas 6A **80**
Wedsley Ct. G41: Glas 1C **102**
Weensmoor Rd. G53: Glas 3H **115**
Weeple Dr. PA3: Lin 5G **75**
Weighhouse Cl. PA1: Pais 1A **98**
Weigh Ho. Rd. ML8: Carl 2E **165**
Weir Av. G78: Barr 5E **115**
Weir Pl. ML8: Law 1H **163**
Weir's La. ML8: Carl. 3F **165**
Weir St. ML5: Coat. 4C **90**
PA3: Pais 6B **78**
Weirwood Av. G69: Bail. 1F **107**
Weirwood Gdns. G69: Bail 1F **107**
Welbeck Rd. G53: Glas. 2B **116**
Weldon Pl. G65: Croy. 2B **34**
Welfare Av. G72: Camb 3D **122**
Welland Pl. G75: E Kil 4A **148**
Wellbank Pl. G71: Udd. 2D **124**
Wellbeck Ho. *G74: E Kil 1H* ***149***
(off Stuart St.)
Wellbrae Hill ML9: Lark 3E **161**
Wellbrae Rd. ML3: Ham 2F **153**
Wellbrae Ter. G69: Mood 5D **52**
Wellcroft Pl. G5: Glas 1F **103**
(not continuous)
Wellcroft Rd. ML3: Ham. 6C **140**
Wellcroft Ter. ML3: Ham. 6C **140**
Wellesley Cres. G68: Cumb 4A **34**
G75: E Kil 4B **148**
Wellesley Dr. G68: Cumb. 4H **33**
G75: E Kil 3B **148**
Wellesley Pl. G68: Cumb 4H **33**
Wellfield Av. G46: Giff 4H **117**
Wellfield St. G21: Glas. 5B **64**
Wellgate Ct. ML9: Lark. 1E **161**
Wellgate St. ML9: Lark. 1E **161**
Well Grn. G43: Glas 5A **102**
Well Grn. Ct. *G43: Glas 5A* ***102***
(off Well Grn.)
Wellhall Ct. ML3: Ham 5F **141**
Wellhall Rd. ML3: Ham 1C **152**
Wellhouse Cres. G33: Glas. 4E **87**
Wellhouse Gdns. G33: Glas 4F **87**
Wellhouse Path G34: Glas. 4F **87**
Wellhouse Rd. G33: Glas 3F **87**
Wellington G75: E Kil 4D **148**
Wellington La. G2: Glas 4E **83** (5B **4**)
(not continuous)
Wellington Path G69: Bail. 1H **107**
Wellington Pl. G81: Clyd 4H **41**
ML2: Wis 3B **158**
ML5: Coat. 6G **89**
Wellington Rd. G64: B'rig. 3D **48**
Wellington St. G2: Glas 4F **83** (6C **4**)
ML2: Wis 4C **144**
Wellington St. ML6: Air 2A **92**
PA3: Pais 5H **77**
Wellington Way PA4: Renf 2E **79**
Wellknowe Av. G74: T'hall 6G **135**
Wellknowe Pl. G74: T'hall. 6F **135**
Wellknowe Rd. G74: T'hall 6G **135**
Well La. G66: Len. 3F **7**
Wellmeadow Cl. G77: Newt M 4D **132**
Wellmeadow Grn. G77: Newt M . . . 3D **132**
Wellmeadow Rd. G43: Glas 1H **117**
Wellmeadow St. PA1: Pais. 1H **97**
Wellmeadow Way G77: Newt M . . . 4D **132**
Wellpark La. G78: Neil 3D **130**
Wellpark Rd. FK4: Bank 1D **14**
ML1: Moth 3E **143**
Wellpark St. G31: Glas. 4A **84**
Wellpark Ter. G78: Neil. 3D **130**
Well Rd. PA10: Kilb 2A **94**
Wellshot Cotts. G65: Kils 4H **11**
Wellshot Dr. G72: Camb 2H **121**
Wellshot Rd. G32: Glas 2H **105**
WELLSIDE. **3D 122**
Wellside Av. ML6: Air. 2A **92**
Wellside Dr. G72: Camb 3C **122**
Wellside La. ML6: Air. 2B **92**
Wellside Quad. ML6: Air 1A **92**
Wellsquarry Rd. G76: Crmck 5E **137**
Wells St. G81: Clyd 4B **42**
Well St. PA1: Pais 6G **77**
PA3: Pais 6G **77**
Wellview Dr. ML1: Moth 3F **143**
Wellwynd ML6: Air. 3H **91**
Wellwynd Gdns. ML6: Air. 3H **91**
Welsh Dr. G72: Blan 3B **140**
ML3: Ham. 4G **153**
Welsh Row ML6: C'bnk. 2C **112**
Wemyss Av. G77: Newt M. 2C **132**
Wemyss Dr. G68: Cumb 4A **34**
Wemyss Gdns. G69: Bail 2G **107**
Wendur Way PA3: Pais. 3A **78**
Wenlock Rd. PA2: Pais. 3B **98**
Wensleydale G74: E Kil. 6E **137**
Wentworth Dr. G23: Glas 6C **46**
Wesley St. ML6: Air 4H **91**
Westacres Rd. G77: Newt M. 5A **132**
WEST ARTHURLIE **6C 114**
West Av. G33: Step. 4D **66**
G71: View 1F **125**
G72: Blan 4C **140**
ML1: New S 5A **128**
ML6: Plain 1G **93**
ML8: Carl 4D **164**
PA1: Pais 1B **96**
PA4: Renf 6F **59**
WEST BALGROCHAN. **3D 28**
W. Balgrochan Rd. G64: Torr 4D **28**
Westbank Ct. *G12: Glas 1C* ***82***
(off Westbank Quad.)
Westbank La. *G12: Glas. 1C* ***82***
(off Gibson St.)
Westbank Quad. G12: Glas. 1C **82**
Westbourne Cres. G61: Bear. 2C **44**
Westbourne Dr. G61: Bear 2C **44**
Westbourne Gdns. La. G12: Glas . . . 5A **62**
Westbourne Gdns. Nth. G12: Glas. . . 5A **62**
Westbourne Gdns. Sth. G12: Glas. . . 5A **62**
Westbourne Gdns. W. G12: Glas. . . . 5H **61**
Westbourne Rd. G12: Glas 5H **61**
Westbourne Ter. La. Nth.
G12: Glas 5H **61**
Westbourne Ter. La. Sth.
G12: Glas 5H **61**
West Brae PA1: Pais. 1H **97**
Westbrae Dr. G14: Glas 5E **61**
Westbrae Rd. G77: Newt M. 3F **133**
West Bridgend G82: Dumb 3E **17**
W. Buchanan Pl. PA1: Pais. 1H **97**
WESTBURN **1E 123**
Westburn Av. G72: Camb 1D **122**
PA3: Pais 6E **77**
Westburn Cres. G73: Ruth 6B **104**
G81: Hard. 6D **22**
Westburn Dr. G72: Camb 6B **106**
Westburn Farm Rd. G72: Camb . . . 1B **122**

Westburn Rd. G72: Camb, Newt . . . 2B **122**
W. Burnside St. G65: Kils 3H **11**
W. Campbell St. G2: Glas 4E **83** (6B **4**)
PA1: Pais 1F **97**
W. Canal St. ML5: Coat 5B **90**
Westcastle Ct. G45: Glas 4H **119**
Westcastle Cres. G45: Glas 4H **119**
Westcastle Gdns. G45: Glas 4H **119**
Westcastle Gro. G45: Glas 4H **119**
W. Chapelton Av. G61: Bear 3F **45**
W. Chapelton Cres. G61: Bear 3F **45**
W. Chapelton Dr. G61: Bear 3F **45**
W. Chapelton La. G61: Bear 3F **45**
Westcliff G82: Dumb 3B **16**
W. Clyde St. ML9: Lark 3F **161**
Westclyffe St. G41: Glas 4C **102**
W. Coats Rd. G72: Camb 3H **121**
West Ct. G81: Clyd 3A **42**
PA1: Pais 1E **97**
WEST CRAIGEND 6E **41**
WEST CRINDLEDYKE 3D **146**
West Cross ML2: Wis 6G **145**
West Dr. ML6: Air 5E **93**
WEST DRUMOYNE 4D **80**
Westend G61: Bear 5G **45**
Westend Ct. ML8: Law 1H **163**
W. End Dr. ML4: Bell 3A **126**
Westend Pk. St. G3: Glas 2D **82**
W. End Pl. ML4: Bell 3B **126**
WESTER AUCHINLOCH 6D **50**
Westerburn St. G32: Glas 5H **85**
Wester Carriagehill PA2: Pais 3H **97**
Wester Cleddens Rd. G64: B'rig . . . 5C **48**
Wester Cochno Holdings
G81: Hard 5D **22**
Wester Comn. Dr. G22: Glas 5E **63**
Wester Comn. Rd. G22: Glas 5E **63**
Westercraigs G31: Glas 4B **84**
Westercraigs Ct. G31: Glas 4B **84**
Westerdale G74: E Kil 6E **137**
Westerfield Rd. G76: Crmck 5H **135**
Westergate Shop. Cen. G2: Glas . . . 6C **4**
Wester Gill ML6: Air 5E **93**
Westergreens Av. G66: Kirk 1B **50**
Westerhill Rd. G64: B'rig 3D **48**
WESTER HOLYTOWN 2G **127**
Westerhouse Ct. ML8: Carl 3D **164**
Westerhouse Path G34: Glas 3G **87**
(off Arnisdale Dr.)
Westerhouse Rd. G34: Glas 3F **87**
WESTERHOUSE ROAD INTERCHANGE
. . . . 3F **87**
Westerkirk Dr. G23: Glas 6C **46**
Westerlands G12: Glas 3G **61**
Westerlands Dr. G77: Newt M 5B **132**
Westerlands Gdns. G77: Newt M . . 5B **132**
Westerlands Gro. G77: Newt M . . . 5B **132**
Westerlands Pl. G77: Newt M 4B **132**
Westermains Av. G66: Kirk 6B **30**
Wester Mavisbank Av. ML6: Air . . . 3G **91**
Wester Moffat Av. ML6: Air 3E **93**
Wester Moffat Cres. ML6: Air 4E **93**
Wester Myvot Rd. G67: Cumb 3C **54**
Western Av. G73: Ruth 5B **104**
Western Baths Club 6B **62**
Western Isles Rd. G60: Old K 1G **41**
Western Rd. G72: Camb 3G **121**
Wester Rd. G32: Glas 1D **106**
Westerton G66: Len 3H **7**
Westerton Av. G61: Bear 1F **61**
G76: Busby 4E **135**
ML9: Lark 4E **161**
Westerton Ct. G76: Busby 4E **135**
Westerton La. G76: Busby 4E **135**
Westerton Rd. G68: Dull 5F **13**
Westerton Station (Rail) 6E **45**
WESTERWOOD 6A **14**
W. Fairholm St. ML9: Lark 6H **155**
WEST FERRY INTERCHANGE 1A **38**
WESTFIELD
Cumbernauld 6B **34**
Kilsyth 2F **11**
Westfield G82: Dumb 3C **16**
Westfield Av. G73: Ruth 6B **104**

Westfield Cres. G61: Bear 5E **45**
Westfield Dr. G52: Glas 6A **80**
G61: Bear 5E **45**
G68: Cumb 6A **34**
Westfield Ind. Area G68: Cumb . . . 1H **53**
Westfield Ind. Est. G68: Cumb . . . 2A **54**
Westfield Pl. G68: Cumb 1H **53**
Westfield Rd. G46: T'bnk 5G **117**
G65: Kils 2F **11**
G68: Cumb 1H **53**
ML1: N'hse 6C **112**
Westfields G64: B'rig 4A **48**
Westgarth Pl. G74: E Kil 6C **136**
West Ga. ML2: Wis 6B **146**
Westgate Way ML4: Bell 3B **126**
W. George La. G2: Glas 3E **83** (4A **4**)
W. George St. G2: Glas 3E **83** (4A **4**)
(not continuous)
ML5: Coat 3C **90**
W. Glebe Ter. ML3: Ham 1G **153**
W. Graham St. G4: Glas 2E **83** (1B **4**)
W. Greenhill Pl. G3: Glas 3C **82**
W. Hamilton St. ML1: Moth 3G **143**
W. High St. G66: Kirk 4C **30**
Westhorn Dr. G32: Glas 4A **106**
Westhouse Av. G73: Ruth 6A **104**
Westhouse Gdns. G73: Ruth 6A **104**
W. Kirk St. ML6: Air 4H **91**
Westknowe Gdns. G73: Ruth 2D **120**
Westland Dr. G14: Glas 6D **60**
Westland Dr. La. G14: Glas 6D **60**
(off Westland Dr.)
Westlands Gdns. PA2: Pais 3H **97**
West La. PA1: Pais 1F **97**
Westlea Pl. ML6: Air 5B **92**
W. Lodge Rd. PA4: Renf 5D **58**
WEST MAINS 1D **148**
W. Mains Rd. G74: E Kil 1D **148**
WEST MARYSTON 4B **88**
Westminster Ter. G3: Glas 3C **82**
(off Royal Cres.)
Westmoreland St. G42: Glas 3E **103**
Westmuir Pl. G73: Ruth 5B **104**
Westmuir St. G31: Glas 6F **85**
W. Nile St. G1: Glas 4F **83** (5D **4**)
G2: Glas 3F **83** (4D **4**)
West of Scotland Indoor Bowling Club
. . . . 3A **104**
West of Scotland R.U.F.C. 5H **25**
Westpark Dr. PA3: Pais 6F **77**
West Pl. ML2: Newm 4E **147**
Westport G75: E Kil 2C **148**
WEST PORTON 3G **39**
W. Porton Pl. PA7: B'ton 3F **39**
Westport St. G65: Kils 3H **11**
W. Prince's La. G4: Glas 1C **82**
W. Prince's St. G4: Glas . . . 1D **82** (1A **4**)
Westray Av. G77: Newt M 2C **132**
Westray Cir. G22: Glas 3G **63**
Westray Ct. G67: Cumb 5G **35**
Westray Pl. G22: Glas 2H **63**
G64: B'rig 5F **49**
Westray Rd. G67: Cumb 5G **35**
Westray Sq. G22: Glas 2G **63**
Westray St. G22: Glas 2G **63**
Westray Wynd ML2: Newm 3D **146**
(off Iona Rd.)
W. Regent La. G2: Glas 3F **83** (4C **4**)
W. Regent St. G2: Glas 3E **83** (3B **4**)
(not continuous)
West Rd. G64: Torr 4D **28**
PA10: Kilb 1A **94**
W. Scott Ter. ML3: Ham 2H **153**
Westside Gdns. G11: Glas 1H **81**
W. Stewart St. ML3: Ham 5G **141**
West St. G5: Glas 1E **103**
G81: Clyd 1G **59**
PA1: Pais 1G **97**
WEST ST. INTERCHANGE 6D **82**
West Street Station (Und.) 6E **83**
W. Thomson St. G81: Clyd 4C **42**
W. Thornlie St. ML2: Wis 1G **157**
W. Westbrae Cres. ML3: Ham 2F **153**
W. Whitby St. G31: Glas 1E **105**

WESTWOOD 3D **148**
Westwood Av. G46: Giff 4H **117**
Westwood Cres. ML3: Ham 1F **153**
Westwood Gdns. PA3: Pais 6F **77**
Westwood Hill G75: E Kil 3D **148**
Westwood Quad. G81: Clyd 6F **43**
Westwood Rd. G43: Glas 1H **117**
G75: E Kil 2D **148**
ML2: Newm 2D **146**
Westwood Sq. G75: E Kil 3D **148**
Weymouth Dr. G12: Glas 3G **61**
Weymouth La. G12: Glas 4H **61**
(off Chelmsford Dr.)
Whamflet Av. G69: Bail 4A **88**
Whamond Twr. ML1: Moth 4G **143**
Wheatfield Rd. G61: Bear 4D **44**
Wheatholm Cres. ML6: Air 2B **92**
Wheatholm St. ML6: Air 2B **92**
Wheatland Av. G72: Blan 1A **140**
Wheatlandhead Ct. G72: Blan 1A **140**
WHEATLANDS 1A **140**
Wheatlands Dr. PA10: Kilb 1A **94**
Wheatlands Farm Rd. PA10: Kilb . . 1A **94**
Wheatley Ct. G32: Glas 6A **86**
Wheatley Cres. G65: Kils 4H **11**
Wheatley Dr. G32: Glas 6A **86**
Wheatley Loan G64: B'rig 1E **65**
Wheatley Pl. G32: Glas 6A **86**
WHIFFLET 6D **90**
Whifflet Ct. ML5: Coat 6D **90**
(off Whifflet St.)
Whifflet Station (Rail) 6D **90**
Whifflet St. ML5: Coat 2C **110**
Whin Av. G78: Barr 3D **114**
Whinfell Dr. G75: E Kil 5C **148**
Whinfell Gdns. G75: E Kil 5C **148**
Whinfield Av. G72: Camb 6G **105**
Whinfield Rd. G53: Glas 3A **116**
WHINHALL 2G **91**
Whinhall Av. ML6: Air 2G **91**
Whinhall Rd. ML6: Air 2G **91**
Whin Hill G74: E Kil 5B **138**
Whinhill Pl. G53: Glas 2A **100**
Whinhill Rd. G53: Glas 2A **100**
PA2: Pais 3D **98**
WHINKNOWE 5C **162**
Whinknowe ML9: Ashg 5B **162**
Whin Loan G65: Queen 2A **10**
Whinney Gro. ML2: Wis 5C **146**
Whinnie Knowe ML9: Lark 4D **160**
Whinpark Av. ML4: Bell 4B **126**
Whin Pl. G74: E Kil 4B **138**
Whins Rd. G41: Glas 4A **102**
Whin St. G81: Clyd 3C **42**
Whirlie Ct. PA6: C'lee 2C **74**
Whirlie Dr. PA6: C'lee 3B **74**
Whirlie Rd. PA6: C'lee 2B **74**
WHIRLIES RDBT., THE. 5A **138**
Whirlow Gdns. G69: Bail 6G **87**
Whirlow Rd. G69: Bail 6G **87**
Whistleberry Cres. ML3: Ham 2F **141**
Whistleberry Dr. ML3: Ham 2E **141**
Whistleberry Ind. Pk. ML3: Ham . . 2E **141**
Whistleberry Pk. ML3: Ham 2E **141**
Whistleberry Retail Pk.
G72: Blan 2D **140**
Whistleberry Rd. G72: Blan 2D **140**
ML3: Ham 2E **141**
Whistlefield Ct. G61: Bear 4E **45**
Whitacres Path G53: Glas 3A **116**
Whitacres Rd. G53: Glas 3H **115**
Whitburn St. G32: Glas 4H **85**
Whiteadder Pl. G75: E Kil 4A **148**
White Av. G82: Dumb 4H **17**
Whitebill Rd. ML3: Ham 4F **141**
Whitebridge Av. PA3: Pais 1D **96**
Whitebridge Cl. PA3: Pais 1D **96**
White Cart Rd. PA3: Glas A. 2A **78**
White-Cart Twr. G74: E Kil 4B **150**
(off Easdale)
WHITECRAIGS 2G **133**
Whitecraigs Pl. G23: Glas. 1C **62**
Whitecraigs Station (Rail) 1G **133**
WHITECROOK 6E **43**

Whitecrook St. G81: Clyd 1D **58**
Whitefield G66: Len 2E **7**
Whitefield Av. G72: Camb 3A **122**
Whitefield Rd. G51: Glas 6A **82**
Whitefield Ter. G66: Len 2E **7**
G72: Camb 2B **122**
Whiteford Av. G82: Dumb 1H **17**
Whiteford Ct. ML3: Ham 5G **153**
Whiteford Cres. G82: Dumb 2H **17**
Whiteford Pl. G82: Dumb 2H **17**
Whiteford Rd. G33: Step 4F **67**
PA2: Pais 3C **98**
Whitehall St. G3: Glas 4D **82**
WHITEHAUGH **6C 78**
Whitehaugh Av. PA1: Pais 6D **78**
Whitehaugh Cres. G53: Glas 3A **116**
(not continuous)
Whitehaugh Dr. PA1: Pais 6D **78**
Whitehaugh Rd. G53: Glas 3A **116**
(not continuous)
WHITEHILL **3F 141**
Whitehill Av. G33: Step 3D **66**
G66: Kirk 4F **31**
G68: Cumb 3F **35**
ML6: Air 2A **92**
Whitehill Ct. G66: Kirk 4F **31**
Whitehill Cres. G66: Kirk 4F **31**
G81: Faif 6G **23**
ML8: Carl 2F **165**
Whitehill Farm Rd. G33: Step 4D **66**
Whitehill Gdns. G31: Glas 4C **84**
Whitehill Gro. G77: Newt M 6F **133**
Whitehill La. G61: Bear 3D **44**
Whitehill Pool **4D 84**
Whitehill Rd. G61: Bear 2D **44**
ML3: Ham 3F **141**
WHITEHILLS **5G 149**
Whitehills PA8: Ersk 5E **41**
Whitehills Dr. G75: E Kil 4G **149**
Whitehills Pl. G75: E Kil 4G **149**
Whitehill Sports Barn **3F 141**
Whitehills Ter. G75: E Kil 5G **149**
Whitehill St. G31: Glas 4C **84**
(not continuous)
Whitehill St. La. G31: Glas 4C **84**
Whitehill Ter. G69: G'csh 5D **68**
Whitehorse Wlk. G75: E Kil 3D **148**
Whitehurst G61: Bear 1C **44**
Whitehurst Pk. G61: Bear 1C **44**
WHITEINCH **6C 60**
Whiteinch Bus. Pk. G14: Glas 1D **80**
Whiteinch Homes *G14: Glas* *6D* ***60***
(off Westland Dr.)
Whitekirk Pl. G15: Glas 5A **44**
Whitelaw Av. ML5: Glenb 4B **70**
Whitelawburn G72: Camb 3G **121**
Whitelaw Cres. ML4: Bell 3F **127**
Whitelaw St. G20: Glas 2A **62**
Whitelaw Ter. G65: Twe 1D **32**
Whitelee G75: E Kil 6F **149**
Whitelee Cres. G77: Newt M 3B **132**
Whitelee Ga. G77: Newt M 3B **132**
Whitelees Rd. G67: Cumb 5E **15**
WHITELEES RDBT. **6F 15**
Whiteloans G71: Both 4F **125**
Whitemoss Av. G44: Glas 3D **118**
G74: E Kil 2H **149**
Whitemoss Gro. G74: E Kil 1A **150**
Whitemoss Rd. G74: E Kil 2H **149**
WHITEMOSS RDBT. **2A 150**
Whitepond Av. ML4: Bell 4B **126**
Whiterigg Ct. *ML6: Air* *3F* ***91***
(off Monkscourt Av.)
Whiteshaw Av. ML8: Carl 3D **164**
Whiteshaw Dr. ML8: Carl 3D **164**
Whiteshaw Rd. ML8: Law 2B **164**
Whitestone Av. G68: Cumb 3D **34**
White St. G11: Glas 1H **81**
G81: Clyd 2F **59**
WHITESTRIPE **3F 147**
Whitevale St. G31: Glas 5C **84**
G40: Glas 5C **84**
Whithope Rd. G53: Glas 3H **115**
Whithope Ter. G53: Glas 3H **115**
Whithorn Cres. G69: Mood 4D **52**
WHITLAWBURN **4H 121**
Whitlawburn Av. G72: Camb 3G **121**
Whitlawburn Rd. G72: Camb 3G **121**
Whitlawburn Shop. Cen.
G72: Camb *4G* ***121***
(off Western Rd.)
Whitlawburn Ter. G72: Camb 3G **121**
Whitriggs Rd. G53: Glas 2H **115**
Whitslade Pl. G34: Glas 2F **87**
Whitslade St. G34: Glas 2G **87**
Whitsun Dale G74: E Kil 6E **137**
WHITTAGREEN **4D 128**
Whittagreen Av. ML1: N'hill 4D **128**
Whittagreen Ct. ML1: N'hill 4D **128**
Whittagreen Cres. ML1: N'hill 4D **128**
Whittingehame Gdns. G12: Glas 4G **61**
Whittingehame Dr.
G13, G12: Glas 4F **61**
Whittinghame La. G13: Glas 4F **61**
Whittington St. ML5: Coat 5C **90**
Whittlemuir Av. G44: Glas 3D **118**
Whitton Dr. G46: Giff 3B **118**
Whitton St. G20: Glas 1A **62**
Whitworth Dr. G81: Clyd 5C **42**
Whitworth St. G20: Glas 3E **63**
Whyte Av. G72: Camb 1G **121**
Whyte Cnr. G82: Milt 4F **19**
Wick Av. ML6: Air 1G **111**
Wickets, The PA1: Pais 2C **98**
Wickham Av. G77: Newt M 3D **132**
Wigton Av. G77: Newt M 2C **132**
Wigtoun Pl. G67: Cumb 1B **36**
WILDMANBRIDGE **4F 159**
Wildman Rd. ML8: Law 5F **159**
Wilfred Av. G13: Glas 2D **60**
Wilkie Cres. ML9: Lark 3F **161**
Wilkie Loan ML4: Bell 1D **126**
Wilkie Rd. G71: Udd 2E **125**
William Dr. ML3: Ham 4H **153**
William Mann Dr. G77: Newt M 5B **132**
WILLIAMSBURGH **1C 98**
Williamsburgh Ct. PA1: Pais 1C **98**
Williamsburgh Ter. PA1: Pais 6C **78**
Williamson Av. G82: Dumb 3G **17**
Williamson Pl. PA5: John 3H **95**
Williamson St. G40: Glas 1E **105**
G81: Clyd 3D **42**
William Spiers Pl. ML9: Lark 4F **161**
William St. G3: Glas 3D **82** (4A **4**)
G65: Kils 3H **11**
G81: Dun, Hard 1C **42**
ML3: Ham 4F **141**
ML5: Coat 1D **110**
PA1: Pais 1G **97**
PA5: John 2F **95**
William Ure Pl. G64: B'rig 2D **48**
WILLIAMWOOD **1B 134**
Williamwood Dr. G44: Neth 5C **118**
Williamwood Pk. G44: Neth 5D **118**
Williamwood Pk. W. G44: Neth 5D **118**
Williamwood Station (Rail) **6B 118**
Willock Pl. G20: Glas 2C **62**
Willoughby Dr. G13: Glas 3F **61**
Willoughby La. G13: Glas 3F **61**
Willow Av. G64: B'rig 1C **64**
G66: Lenz 2C **50**
ML1: New S 5A **128**
PA5: Eld 3A **96**
Willowbank ML9: Lark 6A **156**
Willowbank Cres. G3: Glas 1D **82**
Willowbank Gdns. G66: Kirk 5D **30**
Willowbank St. G3: Glas 1D **82**
Willow Ct. G75: E Kil 5D **148**
G81: Clyd 3B **42**
Willow Cres. ML5: Coat 1C **110**
Willowdale Cres. G69: Bail 1G **107**
Willowdale Gdns. G69: Bail 1G **107**
Willow Dr. FK4: Bank 1E **15**
G66: Milt C 6C **8**
G72: Blan 1A **140**
ML6: Air 4C **92**
PA5: John 4F **95**
Willowford Rd. G53: Glas 3H **115**
Willow Gro. ML1: Holy 2B **128**
Willow La. G32: Glas 3B **106**
Willow Pl. G71: View 5H **109**
PA5: John 3G **95**
Willows, The G76: Crmck 1H **135**
Willow St. G13: Glas 2F **61**
Willow Tea Rooms **3C 4**
Willow Way ML3: Ham 2A **154**
Willox Pk. G82: Dumb 2G **17**
Willwood Rd. ML2: Wis 2A **146**
Wilmot Rd. G13: Glas 3D **60**
Wilsgait St. ML1: Cle 5H **129**
Wilson Av. PA3: Lin 5G **75**
Wilson Ct. ML4: Bell 2B **126**
Wilson Pl. G74: E Kil 5A **138**
G77: Newt M 5C **132**
Wilson St. G1: Glas 4G **83** (6F **5**)
ML1: Moth 2H **143**
ML3: Ham 4E **141**
ML5: Coat 4E **91**
ML6: Air 2H **91**
ML9: Lark 4F **161**
PA1: Pais 1G **97**
PA4: Renf 5F **59**
Wiltonburn Path G53: Glas 3A **116**
Wiltonburn Rd. G53: Glas 3A **116**
Wilton Ct. *G20: Glas* *6C* ***62***
(off Wilton St.)
Wilton Cres. La. G20: Glas 6D **62**
Wilton Dr. G20: Glas 6D **62**
Wilton Rd. ML8: Carl 5G **165**
Wilton St. G20: Glas 5C **62**
ML5: Coat 1H **89**
Wilverton Rd. G13: Glas 1E **61**
Winburne Cres. ML3: Ham 5F **141**
Winchester Dr. G12: Glas 3H **61**
Windemere Gdns. ML3: Ham 5G **153**
Windermere G75: E Kil 6B **148**
Windermere St. ML4: Bell 3B **126**
Windhill Cres. G43: Glas 2H **117**
Windhill Pl. G43: Glas 2A **118**
Windhill Rd. G43: Glas 2H **117**
Windlaw Ct. G45: Glas 5H **119**
Windlaw Gdns. G44: Neth 3D **118**
Windlaw Pk. Gdns. G44: Neth 3D **118**
Windlaw Rd. G76: Crmck 6H **119**
Windmill Ct. ML1: Moth 4H **143**
Windmillcroft Quay *G5: Glas* *5E* ***83***
(off Riverview Pl.)
Windmillhill St. ML1: Moth 3H **143**
Windmill Rd. ML3: Ham 5H **141**
Windrow Ter. ML2: Wis 2A **146**
Windsor Av. G77: Newt M 4F **133**
Windsor Ct. ML8: Carl 3F **165**
Windsor Cres. G81: Clyd 4C **42**
PA1: Pais 5C **78**
PA5: Eld 4H **95**
Windsor Dr. ML6: Glenm 5H **71**
Windsor Gdns. ML3: Ham 3E **141**
Windsor Path *G69: Barg* *5D* ***88***
(off Park Rd.)
ML9: Lark *3G* ***161***
(off Carrick St.)
Windsor Pl. *PA11: Bri W* *3F* ***73***
(off Main Rd.)
Windsor Quad. ML8: Carl 3F **165**
Windsor Rd. ML1: Holy 2A **128**
PA4: Renf 1E **79**
Windsor St. G20: Glas 1E **83**
G32: Glas 5C **86**
ML5: Coat 2A **110**
Windsor Ter. G20: Glas 1E **83**
Windsor Wlk. G71: View 6F **109**
Windward Rd. G75: E Kil 2C **148**
Windyedge & Hareshaw Rd.
ML1: Cle 4H **129**
Windyedge Cres. G13: Glas 4C **60**
Windyedge Pl. G13: Glas 4C **60**
Windyridge ML3: Ham 2A **154**
Windyridge Pl. G72: Blan 2A **140**
Windy Yetts G65: Twe 2D **32**
Wingate Cres. G74: E Kil 5C **138**
Wingate Dr. G74: E Kil 5C **138**
Wingate Pk. G74: E Kil 5C **138**

Wingate St. ML2: Wis 5D **144**
Wingfield Gdns. G71: Both 6F **125**
Winifred St. G33: Glas 5F **65**
Winning Ct. G72: Blan 6C **124**
Winning Quad. ML2: Wis 6D **144**
Winning Row G31: Glas 6F **85**
Winnipeg Dr. G75: E Kil 3D **148**
Winston Cres. G66: Len 3F **7**
Winter Gdns. **6B 62**
Wintergreen Ct. G74: E Kil 5F **137**
Wintergreen Dr. G74: E Kil 5F **137**
Winton Av. G46: Giff 5A **118**
Winton Cres. G72: Blan 2A **140**
Winton Dr. G12: Glas 4A **62**
Winton Gdns. G71: Tann 6D **108**
Winton La. G12: Glas 4A **62**
Winton Pk. G75: E Kil 2C **148**
Wirran Pl. G13: Glas 1G **59**
Wishart Av. G81: Faif, Hard 6E **23**
Wishart St. G31: Glas 4A **84**
WISHAW **5H 145**
Wishaw High Rd. ML1: Cle 1H **145**
WISHAWHILL **5F 145**
Wishawhill St. ML2: Wis 6F **145**
Wishaw Low Rd. ML1: Cle 3G **145**
Wishaw Rd. ML2: Wis 2B **158**
Wishaw Sports Cen. **1F 157**
Wishaw Station (Rail) **1G 157**
Wisner Ct. G46: T'bnk 3F **117**
Wisteria La. ML8: Carl 5F **165**
Wiston St. G72: Camb 2E **123**
Witchwood Ct. ML5: Coat 1H **89**
Witcutt Way ML2: Wis 2E **157**
Wolcott Dr. G72: Blan 1B **140**
Wolfe Av. G77: Newt M 2C **132**
Wolseley St. G5: Glas 2H **103**
Women's Library **6F 5**
Wood Aven Dr. G74: E Kil 5F **137**
Woodbank Cres. G76: Clar 3C **134**
PA5: John 3F **95**
Woodburn Av. G72: Blan 1C **140**
G76: Clar 3C **134**
ML6: Air 5H **91**
Woodburn Ct. G73: Ruth 1D **120**
Woodburn Pl. PA6: C'lee 4E **75**
Woodburn Rd. G43: Glas 2B **118**
ML1: N'hse 6D **112**
Woodburn St. ML1: Moth 1G **143**
Woodburn Ter. ML9: Lark 3G **161**
Woodburn Way G62: Miln 4G **25**
G68: Cumb 3E **35**
Wood Cres. ML1: Moth 1G **143**
Woodcroft Av. G11: Glas 6F **61**
Wooddale ML1: Moth 5F **143**
Woodend G72: Blan 3B **140**
*ML9: Lark 4G **161***
(off Keir Hardie Rd.)
Woodend Ct. G32: Glas 3E **107**
Woodend Dr. G13: Glas 4E **61**
ML6: Air 2C **92**
PA1: Pais 1F **99**
Woodend Gdns. G32: Glas 3D **106**
Woodend La. G13: Glas 4E **61**
Woodend Pl. PA5: Eld 3H **95**
Woodend Rd. G32: Glas 3D **106**
G73: Ruth 3C **120**
ML8: Carl 3G **165**
Wood Farm Rd. G46: T'bnk 5G **117**
Woodfield G71: View 1G **125**
Woodfield Av. G64: B'rig 6D **48**
Woodfoot Path G53: Glas 3B **116**
Woodfoot Pl. G53: Glas 3A **116**
Woodfoot Quad. G53: Glas 3B **116**
Woodfoot Rd. G53: Glas 3A **116**
ML3: Ham 1E **153**
Woodford Pl. PA3: Lin 5G **75**
Woodford St. G41: Glas 6C **102**
Woodgreen Av. G44: Glas 1F **119**
Woodgreen Ct. ML2: Wis 3G **157**
Woodhall ML1: Holy 5A **112**
Woodhall Av. ML1: Holy 2H **127**
ML3: Ham 5F **141**
Woodhall Av. ML5: Coat 2A **110**
ML6: C'bnk 3B **112**
Woodhall Cott. Rd. ML6: C'bnk . . . 4C **112**
Woodhall Mill Rd. ML6: Chap. 4B **112**
Woodhall Pl. ML5: Coat 2B **110**
Woodhall Rd. ML2: Wis 5D **146**
ML6: C'bnk 3B **112**
Woodhall St. G40: Glas 3D **104**
ML6: Chap 4D **112**
Woodhead Av. G66: Kirk 6D **30**
G68: Cumb 6B **34**
G71: Both 1F **141**
Woodhead Ct. G68: Cumb 6B **34**
Woodhead Cres. G71: Tann 6D **108**
ML3: Ham 3E **153**
Woodhead Gdns. G71: Both 1F **141**
Woodhead Gro. G68: Cumb 6B **34**
Woodhead Ind. Est. G69: Chry 3H **67**
Woodhead La. ML3: Ham 3F **153**
Woodhead Path G53: Glas 2A **116**
Woodhead Pl. G68: Cumb 6B **34**
Woodhead Rd. G53: Glas 2H **115**
G68: Cumb 6B **34**
G69: Chry 3H **67**
Woodhead Ter. G69: Chry 2H **67**
Woodhead Vw. G68: Cumb 6B **34**
Woodhill Rd. G21: Glas 3D **64**
G64: B'rig 6E **49**
Woodholm Av. G44: Glas 1G **119**
Woodhouse Ct. G76: Busby 4E **135**
Woodhouse St. G13: Glas 2E **61**
Woodilee Cotts. G66: Lenz 1E **51**
Woodilee Ind. Est. G66: Lenz 1E **51**
Woodilee Rd. G66: Kirk, Lenz 6E **31**
Woodilee Rd. ML1: N'hill 3E **129**
Woodland Av. G66: Kirk 5B **30**
ML6: Air 1C **112**
PA2: Pais 5A **98**
Woodland Cres. G72: Camb 3B **122**
Woodland Gdns. G76: Crmck 2H **135**
ML3: Ham 1B **154**
Woodlands Av. G69: G'csh 2C **68**
G71: Both 4E **125**
ML8: Law 5D **158**
Woodlands Ct. G46: T'bnk 5F **117**
G60: Old K 2F **41**
Woodlands Cres. G46: T'bnk 4F **117**
G71: Both 4D **124**
PA5: John 4D **94**
Woodlands Dr. G4: Glas 1D **82**
ML1: Holy 2H **127**
ML5: Coat 4H **89**
Woodlands Gdns. G71: Both 3D **124**
Woodlands Ga. G3: Glas 2D **82**
G46: T'bnk 4F **117**
Woodlands Gro. G62: Miln 2G **25**
Woodlands Pk. G46: T'bnk 5F **117**
Woodlands Pl. ML5: Coat 4H **89**
Woodlands Rd. G3: Glas 1D **82** (**2A 4**)
G46: T'bnk 5F **117**
ML1: Moth 6H **143**
ML1: N'hse 6D **112**
Woodlands St. G62: Miln 3G **25**
ML1: Moth 5H **143**
Woodlands Ter. G3: Glas 2C **82**
G71: Both 4E **125**
Woodlands, The ML4: Bell 4F **127**
Woodland Ter. ML9: Lark 4G **161**
Woodland Way G67: Cumb 2B **36**
Wood La. G64: B'rig 1E **65**
Woodlea Av. ML6: Air 1C **112**
Woodlea Dr. G46: Giff 3B **118**
ML3: Ham 3H **153**
Woodlea Pl. ML6: Air 2C **92**
Woodlinn Av. G44: Glas 2F **119**
Woodmill Dr. G64: Torr 4E **29**
Woodmill Gdns. G67: Cumb 1B **54**
Woodneuk Av. G69: G'csh 3D **68**
Woodneuk Ct. PA1: Pais 1E **97**
Woodneuk La. G69: G'csh 4D **68**
Woodneuk Rd. G53: Glas 3B **116**
G69: G'csh 4D **68**
Woodneuk St. ML6: Chap 4D **112**
Woodneuk Ter. G69: G'csh 4D **68**
Wood Quad. G81: Clyd 1G **59**
Woodrop St. G40: Glas 3D **104**
Woodrow ML1: Holy 5B **112**
Woodrow Av. ML1: Carf 5B **128**
Woodrow Cir. G41: Glas 1B **102**
Woodrow Pl. G41: Glas 1A **102**
Woodrow Rd. G41: Glas 1B **102**
Woodside ML1: Holy 5G **111**
PA6: Hous 2D **74**
Woodside Av. G46: T'bnk 4G **117**
G65: Kils 3B **12**
G66: Lenz 1D **50**
G73: Ruth 6E **105**
ML3: Ham 1A **154**
PA11: Bri W 2F **73**
Woodside Ct. ML3: Ham 1A **154**
*ML5: Coat 6H **89***
(off Woodside St.)
Woodside Cres. G3: Glas 2D **82**
G78: Barr 5F **115**
ML2: Newm 3F **147**
PA1: Pais 1G **97**
Woodside Dr. G76: Water 6B **134**
ML6: C'bnk 3A **112**
Woodside Gdns. G76: Clar 2B **134**
G76: Crmck 2H **135**
ML5: Coat 1H **109**
Woodside Gro. G73: Ruth 6E **105**
Woodside La. PA5: Brkfld 5D **74**
Woodside Pl. G3: Glas 2D **82**
G71: View 5G **109**
Woodside Pl. La. G3: Glas 2D **82**
Woodside Rd. G76: Crmck 2H **135**
PA5: Brkfld 5C **74**
Woodside St. ML1: Moth 5B **144**
ML1: New S 4A **128**
ML5: Coat 2H **109**
(not continuous)
ML6: Chap 3D **112**
Woodside Ter. G3: Glas 2D **82**
Woodside Ter. La. G3: Glas 2A **4**
Woodside Twr. ML1: Moth 5B **144**
Woodside Wlk. ML3: Ham 1A **154**
Woodstock Av. G41: Glas 4B **102**
G66: Kirk 5F **31**
PA2: Pais 5C **96**
Woodstock Dr. ML2: Wis 5A **146**
Woodstock Way PA2: Pais 5C **96**
Wood St. G31: Glas 3D **84**
ML1: Moth 1H **143**
ML5: Coat 4A **90**
ML6: Air 2B **92**
PA2: Pais 2D **98**
Woodvale Av. G46: Giff 1H **133**
G61: Bear 5H **45**
ML6: Air 1D **112**
Woodvale Dr. PA3: Pais 6E **77**
Woodview G71: View 5H **109**
Woodview Dr. ML4: Bell 6E **111**
ML6: Air 6A **92**
Woodview La. ML6: Air 6A **92**
Woodview Rd. ML9: Lark 5E **161**
Woodview Ter. ML3: Ham 5F **141**
Woodville Pk. G51: Glas 5H **81**
Woodville Pk. Ind. Est. *G51: Glas . . . 5H **81***
(off Woodville Pk.)
Woodville St. G51: Glas 5H **81**
Woodyard Rd. G82: Dumb 4E **17**
Woodyett Pk. G76: Busby 4D **134**
Woodyett Rd. G76: Busby 4D **134**
Wordsworth Way G71: Both 4F **125**
Worsley Cres. G77: Newt M 3C **132**
Wraes Av. G78: Barr 3F **115**
Wraes Vw. G78: Barr 6B **114**
Wraisland Cres. PA7: B'ton 3F **39**
Wrangholm Cres. ML1: New S 4B **128**
Wrangholm Dr. ML1: New S 4A **128**
Wren Ct. ML4: Bell 5A **110**
Wren Pl. ML2: Wis 6H **145**
PA5: John 6D **94**
Wright Av. G78: Barr 5C **114**
Wrightlands Cres.
PA8: Ersk 1A **58**
Wright St. PA4: Renf 1B **78**
Wright Way ML1: New S 4A **128**
Wye Cres. ML5: Coat 2H **89**

Wykeham Pl. G13: Glas 3C **60**
Wykeham Rd. G13: Glas 3C **60**
Wyler Twr. ML3: Ham 6A **142**
Wylie G74: E Kil 4D **138**
Wylie Av. G77: Newt M 2D **132**
Wylie St. ML3: Ham 1H **153**
Wyndford Dr. G20: Glas 4B **62**
Wyndford Pl. G20: Glas 4B **62**
Wyndford Rd. G20: Glas 4A **62**
    G68: Cumb 3D **14**
Wyndford Ter. G71: View 6F **109**
Wyndham Ct. *G12: Glas* *5B 62*
    (off Wyndham St.)
Wyndham St. G12: Glas 5B **62**
Wynd, The G67: Cumb 6B **14**
Wyneford Rd. FK4: Bank 1D **14**
Wynyard Grn. G75: E Kil 3D **148**
Wyper Pl. G40: Glas 5C **84**
Wyvil Av. G13: Glas 6E **45**
Wyvis Av. G13: Glas 1H **59**
    G61: Bear 6C **24**
Wyvis Ct. G77: Newt M 6D **132**
Wyvis Pl. G13: Glas 1H **59**
    G77: Newt M 6C **132**
Wyvis Quad. G13: Glas 1H **59**

X

XS Superbowl 5B

Y

Yair Dr. G52: Glas 5A **80**
Yarrow Ct. G72: Camb 2D **122**
Yarrow Cres. ML2: Wis 5H **145**
    PA7: B'ton 5A **40**
Yarrow Gdns. G20: Glas 6D **62**
Yarrow Gdns. La. *G20: Glas* *6D 62*
    (off Yarrow Gdns.)
Yarrow Pk. G74: E Kil 2A **150**
Yarrow Rd. G64: B'rig 3C **48**
Yarrow Way G72: Blan 1B **140**
Yate St. G40: Glas 6D **84**
Yetholm Gdns. G74: E Kil 5H **137**
Yetholm St. G14: Glas 3G **59**
Yetholm Ter. ML3: Ham 6C **140**
YETT 4C **128**
Yett Rd. ML1: N'hill 4D **128**
Yetts Cres. G66: Kirk 5F **31**
Yetts Hole Rd. ML6: Glenm 6D **54**
Yew Dr. G21: Glas 6C **64**
Yew Pl. PA5: John 4F **95**
Yews Cres. ML3: Ham 4F **141**
Yokerburn Pl. G13: Glas 2G **59**
Yokerburn Ter. G81: Clyd 2F **59**
Yoker Ferry Rd. G14: Glas 3G **59**
Yoker Ind. Est. G14: Glas 3H **59**
Yoker Mill Gdns. G13: Glas 2G **59**
Yoker Mill Rd. G13: Glas 2G **59**

Yoker Station (Rail) 2F **59**
Yoker Sports Cen. 3H **59**
York Dr. G73: Ruth 2F **121**
Yorkhill Pde. G3: Glas 2A **82**
Yorkhill St. G3: Glas 3B **82**
York Rd. ML1: N'hse 5D **112**
    ML6: Chap 5D **112**
York St. G2: Glas 4E **83** (6B **4**)
    G81: Clyd 5F **43**
    ML2: Wis 1H **157**
York Way PA4: Renf 2E **79**
Younger Quad. G64: B'rig 6C **48**
Young Pl. G71: Tann 5E **109**
    G75: E Kil 6A **150**
    ML2: Newm 4F **147**
Young St. G81: Clyd 3D **42**
    ML2: Wis 6H **145**
Young Ter. G21: Glas 5C **64**
Young Wynd ML4: Bell 5C **110**
Yukon Ter. G75: E Kil 3D **148**
Yvetot Ct. ML8: Carl 2E **165**

Z

Zambesi Dr. G72: Blan 6A **124**
Zena Cres. G33: Glas 5E **65**
Zena Pl. G33: Glas 5F **65**
Zena St. G33: Glas 5E **65**
Zetland Rd. G52: Hill 3H **79**

HOSPITALS and HOSPICES
covered by this atlas
with their map square reference

N.B. Where Hospitals and Hospices are not named on the map, the reference given is for the road in which they are situated.

ACCORD HOSPICE —3E **99**
Hawkhead Hospital Grounds
Hawkhead Rd.
PAISLEY
Renfrewshire
PA2 7BL
Tel: 0141 5812000

ACORN STREET DAY HOSPITAL —1B **104**
23 Acorn St.
GLASGOW
G40 4AN
Tel: 0141 5564789

AIRBLES ROAD CENTRE —4H **143**
59 Airbles Rd.
MOTHERWELL
ML1 2TJ
Tel: 01698 261331

ALEXANDER HOSPITAL —3A **90**
Blair Rd.
COATBRIDGE
Lanarkshire
ML5 2EW
Tel: 01236 422661

BLAWARTHILL HOSPITAL —3A **60**
129 Holehouse Dr.
GLASGOW
G13 3TG
Tel: 0141 211 9000

CANNIESBURN HOSPITAL —5E **45**
Switchback Rd.
Bearsden
GLASGOW
G61 1QL
Tel: 0141 2115600

CLELAND HOSPITAL —1A **146**
Bellside Rd.
Cleland
MOTHERWELL
Lanarkshire
ML1 5NR
Tel: 01698 245000

COATHILL HOSPITAL —1C **110**
Hospital St.
COATBRIDGE
Lanarkshire
ML5 4DN
Tel: 01698 245000

COWGLEN HOSPITAL —6D **100**
10 Boystone Rd.
GLASGOW
G53 6XJ
Tel: 0141 2119200

DRUMCHAPEL HOSPITAL —5B **44**
129 Drumchapel Rd.
GLASGOW
G15 6PX
Tel: 0141 2116000

DUMBARTON JOINT HOSPITAL —3C **16**
Cardross Rd.
DUMBARTON
G82 5JA
Tel: 01389 762317

DYKEBAR HOSPITAL —6D **98**
Grahamston Rd.
PAISLEY
Renfrewshire
PA2 7DE
Tel: 0141 8845122

ERSKINE HOSPITAL (PRINCESS LOUISE
SCOTTISH HOSPITAL) —2C **40**
Bishopton
BISHOPTON
Renfrewshire
PA7 5PU
Tel: 0141 8121100

GARTNAVEL GENERAL HOSPITAL —5G **61**
1053 Great Western Rd.
GLASGOW
G12 0YN
Tel: 0141 2113000

GARTNAVEL ROYAL HOSPITAL —4F **61**
1055 Great Western Rd.
GLASGOW
G12 0XH
Tel: 0141 2113600

GLASGOW DENTAL HOSPITAL
—3E **83** (3B **4**)
378 Sauchiehall St.
GLASGOW
G2 3JZ
Tel: 0141 2119600

GLASGOW HOMOEOPATHIC HOSPITAL
—5G **61**
1053 Great Western Rd.
GLASGOW
G12 0YN
Tel: 0141 2111600

GLASGOW NUFFIELD HOSPITAL, THE
—4H **61**
25 Beaconsfield Rd.
GLASGOW
G12 0PJ
Tel: 0141 3349441

GLASGOW ROYAL INFIRMARY —3A **84**
84 Castle St.
GLASGOW
G4 0SF
Tel: 0141 2114000

GLASGOW ROYAL MATERNITY HOSPITAL
—4H **83** (5G **5**)
147-163 Rottenrow
GLASGOW
G4 0NA
Tel: 0141 2115400

HAIRMYRES HOSPITAL —2B **148**
Eaglesham Rd.
East Kilbride
GLASGOW
G75 8RG
Tel: 01355 220292

HAWKHEAD HOSPITAL —3E **99**
Hawkhead Rd.
PAISLEY
Renfrewshire
PA2 7BL
Tel: 0141 8898151

HEALTH CARE INTERNATIONAL HOSPITAL
—5A **42**
Beardmore St.
CLYDEBANK
Dunbartonshire
G81 4HX
Tel: 0141 9515000

JOHNSTONE HOSPITAL —1G **95**
Bridge of Weir Rd.
JOHNSTONE
Renfrewshire
PA5 8YX
Tel: 01505 331471

KIRKLANDS HOSPITAL —3F **125**
Fallside Rd.
Bothwell
GLASGOW
G71 8BB
Tel: 01698 245000

LENNOX CASTLE HOSPITAL —2C **6**
Glen Rd.
Lennoxtown
GLASGOW
G66 7LB
Tel: 01360 329200

LEVERNDALE HOSPITAL —3H **99**
Crookston Rd.
GLASGOW
G53 7TU
Tel: 0141 2116400

LIGHTBURN HOSPITAL —4B **86**
966 Carntyne Rd.
GLASGOW
G32 6ND
Tel: 0141 2111500

MANSIONHOUSE UNIT, THE —5D **102**
100 Mansionhouse Rd.
GLASGOW
G41 3DX
Tel: 0141 2016161

MARIE CURIE CENTRE, HUNTERS HILL
—3B **64**
107 Belmont Rd.
GLASGOW
G21 3AY
Tel: 0141 5582555

Hospitals & Hospices

MERCHISTON HOSPITAL —6E **75**
Bridge of Weir Rd.
Brookfield
JOHNSTONE
Renfrewshire
PA5 8TY
Tel: 01505 328261

MONKLANDS DISTRICT GENERAL
HOSPITAL —4G **91**
Monkscourt Av.
AIRDRIE
Lanarkshire
ML6 0JS
Tel: 01236 748748

PARKHEAD HOSPITAL —6F **85**
81 Salamanca St.
GLASGOW
G31 5ES
Tel: 0141 211 8300

PRINCE & PRINCESS OF WALES HOSPICE
—5F **83**
71 Carlton Pl.
GLASGOW
G5 9TD
Tel: 0141 4295599

PRIORY HOSPITAL, GLASGOW, THE
—5D **102**
38 Mansionhouse Rd.
GLASGOW
G41 3DW
Tel: 0141 6366116

QUEEN MOTHER'S MATERNITY HOSPITAL
—2A **82**
Dalnair St.
Yorkhill
GLASGOW
G3 8SH
Tel: 0141 2010550

RED DEER DAY HOSPITAL —3E **149**
Alberta Av., East Kilbride
GLASGOW
G75 8NH
Tel: 01355 244254

ROADMEETINGS HOSPITAL —5H **165**
Goremire Rd.
CARLUKE
Lanarkshire
NL8 4PS
Tel: 01555 77221

ROSS HALL HOSPITAL —2A **100**
221 Crookston Rd.
GLASGOW
G52 3NQ
Tel: 0141 8103151

ROYAL ALEXANDRA HOSPITAL —3H **97**
Corsebar Rd.
PAISLEY
Renfrewshire
PA2 9PN
Tel: 0141 887 9111

ROYAL HOSPITAL FOR SICK CHILDREN
—2A **82**
Dalnair St.
Yorkhill
GLASGOW
G3 8SJ
Tel: 0141 2010000

ST ANDREW'S HOSPICE —3A **92**
Henderson St.
AIRDRIE
Lanarkshire
ML6 6DJ
Tel: 01236 766951

ST MARGARET'S HOSPICE —2F **59**
East Barns St.
CLYDEBANK
Dunbartonshire
G81 1EG
Tel: 0141 9521141

ST VINCENT'S HOSPICE —6B **94**
Midton Rd.
Howwood
JOHNSTONE
Renfrewshire
PA9 1AF
Tel: 01505 705635

SHETTLESTON DAY HOSPITAL —1H **105**
152 Wellshot Rd.
GLASGOW
G32 7AX
Tel: 0141 3038800

SOUTHERN GENERAL HOSPITAL —3D **80**
Govan Rd.
GLASGOW
G51 4TF
Tel: 0141 2011100

STOBHILL GENERAL HOSPITAL —3C **64**
133 Balornock Rd.
GLASGOW
G21 3UW
Tel: 0141 2013000

STRATHCLYDE HOSPITAL —4F **143**
Airbles Rd.
MOTHERWELL
Lanarkshire
ML1 3BW
Tel: 01698 245000

UDSTON HOSPITAL —5D **140**
Farm Rd.
HAMILTON
Lanarkshire
ML3 9LA
Tel: 01698 245000

VICTORIA INFIRMARY —5E **103**
Langside Rd.
GLASGOW
G42 9TY
Tel: 0141 2016000

VICTORIA MEMORIAL COTTAGE HOSPITAL
—3F **11**
19 Glasgow Rd.
Kilsyth
GLASGOW
G65 9AG
Tel: 01236 822172

WESTER MOFFAT HOSPITAL —3F **93**
Towers Rd.
AIRDRIE
Lanarkshire
ML6 8LW
Tel: 01236 763377

WESTERN INFIRMARY —1A **82**
Dumbarton Rd.
GLASGOW
G11 6NT
Tel: 0141 2112000

WISHAW GENERAL HOSPITAL —6E **145**
Netherton St.
WISHAW
Lanarkshire
ML2 0DP
Tel: 01698 361100